THE LETTERS OF KARL MARX

THE LETTERS
OF KARL MARX

SELECTED and TRANSLATED with EXPLANATORY NOTES and an INTRODUCTION *by Saul K. Padover*

PRENTICE-HALL, INC.
Englewood Cliffs, New Jersey 07632

Book Designer, Linda Huber
Art Director, Hal Siegel

The Letters of Karl Marx: Selected and Translated
with Explanatory Notes and an Introduction by Saul K. Padover

Prentice-Hall International, Inc., London
Prentice-Hall of Australia, Pty. Ltd., Sydney
Prentice-Hall Canada Inc., Toronto
Prentice-Hall of India Private Ltd., New Delhi
Prentice-Hall of Japan, Inc., Tokyo
Prentice-Hall of Southeast Asia Pte. Ltd., Singapore
Whitehall Books Limited, Wellington, New Zealand

FIRST EDITION

10   9   8   7   6   5   4   3   2   1

ISBN 0-13-531525-5 {A REWARD BOOK : PBK.}

Library of Congress Cataloging in Publication Data

Marx, Karl, 1818–1883.
    The letters of Karl Marx.
    Bibliography: p.
    Includes index.
    1. Communists—Correspondence. 2. Communists—
Biography. I. Padover, Saul Kussiel.
HX39.5.A4   1979   335.4'092'4   79-10894
ISBN 0-13-531533-6

INTRODUCTION

In this collection of Marx's personal letters, the first of its kind in English—or perhaps in any language—we see the development of a rich personality in unmatched detail and frankness. The letters, in fact, constitute a kind of intimate autobiography, reflecting a spontaneous honesty, since they were written out of the needs and passions of the moment, without any thought of posterity. In this correspondence we witness Marx as he really was and as he felt in painful and crucial situations. His communications with relatives, friends, and colleagues reveal the many facets of his personality—his immense erudition, his passionate commitments, his peculiar indignations, and his physical sufferings. The light glinting from the correspondence is not always flattering to Marx, but it illuminates the mind and character of one of the seminal figures of modern times.

The letters included here span a period of forty-six years, from Marx's student days, when he was grasping at the Muses (he wanted to be a poet) and grappling with philosophy, to about two months before his death in 1883, when he was literally gasping for breath. They cover the wide range of his interests, his early years when he was an idealistic humanist, his middle life as an embattled communist, and his final period of desperate illness when he could do no creative work. In the letters we see Marx emerging not merely as a fighting intellectual and profound philosopher whose ideas reshaped the modern world, but also as a husband who loved his aristocratic wife and a doting father of three adoring daughters.

Through the letters we can trace the important events of Marx's life. In 1841, at the age of 23, he received his Ph.D. degree with an immensely erudite dissertation on classic Greek philosophy (a study steeped in Greek and Latin sources). Wanting to be a professor of philosophy but finding academic positions closed to him, young Marx became a journalist, the only career he ever had. His first position, that of editor of the *Rheinische Zeitung*, a Cologne daily, was closed by the Prussian censorship, and Marx, after marrying his childhood sweetheart, Jenny von Westphalen, in 1843, moved to Paris to publish a journal, *Deutsch-Französische Jahrbücher*, which failed after one issue.

Marx's residence in Paris, from which he was expelled early in 1845, was a crucial period in his development. Here he met famous writers, among them the self-exiled German lyric poet and satirist, Heinrich Heine, and radical social theorists such as Pierre Joseph Proudhon, whose ideas he was soon to castigate in his first book,[1] *The Poverty of Philosophy* (1847). In addition to being the center of European civilization, Paris was above all the home of European revolutionary ideas. In the French capital, dominated by a triumphant bourgeoisie (a word Marx often used contemptuously), class divisions and class hatreds were frank and inflexible. Marx did not have to invent the idea of the class struggle: he saw it all around him.

A crucial event for Marx in Paris was his meeting with Frederick Engels in the summer of 1844. Engels was on his way back to Germany from Manchester, where he had spent nearly two years working in the English branch of his father's textile firm and had collected materials for his historic book, *The Condition of the Working Class in England*.[2] He was then 24 years old, a handsome young man of a wealthy family in rebellion against his puritanic father, and a dedicated communist. Brilliant and erudite (Engels came to know more than thirty languages), he had an interest in economics and a knowledge of business, subjects of which Marx was then ignorant. The two young Germans—Engels was Marx's junior by two years—found that they were in agreement on all basic questions, philosophic, political and religious, and they decided to become collaborators in their writ-

---

[1]His previously published book, *The Holy Family* (1845), was written in collaboration with Frederick Engels.
[2]Published, in German, in 1845; an English translation came out in 1892.

ings. It was Engels who was instrumental in converting Marx to communism and in stimulating him to a study of political economy, which was to become a lifelong interest.

The destinies of the two men became henceforth entwined. When, after his expulsion from Paris in 1845, Marx moved to Brussels, Engels joined him there. The two men became active in communist organizations and in literary collaboration. They wrote together *The Holy Family* and *The German Ideology*, as well as *The Communist Manifesto*. After revolutions broke out in Europe, including Germany, in 1848, Marx and Engels went to Cologne and founded the *Neue Rheinische Zeitung*, a communist daily of which Marx was editor and Engels chief contributor. Ousted from Germany in 1849, Marx went to Paris, whence he was soon expelled and moved to London, where Engels joined him. They were destined to spend the rest of their lives in England, Marx as an indigent refugee and Engels as a businessman in Manchester, whither he returned in 1850 in order to earn money to support himself and his indigent friend. Without Engels, Marx, his wife and their three surviving daughters would have literally starved in their English exile. The capitalist profits from Engels' business enterprise (among his talents was one for business, which he fundamentally despised) made it possible for Marx to write his classic anti-capitalist work. On the night when Marx finished correcting proofs of Volume I of *Das Kapital* (August 16, 1867), he wrote to Engels with deep emotion:

> "Only YOU alone I have to thank for making this possible! Without your self-sacrifice for me I could never possibly have done the enormous work....I embrace you full of thanks! Greetings, my beloved, dear friend!"

During the twenty years Engels lived in Manchester (he moved to London in September, 1870, after having sold his share of the business), he and Marx were in continuous contact. They often visited each other, in Manchester or in London, but their main communication when away from each other was by mail. Many of Marx's letters consisted of pleas, and not infrequently blunt requests, for money; they also contained the trivia of refugee radical politics (not included in this volume, of course). But a large number of letters had real substance, dealing with ideas, personal feelings, and opinions, expressed in the intimacy of trusted friendship. As Marx told Ludwig Kugelmann (October 25, 1866): "Engels...is my most intimate friend. I have no secrets from him."

Letter writing, be it kept in mind, was the sole means of communication at a distance. It performed the role that the telephone does today, which is fortunate for the history of culture, as it has thus preserved for posterity a frank record of ideas. In a day like ours, when postal services are decaying, it is of interest to recall that a century ago, in Victorian England, a letter mailed in London reached the addressee in Manchester on the following day, and vice versa. Thus epistolary communication between Marx and Engels had, for all practical purposes, a palpable immediacy. Marx's need for constant communication and consultation with his friend in Manchester can be judged from the fact that of a total of 1,523 preserved letters which are published in the *Marx-Engels Werke*,[3] no less than 903—or about 60 percent of the total—are to Engels. This proportion is more or less preserved in our book: Of the 366 Marx letters given here in part or in full, 173—or nearly half—are to Engels.

The other letters are to Marx's other contemporaries, family and friends. He spent more than half of his life in London, an uprooted alien, never really quite at home in England, although an admirer of its literary and scientific culture. His essential contacts were mainly with foreigners like himself. But his three daughters, raised and educated in London, considered themselves English and although they knew German, would not speak it. When away from home, their father wrote them often in English or in his own brand of German-and-English.

For Marx, living in London, with its pervasive air of freedom, had precious advantages. The British capital was then an émigré center, where Germans, Frenchmen, Hungarians, Italians, Poles, and other Continental refugees mingled, worked, and squabbled with each other, without fear of the police. It is to be noted that Marx, the professional revolutionist par excellence, was never bothered by the governmental authorities, although, occasionally afflicted with paranoia, he thought the post office tampered with his mail, which was not true. The European refugees in London supplied Marx with a lifeline to friends and allies across the Channel, not infrequently providing him with titillating gossip about prominent personalities, which he loved to recount with zest.

Of greater importance for Marx as a professional man was the British Museum, then probably the world's greatest library. It possessed,

---

[3]In the monumental collection, *Marx-Engels Werke*, Vols. XXVII to XXXV (Berlin, 1963-1967) contain letters written by Marx and Engels to each other and to third persons.

as Marx wrote in the Preface to his first book on economics, *Critique of Political Economy* (1859), an "enormous amount" of material in the form of essential books in many languages, newspapers, pamphlets, and official government reports. Until chronic illnesses incapacitated him in the 1870's, Marx spent his working days in the reading room of the British Museum, doing research not only for his masterpiece, *Das Kapital*, but also for his journalistic work, especially the *New-York Daily Tribune*, of which he was London correspondent for about a decade, until 1862. He worked long hours in the British Museum during the day and did his writing late at night when the family was asleep.

After the publication of the first volume of *Das Kapital* in 1867, Marx did little serious writing. Much of his time was spent on radical politics, including the First International, of which he was the guiding spirit for about eight years. Friends thought that his absorption in the uncreative polemics of the International was a waste of precious energy. But his intellectual interests continued unabated. Always an avid reader, the nearly always ailing Marx did not give up his lifelong habit of devouring books in a wide variety of fields, not only economics and history, but also mathematics, technology, and natural science, including astronomy, chemistry, and paleontology. His opinions on these and related subjects can be seen in many of the letters included in this volume.

Apart from being revealing of his own personality, Marx's letters often have a special pungency. They show him as a man who could be bawdy, opinionated, and witty. An example is his gossipy report on the Empress Eugénie, whose husband, Napoleon III, he utterly despised. Marx wrote that Eugénie "is given to a very disgusting constitutional inconvenience—uncontrolled *farts*" and that her "strong detonations" at royal receptions made even the hardiest courtiers blush. On another occasion he gleefully mentioned a healthy Russian fellow who after spending twenty-four hours in a nunnery came out dead. "The nuns," Marx wrote, "rode him to death."

Marx's opinions of historic figures could be sharp. Thus he described René de Chateaubriand, the romantic French poet and statesman, as a "literary calligraphist" whose "theatrical" work was a "mishmash of lies." In discussing Charles Darwin, whose work he essentially admired, Marx observed that the famous naturalist viewed the animal kingdom as a reflection of English "bourgeois society." Of another renowned Briton, Benjamin Disraeli, Marx commented that he was "the best proof of how great talent without conviction produces

scoundrels, even though liveried and 'right honorable' scoundrels."
Henry George's famous work, *Progress and Poverty*, Marx dismissed as
"a last attempt—to save the capitalist regime." After studying the
history of the Roman civil wars, Marx concluded that Pompey, the
military opponent of Julius Caesar, was "an utter *Scheisskerl* [shit-
head]" and a dishonest "*Lauskerl* [lousy good-for-nothing]." On the
other hand, in the Roman gladiator Spartacus, Marx discerned a
"most splended fellow" who was a "great general (no Garibaldi), a
noble character."

Even in his misery and sickness, Marx was capable of sardonic
humor. When, by a curious inadvertence, he was ordered to become a
constable of the vestry of St. Pancras, the bemused Marx told Engels
that he was advised by a friend to inform the parish that "I was a
foreigner and that they should kiss me in the arse." A few days before
his fiftieth birthday, the impecunious Marx remarked: "Half a century
behind me and still a pauper! How right my mother was! 'If only
Karell[4] had made capital instead [of writing about it].'" Upon hearing
that Engels was riding horseback recklessly, Marx reminded him that
there were more important occasions for him to risk his neck, adding:
"I don't believe that cavalry is the specialty with which you are most
useful to Germany." On the night Marx finished correcting the last
proofsheets of *Das Kapital*, when he was suffering excruciating pains
from carbuncles on his behind, he wrote to Engels: "I hope that the
bourgeoisie will remember my carbuncles all the rest of their lives."

The criteria for the selection of the letters in this book were
personality, biography, and ideas. Purely political commmunications,
as well as technical economic discussions, have been omitted as being
ephemeral and without enduring qualities. The personal letters,
however, a true reflection of Marx the man and the thinker, continue
to have an abiding freshness and significance.

The presentation of Marx's letters to English readers involved
some special problems. One of them was identification. Many of the
names mentioned in the correspondence, while of meaning and interest to Marx, are obscure or unknown today. This is likewise true of
references to certain events which have passed into oblivion. In the

---

[4]This was how Marx's mother, a Dutchwoman who never fully mastered the German language,
pronounced her son's name.

case of persons, I have made a special effort to identify each one of them, as can be seen in the extensive Biographic Index. As for events, they are, wherever possible, explained briefly in footnotes.

Another problem that had to be solved was linguistic. With few exceptions, Marx wrote his letters in German, but not always totally so. He was in the habit of interspersing his letters with English words and phrases, which I have noted in each instance. In addition, Marx was a polyglot who would mix into his sentences words and expressions from all kinds of languages with which he was familiar, including Danish, Dutch, French, Greek and Latin, to mention but a few. Once, in a letter to Engels from Algiers, he wrote a short sentence in three languages: "... déjeuner [French] findet statt [German] a quarter past 11 [English]." All this *mélange*, which adds colorfulness to Marx's letters, is translated.

Saul K. Padover
New York

I wish to express my appreciation to Robert Sussman Stewart, an inspired editor with an enthusiasm for ideas, whose encouragement stimulated the creation of this book.

I also wish to thank Dorothy Lachmann, production editor, for her expertise and conscientiousness in overseeing the production of this book. My thanks too to Ann Finlayson for her meticulousness and linguistic skill in copy-editing a difficult manuscript.

My thanks are also due to Hal Siegel for his judicious selection of the illustrations and to Linda Huber who designed the book.

CONTENTS

Section Six
FIRST INTERNATIONAL AND *DAS KAPITAL* (*1865-1874*)   *190*

LETTERS TO AND ABOUT FERDINAND LASSALLE
(1849–1868)
INTRODUCTION

THE LETTERS OF KARL MARX

LETTERS TO FAMILY, FRIENDS, AND CONTEMPORARIES

(1837-1883)

Section One
STUDENT

The following is Marx's first letter that has been preserved from his youth. Otherwise, his available correspondence does not begin until 1842, when he was twenty-four-years old.

Upon the death of Marx's mother, on November 30, 1863, the letter was found among her papers by his older sister, Sophie Schmalhausen, who left it to her family. Marx apparently did not know of its existence, or he might have destroyed it, so at least his daughter Eleanor believed.[1]

The letter, an intense reply to his father's insistent advice, hectoring, and criticism[2] is a remarkable document for a nineteen-year old. About 4,000 words long, it took all night to write. An unsparing account of a young student (at Berlin University) in the agony of self-searching, it is memorable in itself. It is a self-portrait of Karl Marx in the throes of his first intellectual development, and

---

1. Eleanor Marx-Aveling, in *Die Neue Zeit*, Vol. I (1897): "The letter submitted here was sent to me a few months ago by my cousin, Frau Karoline Smith, who found it among the papers of her mother Sophie.... Marx himself was in Trier at the time of his mother's death in 1863, but he surely did not know of the existence of the letter and that his sister had it—fortunately so, or he undoubtedly would have destroyed it."
2. For his father's letters to his favorite son, see Appendix I, "Letters from Heinrich Marx to His Son" in the back of this volume.

throws a flood of light on his mind, revealing the strengths and weaknesses associated with the later Marx—a tendency to generalization, a sense of sharp criticism, a relentless chase after ideas and systems.

1

To (father) Heinrich Marx (in Trier).
Berlin, November 10, 1837.

Dear Father:

There are moments in life which stand as landmarks, terminating the past and at the same time pointing firmly toward a new direction.

At such a point of transition we feel compelled to contemplate, with the eagle eye of thought, the past and the present, in order to arrive at a true awareness of our actual situation. Indeed, world history itself loves such a retrospect, seeming to move backward and to stand still, whereas in reality it leans back in the armchair to understand itself and to penetrate intellectually its own action, that of the mind.

The individual, however, becomes lyrical in such moments, because metamorphosis is partly swan song, partly overture to a great new poem and tries to gain shape amid the still hazy, brilliant colors; and yet we should put up a monument to what we have already experienced, so that it should regain in sensibility what it has lost in action; and where could we find a more sacred abode than in the hearts of our parents, the most indulgent judges, the most intimate participants, the sun of love whose fire warms our innermost strivings! What better way is there to correct, and to receive forgiveness for, what is displeasing and blameworthy in our character, than to look at it as a currently necessary condition? In what other way can one remove the reproach of having a twisted heart than by ascribing it as much to adverse luck and to aberration of spirit as to anything else?

If now, at the end of a year spent here, I review the events of that period, and, in doing so, dear Father, answer the affectionate letter you wrote me from Ems, I take the liberty of examining my situation and, in general, my view of life, which I consider an expression of reflection in all directions—in science, in art, in private endeavors.

When I left home, a new world had opened up for me, one of love and, at first, a love drunk with longing and empty of hope. Even the trip to Berlin, which otherwise would have enchanted me to the highest degree, would have inspired me to contemplate nature, and inflamed me to a joy of living, left me cold, indeed, depressed me considerably. For the rocks I saw were no steeper, no harsher than the sensations of my soul, the broad cities no livelier than my blood, the restaurant tables no more overloaded with indigestible food than the contents of my imagination, and, finally, art itself, which was not as beautiful as Jenny.

Upon arrival in Berlin, I broke with all existing connections, paid rare visits and then only with reluctance, and sought to immerse myself in science and art.

In my state of mind then, lyrical poetry was necessarily the first, at least the most pleasant, project I embarked upon, but, in accord with my position and previous development, it was purely idealistic. An equally remote other world, such as my love, became my heaven, my art. Everything real grew blurred, and the vague had no boundaries; attacks on the present, wide and shapeless feeling, nothing natural, everything constructed out of the blue, the complete opposite of that which is and which should be, rhetorical reflections instead of poetic ideas, but perhaps also a certain warmth of feeling and a striving for vigor—all this characterizes the poems in the first three volumes I sent to Jenny. The whole horizon of longing, which sees no limit, assumes various forms and turns "versifying" into "width."

Poetry, however, was to be merely a companion; I had to study law and I felt above all an urge to grapple with philosophy. The two were so closely connected that I studied Heineccius,[1] Thibaut[2] and the sources uncritically, and in schoolboy fashion; thus, for example, I translated the first two books of the Pandect into German, and tried to work out a philosophy of law while studying law. By way of introduction, I preceded it with some metaphysical propositions and then continued this unfortunate opus up to public law, a work of almost 300 pages.

Above all, I was troubled by the same contradictions between the Is and the Ought that is characteristic of Idealism, and this led me to make the following hopelessly inaccurate divisions: First, the metaphysics of law, as I gratuitously termed it, that is, the principles, reflections, and definitions of concepts, divorced from all real law and all real forms of law, as is the case with Fichte,[3] but in my case more modern and less substantial. This—the unscholarly form of mathematical dogmatism, where the subject circles around the matter, reasons to and fro, without the matter itself forming into

---

1

1. Johann Gottlieb Heineccius, *Elementa iuris civilis secundum ordinem Pandectarum* [*Elements of Civil Law According to the Arrangement of the Pandectes*] (Amsterdam, 1728).
2. Anton Friedrich Justus Thibaut, *System des Pandekten-Rechts* [*System of Pandectian Laws*], Vols. I–II (Jena, 1803–05).
3. Johann Gottlieb Fichte, *Grundlage des Naturrechts nach Prinzipien der Wissenschaftslehre* [*Foundation of Natural Law According to Scientific Theory*] (Jena and Leipzig, 1796).

something rich and alive—obstructed an understanding of the truth from the outset. The triangle leads the mathematician to construct and to demonstrate; it remains a mere idea in space, it does not develop into anything else; it has to be set beside something else to assume different positions, and these, when juxtaposed to related ones, yield different relationships and truths. On the other hand, in all concrete expressions in the living world of ideas, such as Law, the State, Nature, and all of philosophy, the object itself has to be observed in its development, arbitrary divisions must not be intruded, and the reason of the thing itself must evolve within its own contending self and find there its own unity.

As a second part, there followed the philosophy of law, that is, according to the opinion I then held about the development of ideas in positive Roman law, as if positive law in its intellectual evolution (I do not mean in its purely finite definitions) could exist at all apart from the shape of the concept of law, which, after all, the first part should have included!

In addition, I had divided that part into formal and substantive theory of law, of which the first was meant to outline the pure form of the system in its progression and context, its structure and scope; whereas the second part was to deal with content and the merging form into content. There is one error which I share with Herr von Savigny,[4] as I was to discover later when I read his erudite work on property—with the difference that, what he called formal definition was something "to find the place which this or the other doctrine has in the (hypothetical) Roman system," and material definition was that which is "the doctrine of the positive which the Romans attributed to a concept defined in this manner";—I, on the other hand, considered form as the architectonics required in the formulation of a concept, and matter as the quality required of these forms. The error was that I believed the one could and should develop independently of the other and thus I did not arrive at true form but merely constructed a writing desk with drawers which I later filled with sand.

Concept is, after all, the mediating element between form and content. In any philosophical treatise on law, therefore, the one must be contained in the other; indeed, form should be but the continuation of content. Thus I arrived at a division that made for simple and superficial classification only, while the spirit of law and its truth were obscured by it. The whole body of law fell into contract and noncontract elements. For better illustration, I take the liberty of presenting here the schema up to the division of the *jus publicum*, which has also been treated in the formal part.

---

4. Friedrich Carl von Savigny (1779–1861), Prussian jurist, professor at Berlin University when Marx was a student there.

I
jus privatum

II
jus publicum

I. *jus privatum*

a. Conditional, contractual private law
b. Unconditional, noncontractual private law
  A. *Conditional, contractual private law*
    a. Personal law
    b. Property law
    c. Personal realty law

a. Personal law

  I. Out of encumbered contract
 II. Out of assured contract
III. Out of charitable contract
    I. Out of encumbered contract
  2. Social contract (*societas*)
  3. Hiring-out contract (*locatio conductio*)
    3. *Locatio conductio*
      1. Insofar as it relates to services (*operae*)
        a. Real *locatio conductio* (not meant to include Roman house- or farm-lease laws)
        b. *mandatum*
      2. Insofar as it relates to the right of use (*usus rei*)
        a. Ground: *ususfructus* (but not also in the purely Roman sense)
        b. Dwellings: *habitatio*
    II. *Out of the assured contract*
  1. Separation or adjustment contract
  2. Insurance contract
    III. *Out of charitable contract*
      1. [missing]
      2. *Consent contract*
  1. *fidejussio* (surety)
  2. *negotiorum gestio* (conducting business without mandate)
    3. *Donation contract*
  1. *donatio* (gift)
  2. *gratiae promissum* (promises of favor)
    b. *Property law*
      I. *Out of encumbered contract*
  2. *permutatio stricte sic dicta* (exchange in the original sense)
    1. Exchange proper
    2. *mutuum usurae* [loan] (interest)
    3. *emptio venditio* (buying and selling)

II. Out of the assured contract
   pignus (pledge)
III. Out of the charitable contract
2. *commodatum* (lending, or loan contract)
3. *depositum* (storing of goods)

But why should I continue to fill the pages with things which I myself have rejected? Trichotomic divisions pervade the whole; it was written with tiresome prolixity, and it abused the Roman concept most barbarously in order to force them into my system. On the other hand, I thereby acquired a love for a general view of the material, at least to a certain extent.

At the end of the part on private law, I saw the falsity of the whole, which in its basis borders on Kantianism, but which deviates entirely from it in its application; and again it became clear to me that without philosophy nothing can be mastered. Thus I could once more throw myself into its arms with clear conscience, and I proceeded to write a new metaphysical system, at the end of which I was again forced to admit its incorrectness as well as those of my own previous efforts in this direction.

In doing this, I acquired the habit of making excerpts from all the books I read—such as Lessing's *Laokoon*,[5] Solger's *Erwin*,[6] Winckelmann's history of art,[7] Luden's German history[8]—and to jot down reflections on the side. At the same time, I translated Tacitus' *Germania* and Ovid's *Libri Tristium*, and began on my own, that is, out of grammars, to study English and Italian, in which I have not yet accomplished anything; I also read Klein's criminal law and his Annals,[9] and all the latest works of literature, the latter on the side, however.

At the end of the semester, I again sought the dances of the Muses and the music of Satyrs; and even in the last notebook which I sent you, Idealism, you will find, plays a role through forced humor *(Scorpion und Felix)* and shines through in an inept and fantastic drama *(Oulanem)*, until finally it

---

5. Gotthold Ephraim Lessing, *Laokoon: oder über die Grenzen der Malerei und Poesie* [*Laocoon: Or About the Borders of Painting and Poetry*] (Berlin, 1766).

6. Karl Wilhelm Ferdinand Solger, *Erwin. Vier Gespräche über das Schöne und die Kunst* [*Erwin. Four Discussions About Beauty and Art*] (Berlin, 1815).

7. Johann Winckelmann, *Geschichte der Kunst des Altertums* [*History of the Art of Antiquity*], 2 Parts (Dresden, 1764 and 1767).

8. Heinrich Luden, *Geschichte des Deutschen Volkes* [*History of the German People*], 12 vols. (Gotha, 1825–1837).

9. Ernst Ferdinand Klein, *Grundsätze des gemeinen deutschen peinlichen Rechts nebst Bemerkung der preussischen Gesetze* [*Common Law Principles of German Criminal Justice, Together with Observations on Prussian Law*], 2d ed. (Halle, 1799). *Annalen der Gesetzgebung und Rechtsgelehrsamkeit in den preussischen Staaten* [*Annals of Legislation and Jurisprudence in the Prussian States*], 26 vols. (Berlin and Stettin, 1788-1809).

changes entirely and moves on to mere art form, mostly without inspired objects or vibrant ideas.

And yet, these recent poems are the only ones in which, suddenly, as if by a stroke of magic,—alas, the stroke was a shattering one at first—the realm of true poetry shone at me like a distant fairy palace and thus all my own creations dissolved into nothingness.

With these manifold activities during the first semester, it is small wonder that many nights were passed in wakefulness, many battles were fought, many a stimulus within and without had to be coped with, so that at the end I did not emerge very enriched; I had neglected nature, art, and the world around me, and I alienated many friends. My physical condition deteriorated, and a doctor recommended the countryside; and thus, for the first time, I traversed the whole spreading city to the gate of Stralow. I did not then anticipate that my stay there would change me from a pale weakling into a physically robust man.

A curtain had fallen, my holy of holies had been torn to shreds, and new gods had to replace it.

From Idealism, which, incidentally, I had compared to and enriched with Kantianism and Fichteism, I moved to investigate the Idea in the reality itself. If the gods had formerly dwelt above the earth, they now became its center.

I had read fragments of Hegel's philosophy,[10] the grotesque, rocklike melody of which did not appeal to me. Once again I wished to dive into the sea, but with the definite intention of finding our spiritual nature as essential, concrete, and solidly rounded as the physical one; no longer would I practice the arts of fencing but hold the pure pearl up to the sunlight.

I wrote a dialogue of approximately twenty-four pages: "Cleanthes, or the Starting Point and Necessary Progress of Philosophy." It combined to a certain extent art and learning, which previously had been separated; and I plunged vigorously into the work itself, into a philosophical-dialectical development of the godhead as it manifests itself as the concept itself, as religion, as nature, as history. My last theme was the beginning of the Hegelian system; and this task, for which I was somewhat prepared by my reading of natural science, Schelling,[11] and history, has caused me endless headaches,

---

10. Georg Wilhelm Friedrich Hegel, *Phänomologie des Geistes* [*Phenomenology of the Mind*], in his *Werke*, Vol. II (Berlin, 1832).

Wissenschaft der Logik [*Science of Logic*], in his *Werke*, Vol. III–V (Berlin, 1833–34).

Vorlesungen über die Geschichte der Philosophie [Lectures on the History of Philosophy], in his *Werke*, Vol. XIV (Berlin, 1833).

Encyclopädie der philosophischen Wissenschaften im Grundrisse [*Encyclopaedia of the Philosophical Sciences in Outline*], 3rd ed. (Heidelberg, 1830).

11. Friedrich Wilhelm Joseph Schelling, *Philosophische Schriften* [*Philosophical Writings*], Vol. I (Landshut, 1809).

being written in such a [words crossed out in manuscript]—(since it was meant actually to constitute a new system of logic), that I myself can scarcely follow it now. This beloved offspring of mine, tended in moonlight, lures me on treacherously, like a false siren, into the arms of the enemy.

I was so angry I was unable to think at all for a couple of days, ran around like a madman in the garden close to the dirty waters of the Spree, a river of which it has been said that it "washes souls and dilutes tea" [Heinrich Heine, "Die Nordsee"]; I even joined my landlord in a hunting party, then hastened back and felt like embracing every loafer at street corners.

Shortly thereafter I pursued only positive studies; I read Savigny's *Property*,[12] Feuerbach's and Grolmann's criminal law,[13] Cramer's *De verborum significatione*,[14] Wening-Ingenheim's Pandect system,[15] and Mühlenbruch's *Doctrina Pandectarum*,[16] the latter of which I have not finished. I also studied some of Lauterbach's works,[17] civil law and in particular ecclesiastical law, including the first part of Gratian's *Concordia discordantium canonum* [Concord of Discordant Laws],[18] of which I have read virtually the whole corpus, including the appendix, and made excerpts, and also Lancelotti's *Institutiones*.[19] Then I translated part of Aristotle's *Rhetoric*, read the famous Bacon's (Baron Verulam) *De augmentis scientiarum*,[20] occupied myself very much with Reimarus, whose book, *Von den Kunsttrieben der Tiere*,[21] I once had studied with great pleasure. I also took up German law, but here I restricted my reading to the capitularies of the Frankish kings and the Popes' letters to them. From grief over Jenny's illness and my fruitless intellectual labors, from a consuming anger over having to make an idol of a view I hated, I fell

---

12. Friedrich Carl von Savigny, *Das Recht des Besitzes* [*The Law of Property*] (Giessen, 1803).

13. Johann Paul Anselm Feuerbach, *Revision der Grundsätze und Grundbegriffe des positiven peinlichen Rechts* [*Revision of the Principles and Basic Concepts of the Statutory Capital Law*], 2 Parts (Erfurt and Chemnitz, 1799–1800); *Lehrbuch des gemeinen in Deutschland gültigen peinlichen Rechts* [*Textbook of the Common Criminal Law Valid in Germany*], 4th ed (Giessen, 1808). Karl von Grolmann, *Grundsätze der Criminalrechts-Wissenschaft* [*Principles of the Science of Criminal Law*], 4th ed. (Giessen, 1825).

14. Andreas Wilhelm Cramer, *De verborum significatione tituli pandectarum et codicis cum variae lectionis apparatu* (Kiel, 1811).

15. Johann Nepomuk Wening-Ingenheim, *Lehrbuch des Gemeinen Civilrechtes* [*Textbook of Common Civil Rights*], 3 vols., 4th ed. (Munich, 1831–32).

16. Christian Friedrich Mühlenbruch, *Doctrina pandectarum. Halis Saxonum 1823 bis 1825*, 3 vols., 3d ed. (Halle, 1838).

17. Wolfgang Adam Lauterbach, *Collegium Theorico-practicum. Ad L pandectarum libros methodo synthetica*, 43 vols. (Tübingen, 1690-1714).

18. In Gratian's *Corpus iuris canonici* (published in the twelfth century).

19. Giovanni Paolo Lancelotti, *Institutiones iuris canonici* (in *Corpus iuris canonici*).

20. Francis Bacon, *De dignitate et augmentis scientiarum* (London, 1623).

21. Hermann Samuel Reimarus, *Allgemeine Betrachtungen über die Triebe der Tiere, hauptsächlich über ihre Kunst-Triebe* [*General Opinion on the Urges of Animals, Chiefly on their Art Urges*] (Hamburg, 1760).

sick, as I have already told you, dear Father. My health restored, I burned all my poems and sketches for short novels, etc., laboring under the illusion that I could abandon them altogether—of which there is as yet no evidence.

During my illness, I came to know Hegel's works, as well as most of his disciples, from beginning to end. As a result of several meetings with friends at Stralow, I got into a doctors' [of Philosophy] club, which had among its members university lecturers [*Privatdozenten*] and my most intimate Berlin friend, Dr. Rutenberg.[22] In the course of our debates, many an opposing opinion came to light and I clung ever more tightly to my own world outlook, of which, in truth, I had believed myself free, but any resounding ideas I might have had were muted; and so I was seized with a rage for irony, as so often happens when there is that much negativism. This was aggravated by Jenny's silence. I could not rest until I had grasped modernity and the point of view of modern scholarship by turning out a few bad productions, such as *Der Besuch* [The Visit], etc.

If perhaps I have failed to convey to you either a clear idea or all the details, as well as the nuances, of the past semester, do please forgive me, dear Father, on account of my eagerness to speak of the present.

Herr von Chamisso[23] sent me a measly note in which he says "he regrets that his Almanac cannot use my contributions, because it has long since gone to press." I swallowed his note in anger. Wigand,[24] the bookdealer, forwarded my plan to Dr. [Karl] Schmidt, publisher of Wunder's Store of Good Cheese and Bad Literature.[25] I am enclosing Wigand's letter; Schmidt has not answered yet. In the meantime, I shall by no means give up this plan, all the more so as all the famous experts on aesthetics of the Hegelian school, through the good offices of Instructor [Bruno] Bauer, who plays a great role among them, as well as my co-adjutor Dr. Rutenberg, have promised to cooperate.

In regard to the question of a government career, my dear Father, I have recently made the acquaintance of Assistant Judge [Assessor] Schmidthänner, who advised me to enter it after passing the third law examination; this would appeal to me all the more since I really prefer jurisprudence to any study of public administration. The gentleman in question told me that from the Münster District Court in Westphalia he himself and many others made it to assistant judge in three years, which, he says, is not difficult to do—provided, of course, that one works hard—since there the stages [of

---

22. Adolf Rutenberg (1808–1869) was a German newspaperman and editor of the *National-Zeitung* in 1848.
23. Adelbert von Chamisso (1781–1838), a French-born German poet, was the author of the famous *Peter Schlemihls wunderbare Geschichte* [*Peter Schlemihl's Amazing History*] (1814).
24. Otto Wigand (1795–1877) was a Leipzig publisher and bookdealer.
25. Julius Wunder had a book business in Leipzig between 1833 and 1841.

promotion] are not as strictly fixed as they are in Berlin and other places. If, as assistant judge, one later attains the doctorate, there are much better prospects for immediate appointment as professor extraordinary, as happened in the case of Mr. Gärtner[26] in Bonn after he wrote a mediocre book on provincial codes of law, his only other title to fame being that he calls himself a member of the Hegelian school of law. However, my dear Father, best of fathers, would it not be possible for us to talk this over face to face? Eduard's [Karl's brother] condition, dear Mother's illness, your own indisposition, which I hope is not very serious—all this makes me wish, indeed makes it virtually a necessity, for me to hurry home. I would, indeed, have been there already, if I had not been in doubt about your permission, your consent.

Believe me, my dear, beloved Father, this is not a selfish wish (although I would be blissful to see Jenny again); I am, however, motivated by a thought which I may not put into words. In some respects it would be difficult for me to come, and yet, as my own sweet Jenny writes, such considerations must give way to the fulfilment of duties, which are sacred.

Whatever your decision, I implore you, dear Father, not to show this letter to Angelic Mother [*Engelsmutter*], or at least not this page of it. My unexpected arrival may perhaps cheer up that great, splendid woman.

My letter to her was written long before the arrival of Jenny's dear letter, and thus, unwittingly, I may have written too much about matters which are not suitable or very little so.

In the hope that the clouds which hang over our family will gradually pass; that I may be permitted to share your sufferings and mingle my tears with yours, and perhaps in your presence demonstrate the deep affection, the boundless love, which often I have expressed poorly; in the hope that you too, dear, eternally beloved Father, mindful of the confused state of my storm-tossed soul, will forgive me where the heart must often have seemed to err as the overburdened spirit stifled it; in the hope that you will soon be fully restored to health so that I shall be able to press you close to my heart and tell you all that I feel,

I remain your ever loving son, Karl

Forgive, dear Father, the illegible handwriting and the bad style; it is nearly four o'clock; the candle has burned out completely, and my eyes are blurred; a true restlessness has taken hold of me; I shall not be able to mollify the specters haunting me until I am in your dear presence.

Please greet for me my sweet, splendid Jenny. I have already read her letter twelve times, and every time I discover new charms in it. In every respect, even in style, it is the most beautiful letter I can imagine a lady to write.

---

26. Gustav Friedrich Gärtner (d. 1841) was a professor of law in Bonn.

Section Two

JOURNALISM
Cologne and Paris · *1842-1845*

After four years at Berlin University, Marx submitted his dissertation on the classic Greek philosophers—*Difference between the Democritean and Epicurean Philosophy of Nature*—to Jena University, which granted him the Ph.D. degree in 1841. Finding it hopeless to obtain an academic position in reactionary Prussia, he turned to journalism for a living. In May, 1842, he began to contribute articles to the recently founded liberal Cologne daily, *Rheinische Zeitung*, of which he became editor in October. Half a year later, Marx resigned from the paper, which was closed by the government censorship on April 1, 1843. He then married his childhood sweetheart, Jenny von Westphalen, and moved to Paris, to publish there the *Deutsch-Französische Jahrbücher*, in collaboration with Arnold Ruge, a Saxon editor and author. The journal, planned to be, as the title suggests, a Yearbook, suspended publication after one issue—in February, 1844—and Marx turned to other writings, including what is now known as *Economic and Philosophic Manuscripts of 1844* (not published until 1932). In January, 1845, Marx, who by then had become a communist, to a considerable extent under the influence of Frederick Engels with whom he struck up what became a permanent friendship while in Paris, was expelled from France and moved to Brussels.

13

2

From letter to Arnold Ruge¹ (in Dresden)
Trier, March 20, 1842

Dear Friend:

Novices are the most pious, as Saxony demonstrates *ad oculos* [visibly]. Bauer²
once had a scene with Eichhorn³ similar to yours with the Minister of Interior. The oratorical figures of these gentlemen are as alike as two eggs. By
contrast, it is exceptional that philosophy should speak intelligibly to the
political wisdom of these highly sworn scoundrels, and even a little fanaticism does not hurt. To these worldly types, nothing is more difficult to make
believable than the belief in truth and spiritual sentiment. They are such
political dandies, such experienced fops, that they no longer believe in true,
disinterested love. How can one reach these roués except by means of what is
called fanaticism there? A lieutenant of the Guards considers a lover, who has
honorable intentions, a fanatic. Should one, therefore, no longer marry? It is
remarkable how the belief in the brutalization of man has become a government article of faith and political principle. But this is no contradiction of
religiosity, for the animal-religion is the most consistent essence of religion,
and perhaps it will soon be necessary to speak of religious zoology instead of
religious anthropology . . . .

Now to the matter at hand: I found that the article "concerning Christian art," which is now changed to "concerning religion and art, with special
reference to Christian art," has to be totally corrected, in that I had sincerely
fulfilled the hosanna tone—"Thy word is a lamp unto my feet, and a light
unto my path."⁴ "Thou through thy commandments hast made me wiser
than mine enemies: for they are ever with me."⁵ "The Lord will roar from
Zion."⁶ This trumpet tone, together with Hegel's presentation, must now be
changed to a more free and, therefore, a more basic treatment. In a few days I
must go to Cologne, where I shall set up my new domicile, because the

---

2

1. Arnold Ruge (1802–1880) was a Young Hegelian German writer and magazine editor to
whose publication, soon closed by the Saxon censorship, Marx hoped to contribute his
first serious articles.
2. Bruno Bauer (1809–1882), a Young Hegelian theologian, was a Marx friend (and later
butt of ridicule) at Berlin University.
3. Johann Albrecht Friedrich Eichhorn (1779–1856), Prussian Minister of Cultural (and
Medical) Affairs, 1840–1848.
4. Psalms, 119:105.
5. Psalms, 119:98.
6. Amos, 1:2.

proximity of the Bonn professors is insupportable to me. Who wants forever to converse with intellectual stink animals, with people who study only for the purpose of finding new boards in all the corners of the world!

Hence under present circumstances I cannot send you the critique of the Hegelian philosophy of law for the next issue of *Anecdota*[7] (because it was also written for "trumpets"), but I promise you that article on religious art by the middle of April, if you want to wait that long.[8] I would prefer this, since I am treating the matter from a new point of view and presenting it also as a supplement to an Epilogue on the Romantics. In the meantime I will work on the subject most energetically, to use a Goethean[9] expression, and await your decision. Would you please write me to Cologne, where I will be as of the beginning of next month.[10] Since I do not have as yet a definite domicile there, please write me at Jung's[11] address.

In my treatment, I must necessarily discuss the general essence of religion, and thus to some extent come into collision with Feuerbach,[12] a collision which does not involve an attack on his principles but on his style. At any rate, religion will not gain by it.

I have not heard for a long time from Köppen.[13] Have you never contacted Christiansen[14] in Kiel? I know him only from his history of Roman law,[15] which also contains some things about religion and philosophy in general. He seems to be a man of superior intelligence, although when he comes to philosophy proper he writes with a formalistic and frightful lack of understanding. Perhaps by now he writes German. Otherwise he seems to be *à la hauteur des principes* [at the top of the principles].

I would be pleased to see you here on the Rhine.

Yours, Marx

---

7. *Anekdota zur neuesten deutschen Philosophie und Publizistik* [*Anecdotes on the Newest German Philosophy and Journalism*], a collective volume of essays published by Arnold Ruge in Zurich and Winterthur, Switzerland, in 1843. The volume contained two articles by Marx: "Remarks on the Latest Prussian Censorship Instruction," and "Luther as Arbitrator between Strauss and Feuerbach."
8. Marx never wrote the article on Christian religious art.
9. Johann Wolfgang von Goethe.
10. Marx gave up his plan to move to Cologne; in April, 1842, he returned to Bonn, where he remained, with some interruption, until the middle of October. In that month he became editor of the *Rheinische Zeitung* and moved to Cologne, where the paper was published.
11. Georg Jung (1814–1886) was copublisher of the *Rheinische Zeitung*.
12. Ludwig Feuerbach (1804–1872), German materialist philosopher, admired by Marx.
13. Karl Friedrich Köppen (1808–1863), young Hegelian historian, friend of Marx at Berlin University.
14. Johannes Christiansen (1809–1853), German jurist at Kiel University.
15. Christiansen, *Die Wissenschaft der römischen Rechtsgeschichte im Grundrisse* [*The Science of Roman History of Law in Outline*], Vol. I (Altona, 1838).

Bauer[16] has just written me that he wants to go North again, in the foolish belief that there he could better pursue his case against the Prussian government. Berlin is too close to Spandau. In any case, it is a good thing that Bauer does not let the matter go. As I learn here from my future brother-in-law,[17] an aristocrat *comme il faut* [proper], Berlin is angry at Bauer mostly over his *bonne foi* [good faith].

3

To Arnold Ruge (in Dresden)
Bonn, April 27, 1842

Dear...

You must not be impatient if I postpone my contributions for a few more days. Bauer will perhaps report to you orally how all manner of external confusions have made work impossible during this month.

Nevertheless, I am almost finished. I will send you four articles: (1) "on religious art"; (2) "on the romantics"; (3) "the philosophic manifesto of the historical school of law"; (4) "the positive philosophy," which I have tickled a bit. The articles hang together in content.[2]

The piece on religious art you will receive in duodecimo form, as the thing has grown almost into a book and I got into all kinds of investigations which will take much more time.

I gave up my plan to settle in Cologne, as life there is too bustling, and through sheer good friends one does not attain philosophy.

I sent a long article to the *Rheinische Zeitung* on our recent Rhenish Landtag with a frivolous introduction on the *Preussische Staats-Zeitung*. On the occasion of the debates on the press I will return with an article on censorship and freedom of the press.[3] For the time being I will remain in Bonn, and it would be a pity if nobody remained here to irritate the holy ones [the theologians on the university faculty].

---

16. Bruno Bauer, who was ousted from his position on the faculty of theology at Bonn University for his critical views of Christianity.
17. Ferdinand Otto Wilhelm von Westphalen, half-brother of Marx's fiancée Jenny von Westphalen, who became Prussian Minister of Interior in 1850.

3

1. Name blotted out in the original.
2. Of the four articles, only one was published: "The Philosophic Manifesto of the Historical School of Law," in *Rheinische Zeitung*, August 9, 1842.
3. Marx published a series of articles on the subject in *Rheinische Zeitung*, May 5, 8, 10, 12, 15, 19, 1842.

Yesterday Hasse[4] came from Greifswald; I never saw anything more in him than a big, booted provincial parson. He also spoke altogether like a booted provincial parson, knew nothing of God and the world, is preparing a multivolume edition of the tedious Anselm of Canterbury on which he had worked for ten years,[5] thinks that the present criticism is a moment that has to be overcome, speaks of religiosity as a product of life experience, by which he probably means his flourishing pedagogy and his fat belly, for fat bellies undergo all kinds of experiences and, as Kant says, when it's behind it's an *F.*, and if above, a religious inspiration. The pious Hasse with his religious constipations!

What we learned here from your letters about Vatke's[6] lack of a "full heart" was highly amusing. This super-clever, diplomatic Vatke, who would so like to be the greatest critic and the greatest believer, and who always knows best, is now viewed by one party as having no heart and by the other as having no head. *Hic jacet* [here rests] Vatke, a memorable example of addiction leading to card playing and to religious music.

Fichte,[7] who wraps himself here in the mantle of his unpopularity, has spread the ambiguous rumor that he has been called to Tübingen. The faculty does not fulfil his wish to keep him here by an increase in salary.

Sack[8] in all his piety is going to Berlin in order to speculate on the madness of his brother and to apply for his place.

Nothing but war and dissoluteness, says Thersites,[9] and even if one cannot reproach this university [Bonn] with war, at least it does not lack dissoluteness.

Would you not once make a trip to the Rhine?

Yours, Marx

4

From a letter to Arnold Ruge (in Dresden)
Trier, July 9, 1842

Dear Friend:

If circumstances had not excused me, I would have given up every attempt at an excuse. It goes without saying that I consider it an honor to contribute to

---

4. Friedrich Rudolf Hasse (1808–1862), professor of theology, Bonn University.
5. Hasse, *Anselm von Canterbury*, 2 vols. (Leipzig, 1843 and 1852).
6. Wilhelm Vatke (1806–1882), professor of theology, Berlin University.
7. Immanuel Hermann Fichte (1796–1879), philosopher, professor at Bonn and Tübingen universities.
8. Karl Heinrich Sack (1789–1875), Protestant theologian at Bonn University.
9. Thersites is a brawling character in Homer's *Iliad*.

Anecdotis[1] and only through unpleasant externalities have I been prevented from sending in my articles.

Since the month of April, I have been able to work at most only four weeks, and even then not without interruptions. I had to spend six weeks in Trier on account of a new death,[2] and the rest of the time was fragmented and put out of tune by the most disagreeable family squabbles. My family put obstacles in my way which, despite their easy circumstances, placed me momentarily under the most pressing [financial] conditions. I can hardly burden you with the tale of these private rascalities; it is truly lucky that the public rascalities make every possible irritation with the private ones impossible for a man of character. . . .

Yours, Marx

5

From letter to Dagobert Oppenheim[1] (in Cologne)
Bonn, c. August 25, 1842

Dear Oppenheim:

Enclosed a manuscript from Ruge. No. 1 will not be usable; no. 2, on conditions in Saxony, you could well use.

Send me the article by Mayer in the *Rheinische Zeitung* on communal organization[2] and, if possible, all the articles by Hermes *against Judaism*.[3] I will then, as soon as possible, send you an article on the latter subject, which, even though not conclusive, will present a different point of view. . . .

If you agree with its viewpoint, send me also the *Juste-milieu*[4] article for criticism. One must discuss the thing dispassionately. In the first, as a rule general theoretical discussions of constitutionalism are more fitting for purely scientific organs than for newspapers. Genuine theory must be made clear and developed within concrete conditions and existing circumstances.

Still, since it has already happened, two things are to be taken into consideration. At every opportunity, whenever we get into conflict with

4

1. *Anekdota zur neuesten deutschen Philosophie und Publizistik*, see Letter 2, Note 7.
2. Ludwig von Westphalen, the father of Marx's fiancée Jenny, who died on March 3, 1842.

5

1. Dagobert Oppenheim (1809–1889), a copublisher of the *Rheinische Zeitung*.
2. Eduard Mayer, a Cologne lawyer, on editorial board of *Rheinische Zeitung*. The reference is to an article published in the newspaper, August 14, 1842.
3. Carl Heinrich Hermes, in *Kölnische Zeitung*, July 6 and 30, and August 23, 1842.
4. "*Das Juste-Milieu*," an article by Edgar Bauer, published anonymously in the *Rheinische Zeitung*, June 5, 16, 18, and 21, and August 23, 1842.

other papers, the thing can be thrown in our teeth. Such a clear demonstration against the foundations of the present political conditions can result in a sharpening of the censorship, and even in a suppression of the paper. It was in this way that the south German *Tribune* was destroyed. But in any case we would discourage a large, and perhaps the largest, number of liberal-minded, practical men who have taken over the painful role of fighting for freedom step by step within the constitutional limits, while we, from our comfortable chairs of abstraction, demonstrate to them their contradictions. It is, to be sure, true that the author of the *Juste-milieu* article calls for criticism; but (1) we all know how governments react to such challenges; (2) it is not enough that someone subjects himself to criticism, for which, moreover, he is not asked permission. What is in question is whether he chooses the proper terrain. Newspapers begin to be the proper terrain for such questions only when they have become questions of the actual state, practical questions.

I consider it unavoidable that the *Rheinische Zeitung* not be managed by its staff, but on the contrary that it manages the staff. Articles like the one mentioned offer the best opportunity for indicating to the staff a definite plan of operations. The individual author cannot in the nature of things have a view of the whole, the way a newspaper does.

Should my views not be in accord with your own, I will, if you do not consider it improper, send my critique to *Anecdotis* as an appendix to my article against Hegel's theory of constitutional monarchy. I consider it better for the newspaper to be its own physician.

Awaiting your prompt reply,

Yours, Marx

6

To Arnold Ruge (in Dresden)
Cologne, November 30, 1842

Dear Friend:

My letter today will confine itself to the "tangle" with the "*Freien.*"[1]

You already know that the censorship is pitilessly mutilating us every day, so that the paper can hardly appear. Thereby a mass of articles by the *Freien* has fallen by the wayside. As much as the censorship itself, I also

---

6

1. "*Freien*"—the Free Ones—was the name applied to a group of Young Hegelian writers in Berlin, whose philosophy was becoming increasingly abstract and divorced from reality. Among the "Freien" were Bruno and Edgar Bauer, Eduard Meyen, Ludwig Buhl, and Max Stirner. The group was later sharply criticized by Marx and Engels in their book, *The Holy Family*, which they published in 1845.

allowed myself to annul them, since Meyen and Company sent us piles of brainless stuff pregnant with world-revolution, scribbled in a slovenly style, permeated with a bit of atheism and communism (which the gentlemen had never studied); under Rutenberg's complete lack of critical sense, independence and competence, they had become accustomed to regard the *Rheinische Zeitung* as their supine organ, but I did not believe in allowing this urine to continue as of old. This omission of a few inestimable productions of "Freedom," which by preference strives "to be free of all thought," was thus the first ground for the darkening of the Berlin sky.

Rutenberg, whom the German article (on which his main activity consisted of punctuation) already warned, and which was provisionally translated only *at my insistence* into French—Rutenberg, in the monstrous stupidity of our political Providence, had the good fortune to be considered dangerous, although he was dangerous to nobody except the *Rheinische Zeitung* and himself. Rutenberg's removal was vigorously pressed. The Prussian Providence, this *despotisme prussien, le plus hypocrite, le plus fourbe* [Prussian despotism, the most hypocritical, the most deceitful], spared the editor an unpleasant scene, and the new martyr, Rutenberg, who, in face, deportment, and speech, already knew how to act martyrdom with virtuosity, exploited this opportunity, wrote to the whole world, wrote to Berlin, that he was the *exiled principle* of the *Rheinische Zeitung*, which was now entering into a different relationship with the government. It goes without saying that here too demonstrations were made by the heroes of freedom on the Spree, "the dirty water, which washes souls and dilutes tea."[2]

Finally, there came your and Herwegh's relation to the "*Freien*," and the measure of the furious Olympians overflowed.[3]

A few days ago I received a letter from little Meyen, whose favorite category is rightly the *ought*, wherein my relationship to (1) you, (2) Herwegh, and (3) to the new editorial principle and attitude toward the government, is put in question. I replied immediately and expressed my frank opinion on the inadequacy of their writings, which find freedom more in licentious, sans-cullottish, and smug form than in *free*, that is, independent and profound content. I demanded from them fewer vague ratiocinations, high-sounding phrases, self-compliant games, and more precision, more analysis of concrete conditions, and more expertise. I stated that I considered communist or socialist dogmas, that is, a new philosophy, smuggled into incidental theater criticisms, etc., as inappropriate, yea, even as unethical, and demanded an entirely different and more thorough discussion of communism, if it is to be discussed at all. I then requested that religion be criticized more in the critique of political conditions than political conditions in re-

---

2. The quotation is from a poem by Heinrich Heine in *Die Nordsee*.
3. *Rheinische Zeitung*, November 29, 1842, stated in a note: "Herwegh and Ruge found that on account of their political romanticism, genius-mania, and bragging, the '*Freien*' are compromising the cause of freedom."

ligion, since the former approach is more in accord with the essence of a newspaper and the formation of public opinion, as religion, in itself without content, lives not from heaven but from earth, and with the dissolution of the reverse reality, whose *theory* it is, it will collapse in itself. Finally, I demanded that if philosophy is to be discussed at all, there should be less toying with the *Firma* [business firm] "Atheism" (which is like children who will tell everybody who will listen that they are not afraid of the bogeyman), and much more content be presented to the public. *Voilà tout* [That is all].

Yesterday I got an insolent letter from Meyen, who had not yet received mine, demanding answers to all possible things: (1) my attitude to their quarrel with [Bruno] Bauer, about which I knew not a word; (2) why I did not let through this and that, and accused me of conservatism; (3) the newspaper ought not to temporize, but must do its *utmost*, that is, quietly, to yield to the police and the censorship, instead of asserting its position through a duty-bound struggle, invisible to the public, but nonetheless stubborn. Finally, he reported insultingly about Herwegh's betrothal, etc., etc.

From all this there shines forth a frightful dose of vanity, which does not comprehend how, in order to save a political organ, one can sacrifice a few Berlin windbags, who think of nothing altogether than their own clique stories. Withal, the little man strutted like a peacock, beat protestingly on his chest and on his sword, dropped something about "his" party, threatened with his displeasure, declaimed à la Marquis Posa but only a bit worse, etc.

Since, from morning till night, we have to endure the most frightful censorship vexations, ministerial scribblings, gubernatorial complaints, Provincial Diet accusations, protests of the shareholders, etc., etc., and since I remain at my post only because I consider it a duty to frustrate the intentions of authority, insofar as I can, you can imagine that I am somewhat irritated and that I answered pretty roughly. It is thus probable that the "*Freien*" will retire for a moment. I urgently appeal to you, therefore, not only to support us with your own articles but also to ask your friends to do the same.

Yours, Marx

7

To Arnold Ruge (in Dresden)
Cologne, January 25, 1843

Dear ...[1]

You probably know that the *Rheinische Zeitung* has been suppressed, prohibited, received a death sentence. It has been given its termination at the end

---

7

1. The name is unclear in the original.

of March. During this gallows reprieve it has a double censorship. Our censor [Wiethaus], an honorable man, has been put under the censorship of Regierungspräsident [Governor] von Gerlach, a passively obedient blockhead, and specifically, our entire paper must be presented to the police nose for sniffing, and when the latter smells something un-Christian, un-Prussian, the paper must not appear.

Several special causes combine in this prohibition: our circulation;[2] my defense of the Mosel correspondent;[3] in which the highest statesmen are brought into disrepute; our stubborn refusal to name the informant of the marriage law;[4] the convocation of the Provincial Estates, in which we could agitate; finally, our criticisms of the prohibition of the *Leipziger Allgemeine Zeitung*[5] and the *Deutsche Jahrbücher*.

The Ministerial Rescript, which is to appear in the newspapers presently, is if possible even weaker than the previous ones. As explanations, the following are given:

1. The *lie* that we had no license, as if in Prussia, where not even a dog can live without a police permit, the *Rheinische Zeitung* could appear even for a day without meeting official conditions essential to life.

2. The Censorship Instruction of December 24 aimed at a *tendency* censorship. Tendency was understood to mean the *fancy*, the romantic belief, of possessing freedom, which in reality one would not be permitted to possess. Where the intelligent Jesuitism which dominated the previous government had a stern intellectual visage, the romantic Jesuitism has the power of imagination as its main requisite. The censored press has to know how to live with imaginary freedom and with that gorgeous man [the King] who graciously permits this imagination. But while the censorship instruction demanded a tendency censorship, the present ministerial rescript declares: *Prohibition, suppression* was invented in Frankfurt for thoroughly bad tendency. Censorship exists only for censoring the excrescences of good tendencies, even though the instruction had said the opposite, namely, excrescences were permitted in good tendencies.

3. The old fiddle-faddle of bad intentions, hollow theory, tweedle-dum, etc.

I was not surprised at anything. You know what I thought of the censorship instruction.[6] Here I see only a consequence, I see in the suppression of the *Rheinische Zeitung* a *progress* in political consciousness, and am

---

2. The *Rheinische Zeitung*, which started with 400 subscribers, ended with 3,400.
3. "Defense of the Mosel Correspondent," January 15, 17, 18, 19, 1843.
4. "The Draft of the Marriage Law," *Rheinische Zeitung*, December 19, 1842.
5. "The Suppression of the *Leipziger Allgemeine Zeitung*," in *Rheinische Zeitung*, January 1, 4, 6, 8, 10, 13,16, 1843.
6. Marx, "Remarks on the Latest Prussian Censorship Instruction" (1843).

therefore resigning. Furthermore, the atmosphere had become very oppressive for me. It is bad to perform menial services even for freedom, and to fight with needles instead of clubs. I became tired of hypocrisy, stupidity, raw authority, and our cringing, bowing, back-turning, and word picking. Thus the government has given me my freedom again.

I have, as I already wrote you, fallen out with my family and, so long as my mother is alive, I have no right to my property. Moreover, I am betrothed and neither can, should, nor will leave Germany without my fiancée.[7] If it were possible for me to co-edit the *Deutsche Boten* in Zurich with Herwegh[8] I would be pleased. In Germany I can no longer begin anything. One falsifies oneself here. Should you therefore give me advice and information in this matter, I would be very grateful.

I am working on a number of things, which could find neither censor nor publisher nor any possible existence at all here in Germany. I await your prompt reply.

Yours, Marx

8

From letter to Arnold Ruge (in Dresden)
Cologne, March 13, 1843

Dear Friend:

... Without any romanticism, I can assure you that I am head over heels seriously in love. I have been engaged now for seven years, and my fiancée[1] has had to fight for me the hardest battles, which practically undermined her health, partly with her pietistic-conservative relatives,[2] for whom the "Lord in Heaven" and the "Lord in Berlin" are equal objects of worship, partly with my own family, in which some parsons and other enemies have nestled. I and my fiancée, therefore, for years have had to fight more unnecessary and exhausting battles than many others who are three times older and who constantly talk about their "life experience.". . .

Yours, Marx

---

7. Jenny von Westphalen.
8. Georg Herwegh (1817-1875), a participant in the German revolution of 1848.

8

1. Jenny von Westphalen.
2. Although Jenny's father, Privy Councillor Ludwig von Westphalen, was not opposed to Marx, the rest of the family objected.

9

From letter to Arnold Ruge (in Dresden)
En route, in Holland, late March, 1843

Dear Friend:

I am now traveling in Holland.[1] As far as I can see from the local and French newspapers, Germany has plunged deep into muck and will go still deeper. I assure you that even if one feels little national pride, still one feels national shame, even in Holland. The smallest Dutchman is nevertheless a citizen compared to the biggest German. And the opinions foreigners have of the Prussian Government! In this there is a frightening unanimity; nobody has any illusions about that system and its simple nature.... The pompous mantle of liberalism has fallen off, and the revolting despotism stands in all its nakedness before the eyes of the whole world.

This is also a manifestation, even if a reverse one. It is a truth that at least teaches us to recognize the hollowness of our patriotism and the un-naturalness of our political system. You look at me with a smile and ask: What is gained thereby? One does not make a revolution out of shame. I answer: Shame itself is a revolution; it is in reality the victory of the French Revolution over German patriotism, which defeated it in 1813. Shame is a sort of anger that turns on itself, and if a whole nation were really ashamed, it would be the lion that recoils in order to leap. I admit that shame is not yet to be found in Germany; on the contrary, those wretches are still patriots. But what system would drive out their patriotism if not this ridiculous one of the new knight?[2] The comedy of despotism being staged for us is as dangerous for him as the tragedy once was for the Stuarts and the Bourbons. And even if for a long time one does not see this comedy for what it is, it is still a revolution. The state is too serious a thing to be made into a buffoonery. One could perhaps for a time sail a ship full of fools before the wind, but it would meet its fate precisely because the fools would not believe the warnings. This fate is the revolution, which awaits us.

Yours, Marx

9

1. After resigning from the editorship of the *Rheinische Zeitung* on March 17, 1843, Marx went on a tour of Holland.
2. Frederick William IV, who became King of Prussia in 1840.

10

To Arnold Ruge (in Dresden)
Cologne, May, 1843

Dear Friend:

Your letter, my dear friend, is a good elegy, a breathtaking dirge; but politically it is altogether nothing. No nation despairs, and if it goes on hoping out of mere stupidity for a long time, nevertheless after many years it does realize its pious wishes out of sudden wisdom.

Still, you have infected me; your theme is not yet exhausted, I want to add the finale; and when everything is over, then give me your hand so that we can start again at the beginning. Let the dead bury and lament their dead. In contrast, it is enviable to be the first vigorously to enter a new life, this should be our destiny.

It is true, the old world belongs to the philistines. But we ought not to treat it like a scarecrow from which one turns away in alarm. We ought, rather, to look it straight in the eye. And it pays to study this master of the [philistine] world.

He is master of the world only, of course, insofar as he fills society with his own kind, as worms fill a corpse. The society of these gentlemen, therefore, needs nothing more than a number of slaves, and the owners of slaves need not be free. Even though as owners of landed property and people they are referred to as eminent masters, they are thereby no less philistinish than those they rule.

Men—means intellectual beings; free men—means republicans. The common philistines do not want to be either. Then what is left for them to be and want to be?

What they want—to live and to propagate their species (and further than that, as Goethe says, nobody can take it)—is also wanted by animals. The most a German politician might add to this is that the human being *knows* what he wants, and the German is so minded that he wants nothing more.

One will have to reawaken in the breast of these people the sense of the self-worth of men—freedom. Only such a sense, which vanished from the world with the Greeks and evaporated into the blue with Christianity, can transform society again into a community of people for their highest ends—a democratic state.

On the other hand, men who do not feel themselves to be men achieve the level of their masters, like a flock of slaves or horses. These hereditary masters are the goal of the whole society. That world belongs to them. They take it as it is and at face value. They take themselves as they find themselves, and stand where their feet grew, on the necks of these political animals who know no other destiny than to be "a vassal, propitiating and expectant."

The philistine world is the *political animal world*, and once we recognize its existence, we have no choice but simply to describe the status quo accurately. Centuries of barbarism have produced it and formed it, and here it stands now as a consistent system whose principle is a *dehumanized world*. The most fully realized philistine world, our Germany, must naturally remain far behind the French Revolution, which restored man again; and a German Aristotle who would derive his political ideas from our situation would have to write at the head of his chapter: "Man is a social, yet a thoroughly unpolitical animal," but he could not explain the German state more correctly than Mr. Zöpfl,[1] author of *Constitutional Law in Germany*, has done already. According to him, Germany is a "union of families," which, to continue, belongs hereditarily and intrinsically to the most-high family, which is called dynasty. The more fertile the families show themselves to be, the more happy the people; the greater the state, the mightier the dynasty; hence in normally despotic Prussia a premium of fifty Reichstaler is paid for every seventh son.

The Germans are such prudent realists that all their desires and high-flown thoughts do not reach beyond a bare existence. This realism, and no more, is accepted by those who rule them. These rulers are realists too; they are far removed from all thought and all human greatness, being mere officers and landowning Junkers; but they are not mistaken in that, being what they are, they are thoroughly efficient in using and dominating this animal kingdom, for domination and usufruct form a single concept, here as elsewhere. And when they permit themselves to receive homage and look over the heads of these teeming brainless creatures, what is closer to their minds than Napoleon[2] on the Berezina River? It is recorded that when Napoleon looked at the swarm of drowning men in the river, he said to his companion: "*Voyez ces crapauds!*" ["Look at these toads!"] This remark is probably a lie, but it is nonetheless true. The only principle of despotism is contempt for man, dehumanized man, and this principle has the advantage over many others of being at the same time a fact. The despot always sees men as degraded. For him they are drowned before his eyes in the slime of abject existence, from which, like frogs, they too always reemerge. If men capable of great goals, as Napoleon was before his dynasty madness, can hold such a view, how can one expect an ordinary king to be an idealist under such conditions?

The general principle of monarchy is the despised, despicable *dehumanized man*; and Montesquieu[3] is very wrong in considering honor to be

---

10

1. Heinrich Maria Zöpfl (1807–1877), a German jurist.
2. Napoleon I.
3. Charles de Secondat, Baron de Montesquieu (1689–1755), French political philosopher.

the principle of monarchy. He makes distinctions among monarchy, despotism, and tyranny. But all these are names for only one idea; at most it is a behavioral difference within the same principle. Where the monarchical principle is in the majority, human beings are in the minority; where there is no doubt, there are no people. Why should a man like the King of Prussia, who has no proof of being a problem, not simply follow his whim? And when he does it, what is the result? Contradictory purposes? Good, so nothing comes of it. Impotent tendencies? They are, nevertheless, the only political reality. Disgraces and embarrassments? There is only one disgrace and one embarrassment, that of abdication. So long as the whim stays in its place, it is right. Be it ever so unstable, brainless, and contemptible, it is always good enough to govern a nation that has never had any other law than the despotism of its kings. I do not say that a brainless system and the loss of respect internally and externally will never have consequences; I do not take this assurance of a ship of fools upon myself. I do maintain, however, that the King of Prussia will remain a man of his time so long as the topsy-turvy world continues to be a reality.

You know, I occupy myself a lot with this man. Even at the time when he still made the *Berliner Politisches Wochenblatt* his organ, I recognized his worth and his destiny. When he took the oath at Königsberg he even then justified my conjecture that now the question would become purely a personal one. He declared himself heart and soul for the future basic laws of the Prussian domains, *his* state, and in reality in Prussia the King is the system. He is the only political person. His personality determines the system this way or that way. What he does or what one lets him do, what he thinks or what one puts in his mouth, in Prussia that is what the state thinks or does. Thus it is really a gain that the present King has declared all this plainly.

The only thing in which I erred for a time was the apparently exalted notion of what wishes and ideas the King needed for show. In fact, this did not matter, since the philistine is the material for the monarchy and the monarch is always only the king of the philistines; he cannot liberate either himself or his people, or make real men out of them, so long as both of them remain what they are.

The King of Prussia has tried to change the system with a theory his father[4] did not have. The fate of this effort is known. It completely miscarried. Naturally. When one arrives at the political animal world there is no further place to go, and no way to advance except by abandoning its basis and crossing over to the human world of democracy.

The old King wanted nothing extravagant; he was a philistine and made no pretense to intellectualism. He knew that the servile state and his posses-

4. Frederick William III, King of Prussia, 1797–1840.

sion of it needed only a prosaic, quiet existence. The young King was more lively and alert, and thought much more about the monarch's absolutism, which is limited only by his heart and his understanding. The old vassal, servant-and-slave state revolted him. He wanted to bring it to life but permeated entirely with his desires, feelings, and ideas; and he could demand this, in *his* state, if it was to succeed. Hence his liberal speeches and heartfelt outpourings. Not dead law, but the full living heart of the King was to rule all his subjects. He wanted to set all hearts and spirits in motion toward his heart's desire, his long-nourished plans. A movement followed; but the other hearts did not beat in unison with his, and the subjugated people could not open their mouths without speaking of the abolition of the old government. The idealists, who had the temerity to want to make men out of the people, seized the word, and while the King fantasized in Old German, they thought it desirable to philosophize in New German. For a moment the old order of things seemed to have been turned on its head; indeed, things began to transform themselves into men; there were, in fact, well-known men, although naming names is not permitted in the Assembly; but the servants of the old despotism soon put an end to this un-German activity. It was not difficult to bring the wishes of the King, who had dreamed of a past full of priests, knights, and retainers, into palpable conflict with the aims of the idealists who wanted simply the consequences of the French Revolution— that is, in the last analysis, a republic and a free human order instead of a dead one. When this conflict became sharp and uncomfortable and the irascible King grew sufficiently enraged, the servants, who had hitherto conducted things so easily, came to him and said: the King was not well advised to encourage his subjects to make useless speeches, for it would be impossible to govern a race of talking men. The lord[5] of all the rear-Russians also became disquieted over the movement in the heads of the fore-Russians and demanded the restoration of the old, quiet conditons. And the consequence was a new edition of the old contempt for all wishes and ideas of the men who desired human rights and duties, that is, a restoration of the old vassal servile state, in which the slave serves silently and the owner of the land and people rules as silently as possible through his well-trained and obedient servants. Neither side can say what it wishes, neither the ones who want to be men nor the other, who has no use for men in his country. Silence is therefore the only recourse. *Muta pecora, prona et ventri obedientia.*[6]

Such has been the unfortunate attempt to elevate the philistine state on its own base; it resulted in making despotism's need for brutality and the impossibility of humanness evident before the whole world. A brutal situa-

---

5. Nicholas I, Czar of Russia, which Marx ironically referred to as "rear-Russia," in contrast to Prussia (Latin: *Borussia*), which he called "fore-Russia."
6. The herd is mute, hangs its head, and is obedient to its stomach.

tion can be maintained only with brutality. And at this point I finish with our common task—to look the philistine and his state firmly in the eye.

You cannot say that I hold the present too high; and if I do not altogether despair, it is only because its own desperate condition fills me with hope. I am not referring at all to the inability of the masters and the indolence of the servants and subjects who let everything go as God pleases; and yet both together already suffice to bring about a catastrophe. I am only calling your attention to the fact that the enemies of philistinism—in short, all thinking and suffering people—have arrived at an understanding, for which previously they lacked the means, and that even the passive continuation of the old vassals brings daily recruits in the service of the new humanity. The system of industry and commerce, of property and the exploitation of people, leads, even more quickly than does an increase in the population, to a breach inside the present society, which the old system will not be able to heal because none of it either heals or produces, but only exists and enjoys. The existence of suffering humanity, which thinks, and of thinking humanity, which is oppressed, must, however necessarily become unusable and indigestible to the passive and brainlessly consuming animal world of philistinism.

From our side, the old world must be fully dragged into daylight and the new, positive one created. The longer the time that events allow for thinking humanity to ponder, and suffering humanity to assemble, the more completely will the product, which the present carries in its womb, enter the world.

Yours, K.M.

11

To Arnold Ruge (in Dresden)
Kreuznach, September, 1843

[No salutation]

I am pleased that you have decided to turn your thoughts from the past to undertake a new venture.[1] So be it in Paris, the ancient university of philosophy, *absit omen* [May it not be an ill omen]! and the new capital of the new world. Necessity finds a way. Hence I do not doubt that all obstacles, the gravity of which I do not ignore, will be overcome.

11

1. The publication of the *Deutsch-Französische Jahrbücher*, which Marx and Ruge had been discussing for some months.

Whether the undertaking comes to fruition or not, I will be in Paris at the end of this month,[2] since the atmosphere here enslaves and I see altogether no room in Germany for any free activity.

In Germany everything is suppressed violently; a true anarchy of spirit, a regime of stupidity itself, has broken out, and Zurich obeys the orders of Berlin. It is, therefore, ever more evident that one has to look for a new rallying point for the truly thinking and independent minds. I am convinced that our plan will correspond to the real needs, and the real needs must end in their fulfillment. Hence I have no doubt about the venture, if it is undertaken seriously.

The internal difficulties seem to be almost greater than the external obstacles. If there is no doubt about the "whence," there is the more confusion about the "whither." It is not only that a general anarchy has broken out among the reformers, but also that, as everybody would admit, none of them has an exact view as to what the future should be. Still, this is the advantage of the new direction, that we do not anticipate the world dogmatically but that we first try to discover the new world from a critique of the old one. Until now the philosophers have had the solution of all riddles lying on their lecterns, and the stupid exotic world only had to open its mouth for the ready-roasted pigeons of absolute knowledge to fly into its mouth. Philosophy has become secularized, and the striking proof thereof is that the philosophical consciousness itself has been pulled into the torment of struggle not only externally but also internally. If the construction and preparation of the future is not our business, then it is the more certain what we do have to consummate—I mean the *ruthless criticism of all that exists*, ruthless also in the sense that criticism does not fear its results and even less so a struggle with the existing powers.

I am, therefore, not in favor of planting a dogmatic flag; quite the contrary. We should try to help the dogmatists to clarify their ideas. Thus communism, in particular, is a dogmatic abstraction, and by this I do not mean some fanciful or possible communism, but the real, existing communism, as Cabet[3]. Dézamy,[4] Weitling,[5] etc., teach and conceive it. This communism is itself separate from the humanist principle, merely a phenomenon affected by its opposite, private existence. Hence abolition of private property and communism are by no means identical, and communism has

---

2. Marx moved to Paris at the end of October, 1843.
3. Étienne Cabet, (1788–1856), French utopian, author of *Voyage en Icarie* (1842).
4. Théodore Dézamy, (1803–1850), a French utopian communist.
5. Christian Wilhelm Weitling, (1808–1871), German utopian communist, rejected by Marx.

different doctrines from those of Fourier,[6] Proudhon,[7] etc., not accidentally, but necessarily in contradiction to them, because it is itself only a special, one-sided consummation of the socialist principle.

And the whole socialist principle is again only one aspect of *reality* as it affects the genuine human being. We have likewise to concern ourselves with the other aspect, the theoretical existence of man, that is, religion, science, etc., and make it the object of our criticism. In addition, we want to have an effect on our contemporaries, and especially our German contemporaries. One asks: How is one to achieve this? Two facts cannot be denied. First, religion, and then politics are the objects which constitute the main interest of present-day Germany. We must link up with these, but not to confront them with some ready-made system like the *Voyage en Icarie*.[8]

Reason has always existed, but not always in reasonable form. Hence the critic can choose any form of theoretical and practical consciousness and develop the true reality in its "ought" and in its final goal out of its *own* forms of existing reality. In regard to real life, the *political state*, even where it is not yet permeated with socialist demands, contains the demands of reason in all its *modern* forms. And it does not stop with that. Everywhere it subordinates reason to reality. But everywhere also it falls into the contradiction between its ideal destiny and its presuppositions.

Out of this conflict of the political state within itself, therefore, social truth can develop everywhere. Just as *religion* is the index to the theoretical struggles of mankind, so the *political state* is the index to its practical ones. Hence the political state expresses within its form *sub specie rei publicae* [as a special political form] all the social conflicts, needs, truths, etc. It is, therefore, definitely not under the *hauteur des principes* [height of principles] to make the most specialized political questions—say, the difference between an estate [*ständisch*] system and a representative one—the object of criticism. For this question expresses only in a *political* way the difference between government by the people and the rule of private property. Hence the critic not only can, but must enter into these political questions (which in the view of the crude socialists is beneath all dignity). In demonstrating the advantage of the representative system over the estate one, the critic *interests* a large party in a *practical* way. In raising the representative system out of its political form to a general form and validating the true significance which lies at its foundation,

---

6. François Marie Charles Fourier (1772–1837), French utopian socialist.
7. Pierre Joseph Proudhon (1809–1865), French social theorist; on Marx's later opinion of Proudhon, see Letter 18 to Annenkov, December 28, 1846; and Letter 129 to von Schweitzer, January 24, 1865.
8. By Étienne Cabet.

he forces that party to rise above itself, for its victory is at the same time its loss.

Hence nothing prevents us from tying in our criticism with a criticism of and participation in politics, that is, in *real* conflicts, and in identifying with them. Thus we do not confront the world dogmatically with a new principle, proclaiming: Here is the truth, here kneel before it! We develop for the world new principles out of the principles of the world. We do not say to the world: Give up your struggles, they are stupid stuff; we will provide you with the true watchword of the struggle. We merely demonstrate to the world why it really struggles, and consciousness is something that it *must* adopt, even if it does not want to do so.

The reform of consciousness consists *only* in making the world aware of its perception, waking it up from its own dream, *explaining* its own actions. Our whole purpose can consist of nothing else than in bringing out religious and political questions in self-aware human form, as did Feuerbach in his critique of religion.[9]

Our slogan must, therefore, be: Reform of consciousness, not through dogmas but through an analysis of the mystical consciousness which is unclear to itself, regardless whether it is religious or political. It will then be shown that the world has long possessed the dream of a thing, of which it only needs to have awareness in order to possess it in reality. It will be shown that what is involved is not a great stroke of thought between past and future, but a *consummation* of the ideas of the past. It will finally be shown that humanity begins no *new* task, but consciously consummates its old task.

Hence we can summarize the tendency of our paper in *one* word: Self-understanding (critical philosophy) of our epoch's struggles and desires. This is a task for the world and for us. It can only be the labor of combined forces. What is involved is a *confession*, and nothing else. In order to have its sins pardoned, mankind only needs to interpret them for what they are.

[Unsigned]

12

From letter to Ludwig Feuerbach (in Bruckberg)
Kreuznach, October 3, 1843

Highly Esteemed Sir!

A few months ago, in passing through your town [Bruckberg], Dr. Ruge informed you of our plan to publish French-German *Jahrbücher* [Annuals] and asked your cooperation. . . .

9. Ludwig Feuerbach, *Das Wesen des Christentums* [*The Essence of Christianity*] (Leipzig, 1841).

From your Preface to the second edition of the *Wesen des Christentums* I am justified in concluding that you are engaged in a comprehensive study of Schelling[1] or have something already prepared *in petto* [secretly] against this windbag. You see, this would be a spendid debut.

Schelling, as you know, is the 38th member of the [German] Confederation. The whole German police is at his disposal, as I know from my experience as editor of the *Rheinische Zeitung*. Hence the censorship cannot permit anything against [word missing] the holy Schelling. In Germany, therefore, it is practically impossible to attack Schelling in anything but in books of more than 21 sheets, and such books are not the books of the people. The work of Kapp[2] is very noteworthy but it is too detailed and is clumsy in its separation of judgment from fact. Furthermore, our governments have found means to make such works ineffectual. One is not permitted to discuss them. They are either ignored or are dismissed in a few contemptuous words by the licensed review institutions. The great Schelling himself pretends that he does not know anything about these attacks, and he has succeeded, through the fiscal noise over the broth of old Paulus,[3] in turning away attention from Kapp's work. That was a diplomatic master stroke!

But now think of Schelling in Paris, exposed before the French literary world! There his vanity will not permit him to remain silent, and the Prussian government will feel itself most painfully injured; it would amount to an attack on Schelling's sovereignty from abroad, and a vain monarch clings more to this sovereignty abroad than he does at home.

Cleverly, Schelling knew how to lure first the weak eclectic Cousin[4] and later the gifted Leroux. To Pierre Leroux[5] and his like, Schelling was the man who replaced transcendental idealism with sensible realism, abstract thought with ideas of flesh and blood, technical philosophy with world philosophy! To the French romantics and mystics he proclaimed: "I am the union of philosophy with theology"; to the French materialists: "I am the union of flesh and Ideal"; to the French skeptics: "I am the destroyer of dogmatism." In brief: "I [am] Schelling!"

Schelling knew how to unite not only philosophy and theology but also philosophy and diplomacy. He made philosophy into a general science of diplomacy, a diplomacy of everything. An attack on Schelling, therefore, is an indirect attack on our whole, and particularly Prussian, policy. Schelling's

---

12

1. Friedrick Wilhelm Joseph von Schelling (1775-1854), German Idealistic philosopher.
2. Friedrich Kapp (1824–1884), German historian, who emigrated to the United States in 1850.
3. Heinrick Eberhard Gottlob Paulus (1761-1851), German Protestant theologian.
4. Victor Cousin (1792-1867), French philosopher.
5. Pierre Leroux (1797–1871), French utopian socialist.

philosophy is Prussian policy *sub specie philosophiae* [in the light of philosophy].

Hence you would perform a great service for our undertaking, and even more for truth, if you would contribute to the very first issue a character study of Schelling. You are exactly the man to do it, because you are the antithesis of Schelling. The honest idea of Schelling's youth—we ought to believe in what is good in our opponent—for the realization of which he offered no material except his imagination, no energy except vanity, no motive force except opium, no organ except the irritability of feminine receptivity—this honest idea of Schelling's youth, which has remained with him as a fantastic youthful dream, has become for you the truth, the reality, the seriousness of manhood. Hence Schelling is your anticipated caricature, and the moment it confronts reality it must vanish in mist and fog. I consider you, therefore, the necessary, the natural and, through your majesty, nature and history, the destined enemy of Schelling. Your conflict with him is the conflict of imagination with philosophy itself.

I expect with assurance a contribution from you at your convenience.[6] My address is: "Herr Mäurer, rue Vaneau No. 23, Paris, attention Dr. Marx." My wife sends her regards without knowing you. You would hardly believe how many followers you have among the weaker sex.

Yours entirely, Dr. Marx

13

To Ludwig Feuerbach (in Bruckberg)
Paris, 38 Rue Vaneau, August 11, 1844

Esteemed Sir:

Since I have this opportunity, I take the liberty of sending you an article of mine in which certain elements of my critical philosophy of law[1]—which I had finished once but rewrote to make it comprehensible to the general public—are indicated. I do not place any special value on this article, but I am pleased to find a chance to be able to assure you of the distinguished respect and—excuse the word—love that I have for you. Your *Philosophie der*

---

6. On October 25, 1843, Feuerbach wrote Marx a letter declining to contribute to the *Deutsch-Französische Jahrbücher*.

13

1. "Toward the Critique of Hegel's Philosophy of Law. Introduction," in *Deutsch-Französische Jahrbücher, 1844.*

Zukunft[2] and the *Wesen des Glaubens*,[3] despite their limited scope, are, at any rate, of more weight than all the present day German literature put together.

In these books—I do not know whether intentionally or not—you have given socialism a philosophical foundation, and the communists too have understood these works in the same way. The unity of man with man, which is also rooted in the actual difference among men, the concept of the human species, pulled down from the heaven of abstraction to the real earth—what else is this than a *societal* concept!

Two translations of your *Wesen des Christentums*,[4] one in English and one in French, are being prepared and are practically ready for the printer. The former will appear in Manchester (Engels has supervised it), the latter in Paris (a Frenchman, Dr. Guerrier, and a German communist, Ewerbeck, have translated it with the help of a French stylist).[5]

At this particular time the French will immediately pounce on the book, for both parties—parsons and Voltaireans and materialists—are looking for outside help. It is a remarkable phenomenon that, in contrast to the eighteenth century, religiosity has descended on the middle and upper classes, while irreligiosity—but an irreligiosity of men sensing their humanness—has reached the French proletariat. You would have to attend one of the meetings of the French *ouvriers* [workers] to be able to realize the virginal freshness and nobility that is generated among these workingmen. The English proletarian also makes giant steps, but he lacks the cultural character of the French. But I must not forget to mention the theoretical services of the German artisans in Switzerland, London, and Paris. The only thing is that the German artisan is still too much an artisan.

At any rate, history is preparing among these "barbarians" of our civilized society the practical element for the emancipation of humanity.

The contrast between the French character and that of us Germans has never struck me so sharply and strikingly as in the Fourierist book,[6] which begins with the following sentences: *"L'homme est tout entier dans ses passions."* *"Avez-vous jamais rencontré un homme qui pensât pour penser, qui se ressouvint pour*

---

2. Feuerbach, *Grundsätze der Philosophie der Zukunft* [*Principles of the Philosophy of the Future*] (Zurich and Winterthur, 1843).

3. Feuerbach, *Das Wesen des Glaubens im Sinne Luther's. Ein Beitrag zum "Wesen des Christentums"* [*The Essence of Faith in Luther's Sense. A Contribution to the "Essence of Christianity"*] (Leipzig, 1844).

4. Feuerbach, *The Essence of Christianity* (Leipzig, 1841). It was translated into English by the novelist George Eliot under the title *The Essence of Religion* (London, 1853). The Engels-supervised translation to which Marx refers was never published.

5. August Hermann Ewerbeck, *Qu'est ce que la religion d'après la nouvelle philosophie allemande* (Paris, 1850).

6. E. de Pompery, *Exposition de la science social, constitutée par C. Fourier* [*Exposition of Social Science, as Constituted by C. Fourier*], 2d ed. (Paris, 1840).

se ressouvenir, qui imaginât pour imaginer? qui voulait pour vouloir? cela vous est-il jamais arrivé à vous même? ... Non, évidemment non!"[7]

The main motive force of nature, as of society, is therefore the *magical*, the *passionate*, the *nonreflecting attraction*, and "*tout être, homme, plante, animal, ou globe, a reçu une somme des forces en rapport avec sa mission dans l'ordre universel.*"[8]

From this it follows: "*Les attractions sont proportionnelles aux destinées.*"[9]

Do not all these sentences seem as if the Frenchman had deliberately contrasted his passion for the *actus purus* [pure act] to the German kind of thinking? One does not think in order to think, etc.

How difficult it is for the German to emerge from the one-sidedness contrasted above has been given new evidence by my friend of many years—but now somewhat estranged—Bruno Bauer, in his critical Berlin *Literatur-Zeitung*.[10] I do not know whether you have seen it. There is much unspoken polemic against you in it.

The character of the *Literatur-Zeitung* can be reduced to this: "Criticism" is transformed into a transcendental essence. Those Berliners do not behave like *human beings* who *criticize* but like *critics* who happen to have the misfortune of being human. Thus they recognize only one real need, the need for theoretical criticism. They reproach people like Proudhon, therefore, for taking their point of departure from a "practical need." This kind of criticism devolves into a sad and supercilious spiritualism. Consciousness or self-consciousness is regarded by it as the *sole* human quality. Love, for example, is denied, because in it the beloved is merely an "object." *À bas* [down] with the object! Hence this criticism considers itself as the only *active* element in history. It views all of humanity as a *mass*, a sluggish mass that has value only as a contrast to the spirit. Thus in a critic the highest crime is *mind* or *passion*; he must, instead, be an ironic, ice-cold σοφός [guide].

Thus Bauer states *literally*: "The critic participates neither in the sufferings nor in the joys of society; he knows neither friendship nor love, neither hatred nor envy; he reigns in solitude, where now and again the laughter of the Olympian gods over the perversity of the world rings from his lips."

The tone of Bauer's *Literatur-Zeitung* is therefore a tone of passionless *contempt*, and he makes this the more facile in that he turns upside down your findings and contemporary findings in general. He discovers only contradic-

---

7. "Man is revealed in his passions." "Have you ever encountered a man who thought for the sake of thinking, who remembered for the sake of remembering, who imagined for the sake of imagining, who wished for the sake of wishing? Did this ever happen to you personally? ... No, obviously no!"
8. "Every being, man, plant, animal, or the globe, has received a sum of forces corresponding to its mission in the universal order."
9. "The forces of attraction are proportional to their destinies."
10. *Allgemeine Literatur-Zeitung* [General Literary Journal], a monthly which Bauer published in Charlottenburg from December, 1843, to October, 1844.

tions, and, satisfied with this business, he leaves it with a contemptuous "Hm." He states that criticism is not in *vogue*, it is much too spiritual for that. Yes, he expresses the hope that: "the time is not far distant when all of decadent humanity will assemble before the critique" —and "the critique" is Himself and Company— "it will separate this mass into various groups and hand out to all of them the *testimonium paupertatis* [pauper's certificate]."

It seems Bauer fought against Christ out of rivalry. I intend to publish a small brochure against this aberration of criticism.[11] It would be of the *highest* value to me if you would let me know *your* opinion, and in general a prompt sign of life from you would make me happy. This summer, twice weekly, the German artisans here—that is, the communist element among them, several hundred of them—have heard lectures on your *Essence of Christianity* by their secret chiefs,[12] and have shown themselves to be remarkably receptive. The short excerpt from a letter by a German lady in a feuilleton in No. 64 of *Vorwärts!*[13] was part of a letter from my wife, who is visiting her mother in Trier, and has been published without the author's knowledge.[14]

With best wishes for your well-being,

Yours, Karl Marx

14

To Heinrich Heine (in Paris)
Paris, January 12, 1845

Dear Friend:

I hope to have time yet tomorrow to see you. My departure takes place on Monday [January 13].[1]

The bookdealer Leske[2] has just visited me. He is publishing a censorship-free quarterly[3] in Darmstadt. I, Engels, Hess,[4] Herwegh, [Georg] Jung,

---

11. *The Holy Family*, a 220-page book (not a "small brochure"), which Marx wrote in collaboration with Engels, and which was published in Frankfurt in 1845.
12. Of the League of the Just, a communist group organized in 1836–38. In 1846 it was succeeded by the Communist League.
13. *Vorwärts!* was a German-language publication that appeared in Paris twice a week. Marx was one of its contributors.
14. On August 10, 1844, *Vorwärts!* published anonymous excerpts from a letter of Jenny Marx to her husband.

14

1. Marx, expelled from France, did not leave Paris until February 3.
2. Karl Wilhelm Leske, a bookdealer and publisher in Darmstadt.
3. *Rheinische Jahrbücher zur Gesellschaftlichen Reform*, an annual of which only two volumes appeared, in Darmstadt in 1845, and near Constance, Switzerland, in 1846.
4. Moses Hess (1812–1875), German democratic socialist thinker, living in Paris.

etc. are contributing. He begged me to intercede for your collaboration—poetry or prose. You will certainly not turn this down, since we must use every opportunity to colonize ourselves in German.

Of all the people I am leaving behind me here, leaving Heine is for me the most unpleasant. I would gladly include you in my packing. My wife and I send our regards to you and your wife.

Yours, K.M.

COMMUNISM
Brussels and Cologne · *1845-1849*

Marx spent three years in Brussels, the first stage in what was to be a life of permanent exile. It was for him a fruitful period. In Brussels, he was instrumental in organizing a communist correspondence committee and in developing communist tactics and policies. He was also productive as a writer. He and Engels collaborated on *The Holy Family* (1845) and on *The German Ideology*, which did not come out until 1932. Marx also wrote, in French, his first book by himself: *La Misère de la Philosophie* [*The Poverty of Philosophy*] (1847), a polemic against Pierre Joseph Proudhon.[1] It was in Brussels that Marx and Engels (mostly Marx) wrote their famous pamphlet, *The Manifesto of the Communist Party*, published in German, in London (February, 1848).

At the outbreak of the European revolutions in 1848, Marx returned to Cologne, where, with the help of Engels and other communists, he published the *Neue Rheinische Zeitung*. It appeared from June 1, 1848, to May 19, 1849. Expelled from Germany, Marx went to Paris early in June, but was soon expelled from there too. Europe was closed to him, as it was to other radicals. On August 24, 1849, he moved to London. His pregnant wife and their three

---

1. For Marx criticism of Proudhon, see letters 18 and 129.

children joined him there on September 17. Marx spent the rest of his life as an exile in London.

15

To Heinrich Heine (in Paris)
Brussels, March 24, 1845

Dear Heine:

Owing to a mass of custom-house worries, you must excuse me that I write only a few lines today.

Püttmann[1] in Cologne has requested me to ask you to send in a few poems (perhaps also your German Fleet[2]) for the censorship-free *Jahrbuch*[3] in Darmstadt. You can send the thing to me. The deadline is three weeks.

My wife sends warm greets to you and your consort. The day before yesterday I went to the *Sûreté Publique* [Police Administration], where I had to declare in writing to publish nothing in Belgium on contemporary politics.

Renouard[4] and Börnstein[5] have printed your "*Wintermärchen*" [*Winter Fairy Tale*] in Paris, datelined New York, and sell it here in Brussels. In addition, this reproduction is said to swarm with misprints. More next time.

Yours, K.M.

16

To Heinrich Heine (in Paris)
Brussels, c. April 5, 1846

My dear Heine:

I am taking advantage of the transit of the man carrying this letter, Herr Annenkov,[1] a very amiable and educated Russian, to send you my best regards.

15

1. Hermann Püttmann (1811–1894), a socialist poet and journalist.
2. Heine, "*Unsere Marine. Ein nautisches Gedicht*" ["Our Fleet. A Nautical Poem"].
3. *Rheinische Jahrbücher.*
4. Jules Renouard, a French publisher.
5. Heinrich Börnstein (1805–1892), German editor in Paris.

16

1. Pavel Vassilyevich Annenkov (1812–1887), liberal Russian writer and landowner, friend of Marx when abroad.

A few days ago I accidentally came across a small libel against you—in the letters Börne[2] left behind[3]. I would never have thought him so tedious, petty and tasteless if I had not seen it black on white. And what wretched rubbish the whole postscript by Gutzkow[4], etc., is. I will write in a German journal an extensive critique of your book on Börne.[5] A more loutish treatment than this book has received from the Christian-German jackasses is hardly to be found in any period of literature, and still no German period lacks in loutishness.

If perhaps you have anything "special" to report about your writing, do it quickly.

Yours, K. Marx

17

Draft of letter to Karl Wilhelm Leske (in Darmstadt) Brussels, August 1, 1846

Dear Sir:

I am replying, by return mail, to your letter concerning doubts about the publication.[1] In regard to your question as to being "scientific," I answer: The book is scientific, but not scientific in the sense of the Prussian government, etc. If you recall your first letter, you will remember your great anxiety about the Prussian admonition and police investigation, which in fact have just now happened to you. I then wrote you immediately that I would look around for another publisher.

I received a second letter from you which on the one hand cancelled the publication and, on the other, agreed to the repayment of the advance by another publisher.

You received no reply, because I thought I would be able to give you positive information about another publisher in a short time. How this dragged out, you will now learn. That I accepted your proposal of the repayment of the advance is self-evident, as you can see from the fact that

---

2. Karl Ludwig Börne (1786–1837), German journalist and critic.
3. *Ludwig Börne's Urteil über H. Heine. Ungedruckte Stellen aus den Pariser Briefen* [*Ludwig Börne's Judgment of H. Heine. Unpublished Selections from the Paris Letters*] (Frankfurt, 1840).
4. Karl Ferdinand Gutzkow (1811–1878), young German Hegelian editor and dramatist.
5. *Heinrich Heine über Ludwig Börne* [*Heinrich Heine on Ludwig Börne*] (Hamburg, 1840).

17

1. On March 31, 1846, Marx, in a letter to Leske, a publisher, agreed to prepare a book, *Critique of Politics and National Economy*. On July 29, 1846, Leske wrote to Marx about his doubts concerning the proposed book.

where I did take steps with another publisher I told him immediately to pay you the 1,500 francs at his acceptance of the manuscript. Proof of this can be made at any time. Furthermore, Engels[2] and Hess are witnesses.

Moreover, you will recall that in Paris as well as in the written contract[3] nothing was said about the more or less revolutionary form of my work, but on the contrary I then meant to issue both volumes simultaneously, because if the *first* volume were banned or confiscated it would affect the second one. Heinrich Bürgers of Cologne was present and can testify. *Legally* speaking, therefore, you were not *entitled* to make new conditions or to abrogate the contract, just as I, on my part, am not compelled, from a *legal* standpoint, to repay the advance or to agree to your new proposals, or to modify my work. That I would not for a moment think of taking a *legal* position, particularly since you were not contractually bound to pay me an advance which I had to consider, and did consider, as an act of *pure friendship*, all this requires no discussion. No matter how often I have hitherto absolved bookdealers (for example, Wigand and Fröbel[4] in connection with the *Deutsch-Französische Jahrbücher*, and other publishers, as you will presently hear) from their legally enforcible obligations, despite great pecuniary loss to myself, it has *never* occurred to me to make any publisher lose a penny, even if I could do it *legally*. That I should make an exception in your case, when you had done me a special favor, is absolutely inconceivable.

In regard to my delayed reply, the following:

Some capitalists in Germany have accepted the idea of publishing several works by me, Engels, and Hess.[5] There was even the prospect of an extensive, formal publishing house, free of all police considerations. Through a friend of the gentlemen,[6] the publication of my *Critique of the Economy*, etc., was, moreover, as good as assured. The same friend stayed in Brussels until May, in order that the manuscript of the first volume by me and Engels[7] be taken safely across the border. Once back in Germany, he was to write definitely about the acceptance or nonacceptance of the *National Economy*. But no news, or uncertain news, came, and after most of the manuscript of the second volume was already sent to Germany, those gentlemen finally wrote recently that owing to their capital being invested elsewhere, the whole history of a publishing house came to *nothing*. A definite reply to you was

---

2. Frederick Engels (1820–1895), Marx's lifelong friend and collaborator.

3. Marx signed a book contract with Leske in Paris, February 1, 1845.

4. Julius Fröbel (1805–1893) a German journalist and publisher.

5. In May, 1846, through the intermediary Joseph Weydemeyer, Marx negotiated with the Westphalian businessmen, Julius Meyer and Rudolf Rempel, for the publication of *The German Ideology* and other communist works.

6. Joseph Weydemeyer (1818–1866), German communist, emigrated to the United States, where he served as colonel in the Union Army during the Civil War.

7. *The German Ideology* (which never did find a publisher in Germany).

thus postponed. After everything was decided, I arranged with a Herr Pirscher from Darmstadt, who was here, to take over a letter to you.

In the discussion with the German capitalists about the publication of the *Economy*, I exposed its plan. For it had seemed to me to be very important to come forth with a polemical work of my positive ideas against the German philosophy and the prevailing German socialism. This is necessary, in order to prepare the public for the viewpoint of my economics, which is directly opposite to the German scholarship existing hitherto. This is, moreover, the same polemical work about which I have already written you in one of my letters and which has to be finished before the publication of the *Economics*.

So much for that.

To your present letter I reply as follows:

I. In case you do not publish the book, I declare that it is self-evident that your advance is to be returned in the manner indicated by you.

But it is equally self-evident that if I should receive from another publisher less than the honorarium you and I had agreed upon, you as well as I should share in the loss, since it was you, and not I, who made me take recourse to another publisher.

II. There has opened a possibility of publication of my book. The day before yesterday I received a letter from Germany informing me of the prospect of establishing a joint-stock company for communist writings, to open with mine. But I consider the matter as still so indefinite that I will necessarily approach other publishers.

III. Since the completed manuscript of the first volume of my book has been lying around for such a long time, I will not let it be published until I have gone over it factually and stylistically. It is self-evident that a working author cannot permit the *literal* publication of anything he had written six months ago.

In addition, the *Physiocrats* in two folio volumes has appeared only at the end of July and will arrive here in a few days, although its publication had been announced while I was still in Paris. The work must now be thoroughly looked into.

My book will be so revised that it could be published even by *your* firm. After having looked over the manuscript, you are of course free to have it brought out by another firm.

IV. As for time, the following:

On account of my seriously affected health, I am obliged to spend the month of August at the Ostend seashore, in addition to being busy with the above-mentioned two volumes. Hence nothing much can occur during August.

The revision of the first volume will be ready for printing at the end of November. The second volume, which is more historical, will follow quickly.

V. I have already written you in a previous letter that, partly due to new material acquired in England[8] and partly to the needs of the manuscript as became clear during the revision, it will be twenty printers' sheets larger than was originally agreed upon.

Once the contract had been concluded, I was determined, as you will recall from a previous letter, to dispense with an addition to the agreed upon advance as a result of the increase of the manuscript by about one-third. It would have harmed the book if I had published the new material separately. I did not for a moment take the position of giving the book a commercial disadvantage. I wanted neither to break the contract nor harm the effect of the book.

But since, according to your letter, the resumption of the contract is laid at my doorstep, I must add the one new condition, that the additional printers' sheets be paid for proportionately. I believe that this demand is less expensive than what I spent on my trip to and stay in England and than what I would have spent by acquiring costly and numerous literature for my book.

Finally, if we can settle some reasonable conditions, I wish that my book would appear in your publishing house, as you have shown yourself liberal and amicable toward me throughout.

If necessary, I could prove to you with numerous letters from Germany and France that the public awaits the book with great excitement.

Your devoted Dr. Marx

I beg you to write me *immediately*[9] at the address: at M. Lannoy. Au Bois Sauvage, Plaine St. Gudule No. 12, Brussels.

18

To Pavel Vassilyevich Annenkov (in Paris) [in French]
Brussels, December 28, 1846

Dear Mr. Annenkov:

You would have received my answer to your letter of November 1[1] long ago but for the fact that my bookseller sent me Mr. Proudhon's book, *The Philoso-*

---

8. During Marx's first trip to England, which he took with Engels in July–August, 1845, he studied economics in the Manchester public library.

9. Nearly seven weeks later, on September 19, 1846, Leske informed Marx that, owing to Prussian police persecutions, he could not publish his book. Marx found no German publisher for his work for more than a dozen years: in June, 1859, the Berlin publisher, Franz Duncker, brought out Marx's *Critique of Political Economy*, his first book on economics.

18

1. On November 1, 1846, Annenkov wrote to Marx about Proudhon's book: "I admit to you that even the plan of the work appears to me to be a witticism showing a morsel of German philosophy, rather than something naturally produced by the subject and the necessities of logical development."

phy of Poverty,[2] only last week. I have gone through it in two days in order to be able to give you my opinion at once. Since I have read it very rapidly, I cannot go into details but give you only the general impression it has made on me. If you wish, I could go into details in a second letter.

I must confess to you frankly that I find the book on the whole bad, very bad. You yourself in your letter make fun of the "morsel of German philosophy" which Mr. Proudhon parades in his formless and pretentious work, but you assume that the economic statement has not been infected by the philosophic poison. I, too, am far from imputing the faults in the economic argument to Mr. Proudhon's philosophy. Mr. Proudhon does not give us a false criticism of political economy because he possesses a ridiculous philosophy, but he gives us a ridiculous philosophy because he fails to understand the present social conditions in their concatenation [*engrènement*]—to use a word which, like much else, Mr. Proudhon has borrowed from Fourier.

Why does Mr. Proudhon speak about God, about universal reason, about the impersonal reason of mankind which never deceives itself, which always remains the same, of which one need only to be correctly aware in order to discover truth? Why does he play with feeble Hegelianism, to pose as a bold mind?

He himself gives you the clue to this enigma. Mr. Proudhon sees in history a certain series of social developments; he finds progress realized in history; he finds, finally, that men, as individuals, did not know what they were doing, that they were deluded about their own movement, that is to say, that their social development appears at first glance a thing distinct, separate, independent of their individual development. He cannot explain these facts, and the hypothesis of a manifest universal reason is pure invention. Nothing is easier than to invent mystical causes, that is, phrases that lack common sense.

But when Mr. Proudhon, in confessing that he understands nothing of the historical development of humanity—and he admits this by using such high-sounding words as universal reason, God, etc.—does he not implicitly and necessarily admit that he is incapable of understanding *economic development*?

What is society, whatever its form may be? The product of men's reciprocal activities. Are men free to choose this or that form of society? Not at all. Presuppose a particular state of development of men's faculties, and you will have a corresponding form of commerce and consumption. Presuppose a certain stage of development of production, commerce, and consumption, and you will have a corresponding form of social constitution, a corresponding organization of the family, orders or classes, in a word, a corresponding civil society. Presuppose such a civil society, and you will have a corresponding political state, which is but the official expression of civil society. This is

---

2. Proudhon, *Système des Contradictions Économiques, ou Philosophie de la Misère* (Paris, 1846).

what Mr. Proudhon will never understand, for he believes he is doing something great when he appeals from the State to the civil society, that is, from the official resumé of society to official society.

It is not necessary to add that men are not free arbiters of *their productive forces*—which are the basis of their whole history—for all productive force is an acquired force, the product of antecedent activity. Thus the productive forces are the result of men's practical energy, but this energy is itself circumscribed by the conditions in which men find themselves, by the productive forces already acquired, by the social form which existed before them, which they do not create, which is the product of the antecedent generation. Thanks to the simple fact that each succeeding generation finds the productive forces acquired by the preceding generation, which serve it as the raw material for new production, there arises a connection in human history, a history of humanity, which is the more the history of humanity as men's productive forces and, in consequence, their social connections, have grown. The necessary consequence: the social history of men is never anything but the history of their individual development, whether they are conscious of it or not. Their material relationships form the base of all their relationships. These material relationships are only the necessary forms in which their material and individual activity is realized.

Mr. Proudhon confuses ideas with things. Men never relinquish what they have won, but this does not mean that they never relinquish the social form in which they acquired particular productive forces. Quite the contrary. In order not to lose the result obtained, in order not to lose the fruits of civilization, men are forced, the moment the mode of their *commerce* [intercourse] no longer corresponds to the acquired productive forces, to change all their traditional social forms. (I use here the word *commerce* in the most general sense, as we say it in German: *Verkehr*.) For example, privileges, the institutions of guilds and corporations, the regulatory regime of the Middle Ages, were social relationships which only corresponded to the acquired productive forces and to the preexisting social state, out of which these institutions arose. Under the protection of the corporate and regulatory regime, capital was accumulated, overseas commerce was developed, colonies were founded—and men would have forfeited these fruits if they had wanted to retain the forms under whose protection these fruits had ripened. Thus there came two thunderbolts, the Revolutions of 1640 and of 1688. All the old economic forms, the social relationships which correspond to them, the political state which was the official expression of the old civil society, were shattered in England. Thus the economic forms under which men produce, consume, exchange, are *transitory* and *historical*. With the acquisition of new productive faculties, men change their mode of production; and with the mode of production, they change all the economic connections, which had been but the relationships necessary for that particular mode of production.

This is what Mr. Proudhon has not understood, still less demonstrated. Mr. Proudhon, incapable of following the real movement of history, gives you a phantasmagoria which has the presumption of being a dialectical phantasmagoria. He feels no need to speak of the seventeenth, eighteenth, and nineteenth centuries, for his history takes place in the nebulous milieu of the imagination and rises high above time and place. In a word, it is Hegelian rubbish [*vieillerie*], it is not history; it is not profane history—history of men—it is sacred history—history of ideas. From his viewpoint, man is but an instrument of which the Idea or eternal reason makes use, in order to develop itself. The *evolutions* of which Mr. Proudhon speaks are understood to be evolutions such as occur in the mystical bosom of the absolute Idea. If you tear the veil from this mystical language, what it comes down to is that Mr. Proudhon is giving you the order in which economic categories arrange themselves inside his own head. It will not require great effort on my part to prove to you that this arrangement is one of a very disordered head.

Mr. Proudhon starts his book with a dissertation on *value*, which is his *dada* [hobbyhorse]. I will not, this time, enter into an examination of this dissertation.

The series of the economic evolutions of the eternal reason begin with the *division of labor*. To Mr. Proudhon, the division of labor is a perfectly simple thing. But the regime of castes, was it not also a certain division of labor? Was not the regime of the corporations another division of labor? And the division of labor of the manufacturing regime, which begins in England in the middle of the seventeenth century and ends in the latter part of the eighteenth, is it not also totally different from the division of labor in large-scale, modern industry?

Mr. Proudhon finds himself so far from the truth that he neglects what even the profane economists attend to. When he talks about the division of labor, he does not feel it necessary to speak about the world *market*. Oh, well! But must not the division of labor have been basically different in the fourteenth and fifteenth centuries, when there were as yet no colonies, when America did not yet exist for Europe, when Eastern Asia existed only for her through the intermediacy of Constantinople, from the division of labor of the seventeenth century, when colonies were already developed?

That is not all. All the internal organizations of nations, all their international relationships, are they anything other than the expression of a certain division of labor? And must not these change with the change in the division of labor?

Mr. Proudhon has so little understood the question of the division of labor that he does not even speak of the separation of town and country, which, in Germany, for example, took place from the ninth to the twelfth centuries. Hence for Mr. Proudhon, this separation becomes an eternal law, since he knows neither its origin nor its development. All through his book, he speaks as if this creation of a particular mode of production would last until the end of time. Everything that Mr. Proudhon says on the division of labor is only a summary, and, moreover, a very superficial and very incomplete summary of what Adam Smith and a thousand others have said before him.

The second evolution is *machinery*. To Mr. Proudhon, the connection between the division of labor and machines is entirely mystical. Each kind of the division of labor had its specific instruments of production. For example, from the middle of the seventeenth to the middle of the eighteenth century, men did not do everything by hand. They possessed instruments, and very complicated instruments, such as looms, ships, levers, etc., etc.

Thus, nothing is more ridiculous than to derive machines from the division of labor in general.

I say to you again in passing that as Mr. Proudhon has not understood the historic origin of machinery, he has still less understood its development. You can say that up to the year 1825—the period of the first general crisis—the general demands of consumption increased more rapidly than production, and the development of machinery was the necessary consequence of the needs of the market. Since 1825, the invention and application of machinery have been merely the result of the war between employers and workers. And this is only true of England. As for the European nations, they were compelled to adopt machines because of English competition, both in their home markets and on the world market. Finally, in North America, the introduction of machinery was brought about both by the competition with other countries and by the scarcity of hands, that is to say, by the disproportion between the population and the industrial needs of North America. From these facts, you can conclude what sagacity Mr. Proudhon develops in conjuring up the phantom of competition as the third evolution, as the antithesis of machinery.

Finally, in general, it is a real absurdity to make *machinery* an economic category alongside the division of labor, competition, credit, etc.

Machinery is no more an economic category than the ox that pulls the plow. The actual application of machines is one of the relationships of our current economic regime, but the mode of utilizing the machines is altogether distinct from the machines themselves. Powder remains the same, whether you use it for wounding a man or to dress his wounds.

Mr. Proudhon surpasses himself when he allows competition, monopoly, taxes or police, the balance of trade, credit, and property to develop inside his head in the order that I quote. Nearly all institutions of credit were developed in England in the beginning of the eighteenth century, before the invention of machines. Public credit was only a new method of increasing taxes, of satisfying the new demands created by the advent of the bourgeois class to power. Finally, *property* constitutes the last category in Mr. Proudhon's system. In the real world, on the contrary, the division of labor and all of Mr. Proudhon's other categories are social relationships, all together forming what one today calls *property*. Outside of these relationships, bourgeois property is nothing but a metaphysical and juristic illusion. The property of a different epoch, feudal property, developed in a series of entirely different social relationships. Mr. Proudhon, in establishing property as an independent relationship, commits more than a mistake in method: he proves clearly that he has not grasped the bond that holds together all the forms of *bourgeois* production, that he has not understood the *historic* and *transitory* character of the forms of production in a particular epoch. Mr. Proudhon, who does not see historical products in our social institutions, who understands neither their origin nor their development, can only make dogmatic criticism of them.

Mr. Proudhon is also obliged to take recourse to a *fiction* to explain developments. He imagines that the division of labor, credit, machinery, etc., were all invented to serve his fixed idea, the idea of equality. His explication is of a sublime naïveté. These things have been invented for equality, but unfortunately they turned against equality. This constitutes his whole argument. That is to say, he makes a gratuitous assumption, and then, because the actual development and his fiction contradict each other at every step, he concludes that there is a contradiction. He conceals from you the fact there is a contradiction only between his fixed ideas and the real movement.

Thus Mr. Proudhon, primarily because he lacks historical knowledge, has not perceived that men, as they develop their productive faculties, that is to say, as they live, develop certain relationships among themselves, and that the nature of these relationships must necessarily change with the modification and growth of these productive faculties. He has not perceived that the *economic categories* are only abstractions of these actual relationships, that they remain true only while these relationships exist. Thus he falls into the error of the bourgeois economists who regard these economic categories as eternal laws and not as historic laws which are only laws for a particular historic development, for a development determined by the productive forces. Thus, instead of considering the economic-political categories as abstractions made out of the actual, transitory, and historic social relationships, Mr. Proudhon, by a mystical inversion, sees in the actual relationships only the incarnations of these abstractions. These abstractions themselves are formulas that have been slumbering in the bosom of God the Father since the beginning of the world.

But here the good Mr. Proudhon falls into large intellectual convulsions. If all these economic categories are the emanations from the heart of God, if they are the hidden and eternal life of men, how comes it that, first, there is development, and secondly, that Mr. Proudhon is not a conservative? He explains to you these obvious contradictions by a whole system of antagonism.

To elucidate this system of antagonism, let us take an example.

Monopoly is good, because it is an economic category, and hence an emanation from God. Competition is good, because it, too, is an economic category. But what is not good is the reality of monopoly and the reality of competition. What is still worse is that monopoly and competition mutually devour each other. What is to be done? Because these two eternal ideas of God contradict each other, it seems obvious to him that in the bosom of God there is equally a synthesis between these two ideas, in which the evils of monopoly are balanced by competition, and vice versa. The effect of the struggle is that the good side comes out. One must extort this secret idea from God, then apply it, and everything will be for the best; one must reveal the synthetic formula hidden in the darkness of the impersonal reason of humanity. Mr. Proudhon does not hesitate for a moment to make himself the revealer.

But look for a moment at real life. In the present economic life you find not only competition and monopoly but also their synthesis, which is not a *formula* but a *movement*. Monopoly produces competition, competition produces monopoly. This equation, however, far from removing the difficulties of the present situation, as the bourgeois economists imagine, results in a situation still more difficult and more embroiled. Thus, in changing the foundation on which present-day economic relationships are based, and in destroying the present-day *mode* of production, you destroy not only competition, monopoly, and their antagonism, but also their unity, their synthesis, the movement which is the real equilibrium of competition and monopoly.

Now I will give you an example of Mr. Proudhon's dialectic.

Liberty and *slavery* constitute an antagonism. I need speak neither of the good nor of the bad sides of liberty. As for slavery, I need not speak of its bad side. The only thing that has to be explained is the good side of slavery. We are not dealing here with indirect slavery, the slavery of the proletariat; we are dealing with direct slavery, the slavery of the blacks in Surinam, in Brazil, in the southern states of North America.

Direct slavery is the pivot of our industrialism today as much as machinery, credit, etc. Without slavery, you have no cotton, without cotton you have no modern industry. It is slavery that has given value to the colonies; it was the colonies that created world trade; it is world trade that is the necessary condition for large-scale machine industry. Also, before the slave-trade in Negroes, the colonies supplied the Old World with but very few products and did not visibly change the face of the earth. Slavery is thus an economic category of the highest importance. Without slavery, North America, the most progressive country, would be transformed into a patriarchal land. You have only to erase North America from the map of nations, and you will have anarchy, the total decay of commerce and of modern civilization. But to let slavery disappear, is to erase North America from the map of nations. And thus slavery, because it is an economic category, is found among all nations since the world began. Modern nations have known how to disguise the slavery in their own countries and how to import it openly into the New World. After these reflections on slavery, what will be the good Mr. Proudhon's attitude? He will search for the synthesis of liberty and slavery, the golden mean, or the equilibrium between slavery and liberty.

Mr. Proudhon has very well understood that men produce cloth, linen, silks, and it is a great merit that he has understood that little! What Mr. Proudhon has not understood is that men, according to their faculties, also produce the *social relationships* in which they produce the cloth and the linen. Still less has he understood that men, who produce social relationships in conformity with their material method of production, also produce *ideas* and *categories*, that is to say, the abstract, ideal expressions of these same social relationships. Thus the categories are no more eternal than the relationships which they express. They are historic and transitory products. For Mr. Proudhon, on the contrary, the abstractions and categories are the primordial cause. According to him, it is they, and not men, who make history. The *abstraction, the category taken as such*, that is to say, separated from men and from their material activities, is of course immortal, unalterable, unmoved; it is only a Being of pure reason, which is merely another way of saying that abstraction taken as such is abstract—an admirable tautology!

Thus, economic relationships, regarded as categories, are for Mr. Proudhon eternal formulas, which have neither origin nor progression.

Let us put it in another way: Mr. Proudhon does not directly state that *bourgeois life* is for him an *eternal truth*; he says it indirectly, by deifying the categories which express bourgeois relationships in the form of thought. He takes the products of bourgeois society for spontaneous existences, endowed with a life of their own, eternal, as soon as they present themselves to him in the form of categories, of thought. Thus he does not rise above the bourgeois horizon. Because he is operating with bourgeois ideas, supposing them to be eternal verities, he seeks a synthesis, an equilibrium, of these ideas, and does not see that the actual method by which they attain equilibrium is the only possible method.

Actually, he does what all good bourgeois do. They all tell you that competition, monopoly, etc., are, in principle, that is, taken as abstract ideas, the only basis of life, but in practice they leave much to be desired. They all want competition without its baneful consequences. They all want the impossible, that is to say, the conditions of bourgeois life with the necessary consequences of these conditions. None of them understands that the bourgeois form of production is an historic and transitory form, just as much as the feudal form was. This error arises from the fact that the bourgeois man is to them the only possible basis of every society, and that they cannot imagine a state of society in which man has ceased to be bourgeois.

Mr. Proudhon is, therefore, necessarily a *doctrinaire*. The historic movement which is overturning the world today reduces itself for him to the problem of discovering the correct equilibrium, the synthesis of two bourgeois ideas. Thus, with subtlety, the clever boy discovers the hidden thought of God, the unity of the two isolated thoughts—which are only isolated because Mr. Proudhon has isolated them from practical life, from present-day production, from the combination of realities which they express. In place of the great historic movement arising from men's productive forces, already acquired, and their social relationships, which no longer correspond to those productive forces; in place of the terrible wars which are being prepared among the different classes within each nation and between different nations; in place of the practical and violent action of the masses which alone can resolve these collisions; in place of this vast, prolonged and complicated movement, Mr. Proudhon produces an evacuating movement out of his own head. Thus, it is the men of learning, men capable of snatching the secret thoughts out of God, who make history. The common people have only to apply their revelations. You will now understand why Mr. Proudhon is the declared enemy of every political movement. The solution of present problems does not consist for him in public action, but in the dialectical rotations in his head. Because to him categories are motive forces, it is not necessary to change practical life in order to change the categories. Quite the contrary. It is necessary to change the categories, and the transformation of the actual society would result.

In his desire to reconcile the contradictions, Mr. Proudhon does not ask himself whether the base itself of these contradictions ought not to be overthrown. He is like all political doctrinaires, who will have it that the king, the Chamber of Deputies, and the Chamber of Peers are integral parts of the social life, eternal categories. Only that he is searching for a new formula to equilibrate these forces, whose equilibrium exists precisely in the actual movement, in which one force is now the conqueror, and now the slave, of the other. Thus in the eighteenth century, a crowd of mediocre minds was busy finding the true formula that would bring the social orders, the nobility, the king, the parliaments, etc., into equilibrium, and tomorrow there was no longer any king, parliament, or nobility. The true equilibrium between these antagonisms was the overthrow of all social relationships which had served as the basis of these feudal existences and their antagonisms.

Because Mr. Proudhon places eternal ideas, the categories of pure reason, on one side, and human beings and their practical life, which according to him is the application of these categories, on the other, you find in him from the beginning a *dualism* between life and ideas, soul and body—a dualism which is repeated in many forms. You see now that this antagonism is nothing but Mr. Proudhon's incapacity to understand the profane origin and history of the categories which he deifies.

My letter is already too long for me to speak of the ridiculous case he makes against communism. For the moment, you will grant me that a man who has not understood the present state of society can still less understand the movement that tends to overthrow it, or the literary expressions of this revolutionary movement.

The *sole point* on which I am in complete agreement with Mr. Proudhon is his disgust for socialist sentimentality. Long before him, I have already brought much hostility upon myself by ridiculing this mutton-headed, sentimental, utopian socialism. But does not Mr. Proudhon delude himself strangely by opposing his own petit bourgeois sentimentality—I am speaking of his declamations about home, conjugal love, and all such banalities—to socialist sentimentality, which in Fourier, for example, is much deeper than are the pretentious platitudes of our worthy Proudhon? He himself is so thoroughly aware of the emptiness of his arguments, his complete incapacity to speak about these things, that he throws himself head over heels into rages, exclamations, *irae hominis probi* [angers of a righteous man], froths at the mouth, swears, denounces, cries infamy and pestilence, pounds his chest and boasts before God and man that he is clean of such socialist infamies! He does not ridicule critically socialist sentimentalities, or what he regards as such. Like a saint, a pope, he excommunicates poor sinners and sings the glories of the petit bourgeois and of the wretched amorous and patriarchal illusions of the domestic hearth. And this is not accidental. Mr. Proudhon is from head to foot the philosopher and economist of the petit bourgeoisie. In an advanced society, the *petit bourgeois*, by the necessity of his position, acts as part socialist and part economist, that is to say, he is dazzled by the magnificence of the big bourgeoisie and sympathizes with the sufferings of the people. He is at once a bourgeois and a man of the people. In his innermost conscience he flatters himself on being impartial, on having found the right equilibrium, which claims to be different from what is common. Such a petit bourgeois deifies *contradiction*, because contradiction is the basis of his existence. He himself is nothing but social contradiction, put in action. He must justify by theory what he is in practice, and Mr. Proudhon has the merit of being the scientific interpreter of the French petit bourgeoisie, a genuine merit, because the petit bourgeoisie will form an integral part of all the impending social revolutions.

I would have wished to be able to send you my book on political economy with this letter, but hitherto it has been impossible for me to get this work, and the criticism of German philosophers and socialists about which I spoke to you in Brussels, printed. You would never believe the difficulties that such a publication encounters in Germany, on the one hand from the police, and on the other, from the booksellers, who are themselves the interested representatives of all the tendencies which I am attacking. And as for our own party, it is not only poor, but also a large portion of the German communist party are angry with me because I oppose their utopias and their declamations.

Devotedly yours, Karl Marx

P.S. You will ask why I am writing you in bad French, instead of good German. It is because I am dealing with a French author. You will greatly oblige me by not delaying your reply too long, so that I may know whether you have understood me in this guise of a barbarous French.

19

From letter to Georg Herwegh (in Paris)
Brussels, August 8, 1847

Dear Herwegh:

... The police magistrate himself stated that these lawsuits[1] are *pour le roi de Prusse* [to no purpose]. On the other hand, the *Deutsche-Brüsseler-Zeitung*—which despite its many weaknesses has always had something meritorious about it, and could be improved, especially now, when Bornstedt has declared himself ready to be on our side in all possible ways—is threatened with sudden financial ruin. And how did the noble Germans behave in this matter? The bookdealers *betrayed* Bornstedt because he cannot prosecute them legally. Instead of doing the slightest thing, either literarily or financially, all shadings of the opposition found it more comfortable to find offense in the name Bornstedt. And would these people ever lack excuses for doing nothing? One time the man is no good, another time it is the wife, a third time it is the tendency, still another time it is the style, and once again it is the format, or the distribution is fraught with more or less danger, etc., etc. The roast pigeons are to fly straight into the mouth of the gentleman. When there is only one censorship-free opposition paper, at which the government takes great offense, whose editor as a result of the enterprise itself, shows himself to be sympathetic to all progressives—shouldn't such an opportunity be used and, if insufficient, be made sufficient? But no! Our Germans always have a

---

19

1. Three lawsuits had been instigated by the Prussian Embassy in Brussels against Adalbert von Bornstedt, a former Prussian officer who was editor and publisher of the *Deutsche-Brüsseler-Zeitung*, a twice-weekly German-language refugee paper in Brussels, to which Marx occasionally contributed articles.

thousand philosophical proverbs *in petto* [in reserve] to show why they must let the opportunity pass unused. An opportunity to do something only embarrasses them.

My manuscripts are in more or less the same state as the *Deutsche-Brüsseler-Zeitung*, and withal jackasses write day after day asking why I am not publishing anything, and even reproach me with preferring to write in French or not at all. One will have to atone a long time for having been born a Teuton....

Marx

20

To the Editor of La Réforme,[1] [in French]
Printed March 8, 1848

Dear Editor!

At present the Belgian Government is politically fully and completely on the side of the Holy Alliance. Its reactionary rage strikes the German democrats with unheard of brutality. If our hearts were not so heavy, owing to the persecutions that especially affect us, we would be heartily amused at how the Rogier[2] Ministry makes itself ridiculous with the accusation that a handful of Germans wanted to force a republic on the Belgians against their wills. But in this special situation, the ridiculous gives way to the hateful.

Above all, dear sir, it is desirable to know that practically all Brussels newspapers are edited by Frenchmen, the majority of whom had fled from France to escape the disgraceful penalties which threatened them there. These Frenchmen have the greatest interest in defending the independence of Belgium, which they have all betrayed in 1833. The king, the ministry, and their party followers have used these papers in order to strengthen the impression that a republican-minded Belgian revolution was nothing but a *Frenchification*, and that the whole democratic agitation, which then stirred Belgium, was aroused by overexcited Germans.

The Germans in no way deny that they have openly allied themselves with Belgian democrats, and they did that without any exaltation. In the eyes of the district attorney, this was tantamount to stirring up the workers against the citizens, creating suspicions among the Belgians against their so very beloved *German* king, and opening the gates of Belgium to a French invasion.

At five o'clock in the evening of March 3, after I received the order to leave the Belgian *Kingdom* within twenty-four hours, and while I was still

---

20

1. *La Réforme* was a radical daily that appeared in Paris from 1843 to 1850.
2. Charles-Latour Rogier (1800–1885), Belgian Premier, Minister of Interior, 1847–52.

making preparations to leave that night, a police commissioner and ten policemen broke into my residence, ransacked the whole house, and finally arrested me on the pretext that I had no papers. Entirely apart from the fact that the papers, which Mr. Duchâtel[3] had given me when he expelled me from France [in 1845], were fully in order, I was also in possession of the Belgian expulsion pass which had been given me a few hours previously.

I would not, dear sir, have informed you of my arrest and the brutalities which I underwent, had it not been for an occurrence that one could hardly imagine even in Austria.

Immediately after my arrest, my wife went to Mr. Jottrand,[4] the president of the Democratic Association of Belgium, asking him to take the necessary steps. Upon returning home, she found, in front of the door, a policeman who told her with exquisite courtesy that she only had to follow him if she wanted to speak to Mr. Marx. My wife gladly accepted the offer. She was led to the police bureau, and the commissioner told her that Mr. Marx was not there. Then he asked her rudely who she was, what she was looking for in Mr. Jottrand's house, and if she had her papers with her. A Belgian democrat, Mr. Gigot,[5] who had followed my wife and the policeman to the police bureau, expressed indignation at the commissioner's senseless and shameless questions, and was silenced by the policemen, who seized him and threw him into jail. Under pretext of vagrancy, my wife was led off to prison in City Hall and locked up in a dark room with prostitutes. At eleven o'clock in the morning, in full daylight, she was escorted by gendarmes to the office of the examining magistrate. For two hours, despite the sharpest protests from all sides, she was kept in single confinement, exposed to the injustice of the season and the most disgraceful talk of the policemen.

Finally, she was brought before the examining magistrate, who was completely surprised that the police, in their capacity as guardians, had not also arrested the children. The interrogation could not be anything but a farce, since my wife's whole crime consisted of the fact that, despite her belonging to the Prussian aristocracy, she shared her husband's democratic ideas.

I do not want to go into any more details about this scandalous occurrence. I only want to mention that after we were released, the twenty-four hours were up and that we had to depart without being able to take with us even the most necessary things.

Karl Marx, Vice-president of the
Democratic Association of Belgium.

---

3. Charles-Marie-Tanneguy, comte de Duchâtel (1803–1867), French Minister of Interior from 1840 to 1848.
4. Lucien-Leopold Jottrand (1804–1877), Belgian lawyer, friend of Marx.
5. Philippe-Charles Gigot (1819–1860), Belgian communist, friend of Marx.

21

To Frederick Engels (in Vevey)
Paris, August 1, 1849

Dear Engels:

I have experienced a great deal of disquiet over you, and was really pleased yesterday to receive a letter from your hand.[1] I had asked Dronke[2] (who is here) to write to your brother-in-law[3] for information about you. Naturally, he knew nothing.

My whole family is here; the government wanted to exile me to Morbihan, the Pontine marshes of Brittany. So far, I have hindered its execution. If, however, I am to write you at greater length about my own, as well as general, conditions, here, you must send me a more definite address, for here everything is atrocious.

You now have the finest opportunity to write a history or a pamphlet on the Baden-Palatinate revolution.[4] Without your own participation in the war, we could not have come forth with our opinions of that frolic. In addition, you can take a splendid bite at the position of the *Neue Rheinische Zeitung* toward the democratic party in general.

I have initiated negotiations to found a political-economic monthly in Berlin, to be written mainly by us both.[5]

Lupus[6] is also in Switzerland, I believe in Berne. Weerth was here yesterday, he is establishing an agency in Liverpool. The red Wolff[7] lives here with me. The financial conditions are, of course, in great disarray.

Freiligrath is still in Cologne. If my wife were not in an *état par trop intéressant* [a too interesting state, i.e.: very pregnant], I would leave Paris the moment it was financially possible.

21

1. Engels wrote to Jenny Marx, July 25, 1849, giving as his return address: "F. Engels, *refugié allemand* [German refugee], Vevey, Suisse."
2. Ernst Dronke (1822–1891), German communist journalist, refugee in London.
3. Karl Emil Blank (1817–1893), a German businessman.
4. In August, 1849, Engels began a series of articles, *Die deutsche Reichsverfassungskampagne* [*The German Reich Constitution Campaign*], published in *Neue Rheinische Zeitung. Politisch-ökonomische Revue*, January, February, and March, 1850.
5. Nothing came of these negotiations, but in December, 1849, Marx and Engels in London founded the *Neue Rheinische Zeitung. Politisch-ökonomische Revue*. A continuation of the *Neue Rheinische Zeitung*, it was the organ of the Communist League, and was printed in Hamburg. Only six issues appeared, the last one in November, 1850.
6. Wilhelm Wolff (1809–1864), German communist, living in England, friend of Marx to whom he bequeathed his estate. *Lupus* is Latin for "wolf."
7. Ferdinand Wolff (1812–1895), German communist journalist in exile. Wilhelm and Ferdinand were not related.

Keep well. Best regards for Willich[8] and write by return post to my address: M. Ramboz, rue de Lille 45.

Yours, K.M.

22

From letter to Frederick Engels (in Vevey)
Paris, August 17, 1849

Dear Engels!

I don't know whether you have received my first letter—the reply to your first, which you sent to my wife—since your address was very unclear. I would have answered your second letter if my whole family here had not been sick and thus I was hindered. I repeat to you again what anxiety my wife and I felt about you and how happy and surprised we were to receive sure news from you.[1]

From the above date you will see that the Ministry of Interior has temporarily heeded my appeal and left me unmolested in Paris. The Département of Morbihan, assigned to me, is fatal in this time of the year—the Pontine Marshes of Brittany....

Maintenant, mon cher, que faire de notre part? Il faut nous lancer dans une entreprise littéraire et mercantile, j'attends tes propositions.[2]

Red [Ferdinand] Lupus is here in the same house as I; Dronke is also in Paris, *mais c'est un tout petit homme de l'école de E. Meyen* [but he is a very little man of the school of (Eduard) Meyen]. [Wilhelm] Lupus is at Zurich; his address: Dr. Lüning.[3] You don't particularly have to write to M. Ramboz. *C'est mon pseudonyme.*[4]

My address simply this:
Monsieur Ramboz, 45, rue de Lille.
Salut.

Ch. M.

---

8. August Willich (1810–1878), Prussian officer, communist, emigrated to the United States, where he served as a general in the Union Army during the Civil War.

22

1. Engels to Mrs. Marx, Vevey, July 25, 1849: "You as well as Marx must have wondered why you did not hear from me so long.... The day that I wrote to Marx (from Kaiserslautern) the news came that Hamburg had been occupied by the Prussians and communications with Paris were therefore cut.... If I only knew for certain that Marx is free! The thought often occurred to me that I amid the Prussian bullets was at a much less dangerous post than the others in Germany and especially Marx in Paris."
2. Now, my dear, what do we do? We should begin some literary or commercial enterprise. I await your suggestions.
3. Otto Lüning (1818–1868), a socialist physician and journalist.
4. It is my pseudonym.

23

To Frederick Engels (in Lausanne)
Paris, August 23, 1849

Dear Engels!

I am to be exiled to the Morbihan Département, the Pontine Marshes of Brittany. You understand that I will not accept this masked attempt at murder. Hence I depart from France.

They will not give me a passport to Switzerland, hence I must go to London, and do so tomorrow. Switzerland will moreover soon be hermetically sealed, so as to catch the mice in one stroke.

Apart from that: in London I have a *POSITIVE* prospect of founding a German journal.[1] A portion of the money is already *assured*.

You must, therefore, come to London immediately. This, moreover, will enhance your security. The Prussians would shoot you for two reasons: (1) because of Baden, and (2) because of Elberfeld.[2] And what business do you have in Switzerland, where you can do nothing?

You will have no difficulties coming to London, be it under the name Engels or be it under the name Mayer. As soon as you declare your readiness to come to England, you will receive from the French Embassy an emergency passport to London.

I *positively* count on it. You *cannot* remain in Switzerland. In London we will do business.

My wife remains here temporarily. You write to her at the same address: 45, rue de Lille, M. Ramboz.

But once again, I count on it that you will not leave me in the lurch.

Yours, K.M.

Lupus is with Dr. Lüning in Zurich. Write him also about my plan.

23

1. *Neue Rheinische Zeitung. Politisch-ökonomische Revue*, which Marx and Engels published in London in 1850.
2. In June–July, 1849, Engels fought in the revolutionary struggles in the Palatinate and Baden; in May, 1849, he had prepared an uprising in Elberfeld.

LONDON
First Years as a Refugee · *1849-1852*

Marx's first years in London were particularly brutal. He was a refugee without means and without a knowledge of the language of the country. His only profession, journalism, was not a salable commodity for a foreigner. A German journal—*Neue Rheinische Zeitung. Politische-ökonomische Revue*—which Marx and Engels published in 1850, was unsuccessful and went out of existence after six issues. Marx, with his wife and four children, lived in the most squalid quarters in Soho, amid other poverty-stricken European refugees. The radicals among them spent much of their time in petty squabbles and intrigues. Marx began a serious study of economics in the British Museum, but was perpetually harassed by misery, family illnesses, and near starvation. The situation was so desperate that Engels, in November 1850, swallowed his pride and entered his father's textile business in Manchester, so as to be able to help Marx and his family financially. Although in subsequent years Marx earned some income as a newspaper correspondent, it was Engels who basically gave him financial support for the rest of his life.

24

To Ferdinand Freiligrath (in Cologne)
London, c/o Karl Blind,¹ 18 Roberts Street, Peterson's Coffeehouse,
Grosvenor Square, September 5, 1849

Dear Freiligrath:
I can write you only a few lines, since I have had a kind of cholera in the last four to five days and am frightfully tired.

My wife wrote me I should acknowledge to you the receipt of your letter with the enclosed 100 francs. Think of the vileness of the Paris police; they have harassed my wife and only with difficulty has she managed to remain in Paris until September 15,² the date up to which we have rented our apartment.

I am now in a truly difficult situation. My wife is very pregnant;³ she must leave Paris on the fifteenth, and I don't know where I can raise the money needed for her trip and for lodgings here.⁴

On the other hand, I have every expectation of being able to begin a monthly review here; but time presses, and the first weeks are the really difficult ones.

Because of my letter to you⁵ and to somebody else, Lassalle seems to be offended. This surely was not my intention, and I would have written to him about it, if my present situation did not make letter writing a real burden.

As soon as I am somewhat up to it, I will write you in more detail about politics. I hope to get a few words from you soon. Best regards for your wife, Daniels,⁶ etc.

Yours, K.M.

24

1. Karl Blind (1826–1907), German refugee writer and journalist, participant of the 1848–49 revolutions. Marx, expelled from France, arrived in London on August 24, 1849; since he had no lodgings, he roomed with Karl Blind.
2. She arrived in London with the three children, Jenny, Laura, and Edgar, on September 17, 1849.
3. On November 5, 1849, she gave birth to Heinrich Guido (called Föxchen).
4. The Marx family moved to a rooming house on Leicester Square.
5. See Letter 299, Marx to Freiligrath, July 31, 1849, in Part II of this volume.
6. Dr. Ronald Daniels (1819–1855), a communist physician in Cologne, close friend of Marx when the latter was editor of *Neue Rheinische Zeitung* in that city.

25

To Joseph Weydemeyer (in Frankfurt)
London, 4 Anderson Street, Kings Road, Chelsea,
December 19, 1849

Dear Weydemeyer:

I am writing you after an unconscionable lapse of time. My long silence is explained by civic vexations of all sorts, running around, and finally the very difficulty I find in letter writing. I have now reached the point, *post tot discrimina rerum*,[1] of getting my *Revue*[2] ready, that is, of having a printer and distributor in Hamburg. Otherwise everything is done on private accounts. The worst of it is that in Germany one loses so much time before one gets anything printed. I hardly doubt that after the publication of three, or perhaps two, monthly issues, the world conflagration will intervene and the opportunity of provisionally coming to terms with the economy will cease.

Since you live in the center of Germany and know the details there more precisely than we do, you would perhaps find time to write something short and concise, in a few main strokes, on the situation in South Germany for our *Revue*.

I am asking you, furthermore, to publish the following announcement [of the *Revue*] in your paper,[3] but *only after* you have seen it announced by the agents of the Hamburg bookdealers in the *Kölnische Zeitung*. Perhaps you could send a copy to Westphalia. From the announcement you will see that in addition to the bookstore circulation, we are planning a second one, and hope that our party comrades would get together subscription lists and send them to us. For the time being, we must keep the price quite high and the number of sheets low. Should our means increase through an extended circulation, we will alter this undesirable condition.

What do you say to the row among Proudhon, Blanc,[4] and Pierre Leroux?

Willich, Engels, the Red Wolff, and Weerth[5] send you their regards.

Here in England a most important movement is taking place at this moment. On the one hand, the Protectionist agitation, supported by the

---

25

1. "After so much caprice of fate," Virgil, *Aenead*.
2. *Neue Rheinische Zeitung. Politisch-ökonomische Revue*, of which Marx and Engels published six irregular issues, the final one in November, 1850.
3. *Neue Deutsche Zeitung*, a daily, published in Frankfurt under the editorship of Joseph Weydemeyer, Otto Lüning, and Georg Günther.
4. Jean Joseph Louis Blanc (1811–1882), French socialist and historian, emigré in London.
5. Georg Weerth (1822–1856), German communist poet who had been on the staff of Marx's *Neue Rheinische Zeitung*.

fanaticized rural population—the results of free trade in corn are beginning to be felt, as I had predicted years ago; on the other hand, the Free Traders, who as financial and Parliamentary reformers are drawing the political and economic consequences of their system internally, and as a peace party externally; finally, the Chartists, who are working together with the bourgeoisie against the aristocracy, but at the same time have resumed their own party movement with greater energy against the bourgeoisie. If, as I hope, and this hope is not without real foundations, the Tories replace the Whigs in the Ministry, the conflict between these parties will assume enormous proportions, and the outward form of the agitation will be stormier and more revolutionary. Another, not yet visible *événement* [event], on the Continent is the approach of an immense industrial, agricultural, and commercial crisis. If the Continent postpones its revolution until the outbreak of this crisis, England may perhaps be, even if reluctantly, an ally of the revolutionary Continent. A premature outbreak of the revolution—provided it is not provoked directly by Russian intervention—would be, in my opinion, a misfortune, for at present, when trade is expanding more and more in France, Germany, etc., the working masses in France, Germany, etc., as well as all the small shopkeepers, may be revolutionary in phrase, but certainly not *en realité*.

You know that my wife has enriched the world with a new citizen.[6] She sends you and your wife best regards. Give your wife my best regards too. Write soon.

Yours, K. Marx

26

To Joseph Weydemeyer (in Frankfurt)
London, 64 Dean Street, October 29, 1850

Dear Weydemeyer:
I beg of you to transact the following business for me:

Borrow from Schuster[1] or anybody else money for redeeming my silver in the Frankfurt pawnshop,[2] then *sell* the silver to a goldsmith or to anybody

---

6. See Letter 24, note 3.

26

1. Theodor Schuster, a local socialist.
2. In her *Short Sketch of an Eventful Life* (written in 1865), Jenny Marx wrote that after the last issue of the *Neue Rheinische Zeitung* (May, 1849), "Karl decided to go to Paris for the time being ... I myself went with the three little ones across Bingen ... to my dear old home, where we spent eight days with my beloved mother. From Bingen, I made a small detour in order to sell the silver dishes, just redeemed from the Brussels pawnshop, for ready cash. [In Frankfurt] Weydemeyer and his wife ... were very helpful to me in the pawnshop transaction."

who buys such things there, pay the man from whom you borrowed, and send the remainder to me.

You and the other man run no risk, since should you be unable to sell the thing at a higher price, you can always return it to the pawnshop.

My situation is now such that I must under any circumstances raise some money in order to be able to continue working.

The only pieces I ask you to return to the pawnshop—since they have little sales value—are a small silver goblet, a silver plate, the small fork and knife in a case—all of them objects belonging to little Jenny.

I approve of your plan for a popular work on economics and hope you will soon effectuate it. Regards for your wife [Louise] and best from me and wife.

Yours, K.M.

27

To Frederick Engels (in Manchester)
London, November 19, 1850

Dear Engels:
I am writing only a couple of lines. At ten o'clock this morning our little Gunpowder plotter, Föxchen,[1] died. Suddenly, from one of the cramps, which he often had. A few minutes earlier, he was still laughing and waggish. The thing came entirely unexpectedly. You can imagine what it is like here. This is also the moment when we are very lonely because of your absence.

In my next letter, I will write you something about Harney,[2] from which you will see in what unfortunate position he finds himself.

Yours, K.M.

If you are in a mood, write a few words to my wife. She is entirely beside herself.

27

1. Heinrich Guido, Marx's fourth child, was born on Guy Fawkes Day, November 5, 1849, and hence nicknamed "Föxchen," Little Fox. He died two weeks after his first birthday.
2. George Julian Harney (1817–1897), Chartist editor.

28

To Frederick Engels (in Manchester)
London, February 11, 1851

Dear Engels:
Iterum Crispinus![1]

I have just learned that tonight there was a meeting in Tottenham Court Road for the death of Bem.[2] On the platform sat: *President* Schapper,[3] etc.; Louis Blanc; and the rest of the members of the new People's League Committee. In the front row of the auditorium were Harney and his wife [Mary]. The main audience consisted of the Great Windmill Street.[4]

Schapper, in English, gave his inevitable, enthusiastically received speech: *War to the knife!* Louis Blanc spoke no better: *Vive la guerre!* Tausenau,[5] also present, spoke about Bem. Harney delivered a long and, as they say, good lecture, in which he finally admitted Blanqui,[6] Barbès,[7] and, at the very end, Louis Blanc into the circle of Socialist Messiahs.

Qu'en dis-tu? [What do you say to that?]

If you appeared at a meeting presided over by Th. Clark Esq.[8] and by your presence and speeches gave that meeting importance, would Friend Harney consider that loyal?

For him, therefore, it is not enough that he puffs Ruge in his publication, *Friend of the People*, he also has to promote the Schapper-Willich crowd.

He [Harney] invited me last Sunday. His object was to persuade Jones[9] to accept the title "Friend of the People." I did not go. He can use for that purpose L. Blanc, Landolphe,[10] Schapper or Willich. I am *fatigué* [tired] of this public incense which Harney never tires of wafting around *les petits grands hommes* [the little great men].

Apart from this incident—that *tu Brute* [thou, Brutus] (Harney), who if he does not take sides against us, at least plays the impartial role, while

---

28

1. "Here we go again!" from the Fourth Satire of Juvenal.
2. Josef Bem (1795–1850), Polish general, fought in various European revolutions.
3. Karl Schapper (1812–1870), German communist refugee in London.
4. Location of the London German Educational Society.
5. Karl Tausenau (1808–1873), an Austrian refugee in London.
6. Louis-Auguste Blanqui (1805–1881), French revolutionary.
7. Armand Barbès (1809–1870), French radical.
8. Thomas Clark (d.1857), founder of the National Charter League.
9. Ernest Charles Jones (1819–1869), left–wing English Chartist, a friend of Marx and Engels.
10. Landolphe was a French socialist refugee in London.

Engels in Manchester works for him, Eccarius[11] writes for his paper, and I occasionally work for Jones through him—apart from this, I am very pleased with the public, authentic isolation in which we two, you and I, now find ourselves. It corresponds fully to our position and our principles. The system of mutual concessions, the toleration of half-truths out of decency, and the duty of participating in public ridiculously for the Party with all these jack-asses, all that has now ceased.

Now, I beg you to reply soon to these lines. Here I see practically nobody except Pieper[12] and live entirely withdrawn. You can understand, therefore, how much the more I miss you and how much need I have to talk things over with you.

Tomorrow you will see in the papers that the endowment has been rejected by a vote of 102.[13]

Yours, K.M.

29

To Frederick Engels (in Manchester)
London, February 24, 1851

Dear Engels:
It is now one o'clock in the morning. About an hour ago, Pieper came rushing in, hatless, disheveled, tattered. The thing was as follows:

Tonight the meeting or banquet[1] was held in the City. Willich presided. Jones, in accord with his promise, did not attend. Our Dear[2] wore a red armband. Present were 700 persons, 150 French more or less, 250 Germans, 200 Chartists, and the rest Poles and Hungarians. Blanc read the addresses he received from his Paris Yes-brothers; Willich, one from La Chaux-de-Fonds. There were none from Germany. In addition, there was one from the Poles in Paris.

The speeches were ridiculously bad; generally, despite all this *fraternité*, the dew of boredom clung to the faces and tongues.

---

11. Johann Georg Eccarius (1818–1889), German communist tailor in London, active, with Marx, in the First International throughout its whole existence, from 1864 to 1872.
12. Wilhelm Pieper (b. *c.* 1826), German communist refugee in London, friend and occasional secretary of Marx.
13. In February, 1851, the French Parliament voted against granting a gift of 1,800,000 francs to President Louis Napoleon (soon to become Napoleon III).

29

1. February 24 was the anniversary of the French revolution of 1848; it was celebrated by French and other radicals in London.
2. George Julian Harney.

Schramm[3] and Pieper obtained cards in order to observe the fun. They were molested from the first. Schramm went up to one of the sergeants-at-arms, the worthy, chivalrous Landolphe, and asked him at least to obtain quiet for them for their money. The worthy replied that this was not the place for quarrels.

By and by, it lasted too long for the Great-Windmill Streeters.[4] They cried out: "spy, spy," Haynau, Haynau, and then Schramm and Pieper were whipped out of the hall, their hats torn, and kicked into the courtyard, stumped upon, their faces slapped, almost torn to pieces, tufts of their hair torn out, etc. Barthélemy came over and said about Schramm: *"C'est un infâme! Il faut l'écraser"* [It's an infamy. He should be crushed]. Schramm replied: *"Vous êtes un forçat libéré"* [You are a released convict].

Two hundred subjects participated in the brawl, Germans, French and the gentlemen fraternals,[5] not less "brave" against two unarmed persons.

Post festum [after the event], the Dear [Harney] let himself be seen, and instead of acting energetically, as he should have, he stammers that he knows the men and wants to begin a long exposition. Naturally a fine intercession at such a moment.

The two defended themselves lion-heartedly.

The Windmillers cried: He has stolen 19 shillings from our treasury.

So much for today. *Qu'en dis-tu, mon cher?* [What do you say, my dear?] If a revolution breaks out in London tomorrow, Willich-Barthélemy will infallibly come to power.

Yours, K.M.

30

To Frederick Engels (in Manchester)
London, March 31, 1851

Dear Engels:

While you pursue war history, I am waging a little war that *by and by* [in English] threatens to defeat me, and from which neither Napoleon, nor even Willich—the communist Cromwell—could have found a way out.

You know that on March 23, I had to pay £31 and 10 shillings to old Bamberger[1] and £10 to the Jew Stiebel,[2] all payable currently. I first inquired

---

3. Rudolf Schramm (1813–1882), anti-Marx German refugee journalist in London.
4. Office of the Communist League, led by Schapper and Willich.
5. The Fraternal Democrats, organized in 1845 by the left-wing Chartists under the leadership of George Julian Harney and Ernest Charles Jones.

30

1. Simon Bamberger, a banker in London.
2. Unidentified.

directly, through Jenny,[3] at my mother-in-law's.[4] The answer was that Herr Edgar[5] with the rest of *Jenny's money* has been expedited to Mexico and I could not squeeze out another centime.

Then I wrote to my mother, threatened to draw a promissory note on her and in case of her nonpayment, to go to Prussia and let myself be arrested. I really meant to do the latter in case of that eventuality, but that recourse of course faded away at the moment when the jackasses in the newspapers began to howl about my being deserted by workers, the decline of my popularity, and such. The thing would then have looked like a theatrical coup, a more or less deliberate imitation of Jesus-Christ-Kinkel.[6] I told the Old Lady that the due date of the note was March 20.

On March 10 she wrote me that she would write to relatives; on March 18 she wrote me that the relatives did *not* answer, which meant: the thing was finished. I wrote her immediately: I would stick by my first letter.

On March 16 I paid Stiebel £10 with the help of Pieper. On March 23, after I had taken a number of fruitless steps, the note for the old Bamberger had, of course, to be protested. I had a frightful scene with the old man, who, moreover, had abused me abominably in the presence of the worthy Seiler.[7] Through his banker in Trier, the jackass had inquired about me of the Banker Lautz there. That fellow, the banker of my Old Lady and my personal enemy, naturally wrote the biggest nonsense about me and, in addition, fanaticized my Old Woman against me.

In regard to old Bamberger, I had no choice but to make out two promissory notes, one to him in London, for four weeks after March 24, and the other, for three weeks, to my Old Woman in Trier, in order to cover the first. I immediately informed the Old Woman. Today, together with the letter from you, I received one from the Old Woman, in which she, with the greatest *impertinence* and full of moral indignation, declares that she would refuse to honor any note on her signed by me.

So on April 21, I have to expect the worst from the now enraged old Simon Bamberger.

At the same time, my wife was confined on March 28. The delivery was easy, but now she is very sick, more for bourgeois than for physical reasons. In addition, I literally don't have a farthing in the house, but only more bills from the small tradesmen—butchers, bakers, and so forth.

In seven or eight days, I will have a copy of the will from Scotland [an inheritance from Mrs. Marx's Scottish kin]. If there is anything to be done

---

3. Marx's wife.
4. Karoline von Westphalen (d. 1856) lived as a widow in Trier.
5. Edgar von Westphalen, Jenny Marx's younger brother, whom she loved.
6. Gottfried Kinkel (1815–1882), a German refugee writer in London, an enemy of Marx.
7. Sebastian Seiler, a communist refugee journalist in London.

there, the little Bamberger[8] will do it, out of his own interest. But I cannot rely on it.

You will admit that all this shit is scarcely pleasant for me and that I am stuck in petit bourgeois muck up to the vortex of my skull. And withal one exploits the workers! And strives for dictatorship! *Quelle horreur* [what horror]!

Mais ce n'est pas tout [But that is not all]. The Trier manufacturer who lent me the money in Brussels is dogging me and demands it back because his foundry is doing poor business. *Tant pis pour lui* [So much the worse for him]. Him I cannot take into account.

But, finally, to cap the climax in a tragicomic way, there comes a secret,[9] which I shall reveal to you *en très peu de mots* [in a very few words]. But just now I am being interrupted and called to my wife's sickbed. Hence this thing, in which you play a role, I will leave for next time.

Yours, K.M.

Apropos. How do merchants, manufacturers, etc., compute that part of their income which they themselves consume? Is that money also borrowed from the banker, or what? I would appreciate an answer.

31

To Joseph Weydemeyer (in Frankfurt)
London, June 27, 1851

Dear Hans:

I don't even know whether I am right in sending you a letter through Fabricius.[1] Who can guarantee that he will not be seized at the frontier, since he has loaded himself here with a knapsack full of letters?

Although your American plan—Engels has perhaps written you about it—is not materializing, there is nothing left for you to do but to come over here and strengthen us. Perhaps something, some common activity—natu-

---

8. Louis Bamberger, son of Simon Bamberger.
9. Two days later, on April 2, 1851, Marx again wrote to Engels: "I will not write you about the secret, since *coûte que coûte* [at any cost], I will in any case visit you at the end of April. I must get away from here for eight days." Marx actually went to Manchester on or about April 17. The "secret" he refers to probably had to do with Helene Demuth's pregnancy—she was in her seventh month. On June 23, 1851, she gave birth to an illegitimate son, Freddy, whom Marx did not acknowledge as his son. He apparently wanted Engels to assume the paternity.

31
1. Franz Fabricius, a Frankfurt businessman.

rally, bourgeois, *car il faut vivre* [it is necessary to live]—will possibly be found.

I now know from a *reliable* source about the treason and denunciation involved in the arrest of our friends. I am *morally* convinced that Herr Willich and Herr Schapper and their contemptible *Lumpenhundenbande* [band of rascally dogs] played a direct role in this infamy. You must understand how important it is for these "great men" *in partibus* [abroad] to eliminate those people in Germany whom they believe to stand directly in their way to power. The asses do not understand that they are considered asses and at most they rate contempt.

Willich, despite his philistine-aristocratic, Spartan-broth noncommissioned officer's hypocritical airs, is a thoroughly ordinary, note well, a *thoroughly ordinary, chevalier d'industrie* [sharpie], *pillier d'estaminet* [four flusher] and—I do not vouch for this, although it has been reported to me by a respectable philistine—*false* gambler. The fellow sits all day long in the tavern, naturally a *democratic* one, where he imbibes gratis, and shills cash customers whom he entertains with his stereotype-revolutionary-future-phrases in which this knight himself no longer believes, since he has repeated them often under such contradictory circumstances and always with the same success. The fellow is a parasite of the commonest sort—and always of course under patriotic pretexts.

The entire communism of this subject amounts to his determination to lead a free life, always at the expense of the public, in communion with other mounted knights. The whole activity of this man consists of gossiping about us in the taverns and lying and boasting about contacts in Germany, which he does not have, but in which the chief buffoon Arnold Ruge, the loutish fellow-traveler Heinzen,[2] and the theatrical, applause-seeking, theological belletrist Kinkel, believe and about which they boast also to the French.

Apropos. While the last-named parsonish Adonis runs around in bourgeois circles, letting himself be fed and pampered by them, etc., etc., he secretly keeps forbidden touch with Schapper and Willich, so that he too should have contact with the "labor party." In every respect, he has the most striking resemblance to Frederick William IV, who is nothing more than a Kinkel on the throne and who possesses the same fine talk and leukorrhea as he.

If you ask me, how you would make a living here, I answer: Follow the footsteps of the brave Willich. He sows not, he reaps not, but the heavenly father doth feed him.

---

2. Karl Heinzen (1809–1880), anti-Marx journalist, emigrated to the United States in 1850.

But now *au sérieux* [seriously]. Should your stay in Germany be endangered—it is good that you come here. Should you be able to remain unmolested in Germany, it would of course be better, for there our forces are more useful than here.

Yours, K.M.

I spend mostly from nine in the morning to seven in the evening in the British Museum. The stuff, on which I work, is so damned ramified that despite all efforts one does not succeed in completing it before six to eight weeks. Added to this, there are always practical interruptions, unavoidable in the miserable conditions under which one vegetates here. Despite all and all, the thing is nearing a conclusion. One simply has to break off forcibly. The democratic "simpletons," for whom enlightenment comes "from above," naturally have no need for such exertions. Why should they bother with economic and historical materials, these Sunday children? Everything is *so simple*, the valiant Willich used to say to me. Everything is simple! In these empty heads. Highly simple fellows!

32

From letter to Frederick Engels (in Manchester)
London, July 31, 1851

Dear Engels:

... For approximately the last fourteen days I have written nothing, because during the time I did not spend in the Library,[1] I was hunted like a dog in such a way that, despite the best will, I was distracted from writing.

After the two Bambergers, father and son, have procrastinated from week to week—first from month-to-month—with promises to discount a promissory note for me, and after I went to that Jew-den on an appointment for that purpose, bringing with me the *stamped paper* [in English], the young one informed me that the old one, who was there too, could not, etc., etc.

That I could not box the ears of these two Jews for this infamous procrastination, waste of time and placing me in a *fausse* [false] position, was most regrettable....

Yours, K.M.

32

1. British Museum.

33

To Joseph Weydemeyer (in Zurich)
London, August 2, 1851

Dear Weydemeyer:
I have just received from Engels your letter and hasten to reply to you. Naturally, I would have wished—even though it was impossible to keep you here—at least to see you and speak to you before your departure.

But if you are going to America, you could not find a more opportune moment for doing so, both for finding ways of making a living and for being useful to our Party.

In fact, it is almost a certainty that you will find a position as editor on the *New-Yorker Staatszeitung.*[1] It had been previously offered to Lupus. He is enclosing here a letter to Reichhelm, the co-owner of the paper. So much for business. But you must not lose time.

For another thing: Herr Heinzen, together with the worthy Ruge, are blowing the trumpets weekly in the New York *Schnellpost* against the communists, especially me, Engels, etc. The whole local democratic vermin deposits its manure in the ditch there, but no seeds or fruits, making the weeds flourish luxuriantly. Finally: Heinzen baits the *Staatszeitung*, which is not capable of facing up to this enemy.

Whatever the American policy of the *Staatszeitung* may be, in the European one you will have *la voix libre* [a free hand]. The American press will be glad to see somebody come over there and rap the knuckles of this loud-mouthed bully [Heinzen].

When you are editor, we will give your department every assistance. Unfortunately, the scamp and jackass Seiler is the London correspondent for the *Staatszeitung*. One should also button up the lips of that member of the European government, Ruge.

Your essay against Christ is good. I have no changes to suggest, but only remark in passing that it is true that workers in factory districts marry in order to squeeze *money* out of their children. This fact is sad but true.

You can imagine that my situation is very gloomy. It will be the end of my wife if this continues. The constant worries, the petty daily struggles are grinding her down. Added to this are the infamies of my enemies, who have *never yet* tried to attack me *factually* but seek to revenge themselves for their impotence by impugning my reputation and spreading the most unspeakable calumnies about me. Willich, Schapper, Ruge, and a number of other mem-

---

33

1. German-language daily in New York, published since 1834.

bers of this democratic rabble make this their business. As soon as some one arrives from the Continent, they start working on him, so that he in turn may take up the same handiwork.

A few days ago, the "illustrious" barrister Schramm met an acquaintance on the street and immediately whispered in his ear: No matter how the revolution comes out, on one thing everybody is agreed—Marx is *perdu* [through]. Rodbertus,[2] who has the best prospect for success, will have him shot at once. Of course, I could laugh over this whole muck; I don't let it disturb me in my work for a moment, but you can understand that my wife, who is ill and is involved in the most dismal bourgeois poverty from morning to night and whose nerves are affected, is not helped when stupid scandalmongers bring her daily the pestiferous effluvia of the democratic sink-holes. The tactlessness of some people in this regard is often colossal.

For the rest, there is no question here about parties. The great men, despite the pretended difference of opinion, do nothing here except mutually guarantee each other's importance. No revolution has ever cast up to the surface a more hollow gang than this.

When you are in New York, go and see A. Dana[3] of the *New-York Tribune* and give him regards from me and Freiligrath. Perhaps he can be useful to you. As soon as you arrive, write me at once, but always at Engels' address, since he is in the best position among us to pay the postage. At any rate, I expect a few words from you before you really sail. When your wife arrives, give her my wife's and my best regards.

If you can remain in New York, you will not be far from Europe, and with the complete suppression of the press in Germany, a press campaign can only be waged from there.

Yours, K. Marx

I have just learned that the great men, Ruge and his clique, Kinkel and his clique, Schapper, Willich and his clique, and the go-betweens of these great men—Fickler,[4] Goegg[5] and clique have combined together into a fungus. You know the story of the peasant who sold every other dozen bushels under the cost price. But, said he, the mass [the big turnover] will do it. So also say these weaklings: the mass will do it. For the rest, the cement that holds together this dough is the hatred for the "clique of the *Neue Rheinische Zeitung*," especially for me. A dozen of them, when together, are true manly fellows.

---

2. Johann Karl Rodbertus (1805–1875), Prussian landowner and economist.
3. Charles Anderson Dana (1819–1897), editor of *New-York Daily Tribune* and *The New American Cyclopaedia*, for both of which Marx wrote.
4. Joseph Fickler (1808–1865), German refugee journalist.
5. Amand Goegg (1820–1897), German refugee journalist.

If you should not become chief of the *Arbeiterzeitung* in New York—which, indeed, would be best—but if you should find it necessary to negotiate with the *Staatszeitung*, do be careful about your friend Kapp,[6] who goes in and out there. We have proof in hand that this character—for reasons which I know not—is one of the chief intrigants against us.

Adieu, mon cher.

34

From letter to Frederick Engels (in Manchester)
London, October 13, 1851

Dear Engels:

... Edgar Bauer is supposed to be here [in London]. I have not seen him yet. A week ago, Blind and his wife (Madame Cohen) arrived here to visit the Exhibition,[1] and left last Sunday. I have not seen him again since [October 6] because of the following tasteless incident, which will show you how very much henpecked that unfortunate fellow is. Today I received from him a city letter announcing his departure. Last Monday, he and his wife visited me. Also present were Freiligrath,[2] "Red" [Ferdinand] Wolff (who, one may remark in passing, has quietly sneaked up and *married* an English bluestocking), Liebknecht,[3] and the unfortunate Pieper. Mrs. Blind is a lively Jewess, and we laughed and chattered quite gaily, when the Father of all Lies introduced the subject of religion. She bragged about atheism, Feuerbach, etc. I attacked Feuerbach, but, of course, in a polite and friendly manner. At first the Jewess seemed to me to be amused by the discussion, and that naturally was the only reason why I entered into this boring theme. In the midst of it, my doctrinaire echo, Herr Pieper, interjected himself oracularly and, to be sure, not very tactfully. Suddenly I see the woman dissolved in tears. Blind threw me an expressive, melancholy glance. She stalked out—and was not seen anymore, *ni lui non plus* [he neither]. In my long experience I have never experienced such an adventure....

Yours, K. Marx

---

6. Friedrick Kapp (1824-1884), German historian.

34

1. The London Industrial Exhibition.
2. Ferdinand Freiligrath (1810–1876), German poet, refugee in London, friend of Marx.
3. Wilhelm Liebknecht (1826–1900), a friend of Marx and later one of the main founders and leaders of the Social-Democratic party in Germany.

35

To Joseph Weydemeyer (in New York)
London, January 16, 1852

Dear Weydemeyer:
Today I got out of bed for the first time in fourteen days. From this you can see that my indisposition—which is not yet entirely over—was a serious one. This is why, with the best will in the world, I could not send you the third installment of my articles on Bonaparte[1] this week. On the other hand, I am enclosing a poem and a private letter from Freiligrath[2]. Now I have to ask you: (1) to have the poem printed carefully, the stanzas separated at adequate intervals, and the whole arranged without an eye for saving space, for poetry loses greatly when it is printed all crowded together; (2) to write a friendly letter to Freiligrath. Don't be afraid of complimenting him too much, for all poets, even the best, are *plus ou moins des courtisanes, et il faut les cajoler, pour les faire chanter* [more or less courtesans, and have to be cajoled to make them sing]. In private life, our Freiligrath is the most amiable, most unpretentious man, who conceals *un esprit très fin et très railleur* [a very subtle and very bantering spirit] underneath his genuine simplicity, and whose pathos is "genuine" without making him "uncritical" and "superstitious." He is a real revolutionary and a thoroughly honest man—praise that I would mete out but to few. Nevertheless, a poet, no matter what he may be as a man, needs applause, admiration. I believe this lies in the very nature of the species. I am telling you all this merely to call your attention to the fact that in your correspondence with Freiligrath you must not forget the difference between "poet" and "critic." Moreover, it is very amiable of him to address his poetic letter to you directly. I believe this will give you *relief* [in English] in New York.

I don't know whether I can still send you another article today. Pieper has promised me an article for you. Up to this moment, he has not yet appeared, and if he does, his article must pass the test whether it should be confined to the flames or is worthy of crossing the ocean. I am *trop faible encore* [still too weak] to write more. Today more than a week. Greetings from house to house.

Lupus has not yet recovered, and hence has not written anything yet.

Yours, K. Marx

35

1. Marx, *The Eighteenth Brumaire of Louis Napoleon*, published serially in *Die Revolution*, a German-language journal, edited by Joseph Weydemeyer in New York, January–May, 1852; later editions, including the second one, brought out in Hamburg, 1869, used the title *The Eighteenth Brumaire of Louis Bonaparte*.
2. Ferdinand Freiligrath's two poems against Gottfried Kinkel were published by Weydemeyer in *Die Revolution* in January, 1852.

36

To Ferdinand Freiligrath (in London)
London, January 26, 1852

Dear Freiligrath:
The stanza[1] which you sent for my consideration is very beautiful and expresses the *corpus delicti* artistically, but I believe it hurts the impression of the whole. *D'abord* [to begin with], *is* Kinkel a "German poet"? I and a number of other *bons gens* [cognoscenti] allow ourselves a modest doubt on this point. Then also: is not the significant contrast between the "German poet" and the "commercial" Babylon diminished by a repetition of the contrast between the "free" and the "servile" poet? The more so as in your "Andersen"[2] part of the poem you have already exhaustively sketched the relationship between the inflated worldly *literateur* and the "poet." In my view there is no need to drag Kinkel into this passage, since it would only give enemies an opportunity to consider this as an expression of personal irritation or rivalry. But since the stanza is very well done and should not be lost, you will surely—assuming that you accept my view—find occasion to use it in another connection, perhaps in a succeeding poetic letter. For the sketch is delightful.

Since Engels and Weerth did not return the copy of your first poem [against Kinkel, written on January 16 and 23], I could only write about it yesterday to "Red" Wolff from memory, which, however, sufficed to move him to a fit of enthusiasm.

As to our friend Ebner,[3] he has at any rate received letters from Pieper. Best proof: Pieper has a reply from him. A few days ago Pieper wrote him fully and excused my silence on the ground of my ill health.

I have received a letter from Bermbach[4] consisting of some thirty lines. He asks why he has not heard from me for such a long time? The answer is very simple. I keep sending half proof sheets to Cologne and, after a long interval, I receive a few lines which never answer my questions. For example,

---

36

1. On January 25, 1852, Freiligrath sent Marx part of a satiric poem on their common enemy, Gottfried Kinkel. It read, in part: "*O deutscher Dichter, wer fragt hier nach Dir? Und prangest Du im Lexicon von Brockhaus, Und druckte Cotta Dich in Miniatur, Und ziertest Du sogar einmal das Stockhaus...?*"

    Freely translated:
    "O German poet, who asks for you here?
    And do you shine in the lexicon of Brockhaus,
    And did Cotta print you in miniature,
    And do you adorn even the jailhouse...?"
2. Hans Christian Andersen (1805–1875), Danish poet.
3. Hermann Ebner, journalist, secret police agent.
4. Adolph Bermbach (1822–1875), Cologne lawyer.

in regard to Daniels' state of health, never a word. I will send you Bermbach's letter as soon as it comes back from Manchester. Engels expects to use it in articles for the English papers. The only important thing in that piece of trash is the following: The arraigning Senate, in view—*remarquez le bien* [note this]—of the fact "that no objective facts have emerged and hence the indictment has no support," decides that the judicial inquiry begin *anew*. Thus one first sits in jail for nine months on some absurd grounds. Then it turns out that there is no legal ground for this imprisonment. Result: You must be jailed again until the examining magistrate sees his way clear to provide the indictment with "an objective fact," and if he cannot find such "objective fact," you can rot in jail.

Such shameless cowardice is unbelievable. The main fault lies with the miserable "press," which does not utter a syllable. A few articles in the *Kölnische Zeitung*, the *National-Zeitung*, the *Breslauer Zeitung*—and the Cologne arraigning Senate would never have dared do anything of the sort. But the dogs of democrats and liberals rejoice over this elimination of their communist opponents. Did we not come to the defense of men like Temme[5] and the whole trashy democratic rabble as often as they were in conflict with the police and the courts? Kinkel, whom Becker[6] had baked and Bürgers[7] had bailed,[8] never mentions them in gratitude in the *Lithographische Correspondenz*, which he fodders with American money. *Les canailles* [the riffraff].

If I knew of a safe bourgeois address in Cologne, I would write to Mrs. Daniels and try to reassure her somewhat about the political conditions. From what Pieper reports, it appears that the "gallant bourgeois" are exploiting every counterrevolutionary device to frighten and anger her.

Enclosed a note from Miss Jenny[9] to Master Wolfgang.[10]

Best regards.

Yours, K.M.

37

From letter to Frederick Engels (in Manchester)
London, February 27, 1852

Dear Engels:
... On February 25, the French celebrated a February banquet, or rather a dry meeting with trimmings of tea and sandwiches. I and my wife were

---

5. Jodocus Donatus Hubertus Temme (1798–1881), judge in Münster.
6. Hermann Heinrich Becker (1820–1885), Cologne journalist.
7. Heinrich Bürgers (1820–1878), Cologne communist journalist.
8. Marx is punning on the names—*Bäcker* is German for baker, and *bürgen* means go bail for.
9. Daughter Jenny Marx.
10. Freiligrath's son.

invited. The general public could enter at a fee of one franc. As I neither could nor would go, I sent my wife there with a Frenchman. Ledru-Rollin,[1] Pyat,[2] Thoré,[3] Martin Bernard,[4] etc., in short, the whole Rollinist clique, who had organized the thing, did not show up, because they considered the admission fee, to be used for refugee relief, too vulgar. L. Blanc had also declined. Only the lowest dregs of the emigration, calling themselves mostly Blanquist, were present. But the treacherous little Corsican [Blanc], who lived in some parlor nearby, only appeared after his spies assured him of the absence of Ledru-Rollin & Co., and in the total absence of talent and authority, the coquettish, steel-blue frock coat was received with *rapturous applause* [in English]. His speech, which he delivered and promptly departed, enchanted his enemies. Carried them away. Won them over.

And what did *that little man* [in English] say, this Johnny Russell[5] of socialism? People abroad wonder about the peculiar events in France; he, however, believes more than ever in the star of *la patrie*. And why? *Je veux*, he says, *vous expliquer le mouvement historique* [I want to explain to you the historic movement],[6] etc. To wit, in the life of all great military men, for example, Frederick the Great and Napoleon the Great, are to be found great victories and great reverses. *Eh bien! La France est une nation militaire* [Well, France is a military nation]. She has her élan and her catastrophes. *Quod erat demonstrandum* [Which was demonstrated]. Whatever she had ever wanted she had always achieved: in 1789, she had driven out the feudality, in 1830 the monarchy. Whom did she want to overthrow in 1848? You think perhaps the bourgeoisie? Not on your life! *La misère, la hideuse misère* [Poverty, the hideous poverty]. Now followed a socialist tearjerker about the *misère*. *La misère n'est pas quelque chose de fixe, quelque chose de saisissable*,[7] but nevertheless the French nation in the new revolution will defeat poverty, and then *la mère ne détruira plus de ses propres main le fruit de ses entrailles, la petite fille de sept ans ne se*

37

1. Alexandre Auguste Ledru-Rollin (1807–1874), French politician and editor, émigré in London.
2. Félix Pyat (1810–1889), French journalist, émigré in London.
3. Étienne Joseph Théophile Thoré (1807–1869), French politician and journalist, émigré in London.
4. Martin Bernard (1808–1883), French revolutionist.
5. Lord John Russell (1792–1878), British Whig statesman.
6. Of Blanc as an historian, Marx wrote in a letter to Engels, February 23, 1851: "Insofar as his historical works are concerned, he produces them the way Alexandre Dumas does his feuilletons. He always studies the materials for the next chapter only....On the one hand, this gives his presentations a certain freshness, for what he reports is at least as new to him as to the reader; on the other hand, the whole thing is weak."
7. Poverty is not a thing that is fixed, not a thing that is seizable.

"*groupera*" *plus sous la machine*,[8] and similar asininities. In his speech he squandered three whole jokes. He called Bonaparte[9] (1) *un aventurier* [an adventurer], (2) *un bâtard* [a bastard], and (3) *le singe de son oncle* [the ape of his uncle, Napoleon I]. This last news threw his audience into a veritable St. Vitus dance. *Qu'en dis-tu* [What do you say to that]? One despairs of these *crapauds* [toads]. Their history in the large is epigrammatic, a genuine dramatic work of art, but the fellows themselves! *Mon dieu*! Herr Blanc's incursion reminds me of a joke told to me by Massol.[10] After midnight, Bonaparte is regularly drunk in the company of male and female creatures whom he assembles for his orgies. He curses and swears then. One of the ladies in his circle excuses him with the words: *Mais c'est un militaire* [But he is a military man]! Adio.

Yours, K. Marx

38

From letter to Joseph Weydemeyer (in New York)
London, March 5, 1852

Dear Weywy:
... When a member of Parliament in England becomes Minister he has to run for his seat again. Thus Disraeli,[1] the new Lord of the Exchequer, writes to his constituents, under the date of March 1:

"We shall endeavor to terminate that *strife of classes* which, of late years, has exercised so pernicious an influence over the welfare of this kingdom."

On which the *Times* of March 2 commented:

"If anything would ever divide classes in this country beyond reconciliation, and leave no chance of a just and honourable peace, it would be a tax on foreign corn."

And so that an ignorant "man of character" like Heinzen should not imagine that aristocrats are *for* and the bourgeois *against* corn laws, because the former are in favor of "*monopoly*" and the latter in favor of "*freedom*"—a simple person knows the contradictions only in this ideological form—one has only to remark that in the eighteenth century the aristocrats in England

---

8. The mother will no longer destroy with her own hands the fruit of her bowels; little girls of seven will no longer have to be "grouped" under the machine.
9. Napoleon III.
10. Marie Alexandre Massol (1805–1875), French socialist journalist.

38

1. Benjamin Disraeli (1804–1881), British statesman, Prime Minister, 1867 and 1874–1880.

were for "freedom" (of trade) and the bourgeois for "monopoly," the same position in regard to "corn laws" that we find at this moment in "Prussia" between the two classes. The *Neue Preussische Zeitung* is the most frantic Free Trader.

Finally, in your place I would remark to the gentlemen democrats in general that they would do better to begin with getting acquainted with bourgeois literature, before they undertake to bellow about contradictions. The gentlemen should, for example, study the historical works of Thierry,[2] Guizot,[3] John Wade,[4] etc., to get an idea about the "history of classes." They should become familiar with elementary political economy. It suffices, for example, to open Ricardo's[5] great work, to find on the first page these words with which he opens the Preface:

> The produce of the earth—all that is derived from its surface by the united application of labour, machinery, and capital, is divided among *three classes* of the community; namely the proprietor of the land, the owner of the stock of capital necessary for its cultivation, and the labourers by whose industry it is cultivated.

How little bourgeois society in the United States has developed intellectually in regard to understanding the class struggle is most brilliantly illustrated by H. C. Carey (of Philadelphia),[6] the only important North American economist. He attacks Ricardo, the classical representative of the bourgeoisie and the most stoical opponent of the proletariat, as a man whose work is the arsenal for anarchists, socialists, and all other enemies of the bourgeois order. He not only reproaches him but also Malthus,[7] Mill,[8] Say,[9] Torrens,[10] Wakefield,[11] MacCulloch,[12] Senior,[13] Whately,[14] R. Jones,[15] etc.—these economic dancing masters of

2. Jacques Nicolas Augustin Thierry (1795–1856), French historian.
3. François Guizot (1787–1874), French historian and statesman.
4. John Wade (1788–1875), English economist.
5. David Ricardo (1772–1823), English economist.
6. Henry Charles Carey's work included *Essay on the Rate of Wages* (1835); *Principles of Political Economy* (1837, 1838, 1840); *Past, Present and Future* (1848); *The Harmony of Interests, Agricultural, Manufacturing and Commercial* (1851).
7. Thomas Robert Malthus (1766–1834), English economist, population theorist.
8. James Mill (1773–1836), English economist.
9. Jean Baptist Say (1826–1896), French statesman and economist.
10. Robert Torrens (1780–1864), English economist.
11. Edward Gibbon Wakefield (1796–1862), British statesman and economist.
12. John Ramsay MacCulloch (1789–1864), Scottish economist.
13. Nassau William Senior (1790–1864), English economist.
14. Richard Whately (1787–1863), English theologian and economist.
15. Richard Jones (1790–1855), English economist.

Europe—for tearing society apart and spreading civil war by their demonstration that the economic foundations of various classes must give rise to a necessary and ever-growing antagonism among them. He attempts to refute them, but not like the fatuous Heinzen, by linking the existence of classes with the existence of political privileges and monopolies, rather by attempting to show that economic conditions—rents (landed property), profit (capital), and wages (wage labor)—instead of being conditions of struggle and antagonism, are rather conditions of association and harmony. Naturally, all he proves is that the "undeveloped" conditions in the United States are, for him, "normal conditions."

Insofar as I am concerned, the merit of having discovered either the existence of classes in modern society or the class struggle does not belong to me. Bourgeois historians have presented the historic development of this struggle of classes, and bourgeois economists the economic anatomy of the same, long before I did. What was new in what I did was: (1) to demonstrate that the *existence of classes* is tied only to *definite historical phases of development of production*; (2) that the class struggle necessarily leads to the *dictatorship of the proletariat*; (3) that this dictatorship is only a transition to the *dissolution of all classes* and leads to the formation of a *classless society*. Ignorant louts like Heinzen who deny not only the struggle but also the existence of classes, only prove that, despite their blood-oozing and humanistically boastful yelping, they consider the societal conditions in which the bourgeoisie rules, to be the final product, the non plus ultra [*sic*], of history, that they are the slaves of the bourgeoisie, a servitude which is the more disgusting the less the louts understand the great and transitory necessity of the bourgeois regime.

From the marginal notes above, you may select whatever appears to be good to you. . . .

Yours, K. Marx

39

From letter to Jenny Marx (in London)
Manchester, June 11, 1852

Dear Heart:[1]
I was very pleased with your letter. Incidentally, you don't have to feel embarrassed reporting everything to me. When you, poor little devil, live

---

39
1. Mrs. Marx. Marx was on a visit with Engels in Manchester from end May to mid-June, 1856.

through bitter reality, it is only fair that I share with you the distress at least in my mind. I know, moreover, how endlessly elastic you are and how the slightest favorable thing revivifies you. Hopefully you will receive this week or at the latest next Monday another £5. . . .

Kiss and greet my little men[2] for me.

Yours, K.M.

---

2. The three children: five-year old Edgar, seven-year old Laura, and eight-year old Jenny.

Karl Marx in London in 1861, at the age of 43

Karl Marx's last picture, in Algiers in 1882, the year before he died. He wrote to his daughter Laura (May 6, 1882): "I am enclosing a photo for you and for Fred [Engels]; no art could make a man look worse."

Marx's grave in London's Highgate Cemetery, where he was buried on March 17, 1883

(Left) Karl Marx in London in 1876, at the age of 58. This portrait, by Mayall of London, hung in Stalin's office

*Marx and Engels and the three Marx daughters
(l. to r.): Jenny, Eleanor, Laura, c.1861*

*(Right) Jenny von Westphalen Marx
Marx's young wife, in the 1840*

Edgar ("Musch"), Marx's only son, who, to the despair of his father, died in 1855 at the age of eight

Marx's daughters: Jenny (1844–1883) and Laura (1845–1911)

Marx and his oldest daughter, Jenny, in 1869

Eleanor ("Tussy"), Marx's youngest daughter (1855–1898), as a young girl

French socialist Paul Lafargue (1842–1911), husband of Marx's daughter Laura, who committed suicide with his wife on November 26, 1911

Section Five

JOURNALISM and ECONOMIC RESEARCH · *1852-1864*

Marx was saved from outright starvation not only by Engels, who in the decade of the 1850's could not yet contribute large sums, but by the *New-York Daily Tribune*, whose London correspondent he became in 1851. The *Tribune* paid £2 per article, generally printing two of them weekly until the late 1850's, when it published fewer and fewer, ceasing altogether in March, 1862. To supplement his meagre income, Marx wrote occasionally for some other journals, such as *The People's Paper* in London, the *Neue Oder-Zeitung* in Breslau, and *Die Presse* in Vienna. But these papers paid even less than the *Tribune*.[1]

At the same time he did systematic research in the British Museum, not only for his journalism (which consisted of solid economic and political fare) but also for his books on political economy, which he considered his real life's work. His first book on the subject, *Critique of Political Economy*, was published in Berlin in 1859, after difficulties with his publisher, Franz Duncker. Misery and illnesses at home, where two children died in infancy and a third in childhood, did not keep him from his dogged economic

---

1. On Marx's journalism, see Saul K. Padover, ed., *Karl Marx on Freedom of the Press and Censorship* (Mc-Graw Hill Book Co., New York, 1974).

research and writing. The dozen years 1852–1864 constituted for Marx a period of remarkable productivity. He wrote hundreds of articles, mostly carefully researched. In the *New-York Daily Tribune* alone he published at least 321 articles, plus another fourteen in collaboration with Engels. He spent most of his nights at the writing table.

40

To Frederick Engels (in Manchester)
London, September 8, 1852

Dear Engels:

Your letter arrived today in a very agitated atmosphere.

My wife is ill, Jennychen[1] is ill, Lenchen[2] has a sort of hysteria. I cannot and could not call the doctor because I have no money for medicine. For the past eight to ten days I have been feeding the family on bread and potatoes, and it is questionable whether I can get any more today. This diet was naturally not beneficial under present climatic conditions. I did not write the article for Dana[3] because I did not have the penny to buy newspapers to read. For the rest, as soon as you have sent me No. 19, I will write No. 20, a summary of the whole current shit.[4]

When I visited you[5] and you told me that up to the end of August you would be able to procure for me a somewhat larger sum, I wrote that to my wife to ease her mind. Your letter of three or four weeks ago[6] indicated that there was not much prospect of this. So I postponed paying all creditors, who, as you know, are always paid in small sums, until early September. Now the storm has broken loose.

I have tried everything, but in vain. First, the dog of a Weydemeyer took me for £15. I wrote to Germany to Streit.[7]... The animal did not even

---

40

1. Daughter Jenny.
2. Helene Demuth (1823–1890), the Marx family housekeeper and lifelong friend.
3. In 1851, Marx became London correspondent for Dana's paper, the *New-York Daily Tribune*.
4. The series of articles, published subsequently under the title *Revolution and Counter-Revolution in Germany*, which Engels wrote and which was published in the *New-York Daily Tribune* under Marx's name.
5. Marx was in Manchester from the end of May to mid-June, 1852.
6. Engels to Marx, August 6, 1952: "...in this month I owe £20 to £25 and am completely strapped."
7. Feodor Streit (1820–1904), a German publisher in Koburg.

answer. I turn to Brockhaus[8] and offer him an article of uncaptious content for *Die Gegenwart*. He refused very politely. Finally, in the last week I have been running around all day with an Englishman [Pönisch] trying to discount Dana's bill. *Pour le roi de Prusse* [in vain].

The best and most desirable thing that could happen would be for the landlady to throw me out of the house. I would then at least be quit for the sum of £25. But so much favor I cannot expect from her. In addition, I still owe the baker, the milkman, the tea fellow, the greengrocer, and an old debt to the butcher. What am I to do with all this devil's muck? Finally—what is to me the most dreadful—in the past eight to ten days, out of necessity, in order not to croak, I have borrowed shillings and pence from philistines [*Knoten*].

From my letters you will have seen that I am wading through the muck, as usual, with great indifference, even though I am stuck in it and don't hear the end of it. Still, *que faire* [what to do]? My house is a lazarette, and the crisis becomes so disturbing that it forces me to give it my utmost attention. *Que faire?*

In the meantime, Mr. Goegg is again on a pleasure tour to America, steamer first class. Mr. Proudhon has pocketed some 100,000 francs from his Anti-Napoleon,[9] and Father Massol is so generous as to leave the *fouiller* [grubbing, rummaging], etc., to me. *Je le remercie bien* [I thank him very much].

Yours, K.M.

41

From letter to Frederick Engels (in Manchester)
London, September 28, 1852

Dear Engels:

For a long time you have not received any letter from me. The main cause is Weerth, who *plus ou moins* [more or less] requisitions the evenings which I otherwise devote to writing. And this to my not too great joy. You know that I am very fond of Weerth, *mais* [but] when one is stuck in the muck up to one's neck, it is painful to be in the presence of such a fine gentleman, *auquel il faut cacher les parties trop honteuses* [from whom one must conceal all the too

---

8. Heinrich Brockhaus (1804-1874) was the head of the Leipzig publishing house, F.A. Brockhaus, which among other things published *Die Gegenwart*, an encyclopedic collection of contemporary history.
9. Proudhon, *La révolution sociale démontrée par le coup d'état du 2 décembre* (Paris, 1852).

shameful things]. Such a relationship brings forth a double *gêne* [embarrassment] and I hope that he will leave for Manchester tomorrow and that, when he comes back, he will find me in circumstances where I can again communicate with him *franchement* [unreservedly]. Incidentally, I think that, apart from the ailing condition of my wife, he has not looked more deeply into my cards.[1]. . . .

Yours, K.M.

42

From letter to Adolf Cluss (in Washington)
London, March 25, 1853

Dear Cluss:

. . . One more *fact* [in English]. It is not my fault if it is unesthetic. The "*blonde souveraine*",[1] Montijo-Lola,[2] is given to a very disgusting constitutional inconvenience—uncontrolled *farts*. One calls it tympoptanomania[3]. Previously, she had tried to resist this "accident" by vigorous riding, something that Bonaparte[4] has now forbidden her as not in accordance with her rank, and so at various "*Réunions*" [gatherings] her "*détonations fortes*" made even the beribboned Décembraillards[5] blush. *Ce n'est qu'un petit bruit, un murmure, un rien; mais enfin, vous savez que les Français ont le nez au plus petit vent.*[6]

Yours, K.M.

41
1. Marx refers to his poverty.

42
1. "Blond Empress": Eugénie Marie de Montijo (1826-1920), Spanish wife of Napoleon III.
2. Lola Montez (1818–1861), Spanish dancer, mistress of King Ludwig I of Bavaria. Marx used her name as a term of contempt for the Empress who was also Spanish-born.
3. The word was apparently invented by Marx.
4. Napoleon III.
5. The Decembrists, involved in Napoleon III's *coup d'état* of December, 1852.
6. 'Tis but a small noise, a murmur, a nothing; but, after all, you know the French have a nose for the smallest wind.

43

From letter to Frederick Engels (in Manchester)
London, June 2, 1853

Dear Frederic!

...The praise you give my "young" English[1] has had a heartening effect on me. What I mainly lack is, first, grammatical sureness, and, secondly, a knack for certain secondary turnings of phrase, without which sharp writing is impossible. Mr. "Tribune" put a headnote on my second article on Gladstone's budget,[2] calling public attention to the "masterly exposition" and stating it had never seen "a more able criticism" and did "not expect to see one." This is all right. But in the succeeding article it embarrasses me again by putting a thoroughly insignificant headline, meant to be by me, under my name, while at the same time it appropriates your "Swiss" article.[3] I will write to Dana that I am very "flattered" when the *Tribune* sometimes uses my things as leaders. But it should please not use my name under insignificant notices....

Vale faveque [Be well and devoted].

C.M.

44

From letter to Frederick Engels (in Manchester)
London, April 22, 1854

Dear Frederic:

...Recently the *Tribune* has again appropriated all my articles as leaders and published only *trash* under *my* name. Thus, for example, it annexed a detailed analysis of Austrian finances,[1] an article on the Greek insurrection,[2]

43

1. Engels to Marx, June 1, 1853: "In an old issue of the *Tribune*, of early April date, I read yesterday your article on the *Times* and the refugees....*Je t'en fais mon compliment* [I compliment you]. Your English is not only good, it is brilliant. Here and there a few catch-words are not woven in fluently enough, but this is the worst that can be said about the article."
2. Marx, "Riots at Constantinople—German Table Moving—The Budget," *New-York Daily Tribune*, May 6, 1853. The first article in which Marx discussed the English Budget was published on May 3, 1853.
3. "The Rocket Affair—The Swiss Insurrection," by Marx and Engels, in *New-York Daily Tribune*, May 14, 1853. This was one part of the article; the rest of it, written by Engels, was published in the *Tribune*, May 17, 1853.

44

1. "Austrian Bankruptcy," *New-York Daily Tribune*, March 22, 1854.
2. "The Greek Insurrection," *New-York Daily Tribune*, March 29, 1854.

etc. In addition, the "constitutionally" achieved reputation with your military stuff. I positively intend—as soon as Dana has replied to my last *monitorium* [reminder]—to propose an increased honorarium, and will specifically refer to the expenses incurred in connection with the *militaria* [military articles]. Don't you think so? The fellows must pay at least £3 per article. Thus they spent £500 to send Taylor[3] to India, and the fellow writes worse and less from there—and what, after all, could he learn on a quick trip in such a country?—than I do from here on the same subject. With £3 per article, I could at last get out of the muck....

Yours, K.M.

45

From letter to Frederick Engels (in Manchester)
London, May 3, 1854

Dear Engels:
...In my spare hours I am now studying Spanish. Began with Calderón, from whose *Magico Prodigioso*[1]—the Catholic Faust—Goethe used not only individual passages but also the whole design of scenes in his *Faust*. Then— *horribile dictu* [terrible to say]—I read in Spanish what would have been impossible in French: *Atala* and *René* by Chateaubriand[2] and a bit of rubbish by Bernardin de St. Pierre.[3] Am now in the middle of *Don Quixote*. I find that in Spanish one needs a dictionary more than in Italian, in the beginning....

Vale faveque [Be well and devoted].

K.M.

46

To Frederick Engels (in Manchester)
London, May 22, 1854

Dear Engels:
It was good that you did not come on Saturday. My story—now fourteen days old—had reached the crisis point. I could talk little, and it hurt even to

---

3. Bayard Taylor (1825–1878), American journalist, correspondent for *New-York Daily Tribune*.

45

1. Pedro Calderón de la Barca, *El Mágico Prodigioso*.
2. François René de Chateaubriand (1786–1848), French author and statesman.
3. Jacques Henri Bernardin de St. Pierre (1737–1814), French writer.

laugh on account of the big abscess between nose and mouth, which this morning has been reduced at least to reasonable proportions. Also, the violently swollen lips are becoming reduced closer to their previous dimensions, etc., in short here are all the symptoms of approaching improvement. May the head of the devil go through such fourteen days. All this stops being a joke. In the last eight days I had to give up reading and smoking completely, and today am awaiting a friend in order to find out whether a cigar may be smoked tentatively.

To the augmentation of the ill luck, all three children have had the measles since Friday (Thursday night), so that the house has been transformed into a veritable lazarette.

Enclosed, Cluss' letter. The closing of *Reform*² is disgusting.

For this whole week I still rely on you to perform the American service³ for me, as I am still totally incapable of writing and have already lost £6 through this shit, which is very bitter for me. In the meantime, I expect a few words from you.

The enclosed letter from Cluss is to be communicated to Lupus only. Heise⁴ seems to have the mission of compromising you in Manchester. Beware of the fellow.

Yours, K.M.

47

From letter to Frederick Engels (in Manchester)
London, July 27, 1854

Dear Engels:

... Pieper, who for two weeks lived with a whore whom he declared to be a *bijou* [jewel], and looks *half-starved* [in English] like a milk-weaned sucking pig, is—*hélas* [alas]—again on my neck, after he has jubilated through some £20 in fourteen days and is now empty in both pockets. In this heat it is inconvenient to have in the house a fellow *du matin jusqu'au soir et du soir jusqu'au matin* [from morning to night and from night to morning]. It also disturbs one's work....

46

1. Adolf Cluss. (*c.* 1820–*c.* 1889), German communist, emigrated to the United States, where he became an employee in the Navy Department, Washington, D.C.
2. German-language labor weekly in New York.
3. Articles for the *New-York Daily Tribune*, which Engels wrote in Marx's name.
4. Heinrich Heise (d. 1860), refugee German journalist.

...A book that has interested me very much is Thierry's *Histoire de la Formation et du Progrès du Tiers État*,[1] 1853. Strange how this gentleman, the father of the "class struggle" in French historiography, in his Preface expresses anger at the "new ones" who likewise see an antagonism between bourgeoisie and proletariat and who discovered traces of this conflict in the history of the Third Estate up to 1789. He takes great pains to prove that the Third Estate embraces all estates that are not noblesse and clergy and that the bourgeoisie plays its role as the representative of all these other elements. He cites, for example, from the Venetian Ambassadorial reports: *"Questi che si chiamano li stati del regno sono di tre ordini di persone, cioè del clero, della nobiltà, e del restante di quelle persone che, per voce comune, si può chiamare populo."*[2] If Thierry had read our writings, he would have known that the decisive antagonism of the bourgeoisie against the people naturally begins as soon as it ceases to oppose the noblesse and clergy as the Third Estate. But in regard to the *racines dans l'histoire* [roots in history], and *d'un antagonisme né d'hier* [an antagonism born yesterday], his book provides the best proof that these *racines* [roots] arise as soon as the Third Estate begins. From the *Senatus populusque Romanus* [Senate and People of Rome], this otherwise intelligent critic in his field should have concluded that in Rome there never was any other antagonism than that between *senatus* and *populus*. What interested me, in the documents which he quotes, is that the word *catalla, capitalia*—capital—arises with the rise of the communes. For the rest, he proved reluctantly that the bourgeoisie was delayed in its victory only until it decided to make common cause with the peasants in 1789. Handsomely presented, even though not summarized: (1) how from the beginning, at least since the rise of the cities, the French bourgeoisie thereby wins so much influence that it constitutes itself as Parliament, bureaucracy, etc., and not, as in England, merely through commerce and industry. (2) From his presentation it is easily seen how class arises, in that the various forms in which it finds its core in various periods and the different fractions that win influence through these forms, go to pieces. This consequence of metamorphoses, until it comes to the rule of class, in my view has nowhere—at least according to the facts—been so presented. Unfortunately, in regard to the *maîtrises, jurandes* [guilds, corporations], etc., in short, the forms in which the industrial bourgeoisie has developed, he has confined himself to well-known general phrases, although he knows this material too. What he has well developed and empha-

---

47

1. Thierry, *Essay on the History of the Formation and Progress of the Third Estate* (Paris, 1853).
2. These, called the various estates of the realm, consist of three orders of persons, namely, the clergy, the nobility and the rest of the persons that are commonly called the *people*.

sized is the conspiratorial and revolutionary character of the municipal movement of the twelfth century. . . .

Yours, K. Marx

48

From letter to Frederick Engels (in Manchester)
London, October 26, 1854

Dear Frederick:
In studying the Spanish shit,[1] I again came across the worthy Chateaubriand, that literary calligraphist who combines in the most offensive way the elegant skepticism and Voltaireanism of the eighteenth century with the elegant sentimentalism and romanticism of the nineteenth. Stylistically, of course, this combination was bound to be the rage in France, even though in the style itself, despite some artistic tricks, the false often leaps to the eye. In regard to the political Chateaubriand, he revealed himself completely in his *Congrès de Vérone*,[2] and the only question is whether he got "cash" from Alexander Pavlovich[3] or was simply bribed by *flatteries* [in English], to which the conceited fop is susceptible as nobody else. *At all instances* [in English], he received the Order of Saint Andrew from Petersburg. *Vanitas* [vanity] peeps from every core of Herr "Vicomte" (?), despite his now Mephisthophelean, now Christian flirting with *vanitatum vanitas* [vanity of vanities]. You know that in the time of the Congress,[4] Villèle[5] was Prime Minister of Louis XVIII and Chateaubriand was French ambassador in Verona. In his *Congrès de Vérone*—which perhaps you may have read once—he reports on the documents, negotiations, etc. He begins with a short history of the Spanish revolution of 1820–23. As far as this "history" is concerned, it suffices to cite that he places Madrid on the Tagus (simply in order to introduce the Spanish proverb that this river *cria oro* [produces gold]); and he says that Riego[6] at the head of *10,000 men* (in reality, there were 5,000) attacked General Freire[7] at

---

48

1. "Revolutionary Spain," a series of eight articles that Marx published in the *New-York Daily Tribune* between September 9 and December 2, 1854; for the text, see Saul K. Padover, ed., *Karl Marx On Revolution* (New York, 1973), pp. 547–629.
2. Chateaubriand, *The Congress of Verona* (Brussels, 1838).
3. Czar Alexander I.
4. The Congress of Verona, assembled by the Holy Alliance, took place in 1822.
5. Jean Baptiste Seraphin Joseph, Comte de Villèle (1773–1854).
6. Rafael de Riego y Nuñez, (1785–1823), Spanish officer, leader of 1820-23 revolution, executed.
7. Manuel Freire (1765–1834), a Spanish general.

the head of 13,000; that Riego was defeated and then retreated with 15,000 men. Instead of retiring to the Sierra de Ronda, he has him retire to the Sierra Morena, in order to compare him with the hero of Mancha.[8] I mention this in passing, in order to characterize his method. Almost not a single fact is correct. ...

When you read the book again, your contempt for the *"crapauds"* ["toads"] and their *"grands hommes"* ["great men"] will hardly decrease. Adieu.

Yours, K.M.

49

From letter to Frederick Engels (in Manchester)
London, November 30, 1854

Dear Engels:
... The day before yesterday I finally received the two volumes of Ripley's *Mexican War*,[1] approximately 1,200 pages, large format. Ripley seems to me—a *pure layman's judgment*—to have fashioned himself *plus ou moins* [more or less] after Napier[2] as a military historian. The book is sensible and, as it seems to me, not uncritical. Dana has surely not read it. Otherwise he would have seen that its [The *Tribune's*] hero, General Scott,[3] by no means appears in a favorable light either as a commander-in-chief or as a gentleman. I was especially interested in the history, as I recently read about the campaign of Fernando Cortez[4] in Antonio de Solis *Conquista de Mexico*[5]. Very interesting comparisons can be made between the two *conquistas* [conquests]. Moreover, although the two commanders—Taylor[6] as well as Scott—appear to me to be very mediocre, the whole war is surely a worthy overture to the war history of the great Yankee land. The enormous spaces in which the action takes place, and the small number of men with which it is waged (among them more volunteers than regular army), give it an "American" originality. As regards Taylor and Scott, their entire merit consists in their being convinced

---

8. Don Quixote.

49

1. Roswell Sabine Ripley, *The War with Mexico*, 2 vols. (New York, 1849).
2. William F. P. Napier, *History of the War in the Peninsula and in the South of France, from the Year 1807 to the Year 1814*, 4 vols. (London, 1828–1840).
3. Winfield Scott (1786–1866), American general, commander in Mexican War, 1846–1848.
4. Hernán (Fernando) Cortes (1485–1547), Spanish conquistador.
5. Antonio de Solis, *Historia de la Conquista de Méjico*, new ed. (Paris, 1844).
6. Zachary Taylor, commanding general in the Mexican War, was elected President of the United States in 1848.

that Yankees will extricate themselves, no matter how deep in the muck they are stuck. Early next week I will send you the two volumes. Let me know whether—since they are voluminous—by post (I am not sure about the recent rates) or Parcel Co.

Adio.

Yours, K.M.

50

From letter to Frederick Engels (in Manchester)
London, December 2, 1854

Dear Engels:
I think not, Sir [in English], that your letter or even your name can be used in connection with the worthy "Freund."[1] (The Jew is so pressing because he brought himself *at the very brink of bankruptcy* [in English] with a *fashionable* school which he had his wife establish in St. John's Wood. I have now learned the details from Cornelius[2]). Following your suggestion, I did as follows: (1) Sent him a letter from A. Dana, from which he can see how the business crisis in America has affected *me* and thereby *him*; (2) to cover the deficit, I have in the meantime made new literary connections on the basis of which I obligate myself in writing to pay him £4 on the tenth of every month, beginning January, 1855. The total sum still amounts to about £17. If Herr Freund does not agree, he can *sue* me. The letter from Dana covers me in every *court* [in English], as he can see himself. If I should drag you in directly, I lose: (1) my whole position vis-à-vis Freund; (2) he tells it (and shows the letter) to the teacher in his institute, Herr Gottfried Kinkel, who tells it to Herr Gerstenberg,[3] who tells it to every German Jew in the City, until it reaches Blanc, which *was by no means* [in English] desirable.

I asked Lassalle[4] if he could procure for me some literary *business* [in English] in Germany, for in *regard* [in English] to a reduced income and increased expenses I must bestir myself earnestly. Lassalle now makes me the following proposition, on which I would like to have your *considered* opinion. At the beginning of this month, his cousin, Dr. Max Friedländer, will be-

---

50
1. Freund (in German: friend), the Marx family doctor to whom he owed medical bills.
2. Wilhelm Cornelius, a German journalist émigré in London.
3. Isidor Gerstenberg, banker in London.
4. Ferdinand Lassalle (1825–1864), German lawyer and jurist, founder of the General German Workers' Association in 1863, who considered Marx a friend. Marx maintained a stormy relationship with him. See Part II of this volume.

come the proprietor of the *Neue Oder-Zeitung*,[5] but in the company of Stein[6] and Elsner.[7] I am to become London correspondent for the paper. Friedländer does not believe that at first he would be able to pay more than 20 *taler* monthly. But Lassalle thinks he can drive him up to thirty. *Voilà la proposition* [Here is the proposition]. The sum is miserable. Also, even a small correspondenceship for a shady German paper is not to be considered highly. Forty to £50 could always be tolerated. But the main snags—Elsner and Stein! This is to be the more maturely weighed, in that these gentlemen are not conservatives but *liberals*, and are more directly opposed to us than to the *Neue Preussische Zeitung*.[8] *That is the question* [in English]. Consider it carefully.[9] . . .

On Monday, I will send you by the indicated Parcel Company, Ripley and also Solis' *Conquista de Mexico*.[10] The latter to be returned to me as soon as you no longer need it, since the Solis book does not belong to me. I have now read all of Ripley (of course hastily, which suffices for my purpose). It is now entirely clear in my mind—and Ripley conveys it often in flat and "restrained" sarcastic form—that the great [Winfield] Scott was a quite ordinary, petty, untalented, nagging, envious dog and humbug, who, conscious that he owed everything to his divisional commanders, pulled cheap tricks to assure himself of fame. He seems to be as much a great general as the many-sided Greeley[11] is a great philosopher. The fellow blundered and made so many fumbles throughout the whole campaign that he deserved to be shot by any court-martial. But he is the *first* (according to *rank*) general of America. This is probably why Dana believes in him. [Zachary] Taylor is surely always worth more than Scott, which is what the American public seems to have sensed, in that it made the former President of the United States and let the latter, despite all his efforts, drop again and again. To me, General Worth[12] seems to be the most outstanding, a matter on which you must give me your opinion as soon as you have read the thing. Is it not curious that Scott is always two to ten miles removed from active operations, *never* appears on the battlefield *himself*, but is always merely "observing the progress of events"

---

5. A daily published in Breslau.
6. Julius Stein (1813–1883), German newspaperman, editor of *Breslauer Zeitung*.
7. Karl Friedrich Moritz Elsner (1809–1894), Prussian journalist and politician.
8. A conservative Berlin daily, organ of Prussian officialdom.
9. Marx accepted the offer and began to write for the *Neue Oder-Zeitung* on January 2, 1855; he terminated his relationship with the paper on October 8, 1855, after having contributed 112 articles.
10. On the books by Roswell Sabine Ripley and Antonio de Solis, see Letter 49, Marx to Engels, November 30, 1854.
11. Horace Greeley (1811–1872), American newspaper publisher, founder of the *New-York Daily Tribune*, of which Marx was the London correspondent, 1851–1862.
12. William Jenkins Worth (1794-1849), American General in campaign against Mexico.

from his safe hind-quarters? He does not even show up, as does Taylor, when the appearance of the commander-in-chief is necessary for the "moral" of the Army. After the very hot battle of Contreras, he comes riding out with his whole staff, when the thing is over. During the fluctuating battle of Molino del Rey, he let the "gallant" men know that they should persevere, that he might perhaps show up himself. Where he shows mistrust, it is always of his more talented divisional commanders, but never of Santa Anna,[13] who leads him by the nose as if he were an elderly child. The characteristic aspect of the war seems to me to be that each division and each small corps of troops, despite false or lacking orders from the chief, always stubbornly pursues its objective and uses every incident spontaneously, so that in the end something complete comes out. It is the Yankee sense of independence and individual efficiency, perhaps even more than among the Anglo Saxons. The Spaniards are already degenerated. But now a degenerate Spaniard, a Mexican, is an ideal. All encumbrances, braggings, loud-mouthedness, and quixoticisms of the Spaniards, here raised to cubic power, but far from having the solidity of the latter. The Mexican guerrilla war is a caricature of the Spanish one, and even the running away of the regular armies endlessly surpassed. But for that, the Spaniards do not have the kind of talent that is shown by Santa Anna.

Vale [Farewell].

Yours, K.M.

51

From letter to Frederick Engels (in Manchester)
London, January 17, 1855

Dear Frederic:

I could not of course write for the *Tribune* today and also not for some time *à venir* [to come], because yesterday between six and seven o'clock in the morning my wife gave birth to a *bona-fide traveler* [in English]—alas of the "sex" par exellence.[1] Had it been a male child, the whole thing would have been nicer. . . .

I now have Heine's[2] three volumes at home. Among other things, he tells in detail the lie that I, etc., went to console him when he was "attacked" by the Augsburg *Allgemeine Zeitung* because of receiving money from Louis

---

13. Antonio Lopez de Santa Anna (c. 1797-1876).

51

1. Marx is referring to the birth of his daughter Eleanor.
2. Heinrich Heine (1797–1856), German poet and wit, friend of Marx.

Philippe.[3] The good Heine deliberately forgets that my intervention in his behalf occurred at the end of 1843 and hence could not be connected with facts that came to light *after* the February 1848 revolution. *But let it pass* [in English]. In the anxiety of his bad conscience, for the old dog has a monstrous memory for all such muck, he tries to cajole.

I am expecting you for Friday. I cannot write any more today, as I have to send out a mass of birth announcements.

Yours, K.M.

52

From letter to Frederick Engels (in Manchester)
London, March 8, 1855

Dear Engels:

The £5 received.

I cannot depart from here until Colonel Musch[1] is clearly improved. In the meantime he took rapid steps for reconvalescence this week, the doctor was *exceedingly pleased* [in English] today, and next week everything is perhaps *all right* [in English]. As soon as I can leave with good conscience, I will write you. I think, next week.

A very happy event [in English], the death of my wife's ninety-year old uncle[2] was reported to us yesterday. Thereby my mother-in-law saves an annual contribution of 200 *taler* and my wife will receive £100, and more if the old dog did not bequeath to his housekeeper part of the money that is not entailed. The question of the manuscript of the Duke of Brunswick[3] on the Seven Years' War, for which old Scharnhorst[4] had already once offered large sums, will also be decided. My wife had promptly sent a protest against any possible attempt by her brother[5] to give the manuscript as a present to the

---

3. Louis Philippe (1773–1850), King of the French, 1830–1848.

52

1. Nickname for Marx's eight-year old son Edgar; the boy died on April 6, a month after this letter was written. See Letter 53, Marx to Engels, April 6, 1855.
2. Heinrich Georg von Westphalen (1768–1855), brother of Mrs. Marx's father.
3. Ferdinand, Duke of Brunswick (1721–1792); a von Westphalen ancestor served under the Duke in the Seven Years' War.
4. Gerhard Johann David von Scharnhorst (1755–1813), Prussian general, military theorist, chief of staff.
5. Ferdinand Otto von Westphalen (1799-1876), who was actually Jenny Marx's half-brother.

"*Allergnädigsten.*"[6] The Prussian State may acquire it for cash, *but not otherwise* [in English]...
    Adieu.

Yours, K.M.

53

To Frederick Engels (in Manchester)
London, April 6, 1855

Dear Engels:

Poor Musch[1] is no more. He fell asleep (literally) in my arms today between five and six o'clock. I will never forget how your friendship has lightened for us this terrible time. You can imagine my sorrow over the child. My wife sends you the friendliest greetings. It is possible that if I go to Manchester I will take her with me for eight days; naturally we will be staying in an inn (or some *private lodging* [in English]). At any rate, I must seek some means to tide her over the next few days.

Yours, K.M.

54

To Frederick Engels (in Manchester)
London, April 12, 1855

Dear Engels:

I am thinking of coming to Manchester with my wife on Wednesday;[1] she must change the locality for a few days. If I don't write you to the contrary, that will remain the date. At any rate, I will write to you again on Monday.

    The house is naturally desolate and empty since the death of the dear child, who was its animated soul. It is indescribable how we miss the child everywhere. I have already experienced all kinds of ill luck, but only now do

---

6. Most Gracious: King Frederick William IV.

53

1. Edgar Marx.

54

1. April 18. On April 16, Marx informed Engels briefly: "Wednesday morning my wife and I will leave for Manchester by parliamentary train." They stayed with Engels in Manchester until May 6, 1855.

I know what real misfortune is. I feel myself broken down. Luckily, I have had such wild headaches since the burial that I have lost the power of thinking, hearing, and seeing.

Amid all the frightful torments I have suffered these days, the thought of you and your friendship has sustained me, as well as the hope that we two still have something good to do together in the world.

Yours, K.M.

My wife writes a few words to you, which I enclose.

55

To Amalie Daniels (in Cologne)
London, September 6, 1855

My dear Frau Daniels:

I find it impossible to describe the pain with which I was filled at the news of the passing of your dear, unforgettable Roland. Although the previous accounts I received through Steffen[1] had by no means been reassuring, I nevertheless did not for a moment lose hope in the recovery of your admirable husband. His was a delicate, finely organized, entirely noble nature—character, talent and aesthetic feeling in rare harmony. Among the Colognese, Daniels always seemed to me to be like a statue of a Greek god, whom capricious accident cast among a troop of Hottentots. His premature passing is not only an irreplaceable loss to his family and friends but also to science, in which he showed the finest promise, and to the great mass of suffering humanity, which had in him a true champion.

I know enough of your heroic nature to be convinced that the imperishable pain will not prevent you from continuing to be the faithful guardian of the precious commitments left behind by your Roland. In the sons, you will twice give the father again to the world.

The news of this loss has so vividly reawakened my wife's remembrance of the death of our only little son[2] that her state of mind does not permit her to write to you. She weeps and wails like a child.

I dare not offer you solace, the less so for being myself unconsoled over the loss of a friend, whom I have personally loved more than any other. Such aches cannot be decreased but only shared. As soon as I have mastered the

---

55

1. Wilhelm Steffen, Prussian ex-officer and a friend of Marx, was a witness in the 1852 communist trial in Cologne; emigrated to England and then to the United States in 1853.
2. On April 6, 1855, Marx's son Edgar (Musch) died at the age of eight.

first fierce emotions, I will send to the *New-York Tribune* an obituary notice on the deceased for his numerous friends in America. I hope that conditions will some day allow me to wreak a more serious vengeance on those who have cut short his career than an obituary notice.

I need not have to assure you that in me you always have a loyal and devoted friend at your disposal.

With inmost sympathy,

Yours, K. Marx

56

From letter to Frederick Engels (in Manchester)
London, December 14, 1855

Dear Frederic:

The house arrest [illness] begins to be tedious. Not a breath of fresh air gulped yet. Still, yesterday I sent off again 1,000 . . . [indecipherable]. Jones is finally supposed to come today.

You would never guess who came to visit me the evening before last. Edgar Bauer—whom I have not seen for about a year—and with him Bruno.[1] Bruno has already been here for a fortnight and wants to remain about six months, "in order to put his ideas to the test," which, considering how he begins it, certainly cannot fail. The man has visibly aged,[2] the forehead has expanded, and he now makes more or less the impression of a pedantic old professor. For the time being, he is staying with Edgar, in a shack *somewhere about* [in English] the end of Highgate, and there he sits in the midst of the deepest petit-bourgeois misery, and sees and hears nothing. This he believes to be London, and believes that except for 30,000 privileged persons all Englishmen live like Edgar Bauer. Hence his hatred and "contempt" for the country are enormous. He feels as if he were living "in Treuenbrietzen."[3] London is a real "prison" when you come from "Berlin." It also came out incidentally that his present ideal is the "East Frisian," "Altenburgian," *and partly* [in English] "Westphalian" peasant—those true aristocrats. He is also convinced that these louts are not to be subtilized away and that the modern

---

56

1. Bruno Bauer.
2. Bauer, to whom Marx had been close when he was a student at Berlin University, was now only forty-six years old.
3. A Potsdam suburb.

rubbish about leveling, wailed over by the "dissolutionist," will shatter on these *rocks* [in English]. It was very curious to hear the "Critique"[4] make the *confession* [in English] that in the last analysis Berthold Auerbach[5] is its real foundation. In his opinion, with the exception of a few "purely commercial cities," the cities in Germany are decaying, but the "countryside" is flourishing splendidly. He did not know a syllable about the industrial growth, but quietly lamented that nothing is now done in Germany except "improvements."

The "English language" is "miserable," entirely Latinized. Hereupon I explained to him as a consolation that the Dutch and Danes say the same thing about the German language and that the only chaps not corrupted by foreign tongues are the "Icelanders."

The old boy has occupied himself much with languages. He *speaks* Polish and therefore declares that the Polish language is "the most beautiful of all." His language studies seem to have been very uncritical. For example, he considers Dobrovsky[6] much "more important" than Grimm,[7] and calls him the father of comparative philology. He has also let himself be hoaxed by the Poles in Berlin that Lelewel,[8] in a most recent work, has refuted Grimm's *History of the German Language.*[9]

Apropos. He also related that there appeared in Germany a thick volume (from the German side) against Grimms' Lexicon.[10] The whole volume consists of blunders ascribed to Grimm.

Despite all efforts to appear humorous, great gloom and melancholy permeated him about the "present." In Germany—*horrible indeed*! [in English]—nothing is read or bought anymore except miserable compilations of the natural sciences. When you visit here,[11] we will amuse ourselves very much with the old boy....

Salut.

Yours, K.M.

---

4. The reference is to the "critical critique" of the Young Hegelians (which Marx and Engels ridiculed in their first book, *The Holy Family* [1845]), of whom Bruno Bauer was the leader, that only select personalities are the bearers of "pure criticism" and the real creators of history.
5. Berthold Auerbach (1812–1882), German novelist who idealized peasant life.
6. Josef Dobrovsky (1753–1829), Czech pioneer philologist.
7. Jacob Grimm (1785–1863), German philologist and culture historian.
8. Joachim Lelewel (1786–1861), Polish historian.
9. Grimm, *Geschichte der deutschen Sprache*, 2 vols. (Leipzig, 1848).
10. Jacob and Wilhelm Grimm, *Deutsches Wörterbuch* [*German Lexicon*], vol. I (Leipzig, 1848).
11. Engels visited London from December 24, 1855, to early January, 1856.

57

From letter to Frederick Engels (in Manchester)
London, February 13, 1856

Dear Fred:

...A few days ago Pieper was in the house here and gave the children instruction, when the postman knocked downstairs. A letter to Pieper in a feminine handwriting. Invitation to a rendezvous. Since he did not know the handwriting or the signature, he cradled himself in great expectations and gave my wife the letter to read. She immediately recognized the signature as that of the fat old Irish pig, our former wet nurse, who does not know how to write and hence had it written by a third person. You can imagine with what laughter our Fridolin [Pieper] was tickled. Nevertheless, he kept his rendezvous with the "cow." Such are his "adventures." Oh, King Wiswamitra, what an ox you are![1]...

Yours, K.M.

58

From letter to Frederick Engels (in Manchester)
London, March 5, 1856

Dear Frederic:

Next week I will examine Heffter[1] more closely. If there is material in it, I will order it. A very miserable book is Eichhoff, *Histoire de la Langue et de la Littérature des Slaves.*[2] Aside from the grammatical part, which I cannot judge, (but it strikes me that the Lithuanians and Letts are declared to be Slavs. Isn't that nonsense?), the rest of it is largely plagiarism from Schaffarik.[3] The fellow also includes texts in the original languages, together with French translations, from the national poetry of the Slavs. Among them I found also

---

57

1. From Heinrich Heine, *"Die Heimkehr"*, in his *Buch der Lieder [Book of Songs]*.

58

1. Moritz Wilhelm Heffter, *Der Weltkampf der Deutschen und Slawen seit dem Ende des fünften Jahrhunderts* ... [*The World Struggle Between Germans and Slavs since the End of the Fifth Century*] (Hamburg and Gotha, 1847); and his *Das Slawentum [The Slavs]* (Leipzig, 1852).
2. Frédéric Gustave Eichhoff, *History of the Language and Literature of the Slavs* (Paris, 1839).
3. Paul Joseph Schaffarik, *Geschichte der slawischen Sprache und Literatur nach allen Mundarten* [*History of Slavic Language and Literature According to All the Dialects*] (Ofen, 1826).

"Igor's Expedition."[4] The point of that poem is a call to the Russian princes for unity, just at the time of the incursion of the Mongolian hordes proper. Most striking is this passage in the poem: "*Voici les jolies filles des Gothes entonnent leur chants au bord de la Mer noire.*"[5] So that, according to this, the Geths or Goths celebrated the victory of the Turkish Polovcens[6] over the Russians. The whole poem is Christian heroic, even though the heathen elements still shine through strongly. By contrast, the Bohemian epic, *Zaboi* (Samo?), in the collection of Bohemian epic poetry published in German translation by Hanka and Swoboda,[7] is polemical and fanatically anti-German. Seems to be aimed at Dagobert,[8] a German capitano, whom the Bohemians defeated. But it is as much a cry of revenge against Christianity as against the Germans, who, among other things, are reproached, in a very naïve poetical form, for trying to force the worthy Bohemians to confine themselves to one wife. Of folk poetry, of which the Poles have none, except for "Adalbert's Prayer" to the Mother of God, I found the following:

[P.O.] Goetze, *Fürst Wladimir und seine Tafelrunde.*[9] *Stimmen des russischen Volkes*[10]

Kapper (Siegfried), *Slavische Melodien* [*Slavic Melodies*]. By the same author: *Die Gesänge der Serben* [*The Song of the Serbs*]. (It is more complete than the book by Jakob.)[11] Finally, Vuk Stephanowitsch, *Serbische Hochzeitslieder* [*Serbian Wedding Songs*]. Translated into German by E. Wesely,[12] Pest, 1826.

Here are some other books that have aroused my attention next to Cyprien[13] and Desprez,[14] and which I will look over next week:

Südslavische Wanderungen im Sommer 1850.[15] (It is also translated into English). *Betrachtungen über das Fürstentum Serbien.*[16] *Die Serbische Bewegung in*

---

4. An old-Russian epic poem dealing with Prince Igor's campaign against the Polovcens in 1185.

5. "Here are the beautiful Gothic girls intoning their chants on the shore of the Black Sea."

6. The Polovcens were nomads who lived in southern Russia up to the thirteenth century, when they moved to Hungary and the Balkans.

7. Vaclav Hanka, *Königinhofer Handschrift* [*Royal Court Manuscript*], a collection of old Bohemian songs, poems and epics, translated into German by Vaclav Alois Swoboda (Svoboda).

8. Dagobert I, Frankish king, A.D. 628–638.

9. *Prince Vladimir and His Round Table* (Leipzig, 1819).

10. By the same author, *Voices of the Russian People* (1828).

11. Therese Albertine Luise von Jakob-Robinson (pseudonym: Talvi), *Volkslieder der Serben . . .* [*Serbian Folk Songs*].

12. Eugen Wesely (1799–1828), Austrian poet.

13. Robert Cyprien, *Le monde slave, son passé, son état présent et son avenir* [*The Slavic World, Its Past, Its Present State and Its Future*], 2 vols. (Paris, 1852).

14. Hippolyte Desprez, *Les peuples de l'Autriche et de la Turquie . . .* [*The Peoples of Austria and Turkey*], 2 vols. (Paris, 1850).

15. *South Slavic Travels in the Summer of 1850*, 2 vols. (Leipzig, 1851); the author was Siegfried Kapper.

16. *Reflections on the Principality of Serbia* (Vienna, 1851).

Südungarn.[17] *Slawismus und Pseudomagyarismus. Von allen Menschen Freunde, nur der Pseudomagyaren Feinde.*[18] *Die Beschwerden und Klagen der Slaven in Ungarn.*[19]...

Father Leo[20] has read a lecture on Münzer[21] before the king[22] (partly printed in the *Neue Preussische [Zeitung]*).[23]... The Reformation must, of course, be cleansed of the reproach to have been the Mother of Revolution. Münzer was a visionary who said: *"Intelligo ut credam"* ["I understand in order to believe"]. Luther said: *"Credo ut intelligam"* ["I believe in order to understand"]. The *Spenersche*[24] replied: In his later years, Luther regretted the miserable role he had played, etc. You can see that the ferment is breaking through even the official ranks.

Apropos the Reformation, from the outset Austria had considered the Slavic tribes as basically dangerous where they tended toward the Reformation. With the Reformation came the translation of the Bible into all Slavic dialects. This, of course, aroused nationalism. On the other hand, a deep alliance with the Protestant German North. If Austria had not suppressed this movement, Protestantism would have become the basis for the preponderance of the German spirit, as well as the bulwark against the Greek-Catholic Russia. Austria shoved the Germans into the muck and worked for the Russians in Germany, as well as in the East....

Salut.

Yours, K.M.

59

From letter to Frederick Engels (in Manchester)
London, April 10, 1856

Dear Frederic:

It is high time that I write again. I have been prevented from doing it by all sorts of household chores....

You know that Heine is dead, but you do not know that Ludwig Simon[1] of Trier has pissed on his grave—I wanted to say, poured his urine—in the

---

17. *The Serbian Movement in South Hungary* (Berlin, 1851).
18. *Slavism and Pseudo-Magyarism. Friends of All Men, Enemies Only of Pseudo-Magyars* (Leipzig, 1842).
19. *The Grievances and Complaints of the Slavs in Hungary* (Leipzig, 1843).
20. Heinrich Leo (1799–1878), right-wing Prussian historian and journalist.
21. Thomas Münzer (*c.* 1490–1525), German Anabaptist, mystic, associate of Martin Luther.
22. Frederick William IV.
23. Berlin conservative daily.
24. *Spenersche Zeitung*, a monarchist Berlin daily, the real name of which was *Berlinische Nachrichten von Staats und gelehrten Sachen*.

59

1. Ludwig Simon (1810-1872), German lawyer and politician, who eventually emigrated to Switzerland.

New York *Neue-Zeit* of the quondam lion[2] of the Parliament of the German Nation who had retired to Stuckert.[3] The poet or minstrel [Simon] of the Jew-woman *Hohenscheissische* [High Shitty] or [Hohen]-linden from Frankfurt naturally finds that Heine was no poet. He had *"kai Gemiet"* ["no feeling"] was full of *"Bausheit"* ["malice"] and slandered not only Kobes but also even Berne's[4] *Fraindin* ["girlfriend"], the *graussen* ["curly-headed"] Berne's "mouse," muse or Möse [She-Moses], the Strauss woman.[5]

There exists here a society for the protection of small tradesmen [mostly in English]. This society issues a weekly paper for protection of same. In this weekly, our friend Seiler "with wife" are pilloried as *"swindlers"* [in English].

But greater things are on the carpet. Pieper, who has lived brilliantly as a freebooter since January and who has, despite that, also received not inconsiderable *subsidies* [in English] from me, and has lived with his *landlady* [in English] every day on the qui vive, suddenly was struck with the idea that what he needs is a little capital in order to be a big man. Seiler's *sister-in-law* [in English], second daughter of *a greengrocer* [in English], a tallow candle who wears big eyeglasses, has for some time been madly in love with said Pieper. The whole creature is green, like verdigris, not even like vegetables, and moreover *greens* [in English] without *any meat* [in English] or *flesh whatever* [in English]. Pieper says she is a picture of ugliness, but has discovered that she is not without brains, which she has indisputably demonstrated by considering our heath sheep from Hanover as a shipwrecked German Byron.[6] So Pieper, to whom the woman clings, not like a barnacle but like a *caterpillar* [in English]—Pieper decided the day before to open his heart to brother-in-law Seiler. He did not want to do it in the presence of the "sweetheart," out of fear that he would have to kiss her, and that is in truth *hard work* [in English] for an Occidental who is not yet used *to feed upon tallow* [in English]. But in a true Pieper fashion he combined his declaration of love with—an attempt to borrow. Pieper could not pump[7] out his heart before the greengrocer without pumping out his *pockets* [in English] and without pumping from him. Specifically, he must have a little capital, say £20 to £40, *to create himself a position* [in English] as a fashionable private teacher. Meanwhile, he thinks of already letting his "sweetheart" enjoy the pleasures of widowhood as a bride and out

---

2. Wilhelm Löwe (Lion), editor of the *Neue-Zeit*, had been a member of the Frankfurt National Assembly in 1848–49.
3. Yiddish for Stuttgart: all the foreign terms in this paragraph are in Yiddish.
4. Yiddish pronunciation of Börne [Ludwig].
5. Jeanette Wohl-Strauss (1783–1861), friend of Ludwig Börne.
6. George Gordon, Lord Byron (1788–1824), English romantic poet.
7. "Pump" in German also means "borrow," "borrowing."

of pity *never* marrying her. The whole affair smells bad, despite all the greens, but Pieper imagines he would come out of it an honorable man, that is, he would repay the *would-be* [in English] father-in-law the "attractive" loan *at a certain epoch looming in the future* [in English] to the last penny, and also generously leave him his daughter in the deal. Since that fateful day he has been in my house once, for one minute, in my absence. Called himself "the lucky one." Jennychen[8] called him *"Benedick the married man"* [in English], but Laurachen[9] said *Benedick was a wit, he is but "a clown,"* and *"a cheap clown" too* [in English]. The children have always read their Shakespeare.

Liebknecht has finally achieved something, namely, a young Liebknecht.

My wife has received, through "His Majesty the All-Highest's special order," a pass from Berlin. In May, she will go to Trier with the whole family for three to four months.

Salut. Regards for Lupus.

K.M.

60

From letter to Frederick Engels (in Manchester)
London, May 23, 1856

Dear Engles:
... I am unable to write today, but I must ask you for an explanation of a philological scruple. In Shakespeare's *Henry IV* one finds Hiren for Syrene, and according to the notes of pedant Johnson[1] the form Hiren also appears in other older English writers. The exchange of H and S is quite in order. But could not Hiren be connected with whore, and thence Syrene? Or with *Hören* [hearing], *auris* [ear], etc.? You see *to which low state of spirit* [in English] I am today *depressed* [in English], for this case interests me very much. ...

Yours, K.M.

---

8. Marx's daughter Jenny.
9. Laura Marx.

60

1. Samuel Johnson.

61

From letter to Jenny Marx (in London)
Manchester, June 21, 1856

My heart's beloved:[1]

I am writing you again, because I am alone[2] and because it troubles me always to have a dialogue with you in my head, without your knowing anything about it or hearing it or being able to answer. Poor as your photograph is, it does perform a service for me, and I now understand how even the "Black Madonna," the most disgraceful portrait of the Mother of God, could find indestructible admirers, indeed even more admirers than the good portraits. In any case, those Black Madonna pictures have never been more kissed, looked at, and adored than your photograph, which, although not black, is morose, and absolutely does not reflect your darling, sweet, kissable *dolce* face. But I improve upon the sun's rays, which have painted falsely, and find that my eyes, so spoiled by lamplight and tobacco, can still paint, not only in dream but also while awake. I have you vivaciously before me, and I carry you on my hands, and I kiss you from head to foot, and I fall on my knees before you, and I groan: "Madame, I love you." And I truly love you, more than the Moor of Venice ever loved. The false and worthless world views virtually all [literary] characters falsely and worthlessly. Who of my many slanderers and snake-tongued enemies had ever reproached me that I am destined to play the role of chief lover in a second-class theater? And yet it is true. If the scoundrels had had wit, they would have painted "the production and direction" on one side, and me lying at your feet on the other. *Look to this picture and to that* [in English]—they would have written underneath. But dumb scoundrels they are and dumb they will remain, in *seculum seculorum* [all eternity].

Momentary absence is good, for in constant presence things seem too much alike to be differentiated. Proximity dwarfs even towers, while the petty and the commonplace, at close view, grow too big. Small habits, which may physically irritate and take on emotional form, disappear when the immediate object is removed from the eye. Great passions, which through proximity assume the form of petty routine, grow and again take on their natural dimension on account of the magic of distance. So it is with my love. You have only to be snatched away from me even in a mere dream, and I know immediately that the time has only served, as do sun and rain for

---

61
1. Mrs. Marx.
2. Marx was then on a visit with Engels in Manchester.

plants, for growth. The moment you are absent, my love for you shows itself to be what it is, a giant, in which are crowded together all the energy of my spirit and all the character of my heart. It makes me feel like a man again, because I feel a great passion; and the multifariousness, in which study and modern education entangle us, and the skepticism which necessarily makes us find fault with all subjective and objective impressions, all of these are entirely designed to make us all small and weak and whining. But love—not love for the Feuerbach-type of man, not for the metabolism, not for the proletariat—but the love for the beloved and particularly for you, makes a man again a man.

You will smile, my sweet heart, and ask, how did I come to all this rhetoric? If I could press your sweet, white heart to my heart, I would keep silent and not say a word. Since I cannot kiss with my lips, I must kiss with language and make words. I could really even make verses and rhymes like Ovid's *Libri Tristium*, which in German means *Bücher des Jammers* [Books of Laments]. But I am exiled from you, which is something Ovid did not conceive.

There are actually many females in the world, and some among them are beautiful. But where could I find again a face, whose every feature, even every wrinkle, is a reminder of the greatest and sweetest memories of my life? Even my endless pains, my irreplaceable losses[3] I read in your sweet countenance, and I kiss away the pain when I kiss your sweet face. "Buried in her arms, awakened by her kisses"—namely, in your arms and by your kisses, and I grant the Brahmins and Pythagoras their doctrine of regeneration and Christianity its doctrine of resurrection. . . .

Good-bye, my sweet heart. I kiss you and the children many thousand times.

Yours, Karl

62

Postcript to letter to Frederick Engels (in Manchester)
London, August 1, 1856

P.S. At Blind's I saw two volumes of the Emigration jeremiad by Simon of Trier.[1] Diluted insipidity, every word a flabby, schoolboyish bungle, foppish rabbit's-foot, affectedly churlish pretention to naïvete, beggars, soup in

---

3. Marx refers to the death of their three young children: Guido (died in 1850), Franziska (died in 1852), and Edgar (died in 1855).

62

1. Ludwig Simon, *Aus dem Exil* [*From the Exile*], 2 vols. (Giessen, 1855).

which are mixed the dissolved Karl Grün's[2] Jew-cherries, wide platitudes—never has anything like it been published. This was still lacking, to give the "German parliament" its last kick in the ass, this self-revelation by one of its heroes.[3] I have of course only browsed through it. I would just as soon imbibe soap-water or drink hot cow piss with the great Zoroaster than read through this stuff. Our specter constantly haunts him and Company. Louis Blanc, Louis Blanqui, Marx and Engels are his hellish quadrinity, which he never forgets. Among other things, we two—the teachers of "economic equality"—are supposed to have preached "*armed* (!) expropriation of capital." Even the jokes which we made about Switzerland in the *Revue* make him "indignant." "No civil list, no standing army, no millionaires, no beggars"—"Marx and Engels hope that Germany will never sink to this level of degradation." Most peculiar is how the fellow views us both in the *singular*: "Marx and Engels *says*," etc.

63

To Jenny Marx (in Trier)[1]
London, August 8, 1856

Sweet, dear, unique heart:

Together with your letter, I received this morning a note from Frederic,[2] containing 15 taler for Lenchen.[3] Acknowledge it, as he is *very exact* in such things. I will write more tomorrow. Today the "immortal Collet"[4] is in my room, and I keep him in check by saying: "*I am obliged to write some lines to Mrs. Marx*" [in English].

Lily-white Sandy[5] is made up in *reality*, not in *fancy*.

Much as I miss the children—and that is *quite* [in English] *indescribable*—I wish you would remain eight days more in Trier. It will do you and the children a world of good. More tomorrow.[6]

Yours, K.M.

---

2. Karl Grün, a German journalist, was a leader of the so-called "true" socialists in the 1840's.
3. Ludwig Simon had been a member of the Frankfurt National Parliament in 1849.

63

1. Mrs. Marx and the children were on a visit to her widowed mother in Trier, Germany.
2. Engels.
3. Helene Demuth.
4. Charles Dobson Collet, English journalist.
5. Not identified.
6. Letter not found.

P.S. The Urquhartites[7] are pushing damn hard. This is financially good. But *politically* I don't know whether I can get mixed up with the fellows. Thousand kisses, dear, sweet heart.

P.S. II. Lina[8] did get the fine position. But she will start weeks later.

But it is dreadful for me that I now have to play the dandy before Liebknecht. *Hang it* [in English]! In addition, Pieper sleeps here instead of you. *Horrible* [in English]! At least in the same room. Engels comes here next week. This is a deliverance. For three weeks now I have been hypochondriacal like the devil.

64

From letter to Frederick Engels (in Manchester)
London, September 22, 1856

Dear Engels:

I would have *acknowledged* [in English] your last letter sooner if, in about the last fourteen days, I had not lost time in looking for lodgings from morning to evening. Cannot remain in the old hole[1] under any circumstances. We have finally found a whole house, which we have to *furnish* [in English] ourselves. It is: 9, Grafton Terrace, Maitland Park, Haverstock Hill, Hampstead Road. Rent: £36. Moving on September 29; this week it is to be furnished. We are in a bit of a quandary, since we have to pay about £26 in the City, and much more for the new furnishing. That is, we are short £10 to £15, even if momentarily, as my wife is to receive a yet larger sum from her brother[2] in Berlin as a result of the Trier inheritance. Yesterday he wrote that he could not yet send the money, because the Lower Silesian railroad bonds in which the capital coming to my wife is invested can, *dans ce moment* [at this moment], be sold only at great loss. In this connection the Herr Minister[3] made the following melancholy observation: "It is now of course precisely an unfavorable moment, in that all such securities have declined as a result of the raging Crédit-mobilier and limited-liability company swindles" [in France].

If you could supply a part of the shortfall, I am thinking of raising the rest in the pawnshop, until the Berlin money arrives. The bad thing is that there is no time to lose.

7. Followers of David Urquhart (1805–1877), publisher of *The Free Press*.
8. Lina Schöler, friend of the Marx family.

64
1. 28, Dean Street, Soho.
2. Ferdinand Otto von Westphalen.
3. Ferdinand Otto von Westphalen was Prussian Minister of Interior, 1850–1858.

The news of Weerth's death has affected me frightfully, and I found it hard to believe the thing. Freiligrath has already written me also about an obituary. But in fact I see no paper in Germany. The one possibility might perhaps be an obituary in the *Tribune*, until the times will make possible something more and better! *What is your opinion* [in English]?

I have been invited to dinner today by the *Putnam* fellow,[4] who is here again. I don't know whether I will go. My bad English speech would embarrass me.

Tribune has returned to me the *unprinted* articles. It is, *all in all* [in English], the Pan-Slavism stuff[5] and my article on the *Danubian principalities* [in English]. Herr Dana writes that if I cannot publish the things elsewhere, they must justly carry the "loss" since they had not objected in time. If I can publish them, they expect part of their *expenses* [in English] back. *Nous verrons* [we will see].

Bruno Bauer is publishing two volumes on England.[6] He will undoubtedly discuss in detail the *pig-sty* [in English] of his *cher frère* [dear brother: Edgar Bauer]. I don't know what else he has seen in England.[7]...

About Heine I received all sorts of details, which Reinhardt[8] has told my wife in Paris. More of this, another time. For now only that

> *"Sie aber schon um achte*
> *Trank roten Wein und lachte"*[9]

has literally [in English] come to pass. His corpse was still in the death house —on the day of burial[10]—when the *maquereau* [pimp] of the Mathilde[11] with the angelic smile stood at the door and actually fetched her. The worthy "Meissner,"[12] who had smeared such soft cow dung on the German public, received cash money from Mathilde to glorify this human swine who had tormented Heine to death.

Now, another story apropos Moses Hess. The fame of that lad was *due to a great part* [in English]—to Sasonov.[13] When Hess and Mösin [She-

---

4. Frederick Law Olmsted (1822–1903), American landscape architect, contributor to *Putnam's Monthly*.
5. Articles on Pan-Slavism on which Engels worked from January to April, 1856, and which Marx sent in to the *New-York Daily Tribune*.
6. Actually, Marx meant Edgar (not Bruno) Bauer, *Englische Freiheit* [*English Freedom*] (Leipzig, 1857).
7. See Letter 56, Marx to Engels, December 14, 1855.
8. Richard Reinhardt (1829–1898), Heine's secretary.
9. "But already at eight, She drank red wine and laughed" (From Heine's "*Ein Weib*" [A Female], in his *Romanzero* (1851).
10. Heine died on February 17, 1856.
11. Mathilde Heine (1815–1883), the poet's wife.
12. Alfred Meissner, *Heinrich Heine. Erinnerungen* [*Recollections*] (Hamburg, 1856).
13. Nicolai Ivanovich Sasonov (1815–1862), Russian émigré journalist.

Moses][14] came to Paris, this Russian was very much down-at-the-heels, very tattered, very penniless and creditless, and consequently very susceptible to plebeian and revolutionary world-transforming ideas. Sasonov heard that Moses was not without "dough." He, therefore, got behind Moses and before Mösin. The latter he screwed and the former he trumpeted about as *a great literary* [in English] *lumen* [light] and introduced him to Revues and newspaper editorial offices. Vladimir,[15] of course, had his hand in every pie and entrée everywhere. So he squeezed out of the stingy Moses enough dough so as to be able to "sparkle" again and used decoys for new credit. And with that he enticed a rich old Jewess into kosher *wedlock* [in English]. From that time on, however, he has become elegant again and turned his back on Moses, declaring him to be a *very common and subordinate fellow* [in English]. But he left the Mösin faithlessly, and now she runs around Paris cursing and blustering, telling everybody who would listen, about the treachery of the perfidious Muscovite. This is to a certain extent the history of the Grandeur et Décadence de la Maison Moses [The Greatness and Decline of the House of Moses]. . . .

Yours, K.M.

65

From letter to Frederick Engels (in Manchester)
London, September 26, 1856

Dear Frederick:

I have first with thanks the receipt of the monish [money] *to acknowledge.*[1] I would have done it yesterday, except that we were in a real hurly-burly with the moving.[2] Moreover, it is still questionable whether we will be able to move out before Monday [September 29], since despite the money you sent us and the pawning of things in the hock shop, we do not quite have the necessary sum. The current crisis on the Continental exchanges is for us personally inopportune.

---

14. Sibylle Hess.
15. Sasonov. "Vladimir" is a nickname for "Russian."

65
1. This sentence was written in Marx's own brand of English.
2. On or about October 1, 1856, Marx moved to larger quarters at 9, Grafton Terrace, Maitland Park, Haverstock Hill, where he lived until 1868.

Nothing new, except what you probably know already, that Stirner[3] died. Also, as I hear from Freiligrath, he received here in London a letter from his "ex-sweetheart"[4] in Australia, in which she reports that she had married again, but at the same time she became religious and through the providence of a "higher life beyond," has managed to bring her *novum homi- nem* [new man] "into the lunatic asylum." The latter is to be understood *verbatim* [literally].

I had supper with the man from *Putnam's*.[5] In addition to him, Freiligrath and an old Yankee were also present. The man from *Putnam's* was a quiet, modest creature, but the other Yankee was a jolly and witty fellow. *Putnam's* asked whether after the Bazancourt article[6] it would be possible to do "Ships Against Walls," as being particularly interesting to America in view of the last war.[7] Afterward, also floating batteries and gunboats, light or heavy artillery, etc. All this seems to point to a war between America and England sooner or later. Apart from this *militaribus* [military articles], I am expected to write about Heine. In short, we can now enter into regular intercourse with this very "good" house.

The house which I have rented is very attractive at the price, and would not be rented so cheaply if it were not for its immediate environment. Roads, etc., somewhat unfinished. But when you come to London you will find a complete home. . . .

Yours, K.M.

66

From letter to Frederick Engels (in Manchester)
London, January 20, 1857

Dear Engels:

I am thoroughly down on my luck. For approximately three weeks now, Dana is sending me the daily *Tribune*, obviously with the intention of only showing me that they no longer print *anything* of mine. With the exception of some forty lines on the moves of the Banque de France,[1] not a single line of

---

3. Max Stirner (pseudonym for Johann Caspar Schmidt) (1806–1856), a German philoso- pher whom Marx and Engels satirized in *The German Ideology*.
4. Marie Wilhelmine Dähnhardt (1818–1902), Max Stirner's wife.
5. Olmsted.
6. Engels' article on the French military writer, Baron César de Bazancourt, entitled "Saint-Arnaud," was returned by *Putnam's Monthly* unpublished.
7. The Crimean War (1853–1856).

66
1. "The Crises in Europe," in *New-York Daily Tribune*, December 6, 1856.

mine has appeared since then. From week to week I have postponed drawing on the *Tribune*, because I believed that the articles would be printed belatedly, *but nothing of the sort* [in English]. My articles on Prussia, Persia, Austria—all equally rejected.[2] After the dogs have printed all my things (and yours too) for about four years under their own name [as editorials], they reached the point of eclipsing my name before the Yankees, a name that was growing and would have enabled me to find another paper or to threaten them with moving to another paper. *Que faire* [What to do]? Good advice is dear *in these circumstances* [in English]. The moment I draw on them, it would serve them as an excuse of giving me notice, and the possibility of writing twice a week and so that of ten articles *perhaps* one would be printed and paid for, is a practice that is too ruinous to continue. And how can I draw [money], when nothing is printed? . . .

So I am completely stuck in the sand, in a house where I put my few belongings and wherein it is impossible to piss through from day to day as in Dean Street, without prospects and with a growing family. I absolutely don't know where to begin, and am in fact in a more desperate situation than I was five years ago. I believed to have already swallowed the quintessence of the muck. *Mais non* [But no]. Moreover, the worst of it is that the crisis is not temporary. I don't see how I can disentangle myself from it. . . .

Yours, K.M.

67

To Frederick Engels (in Manchester)
London, January 23, 1857

Dear Engels:

D'abord [First], my best thanks for the friendliness of your letter.

I wrote Olmsted[1] about ten days ago; am expecting a reply. It seems to me that Dana's anger over Freiligrath's blabbing out his secret[2] had something to do with the behavior of the *Tribune*, or rather that Dana has not used his influence.

---

2. Marx was wrong; the articles *were* published: "The Anglo-Persian War," in *New-York Daily Tribune*, January 7, 1857; "The Maritime Commerce of Austria," January 9, 1857; "The Divine Right of the Hohenzollerns," January 9, 1857.

67
1. About contributing to *Putnam's Monthly*.
2. That a Polish newspaperman, Count Gurowski, influenced Dana to reject Engels' and Marx's articles, especially those dealing with Pan-Slavism.

To write for the *New-York Herald* is impossible; one must try the *New-York Times*. I am thinking of approaching it secretly, through Dr. Abraham Jacobi,[3] who is at least discreet and seems generally to have impressed the Yankees with his quiet demeanor. I will write him next Tuesday, and at the same time also write to Dana, which will put him into a more disagreeable conflict than he imagines. I would appreciate it if you would send me an article on Persian military affairs[4] for Tuesday, for after that day I will probably suspend my correspondence to the *Tribune* until further notice. This time thoroughness is not necessary. Only a few general strategic views. The *Tribune* probably imagines that I—dismissed by it—would be resigned to abandon the American camp entirely. The prospect of seeing its "military" and "financial" monopoly taken over by another paper would hardly be appealing. Hence *today* I sent in a "financial" piece.[5] An introduction to the *Persian war*, no matter how cursory, would be important, because it would indicate that there is still a war on, and thus help the paper in competition with others. The chances (military) of the Russians and English should, of course, be only indicated.

Hence I will postpone a direct break with the *Tribune* until I find out what other arrangement can be made in New York. If it cannot be made, and if the *Tribune* does not change, then, of course, a break must be made. I believe, however, that in such a lousy struggle time is important. It appears to me that, since the "great change" in America,[6] the *Tribune* has come to the conclusion that it can dispense with all extra expenses (at least European ones). It is really disgusting that one is condemned to consider oneself lucky when such a blotting-paper receives one with its boot. Crushing bones, grinding them, and making soup out of them, as the paupers do in the workhouse, this is to what political work is reduced, to what one is richly condemned in such an undertaking. As a jackass, I am at the same time aware, and not only recently but for years now, to have given those fellows too much for their money.

Pieper has accepted a job as tutor somewhere between Portsmouth and Brighton; he has tried to get something like it for months.

How is Lupus' adventure? You forgot to write me about it.

Yours, K.M.

3. Abraham Jacobi (1830–1919), a German doctor from Cologne who emigrated to the United States in 1853.
4. [Friedrich Engels], "Perspectives of the Anglo-Persian War," editorial, in *New-York Daily Tribune*, February 19, 1857.
5. This article was not published by the *Tribune*.
6. The near-victory of the newly founded Republican Party in the Presidential election of 1856.

P.S. I envy the fellows who know how to turn somersaults. It must be a splendid means of casting anger and bourgeois muck out of one's head.

In the *Morning Advertiser*, I saw an excerpt from *Grenzboten*,[7] of strategic content about the Persian shit.[8]

68

From letter to Frederick Engels (in Manchester)
London, March 24, 1857

Dear Engels:

... Now to *private affairs* [in English]. *D'abord* [First], I received a letter from the *Tribune*, which I will send you as soon as I have answered it. My threat to write for another paper has had its effect, at least to some extent. Despite the *very friendly tone*, it shows that I have correctly understood those gentlemen. The proposition is this: They will pay for *one article* a week, whether they print it or not; the *second* article I send at my own risk, and will be paid *if* they print it. Thus *au fait* [in fact] they cut me down to half. I *accept* this, and *must accept* it. Also, when stories develop in England, as I think they will, I ought to manage after a bit of time to regain my old income.

I am very sorry for the time being I still have to press you [for money], because the arrears into which I fell are such that I had to pawn everything that is pawnable, and the gap in my income can be filled only when I find new sources. In addition, since I can no longer conceal the fact from you, my wife finds herself in highly interesting circumstances. Still, my last letter was in *no way* meant to do *anything else* than to explain my long silence. You understand that even the most even-tempered person—and in this muck I do, indeed, possess a lot of equanimity—occasionally loses his patience and lets himself go in the presence of friends. ...

Salut.

Yours, K.M.

---

7. *Die Grenzboten*, a Leipzig weekly devoted to politics and literature.
8. The Anglo-Persian War of 1856–57.

69

To Frederick Engels (in Manchester)
London, April 21, 1857

Dear Engels:

Be so good as to write me by *return mail* how I am to reply to the enclosed letter from Dana.[1] The reply must be mailed with the Friday post.

By following the Christian precepts—"if thy tooth offends you, pull it out"—I have at last obtained relief: at the same time I discovered that this damn tooth was the basic cause of all the other afflictions that had plagued me for months. Our house you have detected correctly. Herr Edgar's[2] book is not called *English Impressions* but *English Freedom*. One-fourth of it is said to contain Mormonism. The whole pretends to present the physiognomy or, *if you like* [in English], the physiology of national character. I have read nothing in it. A letter to you *in some days* [in English].

Salut.

Yours, K.M.

70

From letter to Frederick Engels (in Manchester)
London, May 22, 1857

Dear Engels:

For your consolation,[1] I can report to you that for three weeks now I have been inundated with medicines and pills on account of my old and, as I believe, hereditary *liver complaints* [in English]. Only with the greatest effort have I been able to attend to my "business"—I mean the *Tribune*—and have

---

69

1. Charles Anderson Dana, on April 6, 1857, asked Marx whether he would contribute articles to *The New American Cyclopaedia*, which he and George Ripley were publishing. Marx and Engels contributed sixteen articles, on military personnel in Vols. II to IV (A to B) in 1858–1859.
2. Edgar Bauer.

70

1. Engels to Marx, May 20, 1857: "They tell me that I ate too much roast beef, and in any case, in the last four weeks I have been continuously occupied with my face, first toothaches, then swollen cheek, then toothache again, and now the whole culminated in a furuncle, as the little Heckscher [Dr. Martin] calls the thing."

been otherwise *quite disabled* [in English]. In order not to lose time altogether, I have, *faute de mieux* [for lack of something better], mastered *der dansk sprog* [the Danish language] and started to read an enormous political hemorrhoid: *Af mit Livs og min Tids Historie af* [The History of My Life and My Times by] Orsted (the ex-Minister).[2] It would have been more amusing to read zoology. In the meantime. I have the prospect, according to the doctor's promise, to become human again next week. For the time being, I am still as yellow as a quince but more peevish.

As for your own dolor, it is my *idée fixe* that the whole thing derives from a hollow tooth that should be extracted, for it lies at the root, through a series of interconnections, of all the ill symptoms. Heckscher,[3] of course, will deny it. Still, when you come here, to which I am looking forward, it would do no harm if you accompany me to a really excellent dentist, who would examine your teeth. My opinion is based on the fact that two years ago I suffered from quite similar ailments, that Dr. Freund, too, said that I ate too much meat, and that finally, through a courageous visit to a dentist a few months ago, the source of the trouble was discovered. My opinion, of course, is based mainly on your periodic toothaches.

My wife's confinement is expected to take place at the end of this month,[4] and this time under not quite pleasant circumstances. At best, I will not be able to draw money from the *Tribune* before three weeks, for it now takes a long time to cash a draft. I have tried, for the interim, to sign an I.O.U. but failed splendidly. The household debts proper I can postpone, but with taxes that can be done only up to a point, and, moreover, under present circumstances certain preparations have to be made for which one has to shell out....
      Salut.

Yours, K.M.

71

To Frederick Engels (in Manchester)
London, July 8, 1857

Dear Frederic:

My wife has finally had her confinement. But the child was not viable, it died immediately. In and by itself, this is no misfortune. But partly, because of the

2. Anders Sandøe Ørsted (1778–1860), Danish jurist, statesman, Prime Minister, 1853–1854.
3. Martin Heckscher, German physician in Manchester.
4. Marx miscalculated the month of confinement; see Letter 71, Marx to Engels, July 8, 1857.

circumstances directly connected with it, it has made a frightful impression on my imagination; partly, because the circumstances that led to this result were such that the memory is distressing. One cannot go into this in a letter.[1]

Salut. Give my regards to Lupus and convey the news to him.

Yours, K.M.

72

To Frederick Engels (in Waterloo, near Liverpool)
London, August 15, 1857

Dear Frederick:

I am very glad that the seaside,[1] as was to be expected, is salutary. As soon as your condition permits going into the water, the improvement will be even more rapid.

The sea itself is, of course, the main cure. Still, certain internal medicaments are necessary, partly preventively and partly positively, in order to enrich the blood with substances of which it is deficient; and, supported by all the latest French, English, and German medical literature which I have read for your illness, I am, contrary to the assertions in your letter to my wife,[2] stating the following, which can be submitted to any board of doctors or chemists for examination:

(1) Where liver oil works in three months, iron does so in three weeks.

(2) Liver oil and iron do not cancel but supplement each other in the cure.

(3) The basic cause of your illness is the momentary *lack of iron in the blood*. In addition to sea bathing, you must continue to take iron, even after all the external traces of the illness have disappeared.

(4) For you, the healing element in the liver oil is the iodine, as the fat-producing characteristic of oil itself is unessential. *Iodide of iron*, therefore, combines both elements that you need, and of which the one is supplied by liver oil. At the same time, this prescription avoids filling the stomach with the unnecessary ballast connected with liver oil.

71

1. Marx to Engels, July 14, 1857: "The circumstances connected with my wife's confinement which unnerved me for some days can only be reported orally. I cannot write about them."

72

1. Engels to Marx, July 30, 1857: "Since the day before yesterday, I am at the seaside, three miles further than Newbrighton, but north of Mersey; I arrived here, alas, with a proper cold, which aggravated the glandular swelling, caused great pain, and disturbed my sleep...."

2. Engels' letter to Jenny Marx, written on August 11, 1857, has not been found.

Voilà mes Thèses [here are my theses], and I hope that you will examine them seriously, so that after the cure there would be no later relapses, which could be *exceedingly* [in English] unpleasant....

With best wishes for your health from me and my wife.

Yours, K.M.

73

To Frederick Engels (in Ryde)
London, September 25, 1857

Dear Engels:

You should have received by now my letter from the day before yesterday with its acknowledgment of the receipt of the £5. I do not understand the delay, as I myself had mailed the letter on time.

Your "*Army*"[1] is very well done; but its size made me feel as if I had been hit over the head, for it must be harmful to you to work so much. Specifically, if I had known that you would work far into the night, I would rather have let the whole thing go to the devil.

The history of the *army* [in English] brings out more clearly than anything else the correctness of our conception of the connection between forces of production and social relations. In general, the *army* [in English] is important for economic development. For example, it was in the army that the ancients first fully developed a wage system. Likewise among the Romans the *peculium castrense*[2] was the first legal form in which the right of others than fathers of families to movable property was recognized. So also the guild system among the corporation of *fabri*.[3] Here, too, the first application of machinery on a large scale. Even the special value of metals and their *use* [in English] as money appears to have been originally based—as soon as Grimm's Stone Age was passed—on their military significance. The division of labor *within* one branch was also first carried out in armies. Furthermore, the whole history of bourgeois societies is very strikingly epitomized here. If you can find time someday, you must work the thing out from this point of view.

73

1. Engels' essay, "Army," in *The New American Cyclopaedia*, Volume II, 1858.
2. A Roman legal rule granting the father control over the son's property acquired during the latter's military service.
3. Craftsmen in the Roman military system.

In my opinion, the only points that have been overlooked in your account are: (1) The first appearance of mercenary troops, ready for use on a large scale *and at once* [in English], among the Carthaginians (for our *private use* [in English], I will look up a book by a Berlin man[4] on the Carthaginian armies, which I came to know only later). (2) The development of the army system in Italy in the fifteenth and early sixteenth centuries. At any rate, tactical tricks were developed here. Extremely humorous is Machiavelli's description (which I will copy out for you), in his *History of Florence*,[5] of the way the condottieri fought one another. (But when I come to see you in Brighton—when?[6]—I would rather bring the volume of Machiavelli with me. His *History of Florence* is a masterpiece). And, finally (3), the Asian military system, as it first appeared among the Persians, and then, though modified in a great variety of ways, among the Mongols, Turks, etc.

In preparing my biographies, etc.,[7] I was of course compelled to consult all sorts of encyclopedias, among them, German ones. On that occasion I found articles under the rubrics "Labor," "Classes," "Production," etc., honest but dumb. On the other hand, all of them avoid mentioning us, even though they devote many columns to Herr Edgar Bauer and similar great ones. *Tant mieux pour nous* [so much the better for us]. The biographies in the encyclopedias are written for children under eight years old. The French are partisan but at least worldly wise. The English encyclopedias are in integrity like the French and German. In the German ones, the same fellows seem to deposit the same twaddle with the most varied publishers. Ersch and Gruber[8] are good in the later volumes, to which many scholars contribute.

Salut.

Yours, K.M.

The *Realencyclopädie des Altertums* by Pauly[9] *is solid* [in English].

---

4. Wilhelm Bötticher, *Geschichte der Carthager nach den Quellen bearbeitet* [*History of the Carthaginians, Based on the Sources*] (Berlin, 1827).

5. Niccolo Machiavelli, *History of Florence from 1492 to 1512*.

6. Marx met Engels in Brighton probably on September 30, 1857.

7. For Marx's biographies in *The New American Cyclopaedia* (fifteen of them, seven in collaboration with Engels), see Saul K. Padover, ed., *Karl Marx On History and People* (New York, 1977), pp. 328–91.

8. *General German Encyclopedia of Science and Art*, begun in 1818 by Ersch and Gruber and continued until 1890, when volume 167 was published; the greatest of German encyclopedias, it remains incomplete.

9. August von Pauly, *Encyclopedia of Antiquity*, 6 vols. (1839–1852).

74

From letter to Frederick Engels (in Manchester)
London, December 18, 1857

Dear Frederick:

I am writing these lines in all haste. I have received the *third and last warning* from the lousy tax collector that if I did not pay up by Monday,[1] I would have the *broker* [in English] put into the house that afternoon. If, therefore, it is possible, send me a few pounds until Monday. The money *pressure* [in English] is now greater than usual,[2] because for about three weeks now I have had to pay *cash* for everything *and anything like credit* [in English] has ceased, while at the same time of the money I earn, two-thirds has to go immediately to cover the floating debt. Added to that, my income is very slight, since I have hitherto not been able to send the *Tribune* more than one article [weekly].[3] *So far as to private matters* [in English].

I work quite colossally, mostly until four in the morning. It is a double labor: (1) Working on the foundations of the economics book[4] (it is absolutely necessary for the public to go *au fond* [to the bottom] of the thing and for me, individually, *to get rid of this nightmare* [in English]).

(2) The *present crisis*. On this subject—apart from the articles in the *Tribune*—I merely fill notebooks, which, however, takes up important time. I think that in *about* [in English] the spring you and I *together* should write a pamphlet on the story,[5] as a *re-announcement* to the German public—that we are still here, *always the same* [in English]. I have planned three big books— England, Germany, France. On America, all the materials are in the *Tribune*. One could gather together later. For the rest, I would appreciate it if you would send me the [Manchester] *Guardian* daily. It doubles the work and causes interruption if I have to catch up with a whole week at one time....

If you have time, write me, as you otherwise forget all the necessary *"Chronique scandaleuse"* ["Scandalous chronicle," that is, gossip] of the [world economic] crisis; I will make extracts from your letters and put them in the books.

Salut. Best regards for Lupus. Pieper has the satisfaction that his ex-Principal Saalfeld,[6] with whose wife he has had such a brawl, *has gone to the wall* [in English].

Yours, K.M.

74

1. December 21.
2. Marx wrote in English "usually."
3. See Letter 68, Marx to Engels, March 24, 1857.
4. Marx, *Critique of Political Economy*, published in 1859.
5. This plan did not materialize.
6. Unidentified.

75

From letter to Frederick Engels (in Manchester)
London, January 28, 1858

Dear Frederick:

The great cold that has set in here and the *actual lack of coal in our home* force me—although of all things in the world, this is for me the most disagreeable—to press you again. I have decided to do this only because of *heavy pressure from without* [in English]. My wife has shown me that as a result of a transmission from Jersey, which arrived sooner than usual, you had made an error in calculation and that, therefore, without my writing to you, you will send nothing this month; that she had pawned her *shawl* [in English], etc., etc., and does not know what to do. In short, if this condition continues, I would rather lie 100 fathoms deep under ground than to go on vegetating like this. Always to be a burden on others and constantly to be harassed by the pettiest muck, is unendurable in the long run. I personally work off the misery through intense occupation with ordinary things. My wife, *of course* [in English], does not have the same resources, etc....
Salut.

Yours, K.M.

76

From letter to Frederick Engels (in Manchester)
London, February 14, 1858

Dear Engels:

You promised to send me the [Manchester] *Guardian*. I expected it, therefore, today, since it is left as the only material for the correspondenceship[1] and the fellows prefer anecdotal gossip to *any amount of ideas* [in English]. I believe the promised copies of the *Guardian* will arrive tomorrow, but I urge you in the future always to send the things to me for Thursday or Friday at the latest. They are, *of course* [in English], of no use to me *after* the day of my mailing the correspondence.

For three days I will sit on pins and needles until I know whether my promissory note, which seems to have been sent out from here some weeks *after its drawing* [in English], is being honored or not. At best, I will not be able to draw on the *Tribune* for the articles I already sent out, until the thing

76
1. The weekly articles for the *New-York Daily Tribune*.

is settled with Appleton.[2] I have completely miscalculated my estimate for the wares I sent the latter. In addition, Dana has expressed misgivings about my lengthy article on "Bolivar"[3] because it is written in *a partisan style* [in English], and demands my authorities. I can, of course, supply him with the latter, although it is a strange demand. In regard to the partisan style, I did, it is true, deviate somewhat from the encyclopedic tone. To hail the most cowardly, the most vulgar, the most miserable scamp [Bolivar] as Napoleon I, was too absurd. Bolivar is the true Soulouque.[4]

I congratulate you upon your equestrial performance [in English]. But only don't make any neck-breaking jumps, for soon there will be more important occasions for risking your neck.[5] You seem to *ride somewhat hard this hobbyhorse* [in English]. In any case, I don't believe that cavalry is the speciality with which you are most useful for Germany. I also allow myself some quiet doubts as to whether *over-exertion in any line* [in English] is good for your health. I have been at least assured by doctors that *aurea mediocritas* [the golden mean] in all sorts of exertions must remain the norm for you for some time to come.[6]. . .

Salut.

Yours, K.M.

77

To Frederick Engels (in Manchester)
London, July 15, 1858

Dear Engels:

I beg you, *d'abord* [to begin with], not to be alarmed by the content of this letter, since it is in no way an *appeal* [in English] to the already indecent

---

2. William Henry Appleton (1814–1899), head of the New York publishing house, D. Appleton and Co., which published *The New American Cyclopaedia* to which Marx and Engels contributed.
3. Marx's piece, "Bolivar y Ponte," appeared in Volume III (1858) of *The New American Cyclopaedia.*
4. Faustin Soulouque (*c.* 1782–1867), Emperor of Haiti under the name of Faustin I, 1849–1859.
5. Engels to Marx, February 11, 1858: "Yesterday I was inveigled into riding at a coursing meeting, where rabbits were hunted down by greyhounds, and I was in the saddle for seven hours. This agreed with me splendidly, but it interrupted my work."
6. Engels to Marx, February 18, 1858: "About riding I will write you some other time. *Au fond* [at bottom], the thing is the material basis for my war studies—what do you expect? The louse Bonaparte appears to be a hero to the *crapauds* [toads] because he rides passably well and handsomely.... Furthermore, riding is the only physical accomplishment in which I have at least achieved mediocrity, and in hunting the element of danger is so slight (probability: 1 to 10,000) that its attraction is irresistible. For the rest, *sois tranquille* [don't worry], I will break my neck in another way than falling off a horse."

claims on your purse. On the other hand, it is necessary to take counsel together to see if some solution could be found to the present situation, which is absolutely no longer tenable. Its direct result has been that I am *completely disabled* [in English] to work; partly because I lose the best part of my time in running around in vain attempts to raise money, and partly because my power of thinking no longer holds out, perhaps as a consequence of a further decline in health and the lamentations in the house. My wife's nerves are shattered by this muck, and Dr. Allen, although he does have an idea where the *shoe pinches* [in English] but does not know the real situation, has told me repeatedly and positively that if she is not immediately sent to the seashore, he feared an inflammation of the brain or something like it. For my own part, I do know that, even if it were possible, going to the seashore would be of no use, so long as the daily pressures continue and she is haunted by the specter of an unavoidable final catastrophe. The latter, however, is not to be postponed much longer and even a relief of a few weeks still leaves the unbearable daily struggle for *mere necessaries* [in English] and the general situation unsolved, which must end in the ruin of everything.

Since there are in London so-called *loan-societies* [in English] which offer loans of from £5 to £200 *without securities* [in English] but on *references* [in English] only, I tried out this kind of operation, in which Freiligrath and a grocer offered themselves as *referees* [in English]. The result was that some £2 were wasted on fees. The rejection of the loan came before yesterday. I do not know whether I will make another such attempt.

In order that you have a real insight into the situation, I have had my wife make out an account of how we spent the £20 that you have advanced me and the £24 (of which £2 were overdrawn) which I received from the *Tribune* since June 16. From it you will see that as soon as such a large sum arrives, not a penny remains even for the most pressing daily expenses, not to mention any human gratifications; that on the following day exactly the same loathsome *struggle* [in English] begins anew, and the sparingly reimbursed creditors in a very short time start to press in exactly the same way for the demands which had in the meantime grown bigger. You will also see that my wife, for example, has not spent a single *farthing* [in English] on clothing for herself, while the status of the *summerdresses* [in English] for the children is below proletarian. I consider it necessary that you go through these details, since otherwise it would be impossible to come to a correct decision about *the case* [in English].

Account of the £20 on May 19, from which were paid:

Taxes (water, gas)	£7	
Pawnshop interest	£3	
Redeemed in the pawnshop	£1	10 sh.

Loan	£2	
Tallyman (paid weekly for coat and trousers)		18 sh.
Shoes and hats for the children	£1	10 sh.
Baker	£1	
Butcher	£1	10 sh.
Grocer	£1	
Cheesemonger		10 sh.
Coal		10 sh.

Account of the £24 on June 16, from the Tribune:

School tuition for the February-March-April *quarter* [in English]	£8	
Repayment of loan to Schapper for four-weeks daily expenses	£3	
Linen redeemed from the pawnshop	£2	
Loan	£1	
Tallyman	£1	4 sh.
Butcher	£2	
Grocer	£2	
Greengrocer	£1	
Shirts, dresses, etc., for the children	£2	
Baker	£2	

Thus after June 17 there was again not a penny in the house, and in order to pay the daily expenses for the last four weeks, which had to be paid in cash, we had to borrow £4 from Schapper, of which, however, we had to spend £2 for the miscarried *loan operation in fees* [in English].

The following state of our debt in London will show you how a major part of it consists of debts to small tradesmen, who have extended to us the limit of their credit:

House tax, due June 25	£9	
School, due August 2	£6	
Newspaper delivery man (for one year)	£6	
Tallyman	£3	9 sh.
Butcher	£7	14 sh.
Baker	£6	
Grocer	£4	
Greengrocer and coal	£2	
Milkman	£6	17 sh.
Debt due to the old milkman and baker in Soho	£9	
Dr. Allen (£7 paid with previous *Tribune* money)	£10	
Schapper	£4	
Pawnshop	£30	

Of all these debts, only those owing to Dr. Allen, Lina Schöler, the old creditors in Soho, and part of the pawnshop, are not urgent.

The whole story hinges on the fact that the meagre income is never destined for the next month, but always merely suffices to lighten the debts—after deduction for standing expenses for the house, school, taxes, and pawnshop—only up to the point of not being thrown on the street. In four to five weeks I expect to draw about £24 on the *Tribune*. Of this, I must immediately pay £15 merely for the house tax and rent. Should only a minimum of the other debts be paid—and it is very questionable whether the butcher, etc., will be patient that long—the muck will again increase in the four weeks, which, after all, one has to live through *d'une manière ou d'une autre* [in one way or another]. The *landlord* is himself hounded by creditors and persecutes me like crazy. I don't see what I am to do if I cannot effect a *loan* [in English] at some *loan-society* [in English] or *life-assecurance* [sic] *society*. If I should take the step of reducing the expenses to an extreme—for example, take the children out of school, move into purely proletarian quarters, dismiss the maids, live on potatoes—even the auctioning off my furniture and chattels would not bring enough to satisfy even the neighboring creditors so that I could slip away unhindered into some hiding place. The *show* [in English] of *respectability* [in English] which has been maintained hitherto had been the only means of preventing collapse. For my part, I would even ask the devil if only I could find a peaceful hour to pursue my work, even if I had to live in Whitechapel.[1] But for my wife in her present state such a change would have dangerous consequences, and for the growing girls too it would be hardly appropriate.

I have now made a clean breast of it [in English], and I assure you that it has cost me no small effort. But *enfin* [finally], I have to speak at least to one person. I know that you personally cannot help in the matter.[2] What I request is a communication of your views—*what to do* [in English]? I would not wish my worst enemy to wade through the *quagmire* [in English] in which I have been sitting in the last eight weeks, aggravated by the greatest rage that my intellect by all this lousiness and my ability to work is being broken.

Salut.

Yours, K.M.

I am sending you the things you requested.[3]

77
1. A workingclass slum.
2. But Engels did. Immediately upon receipt of the letter, on July 16, he wrote Marx he would send him £30 right away and would try to raise another £30 through a promissory note.
3. On July 14, Engels asked Marx to send him Hegel's *Naturphilosophie* [*Philosophy of Nature*], as he was then studying physiology and anatomy.

78

From letter to Frederick Engels (in Manchester)
London, July 20, 1858

Dear Engels:

...On Saturday[1] I received a long letter from my mother.[2] I had given Frau Liebknecht,[3] who went to Germany, a picture of the youngest child[4] for *die Alte*[5] with a short letter in which I mentioned my frequent indispositions, but not the rest of the circumstances. The letter from the *Alte* is such that it is possible that a meeting between us is in prospect in a few weeks. *If so, I should arrange things. But I must not press in this respect* [in English]. Otherwise she will immediately draw *back* [in English].

Thanks for the *Tribune* article.[6] More tomorrow.

Yours, K.M.

79

From letter to Frederick Engels (in Manchester)
London, August 8, 1858

Dear Engels:

...After receiving the money,[1] I immediately paid up as much as possible and yesterday I sent my wife to Ramsgate, as not a day can be delayed. She is really extraordinarily ill. If Ramsgate is not too expensive and she can have a few weeks of sea bathing, I believe everything will be *right* [in English] again. *Meanwhile* [in English], I will see what I can get from my mother. It is a very ticklish point as to how I should answer the *Alte* [Old Woman], on account of my relation to Prussia. It is *possible* that she would come forth with her money if she believes that my inheritance is threatened by the Government. But it is also *possible* that—since she seems to be drawing up her will—she would put everything under the guardianship of the Dutchman,[2] which I don't like at

---

78

1. July 17.
2. Henriette Marx.
3. Ernestine Liebknecht (d. 1867), wife of Wilhelm Liebknecht.
4. Eleanor Marx.
5. The Old Woman: Marx's mother.
6. Engels, "How the Indian War Has Been Managed," published in garbled form in *New-York Daily Tribune*, August 13, 1858.

79

1. The sum of £40, arranged by Ferdinand Freiligrath on a promissory note.
2. Lion Philips, Marx's uncle, the executor of his mother's will.

all. *Que faire dans cette situation* [What do you do in this situation]? She writes that her days are numbered.[3] But I consider this mere talk. She probably wanted me to invite her to London, and I would positively have done it, but just now I need the time for myself. For the last two months I have been hardly able to work, and the matter with Duncker[4] is pressing....

Salut. I hope to hear *good* news of your *state of health* [in English].

Yours, K.M.

80

From letter to Frederick Engels (in Manchester)
London, October 8, 1858

Dear Frederick:

...We cannot deny that bourgeois society has experienced its sixteenth century for the second time, a sixteenth century which I hope will knell it to its grave as much as the first had pushed it into life. The special task of bourgeois society is the restoration of the world market, at least according to its outlines and on a production resting on its basis. Since the world is round, this seems to have terminated with the colonization of California and Australia, and the opening of China and Japan. The difficult question for us is this: On the Continent the revolution is imminent and will also immediately take on a socialist character. Will it then not be crushed of necessity in this small corner, while on the much larger terrain the movement of the bourgeois society is still in the ascendant?...

Yours, K.M.

81

From letter to Frederick Engels (in Manchester)
London, December 11, 1858

Dear Engels:

... Here in the house it looks *more dreary and desolate out than ever* [in English]. Since my wife could not herself prepare a Christmas celebration for the children, but instead is being pursued by demand notes from all sides, and works on the manuscript[1] in addition, and has to run to the pawnshops in the

---

3. Actually, Marx's mother did not die until some five years later, on November 30, 1863.
4. Franz Gustav Duncker, the Berlin publisher of Marx's *Critique of Political Economy* (1859).

81

1. *Critique of Political Economy*, of which Jenny Marx made a clean copy (since Marx's handwriting was illegible) for publication in 1859.

City in-between times, the atmosphere is extraordinarily gloomy. Moreover, my wife is quite right when she says that after all the misery she has had to endure already, it will be even worse after the revolution and she will have the dubious pleasure of seeing all the humbugs from here on out celebrate their triumphs. Women are like that. And the feminine behavior of the Freiligraths,[2] etc., and other acquaintances justly embitters her. She says, *à la guerre comme à la guerre* [war is war]. But *there is no* [in English] *guerre.* Everything is bourgeois.

Salut.

Yours, K.M.

82

To Frederick Engels (in Manchester)
London, January 21, 1859

Dear Engels:

The unfortunate manuscript[1] is completed, but cannot be mailed because I don't have a *farthing* [in English] to prepay and insure it. The latter is necessary because I don't have a copy. I must, therefore, beg you to send me a little money by Monday (*Postoffice in Tottenham Court Road corner* [in English]). If you could send me £2, it would be very welcome, as I have postponed some absolutely no longer postponable demands from small creditors until Monday. You understand that it is no way pleasant for me to fall on your neck again now that you have just paid the promissory note to Freiligrath. *But iron necessity* [in English]. I will see next week—as I am giving myself eight days vacation to work on a *continuation* of the manuscript—if I can succeed in making some kind of financial coup. I don't believe that anybody had ever written about "money" while suffering such a lack of money. Most authors on this subject have been in deep peace with the *subject of their researches* [in English].

If the matter works out in Berlin, it is possible that I will extricate myself from all this muck. It is *high time* [in English].

Salut.

Yours, K.M.

---

2. Ferdinand Freiligrath and family.

82

1. Marx, *Critique of Political Economy*, published in Berlin on June 11, 1859; for Marx's difficulties with his publisher, see letters 87 and 88, Marx to Franz Duncker, the publisher, May 28 and June 2, 1859.

If things can be arranged in Berlin, it would perhaps be possible to make a coup for an English translation with a publisher in London, where one is paid differently than in Berlin. In addition, such an *event* [in English] would annoy to death our worthy enemies. The latter canaille believe that we are both dead—and especially now, when Herr *Clown* [in English] "Edgar Bauer," as Gottfried Kinkel tells everybody in the City, has "supplanted" us "among the workers." The canaille, which reveal their own death certificate with every word they print, should wonder what "*sort of life*" [in English] we have preserved.

I hesitate in deciding whether I should inscribe on the muck:[2] "*The Author reserves to himself the right of translation*" [in English]. (You are familiar with the cartel agreement about copyrights between Prussia and England.) My aversion for all humbug and seeming vanity and pretension says No. On the other hand, my interest says Yes, as practically every week there appears in England some dirty story about such money shit. *What do you think, Sir* [in English]? You must write me by return mail about this point, as I have to decide on Monday.[3]

83

From letter to Joseph Weydemeyer (in Milwaukee)
London, February 1, 1859

Dear Weiwi:
Your letter, dated February 28, 1858, came here (or at least reached me) at the end of May, and my reply takes place in February, 1859. The reasons are simple: During the spring and summer months I was constantly ill with liver trouble and only with difficulty did I find time to do the necessary work. Writing, unless absolutely necessary, was therefore *out of the question* [in English]. In the subsequent months, however, the work was overwhelming.

First of all, warm regards to you and yours from all the members of my family, as well as from Engels, Lupus, and Freiligrath. And my special greetings to your dear wife [Louise].

Engels is, as always, in Manchester; Lupus, also there, gives lessons and does tolerably well; Freiligrath is in London, manager of a branch of the Swiss Crédit mobilier; Dronke is a commission agent in Glasgow; Imandt[1] (I

---

2. His book, *Critique of Political Economy*.
3. Engels to Marx, February 14, 1859: "I forgot to write you: State in your book that you reserve the right of translation. Even if only for the reason that some jackass or industrialist doesn't botch it. Furthermore, this is now a purely legalistic formality which anybody can fill out with propriety."

83
1. Peter Imandt, a German communist teacher, refugee in England.

don't know whether you know him) is a professor in Dundee; our dear friend Weerth, alas, died in Haiti, an *irreplaceable* loss.

Things were going badly rather than well with me for the last two years, as on the one hand, the worthy *Tribune* cut my income in half because of the [economic] crisis, although in time of prosperity it never gave me an extra penny; and on the other hand, the time I needed for my studies of political economy (more about that below) forced me to turn down (although with heavy heart) very remunerative offers made to me in London and Vienna.[2] But I must pursue my goal through thick and thin, and not allow bourgeois society to turn me into a money-making machine.

Mr. Cluss was here last May. I happened then to be with Engels in Manchester. Cluss visited my wife and accepted an invitation to return the next day, but he did not show up. He [disappeared] from London and was not seen again. Instead of a visit, he sent my wife a letter, which, out of "embarrassment," had a rather "rude" tone. Nor did he show up in Manchester. Later we learned that he had formed an alliance with Willich. This explains the mysterious breaking off of his correspondence. If we were conceited, we would feel properly chastised by the experience of having a fool like Willich knock us out of the saddle vis-à-vis a sensible man like Cluss. But this whole episode was too comical not to stifle any chagrin.

I have broken with Ernest Jones.[3] Despite my repeated warnings, and though I had predicted exactly what would happen—namely, that he would ruin himself and disorganize the Chartist party—he nevertheless attempted to effect a reconciliation with the bourgeois radicals. Now he is a ruined man, but the damage he has done to the English proletariat is extraordinary. The split will of course be mended again, but a very favorable moment for action has been lost. Think of an army whose general crosses over to the enemy on the eve of battle.

You will have heard that Herr Kinkel has again become a famous man since Frau Kinkel fell out of the window and broke her neck. The "gay" customer—who has never felt as well as he does now since the death of the old Mockel[4]—decided immediately to go around peddling his "grief." Freiligrath permitted himself to be taken in by Gottfried's melodramatic scenes to write a poem on Johanna,[5] which he now regrets, since he has become convinced, first, that Gottfried is as happy as a lark, and secondly, that he has used his poem promptly to spread the lie that Freiligrath had

---

2. One of the offers, made in 1858, was by Max Friedländer, editor of the Vienna *Presse*, to contribute to his paper. Marx, who had doubts about Friedländer's politics, did not become a contributor to the *Presse* until October, 1861.
3. Ernest Charles Jones (1819–1869), a Chartist leader and editor of *Northern Star, Notes to the People*, and *The People's Paper*, was a friend of Marx up to 1858.
4. Johanna Kinkel, née Mockel (1810–1858), committed suicide on November 15, 1858.
5. See Letter 81, Marx to Engels, December 11, 1858.

allied himself with him and broken with us. Gottfried, who immediately wanted to start a Kinkel revival as a result of his wife's death, within a week published a weekly in London, called *Hermann*. As this is not the *Hermann* about whom Schönaich[6] write poetry and Gottsched[7] had crowned, the title should be *Gottfried*. The little sheet preaches peace with God and the world, but this is merely advertisement for Herr Gottfried among the London City German philistines. Anything more wretched has never been published, and we can only congratulate ourselves that in the ten-year exile of our democratic friends their hollowness has never been more exposed. Compared to this, the *Kölnische Zeitung* is witty and daring.

The nicest thing about Kinkel's exploitation of the death of his wife is that the latter, suffering from heart disease, was exasperated because the sweet parson seduced a Jewess named Herz and generally treated her "coldly." The Jewesses in Manchester swear that this was the reason why the deceased Johanna Mockel fell out of the window. In any case, this would prove that, fatuous as Gottfried is otherwise, he possesses enough slyness to exploit the official *credulity* [in English]. But enough of this humbug....

Salut.

Yours, K. Marx

84

Draft of a letter to Eduard Müller-Tellering¹ (in London)
London, March 12, 1859

[No salutation]
I would challenge you, after your letter of yesterday to the Workers Association, if you were still capable of rendering satisfaction after your disgraceful calumnies against Engels motivated by the association's committee to expel you.[2] I await you on a different field, in order to tear off the hypocritical mask of revolutionary fanaticism, behind which you had known how to conceal cleverly your petty interests, your envy, your unsatisfied vanity and your malcontent vexation over the world's oversight in recognizing your great genius—an oversight that began when you failed your examination.

---

6. Christoph Otto Schönaich (1725–1807), author of the epic, *Hermann, or the Liberated Germany* (1751).
7. Johann Christoph Gottsched (1700–1766), German literary critic.

84

1. Eduard von Müller-Tellering (b. *c.* 1808), anti-Marx German journalist, emigrated to the United States in 1852.
2. The association expelled Müller-Tellering on March 3, whereupon he wrote a letter slandering Engels.

After some reflection, you must have assumed that when I was compelled as a *witness* to report an aggravating fact against you, nothing was left
out on my part to avoid a scandal that would compromise me doubly: before
the eyes of the Workers Association, since you were recommended *by me*, and
before the eyes of the public, for which you exist only through your correspondenceship on *my newspaper* [*Neue Rheinische Zeitung*].

Your letters to me, and they are ready for publication, prove that you
had tried everything to force upon me the role of the "democratic Dalai-Lama
and Possessor of the Future." How do you prove that I had ever accepted this
silly role? The only thing you can reproach me with is that I did not immediately break with you and denounce you after the story on Klapka,[3] about
whose compromising character I had immediately expressed my candid opinion to you in the presence of witnesses. I confess my weakness. First,
Becker's statement that four weeks before the publication of your already
completed brochure against the *Westdeutsche Zeitung*[4] you offered yourself as
correspondent to this newspaper; this statement, supported by the testimony
of Freiligrath and Hagen, and now your calumnies against Engels, taken out
of the blue, convinced me that what I had thought to be an occasional
rashness was actually an integral part of a whole system. Moreover, it was
clever of you not to appear yesterday at the final appointment repeatedly
asked by Willich at your request. You knew what you could expect from a
confrontation with me.

K. Marx

85

To Frederick Engels (in Manchester)
London, April 16, 1859

Dear Engels:
I assume that your toothache will be over by the time this letter arrives. It is a
devilish story.

Meanwhile I have taken steps that will double my income in a short
time and thereby end the encrusted muck. Lassalle's cousin, Friedländer[1]

---

3. Georg (György) Klapka, a Hungarian general during the 1848–49 revolution in Hungary.
4. Müller-Tellering, *Westdeutscher Zeitungsjammer* [*West German Newspaper Lamentation*] (Düsseldorf, 1850).

85

1. Max Friedländer (1829–1872), editor of *Neue Oder-Zeitung* and Vienna *Presse*, for both of
which newspapers Marx wrote.

(former editor, together with Elsner et Co., of *Neue Oder-Zeitung*[2]), now editor of the Vienna *Presse* (which, in passing, has 24,000 subscribers), has offered me a correspondenceship for his paper in January, 1858. At that time I refused it, because he had made it a condition that Palmerston[3] should not be attacked, but only Bonaparte.[4] Now, *all conditions laid aside* [in English], he has renewed the offer. Still, this is of secondary importance, since what is involved is one *regular* article (at 20 francs) weekly. But at the same time I am to send telegrams (in French), at 10 francs per telegram, and this, although time-consuming, is profitable.

The only point still involved is the instruction about a banking house in London, as telegraphing involves much expense. The negotiations—ere the conditions are settled—have stretched over three weeks. Only yesterday did I send a reply to the letter I received from Vienna on the same day. It will thus take eight to ten days before the thing goes into effect.

Meanwhile, interest on our best silver, watches, etc., is due in the pawnshop next Tuesday [April 19]. For three weeks now my wife has postponed the due date through private *transactions* [in English] with the *pawnbroker* [in English], but Tuesday is the *ultimus terminus* [ultimate date]. While I am thus asking you to send over a few pounds sterling, I hope at the same time that this time the thing is definitely over and the tax on you has a peremptory end.

Be so good as to send one copy[5] to me. As soon as you have more, Freiligrath and Pfänder[6] must have one copy each.

Salut.

Yours, K.M.

86

From letter to Frederick Engels (in Manchester)
London, May 24, 1859

Dear Engels:
If it were possible for you to send me some "tin" [money], I would be *very* much obliged. The lousy guy [Lauskerl] Duncker,[1] on whom I counted,

2. A Breslau daily.
3. British Prime Minister, Lord Palmerston.
4. Napoleon III.
5. Engels' brochure, *Po und Rhein* (Berlin, 1859).
6. Karl Pfänder (c. 1818–1876), German communist refugee in London, friend of Marx.

86

1. Franz Gustav Duncker, the Berlin publisher at whom Marx was furious for the delay in bringing out his *Critique of Political Economy*, which was actually published on May 11, some two weeks after the above letter was written.

seems to have postponed the matter into the blue yonder. The beast has sent me nothing for the last eleven days. Do you know who blocks my way? Nobody else but Lassalle. First, my work is shunted aside for four weeks because of his *Sickingen*.[2] Now, that his thing has been finished, the fool must interject himself again with his "anonymous" pamphlet,[3] which he wrote only because your own "anonymous" pamphlet[4] did not let him sleep. Doesn't the dog see that decency itself required that my thing be brought out first? I will wait another few days, and then write a very rude [*saugroben*] letter to Berlin....[5]

Salut.

Yours, K.M.

87

To Franz Duncker (in Berlin)
London, May 28, 1859

Dear Sir:

You saw fit not to answer the letter I wrote you, asking for the price of my publication.[1] This has made it impossible for me to answer my friends in America, since mail goes there only twice a week.

It took you fourteen days to acknowledge the receipt of my manuscript.[2] You informed me then that printing would begin within a week. That one week became more than three weeks. About eight weeks ago, Lassalle wrote me that the thing would be finished in the middle of May.[3] More than three weeks ago I received the last three proof sheets. The corrections that needed to be made could have been done comfortably in *one* day. Instead, despite the fact that the printing was *finished*, a complete cessation of activity seems to have taken place during this whole period. I hereby declare to you that I am tired of this *systematic and deliberate obstructiveness* and I hereby

---

2. Ferdinand Lassalle's tragedy, *Franz von Sickingen*, published by Duncker, Berlin, 1859.
3. Lassalle, *"Der italienische Krieg und die Aufgabe Preussens"* ["The Italian War and Prussia's Mission"] (published anonymously, early May, 1859).
4. Frederick Engels, *Po und Rhein*.
5. See Letter 89, Marx's "very rude" letter to Duncker, June 22, 1859.

87

1. Marx, *Critique of Political Economy*. The price was one taler.
2. Duncker received Marx's manuscript on February 1, 1859.
3. Lassalle to Marx, April 8, 1859: " ... For the rest, Duncker told me that your honorarium would be due in the middle of May," upon publication of the book.

Critique of Political Economy was published on June 11, 1859, in an edition of 1,000 copies. Duncker sent Marx the remainder of his honorarium—90 taler—on June 25, and told him at the same time that he no longer wanted to have anything to do with him.

demand, and indeed I do so categorically, that you put an end to these maneuvers, which appear to me to be highly suspicious. All my acquaintances in England share this opinion and have urged me to take this last step.

Yours truly, Dr. K. Marx

88

To Franz Duncker (in Berlin)
London, June 2, 1859

Dear Sir:
I am really sorry to have written you a wounding letter.[1] You will, therefore, permit me to give you my excuse for it in a few words. For one thing, I have been away from Germany too long and have accustomed myself too much to London conditions to appreciate correctly German business methods. For another, as Lassalle already learned from me about eight weeks ago, I am in negotiation with a London bookseller for the English translation of the first *Heft* [Part]. The constantly false information which I, myself being under constantly false assumptions, had to give this man regarding the publication of the book sufficed to create in the mind of this John Bull the idea that I was a regular humbug. The continuous, impatient inquiries of my friends, and finally the rumor, painstakingly spread by a *local* Berlin clique, from motives which I do not understand, that the thing will never appear, put a final end to my patience.

Finally, I hope that, in view of all this, you will see in my letter only a hasty expression of vexation caused by various circumstances and will absolve me from any intent of wanting to hurt your feelings.

Devotedly yours, Dr. K. Marx

89

To Franz Duncker (in Berlin)
Manchester, June 22, 1859

Dear Sir:
I request that you *immediately* send the rest of the honorarium for my book to my wife in London.

88

1. Replying on May 31, to Marx's harsh letter of May 28 (Letter 87), Duncker stated that "your injurious charges of systematic obstructiveness, maneuvers, etc., do not even remotely enter into the question," and explained that there were unavoidable business reasons for the delay. "I must, therefore," Duncker concluded, "decisively reject the various direct and indirect accusations of your last letter."

In your letter of the end of May [31] you wrote that the book would appear "*next week*" and that the honorarium would be paid then. Up to now, June 22, neither the one nor the other has taken place.' It seems to be your principle that a "strictly scientific work" cannot appear late enough and that one must wait for the period when the widening of the war² will restore a "strict scientific" interest.

The circumstances that have caused you to postpone publication could probably justify your delay into the year 1860—particularly since you write me that, in connection with scientific writings whose contract does not specify a publication date, it is the custom of German bookdealers to embargo their distribution whenever the publication of newspaper dailies make it convenient for them to do so.

Since it is impossible for me to answer the private inquiries concerning the postponement of my work, I will wait another few days and then issue a *public declaration*.

Sincerely yours, Dr. K. Marx

90

From letter to Frederick Engels (in Manchester)
London, c. January 11, 1860

[No salutation]
... In my opinion, the biggest things now happening in the world today are, on the one hand, the American slave movement, started by the death of Brown,' and, on the other hand, the slave movement in Russia. You will have seen that the Russian nobility has thrown itself directly into the agitation for a constitution and that two or three people from the most notable families have already wandered to Siberia. At the same time, Alexander² has spoiled things with the peasants with his latest manifesto which literally declares that "*the communistic principle*" [in English] must cease with emancipation. Thus, the "social" movement has begun in the West and in the East. This, added to the impending *downbreak* [in English] in Central Europe, will become grandiose. . . .
Salut.

Yours, K.M.

89
1. The book, *Critique of Political Economy*, actually came out on June 11 in Berlin, but Marx did not know it.
2. The Franco-Sardinian war against Austria, April–July, 1859.

90
1. John Brown, the American abolitionist, hanged on December 2, 1859, for his raid on Harpers Ferry, Virginia.
2. Czar Alexander II (1818–1881).

91

To Frederick Engels (in Manchester)
London, November 28, 1860

Dear Engels:
My wife is now *out of danger.*[1] Tell this *also to Lupus* with my best regards. The thing will last for a *long* time, and after recovery, as [Doctor] Allen says, she must *go away* immediately for at least four weeks.

As for me—since the danger of infection is greatest *at most* ten days from *yesterday*—I have been *vaccinated* anew yesterday. Ditto Lenchen.[2] One circumstance, which turned out to be useful, was a hideous toothache. I had the tooth extracted the day before yesterday. The fellow (his name is Gabriel), after great physical pains he caused me, pulled out the root to be sure, but left a splinter. Now my whole face is in pain and swollen, and half the neck too. This physical pressure furthers very much the ability to think and hence of the power of abstraction, for, as Hegel says, pure thought or pure Being or *Nonbeing* are identical.[3]

During the coming ten days the rigor of isolation will be increased.

Under these conditions, I cannot, of course, do any writing, and as the note for £50 drawn on Dana two and a half months ago has not been properly endorsed, since even before her illness my wife already suffered from all sorts of *nervous complaints* [in English] and thus all sorts of shortages occurred—I am in great straits, and I beg you to write[4] as often as possible in the next two weeks at least. In the present circumstances, it would be seemingly fitting for me to write my Old Woman.[5] But ever since she has had the Prussian corporal[6] in the house, all *intercourse* [in English] between us has ceased, owing to some remarks on my part. The dunning from all sides has increased hideously. I have paid out most of the £10 to appease at least some of the creditors. I should not write about this to you, who does more than is possible, but *que faire* [what to do]? But what to do? Added to this is the fact that, peculiarly enough (explainable by the convalescence), I cannot leave the

91

1. Marx to Engels, November 23, 1860: "What my wife has is—smallpox, and very malevolent to boot, although she had been vaccinated twice."
2. Helene Demuth.
3. Hegel, *Wissenschaft der Logik* [*Science of Logic*], Part I; and his *Encyclopädie der philosophischen Wissenschaften* [*Encyclopedia of Philosophic Sciences*], Part I (1833 and 1840).
4. The weekly articles for the *New-York Daily Tribune*.
5. Marx's mother.
6. Johann Carel Juta, a Dutchman married to Marx's sister Louise, who moved in with the widowed Mrs. Marx in Trier.

house, because precisely now that I should see my wife as little as possible (which, of course, must not be told to her), she wants to have me around constantly.

[Doctor] Allen believes that if she had not been vaccinated twice, she would not have survived. As things stand, he considers the smallpox itself a stroke of luck. For, as he told me yesterday, the state of her nerves was such that he preferred the smallpox to a typhoid fever or something similar, to which it would have come.

The poor children are very worried. On Friday, Allen vaccinated them and the whole Liebknecht family.[7]

You ought to receive the pamphlet, *Herr Vogt*, by Friday. Some delay occurred last week because I could not correct the last sheet on time.

Best thanks for the wine.[8] Even before its arrival, Allen had already prescribed the same wine, in addition to other medicines, which are not as pleasant.

Yours, K.M.

92

From letter to Frederick Engels (in Manchester)
London, December 19, 1860

Dear Frederick:
... In my time of trial [illness]—during the last four weeks—I have read all sorts of things. Among others, Darwin's book on *Natural Selection.*[1] Although it is developed in a crude English way, this is the book that contains the natural-history foundation for our viewpoint. In contrast, A. Bastian's *Der Mensch in der Geschichte*[2] (three thick volumes; the fellow is a young Bremen physician who toured around the world for a number of years), with its attempt at "natural history" presentation of psychology and a psychological presentation of history, is poor, confused, and formless. The only useful

---

7. Marx to Engels, November 23, 1860: "I put up the poor children with the Liebknechts who live nearby and to whom I send the victualers daily. They did not want to go to the boarding school because of the religious rites."
8. Marx to Engels, December 5, 1860: "My wife is convalescing very well, and I believe that the wine helps her more than any medicine."

92

1. Charles Darwin, *On the Origin of Species by Means of Natural Selection, or the Preservation of Favoured Races in the Struggle for Life* (London, 1859).
2. Adolf Bastian, *Der Mensch in der Geschichte. Zur Bergründung einer psychologischen Weltanschauung* [*Man in History. Toward the Founding of a Psychological World View*], 3 vols. (Leipzig, 1860).

things in it are some ethnographic *oddities* [in English] here and there. In addition, a lot of pretentiousness and an atrocious style....
Salut.

Yours, K.M.

93

From letter to Frederick Engels (in Manchester)
London, January 8, 1861

Dear Frederick:
... You see what a *Pechvogel* [unlucky person] I am. Since last Wednesday[1] (*just a week ago* [in English]), I have had, together with a cold and cough, a piercing ache in the liver, so that I felt physical *pains* [in English] not only when I coughed but also when I turned the cadaver to one side. To me, this indicated an inflammation. It is the first time that I have felt such a *dolor* [in English], although [Doctor] Allen has often and urgently inquired about it. This time—particularly since I have in any case a frightening *doctorbill* [in English] in addition to other bills on my back—I have treated myself *so far* [in English]. The treatment was simple—no smoking, *castoroil* [in English], drinking only lemonade, eating little, nothing spirituous, doing nothing, staying in the house (the cold air makes me cough immediately). I am not entirely recovered yet and weak to a certain extent. You can, by the way, ask Gumpert[2] what is to be done in such acute prolapses, if they should recur. I will ask Allen, as soon as I go out and am entirely myself again.
Salut.

Yours, K.M.

94

From letter to Frederick Engels (in Manchester)
London, February 27, 1861

Dear Engels:
Tomorrow I leave for Holland,[1] but not with my own passport but with one made out to Bühring.[2] This, as well as the raising of so much money, had cost

---

93

1. January 2.
2. Dr. Eduard Gumpert, a German doctor in Manchester who treated Marx on his visits there.

94

1. Marx was going to Holland to raise money, especially from his uncle, Lion Philips.
2. Karl Johann Bühring (b. 1820), a communist artisan.

me such enormous *trouble* [in English] that I could barely make it. Paid the most pressing creditors small installment sums; with others (for example, the *grocer* [in English]) I referred to the American crisis[3] and postponed the debts, but only on condition that during my absence my wife pays *weekly*. In addition, she has to pay £2, 8 shillings tax next week.

Notabene. Did you receive my wife's letter (about eight days old) in which she thanks you for the wine? She is a little worried that it might have fallen into the wrong hands. The children, too, are very grateful for the wine. They seem to have inherited a love of drink from their father.

I will probably also go to Berlin—without a passport, to explore the matter of the weekly[4] and to look over the muck in general. (Apropos. William I[5] is called in Berlin "The Handsome William"). . . .

The Colognese have made a fine mess of my library.[6] The entire Fourier is stolen, ditto Goethe, ditto Herder,[7] ditto Voltaire, and what is most awful for me, the *Économistes du 18 Siècle*[8] (quite new, had cost me about 500 francs) and many volumes of the Greek classics, many single volumes of other works. Should I go to Cologne, I will have a word to say to National Union man Bürgers. Hegel's *Phenomenology* and *Logic* ditto.

As a result of the beastly running around in the last fortnight—and it requires real skill to prevent the complete breakdown of the household—I have not been able to read any newspapers, not even the *Tribune* on the *American Crisis* [in English]. For relaxation in the evenings, I have been reading Appian's Roman Civil Wars in the Greek original. A very valuable book. The fellow is an Egyptian by birth.[9] Schlosser[10] says he has "no soul," probably because Appian goes to the roots of the material basis in these civil wars. Spartacus[11] is revealed as the most splendid fellow in all ancient history. A great general (no Garibaldi), a noble character, a *real representative* [in English] of the ancient proletariat. Pompey,[12] an utter shit-head; got his undeserved reputation by *escamotage* [pilfering] the credit, first for the success

---

3. The Civil War, which all but terminated his correspondenceship for the *New-York Daily Tribune*.
4. In a letter of January 19, 1861, Ferdinand Lassalle asked Marx to think about publishing a newspaper in Berlin. For a discussion of Lassalle's proposal when Marx visited him in Berlin, see Letter 338, Marx to Engels, May 7, 1861.
5. King of Prussia.
6. At his expulsion from Cologne in 1849, Marx left his library with Dr. Roland Daniels; after the latter's arrest in 1851, many of the books were lost.
7. Johann Gottfried Herder (1744–1803), German philosopher.
8. Eugène Daire, *Économistes-Financiers du XVIIIe Siècle* [*Financial Economists of the 18th Century*] (Paris, 1843).
9. Appian, a sixth century Roman historian writing in Greek.
10. Friedrich Christoph Schlosser (1776–1861), a German historian.
11. Spartacus (d. 71 B.C.), a Roman gladiator, slave revolt leader.
12. Gnaeus Pompeius Magnus (106 B.C.–48 B.C.), Roman general and statesman.

of Lucullus[13] (against Mithridates[14]), then for the success of Sertorius[15] (Spain), etc., and as Sulla's[16] *"young man"* [in English]. As a general, he [Pompey] was the Roman Odilon Barrot.[17] As soon as he had to show what was in him—against Caesar—a *Lauskerl* [rogue]. [Julius] Caesar made the greatest possible military mistakes, deliberately mad, in order to bewilder the philistine who was opposing him. An ordinary Roman general—say, a Crassus[18]—would have destroyed him six times over during the Epirus campaign.[19] But with Pompey everything was possible. Shakespeare in his *Love's Labour Lost* seems to have had an inkling of what Pompey was like.

Salut.

Yours, K.M.

I will write you from Holland.[20] You know, without my writing you about it, how grateful I am to you for the extraordinary proofs of your friendship.

95

To Antoinette (Nannette) Philips[1] (in Zalt-Bommel)[in English]
Elberfeld, April 13, 1861

My sweet little cousin:
I hope you have received the letter I sent you from Berlin [March 24, 1861], although you were cruel enough to leave your admirer without one single word of acknowledgment. Now, my cruel little witch, how will you be able to defend such a line of conduct? Were you not aware that a world of Philisteans [*sic*] hemmed me in, and that half an army of antiquated beauties and detestable blue stockings, did their best to transform me into an ass? Old Circe, as you are aware, metamorphosed the companions of Ulysses into pigs. These modern Circes have so far civilized themselves as to take the

---

13. Lucius Licinius Lucullus (*c.* 106–*c.* 57 B.C.), Roman general known for his elegant life.
14. Mithridates VI (132–63 B.C.), king of ancient Pontus (Asia Minor).
15. Quintus Sertorius (*c.* 123–*c.* 72 B.C.), Roman general.
16. Lucius Cornelius Sulla (138–78 B.C.), Roman general and dictator.
17. Camille Hyacinthe Odilon Barrot (1791–1873), French monarchist politician.
18. Marcus Licinius Crassus (*c.* 115–53 B.C.), Roman general and politician.
19. The Epirus (Greek) campaign, which began in fall 49 B.C., ended in the summer 48 B.C. with a defeat of Pompey by Caesar in the battle of Pharsalus (Thessaly).
20. Marx visited his uncle Lion Philips in Zalt-Bommel, Holland, from February 28 to March 16, 1861.

95

1. Antoinette (Nannette) Philips (*c.* 1837–1885), daughter of Marx's Dutch uncle, Lion Philips.

asinine line. And was it not your duty, under such circumstances, to come to my rescue? Beware that I take my revenge, and conspire with *Waradje* [Dutch: *truly*, probably a reference to A. Roodhuizen, a Zalt-Bommel pastor whom Nannette married] against the tranquillity of your heart.

"*Ans Vaterland, das theure schliess' dich an,*"[2] is a very fine sentence, but, quite confidentially, I may tell you that Germany is a beautiful country to live out of it. For my own part, if I were quite free, and if, besides, I were not bothered by some thing you may call "political conscience," I should never leave England for Germany, and still less for Prussia, and least of all for that *affreux* [frightful] Berlin with its "*Sand*" and its "*Bildung*" [education] and "*seinen überwitzigen Leuten*" [its superclever people].

At Berlin everybody who has some spirit to loose, is of course extremely anxious for fellow sufferers. If the *ennui*, that reigns supreme at that place, be distributed among a greater lot of persons, the single individual may flatter itself to catch a lesser portion of it. For this reason the countess Hatzfeldt,[3] Lassalle's Egeria, tried everything to prolong my sojourn in the metropolis of tschakos without heads. Yesterday she made her last effort, and we had the following scurrilous conversation:

She. "This, then, is the thanks for the friendship we have shown you, that you leave Berlin so soon as your business will permit?"

I. "Quite the contrary. I have prolonged my stay at this place beyond the due term, because your amiability chained me to this Sahara."

She. "Then I shall become still more amiable."

I. "Then there remains no refuge for me but running away. Otherwise I should never be able to return to London whither my duty calls me."

She. "This is a very fine compliment to tell a lady her amiability is such as to drive you away!"

I. "You are not Berlin. If you want to prove me the sincerity of your amiability, do run away with myself."

She. "But I fear you will abandon me at the first station."

I. "I am not quite sure of not 'leaving the girl behind me' at the next station. You know that when Theseus, having eloped with the Greek beauty, abandoned her at some station or other, there at once the god Bacchus descended from the Olymp and carried the forlorn one in his arms to the abode of eternal pleasures. Now, I do not doubt but a god is already waiting for you at the first railway station behind Berlin, and I would be the most cruel of mortals to frustrate you of such a rendezvous."

---

2. "Join the dear Fatherland" from Friedrich von Schiller's *Wilhelm Tell*, Act. II, Scene 1.
3. Sophie von Hatzfeldt (1805–1881), German countess, intimate friend and client of Ferdinand Lassalle (See Part II of this volume).

But enough of these fooleries. In true real earnest, I feel most happy in the idea of soon seeing again yourself and the whole Bommel family circle. Recommend myself to your "rival,"[4] and tell her that the deepest sentiments are the most difficult of being expressed in words. In that way she ought to interpret my silence, the respectful silence I have till now observed.

And now, my little charmer, farewell and do not altogether forget

Your knight errant, Charles Marx

96

To Lion Philips¹ (in Zalt-Bommel)
London, May 6, 1861

Dear Uncle:
First, I want to express my heartfelt thanks for the great friendship that you have shown me anew and for the kind hospitality that I found in your house.[2] In order not to be suspected of flattery, I want to remark in passing what an extraordinary pleasure the contact with a man of your experience has afforded me—a man, who, on the one hand, views world events with such humanity, lack of prejudice, and originality, and, on the other, has fully preserved the fire and impetuousness of youth.

My trip from Zalt-Bommel went according to the original plan. In Rotterdam, I found Jacques[3] at the landing place, we chattered for a couple of hours and then on the same day hurried off to Amsterdam, where my affairs were quickly arranged on the next day. August[4] and his family—enlarged this time by his wife's Rotterdam niece—were cheerful and well. August gave me a special commission that upon my return to Rotterdam I should shake up Mr. Jacques, who suffers, *plus ou moins* [more or less], from melancholy [*Weltschmerz*]—an illness which is simply explainable by the fact that, unlike the great majority of people, he looks upon himself critically and has not yet arrived at a firm political point of view that would satisfy him. Returning from Amsterdam, I arrived in Rotterdam at ten o'clock in the evening, and then on the next day (Sunday) I had to take the steamer for London at seven o'clock in the morning. In the short time that I spent with Jacques, it was, of

---

4. Nannette's sister Henriette (Jettchen), who was married to the Zalt-Bommel doctor, A. van Anrooy.

96

1. Lion Philips (d. 1866), Marx's uncle, businessman in Zalt-Bommel, Holland.
2. Marx visited the Philips family in the last week of April.
3. Jacques Philips.
4. Marx's cousin, August Philips, an Amsterdam lawyer.

course, impossible for me to answer all the questions he asked me or more than touch upon all the points he raised. Jacques decided, therefore, after agreement with his partners, to continue the discussion in London. I arrived in the world capital on Monday and found the whole family well and cheerful. Jacques surprised us last Wednesday [May 1] and left us again yesterday morning, to the regret of my family who would have gladly had him stay longer. We agreed to engage in a sort of political correspondence.

You will recall, dear Uncle, that we have often joked together that human breeding is nowadays far behind animal breeding. Now that I have seen your whole family I must declare you to be a *virtuoso in human breeding*. I have never in my life met a better family. All your children are independent characters, each is original, each possesses special intellectual talents, and all of them show equally the marks of a humane education....

Lassalle has written me a very friendly letter today. He still has no news from Police President von Zedlitz about my renaturalization.[5] The collision between the police and the public in Berlin, as Lassalle writes me, has entered a new stage.

With the best regards to you and yours from me and my whole family,

Your devoted nephew, K. Marx

97

From letter to Frederick Engels (in Manchester)
London, May 10, 1861

Dear Frederick:
Enclosed, *d'abord* [to begin with], a photograph. Lupus and Gumpert will each receive same, as soon as I have had more copies made. I had the thing taken, partly to please my Rotterdam cousin[1] and partly *in exchange* [in English] for photographs received in Germany and Holland....

What you had to say about the Berlin newspaper project,[2] is absolutely in accord with my views, and I have already indicated these main points, *mutatis mutandis* [with due alteration of details], to Lazarus.[3] Since I had

---

5. Marx's application for a restoration of his Prussian citizenship (March 19, 1861) was rejected by the Prussian Minister of Interior in November, 1861.

97
1. Jacques Philips.
2. For a discussion of the subject, see Letter 338, Marx to Engels, May 7, 1861 (in Part II of this volume).
3. Ferdinand Lassalle. See Letter 339, Marx to Lassalle, May 8, 1861 (in Part II of this volume).

positively declared to him in Berlin that I would undertake nothing of the sort without you and Lupus, I felt absolutely obligated to report the project "earnestly and objectively" to both of you and thereby *salvavi animam meam* [I saved my soul]. . . .

[In Berlin] I witnessed one session of the Lower House from the press gallery. Once, in the summer of 1848, I attended a session of the Prussian National Assembly [in Frankfurt]. *Quantum mutatum ab illis!*[4] Even though those were surely no titans! A narrow meeting room. A meager spectators' lobby. These fellows here sit on benches (the *"Herren"* ["Gentlemen," that is, members of the Upper House], by contrast, sit in armchairs), a peculiar mixture of office and schoolroom. Compared to this, a Belgian [Parliamentary] Chamber is imposing. Simson or Samson, as the president is called,[5] avenges himself for the kicks he used to receive from Manteuffel[6] by bullying the cowering philistines in the brutally grotesque manner of a Ministerial *huisier* [doorkeeper] and with the jawbone of an ass. In any other assembly this unspeakable species of personified flunkey-insolence would have been boxed on the ears.

Disgusting as is the prevalence of uniforms in Berlin, particularly in the theaters, one is still pleased to discover amid the oppressively bureaucratized school youth here and there a lad in uniform who at least keeps his head up straight and sits relaxedly. (Apropos. To insult the royal family, soon after I arrived, the Hatzfeldt woman[7] took me to the theater where I sat in a loge right next to "Handsome William"[8] and Consort. Three hours ballet. This was the only performance of the evening.) Vincke[9] spoke, something he never altogether omits doing at any meeting. Up to then, I had an idealized view of the fellow. If I had heard him speak before, my portrait[10] of him would have been entirely different. In an inferior comedy by Freytag,[11] called *The Journalists*, which I saw in Berlin, there is a fat Hamburg philistine and wine *merchant* [in English] called *Piepenbrink*. Vincke is the stereotype of this Piepenbrink. Revolting Hamburg-Westphalian patois, rapidly chewed words, no sentence properly constructed or entirely completed. And this is the Mirabeau[12] of the rabbits' meadow! The only at least decent-looking

---

4. How different those were from these! (Virgil, *Aenead*).
5. Martin Eduard Sigismund von Simson (1810–1899), a German lawyer and member of the Diet.
6. Otto Theodor von Manteuffel (1805–1882), Prussian statesman; Prime Minister, 1850–1858.
7. Countess Sophie von Hatzfeldt.
8. King William I.
9. Georg von Vincke (1811–1875), a Prussian politician.
10. In Marx's pamphlet, *Herr Vogt* (1860).
11. Gustav Freytag (1816–1895), a German author and journalist.
12. Honoré Gabriel Victor Riqueti, comte de Mirabeau (1749–1791), orator of the French Revolution of 1789.

figures in this stable of pygmies are Waldeck[13] on one side, and Wagener[14] and Don Quixote von Blanckenburg,[15] on the other.

In Elberfeld I visited Siebel.[16] Had dinner with him in Barmen. Has a beautiful young wife [Reinhilde], sings well, admires her Carl, and I liked her to some extent. Siebel Senior.[17] His main acquaintances: a liberal journalist (former Münster correspondent of the *Neue Rheinische Zeitung*), poets, musicians, and painters. Seel[18] seemed to me to be the best of the lot. Siebel took me to the Barmen "California"; insipid boys. They drank a toast to me. I had Siebel explain that I was hoarse, so that he replied for me with a few insipid jokes, which, however, were in the *right place* [in English]. Siebel told me that his father imitates him in everything, verse making and boozing, so that they say: The trunk does not fall far from the apple.

In Cologne, I visited Schneider II[19] and Dr. Klein.[20] Unchanged; rather developed further. Spent a few hours with them in a pub. In one pub I also saw incognito excrement Königswinter (Wolfgang Müller[21]). Visited Frau [Amalie] Daniels. Did not visit the fool and National Assembly Unity man Bürgers. But about this anon. I got so involved in gossip that I did not yet get to the main point. Next time, then.

Totus tuus [Entirely yours].

K.M.

98

From letter to Frederick Engels (in Manchester)
London, July 1, 1861

Dear Frederic:
I was very glad to see Lupus here again; so was the whole family. Despite his gout, the old fellow looked quite youthful. He delivered your letter and £2, which the *taxgatherer* [in English] received immediately. This morning I expect some *supply* [in English] from Germany, but nothing has arrived yet. Since I am temporarily still entirely without *revenue* [in English] and yet "*in a continual course of consumption*" [in English] (which some economists see as

---

13. Benedikt Franz Leo Waldeck (1802–1870), Prussian liberal politician.
14. Hermann Wagener (1815–1889), Prussian conservative politician.
15. Karl Henning Moritz von Blanckenburg (1815–1888), Prussian conservative politician.
16. Carl Siebel (1836–1868), pro-Marx Rhineland poet.
17. Father of Carl, merchant in Barmen.
18. Seel was a German caricaturist.
19. Karl Schneider II, a Cologne attorney who defended the communists in their trial there in 1852.
20. Johann Jacob Klein (*c.* 1818–*c.* 1897), a communist physician.
21. Wilhelm Müller (pseudonym: Wolfgang Müller von Königswinter) (1816–1873), a poet and physician.

"profit," deriving it not from production cost but from consumption cost), all Manchester contributions are most pleasing.

Please write me *soon* what you think of the movements (military) in Virginia. The *blunders* [in English] of the militia officers—Brigadier General Peirce[1] is by trade a "tailor" from the State of Massachusetts—will, of course, be frequently enough repeated by both sides.[2] Is Washington still threatened? Do you believe that the Southern position at Manassas Junction is offensive? Or are the fellows rather in the process of retreat? In Missouri, the defeat of the Southerners seems to be decisive, and there the dreadful "Colonel Börnstein" comes to the surface. From a private letter to Weber,[3] it appears that "Colonel Willich" is at the head of a corps from Cincinnati. He has not yet gone into the field.

A closer study of these American affairs showed me that the conflict between South and North—after the latter has degraded itself by one concession after another for fifty years—has finally erupted in battle (apart from the shameless new demands of the *"chivalry"*[4]) because of the weight that the extraordinary development of the North Western States threw into the scale. This population, richly mixed with new German and British elements, essentially *self-working farmers* [in English], was naturally not as prone to intimidation as the gentlemen from Wall Street and the Quakers from Boston [*sic*]. According to the last census (1860), it grew 67 percent between 1850–1860, and consisted of 7,870,869 in 1860, while the total free population of the seceding slave States was only about five million. These North Western States delivered the *bulk* [in English] of the vote for the victorious party [Republican], as well as the President[5] in 1860. It was also precisely this part of the North which first decided against recognition of any *Southern Confederacy* [in English]. Naturally they cannot abandon the Lower Mississippi and its estuaries to foreign states. It was also this North Western population that in the Kansas Affair (from which the present war is really to be dated) fought at close quarters with the Border Ruffians.[6]

98

1. Ebenezer Weaver Peirce (b.1822), Union general commanding troops in Virginia, 1861–1862.
2. In the confused battle at Big Bethel and Little Bethel, Virginia, both the Union and Confederate troops fired mistakenly on their own troops and both retreated in confusion.
3. Josef Valentin Weber (1814–1895), German watchmaker in London.
4. Southern planters.
5. Abraham Lincoln.
6. The name applied to the proslavery elements from Missouri which fought for the control of Kansas between 1854 and 1858.

A closer look at the history of the Secession movement reveals that Secession, Constitution (Montgomery, Alabama), Congress,[7] etc., are all *usurpations* [in English]. Nowhere did they allow the people *en masse* to vote. Concerning this *"usurpation"* [in English]—which involves not only the secession from the North but also the strengthening and the sharpening of the hold of the oligarchy of 300,000 Southern *slavelords* [in English] over five million *whites* [in English]—there are articles in the Southern *papers* [in English] that are very characteristic of their time....
Salut.

Yours, K.M.

99

From letter to Frederick Engels (in Manchester)
London, July 5, 1861

Dear Engels:
... In regard to the secession history, the matter has been completely misrepresented in the English papers. Except for South Carolina, there was everywhere the strongest opposition to the Secession.[1]

First: *Borderslavestates* [in English]. In the winter of 1861, there was a *Borderstate Convention* [in English]. To it were invited Virginia, Kentucky, Arkansas, Maryland, Delaware, Tennessee, and North Carolina. These States held individual conventions to choose delegates to the *General Convention* [in English].

Delaware refused to hold a convention for that purpose.

Tennessee ditto. Its Democratic legislature took it out of the Union through a *coup de main* [sudden attack]. It is true that it held elections later to ratify this invalid act. That took place under a pure reign of terror. More than

---

7. The Congress of six Confederate States—Alabama, Florida, Georgia, Louisiana, Mississippi, and South Carolina—sat in Montgomery, Alabama, from February 4 to March 16, 1861, and proclaimed the Confederacy, with a new constitution. Texas joined the Confederacy on March 2, 1861, and Arkansas, North Carolina, Tennessee, and Virginia in May, 1861. For an analysis of the pressures in the Secession movement, see Letter 99, Marx to Engels, July 5, 1861.

99

1. In June, 1861, Marx made a special study of the American secession, utilizing local Southern newspapers. He used this material in two articles published in the Vienna *Presse*: "The North American Civil War" (October 25, 1861); and "The Civil War in the United States" (November 7, 1861). See Saul K. Padover, ed., *Karl Marx On America and the Civil War* (New York, 1972), pp.69–78, 87–94.

one-third did not vote at all. Of the rest, one-third was opposed to secession, among them all of East Tennessee, which is presently arming against it.

Kentucky. A hundred thousand for the Union ticket; only a few thousand for secession.

Maryland declared itself for the Union, and has now elected six Union men to Congress.

North Carolina and even Arkansas chose Union delegates, the former even with a strong majority. They were later terrorized.

Virginia. The people chose a Union Convention (according to the majority). Some of those fellows let themselves be bought. At the height of the South fever—the fall of Fort Sumter[2]—*the Ordinance of Secession was passed* secretly *by* [in English] a vote of 88 to 55. All other steps—while the Ordinance was still kept secret—for the *capture* [in English] of the federal navy yard at Norfolk and the federal armory at Harpers Ferry were taken in secret. They were betrayed to the federal authorities before their execution. A secret agreement with Jefferson Davis' government was made and large numbers of Confederate troops were suddenly thrown into the state. Under their protection (very Bonapartelike) only secession was permitted to be voted. Nevertheless, there were 50,000 Union *votes* [in English], despite the systematic terrorism. Northwestern Virginia, as you know, has now openly broken away from the Secession.

Second: *Gulf States* [in English]. Genuine popular voting took place only in a few states. In most of them, the conventions, chosen for the purpose of considering the position of the Southern states in regard to Lincoln's election (they later became *their* delegates to the Montgomery Congress), usurped the power not only to decide on secession but also to recognize the Confederate Constitution, Jefferson Davis, etc. How this was done you can see from the following extracts from the Southern papers.

Texas, where, next to South Carolina, the biggest *slave party* [in English] with the most terrorism was to be found, nevertheless, cast 11,000 votes for the Union.

Alabama. The people voted neither for secession nor for the new constitution, etc. The State Convention passed the Ordinance of Secession with 61 against 39 votes. But the 39 from the northern counties, almost entirely inhabited by whites, represented more *free men* [in English] than the 61; according to the United States Constitution, every slaveholder also votes for three-fifths of his slaves.

Louisiana. At the election of delegates to the convention, more Union than Secession votes were cast. But the delegates went over to the other side.

---

2. April 13, 1861.

In western Carolina, eastern Tennessee, northern Alabama, and Georgia, the mining districts have very different interests from those of the southern swamps....

Yours, K.M.

100 ───────────────────────────

To Antoinette (Nannette) Philips (in Zalt-Bommel) [in English]
London, July 17, 1861

My sweet little Cousin:
I hope you will not have misinterpreted my long silence. During the first time I did not exactly know where to direct my letters, whether to Aachen or to Bommel. Then, there came a heavy pressure of business, and during the last two or three weeks I labored under a most disgusting inflammation of the eyes which very much limited the time I had disposable for writing or reading. So, my dear child, if I must plead guilty, there are many alternating circumstances which I trust you, as a gracious judge, will allow to influence your sentence. At all events, you would do me great wrong in supposing that during all that time one single day had passed away without the remembrance, on my part, of my dear little friend.

My Berlin affair [about his citizenship] has not yet been brought to a definite issue. You will remember that during my stay in the Prussian metropolis the Hohenzollern authorities seemed to yield, and even furnished me with a passport for one year. Yet hardly had I turned my back upon them, when Lassalle, to his utter astonishment, received a letter from the Polizeipräsident von Zedlitz to the purpose that I could not be "renaturalized" because of my "*politische Bescholtenheit*" [political notoriety]. At the same time the Prussian government declared that *all* the Political Refugees, having been absent from Prussia for more than ten years, had lost their right of citizenship, had become foreigners, and would, consequently, like all other foreigners, only be renaturalized at the pleasure of the king. In other words, they declared their so-called amnesty to be a mere delusion, sham and snare. This was a point I had tried to drive them to during my Berlin stay, and it was more than even the Prussian press and the Prussian chamber of deputies were able to bear silently with. Consequently, the case gave rise to bitter discussions in the journals, and to an interpellation of the cabinet in the *Abgeordnetenhaus* [Chamber of Deputies]. For the nonce the ministry escaped by means of some equivocous [*sic*] and contradictory statements, but the whole affair contributed not a little to disillusion people in Germany as to the "new era" inaugurated by what the Berliners irreverently call the "*Schöne*

Wilhelm" [Handsome William].[1] Lassalle, with his usual stubbornness, tried hard to get the better of the authorities. First he rushed to Zedlitz[2] and made him *such a scene* that the Freiherr [Baron] got quite frightened and called his secretary for assistance. A few weeks later, Zedlitz having been removed from his post, in consequence of hostile demonstrations against him by the Berlin mob, Lassalle called upon Geheimrat [Privy Councillor] Winter, the successor of Zedlitz, but the "successor" declared that his hands were bound by the decision of his "predecessor." Lassalle, lastly, caught hold of Count Schwerin,[3] the minister of Interior, who, to escape from the violent expostulations of my representative, promised him to leave the whole case to the decision of the Berlin magistrate—a promise he is, however, not very likely to keep. As to myself, I have attained at least the one success of forcing the Berlin government to throw off its liberal mask. As to my return to Berlin, if I should think proper to go there before May 1862, they could not prevent it because of the passport granted to me. If I should delay my return, things will perhaps have so altered in Prussia, that I shall not want their permission. It is really ridiculous that a government should make so much fuss, and compromise itself so much, for fear of a private individual. The conscience [consciousness] of their weakness must be awful.

At the same time I had the good fortune of being honoured by the singular attention of the French government. A person at Paris whom I do not know, had a translation of my pamphlet *"Herr Vogt"* already in print, when an order on the part of M. de Persigny[4] forbade him going on with the translation. At the same time a general warning was communicated to all the booksellers at Paris against selling the German original of *"Herr Vogt."* I got only acquainted with this occurrence by a Paris correspondence published in the *Allgemeine Augsburger Zeitung* [April 19, 1861].

From the Gräfin [Countess] Hatzfeldt I have received a letter filling sixteen pages.[5] Take an example of this, my dear child. She has gone—of course in the company of Lassalle—to a bathing place near Frankfurt on the Main. Thence they will proceed to Switzerland, and, after a month's sojourn there, to Italy. She feels much *ennuyée* [bored] and thinks herself much to be pitied, because she has no other business on hand save that of amusing

---

100

1. King William I of Prussia.
2. Konstantin von Zedlitz-Neukirch (b. 1813), Prussian official, Berlin chief of police.
3. Maximilian Heinrich Karl von Schwerin (1804–1872), Prussian statesman.
4. Jean-Gilbert-Victor, Duc de Persigny (1808–1872), French Bonapartist, Minister of Interior, and Ambassador to London.
5. Written on June 14, 1861, the letter informed Marx that Berlin rejected his application for renaturalization.

herself. It is in fact a bad plight for an active, stirring and rather ambitious woman whose days of flirtation are gone by.

Apropos. I have sent from Manchester to August [Philips] the two volumes of Lassalle's new juridical work[6] and should like to hear whether the packet has found out its address. From Jacques [Philips] I have heard nothing.

I think not, my dear child, that Mrs. Marx and her daughters will find an occasion of paying this year a visit to Bommel, because the Doctor thinks a seabath during the hot season would be the best she could do for getting rid of the remainders of the terrible disease that befell her last autumn. On the other hand, I hope *you* will not forget your promise to visit London where all the members of the family will feel happy to receive you. As to myself, I need not tell you that nothing in the world would give me greater pleasure.

I hope, my sweet little charmer, you will not prove too severe, but like a good Christian, send me *very soon* one of your little letters without revenging yourself for my too long protracted silence.

Recommend me to your father, to my friend "Jettchen" [Henriette van Anrooy], the Doctor [A. van Anrooy], your brother Fritz [Friedrich Philips] and the whole family, and believe me always

Your most sincere admirer, Charles Marx

I am quite astonished at the news of the *attentat* [attempt] on his Prussian Majesty,[7] alias *"Der schöne Wilhelm."* How could any person of common understanding risk his own head in order to kill a brainless ass?

101

To Antoinette (Nannette) Philips (in Zalt-Bommel) [in English]
London, September 24, 1861

My sweet little Cousin:

You must excuse me for sending you today only a few lines. The fact is that I reserve to myself the pleasure of addressing you a "real letter" in a few days. For the present, I wish only to learn, by your gracious interference, whether August[1] has at last received *Lassalle's work.*[2] Lassalle *bothers me with a new letter*

---

6. Ferdinand Lassalle, *Das System der erworbenen Rechte*, 2 vols. (Leipzig, 1861).
7. In 1861, at Baden-Baden, Oskar Becker, a student, shot at King William I and was sentenced to twenty years in jail.

101
1. August Philips.
2. Lassalle, *Das System der erworbenen Rechte* (1861); see Letter 100, Marx to Nannette Philips, July 17, 1861; also Part II.

as to this subject, he considering of course "his work" as something awfully important. He presses me to answer him by *next post*, and thus I must again call upon you. You will much oblige me by informing me as soon as possible of the real state of the case.

Apropos. The book was to be sent to August from Manchester, not from London, but I have been assured that *it had been* sent from Manchester to Amsterdam. Of course, I don't care a fig for the whole "loss," if loss there be, since August would certainly not much miss "the work." But courtesy obliges me to make these researches.

In writing me, you will be of course so friendly to inform me at the same time of what you are doing and so forth, knowing my deep interest in all that concerns you.

My best compliments to your father and the whole family.

Believe me always your most sincere admirer

K.M.

102

To Frederick Engels (in Manchester)
London, December 9, 1861

Dear Engels:
From my *pertinacious* [in English] silence, you can see with what reluctance I am now writing you altogether. In the face of the great efforts—even beyond your powers—that you make in my behalf, I find it naturally loathsome that I constantly bore you with my Joblike letters.

With the last money you sent me, to which I added another borrowed pound, I paid the school tuition, so as not to have to pay double in January. Butcher and *épicier* [grocer] have forced me to give them promissory notes, one for £10 and the other for £12, to fall due in January. Although I did not know how I would pay them then, I could not refrain from doing it without having the whole household collapse over my head. I owe the *landlord* [in English] £15 now and £21 in January. Ditto the *green grocer* [in English], baker, newspaper dealer, milkman and all the rabble whom I had appeased with part payment since my return from Manchester;¹ finally, also the *tally-man* [in English], since the onset of winter necessitated obtaining clothing, which had to be acquired on credit.

What I expect to take in at the end of the month will reach £30 at most, as the lousy fellows of *Die Presse*² do *not* print some of my articles. I must, of

---

102

1. Marx visited Engels in Manchester from the end of August to the middle of September, 1861.

2. The Vienna *Presse*, for which Marx began to write, for about a year, in October 1861.

course, get used to operating inside the "boundaries of German reason." (Withal, they make a great to-do about my contributions.)

What I owe (including interest in the pawnshop) amounts to £100. It is extraordinary how the decline of income, together with debts that are never quite fully paid, despite occasional help, always bring up the same old muck.

Today, I wrote to Dronke, because he still owes me money. But I reminded him quietly, not dunning him. I took the liberty of telling him that if he could make me an advance, you would guarantee him the repayment.

If I could get out of this shit, I could at least continue to vegetate on the income from my articles in New York[3] and Vienna.

My wife is suffering from a dangerous nervous condition, which frightened Dr. Allen for a few days. He knows, or rather suspects, where the shoe pinches, but is too delicate to say anything improper. The poor woman is still suffering. But from her natural buoyancy I do not doubt that she will recover at the first favorable turn of events.

As I wrote from the very first in the [Vienna] *Presse*, there will be no war [on the part of England] with America, and I only regret that I did not have means to exploit the idiocy of the stock market dominated by Reuter[4] and the *Times* [of London] in this silly period.

Am in agreement with your *strictures on* [in English] Itzig[5] (who wrote me from Florence that he had "a *very* interesting meeting," etc., with Garibaldi).[6] The second volume[7] is more interesting, even if only for the Latin citations. The ideology is acceptable, but the dialectical method is *falsely* applied. Hegel had never subsumed a mass of "*cases*" *under a general principle* [in English] called Dialectic.

My work[8] proceeds, but slowly. It was, in fact, not possible to finish quickly such theoretical matters under such conditions. But it will be treated much more popularly and the method much more concealed than in Part I.

Salut.

Yours, K.M.

---

3. *New-York Daily Tribune*, which ceased publishing Marx's London correspondence in March, 1862.

4. Paul Julius von Reuter (1816–1899), founder of the Telegraphic Agency Reuter in London.

5. Ferdinand Lassalle.

6. Giuseppe Garibaldi (1807–1882), Italian liberator.

7. Lassalle, *The System of Acquired Rights*, 2 vols. (Leipzig, 1861). For Marx's opinion of this major juridical work, see letters 342 and 343, Marx to Lassalle, June 11 and July 22, 1861.

8. After the publication of *Critique of Political Economy* in 1859, Marx was working on a continuation of the book, but gradually decided to change the whole structure; the result of his new approach was *Das Kapital*, published eight years after *Critique*.

103

From letter to Johann Philipp Becker (in Geneva)
London, February 26, 1862

Dear Becker:

... As for the subscription for your book,[1] I will do *my best*, but promise little success. The association gang—with the exception of the Workers Education Association[2] which is in no way funded—is all *constitutional*, yea, Prussian nationalist. The fellows would prefer to give money to suppress a book like yours. You must know that these Germans, young and old, are all overly smart, solid, practical men, who consider people like you and me immature fools who have not yet been cured of their revolutionary fantasies. And the rabble is as bad here, abroad, as it is at home. During my stay in Berlin[3] and elsewhere, I convinced myself that any attempt to influence that canaille by *literary* means is completely futile. The self-complacent stupidity of those scamps, for whom the press, that lamentable press, serves as an extraordinary elixir of life, is simply beyond belief. And then that lassitude of soul. *Cudgeling* is the only means of resurrection of the German Michael[4] who, ever since he lost his philosophical illusions and took to money making, to the idea of "Little Germany" and to "practical constitutionalism," has become nothing but a dull-witted, repulsive clown. Germany seemed to be entirely and ...[5] a room full of old-smart and decrepit children....

Yours, K.M.

104

To Frederick Engels (in Manchester)
London, June 18, 1862

Dear Engels:

It is most loathsome on my part to regale you again with my misery, but *que faire* [what to do]? My wife says to me every day she wishes she and the

---

103

1. Johann Philipp Becker, *Wie und Wann? Ein ernstes Wort über die Fragen und Aufgaben der Zeit* [*How and When? A Serious Word on the Questions and Tasks of the Time*] (Geneva, London, Manchester, 1862).
2. German Education Association for Workers in London, a communist organization founded in 1840.
3. Marx visited Berlin from March 17 to April 12, 1861.
4. The average German bourgeois.
5. Word missing.

children were dead, and I cannot really blame her, for the humiliations, harassments and terrors that one experiences in this situation are in fact indescribable. The £50 were, as you know, spent on debts, of which I could hardly pay half. Two pounds for gas. The lousy money from Vienna[1] will not arrive before the end of July and then it will be damn little, as the dogs don't print even one article per week now. Added to this, new expenses since May. I will not even speak of the really dangerous situation to be without a centime in London for seven weeks, for this has been repeated chronically. But you will know that much from your own experience that there are continuous current expenses that must be paid. This was done at the end of April by pledging again the things taken out of the pawnshop. But for weeks this source has been so exhausted that a week ago my wife made a vain attempt to hock some of my books. I am the more sorry for my poor children, as this is *Exhibition season* [in English] when their acquaintances are having fun, while they themselves experience the dread lest someone visit them and see our filthy situation.

For the rest, I am working vigorously, and curiously enough, despite all the misery around me, my skull is in better shape than it has been for years. I keep on expanding the volume, the more so as the German dogs estimate the value of books according to their cubic content.[2] Incidentally, I have finally cleared up the ground-rent shit (which I will *not* even *indicate* in this Part). For a long time I have had *misgivings* [in English] about the correctness of Ricardo's theory and have finally discovered the swindle. Since we last saw each other, I have also made some fine and surprising new discoveries for this volume.

I am amused at Darwin,[3] into whom I looked again, when he says that he applies the "Malthusian" theory *also* to plants and animals, as if the joke with Herr Malthus did not consist of the fact that he did *not* apply it to plants and animals but only to human beings—in geometrical progression—in contrast to plants and animals. It is remarkable how Darwin has discerned anew among beasts and plants his English society with its division of labor, competition, elucidation of new markets, "discoveries" and the Malthusian "struggle for existence." It is Hobbes'[4] *bellum omnia contra omnes* [war of all against all], and it reminds me of Hegel's *Phenomenology*, wherein bourgeois society figures as a "spiritual animal kingdom," while in Darwin the animal kingdom figures as bourgeois society.

104

1. Marx was correspondent for the *Presse* of Vienna.
2. From August, 1861, until July, 1863, Marx was at work on a continuation of his *Critique of Political Economy*, Part I of which appeared in 1859.
3. Concerning Darwin, see Letter 92, Marx to Engels, December 19, 1860.
4. Thomas Hobbes (1588–1679), English philosopher.

Buckle⁵ has played a trick on Ruge by dying. In his imagination Ruge had seen a library that Buckle would write and Ruge would "negotiate" in German. *Poor* [in English] Ruge! And *poor* [in English] Buckle, whom a "friend" in today's *Times*⁶ has maligned in a *testimonium pietatis* [obituary].

Have you and Lupus received the two copies of *Julian Schmidt*⁷ which I sent you?

Apropos! If you could do it briefly, without taking too much time, I would appreciate a paradigm (together with explanation) of the Italian book business. It would be useful for the illustration of the *Tableau Économique* by Dr. Quesnay.⁸

Nobody visits me, which I like, for the humanity here can _____.A fine bunch!

Salut.

Yours, K.M.

105

From letter to Frederick Engels (in Manchester)
London, September 10, 1862

Dear Engels:
My *family* [in English] has returned from Ramsgate; Jennychen¹ has very much recovered....

As regards the Yankees, I am still of the opinion that the North will win in the end;² the Civil War can, of course, go through all kinds of episodes, perhaps also including truces, and drag itself out. The South would and could conclude a peace only on condition that it retains the *border slave states* [in English]. In that case, it would also get California, followed by the Northwest, and the whole federation, with the exception of the New England states, would again form *one* country, this time under the *acknowledged*

---

5. Henry Thomas Buckle (1821–1862), English historian.
6. John Stuart Glennie, in *The Times* [of London], June 18, 1862.
7. Ferdinand Lassalle, *Herr Julian Schmidt der Literarhistoriker* [*Herr Julian Schmidt, the Literary Historian*] (Berlin, 1862); see Letter 345, Marx to Lassalle, June 16, 1862.
8. François Quesnay, *Analyse du Tableau Économique*, new ed. (Paris, 1846.).

105

1. Daughter Jenny Marx.
2. After the second battle of Bull Run (August 27–September 2, 1862), in which the Confederates won again, Engels wrote to Marx, September 9, 1862: "The Bull Run story No. 2 was a splendid little play by Stonewall Jackson, who is by far the best fellow in America....It is too pitiful, but the chaps in the South, who know least what they want, appear like heroes, compared to the flabby management of the North. Or do you still believe that the gentlemen in the North will be able to 'suppress' the Rebellion?"

supremacy of the slaveholders [in English]. It would be the reconstruction of the *United States* [in English] on the basis demanded by the South. This, however, is impossible and will not happen.

The North, for its part, can conclude peace only if the *Confederacy* [in English] confines itself to the old Slave States between the Mississippi River and the Atlantic. In this case, the Confederacy would soon reach its blessed end. Interim truces, etc., on the basis of the status quo can at most only mean pauses in the progress of the war.

In regard to the North's conduct of the war, nothing else could be expected from a *bourgeois* republic, where swindle has been enthroned for such a long time. But the South, an oligarchy, is better fitted for war, because it is an oligarchy, where all the productive work is done by *niggers* [in English] and the four million *"white trash"* [in English] are filibusterers by profession. Despite all that, I will wager my head that those fellows will get the short end of it, despite "Stonewall Jackson." It is, to be sure, possible that before that, a kind of revolution will take place in the North.

Willich is Brigadier General and, as Kapp said in Cologne, Steffen[3] is now also in the war.

It seems to me that you are a little too much influenced by the military aspect of things.

As for the economic stuff, I don't want to *"ballast"* [in English] you on your trip.

Salut.

Yours, K.M.

106

To Frederick Engels (in Manchester)
London, November 14, 1862

Dear Engels:
Since you have just sent money to Eccarius[1] and paid a large sum for the Lassalle promissory note,[2] you are naturally very *"blanc."* Nevertheless, I

---

3. Wilhelm Steffen.

106

1. Marx to Engels, November 9, 1862: "Three of Eccarius' children died one after the other from scarlet fever. Withal, the greatest distress. Collect a little something among acquaintances and send it to him, 22 Denmark Street, opposite St. Giles Church."
2. Engels to Marx, November 5, 1862: "The £60 will be mailed to Freiligrath tomorrow. As regards the renewal of the note, I will be able to tell only when I know whether it is discountable for *sure*, as soon as Lassalle has accepted it and who is to provide the discounting."

must beg you to send me a trifle *until Monday* [November 17], as I have to buy coal and "provisions," since the *épicier* [grocer] has cancelled my credit for the last three weeks, but so long as I owe the *Schweinhund* money I have to buy from *him* with cash in order not to be haled to court.

Salut.

Yours, K.M.

107

To Frederick Engels (in Manchester)
London, December 24, 1862

Dear Engels:
Since I left you,[1] I had *a most eventful time of it* [in English].

On Monday [December 22] the Manichaens,[2] not all of whom came by prearrangement. I distributed £15 among them. The worst of them I gave a promissory note for £12 for a term of six weeks (actually seven weeks, since I dated it as of the end of this year), entrusting myself to the *chapter of accidents* [in English].

On Wednesday [December 17] my wife had left for Paris. Last night she returned. Everything would have been all right if Abarbanel[3] had not been paralyzed by a stroke just before her arrival, so that, although his mind was clear, he lay helpless in bed. On the whole, the series of mishaps which befell her was tragicomic. A great storm at sea; her ship came through, but one in her vicinity (it was via Boulogne) sank. There was trouble with the locomotive, so that the train was delayed for two hours. Later the omnibus on which she traveled turned over. And yesterday the London cab in which she sat got tangled in the wheels of another one. She got out and came home on foot, with two boys carrying her trunk. However, she did achieve one thing in Paris, where she saw Massol, etc. As soon as my work[4] comes out, it will be published in *French*.

Now I come to the worst *Pech* [tough luck]. Marianne (Lenchen's[5] sister), whom Allen had treated for heart trouble a year ago, began to feel unwell on the day of my wife's departure. Tuesday evening, two hours before my wife's return, she was dead. For the last seven days, Lenchen and I had been her nurses. Allen had misgivings from the first day. Saturday, two o'clock, is

---

107
1. Marx visited Engels in Manchester from December 5 to 13, 1862.
2. The name which German university students applied to pressing creditors.
3. Abarbanel (d. 1863) was a Paris banker whom Marx knew.
4. Marx was then working on *Kapital*, which was not published until 1867.
5. Helene Demuth.

the funeral, when I will have to pay the undertaker £7½ cash. This has to be procured. It is a fine Christmas spectacle for the poor children.

Salut.

Yours, K.M.

108

To Ludwig Kugelmann (in Hanover)
London, December 28, 1862

Dear Sir:

Some time ago Freiligrath communicated to me a letter which he received from you. I would have answered sooner if a series of misfortunes in my family had not made it impossible for me to write for *some time* [in English].

I was very pleased to see from your letter that you and your friends take such a warm interest in my *Critique of Political Economy.* The second part is finally ready, that is, up to copying clean and polishing, for publication.[1] It will contain approximately thirty proof sheets. It is the continuation of Part I, but will appear independently under the title *Das Kapital*, with *Critique of Political Economy* only a subtitle. It contains in reality only what should have been in the third chapter of Part I, that is, "Capital in General." Hence it does not include the competition between capital and the credit structure. This volume contains what the English call "*the principles of political economy*" [in English]. It is the quintessence (together with Part I), and the development of the subsequent one (with the exception of the relationships between the various State forms and the economic structures of society) will be easy to do in other chapters on the basis of this one.

The long delay is due to the following causes: First, in the year 1860 the Vogt scandal[2] took a lot of my time, as I had to undertake a mass of investigations into intrinsically indifferent materials, wage the court case, etc. In the year 1861, owing to the American Civil War, I lost my main source of income, the *New-York Daily Tribune*. My collaboration with that paper is suspended for this moment.[3] I was and am compelled to take on a mass of petty works in order not to be reduced to the streets with my family. I had even decided to

---

108

1. Marx had intended *Critique of Political Economy* (1859) to be the first of a series of six books, but he changed his plan, which took the final form of *Das Kapital*, published eight years later. In this letter, Marx explains some of the reasons for the delay in his work.

2. For Marx's irrational and bitter quarrel with Karl Vogt, about whom he wrote a vituperative pamphlet (*Herr Vogt:* 1860), see Saul K. Padover, *Karl Marx: An Intimate Biography* (New York, 1978), Chapter XVIII.

3. Marx's last article in the *New-York Daily Tribune* appeared on March 10, 1862.

become "practical" and begin work in a railway office at the beginning of next year. Should I call it luck or misfortune? My bad handwriting was the cause of my not getting the job. So you see that I had little time and peace of mind left for theoretical work. It is probable that these causes will delay the final publication longer than I like.[4]

In regard to a publisher, I will under no circumstances give the second volume to Duncker. He received the manuscript of Part I in December, 1858, and it did not appear until July or August, 1859.[5] I have some, but not a very strong, expectation that Brockhaus will publish it. The *conspiration de silence* with which the German literary rabble honors me as often as it notices that abuse does not suffice, is disadvantageous for me as to the selling of the book, even apart from its contents. As soon as the manuscript is cleanly copied (which I will begin to do in January, 1863), I will take it to Germany myself, since it is easier to deal with bookdealers in person.

I have every *expectation* that, soon after the German edition has appeared, a French translation will be prepared. To Frenchify it myself, I have absolutely no time, the less so since I will either write in German the final chapters on capital, competition, and credit, or prepare the first two in a book for the *English* public. I do not believe one can count on any effect in Germany without a previous certificate from abroad. It is true, in any case, that the method of presentation in Part I was very unpopular. This was due to the abstract nature of the subject, the limited space at my disposal, and the purpose of the work. Part II is more easily understood because it treats more concrete relationships. *Scientific* efforts to revolutionize a science can never be really popularized.

However, once the scientific foundation is laid, popularization becomes easy. Should the times become somewhat stormier, one would be able again to choose the colors and inks proper for a popularization of *these* subjects. On the other hand, I should have expected, of course, that the German specialists, if only for the sake of decency, would not ignore my work completely. Moreover, I have had the by-no-means pleasant experience of party friends in Germany, who have long occupied themselves with this subject and who have written me privately exaggerated approvals of Part I, not taking the slightest step to have a critique, or even a notice, appear in the journals to which they had access. If this is a party tactic, I confess that the secret of it is impenetrable to me.

I would be pleased if you would occasionally write me about the conditions in the fatherland. We are obviously approaching a revolution—which I have never doubted since 1850.[6] The first act will by no means include a

---

4. *Das Kapital* was not published until 1867.
5. The book actually appeared on May 11, 1859.
6. Marx expressed this idea in the May–October, 1850, issue of *Neue Rheinische Zeitung. Politisch-ökonomische Revue*, where he wrote: "*A new revolution is possible only as a consequence of a new* [economic] *crisis. But that is as sure to come as this one.*"

refreshed revival of the 1848–49 absurdities. Still, this is the course of world history, and one has to take it as it comes.

With best regards for the New Year.

Yours, K.M.

109

To Frederick Engels (in Manchester)
London, January 8, 1863

Dear Engels:
The news of Mary's death[1] has surprised and dismayed me. She was very good-natured, witty, and devoted to you.

The devil knows that nothing but trouble happens in our circle. I absolutely no longer know where my head is. My efforts to raise money in France and Germany have failed, and naturally it was to be expected that with only £15 I could hold back the avalanche only for a couple more weeks. Apart from the fact that we no longer can get credit, except from the butcher and baker, I am pressed by the school, the rent, and the whole pack. The pair who received two pounds in payment, have pocketed them cunningly in order to get after me with redoubled force. Moreover, the children have no dresses or shoes to go out. In short, the devil is loose, as I foresaw when I went to Manchester and sent my wife to Paris as a last *coup de désespoir* [act of despair]. If I do not succeed through a *loan society or life assurance company* [in English] (and I see no prospect here: with the former I have tried in vain; they demand collateral, and rent and tax receipts, which I cannot provide), then my household can last merely another two weeks.

It is frightfully egoistic on my part that at this moment I tell you about my own horrors. But the means are homeopathic. One evil destroys another. And, *au bout de compte* [in the end], what am I to do? In all of London there is not a single person to whom I can speak freely, and in my own house I play the silent stoic, in order to maintain a calm balance against outbursts. *Under such circumstances* [in English], however, work is completely impossible. Should not my own mother, who is now full of physical infirmities and has

---

109

1. Mary Burns, an Irishwoman who lived with Engels in Manchester. Engels to Marx, January 7, 1863: "Dear Mohr: Mary is dead. Last night she went to bed early, and when Lizzy [Mary's sister] went to bed at midnight, she found her already dead. Quite suddenly, heart attack or apoplectic stroke. I only found it out this morning; Monday evening [January 5] she was still entirely well. I cannot tell you how terrible I feel. The poor girl had loved me with all her heart. Yours, F.E."

already lived her life, instead of Mary? ... You see to what strange notions "civilized" people arrive under the pressure of certain circumstances.

Salut.

Yours, K.M.

How will you arrange your *establishment* [in English] now? It is extraordinarily difficult for you who had a *home* [in English] with Mary, free and withdrawn from all human muck, as often as you pleased.[2]

110

To Frederick Engels (in Manchester) *London, January 24, 1863*

Dear Frederick:

I thought it a good idea to have some time elapse before I replied. Your position on the one hand, and mine on the other, made it difficult to view the situation "coolly."

It was very wrong of me to write you the letter I did,[1] and I regretted it the moment it was mailed. But it was in no way due to heartlessness. My

---

2. Engels, resenting Marx's cool reaction to Mary Burns' death, wrote him on January 13: "Dear Marx: You will find it in order that this time my own misfortune and your icy conception of it have made it impossible for me to answer you sooner.

"All my friends, including philistine acquaintances, have shown me, at this moment which has hit me deeply, more sympathy and friendship than I expected. You found this moment appropriate to display the superiority of your cool intellect. *Soit* [So be it]!

"You know the state of my finances and you also know that I do everything to rescue you from your misfortunes. But I cannot raise now the larger sum of which you speak, as you must know. You have three ways open to you:

"1. Loan society. You have to find out how much my guarantee would be worth, which I believe to be little, since I am no householder.

"2. Life insurance. John Watts is manager of the European Life & Guarantee Society, whose London office is in the directory. I see no obstacles to a £400 life insurance policy, on which he can surely borrow £200. If this is not thoroughly ruinous, it would be the best way. Hence you go there immediately, find out the terms, and let me know right away.

"3. Should everything else fail, I can raise some £25 in February—impossible earlier—and am prepared to sign a promissory note for £60, which *absolutely* can be paid off only after June 30, 1863, hence with a *sure* prolongation until then. For this I must have the necessary guarantees. The rest you must absolutely squeeze out of your Dutch uncle [Lion Philips].

"I see no other way.

"Let me know what steps you take, and I will contribute my own part.

"Yours, F.E."

110

1. Letter 109, Marx to Engels, January 8, 1863.

wife and children will testify that your letter[2] (which came in the morning) shocked me as would the death of anyone closest to me. When I wrote you that night, I did so under the pressure of very desperate circumstances. In the house there was the *broker* [in English] from the *landlord* [in English], protest from the butcher for unpaid bills, a lack of coal and groceries, and Jennychen[3] sick in bed. Under such *circumstances* [in English], I generally fall back on cynicism to help me. What drove me particularly mad was that my wife thought that *I* did not report to you adequately our true situation.

Your letter was welcome insofar as it clarified for her the *"non possumus"* [impossible], for she knows very well that I did not wait for your advice to write to my uncle;[4] that I could not turn to Watts[5] in London, when he lives and has his office in Manchester; that since Lassalle's last demand for payment of the debt, I cannot draw another promissory note in London; and that, finally, £25 in February would enable us neither to live in January nor to overcome the crisis at hand. As it was impossible for you to help out, although I reported to you that I was in the position of Manchester workingmen, she must have realized the *non possumus*; and I *wished* for that, since this roasting at a small fire—whereby head and heart are consumed, and, furthermore, the most precious time is lost in order to maintain false *appearances* [in English], which are harmful to me and the children at the same time—must come to an end. What we have gone through in the last three weeks made my wife finally reach the point where she agreed to a suggestion I made some time ago, which, despite all its unpleasantnesses, is the only way out and preferable to the life we have led in the last three years, particularly the last one, and which, moreover, would restore our *selfesteem* [in English]: I would write the various creditors (except the *landlord* [in English]) that, if they did not leave me in peace, I will declare myself bankrupt through the *failing* [*sic*] *of a bill in the court of bankruptcy* [in English]. This, of course, does not apply to the landlord, who has the right to the furniture, which he could keep. My two oldest daughters[6] would take positions as *governesses* [in English] in the Cunningham[7] family. Lenchen[8] would enter another service, and my wife and I with Tussychen[9] would go to live in the same City Model Lodging House where [Ferdinand] "Red" Wolff and his family once lived.

---

2. Engels to Marx, January 7, 1863; footnote 1 in Letter 109.
3. Daughter Jenny Marx.
4. Lion Philips.
5. John Watts (1818–1887), English philanthropist, founder of the People's Providence Assurance Society.
6. Jenny and Laura Marx.
7. Name unidentified.
8. Helene Demuth.
9. Youngest daughter, Eleanor.

Before I came to that decision, I wrote, of course, to various acquaintances in Germany, naturally without success. In any case, the thing is better than the prolongation of the present situation, which can no longer continue anyhow. I have had enough on my hands fending off the landlord and butcher through all kinds of humiliation, and satisfying the *broker* [in English] with false promises. I could not send the children to school this quarter, because the old bill has not been paid and, in addition, they were not in a presentable condition.

Through the above plan, I hope at least to get some peace without any intervention of a third person.

Finally, something that has nothing to do with the above. For the section on machinery in my book,[10] I am in a great quandary. It has never been clear to me how *selfactors* [in English, meaning the automatic spinning machine] changed the weaving process, or rather, since steam had already been applied before, how the weaver used his own [personal] moving power despite the steam power.

I would appreciate it if you would explain it to me.

Apropos. My wife, without my knowledge, turned to Lupus for £1 for *immediate necessities* [in English]. He sent her £2. The thing is disagreeable to me, but fact is fact.[11]

Yours, K.M.

111

From letter to Frederick Engels (in Manchester)
London, January 28, 1863

Dear Frederick:
Owing to a series of peculiar incidents, it was positively impossible for me yesterday to acknowledge the receipt of the letter and the promissory note.

I know very well how *risky* it was for you to supply me in this way with such big and unexpected help. I cannot be grateful enough, although *I*, deep inside of me, needed no new proof of your friendship to be convinced that it is self-sacrificing. Moreover, if you had seen the joy of my children, it would have been for you a beautiful reward.

---

10. *Das Kapital.*
11. Engels accepted Marx's apology and explanation. He wrote him on January 26: "Dear Mohr: I thank you for your sincerity. You understand yourself what an impression your penultimate letter [of January 8] had made upon me. One cannot live with a woman for so many years without feeling her death dreadfully. I feel as if with her I have buried the last piece of my youth. When I received your letter, she was not yet interred. I tell you, your letter was on my mind for a week, I could not forget it. Never mind, your last letter makes it quits, and I am glad that I did not lose, together with Mary, my oldest and best friend."
Engels then proceeded to suggest practical plans to help Marx financially.

I can now tell you without further ado that despite all the strains of the last few weeks, nothing even remotely oppressed me so much as the fear of the breach in our friendship. I told my wife repeatedly that in this whole muck nothing could compare to my having been capable, as a result of these bourgeois lousinesses and eccentric excitement, of pressing you with my private affairs, instead of consoling you in such a moment.[1] *Consequently* [in English], the peace in the household was very disturbed, and the poor wife had to wallow in the thing, and in truth she was innocent, in that women are accustomed to demand the impossible. Naturally, she had no idea what I wrote to you, but after some reflection she could figure out that something like it would have been written. Women are funny creatures, even those who are equipped with a great deal of sense. In the morning my wife wept over Mary [Burns] and your loss, and she forgot her own trouble which culminated on that day, but by evening she was convinced that nobody in the world knew what suffering was if he did not have the *broker* [in English] in a house with children.

In my last letter,[2] I asked you about the *selfactor* [in English]. Specifically, the question was this: How did the so-called spinner work *before* the *selfactor* [in English]? I understand the *selfactor* [in English], but not the preceding situation.

I am adding something to the section on machinery.[3] There are some curious questions which I ignored in my first treatment. In order to get a clear understanding of it, I have reread all my notebooks (extracts) on technology and am also attending a practical (only experimental) course for workers by Professor Willis[4] (in Jermyn Street, at the Geological Institute, where Huxley[5] also used to give lectures). It is the same for me with mechanics as with languages. I understand the mathematical laws but the simplest technical reality, which demands perception, is harder for me than for the biggest blockheads.

You may or may not know, since the matter is in itself of no importance, that there is a conflict of views on how a *machine* differs from a *tool*. The English (mathematical) mechanists, in their crude way, *call a tool a simple machine* [in English] and a *machine a complicated tool* [in English]. Still, the English technologists, who pay a little more attention to economics (and are followed by many, by most, of the English economists), base their distinction on the fact that in one case the *motive force* [in English] derives from the

111
1. The death of Mary Burns on January 6, 1863.
2. Letter 110, Marx to Engels, January 24, 1863.
3. In *Das Kapital* (on which Marx was then working), Volume I, Chapter XIII, Section 4: "The Development of Machinery."
4. Robert Willis (1800–1875), a lecturer before labor audiences.
5. Thomas Henry Huxley (1825–1895), English scientist, follower of Darwin.

human beings, in the other from *a natural force* [in English]. The jackasses, who are great in such trifles, have, therefore, concluded that, for instance, a plow is a machine, and that the most complicated spinning jenny, etc., insofar as it is worked by hand, is not. But there is no question that if we look at the machine in its *elementary* form, the industrial revolution does not emerge from the *motive power* but from that part of the machinery which the Englishman calls the *working machine* [in English]—not, for example, from the substitution of the foot, which moves the spinning wheel, by water or steam, but by the transformation of the immediate spinning process itself and the displacement of that part of human labor which was not merely an *"exertion of power"* [in English] (as in treading the wheel), but was directly applied to the working up of the raw material. Leaving out the purely *historical* development of machinery, but considering machinery as the basis of the present methods of production, there is little question but that the *working machine* alone (for example, the sewing machine) is the decisive factor; for as soon as this process has been mechanized, everyone nowadays knows, the thing can be moved by hand, waterpower or steam engine according to its size.

For the mere mathematicians these are indifferent questions, but they become very important when one wants to prove the connection between human social relations and the development of these material methods of production.

The rereading of my technological-historical excerpts has led me to the view that, apart from the discoveries of gunpowder, the compass, and the printing press—these necessary preconditions of bourgeois development—the two material bases on which the preparations for machine industry were organized within manufacture, from the sixteenth to the middle of the eighteenth century (the period in which manufacture was developing from handicraft to large-scale industry), were the *clock* and the *mill* (at first the corn mill, that is, a water mill), both inherited from antiquity. (The water mill was introduced into Rome from the Near East in the time of Julius Caesar.) The clock is the first automatic machine applied to practical purposes, and the whole theory of production of regular motion was developed on it. In the nature of things, it is itself based on the connection between part-artistic handicraft and direct theory. Cardano,[6] for example, wrote on (and gave practical formulas for) the construction of clocks. German writers of the sixteenth century called clock making "learned (nonguild) handicraft," and from the development of the clock it would be possible to show how different from handicraft has been the relation between theoretical learning and practice, and large-scale industry, for example. There is also no doubt that in the

---

6. Gerolamo Cardano (1501–1576), an Italian mathematician, astrologer, and physician.

eighteenth century the idea of applying automatic (moved by springs) devices to production was first suggested by clocks. It can be proved historically that Vaucanson's[7] experiments in this field have had an extraordinary influence on the imagination of the English inventors.

In the *mill*, on the other hand, from the very beginning, as soon as the water mill was produced, one finds the essential distinctions in the organism of a machine. Mechanical driving power. The prime motor, on which it depends. *Transmissions* [in English]-mechanisms. Finally, the working machine, which deals with the material. Each of those organisms is independent of the others. The theory *of friction* and with it the investigations into the mathematical forms of wheel work, cogs, etc., were all made at the mill; ditto here first the theory of measurement of the degree of motive power, of the best way of applying it, etc. Practically all the great mathematicians since the middle of the seventeenth century, insofar as they occupied themselves with practical mechanics and theorized about them, start with the simple corn-grinding water mill. Indeed, this was why the word *mill* [in English] came to be applied during the manufacturing period to all mechanical motive power adapted to practical purposes.

But with the mill, as with the press machines, the forge, the plow, etc., the actual work of beating, crushing, grinding, pulverizing, etc., was performed from the very first *without* human labor, even though the *moving force* [in English] was human or animal. Hence this kind of machinery is very ancient, at least in its origins, and actual mechanical propulsion was formerly applied to it. Hence it is also practically the only machinery found in the manufacturing period. The *Industrial Revolution* begins as soon as mechanism is employed where from ancient times on the final result has always required human labor; not, that is to say, where, as with the tools just mentioned, the actual material to be worked on has *never*, from the *beginning*, been touched by the human hand, but where, from the nature of the thing, man has not from the very first acted as mere *power* [in English]. If one is to follow the German jackasses in calling the use of animal power (which is just as much *voluntary movement* as human power) machinery, then the use of this kind of locomotive is at any rate much older than the simplest handicraft tool....

Salut.

Yours, K.M.

---

7. Jacques de Vaucanson (1709–1782), a French inventor.

112

From letter to Frederick Engels (in Manchester)
London, February 13, 1863

Dear Frederick:

... I would have written you sooner, but for approximately the last twelve days *all* reading, writing and smoking have been *strictly* [in English] forbidden. I had a sort of eye inflammation, tied up with very unpleasant effects on the nervous system. The thing is now so far under control that I can again dare to write. In the meantime I had all kinds of psychological reveries, like a person going blind or crazy.

What do you say to the Polish affair?[1] One thing is sure, the *era of revolution* [in English] is now once more *fairly opened in Europe* [in English]. And the general state of things is good. But the comfortable *delusions* [in English] and the almost childish enthusiasms with which we greeted the era of revolution before February, 1848, are gone to the devil. Old comrades like Weerth, etc., are gone, others have fallen away or decayed, and a new generation is not yet in sight. In addition, we now know what role stupidity plays in revolutions and how they are exploited by scoundrels. For the rest, the "Prussian" enthusiasts for "Italian" and "Hungarian" nationalism now come under pressure. Let us hope that this time the lava pours from East to West, and not vice versa, so that we are spared the "honor" of the French initiative. The adventure in Mexico[2] is otherwise a highly classical conclusion of the *farce* [in English] of the Lower Empire.[3] ...

In the United States things go damned slowly. I hope that J. Hooker will dig himself out.[4]

But now write me above all how you are now faring in Manchester. The place must appear to you damned lonely.[5] I know for my own part that the

---

112

1. In January, 1863, a revolt broke out in Poland against the Russian occupants of that country; the uprising was suppressed by March, 1864.
2. In 1861, Napoleon III, whom Marx hated and despised, invaded Mexico with the cooperation of England and Spain. The French puppet, Emperor Maximilian, was finally executed in 1867.
3. A comparison of Napoleon III's French Empire with the Byzantine Lower Empire in its decline.
4. General Joseph Hooker, commander of the Union Army of the Potomac, was defeated at Chancellorsville, May 2–4, 1863, by Generals Robert E. Lee and "Stonewall" Jackson; the latter was killed in the battle. See Saul K. Padover, ed., *Karl Marx On America and the Civil War* (1972).
5. Mary Burns, with whom Engels had lived for several years, died on January 6, 1863. For Marx's cool reaction to the news and his apology, see letters 109 and 111, Marx to Engels, January 8 and 28, 1863.

neighborhood of Soho Square always frightens me when I accidentally come near it.[6]

Salut.

Yours, K.M.

113

To Frederick Engels (in Manchester)
London, December 2, 1863

Dear Frederick:
Two hours ago I received a telegram that my mother[1] is dead. Fate claimed one of my family. I myself stood with one foot in the grave. Under present circumstances, I am at any rate more necessary than the Old Woman.

I must go to Trier to settle my inheritance. What was much in question was what [Dr.] Allen would say, as I have been able to take daily half-hour walks for my health only in the last three days.

But Allen, giving me two enormous bottles of medicine, thought it a good idea that I should go. The wound is not yet drained of pus, but on the trip I should find enough good Samaritan ladies to apply the plaster.

I must beg you to send me, by *return mail* enough money so that I can *immediately* take the trip to Trier.[2]

Salut.

Yours, K.M.

114

From letter to Frederick Engels (in Manchester)
London, December 4, 1863

Dear Frederick:
Best thanks for the £10. Ditto, belatedly, for the port wine. It did me a great deal of good. In addition to the wine, I had to guzzle daily (until this hour) one and a half quarts of the strongest London stout [ale]. It seems to me to be a good theme for a novel. In front, the man who regales his *inner man* [in

---

6. It was while Marx lived in Soho that his beloved eight-year old son, Edgar, died. Marx never got over the shock.

113

1. Henriette Marx, born on September 20, 1788, died on November 30, 1863, in her seventy-sixth year.
2. Upon receipt of money from Engels, Marx left London for Germany on December 7, one week after his mother's death.

English] with port, bordeaux, stout, and the most massive chunks of meat.[1] In front, the glutton. But in back, on the hump of the *outer man* [in English], the damn carbuncle. When the devil makes a pact with a man always to set him a good table in such circumstances, may the devil take the devil. Besides, my head is still weak and my knees wobbly, but I think the trip[2] will put an end to all this. Tussychen[3] said to me apropos the *outer man* [in English]: "*But it is your own flesh* [in English]!" For the rest, I cannot praise enough Dr. Allen's behavior. In connection with the operation [on the carbuncle], he remarked to me that it never changes *German philosophers* [in English]. . . .

Salut.

Yours, K.M.

115

To Jenny Marx (in London)
Trier (Gasthof von Venedig), December 15, 1863

Dear, good Jenny[1] *of my heart:*
It is exactly eight days today since I arrived here.[2] Tomorrow I go to Frankfurt to Aunt Esther[3] (*notabene*: the lady who was in Trier, formerly in Algiers, who lives with the aunt, is also a sister of my father's, is called Babette,[4] vulgarly "Bäbchen," is rich). From Frankfurt, I go to Zalt-Bommel, as I informed my uncle[5] yesterday, probably to his dismay.

If I write so belatedly, it is not out of forgetfulness. On the contrary, I have made daily pilgrimages to the old Westphalen house (on the Römerstrasse)[6] that interested me more than the whole Roman antiquity because it reminds me of my happiest youth and had once harbored my dearest treasure. In addition, I am asked daily on all sides about the former

---

114

1. Engels to Marx, November 24, 1863: "I hope you feel better and that you are through with the abscesses. Keep on drinking wine and eating meat, that is the main thing."
2. To Trier.
3. Eleanor Marx.

115

1. Mrs. Marx.
2. Marx went to Trier to settle the inheritance from his mother, who died on November 30, 1863.
3. Esther Kosel (c. 1786–1865), sister of Marx's father.
4. Babette Blum, another sister of Marx's father.
5. Lion Philips.
6. The house in which Jenny grew up.

"most beautiful girl in Trier" and the "Queen of the Ball." It is damn pleasant for a man when his wife lives in the imagination of a whole city as an "enchanted princess."

I did not write you because I hoped daily that I would have something definite to report, but up to this moment I do not have it yet. The situation is as follows: When I arrived, I naturally found everything sealed up, except for the furniture in daily use. Mother, with her "overmanagement mania," had told Conradi[7] he was to worry about nothing; she had it all arranged in such a way that Uncle[8] would take care of "everything." What she gave Conradi was a notarized copy of a kind of testament which contained nothing but the following provisions: (1) for Emilie,[9] all the furniture and linens, with the exception of the silver and gold things; (2) for her son Carl [*sic*], a cancellation of the 1,100 taler, etc.; for Sophie,[10] father's portrait. This is the whole testament. (*Notabene*: Sophie has 1,000 taler annually, given to her mostly by Philips. You can see that my relatives are, after all, decent "folks.")

In addition to that scrawl, my mother had registered in court another testament (now *invalid*). It goes back to earlier dates and is *nullified* by the last testament. It was drafted before Emilie's marriage. In it, she bequeathed everything which was at her disposal to Emilie in usufruct. She made uncles Martin[11] and Philips the executors. She—or rather the drunken notary Zell (deceased)—forgot to *repeat* those executors in the clause of the present valid and above-mentioned testament, so that the uncle [Philips] is the executor only because of our good will (I have naturally "reasons" for this). As for the actual value of the estate, I have as yet no knowledge, since all the papers are in the *sealed* cupboard. The seals have not yet been removed because of the time-consuming delays awaiting the power of attorney (for Juta[12] and Sophie) from Holland. This lasts too long for me. I, therefore, leave my power of attorney to Conradi. Furthermore, there is nothing left in Trier (Grünberg[13] has been sold long ago) except five cartloads of 1858 wine, which my mother did not want to sell when the time was advantageous, and some gold and silver things. This will be divided equally among the heirs. The actual estate, however, is in the hands of Uncle [Philips].

My mother died on November 30, at four o'clock in the afternoon, on the day and hour of her wedding. She had prophesied that she would die at that time.

---

7. Johann Jakob Conradi (1821–1892), husband of Marx's sister Emilie.
8. Lion Philips was executor of the estate.
9. Emilie Conradi (1822–1888), Marx's sister.
10. Sophie Schmalhausen (1816–1883), Marx's oldest sister.
11. Martin Presburg, a Nijmegen businessman, Marx's mother's brother.
12. Husband of Marx's sister Louise.
13. A small vineyard owned by Marx's father.

I will take care of the things for Mr. Demuth and Lieschen today. I will write you in greater detail from Frankfurt or Zalt-Bommel. Warmest regards for all. Kiss them all for me and especially many thousands of times the Chinese Successor.[14]

Yours, Karl

116

To Frederick Engels (in Manchester)
Zalt-Bommel (Holland), December 22, 1863

Dear Engels:
You see from my address that I am again in Holland,[1] where I arrived safely yesterday. In Trier, my mother's sealed papers and effects could not yet be unsealed,[2] because the powers of attorney, which had to go through a complicated legal process in Holland, had not yet arrived. I left my power of attorney with my brother-in-law Conradi and came to this chief headquarters, because my uncle[3] has by far the most important part of the inheritance in his hands and, secondly, he is the executor of the estate. It will take, in any case, from five to six weeks before I will get my money. Since my wife has to pay a butcher's bill (that is, a promissory note) on January 10, 1864, I would appreciate it if you would take care of it.

The carbuncle has gone the way of all flesh, but my hump is now sorely plagued by furuncles, and because of these scoundrelly dogs I could not sleep—which I justly needed after my trip from Frankfurt to here—a wink last night. The husband[4] of my cousin[5] is the only local doctor and city physician, so that I did not lack Aesculapian help.

All over the Rhine Province, from Trier to Frankfurt and from there to Giessen to Cologne, and up to the Dutch frontier, I heard only cursing of Prussia. Little, very little, Schleswig-Holsteinism. The latter was considered mostly "Prussian piffle."

---

14. Jenny (Jennychen) Marx, oldest daughter of Marx.

116

1. Marx stayed with his relatives, the Philips family, in Zalt-Bommel, Holland, from December 21, 1863, to February 19, 1864. He was waiting to collect his share of inheritance from his mother.
2. Henriette Marx, Marx's mother, died on November 30, 1863, and he went to Germany on February 7, to be present at the settling of her estate.
3. Lion Philips.
4. Dr. A. van Anrooy.
5. Henriette van Anrooy (née Philips).

In Frankfurt (where I visited two old aunts)[6] I spent only one day and hence I could not see any bookdealer. Still, I spoke to an acquaintance, who will write me *here* (after he has negotiated with a bookdealer for me).

When you write your brochure, it would be better to include some events, not forgetting the systematic failures of the Prussian Government, the Progressives, and the regular Schleswig-Holstein humbugs who have been incorrigible since 1815.

Salut.

Yours, K.M.

P.S. Write me a few words. Address: Charles Marx, care of Mr. Lion Philips, Zalt-Bommel, Holland.

"Tu n'es pas un Yankee, s'écria le fanatique. . . . Depuis que tu es ici, je t'observe. Dans la figure du Saxon il y a du taureau et du loup; dans la tienne il y a du singe et du chien. Tu as peur de la liberté, tu parles de ce que tu ne sais pas, et tu fais les phrases. Tu es un Français!"[8] (Edouard Laboulaye, *Paris en Amérique* [Paris, 1863], pp. 195–196.)

117

From letter to Frederick Engels (in Manchester)
Zalt-Bommel (Holland), December 27, 1863

Dear Frederick:

Last Wednesday[1] I wrote you about the furunculosis that has broken out again and about the "bitter" night that I passed. On the following day, Dr. van Anrooy found a damn carbuncle next to the furuncles, coming out anew in precisely the place of the old one. Since—apart from the unpleasant effect this discovery has had on my morale—I have until now experienced great pains, especially at night. My uncle,[2] who is a splendid *Old Boy* [in English], himself puts on my plasters and poultices, and my amiable, witty and dan-

---

6. Esther Kosel and Babette Blum, sisters of Marx's father.
7. Engels to Marx, December 3, 1863: "Them is my sentiments [about Schleswig-Holstein]. I have an urge to write a brochure about it, if you can find me a publisher in Germany."
8. "You are not a Yankee, cried the fanatic. . . . I have observed you since you have been here. In the face of a Saxon there is a bull and a wolf; in yours there is a monkey and a dog. You are afraid of liberty, you talk about things you don't know, and you make phrases. You are a Frenchman!"

117
1. See Letter 116, Marx to Engels, December 22, 1863.
2. Lion Philips.

gerously dark-eyed cousin[3] tends me and takes good care of me. Still, I would gladly have returned home in these circumstances, but for physical reasons I could not think of it. The doctor has opened up the pleasant prospect that I will have to deal with this loathsome disease until late in January. He will tell me when my condition will allow locomotion to London. Still, this second Frankenstein on my hump is *by far* [in English] not so fierce as was the first in London. You can see this from the fact that I am able to write.

I have stopped smoking completely for two and a half months, and it is not likely that I will resume again soon.

If one wants to vomit politics out of nausea, one must take it daily in the form of telegraphic pills, such as are delivered by the small Dutch papers....

My best wishes for the New Year. Convey the same to Lupus.

Yours, K.M.

118

From letter to Frederick Engels (in Manchester)
Zalt-Bommel (Holland), January 20, 1864

Dear Frederick:
You see, I am still here, and "I will tell you more," I am in fact *incapable to move about* [in English]. This is a perfidious Christian illness. When I received your letter, I congratulated myself on the healing of old wounds, but in the same evening a big furuncle broke out on my left chest under the neck, and an antipodal one in the back.... A few days later, another carbuncle broke out on my right leg, directly under the spot to which Goethe refers: And when the nobleman has no posterior, how can he sit? This is the most painful of the known abscesses that I ever had, and I hope that it will finally terminate the series. In the meantime, I can neither walk, nor stand, nor sit, and even lying down is damned hard. You see, *mon cher*, how the wisdom of nature has afflicted me. Would it not have been more sensible if, instead of me, it had been consigned to try the patience of a good Christian, a person, say, of the stripe of Silvio Pellico?[1] Besides the carbuncle on the posterior, you should know that a new furuncle has broken out on the back, and the one on the chest is only beginning to heal, so that like a true Lazarus (alias Lassalle), I am scourged on all sides.

---

3. Antoinette (Nannette) Philips.

118

1. Silvio Pellico (1789–1854), Italian author who spent ten years in prison for opposition to Austrian rule of his country.

Apropos Lazarus, I like Renan's *Life of Jesus*[2] which is in some respects mere romance, full of pantheistic-mystical giddiness. Still, the book has some advantages over its German predecessors, and it is not bulky, you must read it. It is, of course, a result of German research. Highly remarkable: here in Holland the German critical-theological tendency is so very much *à l'ordre de jour* [order of the day] that the parsons acknowledge it openly from the pulpits....

Yours, K.M.

119

To Lion Philips (in Zalt-Bommel)[written in a mixture of German and English]
London, February 20, 1864

Dear Uncle:
I begin with the end. I arrived yesterday[1] about noon in a very cool condition, for it was devilish cold. The more warm was the reception, and so from a complete contradiction I enjoyed unalloyed pleasure. Yesterday and today— *en passant* [in passing]—have been the coldest days in London. It thus seems that I am destined to bring winter not only to Bommel but also to London. I wish the Prussians in Schleswig-Holstein[2] the full enjoyment of this "seasonable weather." If their patriotism, or rather "Untertanenbejeisterung" [enthusiasm of the subjects], is not cooled down by that, then, sir, we must give it up!

The little child[3] *was quite enchanted by the really beautiful dolly, Madame August*[4] *had chosen for her. I enclose some lines on the part of the child. She did not leave off bothering myself till I had promised her to enclose also for you a letter which she pretends to be written in Chinese characters and which an English friend has sent her* [in English].

In Amsterdam I found the whole family well and happy. As August was very busy, I did not tell him anything about money affairs. I received at the *Assecurantiecassa* [insurance bank] thousand-gulden notes, which, with

---

2. Ernest Renan, *Vie de Jésus* (Paris, 1863).

119

1. Marx had stayed with the Philips family in Zalt-Bommel from December 21, 1863, to February 19, 1864.
2. On February 1, 1864, Prussian troops, in alliance with Austrians, invaded the Danish province of Schleswig-Holstein, which was finally ceded to Prussia.
3. Eleanor Marx (1855–1898), Marx's youngest daughter.
4. Wife of Marx's cousin, August Philips.

Jacques's[5] help in Rotterdam, I changed mostly into notes and a fourth of them into banknotes.

During the two days I spent in Rotterdam, Jacques had no free time. On the one day he pleaded a cause in a neighboring town, and on the other, he had to attend an investigation. In general, I had the impression that since his engagement he has had more "an eye to business" than before. I do not doubt that in a few years he will have a suitable practice, the more so as he loves jurisprudence. He told me himself that he wins practically all bad cases, and when he takes the trouble to tell this, one can believe him. I laughed very much with him over a man whom he calls *"the client"* par excellence. The man, he told me, is still young and in thirty years or more he can litigate away a great deal of wealth.

Incidentally: August also has a special opinion of the infallibility of the courts. He believes, for example, that the English lose nothing by the fact that their lawsuits are so expensive. People who do not litigate have precisely as much chance to find justice as those who do. *In point of fact, it seemed his opinion, that dear law is as good as cheap law, and perhaps better; and he is a fellow who knows something about such things* [in English].

August gave me the three parts of the *Aardrijkskunde* [geography], and Jacques provided me with a book on political economy (Dutch) by Vissering,[6] Professor at Leyden, and a copy of *Camera obscura.*[7] So I am abundantly supplied with Dutch literature. Frisian literature was not to be found in Amsterdam, although in one bookstore alone there are works in eighty-eight *modern* languages. Negro languages seem to be of closer interest to the Amsterdamers than the Frisian, *but man always contrives to neglect the things that are nearest to him* [in English].

The *"Sorje Oppenheim,"* which has caused such a sensation in Amsterdam, has already been executed by my daughters to the accompaniment of the pianoforte, *and they hope to perform it one day before their uncle* [in English].

A great heap of newspapers, etc., of all shapes has piled up for me here, *but I am firmly resolved to know nothing of politics until Monday next* [in English].

Now, my dear uncle, I bid you farewell. Despite carbuncles and furuncles, I consider the two months I have lived in your house, as one of the happiest episodes of my life, and I shall always feel thankful for the kindness you have shown me [in English].

You will, of course, tell Rothäuschen[8] that I send him my compliments and that I regret having been forced to give battle to him [in English].

---

5. Jacques Philips, Marx's cousin.
6. Simon Vissering, *Handboek van Praktische Staathuishoudkunde* [*Handbook of Practical Political Economy*] (Amsterdam, 1860–1862).
7. Hildebrand, *Camera obscura.*
8. A. Roodhuizen, a pastor in Zalt-Bommel, husband of Marx's cousin Antoinette Philips.

My best compliments to the whole family, especially Jettchen,[9] *Dr. Anrooy and Fritz.*[10] *Mrs. Marx and the girls send also their compliments. Please to give the enclosed lines to Nettchen*[11] [in English].

Yours truly, Charles M.

120

To Lion Philips (in Aachen)
London, March 29, 1864

Dear Uncle:
I assume that you are already or still in Aachen, and hence I am sending this letter there. If you had wanted to wait for good weather, you would have had to remain in [Zalt-]Bommel until now. Here at least March had been quite abominable, with the exception of two beautiful days, cold, wet, and changing every minute. This is perhaps the reason why, up to this moment, I have not been able to get rid of the *Verdummelinge* [German form of the Dutch word: accursed fellows] furuncles. I curse it, but surreptitiously.

Little Eleanor[1] has been coughing violently for two days, and this prevents her from writing you. But she asks me to be greatly rememberd to you and *in regards to the Danish question begs me to tell you, that "she don't care for such stuff," and that "she considers one of the parties to the quarrel as bad as the other, and perhaps worse"* [in English].

The difficulty in understanding Prussian policy derives merely from people's prejudice which ascribe to it serious and far-ranging aims and plans. In this way, for example, the Mormon Bible[2] is also very hard to understand, because there is not a spark of sense in it. In the first place, Prussia aimed to make the Army popular, an aim which already the 1848 Schleswig-Holstein campaigns had to serve.[3] In the second place, it was designed to bar the German volunteer corps, democrats, and the small states from the terrain. Finally, through pressure from without, Prussia and Austria were to enable the Danish king,[4] who plays with them sub rosa, to force the Danish people

9. Henriette van Anrooy.
10. Friedrich Philips, Marx's cousin.
11. Antoinette Philips.

120

1. Eleanor Marx.
2. Joseph Smith's *Book of Mormon* (1830).
3. In March, 1848, after Schleswig-Holstein began its war of liberation against Denmark, Prussia was asked to aid the revolting provinces, but actually sided with Denmark, which won the war in 1850.
4. Christian IX (1818–1906), King of Denmark.

to certain external and internal concessions. Austria, of course, could not refrain from playing a role and used the opportunity to bring about a more specific alliance for other *peripeties* [solutions].

On April 12, the conference will meet in London.[5] In the most extreme case, it will decide on a *personal union* of Schleswig and Holstein with Denmark, perhaps less than that, but in no way more. How little serious the whole affair is, despite powder, lead, and blood pumping, can be seen from the fact that up to this moment, neither Prussia and Austria have declared war on Denmark, nor Denmark on Prussia and Austria. There is no better means to throw dust in the eyes than by having armies march, horses trample, and cannon roar.

Despite all that, serious conflicts may be imminent [in English]. Bonaparte[6] sees himself practically compelled to make his *troupiers* [soldiers] an export business in "freedom," in consequence of great disaffection which exists not only in Paris but shows up provocatively in the elections.[7] And this time the Prussian dogs have paved the way for him.

Garibaldi's trip to England,[8] and the great ovations he has received here from all sides, are merely, or at least should be, an overture to a new rising against Austria. The latter, as ally of Prussia in Holstein and Schleswig, and ally of the Russians because of the state of siege in Galicia,[9] has greatly facilitated the game of its enemies. A new Holy Alliance, in the present conditions that exist in Poland, Hungary, Italy, the popular mood in Germany, and the thoroughly changed position of England, would enable even Napoleon the Little [Napoleon III] to play the great man. Continuation of peace would be best, for every war postpones the revolution in France.

Gott [God] *verdumm me! if there be anything more stupid than this political chessboard* [in English].

I had really intended to write about two more things, the Roman division and the darkness in interstellar space. But since it is getting dark, the paper has come to an end, and the mail will close soon, I must now end with the best regards for the whole family. Ditto Karl[10] and wife, Jean *enz.*[11]

Your devoted nephew, K. Marx

---

5. The conference of European powers to solve an Austro-Prussian conflict, as well as the problem of Schleswig-Holstein, met from April 25 to June, 1864, but achieved nothing concrete.
6. Napoleon III (1808–1873), Emperor of the French.
7. The elections to the Corps Législatif, May 31 to June 1, 1863.
8. Early in April, 1864, Giuseppe Garibaldi came to London to seek the British government's help in a campaign which he planned against Austrian rule in Venice; he left England at the end of April after Prime Minister Gladstone declared his further stay there to be undesirable.
9. On February 29, 1864, Austria put Galicia in a state of siege after a revolt by that province's Polish population.
10. Karl Philips, a merchant in Aachen, was Marx's cousin.
11. Jean Philips, also a merchant in Aachen, and Marx's cousin, "not excepted."

121

To Lion Philips (in Zalt-Bommel)
London, April 14, 1864

Dear Uncle:
I hope that your cough has gone the way of all flesh. For a few days now I have had no new furuncle, and my doctor thinks that I have definitely got rid of the thing. It would, indeed, be about time. The sun seems finally to break through. But a nasty wind still blows from the east. Eleanor's cough is gone. But in her place her sister Jenny has a bad one, that will only go away with a change in the wind.

Before the arrival of your letter, I received one from Conradi, to whom I replied that he can send the money directly to me here.

In the [British] Museum I looked into Boethius' *De Arithmetica*[1] (an author of the period of the Peoples' Migration) on the subject of the Roman division (naturally he knew *no other*). From this, and from some other writings which I compared, I deduce the following: moderate accounts, such as household and business, were never recorded on the calculating slate with figures but with weights and other similar marks. On that slate they put several parallel lines, marking, by weight or other physical indications, ones on the first line, tens on the second, hundreds on the third, thousands on the fourth, etc. Such calculating boards were used practically throughout the whole Middle Ages and are still in use by the Chinese today. As regards higher mathematical calculations, the Romans, insofar as these appear among them, used the multiplication table or the one-times-one of Pythagoras, then, indeed, still inconvenient and ponderous, for it consisted partly of its own characters and partly of letters from the Greek (later Roman) alphabet. As the whole division dissolved in analyses of the dividends in factors and the multiplication table was carried to considerably high figures, it had to suffice to divide such expressions as MDXL, etc. Every figure, such as M, for example, had to be reduced into factors, which it formed with the divisor, and the results were then added up. Thus, for instance, M divided by two, equals D (500); D divided by two, equals 250, etc. That in major calculations the old method encountered insurmountable obstacles, can be seen from the cunning devices to which the extraordinary mathematician Archimedes had to take recourse.

In regard to the "Darkness of the Outer Space," this necessarily arises from the theory of light. As colors appear only as a result of refraction of light

---

121

1. Anicius Manlius Torquatus Severinus Boëthius (*c.* 480-524 A.D.), a Roman philosopher.

waves from bodies, and as in the *intermediate spaces* between the heavenly bodies there is neither *atmosphere* nor any other substances, they must be pitch black. They let all the light rays pass through, which is another way of saying that they are dark. Moreover, the space outside the atmospheres of the planets, etc., is damn *"kond en kil"* [Dutch: "cold and frosty"], which is also the reason why the higher reaches of our own atmosphere are ice-cold in summer and winter, particularly because of the thinness, hence the weightlessness, of those strata. But

> *"Sollte diese Qual uns quälen*
> *Da sie unsre Lust vermehrt?"*[2]

But why light and heat, *where there is no eye to see the one, and no organic matter to feel the other* [in English]? The worthy Epicurus already had the very sensible idea of banishing the gods to the *intermundi* (that is, the *empty* intermediate spaces), and in truth, R's[3] "perfect dogs" belong in those cold, cool, pitch-dark *"stoffelooze wereldruimte"* [Dutch: "immaterial outer spaces"].

That I have become a good Dutchman, you can see from the fact that, *me docente* [under my supervision], Jennychen has already read half of the *Camera obscura*,[4] Laura has read most of the first volume of the *Aardrijkskunde* [Geography], and even Eleanor knows by heart *"Dans Nonneken dans"* [Dutch: "Dance, Nonneken, Dance"] and *"Klompertjen en zijn wijfjen"* [Dutch: "Klompertjen and His Dear Wife"].[5]

Best compliments from the whole family to you, to Karl,[6] and the general's wife[7] *enz* [Dutch: not excluding]. In this fine weather you will not have to wait long for your own beautiful day.

Your devoted nephew, Karl Marx

122

To Jenny Marx (in London)
Manchester, May 9, 1864

Dear Jenny:
Poor Lupus died today, ten minutes after 5 P.M. I have just returned from seeing the body.

---

2. From Goethe's *Westöstlicher Diwan*: "Suleika." Freely translated: "Should this pain torment us, When it increases our pleasure?"
3. A. Roodhuizen.
4. Hildebrand, *Camera obscura*.
5. Dutch children's songs.
6. Karl Philips, Marx's cousin.
7. Karl Philips' mother-in-law, whose husband was a general.

When I arrived from London,[1] I went to see him that same evening; but he was unconscious. Next morning he recognized me. I saw him together with Engels and the two doctors,[2] and upon our departure he called out (in a weak voice): You will come back again. It was a ray of hope. Soon thereafter he fell into apathy again. Until Thursday[3] evening, actually until Friday evening, the condition so wavered that the outcome seemed to be in doubt. From Friday evening until his demise he was unconscious. That is how long his death struggle—although without pain—lasted. He is beyond doubt the victim of the bombastic quack.[4] Tomorrow I will write more.[5]

In him we lost one of our few friends and comrades-in-arms. He was a man in the best sense of the word. His burial will take place on Friday.[6]

Yours, Karl

123

To Jenny Marx (in London)
Manchester, May 10, 1864

Dear Jenny:

Poor Lupus, it appears—as Borchardt already knew—through incessant work[1] had managed to accumulate an estate.

In his testament (of December, 1863) he named Engels, Borchardt, and me his executors, and the notary has just now read it. He bequeaths therein:

1. £100 to the Manchester Schiller Institute.
2. £100 to Engels.
3. £100 to Borchardt and
4. the residue, consisting of £6 to £700 to me (to you and the children in case I *predecease* him, he thought of all contingencies), likewise his books and other effects.

I must go to his quarters, to arrange his papers. Fortunately, he lived, at least in the last six to seven weeks, with extremely worthy and good people,

---

122

1. On May 3.
2. Louis Borchardt and Eduard Gumpert, German doctors in Manchester.
3. May 5.
4. Borchardt.
5. See letters 123 and 124, Marx to Jenny Marx, May 10 and 13, 1864.
6. May 12.

123

1. Lupus, who never married, supported himself—and saved his money—by giving private lessons.

where he enjoyed excellent care. The silly telegrams about male nurses[2]—about which Gumpert knew nothing—were only big talk and pomposity on the part of the bombastic Borchardt.

Thousand kisses for you and the children.

Yours, Karl

124

To Jenny Marx (in London)
Manchester, May 13, 1864

Dear Heart:

Today was the funeral of our good comrade.[1] There were intentionally no invitations, otherwise we would have had half the city here. So among the participants were Borchardt, Gumpert, Engels, Dronke, Steinthal,[2] Marotzki (the *Lichtprotestantische*[3] parson, in whose house Lupus gave lessons and who came as a private friend), Beneke (one of the leading merchants here), Schwabe (ditto), three other merchants, a few boys, and some fifteen to twenty persons of the "lower classes," among whom Lupus was very popular. I gave, of course, a short funeral oration. It was a function that touched me deeply, so that my voice gave out a couple of times. Freiligrath begged off in a letter. For his boss, Fazy,[4] is now in London. Engels and particularly Dronke did not accept the excuse, and tomorrow Dronke will call him to account in London.

To complete the business, paying inheritance taxes, attestations, etc., I

---

2. Engels to Marx, May 2, 1864: "Dear Marx: The Lupus situation is moving quickly. He has hallucinations, constantly leaps out of the bed, etc. We need a man who could watch over him and prevent him from doing damage. Here there is only one male nurse, and he is engaged. Borchardt, to be sure, could get one from the insane asylum, but so long as there is the slightest possibility of a recovery, he does not, of course, want this sort of people, so that there would be no gossip later that would harm Lupus. He now suggests that perhaps you may know a reliable man who does *not* need to be *a male nurse* by profession and preferably should not be, but would be merely reliable, doing what he is told and does not fall asleep at his job—perhaps you have such a man and could send him here tomorrow morning, for we are covered only until next morning, and *periculum in mora* [danger in delay]. You are to send him, *s'il s'en trouve* [if one is to be found], IMMEDIATELY to Borchardt, Rusholme Road, Manchester. If you have none, Borchardt begs you to telegraph him immediately on Monday morning (it costs one shilling) so that he and Gumpert can look around further. I am just now telegraphing you in this sense, but the telegram requires the explanation in this letter. Yours. F.E."

124

1. Wilhelm Wolff (Lupus).
2. A German merchant in Manchester who employed Georg Weerth, a communist poet, friend of Marx.
3. A Protestant sect.
4. Jean Jacques (James) Fazy (1794–1878), Swiss statesman, founder of the Banque Générale de Suisse; Freiligrath worked as manager of his London branch.

have to remain here for at least three or four days. Of course, I will not leave Manchester until everything is done.

At first it was thought that poor Lupus had suffered from a softening of the brain. But this was wrong. Gumpert had said that he suffered from hyperemia of the brain (*the presence of a large blood supply*). This was confirmed by the autopsy, which at the same time proved that if he had had the most ordinary normal treatment he would still be alive today. Borchardt had thoroughly and unconscionably neglected this. But one can make no to-do about it, particularly because of the Borchardt family, (especially Borchardt's oldest daughter), who were very devoted to Lupus, which did much for him and on whom he leaned greatly. Still, I declined Borchardt's invitation to dinner today (where Engels, etc., was to be present) with the statement that on the day of Wolff's burial I could not accept any hospitality.

Dronke asks to be excused that he did not reply to your letter. The poor little one is too shattered by the death of his own children to be able to write.

Lupus had carefully preserved all the letters of our children, and repeatedly told Frau Borchardt in recent weeks how much pleasure Tussychen[5] gave him by her missives.

The day before yesterday, Marotzki (at the confirmation of the children, among them also a younger Borchardt) delivered a eulogy of Lupus in the church. I do not believe that anybody in Manchester was so generally beloved as our poor little man (who as a child had already both his legs broken and who for years suffered medical treatments). In his papers one finds proofs of the mostly friendly sympathy from all sides, girl students, boy students, and particularly mothers.

My best regards for all.

Yours, Karl

Send immediately photographs of dear Eleanor.

125

From letter to Frederick Engels (in Manchester)
London, June 16, 1864

Dear Frederick:
Thanks for [in English] *Dagbladet.*[1]

Before I begin the letter—so that I don't forget—the question: Are the following word groupings, which I find in a Belgian etymologist,[2] *of any value* [in English]?

---

5. Eleanor Marx, whose nickname was Tussy or Tussychen (little Tussy).

125
1. Copenhagen daily.
2. Honoré Joseph Chavée (1815–1877), Belgian philologist.

Sanskrit Wer (couvrir, protéger, respecter, honorer, aimer, chérir), Adjective: *Wertas* (excellent, respectable), *Gothic*: Wairths, *Anglosaxon* Weorth, *English* worth, *Lithuanian* werthas, *Germanic*: Werth. *Sanskrit* Wertis, *Latin* virtus, *Gothic* Wairthi, *Germanic* Werth. *Sanskrit Wal* (couvrir, fortifier), *Valor*, *Value* (???)....

A Dutch Orientalist, Professor Dozy of Leyden, has published a book[3] to prove that "Abraham, Isaac and Jacob were fantasy-mongers; that the Israelites were idolaters; that they dragged with them a 'stone' in the 'Ark of the Covenant'; that the tribe of Simon (exiled under Saul) moved to *Mecca*, where they built a heathenish temple and worshipped stones; that after the deliverance from Babylon, Ezra invented the legend of the Creation and the history up to Joshua, and, in addition, wrote the law and the dogma for the propagation of reform and monotheism, etc."

So they write me from Holland, and also that the book has caused a great uproar among theologians there, particularly since Dozy is the most learned Dutch theologian—and a professor in Leyden to boot! At any rate, outside of Germany, remarkable movements against religion (Renan, Colenso,[4] Dozy, etc.) are afoot....

Salut.

Yours, K.M.

126

From letter to Lion Philips (in Zalt-Bommel)
London, June 25, 1864

Dear Uncle:
My best thanks for your detailed letter. I know how troublesome writing is for you because of your eyes, and in fact I do not expect at all that you should answer every one of my letters. I was glad to see from your epistle that you are physically well and that your mental gaiety has been unaffected even by the discoveries of Professor Dozy.[1] Since Darwin has demonstrated our common descent from apes, hardly any shock whatever could shake "our anecestral pride" anymore. That the Pentateuch was produced only after the return of the Jews from the Babylonian Captivity, Spinoza had already elucidated in his *Tractatus theologico-politicus*.

---

3. Reinhart Dozy, *De Israelëten te Mekka* (Haarlem, 1864).
4. John William Colenso (1814–1883), English bishop and theologian driven from the church for critical views of the Bible.

126

1. Reinhart Dozy, *De Israelëten te Mekka* (Haarlem, 1864). See Letter 125, Marx to Engels, June 16, 1864.

In the enclosed note, Eleanor thanks you herself for your photograph, which is about as good as any of these silhouettes generally are. The child put "her letter" on my desk three or four days ago already.

I have had relapses of furuncles and have got rid of them only in the last fourteen days. Since the irksome illness has very much hindered my work—in addition, the doctor forbade any strenuous and prolonged mental labor—I did, what will surprise you not a little, speculate partly in American funds, but particularly in English stocks, which in this year grew out of the ground like mushrooms (for all possible and impossible stock-enterprises), are driven up to unreasonable heights and then mostly burst like a bubble. In this way, I won more than £400 and will now, when the entanglement of political conditions offers new scope, begin anew. This sort of operation takes little time, and it is worth risking something in order to take money away from one's enemy.

Everything goes quite well at home. The doctor wants Jennychen[2] to have a "change of air," and if you and fate have nothing against it, I will visit you with my three daughters at the end of the summer....

Best regards for the whole family. My wife also sends her regards to you and family.

Yours truly, Ch. Marx.

127

To Lion Philips (in Zalt-Bommel)   [written in a mixture of German and English]
London, August 17, 1864

Dear Uncle:
I found your letter last night when I returned from the British Museum. It was too late to answer immediately. I need not tell you how the content of your letter scared me and my family.[1] One thing I do not understand. Why did you and Nettchen[2] not leave the house immediately? I advise you still to do it. When the same case occurred in my house, I removed my children right away; and the giantess[3] can be tended to also without you. Why provoke danger uselessly? Forgive me for interfering like that, but my anxiety for all of you is too great to mince words. I am truly sorry that I am not there with

---

2. Marx's oldest daughter, Jenny.

127

1. In the letter, Philips wrote that the housemaid had smallpox and that therefore Marx and his daughters had to give up their projected visit to Zalt-Bommel.
2. Antoinette (Nannette) Philips.
3. The maid employed in the Philips household.

you personally, for, as I know from experience, I am not susceptible to this disease, and, if all of you do not wish to leave the house (but why not?), I could have stood by in this crisis, where two are better than one and three are better than two, *to kill time and rough it* [in English].

About our own recent doings, I have already written to Nettchen, and she will report to you the little that is worth mentioning. In general, everything goes well, and all the members of the family are passably well.

Politically and socially, things are becalmed here. Everyone who can manage it shakes the dust off his feet, going either abroad or to the seashore here. The monotony is interrupted only by daily reports of frightful railway accidents. Capital here is not under as much police surveillance as on the Continent, and hence the *railway directors* do not at all care *how many people are killed during an excursion season, if only the balance looks to the comfortable side.* All attempts to hold these railway kings responsible for their *homicidal neglect of all precautionary measures*, have been hitherto frustrated by the great influence which the *railway interest* exercises in the *House of Commons!* [All italic passages in English.]

Another distraction here is *the anxiety prevailing in mercantile circles because of the rise of the rate of discount!* It is certain that if the *rate of discount* continues for some weeks at the present level, a great *crash* will ensue among the myriad of *swindling joint-stock companies* that have sprung up like mushrooms this year. One or two important bankruptcies in the City already point to the approaching storm. [All italic passages in English].

I have recently looked over a very important work on natural science, Grove's *Correlation of Physical Forces.*[4] He demonstrates that all mechanical forces, heat, light, electricity, magnetism, and *chemical affinity* [in English] are properly only a modification of the same force, and they mutually produce, replace, and transform each other. The repulsive metaphysical-physical chimeras, such as "*latent* heat" (as good as "invisible light"), electric "fluid," and such, *pis aller* [of necessity], words used when ideas fail, these he disposes of very skillfully.

I hope to hear good news from all of you soon. I am so absorbed in thoughts about all of you that today I did not have the peace of mind to read the *American news* [in English].

The whole family sends warm regards. For my part, remember me to Jettchen,[5] the doctor,[6] Fritz,[7] et Co.

Your devoted nephew, K.M.

---

4. William Robert Grove, *The Correlation of Physical Forces* (London, 1855).
5. Henriette van Anrooy, Marx's cousin.
6. Dr. A. van Anrooy, Henriette's husband.
7. Friedrich Philips, Marx's cousin.

128

From letter to Lion Philips (in Zalt-Bommel)
London, November 29, 1864

Dear Uncle:
...A few days ago I received a letter from my friend in America, Weydemeyer, colonel of a St. Louis (Missouri) regiment. He writes, among other things: "Alas, we are detained in St. Louis, because, owing to the 'conservative' elements here, military force is necessary to prevent a breakout of the numerous Southern prisoners of war.... The whole campaign in Virginia is a blunder that has cost us hecatombs of men. Despite all this, the South will not be able to hold out much longer: it has sent its last manpower into the field and cannot raise a new army. The present invasion of Missouri, like the incursions into Tennessee, has only the character of a raid, a marauding expedition; a lasting preoccupation of the lost districts does not come into question."

When you think, dear uncle, that three and a half years ago, at the time of Lincoln's election the problem was to make *no further concessions* to the slave holders, while now the *aboliton of slavery* is the avowed[1] and in part already realized aim, you must admit that *never* has such a gigantic transformation taken place so rapidly. It will have a beneficent effect on the whole world.

Our *Stammgenosse* [member of our tribe], Benjamin Disraeli,[2] has again made a fool of himself this week when, at a public *meeting* [in English],[3] he gave himself airs as the guardian angel of the *High Church* [in English], of *church rates* [in English], the repudiator of critics in religious affairs. He is the best proof of how great talent without conviction produces scoundrels, even though liveried and *"right honourable"* [in English] scoundrels....

Your devoted nephew, K.M.

128

1. President Abraham Lincoln issued his preliminary Emancipation Proclamation on September 22, 1862, and his formal one on January 1, 1863.
2. This is the only occasion known to the editor of this volume that Marx identified himself as a Jew. Like Marx himself, Disraeli was of Jewish origin and was baptized a Christian. But Disraeli was not anti-Semitic, as Marx was.
3. The meeting took place on October 25, 1864, at Oxford.

FIRST INTERNATIONAL and *DAS KAPITAL* · *1865-1874*

In September–October, 1864, Marx helped found the International Workingmen's Association—known as the First International—with the aim of providing Europe's disparate workers with an ideal and a program of action. For seven years he was the mind and spirit of the International, and fought its increasingly bitter internecine struggles. The association absorbed so much of his time and energy that it delayed the completion and publication of *Das Kapital*, a work in which he invested the mature years of his life. Only one volume was published in his lifetime (1867). Marx made great efforts to win attention for *Das Kapital* through reviews and translations. To his dismay and anger, the German-written book was practically ignored in Germany. Translations were also slow in coming. The first was in Russian (1872), but an ardently desired full French translation was delayed until 1875. (An English translation did not appear until twenty years after the original German.)

Marx's life was also embittered by the collapsing First International, which brought him dangerous notoriety, particularly after the savage destruction of the Paris Commune by the French government in 1871. The accumulated troubles further undermined his fragile health and made it all but impossible for him to do constructive intellectual work.

The one bright feature in that period—apart from the marriage of his two older daughters, Jenny and Laura—was a £350 annuity which Engels gave him at the end of 1868. This generous gift freed the final years of Marx's life from crushing penury. In 1870, after Engels sold his business in Manchester, he moved to London to be near Marx. Their written correspondence, therefore, largely ceased, except when either one of them was out of London.

129

To Johann Baptist von Schweitzer (in Berlin)
London, January 24, 1865[1]

Dear Sir:
Yesterday I received a letter in which you ask me for a detailed judgment of Proudhon. Time does not allow me to satisfy your wish. In addition, I have none of his writings at hand. But to assure you of my good will, I am hastily jotting down a short sketch. You can complete it, add to it, cut it—in short, do what you like with it.

Proudhon's earliest efforts I no longer remember. His classroom text on the *Langue Universelle*[2] shows how unembarrassedly he tackled problems for the solution of which he lacked the first principles of knowledge.

His first work, *What Is Property?*,[3] is undoubtedly his best. It is epoch-making, if not from new content, at least from the new and audacious way of stating the old. In the works of French socialists and communists that were known to him, "property," of course, was not only variously criticized but also "repealed" in a utopian fashion. In that book, Proudhon's relation to Saint-Simon[4] and Fourier was about the same as that of Feuerbach to Hegel. Compared to Hegel, Feuerbach is positively inferior. Nevertheless, he was epoch-making after Hegel because he laid stress on certain points that were disagreeable to the Christian consciousness but important for the progress of criticism, which Hegel had left in mystical semiobscurity.

In Proudhon's book, there prevails, if I may say so, a strong musculature of style. And I consider the style its chief merit. Even when he is reproducing old stuff, one can see that Proudhon has found it out for himself, that what he is saying is new to him and considered so by him. Provocative defiance, the questioning of the economic "holy of holies," the brilliant

---

129

1. This letter was published in the Berlin socialist newspaper, *Der Social-Demokrat*, of which von Schweitzer was the editor, February 1, 3 and 5, 1865.

2. Proudhon, *"Essai de grammaire générale,"* in N. S. Bergier's *Les Éléments Primitifs des Langues* [*Primitive Elements of Language*] (Besançon, 1837).

3. Proudhon, *Qu'est-ce que la propriété. Ou recherches sur le principle du droit et du gouvernement* [*What Is Property? Or Inquiries into the Principle of Law and Government*] (Paris, 1840).

4. Claude Henri de Saint-Simon (1760–1825), French social philosopher.

paradox that mocked the ordinary bourgeois mind, the withering criticism, the bitter irony, and here and there a deep and genuine feeling of indignation at the infamy of the existing order, a revolutionary earnestness—all these electrified the readers of *What Is Property?* and produced a great sensation at its first appearance. In any strictly scientific history of political economy, the book would hardly be worth mentioning. But sensational works of this kind play the same role in the sciences as much as they do in the history of the novel. Take, for example, Malthus' book on *Population.*[5] In its first edition it was nothing but a "sensational pamphlet" and a plagiarism from beginning to end, to boot. And yet, what a stimulus was produced by this libel on the human race!

If I had Proudhon's book before me, I could easily give a few examples to illustrate his early style. In the passages which he himself regarded as the most important, he imitates Kant's treatment of the antinomies—Kant, whose works he had read in translations, was at that time the only German philosopher he knew—and he leaves one with a strong impression that to him, as to Kant, the resolution of the antinomies is something "beyond" the human understanding, that is, something about which his own understanding remains in the dark.

But despite all his apparent iconoclasm, one already finds in *What Is Property?* the contradiction that Proudhon is criticizing society from the standpoint of a French small peasant (later petit bourgeois), on the one hand, and, on the other, with the yardstick he derived from the socialists.

The deficiency of the book is indicated by its very title. The question was put so falsely that it could not be answered correctly. "Property relationships" of antiquity were swallowed up by feudal ones and the latter by bourgeois ones. Thus history itself had practiced its criticism on past property relationships. What Proudhon was actually dealing with was the existing modern bourgeois property. The question of what this is could have been answered only by a critical analysis of "political economy," embracing the totality of those property relationships, not in their juridical expression as relations of volition but in their real form, that is, as relations of production. But as he entangled the totality of these economic relationships in the general juristic conception of "property," Proudhon could not get beyond the answer that Brissot,[6] in a similar work, had already given before 1789: "Property is theft."

---

5. Thomas Robert Malthus, *An Essay on the Principle of Population, as It Affects the Future Improvement of Society, with Remarks on the Speculations of Mr. Godwin, Mr. Condorcet, and other Writers* (London, 1798).

6. Jean-Pierre Brissot De Warville, *Recherches philosophiques sur le droit de propriété et sur le vol, considérés dans la nature et dans la société* [*Philosophic Inquiries into the Right of Property and of Theft, Considered in Nature and in Society*] (Berlin, Paris, Lyons, 1782).

The most that can be got out of this is that bourgeois-juristic conceptions of "theft" apply equally well to the bourgeois "honest" earning itself. On the other hand, since "theft" as a forcible violation of property presupposes the existence of property, Proudhon entangled himself in all sorts of fantasies, obscure even to himself, about true bourgeois property.

During my stay in Paris in 1844, I came into personal contact with Proudhon. I mention this here because to a certain extent I am to blame for his "sophistication," as the English call the adulteration of commercial goods. In the course of lengthy debates often lasting all night, I infected him to his great injury with Hegelianism, which, owing to his ignorance of the German language, he could not study properly. After my expulsion from Paris, Herr Karl Grün[7] continued what I had begun. As a teacher of German philosophy, Grün had an advantage over me in that he understood nothing about it himself.

Shortly before the appearance of his second important work, *The Philosophy of Poverty*,[8] Proudhon himself announced it to me in a very detailed letter in which he said, among other things: "*J'attends votre férule critique*" ["I await the lash of your criticism"]. This soon fell upon him (in my book *The Poverty of Philosophy*, Paris, 1847), which ended our friendship forever.

From what I have already said, you can see that Proudhon's *Philosophy of Poverty or System of Economic Contradictions* first actually contained his answer to the question: *What Is Property?* In fact, it was only after the publication of the latter work that he had begun his economic studies; he had discovered that the question he had raised could not be answered by invective, but only by an analysis of modern "political economy." At the same time he attempted to present the system of economic categories dialectically. In place of Kant's insoluble "antinomies," the Hegelian "contradiction" was to be introduced as the means of development.

For an estimate of his work, which is in two fat volumes, I must refer you to the book I wrote against it. There I showed, among other things, how little he had penetrated into the secret of scientific dialectics and how, on the contrary, he shared the illusions of speculative philosophy in his treatment of economic categories; how, instead of conceiving them as the theoretical expressions of historical relations of production corresponding to a particular stage of development of material production, he drivels them into preexisting, eternal ideas, and in this roundabout way arrives once more at the standpoint of bourgeois economy.

I also show, furthermore, how very deficient and sometimes even schoolboyish is his knowledge of the "political economy" that he undertook to criticize, and how he and the utopians are hunting for a so-called science

---

7. Karl Grün (1817–87), a German journalist, spokesman of "true" socialism in the 1840's.
8. Proudhon, *Système des contradictions économiques, ou philosophie de la misère* (Paris, 1846).

by which a formula for the "solution of the social question" is to be excogitated *a priori*, instead of deriving their science from a critical knowledge of the historical movement, a movement that itself produces the material conditions of emancipation. But I show especially how confused, wrong and superficial Proudhon remains with regard to exchange value, the foundation of the whole thing, and how he even views the utopian interpretation of Ricardo's theory of value as the basis of a new science. In regard to his general viewpoint, I made the following comprehensive judgment:

"Every economic relationship has a good and a bad side; this is the only point on which Mr. Proudhon does not give himself the lie. He sees the good side expounded by the economists; the bad one, denounced by the socialists. He borrows from the economists the necessity of eternal relationships; he borrows from the socialists the illusion of seeing in misery nothing but misery (instead of seeing in it the revolutionary, subversive aspect which will overthrow the old society). He agrees with both in wanting to rely on the authority of science. For him, science reduces itself to the tiny proportions of a scientific formula; he is the man hunting for formulas. Hence Mr. Proudhon flatters himself on having given a critique of both political economy and communism—he is way beneath them both. Beneath the economists, because as a philosopher who has a magical formula at hand, he believed he could dispense with going into purely economic details; beneath the socialists, because he has neither courage nor sufficient insight to rise above the bourgeois horizon, even if only speculatively. . . . He wants to soar as a man of science above the bourgeois and the proletarians; he is merely the petit bourgeois who is constantly tossed back and forth between capital and labor, between political economy and communism."

Severe though the above judgment sounds, I must still endorse every word of it today. At the same time, however, it must be remembered that at the time when I declared Proudhon's book to be the petit-bourgeois code of socialism and proved it theoretically, Proudhon was still being branded by the political economists and socialists as an *ultra* archrevolutionist. That is why later on I never joined in the outcry about his "treachery" to the revolution. It was not his fault that, originally misunderstood by others as well as by himself, he did not fulfill unjustified hopes.

In the *Philosophy of Poverty*, all the defects of Proudhon's method of presentation stand out very unfavorably in contrast to *What Is Property?* The style is often what the French call *ampoulé* [bombastic]. High-sounding, speculative gibberish, supposed to be German-philosophical, appears regularly when his Gallic acuteness fails him. A quacking, self-glorifying, boastful tone, especially the pompous drivel about "science," always so stale, continually screams in one's ears. Instead of the genuine warmth that glowed in his first book, here certain passages are systematically worked up by rhetoric into transient heat. Added to this, the clumsy, distasteful erudition of the self-taught, whose natural pride in his original thought has already been broken and who now, as a parvenu of science, feels it necessary to bolster himself up with what he is not and what he has not. Then the mentality of the petit bourgeois, who with indecent brutality—and neither acutely nor profoundly nor even correctly—attacks a man like Cabet, who is respected for his practical attitude toward the proletariat, while he [Proudhon] flatters, for example, a man like Dunoyer[9] (a "State Councillor," to be sure), even though the whole significance of the latter lay in the comic zeal with which he preached, in three thick, unbearably boring tomes, the rigorism [*Rigorismus*] that Helvétius[10] had characterized thus: *"On veut que les malheureux soient parfaits"* ["One expects the unfortunate to be perfect"].

The February Revolution certainly came at a very inopportune moment for Proudhon, since only a few weeks previously he had irrefutably demonstrated that "the era of revolutions" was past forever. His appearance in the National Assembly, however little insight it showed into existing conditions, deserves every praise.[11] After the June insurrection, that was an act of great courage. In addition, it had the fortunate consequence that M. Thiers,[12] in his speech opposing Proudhon's proposals which was later issued in a special publication, proved to the whole of Europe on what a small children's-catechism pedestal that intellectual pillar of the French bourgeoisie stood. Indeed, compared to M. Thiers, Proudhon expanded to the size of an antediluvian colossus.

Proudhon's discoveries of *"crédit gratuit"* [free credit] and the *banque du peuple* [people's bank] based upon it, were his last economic "deeds." In my book *A Contribution to the Critique of Political Economy*, Part I (Berlin, 1859, pp. 59–64), will be found the proof that the theoretical basis of his idea arises from a misunderstanding of the first elements of bourgeois "political economy," namely, the relationship between commodities and money, while the practical superstructure is simply a reproduction of much older and far better developed schemes. That the credit system can serve to hasten the emancipation of the working class under certain economic and political conditions— as, for example, at the beginning of the eighteenth and later again in the nineteenth century in England it served toward transferring the wealth of one class to another—is quite unquestionable and self-evident. But to regard interest-bearing capital as the main form of capital, while trying to use a special form of credit—the alleged abolition of interest—as the basis for a transformation of society, is a thoroughly petit bourgeois fantasy. One al-

---

9. Barthélemy-Charles-Pierre-Joseph Dunoyer (1786–1862), French economist.
10. Claude Adrien Helvétius (1715–1771), French philosopher.
11. In the National Assembly session of July 31, 1848, Proudhon attacked the violence used against the insurrectionists of June 1848.
12. Louis Adolphe Thiers (1797–1877), French historian and statesman.

ready finds this fantasy, padded out further, among the economic spokesmen of the English petit bourgeoisie in the seventeenth century. Proudhon's polemic with Bastiat[13] (1850) about interest-bearing capital is on a far lower level than the *Philosophy of Poverty*. He manages to get himself beaten even by Bastiat and breaks into burlesque rumbling when his opponent drives his blows home.

A few years ago, Proudhon—induced I believe by the Lausanne government—wrote a prize essay on *Taxation*. Here the last vestige of genius is extinguished. Nothing remains but the *petit bourgeois tout pur* [petit bourgeois pure and simple].

In regard to Proudhon's political and philosophical writings, they all show the same contradictory, dual character as his economic works. In addition, they have only a local-French value. Nevertheless, his attacks on religion, the church, etc., were of great merit locally at a time when the French socialists thought it desirable to show by their religiosity how superior they were to the bourgeois Voltaireanism of the eighteenth century and the German atheism of the nineteenth. Just as Peter the Great defeated Russian barbarism with barbarism, so also Proudhon did his best to defeat French phrase-mongering with phrases.

His work on the coup d'état,[14] in which he flirts with Louis Bonaparte and, in fact, strives to make him palatable to the French workers, and his last work, written against Poland,[15] in which to the greater glory of the Czar he expresses cretinous cynicism, must be characterized as not only bad but also base productions, the baseness of which, however, corresponds to the petit bourgeois point of view.

Proudhon has often been compared with Rousseau. Nothing could be more false. He is, rather, like Nicolas Linguet,[16] whose *Theory of Civil Law*, by the way, is a very brilliant book.

Proudhon had a natural inclination for dialectics. But as he never grasped the really scientific dialectics, he never got further than sophistry. In fact, this hung together with his petit-bourgeois viewpoint. The petit bourgeois is, like the historian Raumer,[17] composed of On the One Hand and On the Other Hand. This is so in his economic interests and hence also in his politics, in his religious, scientific and artistic views. It is so in his morals, so in everything. He is a living contradiction. If, like Proudhon, the bourgeois is

---

13. Frédéric Bastiat (1801–1850), French economist.

14. Proudhon, *La révolution sociale démontrée par le coup d'état du 2 décembre* [*The Social Revolution as Demonstrated by the Coup d'État of December 2d*] (Paris, 1852).

15. Proudhon, *Si les traités de 1815 ont cessé d'exister?* [*Did the Treaties of 1815 Cease to Exist?*] (Paris, 1863).

16. Simon-Nicolas-Henri Linguet, *Théories des lois civiles, ou principes fondamentaux de la société* [*Theories of Civil Law, or Fundamental Principles of Society*], 2 vols. (London, 1767).

17. Friedrich von Raumer (1781–1873), German historian.

in addition a gifted man, he will soon learn to play with his own contradictions and develop them according to circumstances into striking, ostentatious, occasionally scandalous and occasionally brilliant paradoxes. Charlatanism in science and accommodation in politics are inseparable from such a point of view. There remains only one governing motive, the vanity of the subject, and the only question for him, as for all vain people, is the success of the moment, the attention of the day. Thus the simple moral sense, which always kept a Rousseau, for example, far from even the semblance of compromise with the powers that be, is necessarily extinguished.

Perhaps future generations will characterize the latest phase of Frenchism by saying that Louis Bonaparte was its Napoleon and Proudhon its Rousseau-Voltaire.

And now you must take upon yourself the responsibility of having imposed upon me the role of this man's judge so soon after his death.

Yours very respectfully, Karl Marx

130

From letter to Frederick Engels (in Manchester)
London, May 1, 1865

Dear Fred:
You must excuse me for not having written until today and thus breaking my *last promise* [in English]. This happened, not because it is "too sweet to break one's word," but because I am in reality *overworked* [in English], trying to finish my work[1] on the one hand, and having my time extraordinarily taken up by the "International Association."[2]

Today is Jennychen's[3] birthday, and this evening I will have in the house Ernest Jones, together with Odger,[4] Cremer,[5] Fox,[6] and Jung,[7] so that the birthday will be celebrated politically. Laura[8] had "*the question popped*" [in English] by a certain Charles Manning, born South American, father Englishman, mother Spaniard. He is rich and otherwise a decent fellow, but Laura "*does not care a pin for him*" [in English]. The southern passion "*she has*

130

1. *Das Kapital*.
2. First International.
3. Daughter Jenny Marx.
4. George Odger (1820–1877), member of First International.
5. William Randall Cremer (1838–1908), member of First International.
6. Peter Fox André (d. 1869), member of First International.
7. Hermann Jung (1830–1901), German watchmaker and member of First International.
8. Laura Marx.

already known how to damp" [in English]. But since my girl is a friend of his sisters, and he is frightfully *in love* [in English], it is a *disagreeable case* [in English]. . . .

The *chivalry of the South* [in English] ends suitably. In this, the *assassination* [in English] of Lincoln was the biggest stupidity it could commit. Johnson[9] is *stern, inflexible, revengeful* [in English] and as a once *poor white* [in English] he has a deadly hatred for the oligarchy. . . .

Salut.

Yours, K.M.

131

From letter to Frederick Engels (in Manchester)
London, July 31, 1865

Dear Engels:
My prolonged silence is not due, as you may perhaps have imagined, to the most pleasant causes.

For two months now I have lived entirely on the pawnshop and have been exposed daily to piled-up and increasingly unbearable stormy demands. This fact will not surprise you when you realize that: (1) throughout this whole period I have been unable to earn a *farthing* [in English], and (2) that the mere paying off of my debts and the furnishing of the house cost me about £500. I have kept a record, *pence* [in English] for *pence* [in English] (*as to this time* [in English]), because it was incredible to me too how the money disappeared. In addition, all kinds of antediluvian demands were made on me from Germany, where they spread God knows what news about me.

At first I wanted to visit you in order to discuss the matter personally. But at this moment every bit of lost time is irreplaceable, since I cannot very well interrupt my work. Last Saturday I announced my resignation from the subcommittee of the [First] International so that at least I would have free time every fourteen days and be in a position for *pushing on* [in English] my work[1] undisturbed.

I assure you I would rather have cut off my thumb than to write you this letter. It is truly shattering to have remained dependent half of one's life. The only thought that keeps me going is that we two are running a joint-partnership, to which I contribute my time for theoretical and party *business*

---

9. Andrew Johnson.

131

1. Marx was then at work on *Das Kapital* which, however, he did not complete for nearly another two years.

[in English]. I do, indeed, live too expensively for my conditions, and, furthermore, this year I have lived better than usual. But it is the only means whereby the children, apart from the fact that they have suffered so much and for which they have been compensated for at least a short period, can maintain contacts and relationships to assure their future. I believe that you yourself will agree that, even from a mere business point of view, a purely proletarian household establishment, while quite acceptable to me and my wife or even the girls when they were young, would be unbecoming now.

Now in regard to my work, I will tell you the undiluted truth.[2] There are still three chapters to be written in order to complete the theoretical part (the first three books). Then there is still the fourth book, the historical-literary one, to write, which is for me relatively the easiest part, since all the problems have been solved in the first three books, and this last one, there-fore, is more of a repetition in historical form. But I cannot bring myself to send off anything until I have the whole before me. Whatever shortcomings they may have, the merit of my writings is that they are an artistic whole, and that can only be attained by my method of not having them printed until they lie before me in their *entirety*. This is impossible with the Jacob Grimm method,[3] which is in general more suited for writings that are not dialec-tically constructed. . . .

As a result of the hot weather and the spleen conditions connected with it, I have been vomiting almost daily for the last three months, as previously in Brussels.

Salut.

Yours, K.M.

132

From letter to Frederick Engels (in Manchester)
London, August 9, 1865

Dear Fred:
. . . Edgar[1] is vegetating. In his life as a hermit, he had become accustomed to the narrowest sort of egoism, thinking of the needs of the stomach from morning till night. Since he is naturally good-hearted, his egoism is that of a *kind-natured cat* [in English] or well-meaning dog. The devil take the her-

---

2. Marx used the expression: *"reinen Wein einschenken"* [serve you pure wine].
3. The brothers Jacob and Wilhelm Grimm published their classic *German Dictionary* in separate installments; the first volume, "A," appeared in 1852.

132
1. Edgar von Westphalen.

mitage. He even got disused to women, and the sexual drive has gone to his stomach. In addition, there is the constant anxiety for his precious health—the same lad who used to feel "himself safe" among snakes, tigers, wolves, and leopards.[2]

He now wants to return to Texas again.[3] But he will not be able to avoid the confrontation with the *cher frère*.[4]

You can judge his primitive notions from the fact that the opening of a *store* [in English]—a cigar- or *wine-store* [in English]—is now his ideal, with the obviously cunning intention of making sure of having cigars and wine for himself.

He loves to "strike the pose" of an *old gentleman* [in English] who had settled accounts with life, has nothing to do any more, and only lives "for his health."

In addition, he occupies himself with his *toilette*, and the *"old gentlemen"* [in English] in Rotten Row cause him great sorrow, because he is unable to imitate them. A curious owl! Laura,[5] who has a small *carbuncle* [in English] on her cheek *just now, says that "her mother's brother is an exceedingly bright fellah,"* Tussy,[6] *that "she likes him, because he is so funny,"* and Jennychen,[7] *that Lina Schöler[8] and he should mutually congratulate themselves "to have safely got rid of each other."* Well, *they are a bad lot.* The girls have also *severely crossexamined me as to the "Mrs. Burns"* [in English].[9]

Salut.

Yours, K.M.

133

From letter to Frederick Engels (in Manchester)
London, August 19, 1865

Dear Fred:

Since you are going on a trip, I *must* report to you that on August 28 I have to pay a *bill* [in English] to the *butcher* [in English] of £10 and that the *landlord* [in English] is also becoming very *troublesome* [in English]. *By the by* [in English],

---

2. Edgar had once roughed it as a cowboy in Texas.
3. Marx could hardly wait to see his brother-in-law depart, as he wrote to Engels, July 31, 1865: "Edgar is just now a very expensive guest for us and in no way seems inclined to decamp."
4. Ferdinand von Westphalen, who was the half-brother of Jenny Marx and Edgar.
5. Laura Marx.
6. Eleanor Marx.
7. Jenny Marx (daughter).
8. Lina Schöler had once been engaged to Edgar von Westphalen.
9. "Mrs. Burns" was Lydia (Lizzy) Burns, Engels' mistress whom he married just before her death in 1878.

the English government seems *hardpressed for money* [in English]. This *month* [in English] at least the *taxgatherers* [in English] were more pressing than ever and have "relieved" me unexpectedly.

I am still *sick* [in English], even though [Dr.] Allen has cured the *liver* [in English] trouble. But now came a kind of influenza, which he promises would be over in five or six days, but is in reality most troublesome, *as far as mental activity is concerned* [in English]. I hope that with this, I will have paid *my debt to nature* [in English].

Laurachen[1] is also not quite well. For a year now she has been much thinner than she should be. But she is an independent child, and only today did she decide to go to the doctor with my wife. *I hope it is nothing serious* [in English]. Jennychen[2] and Tussy[3] are very well. (Ditto Edgar,[4] whose *state of health* [in English] has very much improved.) My wife broke two front teeth in the lower jawbone and yesterday she had them replaced with four [*sic*] others. These are approximately the only "events" that have occurred in our house. house.

In my state of ill health, I can do little writing, and then only *by fits and starts* [in English]. In the meanwhile I fool around, although even reading is not compatible with influenza. "On occasion," I again "pursued" a little astronomy, among other things. And here I want to mention something that was new, at least to me, but has probably been known to you for some time. You know Laplace's[5] theory of creation of *the Celestial System* [in English] and how he explains the *rotation* [in English] of the various bodies around each other. Starting from there, a Yankee, Kirkwood,[6] discovered a kind of law on the *difference* in the *rotation* [in English] of the planets, which had hitherto seemed abnormal. The law is this: "The *square of the number of times* that each planet rotates during one revolution in its orbit, is proportioned to the *cube of the breadth of a diameter of its sphere of attraction*" [in English].

Specifically, between the two planets there is a point where their force of attraction is in equilibrium; hence a body remains motionless at this point. On the other hand, on each side of this point, a body will fall to one or the other planet. This point, therefore, forms the limit for the *sphere of attraction* [in English] of the planet. This *sphere of attraction* [in English] again is the

---

133
1. Daughter Laura.
2. Daughter Jenny.
3. Daughter Eleanor.
4. Edgar von Westphalen.
5. Pierre Simon de Laplace, *Exposition du Systéme du Monde* [*Exposition of the Celestial System*], 2 vols. (Paris, 1795–1796).
6. Daniel Kirkwood (1814–1895), professor of astronomy at Indiana and Stanford Universities.

measure of the width of the *gazeous ring* [in English], from which, according to Laplace, the planet was formed at the time of its *first separation from the general gazeous mass* [in English]. Therefrom Kirkwood concluded that, if Laplace's hypothesis was correct, there must exist a definite relation between the *velocity of the planet's rotation* [in English] and the *breadth of the ring* [in English] from which it was formed, or its *sphere of attraction*. And this he has expressed in the above law, based on analytical calculations.

Old Hegel made some very good jokes about the "sudden change" that took place in the centripetal and centrifugal force precisely at the moment when one achieves preponderance over the other. For example, the centripetal force is greatest near the sun; *thus*, says Hegel, the centrifugal force is the greatest, since it overcomes the *maximum of centripetal* force, and *vice versa* [in English]. Moreover, the forces are in *equilibrium* in the middle distance of the apsises. *Hence* they can *never again* get out of this equilibrium, etc. For the rest, in his polemic,[7] Hegel concludes that Newton,[8] with his "proofs," added nothing to Kepler,[9] who had the "conception" of movement—something that is now pretty universally recognized....

Yours, K.M.

Regards for Mrs. Lizzy.[10] The children expect that upon your return [from the Continent] you will not bypass London.

134

To Frederick Engels (in Manchester)
London, November 8, 1865

Dear Frederick:
I arrived here Friday evening.[1] Strohn[2] had urged me to stay with him for a few days, but I had no peace of mind. I knew that the affairs in London were on a slope and I wanted to be on the spot.

---

7. George Wilhelm Friedrich Hegel, *Vorlesungen über die Naturphilosophie als der Encyclopädie der philosophischen Wissenschaften im Grundrisse* [*Lectures on Natural Philosophy as the Encyclopedia of Philosophic Sciences in Outline*], ed. by C. L. Michelet, in Hegel's *Werke*, volume VII, Part I (Berlin, 1847).
8. Sir Isaac Newton.
9. Johannes Kepler (1571–1630), German astronomer and mathematician.
10. Lydia Burns (Mary Burns' sister), who lived with Engels.

134

1. November 3. Marx was with Engels in Manchester from October 20 to November 2, 1865.
2. Wilhelm Strohn, a German communist in Bradford.

There was no lack of *disappointments* [in English] that Mrs. Lizzy[3] had prophesied for me. *D'abord* [To begin with], at my arrival at King's Cross I found my coffer missing, and until this moment it has not yet been found, which is unfortunate as it contained "papers" for which I am responsible. In addition, I found the child[4] still unwell. Finally, the *landlord* [in English] was there, threatening, and my wife could appease him only with the *promise of my return*. The fellow threatened to put a *"broker"* [in English] into the house and suspend the *lease* [in English], which, of course, he has a legal right to do. After the *landlord* [in English], there came the rest of the rabble, some in person and some by sending threatening letters. I found my wife so *desolate* [in English] that I did not have the courage to explain to her the *true state of things* [in English]. And in fact I *do not know what to do!* Also, coal, etc., must be obtained for the house.

Alongside these *disappointments, one good news* [in English]. One of my two aunts in Frankfurt (the seventy-three year old one, the other one is two years younger[5]) has passed away, but *ab intestato* [intestate] (because she feared that she would die if she made a will). I have, therefore, to share the inheritance with the other heirs, which would not have been the case if there had been a will, as she did not care for the others. Added to that, the pleasant [*sic*] circumstances that one must wait for Herr Juta's power-of-attorney from Cape of Good Hope.[6]

All these pleasant conditions have to some extent affected my stomach, so that I immediately renewed Gumpert's medical prescription.

Salut (also to Mrs. Lizzy).

Yours, K.M.

135

From letter to Frederick Engels (in Manchester)
London, February 10, 1866

Dear Fritz:
This time my life was in danger. My family did not know how *serious* [in English] the *cas* [case] was. If the thing recurs three or four more times in the same form, I am a dead man. I have lost much weight and am still damned weak, not in the head but in the hips and legs. The doctor is quite right: the

---

3. Lydia Burns, who lived with Engels.
4. Ten-year-old daughter Eleanor (Tussy).
5. Esther Kosel, sister of Marx's father who was actually seventy-nine years old, and Babette Blum, actually five years younger than Esther.
6. The whole inheritance from Marx's Aunt Esther, which he finally received in the summer of 1866, amounted to only £80. See Letter 150, Marx to Engels, November 8, 1866.

excessive nightwork was the main cause of the relapse. But I cannot tell the gentleman the reasons that *force* me to this extravagance—and it would be entirely purposeless to do so. At present I have all kinds of after growths on the body; they are painful, but in no way dangerous.

The most disgusting thing for me was the interruption of my work,[1] which had proceeded splendidly since January, when my liver illness went away. Of course, there was no question about my "sitting." It still inconveniences me now. But I have drudged on, lying down, even if only at short intervals during the day. I could not proceed with the purely theoretical part. The brain was too weak for that. Hence I have enlarged the historical part on the "work day," which lay outside the original plan. This "insert" of mine now forms the supplement (sketch) to your book[2] up to the year 1865 (which I also mention in a Note[3]), and the complete vindication of your evaluation of the future and present reality. As soon as my book appears, the second edition of your book is, therefore, necessary and at the same time easy. The necessary theoretical part I will supply. As regards further historical additions, which you must give in your book as an *Appendix* [in English], all material is pure trash and scientifically inapplicable, except for the *Factory Reports*, the *Children's Employment Commission Reports*, and the *Board of Health Reports*.[3] With your energy, which is not undermined by carbuncles, you can easily master these materials in three months....

Your wine does wonders for me. During the height of my sickness, I had to buy poor port wine, as the latter is the only wine fit for an acute carbuncle condition....

Salut.

Yours, Mohr[4]

136

From letter to Frederick Engels (in Manchester)
London, February 13, 1866

Dear Fred:

... Yesterday I lay fallow again, since a wicked dog of a carbuncle broke out on the left loin. If I had enough money, that is more $>$-$\bigcirc$ for my family,

---

135

1. On *Das Kapital*.
2. Engels, *Die Lage der arbeitenden Klasse in England* [*The Condition of the Working Class in England*], (Leipzig, 1845).
3. *Das Kapital*, vol. I, chapter VIII, footnote 48.
4. "Mohr" (German for "Moor") was Marx's nickname, used by him and by his family and friends.

and if my book[1] were ready, it would be for me a matter of the greatest indifference if today or tomorrow I were thrown to the place of execution, alias croaked. Under the said circumstances, however, it cannot be done yet.

As to this "damn" book, the position is as follows: It was ready at the end of December. According to the present arrangement, the discussion of the ground rent alone, the chapter before the last, constitutes nearly a whole book. I went to the [British] Museum in the daytime and wrote nights. I had to wade through the new agricultural chemistry in Germany, especially Liebig[2] and Schönbein,[3] who are more important in this matter than all the economists put together, and also the enormous amount of material that the French have produced since I last occupied myself with this point. I completed my theoretical investigation of ground rent two years ago. And just in that interval a lot has been done, entirely confirming my theory, moreover. The opening of Japan (generally, if not obliged professionally to do so, I never read travel descriptions) was also important here. Hence the "shifting system," which the English factory dogs used to apply to the *same* person in 1848–50, has been applied to me by myself.

Although finished, the manuscript, gigantic in its present form, could not be made ready for publication by anybody but me, not even by you.

I began the copying and *styling* precisely on January 1, and the thing proceeded very smartly, as I naturally enjoyed licking the child clean after so many birth pangs. But then the carbuncle interfered again, so that up to now I could not go any further except only to fill out what was already finished according to the plan.

For the rest, I agree with your view and will take the first volume, as soon as it is ready, to Meissner.[4] But to finish it I must at least be able to *sit....*

Salut.

Yours, K.M.

137

To Frederick Engels (in Manchester)
London, February 20, 1866

Dear Fred:
You can imagine how opportunely the £10 came. I had received two threatening notices—£6/9 pence for swinish municipal *taxes* [in English], and 1

136

1. *Das Kapital.*
2. Justus von Liebig (1803–1873), German pioneering agricultural chemist.
3. Christian Friedrich Schönbein (1799–1868), a German chemist.
4. Otto Meissner (1819–1902), the Hamburg publisher of *Das Kapital.*

shilling/16 pence for the *Queen's Taxes* [in English]. And they were due on Friday.[1]

In regard to the carbuncles, the situation is this:

The one at the *top*, as I wrote you from my long experience, would have to be *cut*. Today (Tuesday), after receipt of your letter, I took a sharp razor, *relict of dear Lupus* [in English], and *cut the dog in its own body*. (I can't bear doctors between or near my sexual organs. For the rest, [Dr.] Allen gave me the testimony that I am one of the best subjects to be operated upon. I always recognize *necessity*.) The *sang brulé* [putrid blood], *as Mrs. Lormier[2] says* [in English], gushed, or rather spouted up high, and now I consider this carbuncle as buried, although *it still wants some nursing* [in English].

In regard to the *bottom* dog, it is malevolent and beyond my control, and has not let me sleep the whole night. If this swinishness continues, I must, of course, have Allen come, since, considering the locus of the dog, I am unable *to watch and cure* [in English] it myself. For the rest, it is clear that, *on the whole* [in English], I know more about the carbuncle disease than most doctors.

I am still of the same opinion that I *indicated* to Gumpert during my last *stay* [in English] in Manchester; that is, that the itching and scratching between the testicles and the posterior for the last two and a half years, and the resulting *peeling of the skin*, have irritated my body more than anything else. The thing began half a year ago with the first monster-carbuncle which I had on my back, and has continued *until now*.

Dear *boy* [in English], under all these circumstances one feels *more than ever* the good fortune of the kind of friendship that exists between us. For your part, you know that for me *no* relationship stands as high as this one.

Tomorrow I will send you the Zaches[3] and the *Factory Reports*. You understand, *my dear fellow* [in English], that in a work like mine, some *shortcomings* [in English] in detail must exist. But the *composition*, the connection, is such a triumph of German science that an individual German can admit that it is *in no way* [in English] HIS merit but rather that of the *nation*. This is the more gratifying, as it is otherwise the *silliest nation* [in English] under the sun!

The fact that Liebig had "denounced" and that gave Schönbein the reason for his investigations was this:

The *upper* strata of the soil always contain more ammonia than the *deeper* ones, so that because of plant cultivation they become poorer and retain less

---

137

1. February 23.
2. Marie Lormier, a Marx family acquaintance.
3. *Klein-Zaches*, a fairy tale by Ernst Theodor Amadeus Hofmann.

ammonia. This *fact* had been known to all chemists. Only the cause was *unknown*.

To date, decomposition was considered the only source of ammonia. All chemists (also Liebig) denied that nitrogen in the air could serve plants as nourishment.

Schönbein (through experiments) proved that every flame that burns in the air produces a certain amount of nitrogen in the air in the form of nitrous ammonia, that every process of decomposition is a source of nitrous ammonia as well as ammonia, that the evaporation of water is a means of bringing about plant nourishments.

Finally, here is Liebig's "jubilation" over this discovery:

"Through the burning of one pound of bituminous coal or wood the air receives back not only the elements for the reproduction of this pound of wood or, under conditions, coal, but also the process of burning transforms *in itself* (note the Hegelian category) a certain amount of nitrogen in the air into the production of indispensable nourishment for bread and meat."[4]

I feel proud of the Germans. It is our duty to emancipate this "deep" people [in English].

Yours, K.M.

138

To Antoinette [Nannette] Philips (in Zalt-Bommel) [in English]
Margate, March 18, 1866

My dear child:
From the address[1] you will see that I have been banished, by my medical adviser, to this seaside place, which, at this time of the year, is quite solitary. Margate lives only upon the Londoners, who regularly inundate it at the bathing season. During the other months it vegetates only. For my own part right glad I am to have got rid of all company, even that of my books. I have taken a private lodging which fronts the sea. In an inn or hotel one might have been exposed to the danger of falling in with a stray traveller, or being pestered by local politics, vestry interests, and neighbourly gossip. As it is, "I care for nobody and nobody cares for me." But the air is wonderfully pure and reinvigorating, and you have here at the same time sea air and mountain

---

4. Justus von Liebig, *Die Chemie in ihrer Anwendung auf Agricultur und Physiologie* [*Chemistry in Its Application to Agriculture and Physiology*] (Brunswick, 1862).

138

1. No. 5, Lansell's Place, Margate, where the ailing Marx spent from March 14 to the middle of April.

air. I have become myself a sort of walking stick, running up and down the whole day, and keeping my mind in that state of nothingness which Buddhism considers the climax of human bliss. Of course, you have not forgotten the pretty little diction: "When the devil was sick, the devil a monk would be; when the devil was well, the devil a monk was he."

Withdrawing a little from the seaside, and roaming over the adjacent agricultural districts, you are painfully reminded of "civilization," because from all sides you are startled by large boards, with governmental proclamations on them, headed: *Cattle disease.* The ruling English oligarchs were never suspected to care one farthing for "*der Menschheit ganzes Weh*" [the suffering of humanity], but as to cows and oxen, they feel deeply. At the opening of Parliament, the horned cattle gentlemen of both houses, commoners and lords, made a wild rush at government. All their talk sounded like a herd of cows' lowing, translated into English. And they were not like honest king Wiswamitra, "*der kämpfte und büsste für die Kuh Sabalah.*"[2] On the contrary. They seized the opportunity to "*battre monnaie*" [strike coins] out of the cows' ailings at the expense of the people. By the by, the East sends us always nice things—Religion, Etiquette, and the Plague in all forms.

I am very glad to hear of *Warratjes*' [the same as *Waradje*: a reference to A. Roodhuizen, whom Nannette married] winding up adventure. Verily, verily, I tell thee, my sweet little cousin, I always felt deep sympathy for the man, and always hoped that one day or other he should fix his melting heart in the right direction, and not persevere performing the nasty part in the children's tale: "The Beast and the Beauty."[3] I'm sure he will make a good husband. Is his inamorata a "Bommelerin" or an importation?

A few days before leaving London, I made the acquaintance of Mr. [Cesare] Orsini, a very fine fellow, the brother of the Orsini who was sent to the grave for sending Bonaparte to Italy.[4] He has now left England for the U. States, in commercial matters, but during the few days of our acquaintance, he did me good service. Although an intimate friend of Mazzini's,[5] he is far from sharing the antiquated antisocialist and theocratical views of Mazzini. Now, during my forced and prolonged absence from the Council of the International Association, Mazzini had been busy in stirring a sort of revolt against my leadership. "Leadership" is never a pleasant thing, nor a thing I ambition. I have always before my mind your father's saying in regard to Thorbecke[6] that "*der Eselstreiber den Eseln immer verhasst ist*" ["the donkey

---

2. "Who fought and expiated for the cow Cabalah," an episode from the Ramayana, cited from Heinrich Heine's "*Die Heimkehr*," in his *Buch der Lieder*.
3. "*La Belle et la Bête*," a French fable by Jeanne-Marie Le Prince Beaumont.
4. Felice Orsini, born 1819, an Italian republican, was executed in 1858 for attempting to assassinate Napoleon III. Cesare, his brother, was an emigré in London.
5. Giuseppe Mazzini (1805–1872), Italian nationalist statesman.
6. Johan Rudolph Thorbecke (1798–1872), a Liberal Dutch statesman, was Prime Minister on three different occasions.

driver is always hated by the donkeys"]. But having once fairly embarked in an enterprise which I consider of import, I certainly, "anxious" man as I am, do not like to give way. Mazzini, a most decided hater of freethinking and socialism, watched the progress of our society with great jealousy. His first attempt of making a tool of it and fastening upon it a programme and declaration of principles of his hatching, I had baffled. His influence, before that time very great with the London working class, had sunk to zero. He waxed wroth, when he saw that we had founded the English *Reform League* [in 1865] and a weekly paper, *The Commonwealth* [which appeared in London in 1865–66], to which the most advanced men of London contribute, and of which I shall send you a copy after my return to London. His anger increased, when the editor of the *Rive Gauche* (the journal of the *jeune* [young] France, directed by Rogeard,[7] author of the [pamphlet] "*Propos de Labienus*" ["The Purpose of Labienus"], Longuet,[8] etc.) joined us, and when he became aware of the spread of our society on the Continent. He improved [used] my absence, to intrigue with some English workingmen, raise their jealousies against "German" influence, and even sent his bully, a certain Major Wolff (a German by birth)[9] to the Council there to lodge his complaints and more or less directly to denounce me. He wanted to be acknowledged as "the leader (I suppose *par la grace de Dieu* [by the grace of God]) of the continental democratical movement." In so doing, he acted so far quite sincerely, as he utterly abhors my principles which, in his eyes, embody the most damnable "materialism." This whole scene was enacted behind my back, and after they had made sure that my malady would not allow me to be present. The English wavered, but, although still very weak, I rushed to the following séance, Mr. Orsini accompanying me. On my interpellation, he declared then that Mazzini had lost his influence even in Italy and was, from his antecedents and prejudices, quite disabled from understanding the new movement. All the foreign secretaries declared for me, and, if you, our Dutch secretary [of the International], had been present, I hope you would have also cast your vote for your humble servant and admirer. As it was, I carried a complete victory over this redoubtable adversary. I think that Mazzini has now had enough of me and will make *bonne mine à mauvais jeu* [the best of a bad situation]. I hope to receive a few lines from you. Don't forget that I am quite an insulated hermit.

Your most sincere friend, Bloch[10]

---

7. Louis-Auguste Rogeard (1820–1896), French radical journalist.
8. Charles Longuet (1839–1903), French socialist journalist, married Marx's daughter Jenny in 1872.
9. Luigi Wolff, a member of the International in London, later (in 1871) exposed as a Bonapartist police spy.
10. Probably a Marx alias, to remain anonymous in Margate.

139

To Laura Marx (in London) [in English]
Margate, March 20, 1866

My dear Cacadou:

Very good news indeed! I prefer Mrs. Grach to the mother of all the Gracchi.[1] I am right glad that I have taken my lodgings in a private House, and not in an Inn or Hotel where one could hardly escape being pestered with local politics, vestry scandals, and neighbourly gossip. But still I cannot sing with the miller of the Dee,[2] that I care for nobody and nobody cares for me. For there is my landlady, who is deaf like a post, and her daughter, who is afflicted with chronic hoarseness, but they are very nice people, attentive, and not intruding. As to myself, I have turned into a perambulating stick, running about the greatest part of the day, airing myself, going to bed at ten o'clock, reading nothing, writing less, and altogether working up my mind to that state of nothingness which Buddhism considers the element of human bliss.

However, with all that, I shall not turn out, on Thursday [March 22], that paragon of beauty which the worthy By Bye,[3] in her fantastic mood, seems to expect. The toothache on the right side of the face has not yet altogether disappeared, and the same side is afflicted with an inflammation of the eye. Not that there is much to be seen of it, but that eye has taken to the vicious habit of shedding tears on its own account, without the least regard to the feelings of his master. But for this state of things, I should have my photograph already taken, since you get here 12 cartes de visite for 3. dd. and 48 cartes for 10 sh. Mummelchen[4] will oblige me by pacing her steps to Mr. Hall and ordering him to prepare a solution of zinc (he will know the composition of the drug) for my eye which I expect to find ready on my arrival at London. This bad eye interferes with my nightrest. Otherwise, I am turning a new leaf.

Away somewhat from the seaside, and roaming over the adjacent rustic district, you are painfully reminded of "civilization" by large boards, staring at you everywhere, headed "Cattle Disease," and placarded over with a government proclamation, the result of the wild rush which the horned cattle gentry, lords and commoners, made at the government, on the opening of Parliament.

139

1. Frau Grach, the widow of a bankrupt Trier banker with whom Mrs. Marx had deposited 1300 taler in 1855, promised to make good the loss.
2. "The Miller of the Dee," an English folksong.
3. Nickname for Marx's daughter Jenny.
4. Mrs. Marx.

Oh, oh King Wiswamitra
What fool an oxen art thou,
That thou so much wrangl'st and suffer'st
And all that for a cow.[5]

But if honest Wiswamitra, like a true Indian, tormented himself for the salvation of the cow Cabala, those English gentry, in the true style of modern martyrs, bleed the people to compensate themselves for their cows' ailings. The horn plague upon them! The horn, the horn, as discreet By Bye rings it lustily.

On Sunday, I made up my mind to walk *per pedes* [on foot] to Canterbury. Unhappily, I only formed this grand resolution, after having already measured for two hours the length and breadth of the piers and so forth. So I had already expended too much physical power, when I set out for the archbishop's seat or see, as you like. And from here to Canterbury are fully sixteen miles. From Canterbury I returned to Margate by rail, but I had overworked myself, and could not sleep during the whole night. Limbs and loins were not tired, but the plants of my feet turned out tenderhearted rogues. As to Canterbury, you know, of course, all about it, and more than I can boast, from your Eves,[6] the trusted source of knowledge of all English Eves. (One cannot help, in your company, bad punning. But mark, Thackeray did worse, by playing upon Eves and Ewes.) Happily, I was too tired, and it was too late, to look out for the celebrated cathedral. Canterbury is an old, ugly, medieval sort of town, not mended by large modern English barracks at the one, and a dismal dry Railway Station at the other end of the oldish thing. There is no trace of that poetry about it, which you find in continental towns of the same age. The swaggering of the private soldiers and the officers in the streets, reminded me somewhat of "*Vaterland.*" In the inn, where I was scantily purveyed with some slices of cold beef, I caught the newest scandal. Captain Le Merchant, it seems, had been taken up by the police on Saturday night, for systematically knocking at the doors of all the most respectable citizens. And a summons will be taken out against the Captain because of this innocent pastime. And the redoubtable Captain will have to bend down his diminished head before aldermanic majesty. This is my whole packet of "Canterbury Tales."

And now, Cacadou, pay my compliments to Elly[7] to whom I shall write one of these days, and whose little letter was very welcome. As to Möhmchen,[8] she will hear of me by the by.

That damned boy Lafargue[9] pesters me with his Proudhonism, and will

---

5. From Heinrich Heine's "*Die Heimkehr,*" in *Buch der Lieder*.
6. Charles Eves, an English textbook writer.
7. Marx's youngest daughter Eleanor.
8. Mrs. Marx.
9. Paul Lafargue (1842–1911), who became engaged to Laura on August 6, 1866, and whom he married on April 2, 1868.

not rest, it seems, until I have administered to him a sound cudgeling of his Creole pate.

My good wishes to all.

Your Master

Has Orsini yet received the letter I sent him?

140

From letter to Frederick Engels (in Manchester)
Margate, March 24, 1866

Dear Fred:
From the delayed appearance of this letter you can see how "professionally" I use my time here.[1] I read nothing, write nothing. If only for the three-times daily arsenic,[2] one has so to arrange the time for meals and the strolling along the coast and the neighboring *hills* [in English] that there is "no time" left for other things. And evenings one is too tired to do anything but sleep. The weather is in general somewhat raw, and specifically a *somewhat chilling* [in English] wind often blows from the east, but one soon gets used to it. How well I have recovered, you can see from the fact that last Sunday I made Canterbury (seventeen miles from here) *per pedes* [on foot] in less than four hours. As for social life here, it does not exist, of course. I can sing with the *miller of the Dee: "I care for nobody and nobody cares for me"* [in English].

The day before yesterday, in the evening, I had to go to London, in order to participate in my daughters' "social." For Christmas, my uncle[3] had sent them £5 which, however, was "borrowed" from them for *general purposes* [in English] and which they received back as soon as your money arrived. With their money, they arranged their yearly *"party"* [in English] and bombarded me so with letters that I "made it" to London, as Herr Nothjung[4] used to say. But I returned the next morning (that is, yesterday) to my hermitage. . . .

Before I came back here, I paid, of course, the most urgent house debts, otherwise I would not have had a peaceful hour. If at the end of the month you could send me a little something, I would appreciate it. In the meantime,

---

140

1. Marx was on a cure in Margate from March 15 to April 10, 1866.
2. Used for carbuncle treatment.
3. Lion Philips.
4. Peter Nothjung (1821–1866), a Cologne communist.

the power of attorney should finally arrive from the Cape[5] and, while it may not amount to much, it will still be something for the treasury.

My compliments to Mrs. Lizzy[6] [in English].

Yours, K.M.

141

Postscript to letter to Frederick Engels (in Manchester)
London, July 7, 1866

Bonaparte[1] naturally does not want war now, before he introduces the *needle gun* [in English] or its equivalent. A Yankee[2] here has offered to the War Ministry a gun which, as a Prussian *refugee* [in English] officer (Wilke) assures me, in its absolute simplicity of construction, its not heating up, its less need for cleaning, and cheapness, is as superior to the needle gun as the latter is to "Old Bess."[3] Is our theory that the organization of labor is determined by the means of production, confirmed more brilliantly anywhere than in the human slaughter industry? It would be truly worth your while to write something about it (I lack the necessary knowledge) and I could insert it under your name as an *Appendix* [in English] in my book.[4] Think it over. But if it is to be done, it must be done *pour le premier volume* [for the first volume] where I treat the theme *ex professo* [especially]. You will understand what great pleasure it would give me if you were also to appear in my main work (hitherto I have only done small things) as a direct collaborator instead of merely through quotations.

I am now studying Comte[5] as a sideline, because the English and French make such a fuss over the fellow. What they are attracted by is the encyclopedic, *la synthèse*, but this is lamentable compared to Hegel (although Comte, as a professional mathematician and physicist is superior to him, that is, superior in matters of detail, but even here Hegel is infinitely greater as a whole). And this shit-Positivism appeared in 1832!

---

5. From Johann Carel Juta, Marx's brother-in-law, who lived in South Africa.
6. Lydia Burns.

141

1. Napoleon III.
2. Jacob Snider (d. 1866), American inventor.
3. "Old Bess" or "Brown Bess" was the name of the English army's muzzle-loader.
4. *Das Kapital*.
5. Auguste Comte (1798–1857), French mathematician and philosopher, founder of Positivism.

142

To Frederick Engels (in Manchester)
London, August 7, 1866

Dear Fred:

From my last letter you will have rightly recognized that my health has improved, although it vacillates daily. Still the feeling of being able to work again *does much for a man* [in English]. Unfortunately, I am constantly interrupted by *social troubles* [in English] and lose much time. Thus, for example, the butcher has suspended meat delivery, and even my supply of paper will come to an end on Saturday.[1]

Since yesterday, Laura[2] has become engaged to Monsieur Lafargue, my medical Creole.[3] She treated him like the others, but the mood excesses of such Creoles, a little fear that the *jeune homme* [young man] (he is twenty-five years old) would do away with himself, some affection for him, although cool, as is usual with Laura (he is a handsome, intelligent, energetic, and gymnastically developed lad), have resulted more or less in a half compromise. The young man had first attached himself to me, but soon transferred the *attraction* [in English] from the Old Man to the daughter. His economic condition is middling, as he is the only child of a former planter family. He is *rayé de l'université de Paris pour deux ans* [scratched from the university of Paris for two years] on account of the Congress at Liège,[4] but hopes to take his examination at Strassburg. In my judgment, he has an extraordinary talent for medicine, about which, however, he is infinitely more skeptical than our friend Gumpert. Medical skepticism seems to be the order of the day among professors and students in Paris. For example, Magendie[5] declares the old therapeutics in its present *state* [in English] to be charlatanism. As always, such skepticism not only excludes *crotchets* [in English] but also includes them. Lafargue, for example, believes in alcohol and electricity as chief

---

142

1. August 11.
2. Laura Marx, later Laura Lafargue.
3. Paul Lafargue was born in Santiago de Cuba of a partly French father. His paternal grandmother had been a Santo Domingo mulatto, his paternal grandfather French. His maternal grandmother had been a Caribbean Indian. Marx came to refer affectionately to Lafargue, who became his son-in-law, as "Creole," and sometimes as "nigger."
4. An international student congress, held in Liège in October, 1865; among the French delegates, protesting against the régime of Napoleon III, were Paul Lafargue and Charles Longuet, both of whom became Marx's sons-in-law.
5. François Magendie (1783–1855), French physiologist, member of the Academy of Sciences.

remedies. Fortunately, in Professor Carrère,[6] refugee (higher mathematics, physics and chemistry), he has a good adviser and will acquire much practical experience in the London hospitals.

A very important work which I will send you (but on condition that you return it, as it does not belong to me) as soon as I have finished making the necessary notes, is: P. Trémaux, *Origine et Transformations de l'Homme et des autres Êtres*[7] (Paris, 1865). Despite all shortcomings that strike me, it is a very important advance over Darwin. The two main points in it are: the *croisements* [crossbreedings] do not, as is believed, produce a different but, on the contrary, a typical unity of the *espèces* [species]. In contrast, the formation of the earth does *differentiate* (not in itself, but as main basis). Progress, which in Darwin is purely accidental, is here a necessity, on the basis of the periods of development of the earth; *dégénérescence* [degeneration] which Darwin cannot explain, is here simple; ditto the rapid extinction of mere transitional forms, compared with the slowness of the development of *espèces* types, so that gaps in paleontology, which bother Darwin, are here a necessity. Similarly, fixity is developed as a necessary law (apart from individual *variations* [in English], etc.) in the once-constituted *espèce*. The difficulties of hybridation in Darwin are here, on the contrary, supports of the system, as it is demonstrated that in fact an *espèce* is constituted only when *croisement* with another ceases, becomes fruitful or possible, etc.

In its historical and political application, the book is much more important and copious than Darwin. For certain questions, such as nationality, etc., a natural basis is found only in this work. For example, the author corrects the Pole Duchinski,[8] whose findings in regard to the geological differences between Russia and the West Slavs he generally confirms, that, contrary to the Pole's belief, the Russians are not only no Slavs but, rather, Tartars, etc., but also that on the existing soil formation of Russia the Slavs became Tartarized and Mongolized, just as he (he has been in Africa for a long time) proves that the common Negro type is only a degeneration of a much higher one:

"Outside the grand laws of nature, man's plans are mere calamities; this is shown by the efforts of the Czars to make Muscovites out of the Polish people. The same nature, the same abilities, will be reborn on the same soil. The work of destruction cannot last forever, the work of rebuilding is eternal.... The Slavic and Lithuanian races have, *vis-à-vis* the Muscovites, their real limit in the great geologic line which runs north of the Niemen and

---

6. Unidentified.
7. Pierre Trémaux, *Origin and Transformations of Man and Other Beings*.
8. Franciszek Duchinski (1817–1893), Polish historian, living in Paris.

Dnieper basins.... To the south of this great line, the abilities and the types typical of that region are and will always remain different from those of Russia."[9]

Salut.

Yours, K.M.

143

From letter to Paul Lafargue (in London) [in French]
London, August 13, 1866

My dear Lafargue:

Permit me the following observations:

1. If you want to continue contact with my daughter [Laura], you must give up your manner of "paying court" to her. You know well that there is as yet no promise of marriage, that it is still up in the air. And even if you were formally her betrothed, you must not forget that a lengthy business is involved here. The habits of all too intimate relationship are even more inappropriate here in that both lovers will have to live in chastity in the same place for a necessarily prolonged period under strong temptations. In the course of a geologic era of a single week, I have observed with shock the change in your conduct. In my opinion, true love is expressed in reserve, modesty, and even shyness of the lover toward his idol, and never in temperamental excesses or too premature intimacy. When you invoke your Creole temperament, then I consider it my duty to step in between your temperament and my daughter with my healthy common sense. If you are unable to show your love for her in the form consonant with the London latitude, then it is advisable that you love her from a distance. I don't have to elaborate further.

2. Before your relations with Laura are definitely settled, I must be completely clear about your economic circumstances. My daughter believes that I know about your affairs. She is mistaken. I have not talked about these things because it is my opinion that it was your duty to take the initiative. You know that I have sacrificed my whole fortune to the revolutionary struggle. I do not regret it. Quite the contrary. If I had to start my life over again, I would do the same. But I would not marry. Insofar as it is in my power, I want to protect my daughter from the kind of rocks on which her mother's life has been wrecked. Since this affair would never have reached this stage without my inaction (a weakness on my part!) and without the influence that my friendship for you had on my daughter's attitude, a heavy personal responsibility rests upon me. In regard to your present circumstances, the information, which I did not seek but received only accidentally, is not

---

9. Translated from the French (Trémaux, *op. cit.*, pp. 402, 420). For further comments on the subject, see Letter 147, Marx to Engels, October 3, 1866.

reassuring. But let us leave that. As for your general position, I know that you are still a student, that on account of the Liège event[1] your career in France is half wrecked, that you still lack the English language—an indispensable condition for your acclimatization in England—and that your chances are at best altogether problematical. Observation has proved to me that you are not diligent by nature, despite occasional feverish activity and good intentions. Under these circumstances, you are destined to depend upon others to help in your making a common life with my daughter. I know nothing about your family. Even if they live in prosperous circumstances, it does not prove that they are willing to bear sacrifices for you. I do not even know how they feel about your proposed marriage. It is necessary for me, I repeat, to have a positive clarification of all these questions.[2] For the rest, a professed realist like you cannot expect that I should behave like an idealist where the future of my daughter is concerned. A positive person like you, one who wants to abolish poetry, would not want to make poetry at the expense of my child.

3. In order to anticipate every false interpretation of this letter, I call your attention to the fact that—should you feel tempted to enter into the marriage today—you will not succeed. My daughter would refuse. I would protest. You ought to have achieved something in life before you can think of marriage, and this will require a long testing period for you and Laura.

4. I would appreciate it if this letter remained between us. I await your reply.

Entirely yours, Karl Marx

144

To Frederick Engels (in Manchester)
London, August 23, 1866

Dear Fred:

Today, a few words only. The matter with Lafargue[1] is arranged to the extent that the Old Man[2] wrote me from Bordeaux, asking me for the title of *promesso*

143

1. In October, 1865, Lafargue attended an international student congress in Liège, for which he and other students were suspended from French universities.
2. See Letter 144, Marx to Engels, August 23, 1866, on Lafargue's father's acceptance of Laura as Paul's bride.

144

1. Paul Lafargue's engagement to Laura Marx. On August 13, 1866, Marx wrote to Engels: "Today I wrote to Lafargue a long letter in French in which I told him that I must have *renseignements positifs* [positive information] about his economic situation before the matter [with Laura] can continue or develop further."
2. François Lafargue, Paul's father.

sposo [Italian: betrothed] for his son and stating his very favorable economic situation. Apart from that, it is agreed that Lafargue *jeune* [junior] must take his doctoral examination in London and then in Paris before he can think of marrying. *So far the thing is settled* [in English]. But yesterday I informed our Creole that if he cannot calm himself down to English manners, Laura will give him his congé without further ado.[3] This he must fully realize, or nothing will come of the thing. He is an extremely good chap, but an *enfant gaté* [spoiled child] and too much a child of nature.

Laura states that before she becomes engaged formally, she must have your *consent* [in English].

Here and there I have the beginnings of new carbuncles, which keep on disappearing, but they force me to keep my working hours *within limits* [in English].

Best regards for Lizzy.[4]

Salut.

Yours, K.M.

145

From letter to Ludwig Kugelmann (in Hanover)
London, August 23, 1866

My dear friend:
You must be justly indignant at my long silence, despite your many friendly letters.

But you must excuse me on account of the unusual conditions in which I find myself.

As a result of my long illness, my economic position has reached a point of crisis. I have piled up debts which weigh heavily on my mind and make me incapable of doing any work except the one which absorbs me. If I do not succeed in getting a loan of at least 1,000 taler, say at 5 percent, I really can see no way out. And despite the numerous letters of acknowledgment which I receive from Germany, I don't know where to turn. I can only use the help of private friends, not anything public. You will understand that under such circumstances letter writing becomes difficult.

I have not yet been able to restore my old lucrative connections with America.[1] They are so busy with their own movement there that any expenditure on European correspondence is considered *faux frais de production* [superfluous expenses of production]. I could remedy that if I myself emi-

---

3. See Letter 143, Marx to Lafargue, August 13 (not August 22, as Marx states), 1866.
4. Lydia Burns.

145
1. Marx was correspondent of the *New-York Daily Tribune* from 1851 to March, 1862.

grated there. But I consider it my vocation to remain in Europe to complete the work[2] in which I have been engaged for so many years.

As for that work itself, I do not believe that I will be able to bring the manuscript of the first volume (there will be three) to Hamburg before October. I cannot work productively more than a very few hours daily without feeling the effect physically, and out of consideration for my family I must reluctantly observe hygienic limits until I am fully restored to health. Besides that, my work is often interrupted by adverse external circumstances.

Although I am devoting much time to the preparations for the Geneva Congress,[3] I cannot, and do not want to go there, since such a prolonged interruption of my work is not possible. I think that this work which I am doing is much more important for the workingclass than anything I could do personally at a Congress *quelconque* [of any kind]. . . .

Devotedly yours, K. Marx

146

To Laura Marx (in Hastings) [in English]
London, August 28, 1866

My dear Cacadou:
I have received your letter, but not unopened, since it had to pass through the fingered hands of the Emperor.[1]

It was always my opinion that to give the last finishing stroke to your "heducation," some sort of boarding school was still wanted. It will do you a great deal of good.

Il hidalgo della figura trista [sic] [the knight of the sorrowful face][2] left me at the corner of his house. His heart having been considerably shaken before, he seemed to bear his separation *from me* with a rather heroic indifference.

My best wishes to $\pm \infty \mp$.[3]

I enclose £5, the remainder to be sent in the second week.

Yours humbly, Old One

Mama will start upon her own expedition tomorrow or after-tomorrow. A great push was wanted to set her amoving.

---

2. *Das Kapital.*
3. The Congress of the International, September 3–8, 1866. See Saul K. Padover, ed., *Karl Marx on the First International* (New York, 1973).
146
1. Nickname for his daughter Jenny.
2. Paul Lafargue.
3. Daughter Jenny.

147

From letter to Frederick Engels (in Manchester)
London, October 3, 1866

Dear Engels:
... *Ad vocem* [Regarding] Trémaux:[1] Your opinion that "there is nothing to his whole *theory*, since he neither understands geology nor is capable of understanding the most ordinary literary-historical critique,"[2] you can find *almost literally* in Cuvier's *Discours sur les Revolutions du Globe*,[3] wherein he makes fun of the German nature-fantasists about the doctrine of *Variabilité des espèces* [variability of the species], which expressed Darwin's basic idea insofar as they can *prove* it. This, however, did not prevent Cuvier, who was a great geologist and, for a naturalist, also an exceptional literary-historical critic, from being wrong and the people who expressed the new ideas, right. Trémaux's basic idea regarding the *influence of the soil* (although he naturally does not evaluate the historic modifications of this influence, and in these historic modifications I include also the chemical changes of the topsoil through agriculture, etc., and in addition the varied influence that is caused by the various methods of production of such things as coal beds, etc.) is, in my view, an idea that only has to be *expressed* in order to earn for ever a citizen's right in science, and this apart from Trémaux's method of presentation.
  Salut.

Yours, K.M.

148

From letter to Ludwig Kugelmann (in Hanover)
London, October 13, 1866

Dear Friend:
... My economic position has become so bad as a result of my long illness and the many expenses it necessitated that I am faced with a financial crisis in

---

147
1. See Letter 142, Marx to Engels, August 7, 1866.
2. Engels to Marx, October 2, 1866: "I have come to the conclusion that there is nothing to his whole theory even if for no other reason than that he neither understands geology nor is capable of understanding the most ordinary literary-historical critique. His history of the Nigger of Santa Maria and of the transformation of the whites into Negroes is enough to laugh oneself sick. Specifically, that the traditions of the Senegal niggers deserve absolute credibility, *precisely because the fellows cannot write*! It is also cute [on Trémaux's part] to shove the differences between a Basque, a Frenchman, a Breton, and an Alsatian, on the soil formation, which is naturally also responsible for the fact that those people speak four different languages."
3. Georges Cuvier, *Discourse on the Revolutions of the Surface of the Globe* (Paris, 1826).

the *immediate* future, a matter which, apart from the direct effect on me and my family, would also be ruinous for me politically, especially here in London, where one must keep up *appearances*. What I wanted to know from you was this: Do you know anybody, or a few persons (for the matter must not become *public under any circumstances*), who would lend me about 1,000 taler at 5 or 6 percent interest for at least two years? I am now paying 20 to 50 percent interest for the small sums I borrow, but with all that I cannot put off my creditors much longer and I am therefore faced with the breakup of my household.

Since my last letter but one to you,[1] I have again had constant relapses and have therefore been very interrupted in my theoretical work. (The practical work for the International Association continues its course, and there is a great deal of it, for I really have to lead the whole society.)[2] Next month I shall send the first sheets[3] to Meissner and will continue doing so until I bring the remainder to Hamburg myself. I shall then visit you in any case....

Salut.

Yours, K. Marx

149

From letter to Ludwig Kugelmann (in Hanover)
London, October 25, 1866

Dear Friend:
... You misunderstand my relationship with Engels.[1] He is my most intimate friend. I have no secrets from him. Without him, I would have been compelled to enter some "business." Hence under *no* circumstances do I wish to have any third person intervene with him....

Yours, K.M.

148

1. See Letter 145, Marx to Kugelmann, August 23, 1866.
2. See *Karl Marx on the First International*, ed. by Saul K. Padover.
3. Of *Das Kapital*.

149

1. On October 23, 1866, Kugelmann replied to Marx's letter of October 13 that his efforts to help were "in vain." He asked for Engels' address in order to appeal to him on Marx's behalf. The above letter shows how annoyed Marx was with Kugelmann's attempted meddling.

150

To Frederick Engels (in Manchester)
London, November 8, 1866

Dear Engels:
You will have been struck by my silence. I thought the receipt of the £5 had been acknowledged, as Laura[1] had undertaken to do so, but as it turned out later, she forgot. For the rest, desperate circumstances prevented me from writing. You know that the £10 that you sent me before you went on your trip were used only to pay taxes, and the £50 later were for the payment of rent. The so-called inheritance[2] had to be divided up among at least twenty people, and so my part, which arrived early this summer, amounted to—£80! My efforts to raise money in Germany or Holland all failed. The pawnshop (and my wife has pawned practically everything, so that she can hardly go out) exists only to collect the interest. Hence, as it was in the worst refugee days, I had to borrow small sums right and left in London—and this from a confined circle that has no means itself—in order to pay for the most urgent necessities. Otherwise, the suppliers are threatening, and some creditors have already given me notice and threatened to sue. These circumstances are the more disagreeable in that Lafargue[3] (up to his departure for Bordeaux in a few days) is constantly in the house and the *real state of things* [in English] has to be anxiously concealed from him. All this has not only interrupted my work but also, because I have to make up at night for loss of time during the day, caused a carbuncle to develop not far from the *penis* [in English]. I know that you have done everything in your power, and more. But some sort of remedy has to be created. Is the raising of a *loan* [in English] or some other similar transaction possible?[4]
    Salut.

Yours, K.M.

150

1. Laura Marx.
2. From Marx's aunt, Esther Kosel, who died in 1865. See Letter 134, Marx to Engels, November 8, 1865.
3. Paul Lafargue, who was engaged to Laura Marx, seemed to have been unaware of the desperate poverty of the Marx household.
4. Engels, as always, came through with financial assistance. On November 10, Marx wrote him: "My best thanks for the quick help and ditto for the port wine. I know your situation clearly, and this makes my own pressure on you doubly painful. The thing must of course finally come to an end, but this will be possible only when I move to the Continent and can personally take action there."

151

To François Lafargue (in Bordeaux) [in French]
London, November 12, 1866

My dear Mr. Lafargue:

I hope very much that *Monsieur il amoroso*[1] has excused to you my unforgivable silence. For one thing, I was plagued by relapses of my illness; for another, I was so occupied with my laborious work[2] that I neglected the correspondence with my closest friends. If I did not count you among the latter, I would never have dared offend the normal courtesies.

I thank you heartily for the wine. Since I come from a wine-growing region and am an ex-owner of a vineyard,[3] I know well how to appreciate the value of wine. I even agree a little with old [Martin] Luther, who said that the man who does not love wine would never amount to anything much. (No rule without an exception.) But one cannot, for example, deny that the political movement in England has been hastened by the commercial treaty with France and the import of French wines.[4] This is one of the good things that Louis Bonaparte brought about, while poor Louis-Philippe had been so intimidated by the Northern manufacturers that he did not dare to conclude any commercial treaties with England. It is only to be regretted that such regimes as those of Napoleon, which are based on the exhaustion and impotence of both antagonistic social classes, bought some material progress at the price of general demoralization. Fortunately, the masses of workers cannot be demoralized. Manual work is the great antidote against every social infection.

You will have rejoiced, as I did, at the defeat of President [Andrew] Johnson at the last election.[5] The workers of the North have finally come to understand very well: that a white skin cannot emancipate itself so long as a black skin is branded.

On Saturday evening I received, through Citizen Dupont,[6] a letter from the secretary of the medical faculty addressed to Paul [Lafargue]. It demanded papers which (with the exception of the doctoral diploma) could be

---

151

1. Paul Lafargue. François Lafargue (d.1870 or 1871) was the father of Paul.
2. *Das Kapital*.
3. It was Karl Marx's father, Heinrich Marx, who owned a small vineyard on the Moselle.
4. On January 23, 1860, England and France concluded a commercial treaty wherein the tariff was reduced to a maximum of 30 percent and most French goods were permitted to enter England free of duty.
5. The Congressional elections of 1866 resulted in a Republican victory.
6. Eugène Dupont (*c.* 1831–1881), French watchmaker, member of the First International, friend of Marx, emigrated to the United States in 1874.

found neither at my daughter's [Laura] nor at your son's representative. You must send those documents *immediately*.

Please tell your son that he would oblige me very much if he did not carry on any propaganda in Paris. The times are too *dangerous*. The best he can do in Paris is to use his time to profit from his contact with Dr. Moilin.[7] He does not lose anything by being sparing with his polemical gift. The more he restrains himself now, the better fighter he will be at the appropriate moment.

My daughter begs you to send her, through Paul, yours and Mme. Lafargue's photographs.

My whole family joins me in sending our warmest greetings to the whole Lafargue family.

Entirely yours, Karl Marx

152

From letter to Frederick Engels (in Manchester)
London, April 2, 1867

Dear Engels:
I had decided not to write you until I could announce the completion of the book,[1] which is now the case.[2] Also I did not want to bore you with the reasons for the frequent delays, namely, carbuncles on my posterior and in the vicinity of the *penis* [in English], the remains of which are now fading and which permit me to assume a sitting (that is, writing) position only at great pain. I do *not* take arsenic, because it makes me too stupid and at least for the little time that I have when writing is possible, I want to have a clear head.

Next week, I must go myself with the manuscript to Hamburg.[3] I did not like the tone of Meissner's last letter. In addition, yesterday I received the

---

7. Jules Antoine Moilin, known as Tony (1832–1871), French physician, member of the Paris Commune, for which he was executed.

152

1. *Das Kapital.*
2. Engels replied by return mail, April 4, 1867: "Hurrah! This exclamation was irrepressible when I finally read black on white that Volume One *is* finished.... So that you do not lack *Nervus Rerum*, I am enclosing seven half-pound notes—a total of £3.5—the other half to be sent upon receipt of the acknowledging telegram."
3. On April 10, Marx left London for Hamburg to discuss the publication of *Das Kapital* with his publisher there. For a description of Marx's sea voyage to Hamburg, see Letter 153, Marx to Engels, April 13, 1867.

enclosed scrap of paper from Borkheim.[4] I have every reason to believe that the "Continental friend" is Privy Councillor Bucher.[5] Borkheim had written him a letter, which he read to me, about his projected trip to Silesia, where he has family business. Bucher answered him immediately. Hence behind this canard [hoax] I smell an intrigue, and I must personally put the knife to Meissner's breast. Otherwise, the fellow would be capable of holding back my manuscript (which I estimate at twenty-five big proof sheets) and at the same time *not printing* the book under the pretext of "waiting" for the second volume.

I must, first of all, get my clothes and watch out of the pawnshop. Also, I can hardly leave my family in its present circumstances, when they are without a sou and the creditors are becoming daily more impudent. Finally, so that I don't forget it, all the money which I could have used for Laura's[6] champagne cure went the way of all flesh. She now must have red wine, and a better quality than I can command. *Voilà la situation* [Such is the situation]....

Salut.

Yours, K.M.

153

To Frederick Engels (in Manchester)
Hamburg, April 13, 1867

Dear Fred:
I arrived here at noon yesterday. The ship sailed from London on Wednesday,[1] at eight in the morning. In this you can see the whole story of the sea voyage. Crazy weather and storm. After having been cooped up for so long, I felt as tremendously jolly as the five hundred hogs [on board]. Still, the thing would have been boring in the long run, with all the sick and the deserting crowd right and left, if a small *nucleus* [in English] had not held firm. This was a very "mixed" circle—to wit, a German sea captain, a small fellow, but one who resembled you facially, with your kind of humor and the same good-natured, flippant twinkle in his eyes; a London cattle dealer, a real John Bull,

---

4. Sigismund Ludwig Borkheim (1825–1885), a German businessman in London, wrote Marx on April 1, 1867, that a "Continental friend" had written him he was worried about Marx's financial difficulties.
5. Lothar Bucher, a German official, supporter of Bismarck.
6. Laura Marx.
153
1. April 10.

bovine in every respect [in English]; a German watchmaker from London, a fine chap; a German from Texas; and, the main personality, a German, who for the last fifteen years had knocked about in Eastern Peru, a geographic area only recently explored, where, among other things, human flesh is being eaten heartily. A mad, energetic, and gay fellow. He had with him a very valuable collection of stone axes, etc., which were of a calibre to have been found in "caves." As an appendage, one female (the other ladies all *seasick* [in English] and vomiting in the ladies' cabin), an ancient nag with a toothless mouth, speaking refined Hanoverian [German], daughter of an ancestral Hanoverian minister, named von Baer or something, now for a long time a do-gooder, an exalter of labor, an acquaintance of Jules Simon,[2] full of soulfulness, with which she bores our *bovine friend* [in English] to death. Well! Thursday evening, when the storm was at its worst, so that all the tables and chairs were dancing, we drank *en petit comité* [in a small circle], while "the" old female nag lay on the sofa, from which the movement of the ship tossed her from time to time on the floor in the middle of the cabin—to divert her a little. What captivated this beauty here under these difficult conditions? Why did she not retire to the female chamber? Our German wild man recounted with real gusto the sexual filthiness of the primitives. *Voilà la charme* [here was the attraction] for the delicate, pure, refined lady. One example: he was entertained in an Indian tent on the very day when the woman lay in confinement. The placenta was roasted and—as the highest expression of hospitality—he was given a piece of this *sweetbread* [in English] to share in the celebration.

Immediately upon arrival, I went to see Meissner. The clerk told me he would not be back before three o'clock (afternoon). I left my card with an invitation to Herr Meissner for *dinner* [in English]. He came with another person and asked that I come with him, as his wife expected him. I refused, and we agreed that he visit me at seven in the evening. He told me in passing that [Wilhelm] Strohn was probably still in Hamburg. Hence I went to see Strohn's brother [Eugen]. *The very same morning* [in English] our man had gone to Paris. Meissner came in the evening. A decent fellow, although somewhat Saxonish, as the name indicates. After a brief *pourparler* [palaver], he was *all right* [in English]. I promptly brought the manuscript to his publishing house and put it in *safe* [in English] there. Printing will begin *in a few days* [in English] and proceed quickly. We had some drinks then, and he expressed his great "delight" in making acquaintance with my work. He now wants to have the work[3] appear *in three volumes*. He is against a separate issue of the last book (*the historical-literary part*), as I had planned. He said that, from the point of view of sales and for the "superficial" readers, he counted most on that part. I told him, I would go along with him in this regard.

---

2. Jules Simon (1814–1896), a French politician and editor.
3. *Das Kapital.*

At all events [in English], in Meissner *we* have a man entirely at our disposal; he has great contempt for the entire literary-rascal-pack. I found it wise not to present to him your *little bill* [in English]. The most pleasant surprises should always be kept for the last.

And now Adio, *old boy* [in English].

Yours, K.M.

Best compliments to Mrs. Burns [in English]!

154

From letter to Frederick Engels (in Manchester)
Hanover, April 24, 1867

Dear Fred:

For eight days now I have been the guest of Dr. Kugelmann.[1] For, on account of the publication of the book,[2] I am obliged to remain in Hamburg or nearby. The matter stands like this. Meissner, who wants to have the whole thing done in four or five weeks, cannot do the printing in Hamburg, where there are neither enough printers nor skilled proofreaders. Hence he prints at Otto Wigand's (*rather* [in English], Wigand's son [Hugo], since the renowned old dog is connected with the business only nominally). Eight days ago, Meissner sent the manuscript to Leipzig. Now he wants me *to be on hand*, in order to revise the first two proof sheets and *at the same time to decide* if quick publication would be "POSSIBLE" with *only one revision on my part*. If so, then the whole business would be finished in four or five weeks. But Easter week has come in between. Wigand Junior wrote to Meissner that he can begin only at the end of *this* week. At Kugelmann's urgent invitation, I went to stay with him in the interim (which is also better for economic reasons).[3] . . .

Now as to Hanover.

Kugelmann is a very eminent physician in his specialty, namely, gynecology. Virchow[4] and the other authorities (among them a certain

---

154

1. On April 10, 1866, Marx left London for Hamburg to see his publisher there. While waiting for his book to come out, he visited Dr. Ludwig Kugelmann in nearby Hanover. In this letter he describes Kugelmann, who became a devoted friend for almost a decade.
2. *Das Kapital.*
3. Marx stayed with the Kugelmanns for a whole month, from April 17 to May 15, 1867; these were the among the happiest weeks of his life. See also Letter 157, Marx to Laura Marx, May 13, 1867.
4. Rudolf Virchow (1821–1902), pioneer German pathologist.

Meyer[5] in Berlin), formerly von Siebold[6] in Göttingen, and, until his insanity, Semmelweis[7] in Vienna, have corresponded with him. When there is a difficult case in this specialty here, he is always brought in as a consultant. To give me an idea of professional jealousy and local stupidity, he told me that at first he was blackballed, that is, not admitted to the doctors' association, because "gynecology" was "immoral obscenity" [*Schweinerei*]. Kugelmann also has a lot of technical talent. He has invented many new instruments in his speciality.

He is, secondly, a fanatical supporter (and for my taste, too much of a Westphalian admirer) of our theory and of us both personally. He sometimes bores me with his enthusiasm, which is in contradiction to his cool objectivity as a medical man. But he *understands* and he is *thoroughly upright*, ruthless and capable of self-sacrifice, and, what is the main thing, *convinced*. He has a nice little wife [Gertrude] and an eight-year-old daughter[8] who is most delightful. He possesses a much better collection of our works than the two of us together....

Yours, Mohr

155

To Sigfrid Meyer[1] (in New York)
Hanover, April 30, 1867

Dear Friend:
You must think very badly of me, the more so if I tell you that your letters have not only given me *great pleasure* but have also been a *true comfort* during the very painful period when they came. To know that a competent man, *à la hauteur des principes* [at the top of his principles], is secure for our party, that is for me compensation for the worst. In addition, your letters have been full of the most amiable friendship for me personally, and you understand that I, who am engaged in the most bitter conflict with the world (the official one), can least underestimate that.

Why did I not write you for such a long time? Because I have been continuously suspended over the edge of the grave. I had to utilize EVERY

5. Ludwig Meyer (1827–1900), a physician.
6. Eduard Kaspar Jakob von Siebold (1801–1861), Göttingen professor of gynecology.
7. Ignaz Philipp Semmelweis (1818–1865), Hungarian, professor of gynecology in Vienna and Budapest.
8. Franziska Kugelmann (1858–c. 1930).

155

1. Sigfrid Meyer (c. 1840–1872), a German communist mining engineer, who emigrated to the United States in 1866.

possible moment when I was capable of working, in order to complete my work, for which I have sacrificed health, happiness, and family. I hope that this explanation needs no further elaboration. I laugh at the so-called "practical" men and their wisdom. If one wants to be an ox, then one can, of course, turn one's back on man's torments and tend only to one's own skin. But I would really have considered myself *impractical* if I had croaked without having finished my book, at least in manuscript.

The first volume of the work will be published by *Otto Meissner* in Hamburg in a few weeks. The title is: *Capital. Critique of Political Economy.* I went to Germany to bring over the manuscript, and on the way back to London, I stopped for a few days with a friend in Hanover.[2]

Volume I contains the *"Production Process of Capital."* Next to the general scientific development, I present in detail, from the hitherto unused *official* sources, the conditions of the English—agricultural and industrial—proletariat *during the last twenty years.* You understand as a matter of course that all this serves me only as *argumentum ad hominem* [an evasive argument].

I hope that a year from today the whole work will have appeared. *Volume II* will contain the continuation and conclusion of the theory; *Volume III, The History of Political Economy from the Middle of the 17th Century.*

In regard to the "International Working Men's Association," it has become a power in England, France, Switzerland, and Belgium. Try to organize many branches in America. Contribution per member is one penny (about one silver groschen) annually. Still, every community contributes what it can. This year the congress takes place at Lausanne on September 3. Each community is entitled to one representative. Write me about this, about your own life in America and about conditions in general. If you remain silent, I will take it as proof that you have not forgiven me.

My heartiest regards.

Yours, Karl Marx

156

To Ludwig Büchner (in Darmstadt)
Hanover, c/o Dr. Kugelmann, May 1, 1867

Honored Sir:
If I, a complete stranger, take the liberty of writing to you personally in a personal, although at the same time scientific, matter, you must excuse it

---

2. Dr. Ludwig Kugelmann.

because of the confidence which I place in you as a man of science and party man.

I came to Germany to bring the first volume of my work, *Das Kapital: Critique of Political Economy*, to my publisher, Herr Otto Meissner in Hamburg. I must remain here a few more days,[1] to see if there is a possibility of printing it rapidly, as Herr Meissner intends, that is, if the proofreaders are sufficiently competent for such an operation.

The reason I am turning to you is this: I want the book, after its publication in Germany, to appear also in Paris, in French. I cannot go there personally, at least not without danger, since I have been expelled from France, first under Louis-Philippe[2] and the second time under Louis Bonaparte (President),[3] and during my exile in London I have constantly attacked Mr. Louis.[4] Hence I cannot go there personally to look for a translator. I know that your book, *Stoff und Kraft* [*Energy and Matter*, 1855], has appeared in French,[5] and I assume, therefore, that, directly or indirectly, you could arrange a proper person for me. As I must have the second volume in the summer and the third and final one in the winter ready for the publisher, I do not have the time to undertake the French translation myself.[6]

I consider it of the highest importance to emancipate the French from the false views in which they have been buried by Proudhon and his idealized petit bourgeoisness. At the recent congress in Geneva,[7] as well as in the contacts which I, as a member of the General Council of the International Association, have with the Paris branch, one constantly collides with the most revolting consequences of Proudhonism.

As I do not know how much longer I shall remain here, I would be obliged for a prompt reply. If, on my part, I can be of any service to you in London, I would do so with the greatest pleasure.

Your most devoted, Karl Marx

156

1. Marx stayed with Kugelmann in Hanover from April 17 to May 15, 1867, while waiting for the proof sheets of *Das Kapital* to come from the publisher in nearby Hamburg.
2. In January, 1845.
3. In August, 1849.
4. Napoleon III. In 1852, Marx published a vitriolic criticism of him, entitled *The Eighteenth Brumaire of Louis Napoleon*. In later editions, including the second German one (1869), the title was changed to: *The Eighteenth Brumaire of Louis Bonaparte*.
5. A French translation of Büchner's work, *Force et Matière*, came out in Paris and Brussels in 1863.
6. The French translation of Marx's *Das Kapital* was published serially in Paris between 1872 and 1875.
7. The second congress of the First International was held in Geneva, September 3 to 8, 1866.

157

To Laura Marx (in London) [in English]
Hanover, May 13, 1867

My pretty little Cacadou:
My best thanks for your letter and that of the worthy Quoquo.[1] You complain that I had given no signs of life, but on reviewing the question you will find that, on the whole, I have given weekly signals. Moreover, you know that I am not of a very "demonstrative" character, of rather retiring habitudes, a slow writer, a clumsy sort of man or, as Quoquo has it, an anxious man.

I shall leave Hanover the day after tomorrow, and probably leave Hamburg by first steamer for London. Yet, you must not expect me to settle the day and the hour. I have still some business to transact with my publisher. At all events, this is the last week of my continental stay.[2]

I am very glad that my photograph has met with such good reception. The shadow is at all event less troublesome than the original.

As to Mme. Tenge,[3] I wonder that you ask me how she looks, whether she is pretty? I have sent Jenny her photogram, hidden behind my own. How could it have been lost? Now; to answer your questions, she is thirty-three years of age, mother of five children, rather interesting than pretty, and certainly no professional wit. But she is a superior woman. As to "flirting," he would be rather a bold man who were to try it. As to "admiration," I owe it, and there may, perhaps, have been on her side, some overestimation of your most humble and "modest" master. You know, if no one is a prophet on his own dunghill (speaking symbolically), people are easily overvalued by strangers who, *legen sie nicht aus, so legen sie doch unter* [if they do not interpret you correctly, they interpret you anyhow], and find what they were resolved upon to find in a fellah. She has left Hanover Thursday last.

Eight days since, the weather was still frosty and rainy. Now summer has at once burst into full bloom. On the whole, the weather, since my departure, was here as bad and changeable as it used to be in London. Only, and this is a great thing, the air is thinner.

These continentals have an easier life of it than we on the other side of the Northern sea. With 2000 taler (300 £) you can live here most comfortably.

157

1. Nickname of Marx's daughter Eleanor, who was generally called Tussy.
2. From May 15 to 18 Marx was in Hamburg, discussing *Kapital* with his publisher, Meissner, returning to London on May 19.
3. Madame Tenge (b.c. 1833), a friend of the Ludwig Kugelmanns', in whose house Marx stayed when he was in Hanover.

For inst., there exist here different gardens (à la Cremorne,[4] but "respectable," and where all sorts of people meet), much more artistically arranged than any in London, good music being played every evening, etc., where you can subscribe for self and family—for the whole year—at the price of 2 talers, 6 sh! This is only a specimen of the cheap life the Philister indulge in at this place. Young people amuse themselves more freely and at almost no expense, comparatively speaking. There is of course one great drawback—the atmosphere is pregnant with dullness. The standard of existence is too small. It is a lot of pigmees amongst whom you want no very high frame to feel like Gulliver amidst the Lilliputians.

There arrive[d] this morning rather "excited" letters from Berlin. It seems that a collision between the workmen and the *Pickelhauben* [spiked helmets, the nickname of the Berlin police] is apprehended. I do not expect much for the present, but there is something brewing. The working class in the greater centers of Germany, are commencing to assume a more decided and threatening attitude. One fine morning there will be a nice dance!

And now my dear little birdseye, Cacadou, secretary, cook, equestrian, poet, *auf Wiedersehen*. Regards to Möhmchen[5] Quoquo and Queque, Helen,[6] and last not least, our "mutual friend."[7]

Adio.

Your master, Old Nick[8]

Enclosed Hegel, presented by Kugelmann to Mons. Lafargue.

158

To Ludwig Kugelmann (in Hanover)
London, June 10, 1867

Dear Friend:

The belatedness of this letter puts me under the more or less "justified suspicion" of being a "bad fellow." By way of mitigation, I can only mention that it is only in the last few days that I "live" in London. In the interim, I have been in Manchester with Engels.[1] But you and your dear wife now know me well enough to consider my epistolary insufficiency as normal. Neverthe-

---

4. The Cremorne Gardens, on the Thames in Chelsea, open for public amusements from 1845 to 1877.
5. Mrs. Marx.
6. Helene Demuth.
7. Paul Lafargue.
8. One of Marx's family nicknames.

158

1. Marx was in Manchester from May 21 to June 2, 1867.

less, I have been with you every day. I count my stay in Hanover[2] as among the most beautiful and delightful oases in the desert of life.

In Hamburg, I had no other adventure except to become acquainted, despite all precautions, with Herr Wilhelm Marr.[3] Judging by his personal manner, he is a Christian-translated Lassalle, although worth much less. Also, during the few days I was there, Herr Niemann[4] gave a performance. But I have been too spoiled by the society in Hanover to want to attend the theater in inferior company. So I missed Herr Niemann.

Apropos. Meissner is prepared to print your medical brochure. All you have to do is send him the manuscript and refer to me. As for the detailed conditions, you have to arrange them yourself.

The crossing from Hamburg to London, apart from a bit of rough weather on the first day, was generally favorable. A few hours before arrival at London, a German girl, whose military bearing had already struck me, declared that she wanted that same evening to go from London to Weston supra Mare and did not know how she would manage it with her many pieces of luggage. The matter was the worse in that on the Sabbath day helpful hands are in short supply in England. Friends had warned her about it in a postal card. She had to go to the North Western Station, which I also had to pass. As a good knight, I, therefore, offered to drop her off there. She accepted. Thinking it over, it occurred to me, however, that Weston supra Mare is to the southwest, while the station which I was to pass and to which she was going, was in the northwest. I consulted the sea captain. Correct. It turned out that she was to be let off at a station at the opposite end of London from my direction. But I had made the promise, and now I had to make *bonne mine à mauvais jeu* [a good face at a bad play]. We arrived at two o'clock in the afternoon. I brought *la donna errante* [errant lady] to her station, where I learned that her train would not leave until eight in the evening. *So, I was in for it* [in English], and had to kill six hours walking in Hyde Park, sitting in ice-shops, etc. It turned out that her name was Elisabeth von Puttkamer, *Bismarck's niece*, with whom she had just spent a few weeks in Berlin. She had the whole Army list with her, as her family supplies our "brave Army" with Gentlemen of Honor and *Taille* in superabundance. She was a gay, educated girl, but aristocratic and black-and-white [the colors of the royal flag] to the tip of her nose. She was not a little surprised to discover that she had fallen into "red" hands. I consoled her, however, that our rendezvous would end "without bloodshed," and I saw her depart for her destination *saine et sauve* [safe and sound]. Think what food this would supply to Blind and other vulgar democrats—my *conspiracy with Bismarck* [in English]!

---

2. Marx stayed with the Kugelmanns in Hanover from April 17 to May 15, 1867.
3. Wilhelm Marr (1819–1904), Hamburg journalist, Prussian police spy in the 1860's.
4. Albert Niemann (1831–1917), German opera singer.

Today I sent off fourteen corrected proof sheets. Most of them I received from Engels, who is extraordinarily pleased with the thing, with the exception of sheets two and three, which he finds written *too* simply. His opinion put my mind at rest, since my printed things always displease me, at least at first glance.

I am sending your dear wife, to whom please convey my specific thanks for her most friendly and amiable reception of me, a photogram of my second daughter Laura, as the photograms of the others are depleted and new ones must be taken. Engels is likewise having copies of photograms made of himself and of [Wilhelm] Wolff. Your packets have amused him very much.

Give my best regards to "Madämchen."[5] Eleanor is at school, but she will write you herself.

And now, Adio!

Yours, Karl Marx

159

From letter to Frederick Engels (in Manchester)
London, June 22, 1867

Dear Fred:

Enclosed hereby are four more proof sheets[1] which came yesterday. The fellows let stand a number of typos, which I had corrected very legibly. . . .

I hope that you are satisfied with the four proof sheets. Your satisfaction up to now is more important to me than anything the rest of the world may say of it. At any rate, I hope that the bourgeoisie will remember my carbuncles all the rest of their lives. . . .

As for the development of the *form of value*, I did and did *not* follow your advice, so as to behave dialectically in this respect too. That is to say, (1) I have written an *appendix* in which I describe the *same thing* as simply and as much like a schoolmaster as possible, and (2) I have followed your advice and divided each step in the development into paragraphs, etc., *with separate headings*. In the *Preface*, I then tell the *"non-dialectical"* reader that he should skip pages x-y and read the appendix instead. This is not merely a question of the philistine, but of youth eager for knowledge, etc. Besides, the matter is too decisive for the whole book. Messieurs the economists have hitherto overlooked the extremely simple point that the form: *20 yards of linen = 1 coat* is only the undeveloped basis of *20 yards of linen = £2*, and that, therefore, the

---

5. Franziska Kugelmann, Dr. Ludwig Kugelmann's daughter.

159

1. Of *Das Kapital*.

simplest form of commodity, in which the value is not yet expressed as a relation to all other commodities but only as *differentiated* from the commodity in its own natural form, contains the *whole secret of the money form* and with it, in *nuce* [a nutshell], *all the bourgeois forms of the product of labor*. In my first account (Duncker[2]), I avoid the difficulty of the development by only giving an actual analysis of the *expression of value* when it appears already developed and expressed in money.

You are quite right about Hofmann.[3] For the rest, you will see from the conclusion of my Chapter III, where the transformation of the handicraft-master into a capitalist—as a result of purely *quantitative* changes—is touched upon, that *in the text* I refer to the law that Hegel discovered, of *purely quantitative changes turning into qualitative changes*, as applicable alike in history as in natural science. In a *note* to the text (at that time I was hearing Hofmann's lectures), I mention the *molecular theory* but not Hofmann, who discovered *nothing* exceptional in this matter, but instead I mention Laurent,[4] Gerhardt,[5] and Wurtz,[6] of whom the last is *the real man*. Your letter brought a dim recollection to my mind and I, therefore, looked up my manuscript.

In the last two weeks the printing (only four sheets) has been going slowly, probably due to Whitsuntide. But Herr Otto Wigand must catch up. Apropos. *Your* book[7] is still available. The [London] Workers' Association has ordered two *new copies* [in English] from Wigand and received them (2d edition, 1848).

Now, private things.

My children are obliged to invite, for July 2, other girls for a dance at home, as they do not invite anybody in the whole year they could not reciprocate invitations, and thus were about *to lose cast* [*sic* in English]. So, though depressed at the moment, I had to agree, and count on you for the wine (claret and Rhine), that is, that you will provide it for me in the course of next week.

Secondly, since "misfortune" never comes alone, Lina[8] announced her coming next week. My wife then has to repay her the £5 she owes her, and you can understand that after my defense against the first storm of creditors, I cannot *afford* [in English] this.

I am in reality most furious at the people who had promised me money and from whom (at least until now) I have not heard. They are personally

2. Marx, *Critique of Political Economy*, published by Duncker in 1859.
3. August Wilhelm von Hofmann, *Einleitung in die Moderne Chimie* [*Introduction to Modern Chemistry*] (Brunswick, 1866).
4. Auguste Laurent, *Méthode de Chimie* [*Method of Chemistry*] (Paris, 1854).
5. Charles Frédéric Gerhardt and G. Chancel, *Précis d'Analyse Chimique Qualitative* [*Summary of Qualitative Chemical Analysis*] (Paris, 1862).
6. Adolphe Wurtz, *Leçons de Philosophie Chimique* [*Lessons of Philosophical Chemistry*] (Paris, 1864).
7. Engels, *The Condition of the Working Class in England*.
8. Lina Schöler.

interested in me. I know that. They also know that I cannot continue to work without a measure of peace. And yet they never let me hear from them.

The "noble" poet Freiligrath will after all receive a substantial collection.[9] For the begging among the rich Germans in South America and— China! and the West Indies! attracts, since those fellows consider this as *national*. Meanwhile, the Freiligraths live as before in *relatively* great style, give constant parties, go out constantly. This is one reason why the London German businessmen are very inflexible. He, the fat one (so says my wife, who was there), is very irritable and looks sickly and depressed. But Ida[10] blooms like a cornpoppy and has never been more faithful in her life.

Best regards for Mrs. Lizzy.[11]

Yours, K.M.

160

To Ferdinand Freiligrath (in London)
London, July 20, 1867

Dear Freiligrath:

I do not read German belletristic trash, but cannot escape having friends in Germany send me occasional personalia excerpts. Thus yesterday I received a reference relating to me, from a piece by a certain Rasch,[1] entitled "Twelve Champions of Revolution." I ask you to explain the following passage:

"Freiligrath's relations with Marx have completely ceased, etc.; *a thoroughly inexcusable action on the part of Marx*, about which I want to keep silent here, has given them their last push. It can only be explained by the hatefulness of a character like Marx. When, in my indignation, I asked Freiligrath one day about the *details*, he considerately passed it over."[2]

Yours, K.M.

---

9. In the spring of 1867, after Ferdinand Freiligrath lost his job with the Swiss bank in London, committees were set up in London and abroad to raise money for the poet in need.
10. Ferdinand Freiligrath's wife.
11. Lydia Burns.

160

1. Gustav Rasch (d.1878), a German socialist.
2. Freiligrath replied on July 20, 1867: "Dear Marx: One would have a great deal to do if one listened to every bit of gossip. It is now about four or five years since Rasch visited me here, and I do not recall having spoken to him about you. If he did mean to refer to your and my disagreement over the Vogt-Kolb-Liebknecht affair, you can see from the appropriate passages that I did not enter into the discussion. What he means by that "action" I do not know. At any rate, he himself is the proper person to give you an explanation about it."

161

To Frederick Engels (in Manchester)
London (2 o'clock in the morning), August 16, 1867

Dear Fred:
Have just finished correcting the *last sheet* (forty-nine) of the book. The appendix—*form of value*—in *small print*, takes up one and a quarter sheets.
  Preface ditto. Corrected and returned yesterday. So *this volume is finished.* Only YOU alone I have to thank for making this possible! Without your self-sacrifice for me I could never possibly have done the enormous work for the three volumes. *I embrace you, full of thanks* [in English]!
  Enclosed two sheets of clean proofs.
  The £15 received with best thanks.
  Greetings, my dear, beloved friend!

Yours, K. Marx

I shall only need the corrected proofs back *as soon as the whole book has appeared.*

162

From letter to Ludwig Kugelmann (in Hanover)
London, October 11, 1867

Dear Kugelmann:
... The completion of my second volume depends largely on the success of the first. This is necessary for me so that I can find a publisher in England, and *without the latter*, my material conditions remain so difficult and disturbing that I can find neither time nor peace for its completion. These are, of course, things that I do *not* want Herr Meissner to know. Now, therefore, it depends on fate and the activities of my party friends in Germany whether the second volume will take a long or a short time to appear. A solid critique—whether from friend or foe—can be expected only by and by, as so voluminous and in part difficult a work requires time to read and digest. But its success is not going to be determined by solid criticism but, to speak plainly, by sounding the alarm and striking the drum, which would also force the enemies to speak out. Chiefly, *what* is being said is not as important as that it is *said. Above all, no time is to be lost!*...

Yours, K.M.

Keep me informed of everything that is connected with Volume I in Germany....

163

From letter to Frederick Engels (in Manchester)
London, October 19, 1867

Dear Fred:

... In recent weeks it has been positively impossible for me to write even two hours a day. Apart from pressure *from without* [in English], there are the household headaches which always affect my liver. I have become sleepless again and have had the pleasure of seeing two carbuncles bloom near the *membrum* [penis]. Fortunately, they faded away. My illness always comes from the head. Since I mention the *membrum*, I recommend to you, *for Moore*,[1] the following verses from the sixteenth century French satirist, Mathurin Régnier.[2] Despite my extensive reading in this field, I do not believe that the *chaude pisse* [warm piss] has ever been described more poetically anywhere else:

> "Mon cas, qui se lève et se hausse,
> Bave d'une estrange façon;
> Belle, vous fournistes la sausse
> Lors que je fournis le poisson.
>
> Las! si ce membre eut l'arrogance
> De fouiller trop les lieux sacrez,
> Qu'on luy pardonne son offence,
> Car il pleur assez ses péchez."[3]

No ill turn comes from the same:

> *Fluxion D'Amour*
> "L'amour est une affection
> Qui, par les yeux, dans le coeur entre,
> Et, par la forme de fluxion,
> S'éxcoule par le bas du ventre."[4]

163

1. Samuel Moore (*c.*1830–1912), a Manchester lawyer, cotranslator of *Das Kapital* into English.
2. Mathurin Régnier (1573–1613), French satirist.
3. Freely translated: "My dingus, which rises and gets higher, Foams in a strange fashion; Beauty, you furnish the sauce, while I furnish the fish. Alack! if this member had the arrogance to dig too much in sacred places, his offence should be pardoned, because he weeps enough over his sins."
4. *The Swelling of Love*. "Love is a disease that enters the heart through the eyes, and, by the form of the swelling, flows through the bottom of the belly."

Finally:

> *Lisette tuée par Régnier*
> "Lisette, à qui l'on faisait tort,
> Vint a Régnier tout éplorée,
> Je te pry, donne moi la mort
> Que j'ay tant de fois desirée!
> Luy, ne lea refusant en rien,
> Tire son ... , vous m'entendez bien,
> Et dedans le ventre la frappe.
> Elle, voulant finir ses jours
> Luy dit: Mon coeur pousse toujours,
> De crainte que je n'en rechappe.
> Régnier, las de la secourir,
> Craignant une second plainte,
> Lui dit: Hastez-vous de mourir,
> Car mon poignard n'a plus de pointe."[5]

...

Yours, K.M.

164

Postscript to letter to Frederick Engels (in Manchester) *London, November 7, 1867*

The old Urquhart[1] with his Catholicism, etc. *grows more and more disgusting* [in English].

   On lit dans un registre d'une inquisition d'Italie cet aveu d'une religieuse; elle disait innocemment à la Madonne: "Degrâce, sainte Vierge, donne moi quelque'un avec qui je puisse pécher."[2] But in this respect too the Russian are *plus forts*

---

5. *Lisette Killed by Régnier.* "Lisette, whom one has done wrong, comes to Régnier all in tears, I beg you, give me the death that I have wished for so many times! He, refusing her nothing, pulls out his ... , you know what I mean, and strikes inside the belly. She, desiring to finish her days, says to him: My heart always beats with the fear that I will not escape it. Régnier, tired of helping her, fearing a second complaint, says to her: Hurry up and die, because my dagger no longer has a point."

164

1. David Urquhart (1805–1877), British diplomat, Tory member of Parliament, publisher of the *Free Press.*
2. One reads in an Italian Inquisition record the following avowal of a nun, who innocently prays to the Madonna: "I beseech you, Holy Virgin, give me somebody with whom I could sin."

[stronger]. It has been established that a thoroughly healthy fellow who spent only twenty-four hours in a Russian nunnery came out dead. The nuns rode him to death. Of course, there *le directeur des consciences n'entre pas tous les jours!*[3]

165

From letter to Frederick Engels (in Manchester)
London, December 7, 1867

Dear Fred:
Yesterday I was at the Loan Society,[1] to be examined *bodily* [in English]. This is no mere formality, because if I should die *before* September, the Society would not get back *a farthing* [in English]. I feared to undress (a fate which an Englishman, who was there at the same time, had to undergo). First, I don't like this inocular speculation, and secondly, at this moment, apart from various furuncles, I still have a carbuncle on the left loin, not far from the propagation center. Fortunately, the fellow was so impressed by my chest that he did not want to know anything more. Monday[2] noon I will receive the money....

Yours, K.M.

166

From letter to Frederick Engels (in Manchester)
London, December 14, 1867

Dear Fred:
... Would you do me a favor and inquire of Ernest Jones where one can most suitably have a civil marriage in London, in Doctor's Commons or where? For Laura is to marry in early April. Since there is to be no church wedding, it was originally decided that it should take place in Paris. This, however, is complicated. I would have to prove my identity there and could thereby get to be too known to the police. On the other hand, if the civil wedding is to take place in London, my wife wishes it to be in secret, as she wants to avoid gossip among our English acquaintances. Also ask Jones about the consent of Lafargue's parents. Would they have to sign something at the Embassy (possi-

---

3. The father confessor does *not enter* every day!

165

1. Engels wrote a reference for the loan. He informed Marx, December 4, 1867, that he wrote the loan company: "From confidential information I am convinced that Mr. Marx will be in a position to repay the loan when due."
2. December 9, 1867.

bly British?) in Paris? It is essential that the marriage be valid also under *French* law. Hence no formality in this regard should be overlooked. . . .[1]
Salut.

Yours, K. Mohr

167

To Ludwig Kugelmann (in Hanover)
London, January 11, 1868

Dear Kugelmann:
D'abord [First], my best *happy new years* [in English] for your dear wife, Fränzchen[1] and yourself. And then my best thanks for the Jupiter[2] and for the interest you display in doing propaganda and leading the German press by the nose.[3] As our friend Weerth, who, alas died prematurely, used to sing:
> *"Es gibt nichts Schönres auf der Welt*
> *Als seine Feinde zu beissen,*
> *Als über all die plumpen Gesellen*
> *Seine schlechten Witze zu reissen!"*[4]

With all due respect for your medical authority, you have too low an opinion of the English, German, and French doctors, whom I have consulted and still consult here, if you think that they cannot distinguish anthrax (carbuncles) from furuncles, particularly here in England—the land of carbuncles, which is actually a proletarian illness. And even if the doctors could not distinguish between the two, the patient who, like myself, knows both sorts of horrors, could do so; for the subjective impression they make is quite different, although, so far as I know, no doctor has yet succeeded in making

---

166

1. Engels to Marx, December 16, 1867: "The marriage story is very simple. The marriage is performed before the Registrar for the District, who also posts the banns in his office a fortnight before. Two or more witnesses are necessary. You will get all the information in the Registrar's office. This is all that is necessary *for England*; in regard to the validity in France, even Jones can't tell you. Old Lafargue must inquire about this of *his lawyer in Bordeaux*. For the rest, I will look up the civil code. Gumpert also married this way. As for the philistine neighbors, your wife can tell them that a civil marriage was due to the fact that Laura is Protestant and Paul Catholic."

167

1. Franziska, Kugelmann's daughter.
2. The Kugelmanns sent Marx for Christmas an antique marble bust of Jupiter, which was supposed to resemble him.
3. Kugelmann was active in placing Engels' review of *Das Kapital* in German newspapers.
4. Freely translated: "There is nothing nicer in the world,/Than one's enemies to bite on,/Than to inflict on the ill-bred blokes/His bad jokes."

an exact *theoretical* separation of the two. It is only in the last few years that I have been persecuted by the thing. Before that, it was entirely unknown to me. At the moment of writing to you, I am not yet fully recovered and not yet able to work! Again several weeks lost and not even *pour le roi de Prusse!*[5]

From the critique of Herr Dühring,[6] what appears above all is—fear! I should be glad if you could get for me Dühring's book, *Gegen die Verkleinerer Carey's*,[7] and ditto, von Thünen's *Der isolirte Staat mit Bezug auf die Landwirtschaft* (or something like that)[8] (together with a note on the price). From here such orders take too long.

Finally, I must ask you to be good enough to send me about twelve copies of my photograph (only the *fullfaced* [in English]). About a dozen friends are pestering me for them.

Enclosed, for Mrs. Kugelmann the photographs of my eldest daughter Jenny and of Eleanor, who sends her best greetings to Fränzchen.

Ad vocem [regarding] Liebknecht: Let him play *le petit grand homme* [little great man] for a *little while* [in English]. *Tout s'arrangera pour le mieux dans le meilleurs des mondes possibles.*[9]

I had all sorts of personal anecdotes to relate, but shall save them for the next time, when the writing position no longer troubles me.

Salut.

Yours, K.M.

One of my friends here, who dabbles a lot in phrenology, said yesterday when looking at the photograph of your wife: A great deal of wit! So you see, phrenology is not the baseless art which Hegel imagined.

168

From letter to Ludwig Kugelmann (in Hanover)
London, January 30, 1868

Dear Kugelmann:
Cut, lanced, etc., in short treated in every respect *secundum legem artis* [according to all rules of the art]. In spite of this, the thing [carbuncles] is continually breaking out anew so that—with the exception of two-three days—I have been lying quite fallow for eight weeks. Last Saturday I went

---

5. Literally: For the King of Prussia! Actual meaning: For nothing.
6. Eugen Dühring's review of *Das Kapital* appeared in *Ergänzungsblättern zur Kenntnis der Gegenwart* [*Supplements to Our Knowledge of the Present*], Volume III, Book 3 (1867).
7. *The Belittlers of Carey* (Breslau, 1867).
8. Johann Heinrich von Thünen, *The Isolated State in Relation to Agriculture* (3 vols., Rostock, 1842–1863).
9. All that will turn out for the best in the best of all possible worlds.

out again for the first time—Monday another relapse. I hope it will end this week, but who can guarantee me against another eruption? It is dreadful. Moreover, the thing attacks my head. My friend, Dr. Gumpert in Manchester, urges me to apply arsenic. What do you think of it? ...

Last week, *The Saturday Review*[1]—the *"blood and culture" paper* [in English]—had a notice about my book[2] in a review of various German books. I have come off relatively very well, as you will see from the following passage:

"The author's views may be as pernicious as we conceive them to be, but there can be no question as to the plausibility of his logic, the vigor of his rhetoric, and the charm with which he invests the driest problems of political economy."

Ouff!

My best regards for your dear wife and Fränzchen.[3] You will get other photographs from here, for we have now discovered that the *watercolors* [in English] which looked good the first day dissolved *in patches* [in English] immediately after.

Write me as often as your time permits. During illness and the many occasions for vexations, letters from friends are very welcome.

Salut.

Yours, K.M.

169

From letter to Ludwig Kugelmann (in Hanover)
London, March 6, 1868

Dear Friend:

The peculiarly embarrassed tone of Herr Dühring's criticism[1] is now clear to me. For he is a very noisy and insolent lad, who poses as a revolutionist in political economy. He did two things. First (with Carey as a starting point), he published a *Kritische Grundlage der Nationalökonomie*[2] (about 500 pages) and a new *Natürliche Dialektik*[3] (against the Hegelian). My book has buried him on both counts. He has advertised it out of hatred for Roscher,[4] etc. Secondly,

---

168

1. London conservative weekly; the notice appeared on January 18.
2. *Das Kapital.*
3. Franziska, Kugelmann's daughter.

169

1. Eugen Dühring's review of *Das Kapital.*
2. *Critical Foundation of National Economy* (Berlin 1866).
3. *Natural Dialectic* (Berlin, 1865).
4. Wilhelm Georg Friedrich Roscher (1817–1914), German economic historian.

partly intentionally and partly because of lack of insight, he commits frauds. He knows very well that my theory of development is not Hegelian, since I am a Materialist and Hegel an Idealist. Hegel's dialectic is the basis of all dialectic, but only after it has been stripped of its mystical form, and this precisely is what differentiates my method. *Quant à* [as to] Ricardo, Herr Dühring was annoyed precisely because the former's weak points, which Carey and 100 others before him had pointed out, did not exist in my presentation. Hence, with *mauvaise foi* [bad faith], he tries to burden me with Ricardo's limitations. But never mind. I must be grateful to the man for being the first specialist to have discussed my book at all....

Regards to Fränzchen.[5]

Yours, K.M.

170

From letter to Ludwig Kugelmann (in Hanover)
London, March 17, 1868

Dear Friend:
Your letter has affected me both unpleasantly and pleasantly (you see, I always move in dialectical contradictions).

Unpleasantly, because I know your circumstances and it would be miserable of me if I were to accept such presents at the *expense of your family*. I therefore consider these £15 as a *loan*, which I shall repay in time.

Pleasantly, not only as a mark of your great friendship (and in the bustle of the world, friendship is the only thing of personal importance), but also because you have helped me out of a great embarrassment in regard to the forthcoming marriage.[1] Apart from medicaments and doctors, in the last four months I have spent so much money on Blue Books,[2] investigations and Yankee reports, etc., on banks, that I really had nothing left for my daughter.

You may be sure that I have often discussed leaving London for Geneva, not only with myself and my family, but also with Engels. Here I have to spend from £400 to £500 annually. In Geneva, I could live on £200. But *considered all in all* [in English], it is for the time being *impossible*. Only in London can I finish my work. And *only here* can I hope to draw an appropri-

---

5. Franziska Kugelmann.

170

1. On April 2, 1868, Laura Marx married Paul Lafargue, at a time when there was not a penny in the Marx household.
2. Official British Government publications, which Marx used in his researches for *Das Kapital*.

ate, at least decent, monetary profit from this work. But for this, it is necessary that *I remain here* for the time being. Apart from the fact that, if I were to leave here at this critical time, the whole labor movement, which I influence from behind the scenes,[3] would fall into very bad hands and go the wrong way.

So, for the time being, *all drawbacks notwithstanding* [in English], *fate* ties me to London. *Quant à* [As for] Coppel,[4] you do him wrong. If I had not been ill, he would have amused me and such a diversion never hurts the family. . . .

With warmest greetings to your dear wife,

Yours, K.M.

171

To Frederick Engels (in Manchester)
London, March 18, 1868

Dear Fred:
The £5 gratefully received.

Laura and Lafargue will first go to Paris (after the wedding), then rent an apartment (on Hampstead Heath, if one is to be found), and after Lafargue's final examination (he took all the others in St. Bartholomews Hospital) they will again go to France, and then move to America, where old Lafargue has a house and property.

Whence the word[1] *higid, hid, hiwisc (hida autem Anglice vocatur terra unius aratri culturae sufficiens* [In English one also calls *hida* the amount of land that can be sufficiently cultivated with one plow]). Furthermore, the German word, *wiffa.* (*Qui signum, quod propter defensionem terrae* [Here a mark, to protect the land]—that is, to declare the land is enclosed, hence a sign, instead of a real fencing in—*ponitur, quod signum wiffam vocamus* [Is put up, this sign we call *wiffa*]).

Salut.

Yours, K.M.

---

3. Marx is referring to his dominant role in the General Council of the First International, which had contacts with British trade unions. His influence on them, however, may be questioned.
4. Carl Coppel, a Hanover banker.

171

1. The citation is from the eighth century Bavarian law codex, *Lex Baiuvariorum*, Law X, Paragraph 18.

172

To Frederick Engels (in Manchester)
London, March 25, 1868

Dear Fred:
I wanted to write you yesterday from the [British] Museum, but I suddenly became so unwell that I had to close the very interesting book that I held in my hand. A dark veil fell over my eyes. Then a frightful headache and a pain in the chest. I strolled home. Air and light helped, and when I got home I slept for some time. My condition is such that I really should give up all working and thinking for some time to come; but that would be difficult, even if I could afford it.

In regard to Maurer. His books are extraordinarily important.[1] Not only primeval times, but also the whole later development of the free imperial cities, the immunity of landowners, the public authority, and the struggle between the free peasantry and serfdom, are given an entirely new form.

In human history it is as in paleontology. On account of a certain judicial blindness, even the best intelligences absolutely fail to see the things that lie in front of their noses. Later, when the moment has arrived, one is surprised to find traces everywhere of what one had failed to see. The first reaction against the French Revolution, and the period of Enlightenment bound up with it, was, of course, to regard everything medieval as romantic, and even people like Grimm[2] are not free from this. The second reaction—and this corresponds to the socialist tendency, even though those learned men have no idea that the two are connected—is to look beyond the Middle Ages into the prehistoric period of each nation. They are, therefore, surprised to find the newest in the oldest and even *egalitarian to a degree* [in English], which would have made Proudhon shudder.

To show how much they are caught up in this *judicial blindness* [in English]: right in my own neighborhood [in Trier], on the *Hunsrücken*, the old Germanic system survived up till the last few years. I now recall my father talking to me about it as a lawyer! Another proof: just as geologists,

---

172

1. Georg Ludwig von Maurer, *Einleitung zur Geschichte der Mark-, Hof-, Dorf-, und Stadt-Verfassung und der öffentlichen Gewalt* [*Introduction to the History of the Border-Land, Farm, Village, and City Constitution and Public Authority*] (Munich, 1854); *Geschichte der Dorfverfassung in Deutschland* [*History of the Village Constitution in Germany*], 2 vols. (Erlangen, 1865–66); *Geschichte der Fronhöfe, der Bauernhöfe und der Hofverfassung in Deutschland* [*History of Villeinages, Peasant Farms and Farm Constitution in Germany*], 4 vols. (Erlangen, 1862–63); *Geschichte der Markenverfassung in Deutschland* [*History of the Border-Lands Constitution in Germany*] (Erlangen, 1856).
2. Jacob Grimm, *Deutsche Rechtsalterthümer* [*German Legal Antiquities*], 2d ed. (Göttingen, 1854).

even the best, like Cuvier,[3] have explained certain facts in a completely dis-
torted way, so philologists of the importance of a Grimm have mistranslated
the simplest Latin sentences because they were under the influence of Möser[4]
(who, I remember, was enchanted by the fact that among the Germans
"freedom" had never existed but that "*Luft macht eigen*" [the environment
makes the serf]) and others. For example, the well-known passage in Tacitus:
"*arva per annos mutant, et superest ager*,"[5] which means: they exchange the
fields (*arva*) (by lot, hence also *sortes* [lots] in all the later law codes of the
Barbarians) and the common land remains over (*ager* as contrasted with *arva*
as public land)—is translated by Grimm, etc.: "They cultivate fresh fields
every year and still there always remains (uncultivated) land!"

Likewise the passage "*Colunt discreti ac diversi*" [their tillage is individual
and scattered] is supposed to prove that from times immemorial the Germans
carried on cultivation on individual farms, like Westphalian *Junkers*. But in
the same passage it says: "*Vicos locant non in nostrum morem connexis et cohaeren-
tibus aedificiis: suum quisque locum spatio circumdat*" ["They do not, as we do, lay
out villages with buildings connected and joined together: each surrounds his
place with a strip of land"]; and primitive Germanic villages, in the form
described, still exist here and there in Denmark. Obviously Scandinavia
must become as important for German jurisprudence and economics as for
German mythology. And only by starting from there shall we be able to
decipher our past again. For the rest, even Grimm, etc., found in Caesar[6] that
the Germans always settled as *Geschlechtsgenossenschaften* [kindred associations]
and not as individuals: "*gentibus cognationibusque, qui uno coireant*" [according
to clans and kindreds who settled together].

But what would old Hegel say in the next world if he heard that the
word *Allgemeine* [common, or general] in German and Norse means nothing
but *Gemeindeland* [communal land] and *Sundre, Besondre* [particular], nothing
but the separate property divided off from the communal land? Here are the
logical categories coming damn well out of "our dealings" after all.

Very interesting is Fraas's *Climate and the Vegetable World in Time, a
Contribution to the History of Both*,[7] particularly as it proves that climate and
flora changed in historic times. He is a Darwinist before Darwin and makes
even the species arise in historic times. But he is also at the same time an
agronomist. He maintains that as a result of cultivation—in proportion to its

---

3. Georges Léopold Chrétien Frédéric Dagobert, Baron de Cuvier (1769–1832), French zoologist
and geologist.
4. Justus Möser, *Osnabrücksche Geschichte* [*Osnabrück History*] (Berlin and Stettin, 1780).
5. *Germania*, Chapter 26.
6. Julius Caesar, *De Bello Gallico*, Liber VI.
7. Karl Fraas, *Klima und Pflanzenwelt in der Zeit, ein Beitrag zur Geschichte beider* (Landshut, 1847).

degree—the "dampness" so very much beloved by the peasant is lost (hence plants, too, emigrate from South to North) and eventually the formation of steppes begins. The first effect of cultivation is useful but is eventually devastating on account of deforestation, etc. This man is as much a thoroughly learned philologist (he has written books in Greek) as he is a chemist, agronomist, etc. The sum total is that cultivation—when it progresses naturally and is not consciously controlled (as a bourgeois, of course, he does not arrive at this)—leaves deserts behind it, Persia, Mesopotamia, etc., Greece. Here again another unconscious socialist tendency!

This Fraas is also interesting for Germanism. First, Dr. Med., then inspector and teacher of chemistry and technology. Now chief of the Bavaria Veterinary Institute, university professor, head of the State agronomical experiments, etc. In his latest writings one notices his advanced age, but he is still a jolly lad. Has knocked around a good deal in Greece, Asia Minor, Egypt! His history of agriculture is important too.[8] He calls Fourier "this pious and humanistic socialist." Of the Albanians, etc.: "Every kind of scandalous lewdness and rape."

It is necessary to look over carefully the recent and latest writings on agriculture. The physical school is opposed to the chemical school.

Don't forget to send me back the letter of Kugelmann's manufacturer.[9]

Nothing has given me greater pleasure than the expectation of seeing you here.

Yours, K.M.

173

From letter to Ludwig Kugelmann (in Hanover)
London, April 6, 1868

Dear Kugelmann:
The young pair[1] were married at the registry office[2] (since a *church* ceremony is not legally necessary here) and have left for France on their honeymoon. They send you and Frau Gertrude their best regards....

---

8. Fraas, *Geschichte der Landwirtschaft* (Prague, 1852).
9. Gustav Meyer, a Bielefeld manufacturer. On March 17, 1868, Marx wrote to Kugelmann: "Meyer's letter pleased me very much. Still, he partly misunderstood my theory of development. Otherwise he would have seen that I have presented *big industry* not only as the mother of antagonisms but also as the producer of the material and intellectual conditions for the solution of these antagonisms, which, indeed, cannot take place in *a comfortable way*."

173

1. Laura Marx and Paul Lafargue.
2. They were married in London on April 2, 1868.

The day before yesterday I received a letter from Freiligrath (wedding cards were of course sent to him) in which the following curious sentence occurs.[3] But it will perhaps amuse you more if I enclose the letter itself, which I now do. But you must return it. So that you may understand the letter properly, just the following: Shortly before the appearance of my book,[4] *Zwölf Streiter der Revolution*,[5] by Gustav Struve[6] and Gustav Rasch, was published in Berlin. In this publication Freiligrath is acclaimed as "one" of the twelve apostles and at the same time it is demonstrated to a nicety that he *never* was a communist, and in fact only came to be associated with such monsters as Marx, Engels, [Wilhelm] Wolff, etc., by *too great a condescension* [in English]. Since Wolff was also attacked, I wrote to Freiligrath for an explanation, the more so as I knew that G. Rasch (a scoundrel) was head of his Begging Committee in Berlin.[7] He answered me very drily and with evasive philistine cunning. Later I sent him my *book* [in English], without, however, inscribing my name, as had been formerly our mutual custom. He seems to have taken the *hint* [in English].

Best regards to your dear wife and Fränzchen. If it is at all possible, I shall come *under all circumstances* [in English] and pay you a visit.[8]

Yours, K.M.

174

To Laura Lafargue (in Paris) [in English]
London, April 11, 1868

My dear Cacadou:
You know I am a slow hand at writing, but this time the shortcomings of my left arm are responsible for the sins of my right hand. Under those circum-

---

3. In his letter of congratulations, April 3, 1868, Freiligrath also thanked Marx for sending him a copy of *Das Kapital*, on which he commented thus: "It is really a book that should be studied and therefore its success will not, perhaps, be very rapid or loud; but it will quietly produce an effect that will be all the more profound and lasting. I know that in the Rhineland many young businessmen and factory owners are enthusiastic about the book. In these circles it will accomplish its real purpose—and, in addition, will be an indispensable source work for the scholar."
   Marx thought this comment "curious."
4. *Das Kapital*.
5. *Twelve Fighters of the Revolution* (Berlin, 1867).
6. Gustav Struve (1805–1870), German lawyer, emigrated to the United States where he fought in Union Army during the Civil War.
7. In spring, 1867, after Freiligrath lost his bank job in London, Freiligrath Committees were organized to collect money for his support.
8. Marx, accompanied by his daughter Eleanor, visited the Kugelmanns in Hanover from September 18 to October 7, 1869.

stances I missed the more my secretary[1] who might have addressed to himself, on my behalf, the most charming letters.

I am happy to see from your scribblings (you excuse the "turn," Borkheim with his *"scribaille"* [scribbling] is still dinning [into] my ears) and those of your helpmate that you are thoroughly enjoying your *Brautfahrt* [bridal trip, or honeymoon], and that all the outer circumstances, spring and sun and air and Paris jollities, conjure in your favour. As to that said helpmate, his sending books to me, at such a critical juncture, speaks volumes for the innate kindness of the "young man." This simple fact would go far to prove that he must belong to a better than the European race.[2] By the by, as we have just touched, the chapter of books, you might pay a visit to Guillaumin (14 rue Richelieu) and get his (economical) *bulletins de librairie* for 1866–1868. You might also wend your steps to the *Librairie Internationale* (15 Boulevard Montmartre) and ask for their catalogues (1865–68). Of course, if you get these desiderata, you will not *send* them, but bring them on your return to this dreary place.

I am expecting, from Meissner, three copies of my book.[3] On their arrival, I shall send two to César de Paepe,[4] one for himself, the other for Altmeyer.[5] Meanwhile, if you should find the time to see Schily[6] (that is to say if you write to him 4, rue St. Quentin to come and see you) be so kind to ask him what has become of the three copies, I sent to Jaclard,[7] one for Taine,[8] one for Reclus?[9] If Jaclard was not to be found, you might give his copy to Altmeyer, since Meissner is VERY SLOW in forwarding the copies. In that case, however, I ought to be informed.

You'll certainly fancy, my dear child, that I am very fond of books, because I trouble you with them at so unseasonable a time. But you would be quite mistaken. I am a machine, condemned to devour them and then, throw them, in a changed form, on the dunghill of history. A rather dreary task, too, but still better than that of Gladstone's[10] who is obliged, at a day's notice, to work himself into "states of mind," yclept "earnestness."

We feel here rather somewhat lonely. First you disappeared together with the meridional "silent man," and then Engels left us. In lieu of an "excitement" we had the Lormiers yesterday evening. I played with Louis

---

174

1. Laura had acted as her father's secretary.
2. Laura's husband, Paul Lafargue, was a Creole born in Cuba.
3. *Das Kapital*, published in September, 1867.
4. César de Paepe (1842–1890), Belgian doctor and labor leader.
5. Jean Jacques Altmeyer (1804–1877), Belgian historian.
6. Victor Schily (1810–1875), German lawyer in Paris.
7. Charles Victor Jaclard (1843–1903), French Blanquist, Communard.
8. Hippolyte Adolphe Taine (1828–1893), French philosopher.
9. Jean Jacques Elisée Reclus (1830–1905), French sociologist.
10. William Ewart Gladstone (1809–1898), British statesman.

two parties of chess and allowed him to win one. What do you think the strange Caliban boy told me, in the most solemn manner of the world, on taking leave? *"Sans rancune, j'espère* [Without rancor, I hope]!"

And now, my dear Cacadou, Adio. Old Nick

175

From letter to Frederick Engels (in Manchester)
London, April 30, 1868

Dear Fred:
... In a few days I will be fifty.[1] As that Prussian lieutenant had said to you, "Already twenty years in the service and still a lieutenant," so I can say: Half a century on my back and still a pauper! How right my Mother was! "If only Karell had made capital instead of [writing about it], etc.!"
　　Salut.

Yours, K. Marx

176

From letter to Frederick Engels (in Manchester)
London, May 16, 1868

Dear Fred:
My week-long silence has probably already been explained by Schorlemmer.[1] Two carbuncles on the scrotum would probably irk even a Sulla. How greatly that man, despite his Palmerstonian *temper* [in English], was affected by his mythical but in any case lousy illness, can be seen from the fact that ten days before his death he seized the Decurion [municipal senator] of a neighboring town and, one day before he croaked himself, had him strangled in his own house.[2]
　　Added to this, all kinds of worries. For example, a butcher's note for £15 falls due on the twenty-eighth of this month. No answer to my incendiary letters to Holland.[3] ...
　　Salut.

Yours, K.M.

175
1. Marx was born on May 5, 1818.
176
1. Carl Schorlemmer (1834–1892), German chemist in Manchester, friend of Marx and Engels.
2. The incident is mentioned in Plutarch's *Lives*.
3. Marx's relatives, the Philips family, in Holland.

177

To Frederick Engels (in Manchester)
London, June 27, 1868

Dear Fred:
The £5 received with thanks.

The children are doing very well. The suppuration and swelling in the throat have improved so that today the doctor ordered for them a simple dinner (until now only port *wine* [in English] and broth). They have devoured the dinner with *zest* [in English]. [Dr.] Korklow[1] had already previously prescribed fresh *air*. Instead of *chloride of lime* [in English], he ordered other (newer) disinfections, as he considered the former harmful to the lungs. Fortunately, our house is so built and the children's rooms especially are so located that they have the fullest breezes blowing from various sides.

Tell Mrs. Lizzy[2] (*to whom Tussy*[3] *sends her love* [in English]) that not for a moment must Manchester be held responsible. The *scarlatina* [in English] and *measles* [in English] are now epidemic in London. Tussy had probably caught the infection from the daughter of Professor Frankland.[4]

Best regards for Lizzy from me.

Yours, Mohr

Today I received a curious official document. I am summoned, for next Wednesday,[5] before the *vestry* [in English] of St. Pancras *to show cause why my goods and chattels should not be distrained* [in English]. Specifically, the accursed vestry had elected me, *bon gré mal gré* [willy-nilly], "*constable of the vestry of St. Pancras*" [in English] and I went to Manchester, instead of taking up the post and taking the proper oath of office. Dr. Korklow, whom I showed the *summons* [in English] today, told me it was *an honour much valued by the philistines of St. Pancras. I should tell them that I was a foreigner and that they should kiss me in the arse* [in English].

177

1. About Korklow, Marx wrote to Engels, June 26, 1868: "Our physician is our neighbor, Dr. Korklow, an Irishman, who is known in the neighborhood (also in my children's school) as a scarlet-fever specialist."
2. Lydia Burns.
3. Eleanor Marx.
4. Name not identified.
5. July 1.

Engels reacted mockingly to Marx's vestryship. He wrote him on June 28, 1868: "Salut, ô *connétable de Saint Pancrace*! [Greetings, O Constable of St. Pancras!] Get yourself a dignified outfit, a red dressing gown, a white nightcap, worn-down slippers, white shorts, a long earthenware pipe, and a pot of porter ale. Lafargue, your Esquire, can choose his own uniform."

Leading members of the Paris Commune of 1871, most of them Marx's associates or acquaintances: (top) Gustave-Paul Cluzeret, (center, left to right) Raoul Rigault, Louis-Charles Delescluze, Félix Pyat, (bottom) Pascal Grousset, Charles-Théophile Ferré, and Adolphe-Alphonse Assi

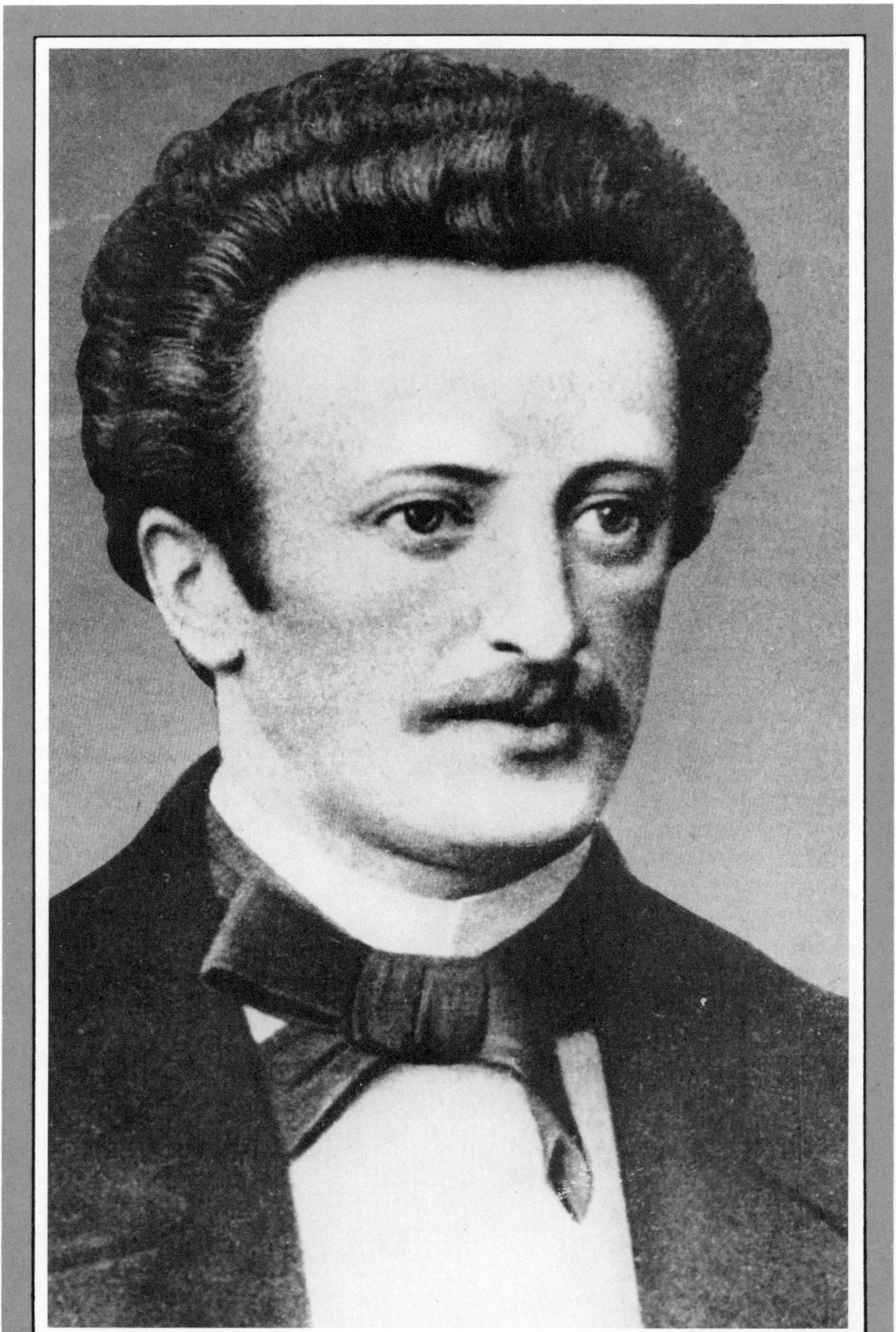

COURTESY GERMAN INFORMATION CENTER

Wilhelm Liebknecht (1826–1900), a founder and leader of the German Social Democratic Party, Marx's friend and disciple

*Left) Ferdinand Lassalle (1825–1864),
ounder of the General German Workers
Association, with whom Marx maintained
a stormy love-hate relationship*

*Georg Wilhelm Friedrich Hegel
(1770–1831), German philosopher whose
writings Marx studied at Berlin University
and who had a profound influence upon him.*

*(Right) François Marie Charles Fourier
(1772–1837), French utopian socialist whose
writings influenced a whole generation of
Europeans, including Marx as a young man.*

Otto Karl Meissner (1819–1902),
Hamburg publisher of Marx's
Das Kapital

Georg Herwegh (1817–1875),
German revolutionary poet, friend of
Marx, lived in exile in Switzerland

(Left) Pierre Joseph Proudhon
(1809–1865), French social
philosopher about whom Marx
wrote devastating criticisms.
Portrait by the French painter
Gustave Courbet (1853)

Frederick Engels (1820–1895), in his fifties. Portrait taken in London in the 1870's

178

From letter to Frederick Engels (in Manchester)
London, July 11, 1868

Dear Fred:
The £10 received with *best thanks* [in English]. I immediately paid £3/5 shillings in taxes, £3 to the *cheesemonger* [in English] (whom, for that matter, I have been paying cash for weeks, since, like the *teagrocer* [in English], he no longer delivers on credit), £1/10 shillings to the apothecary. I owe the baker £17, and the man who is always friendly, is now hard pressed. It is abominable for me to press you so hard. If only I could find some *immediate* way out!

The children are well, although Jennychen[1] is still very weak. The prevailing *temper* [in English] in the house here is not precisely conducive to convalescence. My wife is also not well, and thus needlessly irritable....

The farce of *Mannequin Pisse*[2] Faucher[3] of making me a pupil of Bastiat, you cannot understand in all its humor. In his *Harmonies*,[4] Bastiat states: "If, in the determination of value through work-time, anyone would explain to him why air has *no* value and *diamonds* have a *high* one, he would throw his book into the fire." Since I have just achieved this terrible trick, Faucher must prove that I in fact accept the Bastiat who states that there is "no measure" of value.

The manner in which Bastiat deduces the diamond-value is seen in the following *commis-voyageur* [traveling salesman] conversation:

"*Monsieur, cédez-moi votre diamant.—Monsieur, je veux bien; cédez-moi en échange votre travail de toute une année.*"[5] Instead of the business friend answering: "*Mon cher, si j'étais condamné à travailler, vous comprenez bien que j'aurai autre chose à acheter que des diamants,*"[6] he says: "*Mais, monsieur, vous n'avez pas sacrifié à votre acquisition une minute.—Eh bien, monsieur, tâchez de rencontrer une minute semblable.—Mais, en bonne justice, nous devrions échanger à travail égal.—Non, en bonne justice, vous appréciez vos services et moi les miens. Je ne vous force pas; pourquoi me forceriez-vous? Donnez-moi un an tout entier, ou cherchez vous même un diamant.—Mais cela m'en entraînerait à dix ans de pénibles recherches, sans compter*

178
1. Daughter Jenny Marx.
2. The name of a statue of a urinating boy in a Brussels fountain.
3. Julius Faucher's review of *Das Kapital* in his *Vierteljahrschrift für Volkswirtschaft und Kulturgeschichte* [*Quarterly for Political Economics and Cultural History*], Volume XX (1868).
4. Frédéric Bastiat, *Harmonies Économiques* [*Economic Harmonies*] (Paris, 1861).
5. "Sir, give me your diamonds.—Gladly, sir; give me in exchange your labor for a whole year."
6. "My dear, if I were condemned to work, you can well understand that I would have other things to do than to buy diamonds."

une déception probable au bout. Je trouve plus sage, plus profitable d'employer ces dix ans d'une autre manière.—C'est justement pour cela que je crois vous rendre encore service en ne vous demandant qu'un an. Je vous en épargne neuf, et voilà pourquoi j'attache beaucoup de valeur à ce service."[7]

Is this not like the wine salesman as he lives and breathes?

Moreover—what the German Bastiatites do not know—is this unfortunate expression that the value of commodities is determined by the labor, not what it costs, but what it *saves* the buyer (childish phrase to introduce into the connection between exchange and the division of labor), is as little the invention of Bastiat as any other wine-salesman category.

The old jackass Schmalz, the Prussian demagogue-catcher, says (German edition, 1818; French 1826):[8] *"Le travail d'autrui en général ne produit jamais pour nous qu'une économie de temps, et cette économie de temps est tout ce qui constitue sa valeur et son prix. Le menuisier, par exemple, qui me fait une table, et le domestique qui porte mes lettres à la poste, qui bat mes habits, ou qui cherche pour moi les choses qui me sont nécessaires, me rendent l'un et l'autre un service absolument de même nature: l'un et l'autre m'épargne et le temps qui je serais obligé d'employer moi-même à mes [ces] occupations, et celui qu'il m'aurait fallu consacrer à m'acquérir l'aptitude et les talents qu'elles exigent."*[9]

The old Schmalz was the epigone of the Physiocrats. He says this in his polemic against Adam Smith's *travail productif* [productive labor] and *improductif* [unproductive], and proceeds from the basic principle that only agriculture produces real value. He found the stuff in Garnier.[10] Similar things are to be found in the epigones of the Mercantilist Ganilh.[11] Ditto in the polemic against that differentiation in Adam Smith. Hence Bastiat copies

---

7. "But, sir, you have not sacrificed a single minute for your acquisition.—Well, sir, try to meet such a minute.—But, in fairness we ought to exchange *equal labor.*—No, in fairness, you appreciate your services and I appreciate mine. I do not force you; why should you force me? Give me a whole year, or search for a diamond yourself.—But this would involve me in ten years of painful search, apart from the probable disappointment at the end. I find it wiser and more profitable to employ those ten years in another way.—This is precisely why I believe I am rendering you still another *service* when I demand only one year from you. I am saving you nine, and this is why I attach so much *value* to this service."
8. Theodor Anton Heinrich Schmalz, *Staatswirtschaftslehre in Briefen an einen deutschen Erbprinzen* [*Political Economy in Letters to a German Crown Prince*] (Berlin, 1818); translated in French: *Économique Politique, Ouvrage traduit de l'Allemand* (Paris, 1826).
9. "The labor of others in general never produces anything for us except a *saving of time*, and this saving of time is all that constitutes its *value* and its *price*. The carpenter who makes a table for me, for example, and the servant who takes my letters to the post, cleans my clothing and fetches the necessary things for me, each of them performs for me a *service* of absolutely the same nature; the one and the other *save me* the time that I would have needed to apply and to acquire the aptitudes for those occupations."
10. Germain Garnier, *Abrégé Élémentaire des Principes de l'Économie Politique* [*Elementary Compendium of the Principles of Political Economy*] (Paris, 1796)
11. Charles Ganilh, *Des Systèmes d'Économie Politique* [*Of Systems of Political Economy*], 2d ed. (Paris, 1821).

the epigones' polemic from two standpoints—that do not have the slightest conception of value! And this is the newest discovery in Germany! It is a pity that there is no journal in which one could expose this Bastiat plagiarism.

Salut.

Yours, K.M.

179

To Ludwig Kugelmann (in Hanover)
London, August 10, 1868

Dear Kugelmann:
On receiving your letter I did what I could, but in vain. At the moment it is impossible to raise money for foreign strikes from the unions here.[1] I find the variety of information about the Linden factory contained in the Hanoverian papers recently sent to me, very interesting.

My family is at present at the seaside, which was the more necessary as both girls[2] seemed weak after their illness. Lafargue, after having passed his surgery examination, will perform operations in a hospital as assistant surgeon for a few more weeks and then move to Paris, where he still has to take his French medical examination.

I am at the moment more concerned with private than with public economy. Specifically, Engels has offered to guarantee a loan of £100 to £150 for me at 5 percent interest, the first half to be paid in January, the second in July. Up to the present, however, I have not succeeded in finding a lender.

I hope "very much" that the *state of my work* will permit me to leave London for good and go to the Continent next year, at the end of September. I shall depart as soon as I can dispense with the [British] Museum here. The high cost of living here is becoming more and more burdensome as time goes on. To be sure, the pettiness of conditions there [in Europe] is not much to my taste. However, *"Ruhe is die erste Bürgerpflicht"* ["Tranquillity is the first duty of the citizen"] and it is the only way of attaining peace. There are all sorts of scandals here in and about the so-called French Branch of the International Workingmen's Association, about which I shall report in my next letter.

I am now *solus* [alone], and it appears strange to me that I miss all the noise of the children.

Salut.

Yours, K. Marx

179

1. On August 2, 1868, Kugelmann wrote to Marx about raising funds for 1,000 weavers on strike in a factory at Linden near Hanover.
2. Jenny and Eleanor Marx.

180

From letter to Frederick Engels (in Manchester)
London, September 26, 1868

Dear Fred:
Best thanks for [in English] the £5.[1] These lousy small *shopkeepers* [in English] are a pitiable class. My wife immediately took the money to the creditor. The man himself was momentarily "all in" (and in his own way he is quite a respectable fellow); his wife, full of tears, accepted the money for him. A large, the largest, portion of these *shopkeepers* [in English] are experiencing all the miseries of the proletariat, aggravated by "anxiety" and "enslavement to respectability," without the *compensating* [in English] self-respect of the better class of workers....
    Salut.

Yours, K.M.

181

From letter to Ludwig Kugelmann (in Hanover)
London, October 12, 1868

My dear friend:
Your stubborn silence is quite incomprehensible to me. Did I give cause for it in my last letter?[1] I hope not. In any case, it was unintentional. I need not tell you explicitly, you *know*, that you are my most intimate friend in Germany, and I do not see that, *inter amicos* [among friends], one must keep such a sharp watch over one another for any trifle. Least of all do you have *this right* in regard to me, because you know how much I am obliged to you. You have

---

180

1. Marx to Engels, September 24, 1868: "Could you send me £5 by Saturday [September 26]? One of the tradesmen has just been here and told me he is on the verge of bankruptcy and that he would incur great expenses if he did not raise a certain sum by Saturday."

181

1. See Letter 179, Marx to Kugelmann, August 10, 1868.

done more—apart from everything personal—for me than all of Germany put together.[2]

But perhaps you are so energetically silent in order to prove to me that you are not like the crowd of so-called friends who are silent when things go badly and speak when they go well. Still, there was no need for such a "demonstration" on your part.

When I speak of a "good state of affairs" I mean, first, the propaganda which my book has been making and the recognition it has found among the German workers, since you wrote me last. And, secondly, there is the wonderful progress which the International Workingmen's Association [First International] has made, especially in England.[3]

A few days ago a Petersburg publisher[4] surprised me with the news that a Russian translation of *Das Kapital* is now being printed.[5] He asked for my photograph for the title page and I could not deny this trifle to "my good friends," the Russians. It is an irony of fate that the Russians, whom I have fought for twenty-five years, not only in German, but in French and English, have always been my "patrons." In Paris in 1843 and 1844 the Russian aristocrats there carried me on their hands. My book against Proudhon (1847)[6] and the one published by Duncker (1859)[7] have had a greater sale in Russia than anywhere else. And the first foreign nation to translate *Das Kapital* is the Russian. But too much should not be made of all this. The Russian aristocracy, in its youth, is educated in German universities and in Paris. It always snatches at the most extreme that the West has to offer. It is pure *gourmandise* [gluttony], such as part of the French aristocracy practiced during the eighteenth century. *Ce n'est pas pour les tailleurs et les bottiers*,[8] Voltaire said then of his own Enlightenment. This does not prevent the same Russians, once they enter government service, from becoming scoundrels. . . .

I have suffered a good deal from the heat, because of my liver, but at the moment I am well.

Salut.

Yours, Karl Marx

---

2. Kugelmann was most active in distributing Engels' prepared reviews of *Das Kapital* among German newspapers.
3. See Saul K. Padover, ed., *Karl Marx on the First International* (New York; McGraw-Hill Book Co., 1973).
4. Nicolai Petrovich Polyakov (1841–1905).
5. The translation, mostly by Nicolai Danielson, was not published until March, 1872; even then it was the first foreign-language translation of *Das Kapital* to appear.
6. Marx, *The Poverty of Philosophy*.
7. Marx, *Critique of Political Economy*.
8. This is not for tailors and cobblers.

182

To Frederick Engels (in Manchester)
London, November 30, 1868

Dear Fred:

I am completely *knocked down* [in English] by your too generous goodness.[1]

I had my wife show me all the *bills* [in English], and the sum of debts is much greater than I thought, £210 (of which *about* [in English] £75 due to the pawnshop and interest). This does not include the doctor's *bill* [in English] for the cure of the scarlet fever[2] which he has not yet sent in.

In the last years we needed more than £350, but this sum is entirely sufficient, because (1) in recent years Lafargue has lived in our house and through his presence our expenses were increased; (2) the debt-system made everything much too expensive. Only with the full *clearance* [in English] of the debts, will I be able to put through a *strict* [in English] administration.

How unpleasant the conditions were in the house in recent months, you can see from the fact that Jennychen[3]—behind my back—has engaged herself to give *private lessons* in an English family. The thing begins only in January, 1869. I have subsequently agreed to the thing on condition (the woman of the house and her husband, Dr. Monroe,[4] came to see my wife about it) that the engagement *be binding for only one month* and that at the end of the month each side have the *right to give notice*. Annoying as the matter was (the child[5] has to teach small children practically the whole day)—I don't

---

182

1. On November 29, 1868, Engels, then negotiating with his partner, Gottfried Ermen, for the sale to him of his share of the business in Manchester, wrote to Marx a letter containing an offer of extraordinary generosity. Engels wrote: "Give me a *precise* answer to these questions by return mail . . . (1) How much money do you need to pay *all* your debts, so as to have a clear start? (2) Can you manage with £350 a year for ordinary, regular needs (I exclude extra costs due to illness and other unforeseen events), that is, so that you would not have to incur debts?"

The always impecunious and debt-ridden Marx, who never earned that much money in his professional life, was understandably "knocked down" by his friend's offer. Although Marx overspent his £350 yearly, and Engels always made up the deficit, nevertheless he was thenceforth, until his death fifteen years later, free from the terrible oppression of poverty.

2. See Letter 177, Marx to Engels, June 27, 1868.
3. Jenny Marx, daughter.
4. A Scottish doctor.
5. The "child," Jennychen, was then twenty-four years old.

have to tell you this—I agreed because I thought it good, above all, that Jennychen be diverted by some occupation and specifically to get out of the four walls here. For years, my wife—understandable in our conditions but not the less disagreeable therefor—has thoroughly lost her *temper* [in English] and with her complaints and irritability and *bad humour* [in English] torments the children to death, although no other children could bear all this *in a more jolly way* [in English]. But *sunt certi denique fines* [There are after all certain limits]. It is, of course, *unpleasant* [in English] to write you this. It is easier to say such things. But it is necessary to explain to you why I did not cancel Jennychen's move.

Yours, K.M.

183

From letter to Ludwig Kugelmann (in Hanover)
London, December 12, 1868

Dear Friend:
... Tell your dear wife I never "suspected" her of serving under Lady-General Geck.[1] My question was only a joke. In any case, ladies cannot complain about the [First] International, for it has elected a lady, Madame Law,[2] to membership in the General Council. Joking aside, great progress was shown in the last congress of the American labor union,[3] which, among other things, treated working women with complete equality, whereas in this respect the English, and still more so the gallant French, are burdened with a narrow-minded spirit. Anybody who knows anything of history also knows that great social changes are impossible without the female ferment. Social progress can be measured exactly by the social status of the beautiful sex (the ugly ones included). ...

With best regards,

Yours, K.M.

183
1. Marie Gögg (b.1826), head of the women's section of the First International.
2. Harriet Law (1832–1897), English atheist leader.
3. The National Labor Union, founded in Baltimore in August, 1866.

184

From letter to Frederick Engels (in Manchester)
London, March 20, 1869

Dear Fred:
... I am thinking of becoming *naturalized* as an Englishman, for the purpose of being able to travel to Paris in safety.[1] Without such a trip, the French edition of my book[2] will never come to pass. My presence there is positively necessary. Under the Palmerston law, one could, if one wishes, drop the English citizenship in six months. The law does not protect a naturalized citizen against a crime which he committed in his native land *before* his naturalization, upon his return there. With this exception, the naturalized citizen is equal to a native Englishman vis-à-vis foreign *governments* [in English]. In truth, I see no reason why I should not visit Paris without the permission of Herr Bonaparte,[3] if I have the means to do so....
Adio.

Yours, Mohr

"who daily presents more and more
the picture of a Moor turned white."

185

To Jenny Marx (in London) [in English]
Manchester, June 2, 1869

My dear Emperor:[1]
The thing under the arm was no carbuncle, but another sort of abcess [*sic*], which bothered me much but, since yesterday, is quickly healing. It was a fortune I was at Manchester.[2] Otherwise, it might have turned out a troublesome affair, I am now quite in good health.

I hope to be with you in the course of next week. Tussy will probably somewhat prolong her stay at Manchester. After the restraint at Paris, she feels here quite at her ease like a newfledged bird.

184

1. Marx, however, did not apply for British citizenship until August, 1874, and then he was turned down as a communist who had "not been loyal to his own King and Country."
2. *Das Kapital.*
3. Napoleon III.

185

1. Nickname for daughter Jenny.
2. Marx and his daughter Eleanor visited Engels in Manchester from May 25 to June 14, 1869.

I hope Lessner's[3] departure to Brasil is not yet definitively decided upon. I regret very much being not able to do something for him. With your usual kindness you seem to have sacrificed yourself in the interminable tête à tête of Sunday last. As to Lafargue's paper,[4] I feel rather uneasy. On the one hand, I should like to oblige Blanqui.[5] On the other hand, my other occupations will not allow me to do much for them, but, above all things, I fear lest *old* Lafargue should suspect me to push his son to premature political action and make him neglect his professional duties. As it is, he has not much reason to delight in his connection with the Marx family.

And now, dear By Bye, good-by and my compliments to all.

Your retainer, Old Nick

186

To François Lafargue (in Bordeaux) [in French]
Paris, July 10, 1869

My dear friend:
I arrived here Thursday evening and will return to London on Monday.[1]

Judging by your letter, which I have reread, you seem to assume that my wife is still here. This is an error.

I was particularly shaken by the fact that Laura is still in pain and that her health is so deeply affected.

I start with this because it explains the seeming indifference of our Paul [Lafargue]. He has not interrupted his studies,[2] but has nevertheless neglected to take the necessary measures for his examinations.

To the reproaches that I made him, he replied, and I must say that he had a right to answer so: "Before I could think of the future, I had to concern myself with the present. Laura's health required of me the most attentive care. It does not even permit me to absent myself for a somewhat longer time. Not to worry you and my family, I wanted to keep the thing secret. Laura and I have done everything so that Mrs. Marx should not suspect."

I have spoken with a very good physician, who visits Paul's house. He told me that Laura must absolutely go to the seashore, and suggested Dieppe, because a longer trip would be harmful to her health.

---

3. Friedrich Lessner (1827–1910), German communist tailor in London.
4. *La Renaissance*, a political weekly which Lafargue unsuccessfully planned to publish in Paris.
5. Louis Auguste Blanqui (1805–1881), French revolutionist, communist.

186
1. Worried about his daughter Laura Lafargue's health, Marx, using the alias "A. Williams," visited Paris from July 1 to 12, 1869.
2. He was a student of medicine.

Moreover, Paul has assured me that he would do his best, after his return from Dieppe, to shorten the time needed for his doctor's examination, etc.

I must tell you frankly that my daughter's state of health gives me serious misgivings.

Our grandson[3] is an enchanting boy. I have never seen such a beautifully formed child's head.

My compliments to your wife.

Accept, my dear friend, the heartiest greetings from

Yours, Karl Marx

187

From letter to Frederick Engels (in Manchester)
London, July 22, 1869

Dear Fred:
... I have had another "family" unpleasantness. For some time now I noticed that my wife does not make ends meet with the money I give her weekly, although our expenses have not increased in any way. Since I absolutely don't want to get into debt again, and since the money I gave her last Monday was "all gone" today [Thursday], I asked for an explanation. Then the folly of women came out. In the list of debts which she had drawn up for you, she had suppressed about £75, which she has been trying to pay off *by and by* [in English] from her house allowance. I asked, why this? Reply: She was afraid to tell me about such a big sum! Women obviously always need a guardian![1]...

Salut.

Yours, Mohr

---

3. Charles-Étienne Lafargue, nicknamed Schnappy (1868–1872).

187

1. Engels to Marx, July 25, 1869: "As for the £75, don't let it cause you any gray hair; as soon as Gottfried [Ermen: Engels' partner] has paid me my next installment ... , I will send it to you. Only see to it that this does not happen again in the future; you know that our estimates have been tightly calculated, leaving absolutely no margin for extravagances."

Marx replied, August 4, 1869: "Dear Fred: The £100 received with best thanks. I shall now watch the proceedings so closely that similar mistakes, etc.... "

188

To *Laura Lafargue (in London) [in English]*
Hanover,[1] *September 25, 1869*

My dear Cacadou:
I regret that I cannot celebrate to [*sic*] home of my dear bird's eye,[2] but Old Nick's thoughts are with you.

> *Du bist beslozen*
> *In minem Herzen.*[3]

I was happy to see from Möhmchen's[4] letter (written in her usual amusing way, she is a real virtuoso in letter writing) that your health is improving. Our dear little Schnappy,[5] I hope, will soon get better. At the same time, I fully share Kugelmann's opinion that Dr. West[6] ought to be consulted *at once* (or another medical man if he be absent).

I trust you and Lafargue will in this case yield to my paternal authority, a thing, you know full well, I am not in the habit of appealing to. Nobody is more difficult to treat than a baby. In no case more immediate action is wanted, and any delay more hurtful. You must under no circumstances accelerate your departure from London.[7] It would be really dangerous to the child and do no good to yourself. On this point, every medical man will give you the same advice.

I am glad the Basel congress[8] is over, and has, comparatively speaking, passed off so well. I am always fretting on such occasions of public exhibition of the party *mit allen ihren Geschwüren* [with all its ulcers]. None of the actors was *à la hauteur des principes* [up to high principles], but the higher class idiocy effaces the working class blunders. We have passed through no little German town the *Winkelblatt* [local newspaper] of which was not full of the doings of "that formidable Congress."

We are here in a sort of fix. The Kugelmanns will not hear of an early leave-taking. At the same time, Jenny is much improving in health upon the change of air and circumstances.

188
1. Marx, in the company of daughter Jenny, visited Dr. Ludwig Kugelmann in Hanover from September 18 to October 7, 1869.
2. Laura was born on September 26, 1845, in Brussels.
3. From a medieval folk song; the words mean: "Thou art locked in my heart."
4. Mrs. Karl Marx; the word is diminutive for "mother."
5. Charles-Étienne Lafargue.
6. Dr. Charles West (1816–1898), a London pediatrician.
7. Laura had come to London from Paris in mid-August.
8. The congress of the First International, September 6 to 12, 1869.

With Liebknecht I am likely to meet, within a few days, at Braun-schweig [Brunswick]. I decline going to Leipzig, and he cannot come to Hanover, since the Prussians would probably give him the advantages of free lodging during the present prorogation of the Reichstag.

My best thanks to Paul for his elaborate letter. *Meine herzlichsten Grüsse an das ganze Haus* [My heartiest regards to the whole family] and hundred kisses to yourself and my dear little Schnappy.

Adio, dear child.

Ever yours, Old Nick

189

To Paul and Laura Lafargue (in Paris)[1] [in English]
London, October 18, 1869

My dear Paul and Laura:
I send you today the manuscript of Mr. Keller.[2] I cannot find his address. So you through the aid of Schily get it out from M. Hess.

Tell Mr. Keller that he shall go on. On the whole, I am satisfied with his translation, although it lacks elegance and is done in too negligent a way.

He will do best to send me every chapter *through you*. As to Chapter IV I shall subdivide it.[3]

The changes I have made in his Chapter II need not be maintained, but they show the direction in which I want the corrections to be made.

As to the word "*Verwertung*" [utilization] see my note p.12 of his man-uscript. He must make a note on it for the French reader.

I doubt whether the frequent *large printing of words* will do for the French printers. In German we use the word "Process" (*procès*) for economical movements, as you say chemical *procès, si je ne me trompe pas* [if I am not mistaken]. He translates by phenomena which is nonsense. If he can find no other word, he must always translate by "*mouvement*" [movement] or some-thing analogous.

Kiss dear Schnappy on my behalf.

Yours, Old Nick

189

1. The Lafargues returned to Paris at the end of September; they lived at 47 rue du Cherche-Midi.
2. Charles Keller translated the first chapters of *Das Kapital* from German into French.
3. Chapter IV of the German edition of *Das Kapital* corresponds to Chapters IV, V and VI in the French translation, which came out in November, 1875.

I have received a letter from St. Petersburg. A Russian sent me his work (in German[4]) on the situation of the peasantry and the workingclass generally in that benighted country.[5]

Yours, Old Nick

[*Note to Paul Lafargue in French*]
Point out to Keller that the dotted lines are to be kept in the text.

190

From letter to Frederick Engels (in Manchester)
London, February 10, 1870

Dear Fred:
... I have read the first 150 pages of Flerovsky's book[1] (covering Siberia, North Russia and Astrakhan). This is the first work in which the truth is told about economic conditions in Russia. The man is a decided enemy of what he calls "Russian optimism." I never had very glowing views of this communist Eldorado, but Flerovsky exceeds all expectations. It is, in truth, marvelous and in any case a sign of change, that such a book could be printed in Petersburg.

"In our country there are few proletarians, but the mass of our workingclass consists of workers, whose lot is worse than that of any proletarian."[2]

His method of presentation is quite original, mostly reminiscent at times of Monteil.[3] One can see that Flerovsky has himself traveled everywhere and made observations. Burning hatred of landlords, capitalists and government officials. No socialist doctrine, no soil mysticism (although he favors the form of communal property), no Nihilist extravagance. Here and there some well-meaning twaddle which, considering the stage of development of the people to whom the work is addressed, is suitable. In any case, this is the most important book that has appeared since your *Condition of the*

---

4. Marx obviously meant "Russian."
5. N. Flerovsky (pseudonym for Vassily Vassilyevich Berwi), *The Condition of the Working Class in Russia* (St. Petersburg, 1869). In a letter to Paul and Laura Lafargue, March 5, 1870, Marx called it "an extraordinary book," which he read in the original, "quite fluently with the help of a dictionary." The book, he wrote, convinced him that "a frightful social revolution" was "inevitable in Russia and imminent."

190

1. N. Flerovsky, *The Condition of the Working Class in Russia* (1869). A copy of this book was sent to Marx by N. F. Danielson on September 30, 1869.
2. Quoted by Marx in the Russian original.
3. Amant-Alexis Monteil, *Histoire des français des divers états aux cinq derniers siècles* [*History of the French of Various Conditions in the Last Five Centuries*], 10 vols. (Paris, 1828–1844).

Working Class in England. The family life of the Russian peasants—with its hideous whipping-to-death of their wives, vodka-drinking, and concubines—is also depicted well. So it would be quite appropriate if you would now send me the lying fantasies of Citizen Herzen....[4]

My compliments to Mrs. Lizzie[5] and friends [in English].

K.M.

191

From letter to Frederick Engels (in Manchester)
London, February 12, 1870

Dear Fred:

[Dr.] Allen paid me a visit yesterday. Nothing but a simple cold. Still, he counseled my continued staying indoors, until the Russian wind, "which blows no good to anybody," ceases....

The title of N. Flerovsky's book is: *Polozhenie Rabotshago Klassa v Rossyi*, [*The Condition of the Working Class in Russia*], Publishers, N. P. Polyakov, St. Petersburg, 1869.[1]

What, among other things, amuses me greatly in Flerovsky is his polemic against the *direct dues* paid by the peasantry. It is entirely a reproduction of Marshal Vauban and Boisguillebert.[2] He also feels that the situation of the country people has its analogy in the period of the old French monarchy (after Louis XIV). Like Monteil, he has a great feeling for national characteristics—the "honest Kalmuck," "the Mordwin, poetic despite his filth" (he compares him to the Irish), the "nimble, epicurean, lively Tartar," the "talented Little Russian," etc. Like a good Russian, he teaches his fellow countrymen what they should do to turn the *hatred* all these races have for them into its opposite. As an example of this hatred, he cites, among other things, a genuinely *Russian* colony which had emigrated from Poland to Siberia. These people know only Russian and not a word of Polish, but consider themselves Poles and devote a Polish hatred to the Russians, etc.

From his book it follows irrefutably that the present conditions in Russia are no longer tenable, that the emancipation of the serfs, of course,

---

4. Alexander Ivanovich Herzen (1812–1870), a Russian writer, living abroad since 1852.
5. Lydia Burns.

191

1. Marx wrote the names of the author, publisher, and publishing place, as well as the title, in Russian.
2. Sébastien le Prêtre de Vauban, *"Project d'une dime royale"*; Pierre Le Pesant Boisguillebert, *"Dissertation sur la nature des richesses, de l'argent et des tributs"*—both in *Économistes financiers du XVIIIe Siècle* (Paris, 1843).

only hastened the process of disintegration, and that a frightful social revolution is imminent. Here one also sees the real basis of the schoolboy-nihilism that is now fashionable among Russian students, etc. In Geneva—by the by—exiled students have formed a new colony, whose program proclaims opposition to Pan-Slavism and its replacement by the "International."

In a special section, Flerovsky shows that the "Russification" of alien races is a pure optimistic delusion, *even in the East....*

Salut.

Yours, K.M.

192

From letter to Ludwig Kugelmann (in Hanover)
London, February 17, 1870

Dear Kugelmann:

... Of the brochures that you sent me, one is a special plea with which the privileged classes of the German-Russian-Baltic provinces are currently appealing for German sympathies. This riffraff, which has always distinguished itself for its eager services in Russian diplomacy, Army and Police, and which, since the transference of those provinces from Poland to Russia, has gladly haggled away its nationality in exchange for a legal legitimation of its exploitation of the peasants—is now crying out because it sees its privileged position threatened. The old system [*Ständewesen*], orthodox Lutheranism and extortion of the peasantry, is what they call *German culture*, which Europe is now supposed to defend. Hence the last word of that brochure—*Grundeigentum als Basis der Zivilisation* [Ownership of Landed Property as the Basis of Civilization] and, according to the confession of the miserable pamphleteer, landed property consisting largely of manorial estates or of tribute-paying peasant farms, at that.

In his citation—insofar as Russian communal property is concerned—the fellow shows his ignorance as well as his cloven hoof. Schédo-Ferroti[1] is one of the chaps who claims that communal property is the cause of the miserable condition of the Russian peasants (naturally in the interests of landlordism), just as formerly the *abolition of feudalism* in Western Europe—instead of the serfs' loss of their land—was decried as the cause of pauperism. Of the same calibre is the Russian book, *Land and Freedom*. Its author is von Lilienfeld,[2] a Baltic bumpkin squire [*Krautjunker*]. What has made the Rus-

---

192

1. Pseudonym for Baron Fyodor Ivanovich Firks (1812–1872), a writer on agrarian questions in Russia.
2. Pavel Fedorovich Lilienfeld-Toal (1829–1903), a Baltic landowner and czarist official.

sian peasantry miserable was the same that made the French under Louis XIV, etc., wretched—namely, *State taxes and the Obrok* [land tax] *paid to the big landed proprietors.* Instead of creating misery, communal ownership alone actually mitigated it.

It is, furthermore, an historic lie that *communal property is Mongolian.* As I have pointed out in a number of my writings, it is of *Indian* origin and is, therefore, to be found among all nations of European culture at the beginning of their development. Its specific *Slavic* (not Mongolian) form in Russia (which is repeated also among *non-Russian South Slavs*) even has most resemblance, *mutatis mutandis* [all things considered], to the *old-German* modification of the Indian type of communal property.

That the Pole Duchinski, in Paris, attempted to show, with a great display of erudition, that the Great Russian tribe was *not Slavic* but *Mongolian*—was, from the point of view of a Pole, understandable. Nevertheless, the thing is false. It is not the Russian peasantry, but the Russian nobility that is strongly permeated with Mongol-Tartar elements. The Frenchman Henri Martin[3] took his theory from Duchinski, and the "inspired Gottfried Kinkel" translated Martin[4] and showed up as a Polish enthusiast in order to make the democratic party forget his servile homage to Bismarck.

That, on the other hand, the Russian State in its policy toward Europe and America represents *Mongolianism*, has now, of course, become a commonplace truth, obvious even to Baltic bumpkin squires, philistines [*Spiessbürger*], parsons and professors. The Baltic German cry-for-help scandal must, therefore, be exploited because it puts Prussia's great-German power in a "ticklish" position. Everything on our side that expresses antipathy for that "representative of German culture," in the eyes of Prussia makes it precisely worthy of protection.

Another example of the crass ignorance of the pamphlet-writer! In his eyes, the sale of Russian North American territory[5] was nothing more than a diplomatic trick on the part of the Russian government, which, be it said in passing, *was very hard pressed for costs* [in English]. But the main point is this: The American Congress has recently published the documents on that transaction. There one finds, among other things, a report by the American *Geschäftsführer* [business manager; the identification is not clear] who specifically writes to Washington: The acquisition is for the moment not worth a cent, but—but England will thereby be cut off from the ocean by the

---

3. Bon-Louis-Henri Martin (1810–1883), French historian and member of the First International.
4. Gottfried Kinkel translated Martin's *La Russie et l'Europe* (Paris, 1866) into German in 1869.
5. By a treaty of March 30, 1867, the United States bought Alaska from Russia for $7,200,000 (11,000,000 rubles).

Yankees on one side and thereby the reversion of all of British North America to the United States would be accelerated. *There it is in a nutshell* [in English]!

I approve in essence your correspondence with Jacoby,[6] but the exaggerated praises of my efficacy have absolutely shocked me. *Est modus in rebus* [There is a measure in all things], if you must praise. The old Jacoby himself is very praiseworthy. What other *old radical* [in English] in Europe possesses the uprightness and courage to place himself so directly on the side of the proletarian movement? That his transition measures and detailed proposals are of little value is an entirely unimportant matter. Between ourselves—*take all in all* [in English] I expect more for the social movement from Germany than from France.

I had a big row with that intriguer Bakunin.[7] But more about that in my next letter.

My best compliments to Madame la Comtesse[8] and Fränzchen.[9]

Yours, K.M.

193

From letter to Laura and Paul Lafargue (in Paris) [in English]
London, March 5, 1870

Dear Laura and Paul:

You feel certainly great and just indignation at my prolonged silence, but you ought to excuse it as the natural consequence, first, of illness, then of extra work to make up for the time lost.

The sad news Paul [Lafargue] communicated to us did not take me by surprise. The evening before the arrival of his letter I had stated to the family my serious misgivings as to the little child [a Lafargue infant girl who died in February, 1870, at the age of two months]. I have suffered myself too much from such losses to not profoundly sympathize with yours. Still, from the same personal experience I know that all wise commonplaces and consolatory speech uttered on such occasion increase real grief instead of soothing it.

... I hope you will send us good news of little Schnappy,[1] my greatest favorite. The poor dear little fellow must have suffered severely from the cold

---

6. Johann Jacoby (1805–1877), German socialist physician in Königsberg and member of Parliament.
7. Michael Bakunin (1814–1876), Russian revolutionist, Anarchist leader.
8. Gertrud Kugelmann, wife of Dr. Ludwig Kugelmann.
9. Franziska Kugelmann, daughter.

193
1. Charles-Étienne Lafargue.

so adverse to "*la nature mélanienne* [dark-skinned nature].[2] Apropos, *un certain M. de Gobineau* [a certain M. de Gobineau] published, *il y a à peu près dix ans* [about ten years ago], a work in four volumes, *Sur l'Inégalité des races humaines*,[3] written for the purpose of proving above all that "*la race blanche*" [the white race] is a sort of God among the other human races and, of course, the noble families within the "*race blanche*" are again *la crème de la crème* [the elite]. I rather suspect that M. De Gobineau, *dans ce temps-là* "*premier secrétaire de la légation de France en Suisse*" [at that time "first secretary of the French legation in Switzerland"], to have sprung himself not from an ancient Frankish warrior but from a modern French *huissier* [doorman]. However that may be, and despite his spite against the "*race noire*" [black race] (for such people it is always a source of satisfaction to have somebody they think themselves entitled to *mépriser* [despise]), he declares "*le nègre*" [the Negro] or "*le sang noir*" [black blood] to be the material source of art and that all the artistic creativity of the white nations depends on their mixture with "*le sang noir.* . . ."

Old Nick

194

From letter to Frederick Engels (in Manchester)
London, March 24, 1870

Dear Fred:
. . . Enclosed a letter from the *Russian colony* in Geneva. We admitted it to membership; I *accepted* its request to be its representative in the [International's] General Council, and I wrote a brief reply (officially, in addition to a letter *privée* [private]), giving permission to publish it in its newspaper.[1] *Drôle de position* [funny position] for me, to function as the representative *de jeune Russie* [young Russia]! A man never knows what will happen to him, and what strange fellowship he may subject himself to. In the official reply, I praised Flerovsky and emphasized that the main task of the Russian Branch was to work for Poland (that is, to liberate Europe from its own neighbor). In regard to Bakunin, I thought it safer not to say a word, neither in the public nor in the private letter. But what I can never forgive the fellows is that they make me a "Venerable." Obviously they believe that I am between eighty and a hundred years old. . . .

Yours, K.M.

---

2. Paul Lafargue's paternal grandmother was a mulatto and maternal grandmother an Indian; he himself was dark-skinned.
3. Joseph Arthur de Gobineau, *Essai sur l'Inégalité des races humaines* [*Essay on the Inequality of the Human Races*], 4 vols. (Paris, 1853–55).

194
1. *Narodnoye Delo* [*The People's Affairs*].

195

From letter to Paul and Laura Lafargue (in Paris) [in English]
London, April 18, 1870

Dear Paul-Laurent:[1]
... I am now forced to say a few words which Paul-Laurent will a little fret at, but I cannot help doing so.

Your father wrote me a letter to Hanover which I have not yet answered, because I did not know what to say.

I feel quite sure that Paul has discarded all notion of finishing, or occupying himself with, his medical studies. When at Paris I wrote to his father[2] in a different sense, and I was warranted in doing so by Paul's own promises. Thus I am placed in quite a false position towards M. Lafargue *ainé* [senior]. I cannot remain in that fix. I see no other prospect of getting out of it but by writing to him that I have as little influence with his beloved son as himself. If you see any other way of escape for me, any other means of clearing my position, please communicate it to me.

In my opinion, which however I neither pretend nor hope to see accepted and acted upon, Paul-Laurent *cum figlio* [with son] ought to pay a visit to their parents at Bordeaux and try to coax them by the many means personal intercourse permits of.

Yours truly, [no signature]

196

From letter to Frederick Engels (in Manchester)
London, May 10, 1870

Dear Fred:
... For my birthday, Kugelmann sent me two pieces of tapestry from Leibniz's[1] study, which amused me very much. Specifically, last winter Leibniz's house [in Hanover] was torn down and the stupid Hanoverians—who could have made a good business with the relics in London—have thrown away everything. These two pieces represent something mythological—one, Neptune in his waves, etc., and the other, Venus, Amor, etc., both in poor Louis

---

195

1. Lafargue's literary pseudonym: a combination of Paul and Laura.
2. See Letter 186, Marx to François Lafargue, July 10, 1869.

196

1. Gottfried Wilhelm von Leibniz (1646–1716), German philosopher, mathematician, scientist; founder of the Berlin Academy of Sciences.

XIV taste. Nevertheless, the excellence (solidity) of the manufactured products of those days compares favorably with those of today. I hung both pieces in my study. *You know my admiration for Leibniz* [in English]....
   Salut.

Yours, K.M.

197

From letter to Frederick Engels (in Manchester)
London, May 11, 1870

Dear Fred:
   ... In regard to the Welsh,[1] I do not find the main subject in my notebooks. But here are some notes:
   "Communal property went out with the loosening of the marriage bond, but at the same time there was the *women's right to vote* in the tribal assembly" (W. Wachsmuth,[2] *Europäische Sittengeschichte*, Part II, Leipzig, 1833).
   Wachsmuth bases his statement on the laws of Kings Dyonwall Moelmud[3] and Howel Dda.[4] *Leges Molmutinae* (translated by William Probert):[5] *The ancient laws of Cambria*, containing the institutional triads of D. Moelmud, the laws of Howel the Good, triadical commentaries, code of education, and the hunting laws of Wales (London, 1823); and Edward Davies,[6] *Celtic Researches* (London, 1804).
   I find these curiosa in my notebooks:
   "Statutes on the testing of virginity. An individual's testimony suffices; for example: the girl's statement about her own virginity." "A man who repudiates his bedmate in favor of another has to pay a fine of enough denarii to cover the plaintiff's behind." "A woman who accuses a man of rape swears out her deposition by seizing his penis with her left hand and placing her right hand on a reliquary."
   "*Lewdness with the Queen* cost double *mult* [fine] to the king."
   The first chapter of the book on the civil code deals with women. "If a wife sleeps with another man and *he beats her*, he [the husband] loses his

---

197

1. Engels to Marx, May 11, 1870: "Can you put together for me a note, with sources, on the Welsh phanerogamic system? I can use it just now, to write about it in the next few days."
2. Wilhelm Wachsmuth, *History of European Morals.*
3. Dyonwall Moelmud, fifth century legendary lawgiver of ancient Britain.
4. Howel Dda ("the Good") (d. A.D. 950), Welsh king and lawgiver.
5. William Probert (1790–1870), English scholar of old Welsh.
6. Edward Davies (1756–1831), English scholar of Celtic.

claims for compensation.... What the woman may sell [alienate]—depending upon her status—is clearly stated. The wife of a peasant (*taenigh*) may sell only her necklace and *hide* only the sieve, and ask for their return only within the reach of her voice. The wife of a nobleman (*nihelms*) may sell coat, shirt, shoes, etc., and *hide* the whole household stuff. *For the woman, sufficient grounds for divorce* were the husband's impotence, body scabs, and *bad breath*."

Very gallant fellows, those Celts! Also born dialecticians, because everything is constructed in *triads*. As for phanerogamy, as soon as I am able to leave the house I will look up Wachsmuth in the British Museum....

Yours, K.M.

198

To Ludwig Kugelmann (in Hanover)
London, June 27, 1870

Dear Kaiser Wenceslaus:
I returned this week after a month's stay in Manchester[1] and found your last letter[2] awaiting me.

I cannot tell you when I will be leaving, not even answer the question—which you did not ask—whether I shall go at all.

Last year I counted on a second edition of my book,[3] after Easter, and *consequently* [in English] on the *income* from the first edition. But you see from the enclosed letter from Meissner, which came today, that all this is still in the future. (Please send the letter back to me.)

The German professorial gentlemen have recently found themselves obliged to take notice of me here and there, even if in a stupid fashion. For example, A. Wagner[4] in a booklet on landed property and Held[5] (Bonn) in one on the agricultural credit banks in the Rhine province.

Herr Lange[6] (*Über die Arbeiterfrage*, etc., 2d edition[7]) sings my praises loudly, but with the object of making himself important. Herr Lange, you see, has made a great discovery. The whole of history can be subsumed under a single great natural law. The natural law is the *phrase* (in this application Darwin's expression becomes merely a phrase) "the struggle for life," and the

---

198
1. From May 23 to June 23, 1870.
2. On June 13, 1870, Kugelmann asked Marx whether, and how many, rooms he should book for him in Karlsbad. Marx, however, did not go to Karlsbad until August, 1874.
3. *Das Kapital*.
4. Adolph Wagner (1835–1917), German economist.
5. Adolf Held (1844–1880), German economist, professor at Bonn University.
6. Friedrich Albert Lange (1828–1875), German social economist.
7. Lange, *The Labor Question* (Winterthur, 1870).

content of this phrase is the Malthusian law of population, or, rather, over-population. Thus, instead of analysing the struggle for life as represented historically in varying and definite forms of society, all that has to be done is to translate every concrete struggle into the phrase, "struggle for life," and this phrase itself into the Malthusian "population fantasy." One must admit that this is a very impressive method—for bombastic, sham-scientific, pompous ignorance and intellectual laziness.

What this same Lange has to say about the Hegelian method and my application of it is truly childish. First, he understands *rien* [nothing] of Hegel's method, and thus, secondly, even much less of the critical way I applied it. In one respect he reminds me of Moses Mendelssohn.[8] That archetype of a windbag once wrote to Lessing,[9] asking him how he could take *au sérieux* [seriously] "the dead dog Spinoza"![10] Similarly, Herr Lange wonders why Engels, I, etc., take the dead dog Hegel seriously, long after Büchner,[11] Lange, Dr. Dühring,[12] Fechner,[13] etc., had agreed that they had buried him—*poor deer* [sic, in English]—long ago. Lange is naïve enough to say that in the empirical material I "move with rare freedom." He has not the least idea that this "free movement in material" is altogether nothing but a paraphrase for the *method* of treating the material—namely, the *dialectical method*.

My best thanks to Madame la Comtesse[14] for her kind note. It is truly comforting at a time "when more and more of the good are vanishing." Still, *sérieusement parlant* [seriously speaking], I am always glad when some lines from your dear wife remind me of the cheerful times I spent in your circle.

As to Meissner's pressure for the second volume,[15] I have not only been interrupted by illness throughout the winter; I also found it necessary to learn Russian, because in dealing with the land question it became essential to go to the original sources in studying the relations of Russian landed property. Moreover, in connection with the Irish land question, the English government published a series of Blue Books (soon concluded) on the land question *in all countries* [in English]. Finally, *entre nous* [between ourselves], I wanted the second edition of the first volume to appear first. If that were to come out while I was finishing Volume II it would only be disturbing.

---

8. Moses Mendelssohn (1729–1786), German-Jewish philosopher.
9. Gotthold Ephraim Lessing (1729–1781), German literary figure of the Enlightenment.
10. Baruch (Benedict) Spinoza (1632–1677), great Dutch-Jewish philosopher.
11. Ludwig Büchner (1824–1899), German physiologist.
12. Eugen Dühring. (1833–1921), German economist.
13. Gustav Theodor Fechner (1801–1887), German physicist and psychologist.
14. Gertrud Kugelmann.
15. Of *Das Kapital*.

Best compliments on Jenny's part and my own to all the members of the Kugelmann family [in English].

Yours, ‍*K.M.*

199

From letter to Frederick Engels (in Manchester)
London, July 20, 1870

Dear Fred:

... Finally, I am enclosing a criticism of my book in Hildebrand's *Journal for Economics and Statistics.*[1] My physical condition hardly disposes me to merriment, but I have cried with laughter over this essay, bona fide tears of mirth. With the reaction and the *downfall* [in English] of the heroic epoch of philosophy in Germany, the *"petit bourgeois"* innate in every German citizen has again asserted himself—in philosophic twaddle worthy of Moses Mendelssohn, shit-smart, peevish, know-it-all nitpicking. And so now even political economy is to be dissolved in drivel about *conceptions of justice!* This goes even beyond "the logarithm of attractions."[2] As Schiller,[3] a competent judge in this field, remarked, the philistine solves all problems by shoving them into "his conscience." ...

Yours, K.M.

200

To Paul and Laura Lafargue (in Paris) [in English]
London, July 28, 1870

My dear children:

You must excuse the long delay of my answer. You know I cannot stand heat. It weighs down my energies. On the other hand, I was overwhelmed with business, the German "friends" firing at me a Mitrailleuse of letters which, under present circumstances, I could not decline answering at once.

199

1. Marx's *Das Kapital* was reviewed (by Karl Friedrich Rösler) in *Jahrbücher für Nationalökonomie und Statistik*, published by Bruno Hildebrand in Jena between 1863 and 1897.
2. The experimental psychologist Gustav Theodor Fechner applied logarithms to the intensity of emotions.
3. Friedrich von Schiller (1759–1805), German poet, dramatist, philosopher of the Enlightenment.

You want of course to hear something of the war.[1] So much is sure that L. Bonaparte[2] has already missed his first opportunity. You understand that his first plan was to take the Prussians unawares and get the better of them by surprise. It is, in point of fact, much easier to get the French army—a mere soldiers' army till now—ready than the Prussian one which consists largely of the civilian element forming the Landwehr. Hence, if Bonaparte, as he at first intended, had made a dash even with half-collected forces, he might have succeeded to surprise the fortress of Mayence, to push simultaneously forward in the direction of Würzburg, thus to separate Northern from Southern Germany, and so throw consternation amidst the camp of his adversaries. However, he has allowed this opportunity to slip. He saw unmistakable signs of the *national* character of the war in Germany and was stunned by the unanimous, quick, immediate adhesion of Southern Germany to Prussia. His habitude of hesitation, so much adapted to his old trade of conspirator planning coup d'état and plebiscites, got the upper hand, but this method will not do for war, which demands quick and unwavering resolution. He let his first plan slip and resolved to collect his full forces. Thus he *lost his advantage of a first start*, of surprise, while the Prussians have *gained* all the time necessary for mobilizing their forces. Hence you may say that Bonaparte has already lost his first campaign.

Whatever may now be the first incidents of the war, it will become extremely serious. Even a first great French victory would decide nothing, because the French army will now find on its way three great fortresses, Mayence, Coblentz, and Cologne, ready for a protracted defense. In the long run, Prussia has greater military forces at her disposal than Bonaparte. It may even be that on one side or the other she will be able to cross the French frontier and make "*le sol sacré de la patrie* [the sacred soil of the fatherland]"— according to the Chauvinists of the Corps Législatif this *sol sacré* is situated only on the French side of the Rhine—the theater of war!

Both nations remind me of the anecdote of the two Russian noblemen accompanied by two Jews, their serfs. Nobleman A strikes the Jew of Nobleman B, and B answers: "*Schlägst Du meinen Jud, schlag ich deinen Jud.*"[3] So both nations seem reconciled to their despots by being allowed, each of them, to strike at the despot of the other nation.

In Germany the war is considered as a *national* war, because it is a war of defense. The middle class (not to speak of the *Krautjunkertum*) overdoes itself in manifestations of loyalty. One believes himself taken back to the

200
1. On July 19, 1870, France declared war on Prussia, but military operations did not begin until July 29.
2. Napoleon III.
3. "If you beat my Jew, I will beat your Jew."

times of 1812 *"für Gott, König und Vaterland"* with the old donkey Arndt's:[4] *"Was ist des Teutschen Vaterland!"*[5]

The singing of the *Marseillaise* at the bidding of the man of December[6] is of course a parody, like the whole history of the second Empire. Still it shows that he feels that *"Partant pour la Syrie"*[7] would not do for the occasion. On the other hand, that old damned ass, Wilhelm "Annexander"[8] sings *"Jesus meine Zuversicht,"* flanked on the one side by *larron* [thief] Bismarck and on the other, by the *policier* Stieber![9]

On both sides it is a disgusting exhibition.

Still there is this consolation, that the workmen protest in Germany as in France. In point of fact the war of classes in both countries is too far developed to allow any political war whatever to roll back for long time the wheel of history. I believe, on the contrary, that the present war will produce results not at all expected by the "officials" on both sides.

I enclose two cuts from Liebknechts *Volksstaat.*[10] You will see that he and Bebel[11] behaved exceedingly well in the *Reichstag.*[12]

For my own part, I should like that both, Prussians and French, thrashed each other alternately, and that—as I believe will be the case—the Germans got *ultimately* the better of it. I wish this, because the definite defeat of Bonaparte is likely to provoke Revolution in France, while the definite defeat of the Germans would only protract the present state of things for 20 years.

The English upper classes are full of moral indignation against Bonaparte at whose feet they have fawned for 18 years. Then they wanted him as the saviour of their privileges, of rents and profits. At the same time, they know the man to be seated on a volcano the which unpleasant position forces him to trouble peace periodically, and makes him—beside his parvenuship—an unpleasant bedfellow. Now they hope that to solid Prussia, Protestant Prussia, Prussia backed by Russia, will fall the part of keeping down revolution in Europe. It would for them be a safer and more respectable policeman.

As to the English workmen, they hate Bonaparte more than Bismarck, principally because he is the aggressor. At the same time they say: "The

---

4. Ernst Moritz Arndt (1769–1860), German nationalist writer.
5. "What is the Fatherland of the Germans?"
6. In the coup d'état of December 2, 1851, Napoleon III made himself dictator.
7. "On to Syria"—an official song of Napoleon III's Second Empire.
8. Marx's ironic name for Prussian King William I, combining the words Annexation and Alexander the Great.
9. Wilhelm Stieber (1818–1882), Prussian police chief.
10. *Der Volksstaat*, a socialist publication that appeared three times weekly in Leipzig under the editorship of Wilhelm Liebknecht.
11. August Bebel (1840–1913), a leading founder of the German Social Democratic party.
12. At the Reichstag meeting of July 21, 1870, the socialist deputies Liebknecht and Bebel abstained from voting for the Prussian government's war credits.

plague on both your houses," and if the English oligarchy, as it seems very inclined, should take part in the war against France, there will be a "tuck" at London. For my own part, I do everything in my power, through the means of the *International*, to stimulate this "Neutrality" spirit and to baffle the *"paid"* (paid by the "respectables") leaders of the English working class who strain every nerve to mislead them.

I hope the measures as to the houses within the fortification rayon will not hurt you.[13] Thousand kisses to my sweet little Schnaps.[14]

Yours devotedly, Old Nick

201

From letter to Frederick Engels (in Manchester)
London, September 2, 1870

Dear Fred:
... The exchange of letters[1] between the Swabian ex-seminarian D. Strauss[2] and the French ex-Jesuit pupil Renan[3] is a hilarious episode. Parson remains parson. Herr Strauss's lecture course in history seems to have its roots in some cabbage-delirium or some similar schoolbook.
Adio!

Yours, K.M.

202

From letter to Sigfrid Meyer (in New York)
London, January 21, 1871

Dear Meyer:
... I don't know whether I have already informed you that since the beginning of 1870 I had to teach myself Russian, which I now read quite fluently. The thing came about when they sent me Flerovsky's very significant work on the *Condition of the Working Class* (esp. peasants) *in Russia* and when I also

---

13. Paul and Laura Lafargue lived in the Paris suburb of Levallois-Perret, near the fortifications.
14. Nickname of grandson Charles-Étienne Lafargue.

201

1. On August 18, 1870, the Supplement to *Allgemeine Zeitung*, an Augsburg daily, published a letter, "To Ernest Renan," by David Friedrich Strauss, dated August 12, 1870.
2. David Friedrich Strauss was the author of *Das Leben Jesu* [*The Life of Jesus*], 2 vols. (1835–1836).
3. Ernest Renan, the French philosopher, was the author of an eight-volume *History of the Origins of Christianity* (1863–1883), of which Volume I was *The Life of Jesus.*

wanted to become acquainted with the (splendid) economic works of Chernyshevski[1] (rewarded by being condemned to the Siberian mines for seven years). The work is worth the effort that a man of my years[2] has to exert to master a language that lies so far removed from the classical, Germanic and Romance language-stocks. The intellectual movement that is now taking place in Russia shows that it is a deep ferment. The heads are still connected by invisible threads with the body of the people....

Yours, Karl Marx

203

From Letter to Paul Lafargue (in Bordeaux) [in English]
London, February 4, 1871

Dear Paul:
Il faut créer des nouveaux défenseurs à la France.[1] You and Laura seem seriously and successfully engaged in that patriotic business. The whole family was delighted to hear that our dear Laura has passed victoriously through the critical juncture and we hope the progress will prove no less favorable. Embrace little Schnappy on my part and tell him that Old Nick feels highly elated at the two photographs of his successor. In the "serious" copy the stern qualities of the little man protrude, while in his attitude as *franc-fileur*[2] there is a charming expression of humor and *espièglerie* [roguishness]....

Yours, Old Nick

204

From Letter to Ludwig Kugelmann (in Hanover)
London, April 12, 1871

Dear Kugelmann:
Your "medical advice" was effective insofar as I consulted my Dr. Maddison and have for the present put myself under his care. He says, however, that my lungs are in excellent condition and the coughing is connected with bronchitis. Ditto it may affect the liver.

202
1. Nicolai Gavrilovich Chernyshevski (1828–1889), Russian socialist author and critic.
2. Marx was then in his fifty-second year.

203
1. "It is necessary to produce new defenders of France." The reference is to Laura Lafargue's third child, a boy, who died later, on July 26, 1871.
2. *Franc-fileur* was the epithet applied to those who fled from Paris during the siege. Laura called her infant son a *franc-fileur* because he was frightened of unaccustomed things.

Yesterday we received the by-no-means reassuring news that Lafargue (not Laura) is momentarily in Paris.[1]

If you look at the last chapter of my *Eighteenth Brumaire*, you will find that I say that the next attempt of the French revolution will be no longer, as before, to transfer the bureaucratic-military machinery from one hand to another, but to *smash* it, and this is the prerequisite for every real people's revolution on the Continent. This is also what our heroic Paris party comrades are attempting.[2] What elasticity, what historical initiative, what a capacity for sacrifice in these Parisians! After six months of hunger and ruin, caused by internal treachery more than by the external enemy,[3] they rise, beneath Prussian bayonets, as if there had never been a war between France and Germany and the enemy were not at the gates of Paris! History has no example of similar greatness! If they are defeated, only their "good nature" will be to blame. They should have marched at once on Versailles, after first Vinoy[4] and then the reactionary section of the Paris National Guard itself had cleared the field. The right moment was missed because of conscientious scruples. They did not want to *start the civil war*, as if the *mischievous* [in English] *avorton* [dwarf] Thiers[5] had not already started the civil war with his attempt to disarm Paris. Second mistake: The Central Committee surrendered its power too soon, to make way for the Commune. Again from a too "honorable" scrupulousness! However that may be, the present rising in Paris—even if it be crushed by the wolves, swine, and vile dogs of the old society—is the most glorious deed of our Party since the June insurrection in Paris. Compare the heaven stormers of Paris with the heaven slaves of the German-Prussian Holy Roman Empire, with its posthumous masquerades, reeking of the barracks, the Church, cabbage-Junkerdom and above all, of Philistinism....

Best greetings to the Lady Countess[6] and Käuzchen.[7]

Yours, K.M.

204

1. Paul Lafargue had come to Paris to obtain powers from the Commune to organize an armed uprising in Bordeaux, where he then lived.

2. The Paris Commune was organized in March 26, 1871, by a group of assorted radicals in defiance of the recently established French republican government, with its seat in Versailles.

3. The Prussians, having defeated the French Army at Sedan in September, 1870, and taken Napoleon III prisoner, encamped outside Paris while negotiating a peace with the new French government.

4. Joseph Vinoy (1800–1880), French general who helped crush the Commune, which was finally destroyed by the end of May, 1871.

5. Louis Adolphe Thiers, became President of the new republic in 1871.

6. Gertrud Kugelmann.

7. Franziska Kugelmann ("Käuzchen" means "little kitten").

205

To Ludwig Kugelmann (in Hanover)
London, April 17, 1871

Dear Kugelmann:
Your letter arrived all right. At this moment I have my hands full. Hence only a few words. How you can compare the petit bourgeois demonstrations *à la* June 13, 1849,[1] etc., with the present struggle in Paris is completely incomprehensible to me.

World history would indeed be very easy to make if the struggle were taken up on condition of infallibly favorable chances. On the other hand, it would be of a very mystical nature if "chances" played no role. These accidents themselves naturally fall in to the general course of development and are again compensated by other accidents. But acceleration and delay are very dependent upon such "accidents"—which include the "accident" of the character of those who at first stand at the head of the movement.

The decisive, unfavorable "accident" this time is in no way to be found in the general conditions of French society but in the presence of the Prussians in France and their position right near Paris. Of this the Parisians were well aware. But the bourgeois *canaille* in Versailles were also well aware of it. Precisely for that reason, they presented the Parisians with the alternative either of taking up the fight or of succumbing without a fight. In the latter case, the demoralization of the working class would have been a much greater misfortune than the fall of any number of "leaders." The struggle of the working class with the capitalist class and its State has entered upon a new phase through the struggle in Paris. Whatever the immediate outcome, a new point of departure of world historic importance has been gained.

Adio, K.M.

206

To Ludwig Kugelmann (in Hanover)
London, July 27, 1871

Dear Kugelmann:
Be so good as to send the enclosed note immediately to Liebknecht.

I find your silence extremely strange. I cannot assume that the various packages of printed matter have all failed to reach you.

205

1. On June 13, 1849, the "Mountain," a Left-wing bourgeois party in the National Assembly, organized a quickly defeated demonstration against the suppression of the Roman Republic by French troops.

On the other hand, it would be very foolish if you—on the old principle of an eye for an eye, a tooth for a tooth—wanted to punish me in this way for not writing. Remember, *mon cher*, that if the day had forty-eight hours, in the last few months I would still not have finished my day's work.

The work for the [First] International is immense, and in addition London is overrun with *refugees* [in English], whom we have to look after.[1] Moreover, I am overrun by other people—newspapermen and others of every description—who want to see the "monster"[2] with their own eyes.

Up to now it has been thought that the Christian myth-building during the Roman Empire was possible only because printing had not yet been invented. Precisely the contrary. The daily press and the telegraph, which spread their inventions over the whole earth in a second, fabricate more myths (and the bourgeois cattle believe and spread them) in one day than could formerly have been done in a century.

My daughters have been for some months in the Pyrenees. Jennychen, who was still suffering from the after-effects of pleurisy, is getting visibly better, as she writes me.

Best thanks for your Germanic despatches.

I hope that you, as well as your dear wife and Fränzchen[3]—whom I ask you to greet cordially—are well.

Apropos. You were probably astonished that in my missive to the *Pall Mall*[4] I made references to a duel. The matter was quite simple. Had I not given the editor[5] this excuse for making a few cheap jokes, he would simply have suppressed the whole letter. As it was, he fell into the trap and achieved my real purpose—he published word for word the accusations against Jules Favre[6] et Co. contained in the Address.[7]

Salut.

Yours, K.M.

206

1. In July, 1871, the General Council of the First International set up a committee, of which Marx was a member, to help the refugees of the Paris Commune.
2. Marx's name became so notorious in connection with the Paris Commune that he was viewed by its enemies as a "monster."
3. Franziska Kugelmann.
4. *The Pall Mall Gazette*, a London daily.
5. Frederic Greenwood (1830–1909).
6. Jules Favre (1809–1880), French politician, negotiated peace treaty with Germany in 1871.
7. Marx, *The Civil War in France* (April–May, 1871), a pamphlet in defense of the Paris Commune.

207

To Jenny Marx (in London)
Brighton, August 25, 1871

Dear Jenny:[1]

Yesterday, I forgot to write you about a peculiar event. On the second day of my arrival here,[2] I found waiting at the corner of my street the same fellow about whom I wrote you that he had followed Engels and me several times and whom Engels thought to be a spy and whom we once "winked" at. You know that, generally speaking, I am no spy smeller. But this fellow has openly and undeniably followed me around. Yesterday I got bored with the thing, stopped, and fixed the chap with my notorious monocle. What did he do? He humbly donned his hat, and today he no longer honoured me with his presence.

Today I wrote a detailed letter to Dana, in which I wrote him in detail about the adventure in Luchon and Spain. He will certainly use it in his *Sun*. *It is exactly that sort of thing the Yankees are fond of* [in English]. Naturally, I have stated the matter in such a way as not to hurt the children—in case they remain there much longer.

Nobody is as deaf as he who does not want to hear! And this is the case with old Stepney[3] in regard to the refugees! Jung and I have treated him to pure wine. Hales[4] has sent him subscription lists. I reported to him Davyson's[5] letter, and finally I initiated him into the ways of getting subsidies. *Despite all this, the old jackass till now has not loosened his purse-strings nor seems he at all willing to do so* [in English]. Yesterday he told me in his eunuch voice that—he sent the subscription lists to Boston and showed me a letter he wrote to a local lady for contributions. But he himself! Not he!

The fellow is altogether "nuts," as Jung says. Jung arrived here last Saturday and left on Monday. He had brought with him his two boys, and before leaving he told Stepney that he was going to leave the boys with a family he knew. Stepney went along with him, and after Jung has *"gesettled"* [in English] everything with the landlady, Stepney said: *"But I want for eight days to take care of the boys myself* [in English]!" and so everything became again unsettled.

207

1. Mrs. Marx.
2. Marx was in Brighton from August 16 to 29 for his health.
3. Cowell William Frederick Stepney (1820–1872), a member of the Reform League and of the General Council of the International.
4. John Hales, a British trade union leader.
5. Real name, Anatoli Davydov (b. 1823), a Russian revolutionary living in London.

Altogether, I have had stormy and rainy weather here, so that the snuffling and coughing did not stop. But the wonderful air and the bath which I take daily have had a beneficent effect on the general state of health. The only thing I have regretted during the whole period is that you are not with me here. But, come what may, you must at any rate have, if not your summer journey, then the autumn one.

In regard to the Swiss vulgarians [*Knoten*: one of Marx's favorite epithets] Schneider[6] and Zichlinsky,[7] (The *"Schneider"* [tailor] is already a notorious individual in Germany), the fellows will soon discover that this is *not* Germany.

I found that too many Proudhonists are let into the General Council [of the International], and upon my return I will insist upon an antidote for the admission of Martin[8] and LeMoussu.[9]

Brighton—where I, for the rest, live like a native—is naturally absorbed in the great poisoning case, clearly a pure outbreak of hysterical boredom on the part of a sickly, silly, thirty-five-year-old spinster living in comfortable circumstances.

The report of the Paris correspondents in the *Daily News* and *Daily Telegraph* about the Versailles trial[10] are truly revolting, penny-a-liner vile.

Adio.

Yours, Karl

208

To Jenny Marx (in Ramsgate)
London, September 23, 1871

Dear Jenny:[1]
At last, the conference[2] comes to an end today. It was hard work. Morning and evening sessions, in-between committee sessions, hearing of witnesses, reports to be drawn up, and so forth. But more was accomplished also than in all previous conferences together, because it was not open to the public—before which to play rhetorical comedies. Germany was not represented, and

---

6. Joseph Schneider, an opponent of the General Council of the International.
7. Zichlinsky (or Zilinski), a German refugee in London, and, like Schneider, an opponent of the International.
8. Constant Martin, a French member of the General Council of the International.
9. Benjamin LeMoussu, another French member of the International.
10. The court-martial against the Communards which began on August 7, 1871, in Versailles.

208

1. Mrs. Marx.
2. The conference of the First International, held in London from September 17 to 23, 1871.

from Switzerland only Perret[3] and Outine.[4]

Last week in Rome the revolutionary party gave a banquet for Ricciotti Garibaldi,[5] the report of which in the Roman journal, *La Capitale*, was sent to me. A speaker (il signore Luciani)[6] proposed a toast, which was received with great enthusiasm, to the working class and *"a Carlo Marx che ne è fatto l'instancabile instrumento* [to Carl Marx who has made it into an indefatigable instrument]." Bitter, this, for Mazzini!

In New York, the news of my death led to a meeting of the "Cosmopolitan Society," the resolution of which, printed in the *World*, I am sending you.[7]

Tussy[8] has also received an anxious letter from a friend in St. Petersburg.[9]

Things were hard here [at the conference] for Robin[10] and Bastelica,[11] the friends and fellow-intrigants of Bakunin. The revelations of Robin's activities in Geneva and Paris were, indeed, strange. Jennychen's article went off to America today.[12]

Yours, Karl

209

To Laura Lafargue (in San Sebastian)[1] [in English]
London, December 18, 1871

My dear Laura:
In the first instance my best thanks for the offer[2] of Toole [Lafargue]. I accept it under two express conditions.

---

3. Henri Perret, Swiss member of the First International, a Bakuninist.
4. Nicolai Outine (or Utin) (1845–1883), Russian Populist.
5. Son of Giuseppe Garibaldi.
6. Giuseppe Luciani, Italian journalist.
7. The "Cosmopolitan Society," an organization founded in 1870, passed a resolution, stating that Marx was "one of the most faithful, fearless, and selfless defenders of all oppressed classes and peoples."
8. Eleanor Marx.
9. On September 12, 1871, Nicolai Frantzevich Danielson (1844–1918), cotranslator of Marx's *Das Kapital*, wrote to Eleanor Marx that the Russian newspapers reported that Marx was gravely ill; he wanted to know whether it was true.
10. Paul Robin (1837–1912), French teacher, Bakuninist.
11. André Bastelica (1845–1884), French printer, Bakuninist.
12. Jenny (Jennychen) Marx's piece, telling her experiences with the French police at the Pyrenees border, was printed in *Woodhull & Claflin's Weekly*, October 21, 1871.

209
1. The Lafargues were in Saint-Sebastian, Paul being a refugee from the Paris Commune.
2. On December 12, 1871, Laura informed Marx that she and her husband had negotiated with Maurice Lachâtre a French edition of *Das Kapital*; the question was whether it should be a popular edition of 3 francs or a luxury one at 6 francs, and that an outlay of 4,000 francs would be necessary at the beginning.

(1) that if the enterprise fails, I have to pay the sum advanced with the usual interest upon it,

(2) that Toole does not advance more than 2,000 francs. The expression of the Editor[3] that this is only wanted for the beginning seems to me *ominous*. At all events Toole must *stipulate* that his obligations refer only to this "beginning." I prefer in every respect a *cheap popular* edition.

It is a fortunate combination that a *Second German edition*[4] has become necessary just now. I am fully occupied (and can therefore write only a few lines) in arranging it, and the French *translator* will of course have to translate the amended German edition. (I shall forward him the old one with the changes inserted.) Möhmchen[5] is just trying to find out the whereabouts of Keller. She has written for that purpose to his sister. If he is not to be found (and in due time), the translator of Feuerbach would be the man.[6]

The Russian edition (after the first German edition) will appear January next in St. Petersburg.[7]

Many kisses to you añd Schnappy, happy new year to Toole and all.

Cacadou's Old Master

210

To Laura Lafargue (in Madrid) [in English]
London, February 28, 1872

My dear child:
You can judge of the overwork[1]—I am being bothered with ever since December last—from my negligence in replying to your own and Paul's letters. Still my heart was always with you. In fact, the health of poor little Schnappy[2] occupies my thoughts more than everything else, and I feel even a little angry

---

3. Maurice Lachâtre, publisher of the French translation of *Das Kapital*.
4. The first German edition of *Das Kapital* was nearly exhausted by November, 1871; the second, and improved, German edition came out in 1873 (but under an 1872 date).
5. Mrs. Marx.
6. Joseph Roy, French translator of *Das Kapital*.
7. The Russian translation of the first volume of *Das Kapital* was published in March, 1872, in an edition of 3,000 copies.

210

1. Marx was busy preparing the second German edition of *Das Kapital*, as well as organizing the last congress of the First International, which met in The Hague, September 2 to 7, 1872.
2. Charles-Étienne Lafargue, who died in July, 1872, at the age of four.

at Paul's last epistle, full of interesting details as to the "movement," but a mere blank in regard to that dear little sufferer.

In consequence of uninterrupted reading and writing, an inflammation of my right eye has set in since a few days, so that it forsakes service for the moment and obliges me to limit even this letter to the most necessary matter-of-fact communications.

In the first instance, Keller is *not* the translator of my book.[3] When, at last, I had found out his whereabouts, I wrote at once. In his reply, he told me that he had till then only translated about two hundred pages, and that, moreover, he could not proceed with the work before the month of May, being bound by contract to finish the translation of a medical work. This would not do for me. I have found in Roy, the translator of Feuerbach, a man perfectly suitable to my purpose. Since the end of December, he has received from me the correction manuscript of the Second German edition [of *Das Kapital*] up to pagina 280. Today I have written him to send at once to Paris what manuscript may be ready.

As to the biography,[4] I have not yet made up my mind as to whether it be at all opportune to publish it in connection with this work.

As to the preface for Proudhon,[5] *j'y penserai* [I will think about it].

The printings Paul wants I shall send tomorrow and should have done so before, if I had found the time to look after some statistical facts in *The Eighteenth Brumaire*,[6] which, I apprehend, are not quite correct.

To Liebknecht I shall write.[7]

As to Lara,[8] making him—a man who is a perfect stranger to our party—a contributor to our party prints, is quite out of the question. At the same time you ought not to neglect all relations with his family. Under certain circumstances they might prove useful.

I regret that you have written to Woodhull et Co.[9] They are humbugs that compromise us. Let Paul write to Charles A. Dana, editor of the *Sun* (New York) and offer him Spanish correspondence, and ask him at the same time (such thing must be settled beforehand with the Yankees), as to the

---

3. On Charles Keller, see Letter 189, Marx to Paul and Laura Lafargue, October 18, 1869.

4. Maurice Lachâtre, the French publisher, had made the suggestion that a biography of Marx be appended to the French translation of *Das Kapital*, but dropped the idea.

5. Lafargue had suggested that Marx write a preface to his Spanish translation of *The Poverty of Philosophy*. Marx never wrote it.

6. Marx, *The Eighteenth Brumaire of Louis Napoloen*, German edition (New York, 1852).

7. Lafargue had asked that Wilhelm Liebknecht send him to Madrid his Leipzig triweekly, *Der Volksstaat*.

8. Lopez de Lara, a Spanish businessman in London.

9. Victoria Woodhull (1838–1927) and her sister, Tennessee Claflin (1845–1923), American suffragettes.

money terms. I enclose a few lines to Dana. If he should not accept, I shall find another paper at New York. (The *Herald* or something else.)

The *New Social Demokrat*[10] is the continuation of Schweitzer's paper[11] under another editorship. He observed still a certain decorum. It is now a mere police caper, Bismarck's paper for the Lassalleans, as he had his feudal, his liberal, his all sort of colour papers.

Apropos. Misled by one of your letters I had put in the contract with Lachâtre "*somme de . . . sera remise à Paris . . . quinze jours après demande* [the sum of . . . to be paid in Paris . . . fifteen days after demand]." I shall write him tomorrow, that I prefer the payment on 1st July. In case of need, I can find the money, but I must be informed beforehand.

And now, my dear child, adio, with thousand kisses for little Schnappy and yourself, and my greetings to Paul.

Yours most devotedly, Old Nick

211

To Maurice Lachâtre (in San Sebastian) [in French]
London, March 18, 1872

To Citizen Maurice Lachâtre
Dear Citizen:
I applaud your idea of publishing the translation of *Das Kapital* in periodical numbers.[1] In this form, the work will be more accessible to the working-class, and for me this consideration outweighs all the others.

This is the good side of your medal, but there is also the reverse side: The method of analysis which I have used and which has never been applied to economic subjects make the reading of the first chapters quite arduous, and it is to be feared that the French public, which is always impatient for conclusions and avid to know the connection between general principles and immediate questions, will be frightened off if it cannot penetrate any further.

This is a disadvantage about which I can do nothing more than to alert and prepare the readers interested in the truth. There is no royal road to

10. *Neuer Social-Demokrat*, a Berlin publication of the Lassallean General German Workers' Association, 1871–1876.
11. *Der Social-Demokrat*, a Berlin publication of the General German Workers' Association, 1864 to 1871, under the editorship of Johann Baptist von Schweitzer.

211
1. Lachâtre, the publisher, brought out the French translation of *Das Kapital* in installments, the first of which appeared in September, 1872.

science, and only those have a chance to reach the luminous summits who are not afraid to make the effort to climb their steep escarpments.

Accept, dear Citizen, the assurance of my devoted sentiments.

Karl Marx

212

To Ludwig Kugelmann (in Hanover)
London, July 9, 1872

Dear Kugelmann:
My best thanks for the gift of £15 for Jennychen. I have worked like a dog so that today (in two hours) I am leaving London with Engels for four or five days and going to the sea (Ramsgate).[1] From the day of my return until September 2 (the International Congress at the Hague) I shall have my hands full, but from then I shall again be more free. But this freedom begins only in the middle of September, as I myself will go to The Hague.[2]

Perhaps we could see each other later (that is, you could see me, for I would not be safe in Germany).

Adio.

Yours, Karl Marx

As soon as the first installments (German[3] or French[4]) are out, you will of course receive them. *I am highly dissatisfied with Meissner.* He has led me by the nose—first overworked me by the sudden and unexpected haste with which he announced the second edition (end of November, 1871), then lost months and let the best time slip by. He is a rotten little philistine.

To punish Meissner, it would be good if *you were to write him on the pretext* of wanting to know when the "first" installment will finally appear. On that occasion, you can remark, *en passant* [in passing], that from my last letter it seemed to you that I am *very embittered against Meissner* and very *dissatisfied with him;* what is the reason for that? It is not my usual manner! The fellow has actually angered me very much by his "if you don't come today, come tomorrow" manner.

212
1. Marx and Engels were in Ramsgate from July 9 to 15, 1872.
2. The congress of the First International met in The Hague from September 2 to 7, 1872. At this session, which Marx attended as delegate, the congress expelled Michael Bakunin and his Anarchist followers, and decided to remove its headquarters to New York City. It was the end of an organization that Marx had led for eight stormy years, since 1864.
3. The second edition of *Das Kapital*, dated 1872, was actually published, by Meissner in Hamburg, in nine installments between June, 1872, and May, 1873.
4. The French translation of *Das Kapital* was published, by Maurice Lachâtre in Paris, in nine installments between 1872 and November, 1875, the bulk of them in the latter date.

213

From letter to Frederick Engels (in Ramsgate)
London, August 30, 1873

Dear Fred:
... Yesterday, *a few hours* [in English] before I wrote you, *je l'ai échappé belle* [I had a narrow escape], and I still feel it in my bones today. I drank a spoonful of raspberry vinegar, of which some got into my windpipe. I had a real choking spasm, the face turned dark, etc., and in another second my temporal days would have been over. What occurred to me immediately *post festum* [after the event] was whether one could not produce such *accidents* [in English] artificially. It would be the most decent and the least suspicious manner, and, moreover, very expeditious, for a man to do away with himself. One would perform a great service for the English to recommend such experiments publicly.[1] ...
Salut.

Yours, K.M.

214

From letter to Frederick Engels (in London)
Harrogate, November 30, 1873

Dear Fred:
On Thursday[1] I visited Gumpert, whom I found very bald and aged. The poor fellow suffers greatly from a hemorrhoid convolution which has grown up with him and which he finally wants to have operated on, something, as he himself admits, that is always fraught with a certain amount of danger. I dined with him (except for him, I could not, of course see anybody else during my brief visit to Manchester) and the four children made by him, and their *governess* [in English].

Gumpert examined me *bodily* [in English], and found a certain elongation of the liver, which, he believed, I could cure entirely only in Karlsbad. I

213

1. Engels to Marx, September 3, 1873: "My congratulations on your narrow escape. Alas, such spasms cannot be produced with any assurance, as raspberry vinegar and even more solid substances could get into the windpipe a hundred times without bringing forth such symptoms."

214

1. November 27.

am to take the same waters as Tussy[2] (here they call it Kissingen because of its kindred nature), but no mineral baths. For the rest, Tussy's and my regime are somewhat different. Mine is to be very moderate—a point with which Gumpert is entirely in agreement with the local Dr. Myrtle (a very fragrant name, the man is a Scot and boasts of being a *Jacobite*[3] even now; is said to turn to Colonel Stuart[4] who is with Don Carlos[5]); but, on the other hand, I must take vigorous walks. Gumpert's advice that I should be little active was hardly necessary, since until now I have in fact done nothing, not even written letters. I thought that two weeks here would suffice, but Gumpert insists on three.[6] In reality, only by the middle of the coming week will Tussy also need much stronger mineral baths than hitherto. . . .

Last night, Tussy and I took refuge in chess. For the rest, I read Sainte-Beuve's book on Chateaubriand,[7] a writer whom I have always found distasteful. If he has become so famous in France, it is because in every respect he is the classic incarnation of French vanity, and he embodies this vanity not in a light and frivolous eighteenth century sense, but in romantic garb, flaunting new-baked expressions, false depth, Byzantine exaggeration, toying with emotions, motley sheen, word painting, theatrical, sublime, in a word a mishmash of lies, as never before rendered in such form and content. . . .

Adio.

Yours, K.M.

215

To Ludwig Kugelmann (in Hanover)
London, January 19, 1874

Dear Wenceslaus:
Engels has reported to me your letter to him.[1] Hence these few lines. After my return,[2] a carbuncle broke out on my right cheek, which had to be

---

2. Eleanor Marx.
3. Follower of the Stuart king, James II.
4. Charles Edward Stuart (1824–1882), a Stuart Pretender.
5. Don Carlos (1848–1909), Pretender to the Spanish throne.
6. Marx, with his daughter Eleanor, stayed in Harrogate from November 24 to December 15, 1873.
7. Charles Augustin Sainte-Beuve, *Chateaubriand et son Groupe Littéraire sous l'Empire* [*Chateaubriand and His Literary Group Under the Empire*], 2 vols. (Paris, 1861).

215

1. Worried by a report about Marx's health in the *Frankfurter Zeitung*, Kugelmann, on January 13, 1874, asked Engels for information about it.
2. Marx, with his daughter Eleanor, were on a cure in Harrogate from November 24 to December 15, 1873.

operated on; then it had several smaller successors, and I think that at the present moment I am suffering from the *last* of them.

For the rest, don't worry at all about newspaper gossip; *still less answer it*. I myself allow the English papers to announce my death from time to time, without giving a sign of life. Nothing annoys me more than to appear to be supplying the public with reports on my state of health through my friends (*you are the greatest sinner in this respect*). I don't give a farthing for the public, and, if my occasional illness is exaggerated, it at least has this advantage, that it keeps away all sorts of requests (theoretical and otherwise) from unknown people from all corners of the world.

My best thanks for the kind words from the lady Countess[3] and Fränzchen.[4]

I am very glad to receive the *Frankfurter Zeitung*, in which I found many interesting things.

The relative victory of the Ultramontanes and Social Democrats in the elections[5] *serves Mr. Bismarck and his middle class tail right* [in English]. More another time.

Yours, K.M.

Apropos: On the advice of my friend, Dr. Gumpert (in Manchester), I now use quicksilver ointment at the first carbuncle-itch and find that it works quite specifically.

What has happened to your friend, "Dr. Freund" of Breslau, who in your opinion was such a promising man? It appears that, *après tout, que c'est fruit sec* [after all, that's dessicated fruit—that is, a failure].

216

To Jenny Marx (in London)
Ramsgate, April 19, 1874

Dear Jenny:[1]
16, Abbot's Hill—vis-á-vis Mad[ame] Williams—this is the "Cliff" where I live.[2] But never mind! The rate also has not yet been decided. The landlady

---

3. Gertrud Kugelmann.
4. Franziska Kugelmann.
5. In the Reichstag elections of 1874, the Ultramontanes, or the Catholic Center Party, won a victory with 1,500,000 votes (ninety-one seats); while the Social-Democrats polled 351,670 votes, winning nine seats.

216
1. Mrs. Marx.
2. Marx was in Ramsgate for his health from mid-April to May 5, 1874.

first asked £1 and then came down to 12 shillings. These are otherwise decent "folks"; the husband, a coach builder, seems also to dabble in art. On the very idealized and rather enigmatic figure of a sentinel at the entrance-gate, he not only sketched out but painted in a certain spot. In the middle of the little garden in front of the house, on a brick pedestal there also stands the statue of Napoleon the First, in Tom-Thumb edition, made of clay, dressed in black, yellow and red, etc., a very manly man, and well done. In addition to other children, the landlady also has a six-weeks old baby, which often makes itself unpleasantly audible.

The air here is excellent, but, despite all my walking, I have hitherto not yet succeeded in sleeping at night.

The place is not entirely empty, but *the home-brewed people* [in English, probably meaning "home-bred"] still play the main role.

I hope that Jennychen feels better and that the excellent little man[3] does not suffer too much from teething. Mother and little son are much in my mind.

Apropos. Tell Tussychen,[4] who had so amused herself over Tennyson's poem, "*Alexandrovna!*" that there is nothing new under the sun, which, for that matter, is known to a Bible-rooted man like him—namely, in June, 1782, the *Comte du Nord* (the later Czar Paul, the madman, who traveled under that incognito) was in Paris wth his young wife. There he attended a session of the French Academy, where M. de La Harpe read a poetic-letter to the *Altesse Imperiale* [Imperial Highness]; every stanza ended with "*Petrovich*" [son of Peter]. Grimm[5] commented on this: "*apostrophe répetée, plus ridicule encore pour les oreilles russes qu'elle n'est étrange pour les notres. Ce mot, lorsqu'il n'est pas précedé de quelque épithète qui le distingue, est aussi familier en russe que le serait celui de Toinette ou de Pierrot en français.*"[6] If Tussy sent this paragraph to the *Quiddities and Oddities Journal*, it would perform an admirable service for Tennyson.

Give my thanks to Engels for his letter. One does not often find another such an exact letter writer in our *temps corrompu* [corrupt time].

Adio and regards for all.

Yours, Karl

---

3. Charles Longuet, Marx's grandson.
4. Eleanor Marx.
5. Friedrich Melchior von Grimm (1723–1807), a Franco-German writer and Encyclopedist.
6. "Repeated apostrophizing, even more ridiculous to Russian ears than it is strange to our own. This word [Petrovich], if it is not preceded by some epithet which distinguishes it, is about as familiar in Russian as is Toinette or Pierrot in French."

217

To Jenny Longuet (in London)
Ramsgate, between April 20 and 24, 1874

Dear Jennychen:
I am sending you today the proofs [of the French translation of *Das Kapital*], which you would oblige me by returning after Longuet has gone through them. Then I would send the definitive corrections back to Paris.

Today is the first day that I have been able to do anything at all. Until now, despite baths, walking, splendid air, careful diet, etc., my condition has been worse than in London. Proof that my condition had reached a dangerous point and that it was high time to shake the [London] dust off and come here. This is also the reason why I am postponing my return, because it is absolutely necessary to return in a *condition for work* [*arbeitsfähig*]. Engels' letter, which indicates that he is arriving today, reminds me, I suppose, of one of the reasons why you do not come here. How is your health? I am convinced that a few weeks at the seaside would completely restore you. In reality, it is here now more agreeable and beneficent than during the proper season.

My beloved Putty[1] will, I hope, recognize me again.

Tell Tussychen that the "sacred music"—"*sacrée musique*," as she translates it—is not known to the frivolous Parisians under quite that name, but that the thing itself, which came from Italy, where they make divine comedy from way back, has been called "*concerts spirituels*" in Diderot's[2] time[3].

Pour la bonne bouche [for the best last], here is a witticism by the Chevalier de Boufflers, taken from Grimm: "*Les princes ont plus besoin d'être divertis qu'adorés; il n'y a que Dieu qui ait un assez grand fonds de gaieté pour ne pas s'ennuyer de tous les hommages qu'on lui rend.*"[4]

Adieu, my heart's child.

Yours, Old Nick

217

1. Charles Longuet, Marx's 8-month-old grandson.
2. Denis Diderot (1713–1784), French Encyclopedist.
3. An interesting illustration of Marx's accuracy in this matter is Thomas Jefferson's report that when he lived in Paris (1784–1789), he used to attend such "*concerts spirituels*" in the Tuileries; see Saul K. Padover, "Thomas Jefferson—Philosopher, Statesman, and Musician," in *Stereo Review*, November, 1968, pp. 82–86.
4. "Princes have greater need to be entertained than adored; only God possesses a large storehouse of gaiety so that he would not be bored during all the homages that are shown him."

218

From letter to Ludwig Kugelmann (in Hanover)
London, May 18, 1874

Dear Kugelmann:
I have received everything: your letters (including some friendly notes from your dear wife and Fränzchen[1]), the "Meyer"[2] (police-socialist, *faiseur* [mountebank], literary scribbler), the clippings from the *Frankfurter* [*Zeitung*], etc., and finally a letter from Madame Tenge.[3]

I am very grateful for your, your family's and Madame Tenge's friendly interest in my progress. But you do me an injustice if you ascribe my failure to write to any other cause than an uncertain state of health, which constantly interrupts my work, then goads me to make up for the time lost by neglecting all other duties (letters included), and finally puts a man out of humor and makes him disinclined to activity.

After my return from Harrogate,[4] I had *d'abord* [to begin with] an attack of carbuncles, then my headaches returned, sleeplessness, etc., so that I had to spend from the middle of April to May 5 at Ramsgate (*seaside* [in English]). Since then I have been feeling much better, but am far from being quite well. My special physician (Dr. Gumpert in Manchester) insists upon my going to Karlsbad[5] and would like to make me travel there as soon as possible, but I must finally see to the completion of the French translation,[6] which has come to a complete stop, and apart from that, I should much prefer if I could meet you there.

In the meantime, while unable to write, I worked through a lot of important new material for the second volume.[7] But I cannot start on its final working out until the French edition is completed and my health fully restored...

With my warmest greetings to your dear wife and Madame Tenge.

Yours, K.M.

218

1. Franziska Kugelmann.
2. Rudolph Hermann Meyer (1839–1899), German conservative economist.
3. Madame Tenge and Marx became friends when the latter visited Hanover in the spring of 1867. See Letter 157, Marx to his daughter Laura, May 13, 1867.
4. December 15, 1873.
5. Marx, accompanied by his daughter Eleanor, arrived for a cure in Karlsbad on August 19, 1874, and remained there until September 21.
6. The translation of *Das Kapital* by Joseph Roy was thoroughly gone over by Marx, who had a perfect knowledge of French.
7. Of *Das Kapital;* the second volume was brought out by Engels in 1893, ten years after Marx's death.

219

From letter to Frederick Engels (in Ramsgate)
Ryde, July 15, 1874

Dear Fred:

It is a real shame that I have not written to you, but as is well known, in one's idleness it is very difficult to find time. This *island* [in English][1] is a little paradise, particularly for the gentlemen who had fenced in the best-located land. We made a *tour* [in English] of the island by boat, to Ventnor, Sandown, Cowes, Newport, as well as various tours on foot. It is too warm to do the latter thoroughly, although the temperature is temperate compared to London.

Religion flourishes among the *natives* [in English] here everywhere, but in addition, they are practical people. "*Vote for Stanley, the rich man* [in English]," was a poster we found everywhere in the vicinity. The Town Council of Ryde, on which sit various members of the Ryde Pier and Railroad Company and whose proceedings replace the English House of Commons in the local press, is a veritable model of *jobbing* [in English].

Our *landlord* [in English] is a Scripture reader for the poor, and his theological library, *about two dozen volumes* [in English], adorns the *sitting room* [in English]. Although he belongs to the Church of England, I found among his books Spurgeon's[2] sermons. In Sandown, where I took a warm bath, I found a similar *library* [in English] in the bathhouse, and one cannot take a step without seeing announcements of pious *Meetings* [in English]. In reality, the plebs here are very poor and seem to find in the church their main diversion. It would be interesting to investigate how this original fishermen-population was crushed down to this idol-grinding condition in no time. "Overpopulation" certainly did not do it, for altogether there are not even 100,000 permanent inhabitants here.

My state of health is better, that is, I do not need any pills, but despite all this, the head is not altogether in order.

Laurachen[3] gave us great joy with her visit here last Saturday;[4] unfortunately, she had to leave Monday evening. As we accompanied her to the

---

219

1. Marx was on a cure in Ryde, Isle of Wight, from early to the end of July.
2. Charles Haddon Spurgeon (1834–1892), an English Baptist preacher.
3. Laura Lafargue.
4. July 11.

pier, a temperance-excursion gang arrived from Brighton. Half of them were drunk. It was, as an old Englishman near me said, "*the worst lot he had ever met with in his life* [in English]," and in reality I have never seen such a lot of stunted, churlish, filthy idiots together, the women, moreover, thoroughly repulsive, all of them "young folks." For *foreigners* [in English], this *sample of freeborn Britons* [in English] would be a striking sight....

With best regards for Madame Lizzy and Pumps.[5]

Yours, Mohr

220

To Ludwig Kugelmann (in Hanover)
London, August 4, 1874

Dear Kugelmann:
About eight days ago I wrote your dear wife a few lines, telling her of the death of my only grandson[1] and the severe illness of my youngest daughter.[2] The latter was not an isolated case but rather an outbreak of an illness from which she has long suffered. Eleanor is now up again, much sooner than her doctor (Madame Dr. Anderson-Garrett[3]) had hoped. She is able to travel, although of course still delicate. Madame Anderson thinks the Karlsbad waters very desirable for her complete cure, just as did Dr. Gumpert when he ordered, rather than recommended, me to go there. It is of course difficult for me to leave Jenny[4] now (I mean in about two weeks). In this respect I am less stoical than in other things, and the family afflictions always hit me hard. The more one lives, as I do, almost cut off from the outside world, the more one is caught in the emotional life of one's most intimate circle.

You must send me your exact Karlsbad address and, in particular, make my excuses to your wife and Fränzchen for not answering their friendly and affectionate letters.

Yours, K.M.

---

5. Lydia Burns and niece Mary Ellen.

220
1. Charles Longuet, died July, 1874, aged ten months.
2. Eleanor Marx.
3. Elisabeth Anderson-Garrett (1836–1917), English doctor and physicist.
4. Daughter Jenny Longuet.

221

From letter to Friedrich Adolph Sorge (in Hoboken, N.J.)
London, August 4, 1874

Dear Sorge:[1]
My long silence is not to be excused at all; *cependant il y a des circonstances atténuantes* [yet there are extenuating circumstances]. The damned liver illness has made such headway that I was positively unable to continue the French translation (which in reality amounts almost to a complete rewriting), and I reluctantly submitted to the doctor's order that I go to Karlsbad. I am being assured that after I return I shall be fully able to work, and being *unable* to work is indeed death sentence for any man who is not an animal. It is an expensive trip and it is expensive to stay there, and what is more, it is uncertain whether the foolish Austrian government will expel me or not! The Prussians would hardly be so stupid, but they love to mislead the Austrians into such compromising steps; and I really believe that the false newspaper reports that Rochefort[2] wants to go to Karlsbad, etc., stem from Herr Stieber[3] and are, in the last analysis, coined for me. I have neither the time nor the money to lose and have, therefore, decided to apply for British citizenship, but it is very likely that the British Home Minister[4] who, like a Sultan, disposes over naturalization, will nullify this. The matter will probably be decided this week.[5] In any case, I am going to Karlsbad, if only because of my youngest daughter[6] who has been seriously and dangerously ill, and is only now able to travel again, and has also been advised by her doctor to go to Karlsbad.

A great misfortune has befallen us about a week ago, the death of Jenny's (Frau Longuet) eleven-month-old baby, a most darling little boy. He fell victim to a frightful diarrhea....

My wife and children send you their best regards.

Yours, Karl Marx

221

1. Friedrich Adolph Sorge (1828–1906), German-born American labor leader, member of the First International in America; a friend of Marx, with whom he corresponded frequently.
2. Victor Henri Marquis de Rochefort (1830–1913), French Left-wing newspaper publisher, exiled to New Caledonia after the defeat of the Paris Commune.
3. Police spy Wilhelm Stieber.
4. Robert (Bob) Lowe, Viscount Sherbrooke (1811–1892), British statesman, Liberal.
5. On August 24, 1874, the British government rejected Marx's application for citizenship on the ground that he had not been loyal to his own king and country [Prussia].
6. Eleanor Marx.

222

To Jenny Longuet (in Ramsgate)
London, August 14, 1874

My darling child:
I believe you must have finally received the letter I addressed to Engels last Tuesday. If not, one should have recourse to the post office, for such disorders ought not to be permitted to pass unnoticed.

It was wrong on Longuet's part to worry you about my carbuncles. Yesterday morning the wadding finally came out and the suppuration ended; I immediately put on a sticking plaster, which soon began to have its regular effect. You see, therefore, my dear child, that everything is in order here.

In regard to the naturalization,[1] my *solicitor* [in English] informed me last night that there is no further *news* [in English] from the *Home Office* [in English]. I am going there again today. Regardless of anything, I shall depart tomorrow evening.[2] At worst, I will have to return from Karlsbad via Hamburg, which would be annoying because of the expense. It is very curious that after there having been no talk about the [First] International or about me for such a long time, my name should again *just now* [in English] figure in trials in Petersburg and Vienna, and that ridiculous *riots* [in English] in Italy[3] should be connected not only with the International but also directly with me (see today's report from Rome in the *Daily News*).[4] The insinuation by the Rome correspondent that the *international* [in English] agitators are working for the Pope, is something that smells altogether of a recipe cooked up by Bismarck.[5]

Yesterday's *Evening Standard*[6] carried a small *leader* [in English] which began thus: "*The International has been scotched, but not killed* [in English]." This in relation to the imprisonment of eight hundred men in Versailles, who were supposed to have been in secret contact with the Italian farce, although the connection was very *palpable* [in English]: Bazaine *s'est échappé* [has escaped].[7]

222

1. To obtain a passport for travel on the Continent, the stateless Marx applied for British citizenship on August 1, 1874; the application was rejected on August 24.
2. On August 15, Marx, accompanied by his daughter Eleanor, left London for Karlsbad, where they stayed from August 19 to September 21, 1874.
3. In August, 1874, Italian Anarchists attempted uprisings in Bologna and Apulia.
4. A London newspaper.
5. Otto von Bismarck (1815–1898), German statesman, Chancellor of the German Empire.
6. A London daily.
7. In October–December, 1873, Marshal François Achille Bazaine (1811–1888), was tried by a court martial in Versailles for having surrendered Metz to the Germans in the Franco-Prussian War (1870) and condemned to death for high treason; the sentence was commuted by Marshal MacMahon to exile on the island of Ste. Marguerite, whence Bazaine escaped to Spain in August, 1874.

Donc [Hence]—as a MacMahonist[8] compensation—80 Communards *sont arretés* [are arrested] in Marseilles. The *Standard*, which in police vileness surpasses the *Daily News*, comments further that these *revolutionists* [in English] always become very conservative the moment they acquire the least bit of property, and are all have-nothings, etc. In the same issue, the *Standard* prints a telegram from Marseilles, reporting that one of those arrested was a millionaire. *Brave fellows, those British gentlemen of the "freest press in the world"* [in English]! It is also strange that the various French (Parisian) Journals I have seen—among them some very conservative ones—make no connection whatever between the Italian farce and the International.

Now for another picture. Frankel[9] and Outine were here last night. The latter brought the news that Madame Tomanowski[10] is *married*. (What he did not know exactly was whether her imminent confinement—keep this among ourselves—was prepared before or after the marriage. Nor does he have any further details about the lucky couple.) Frankel suffered greatly from this unexpected blow.

Mr. General Cecilia[11] bored me the day before yesterday for three or four hours. Among other things, he informed me that they (*id est* [that is], as we already knew, he and C. Martin) are planning to set up a school for refugee children. The curriculum, he said, would include *enseignement de l'hygiène* and *économie sociale* [social economics]—for the latter of which I am chosen graciously to prepare a *primer* [in English] on the English model. With great indignation he told me that *Figaro*,[12] in one of its recent issues, made the charge that the Republic ruined France by its having created four generals, *et qui s'appellent* [whose names are]: Crémieux,[13] Glais-Bizoin,[14] Cecilia, and Lissagaray![15] That same evening I whispered that bit of flattery in the latter's ear.

I am gossiping this way because I hardly dare to speak of that which is of most concern to you. The house died with the death of the little angel.[16] I miss him at every step. My heart bleeds when I think of him, and how can one get out of one's mind such a sweet and clever little man! But I hope, my child, that you remain brave for the sake of your Old Man.

Adieu, my dear, beloved, dark darling.

Your faithful Old Nick

---

8. Marie Edme Patrice Maurice MacMahon (1808–1893), French marshal, President of the Third Republic, 1873–1879.
9. Leo Frankel (1844–1896), Hungarian revolutionist, member of the Paris Commune.
10. Elizabeth Tomanovskaya (1851–*c*. 1898), Russian revolutionist, living in Geneva.
11. Napoleone La Cecilia (1835–1878), an Italian Garibaldist, general in the Paris Commune.
12. *Le Figaro*, a Paris conservative daily.
13. Adolphe Crémieux (1796–1880), French lawyer and politician.
14. Alexandre Olivier Glais–Bizoin (1800–1877), French lawyer and politician.
15. Prosper Olivier Lissagaray (1838-1901), a French journalist in London.
16. Charles Longuet, Marx's grandchild.

223

To Frederick Engels (in London)[1]
Karlsbad, September 1, 1874

Dear Fred:

Next Wednesday it will be two weeks since I am here,[2] and my gunpowder, *alias money* [in English], will last me just for the third week. When you write me, please do so to the above address [Hotel Germania, am Schlossberg, Karlsbad, Austria], but c/o Eleanor Marx on the envelope. The cure has done wonders for Tussy;[3] I feel better, but the insomnia is not yet conquered.

Both of us live strictly according to the regulations. Mornings, at six, we go to our respective springs, where I have to drink seven glasses of water. Between each glass there is a fifteen-minute interval, during which one strolls up and down; after the last glass, a *walk* [in English] of one hour, then coffee. Evenings, before going to sleep, another cold glass.

For profane drink, I have been hitherto reduced to Pumpenheimer; Tussy, on the other hand, gets *daily* [in English] one glass of Pilsener beer, at which I leer enviously. Östreicher,[4] the doctor recommended to me by Kugelmann and who in his manners, speech, etc., resembles the famous Cecilia, was at first not without worry about my being here. At his advice, I registered as Charles Marx, *Privatier* [gentleman of private means], London, the consequence of this "*Privatier*" being that I had to pay, both for me and for Eleanor, a double spa tax to the worthy city treasury, but it served to keep away the suspicion that I was the notorious Karl Marx. Yesterday, however, I was denounced as such in the Vienna scandalsheet *Sprudel* (spa journal), together with the Polish patriot, Count Plater[5] (good Catholic, liberal aristocrat), he as the "chief of the Russian Nihilists." But this denunciation now probably comes too late, since I have the city's receipt for the paid-up spa tax to show. I could also have lived more cheaply than the way Kugelmann had arranged it, but given my particular situation which makes a respectable appearance useful, this was useful, perhaps necessary. *Under no circumstances* will I return via Hanover, although Kugelmann does not know it yet, but I will rather take the southern route, the way I came. The man bores me with his depressing naggings-or boorishnesses with which he embitters the life of

---

223

1. On September 22, 1870, Engels moved to London from Manchester, where he had lived for twenty years. From that time on, until Marx's death in 1883, the two men saw each other nearly every day, unless one or the other was out of the city. In consequence, their written correspondence was sharply reduced.
2. Marx, accompanied by his daughter Eleanor, was on a cure in Karlsbad from August 19 to September 21, 1874.
3. Eleanor Marx.
4. Unidentified.
5. Wladyslaw Plater (1806–1889), a Polish politician who lived in exile.

his family completely without cause.[6] On the other hand, it is possible that I may be obliged to remain in Karlsbad five weeks.

The environs here are very beautiful, and one cannot have enough of walking through and over the wooded granite hills. But no bird lives in these woods. Birds are healthy and don't like mineral vapors.

I hope that Jennychen[7] has recovered to a certain extent.

Best regards for all from

Mohr

224

To Frederick Engels (in London)
Karlsbad, September 18, 1874

Dear Fred:
On Monday[1] we depart; we go via Leipzig, where I will stay a bit[2] and see Wilhelm [Liebknecht] and then to Hamburg.

You know that I am a very lazy correspondent; but this time this was not the reason for my obstinate silence. I spent the first three weeks *practically sleepless*; this, together with the exertions here, will explain everything.

Although one drinks the waters only in the morning (evenings before retiring, one has brought into the house a cold glass from a special spring), all day long one finds oneself being a kind of machine that leaves not a moment of freedom.

Up at five or five-thirty in the morning. Then one drinks six glasses one after the other at various fountains. At least fifteen minutes must elapse between glasses.

Then breakfast is prepared, followed by a purchase of pastry appropriate to spas. Afterward a walk of at least an hour, finally coffee, which is splendid here, in one of the coffee houses outside the city. Thereupon a tour on foot of the surrounding hills; at about twelve noon, one returns to the house, then a daily bath, which takes another hour.

Followed by a change of toilette; then dinner in some favorite inn.

Sleeping *after* the meal (it's permitted before the meal) is strictly forbidden, and rightly so, as a few attempts to do so have convinced me. Thus

---

6. For a further description of his break with Kugelmann, see Letter 224, Marx to Engels, September 18, 1874.

7. Jenny Longuet.

224

1. September 21.

2. Marx stayed in Leipzig from September 23 to 25.

another foot tour is undertaken, alternating with a ride. Return to Karlsbad between six and eight in the evening, a light evening snack, and—to bed. This is varied by going to the theater (which always closes at nine o'clock, as do all other entertainments), a concert, or reading room.

As a result of the water cure, the head is very irritable. You will understand, therefore, that in the long run Kugelmann became unbearable. Out of good nature, he gave me a room between his and Tussy's, so that I had his company not only when we were together but also when I was alone. His constant chattering in a deep, earnestly lecturing voice, I bore with patience; but less so the Hamburg-Bremen-Hanover philistine gang, male and female, that would not leave me alone. Finally my patience broke when he became very boring with his domestic scenes. This archpedantic, bourgeois-petty-tradesman philistine imagines that his wife does not understand his Faustian, higher world-philosophic nature, and he most revoltingly torments the little lady, who is in every way superior to him. Hence we had a row; I moved to an upper floor, emancipated myself entirely from him (he genuinely spoiled the cure for me) and became reconciled only at his departure (which took place last Sunday). But I declared positively that I would not visit Hanover.

A quite agreeable contact with Simon Deutsch[3] (the same with whom I had a brawl in Paris, but who immediately sought me out here). Also, about half the local medical faculty soon grouped itself around me and my daughter; for my local purpose, when one must think little and laugh much, entirely suitable persons. Also, Knille,[4] the Berlin painter, an amiable companion.

About my adventure with Hans Healing Kugelmann, I will tell you some amusing things in London.

The more details one hears "about the Austrians" the more convinced one becomes that this State is coming to an end.

I have hitherto lost about four pounds (customs weight) and can feel with my own hand that the liver-enlargement is in *status evanescens* [a vanishing state]. I believe that I have achieved my purpose in Karlsbad, at least for a year. I would appreciate receiving a few words from you in Hamburg, care of Meissner.

With best regards from Tussy and me for Madame Lizzy and Pumps.[5]

Yours, Mohr

---

3. Simon Deutsch (1822–1877), Austrian bibliographer.
4. Otto Knille (1832–1898).
5. Mrs. Lydia Burns and her niece, Mary Ellen.

IN SEARCH
of HEALTH · *1875-1881*

The final years of Marx's life were plagued by almost unceasing ill health. He suffered from a variety of illnesses which would have tried the patience of Job.[1] His carbuncles were chronic; his whole skin became a mass of scars, resulting from the arsenic rubbings which were then prescribed by doctors. But Marx also suffered from toothaches, headaches, hereditary liver ailment, bronchitis, insomnia, and almost constant coughing. He went to various spas, including Karlsbad three times (1874, 1875, 1876), in search of a cure, which always turned out to be temporary. His personal sufferings were aggravated by the illnesses of his daughters and his wife, who died of intestinal cancer (as did also his oldest daughter Jenny in January, 1883) in December, 1881. Unable to do serious work, he read a great deal, books on history (of which he made voluminous extracts), economics, mathematics, and natural science.

---

1. For Marx's illnesses and medical record, see Saul K. Padover, *Karl Marx: An Intimate Biography* (McGraw-Hill Book Co., New York, 1978), especially pages 639–43.

225

To Max Oppenheim[1] (in Prague)
London, January 20, 1875

Dear Friend:

Forgive the delay in my letter. I have been very busy, since it is only today that I finished with the translation (French) of those *livraisons* [separate sheets] of *Kapital* that had not yet appeared. As soon as the whole thing is out, I shall send it to you, as I have changed much and added much, specifically in the parts of the French edition.

Your consignment of pheasants and livers arrived in time and was received here with genuine enthusiasm.

I am not familiar with the Berlin paper about which you wrote me;[2] but one of my followers might well be its correspondent, without my knowing it.

Now I have a favor to ask of you. The doctors have forbidden me to smoke without a cigar holder. I would therefore like to have, for me and my friends, 200 holders, which I got to know in Karlsbad, which one can throw away after each smoked cigar, when they are no longer useful, which cannot be obtained here. But note well, this is a commercial order, the cost of which you must let me know, otherwise I would be embarrassed to turn to you for similar favors in the future.

My daughter[3] sends her warmest regards. She corresponds with Frau Kugelmann and daughter, from whom she has received letters recently.

When you write to me next, please let me know a few more details about business conditions in Bohemia.

I am looking forward with pleasure to the time when I can see you here.

Most cordially yours, Karl Marx

226

From letter to Frederick Engels (in Ramsgate)
Karlsbad, Hotel Germania, Schlossplatz, August 21, 1875

Dear Fred:

I arrived here last Sunday.[1] Dr. Kraus[2] has been away again at Gmund, with his family; he has rearranged his relations with his wife.

225

1. Max Oppenheim, brother of Mrs. Ludwig Kugelmann.
2. *International Gazette*, a Berlin English-language paper.
3. Eleanor Marx.

226

1. On his second visit to Karlsbad, Marx stayed there from August 15 to September 11, 1875.
2. Bernhard Kraus (1828–1887), Austrian doctor and medical publisher.

As I had assumed, I am now my own doctor, and as Dr. Gans[3] has told me with quiet sorrow, this is the case with a third of the older guests here. The absence of my personal physician Kugelmann is also very healthful for me.[4]

Despite the change of personnel, the public looks about the same as last time: the *average man* [in English] of Quételet[5] constitutes the exception; instead, the preponderance consists of the extreme, barrel-thick and spindle-thin.

I spend at least twelve hours in the open, and after completion of the routine, my main pleasure consists in discovering new paths, points, and outlooks in the forested hills, and am the more exposed to surprises the less sense of direction I possess.

From today on—when I received the receipt for my payment of the cure tax, I feel secure from the police. My namesake, the police director of Vienna, is so artful as always to arrive here at the same time as I.

Last night I went to the Hopfenstock, which is famous for its beer, to drink my glass of Giesshübler mineral water. There were Karlsbad philistines, and the whole conversation revolved around what is here the *inexhaustible* wrangle and partisan-question, the respective advantages of the old Pilsener, the plain and the Aktien beers. Yep, said one, in the old one I consumed fifteen glasses (and they are big) like nothing. Nope, said the other, I also was a partisan, but now I am above these squabbles. I drink all of them through with the same result, etc. But next to these wise *natives* [in English] there were also two Berlin *swells* [in English], junior trainees or something like that. They argued over the advantages of the coffees in the various famous Karlsbad restaurants, and one of them assured the other with solemn earnestness: It is *statistically* proven that the coffee in the Garden of Schönbrunn is the best. In between a *native* [in English] cried out: But our Bohemia is great, achieves great things. Its Pilsener beer is being exported to all countries; in Paris, the great brewer Salzmann[6] has a branch; the beer also goes to America! Unfortunately, we cannot send along our great stone cellars which belong with Pilsener!

Now that I have reported to you newly won insights into world trade *in nuce* [in a nutshell], some items about my travel experience.

In London, a cunning-looking Jew-boy [*Jüdel*] entered our wagon in great haste, carrying a small trunk under his arm. Shortly before Harwich,

---

3. Unidentified.
4. On Marx's break with Kugelmann, see Letter 224, Marx to Engels, September 18, 1874.
5. The Belgian statistician Lambert Adolphe Jacques Quételet (1796–1874) developed the concept of the "average man."
6. Unidentified.

he searched for his keys to see, as he said, if his clerk had packed his necessary clothing. "In my brother's shop I received a telegram from Berlin," he said, "to go there immediately, and so I sent the clerk home to bring the necessary stuff." After much rummaging, he finally located, not the real key, but a key that did open the trunk and found that pants and coat did not match, that nightshirts, overcoat, etc., were missing. On the boat, the Jew-boy opened up his heart to me. "Such cheating," he exclaimed again and again, "has never been seen in the world before." This was his story: A German Yankee named Börn- or Bernstein, recommended to him by his Berlin friend Neumann, swindled him out of £1,700—him, considered to be one of the shrewdest businessmen! The swindler, presumably in the African trade, had shown him bills of goods, worth thousands of pounds sterling, which he bought from the best firms in Bradford and Manchester; the ship with the goods lies at anchor in Southampton. He gave him [the swindler] the advance payment he asked for. As he does not hear anything from him, he becomes anxious. He writes to Manchester and Bradford; and he shows me the replies: Börnstein had taken samples and bought goods from them, the price to be paid upon *receipt of the goods*; the bills were, therefore, merely forms; the goods were never picked up. They were seized in Southampton and it was found that the bales were filled with straw mattresses.

What chagrined our Jew-boy most, apart from the loss of the £1,700, was that a sharp dealer like himself could be so diddled. He wrote to his friend Neumann and to his brother in Berlin. The latter informed him by telegram that Börnstein was found in Berlin, was denounced to the police, which keeps an eye on him, but he is preparing to take to his heels. Do you want, I asked him, to haul him to court? "Not his carcass I want," he replied, " 'tis the money I want back." I: "He will have squandered it by now." He: "Not his carcass I want! He may have tricked those gents in the City [he mentioned all possible characters there] out of £12,000, but me he must pay. The others can see where they can nab him." The best of it was that at our arrival in Rotterdam it turned out that he had a ticket only to Minden and that he had to wait until eleven o'clock next morning before he could take off. The fellow cursed the Railway Administration like mad. Did him no good. . . .

And now *vale faveque* [be well and devoted to me]. I must go to my routine. Best regards for Madame Lizzy.[7]

Yours, Mohr

---

7. Lydia Burns.

227

To Frederick Engels (in Ramsgate)
Karlsbad, Hotel Germania, September 8, 1875

Dear Fred:
You will probably have already known from Tussy that my first letter, which, in the presence of Dr. Gans junior, I personally handed in at the main post office here, has been intercepted, undoubtedly through the Prussian post. The later ones did arrive; the last one, which I mailed to her in the past week, seems again to have shared the fate of the first, since otherwise I would already have received a reply from her.

The cure agrees with me excellently; with few exceptions, I also have good nights. But, according to the assertions of the numerous doctors with whom I am friendly, I am also the model guest of Karlsbad. These gentlemen have themselves tried here and there to turn me away from the path of the "cure," under the pretext of *"praesente medico"* ["in the presence of a doctor"], etc., but without success.

As a second-year patient, I have moved up to the rank of the *Brunnen* [wells of mineral water]. Last year, the Theresienbrunn (41°*R*), Marktbrunn (39°), and Mühlbrunn (43.6°) were my sources of supply, while I took a glass of bubbling water only twice. This year, since the beginning of the second week, Felsenquelle (one glass daily) (45°*R*), Bernardsbrunn (53.8°) (two glasses), and bubbling (two glasses) (59-60°*R*); this makes five glasses of hot water every morning, to which are also added one cold glass from Schlossbrunn in the morning and one when going to sleep.

The bubbling water, according to Professor Ferdinand Ragsky's analysis, consists of:

In 16 ounces—7,680 grams

Calcium sulphate potassium	1,2564
Calcium sulphate sodium	18,2160
Sodium chlorite	7,9156
Carbonate of soda	10,4593
Carboniferous limestone	2,2870
Carbonate of magnesia	0,9523
Carbonate of strontion	0,0061
Carbonate of ferrous oxide	0,0215
Carbonate of manganese oxide	0,0046
Phosphoric alumina	0,0030
Phosphoric limestone	0,0015
Fluorspar	0,0276
Silica	0,5590
Total of the fixed ingredients	41,7099
Free and half-agglutinated carbonates	5,8670

Among the fellows here who called for a Sedan celebration[1] was Gustav Köttgen, merchant from Barmen; does he have any connection with the old fool?[2]

You must look out; Karl Grün is giving you competition; next spring, he will publish a work on natural philosophy, which has already been preluded in the Berlin *Wage*,[3] which Weiss sent me from Berlin.

I am leaving here on Saturday,[4] first for Prague, as I received today a letter from Oppenheim there. From Prague, I go home via Frankfurt.

Dr. Fleckles[5] has just arrived, to take me out to eat. Thus, no long letter; Fleckles also says it is not in accord with a cure. Best regards for Madame Lizzy.[6]

Yours, Mohr

228

To Frederick Engels (in Ramsgate)
Karlsbad, Hotel Germania, August 19, 1876

Dear Fred:
I am writing you at the London address, since I do not know whether you are still at the sea resort.

First of all, our travel adventure.[1] In accord with my plan, we stayed overnight in Cologne—left there at six in the morning for Nuremberg, our next resting place. About five o'clock in the afternoon, we arrived at Nuremberg, which we wanted to leave only the following evening (it was the fourteenth [of August] and we had informed our Karlsbad hostess that the fifteenth would be our day of arrival). The trunks were unloaded, handed

---

227

1. To commemorate the decisive German victory over the French at Sedan, on September 1–2, 1870.
2. Marx and Engels had contact with Gustav Adolph Köttgen [1805-1882], an Elberfeld socialist, in 1845–46.
3. Grün published a series of articles, "*Über Weltanschauungen*" [*On the Philosophies of Life*], in the Berlin weekly, *Die Wage*, between August 20 and September 17, 1875. The complete work appeared under the title, *Die Philosophie der Gegenwart. Realismus und Idealismus* [*Philosophy of the Present Time. Realism and Idealism*] (Leipzig, 1876). Engels was then at work on his *Dialectics of Nature*, which he began in 1873, which was published posthumously in German and Russian editions in 1925; enlarged editions came out in Moscow in 1941 and 1961.
4. September 11.
5. Ferdinand Fleckles (d. *c.* 1894).
6. Lydia Burns.

228

1. Marx went to Karlsbad for the third consecutive year; in 1876, he stayed there from August 15 to September 15.

over to a man with a cart who was to accompany us to an inn in the city nearest to the railroad. But that inn had only one free room, and at the same time the host told us the chilly news that we would have difficulty finding accommodations elsewhere, since the city was overflowing, partly because of a congress of millers and bakers, and partly because people from all over the world came for the Bayreuth Fool's Festival of the State Musician, Wagner.[2] And so it was. We wandered through the city for a long time with the cart; neither the smallest pub nor the biggest hotel offered any asylum; all that we achieved was a superficial acquaintanceship with the ancestral home (highly interesting) of German *Knotentums* [loutishness, or philistinism]. Thus, back to the railroad; there we were told that the city nearest to Karlsbad whither we could still be transported was Weiden; we bought tickets for Weiden. But the Herr Conductor already had a drop (or more) too many in the head; instead of making us get out near Neunkirchen, where there was a recently built branch line to Weiden, he let us go as far as Irrelohe [Irrenlohe] (this is more or less the name of the nest), whence we had to travel back (in the opposite direction) for two whole hours, in order to get to Weiden, where we finally arrived at midnight. Here, too, the only existing inn was filled, so that we had to sit on the hard benches of the railroad station until four o'clock in the morning. Altogether, the trip from Cologne to Karlsbad took twenty-eight hours! And with it, an indecent heat!

What we heard from all sides on the next day in Karlsbad (where it had not rained for six weeks), and experienced the same on our own skins—was an excess of warmth! In addition, a shortage of water; the Tepl appears to be entirely drained. The deforestation had put it in such a condition that in a rainy period (as in 1872) it overflows, and in hot years becomes entirely dried up.

For the rest, the excessive heat has let up in the last three days, and even during the very hot days we found forest glens, known to me from before, where it was bearable.

Tussychen, who has been quite ill during the trip, is visibly mending here, and on me Karlsbad has a wonderful effect, as always. The unnatural headaches, which had returned in the last few months, have now completely disappeared.

Dr. Fleckles has told me a highly striking bit of news. I asked him if his cousin, Madame Wollmann[3] of Paris, a very interesting lady whom I met last

---

2. Richard Wagner's operatic tetralogy, *The Ring of the Nibelungen*, was performed in Bayreuth, about thirty-five miles from Nuremberg, August 13–17, 1876.
3. First name unknown.

year, was here. He answered that her husband had lost his whole fortune, and also that of his wife, speculating on the Paris Exchange, so that the family had to retire in a hopeless condition to a corner of Germany. What is curious about the affair is this: Herr Wollman[3] had made a great fortune in Paris as a paint manufacturer; he had never played on the Exchange, but had quietly invested the money he did not need in his business (as well as that of his wife) in Austrian government securities. Then one day he had a crazy idea; he considered the Austrian state as unsafe, sold all his securities; and *entirely in secret*, without the knowledge of his wife or his friends Heine and Rothschild,[3] he speculated on the Exchange on a rise—of Turkish and Peruvian securities—until the last penny went to the devil! The poor wife was in the process of fixing up their newly rented house in Paris, when one fine morning, without any forewarning, she heard that she had become a beggar.

Professor Friedberg[4] (on the medical faculty of Breslau University) told me today that the great Lasker[5] has published anonymously a semiromance, entitled, *Erfahrungen einer Mannesseele [Experiences of a Male Soul]*. These high-breasted experiences are introduced in a fulsome Preface or Introduction by Herr Berthold Auerbach. What Lasker experienced was that all females (including a daughter of Kinkel) fell in love with him and he now explains why he did not marry all of them together, and why he did not finally settle with even one of them. The book was said to be a genuine dishrag odyssey. Soon there appeared a parody (equally anonymous[6]), so horrible, that Otto's [Bismarck's] big brother,[7] with a painful loss of money, bought up every possible copy of the *Erfahrungen*. "Duty" now calls me away from the writing desk. Thus, until next time—insofar as the magically stupefying effect of the hot alkali drink will allow me to scribble a few more lines.

My best regards to Madame Lizzy.[8]

Yours, Mohr

It swarms with Russians here.

My wife has just written me that you are still in Ramsgate. Hence I am sending the letter direct there.

---

4. Hermann Friedberg (1817–1884).
5. Eduard Lasker (1829–1884), German jurist and politician.
6. Heinrich Joachim Gehlsen, *Das Buch vom 'grossen' Lasker oder Leiden und Freuden einer schönen Mannes-Seele [The Book of the 'Great' Lasker or Sorrows and Joys of a Beautiful Male Soul]* (Berlin and Leipzig, 1874/1875).
7. Eduard Lasker.
8. Lydia Burns.

229

To Jenny Longuet (in Hastings)
Karlsbad,¹ end August–early September, 1876

My dear heart:
I was very pleased to see from your letters, of which one, alas, got lost, that your health has improved and that your fine little one² enjoys Hastings and already begins to play his role. *Macte puer virtute!*³

We live here day after full day, as mindless as the success of the cure requires. In the last few days our walks through the woods have been interrupted through the sudden changes in the weather, now April rain, now cloudburst, then again sunshine. But the cold weather, which came suddenly after the heat, has gone entirely.

We have made many acquaintances recently; excepting a few Poles, mostly German university professors and physicians.

Everywhere one is pestered with the question: What do you think of Wagner?⁴ Highly characteristic of this new-German-Prussian Empire-musician: He and wife (she who divorced von Bülow⁵), with Hahnrei Bülow and their common father-in-law Liszt,⁶ all four of them live in harmony together in Bayreuth, hugging, kissing, adoring, and enjoying each other. When you think, moreover, that Liszt is a Roman monk and Madame Wagner (first name, Cosima) is his "natural" daughter by Madame d'Agoult (Daniel Stern)—you can hardly imagine a better text for an opera by Offenbach⁷ than this family group with its patriarchal relationships. The adventures of this group—like the Nibelungen—would lend themselves to a tetralogy.

I hope, dear child, that I will find you well and gay again. Give my best regards to Longuet and my little grandson a dozen kisses from his *granny* [in English].
Adio.

[No signature]

229

1. From August 15 to September 15, Marx, accompanied by his daughter Eleanor, was on a cure in Karlsbad for the third (and last) time.
2. Jean-Laurent-Frederick Longuet ("Johnny"), born in that year.
3. Correctly: *Macte nova virtute, puer.* "Hail, Youth in your hero's career"; from Virgil, *Aenead*, Book IX.
4. Richard Wagner (1813–1883).
5. Hans Guido von Bülow, (1830–1894), pianist and conductor.
6. Franz Liszt (1811–1886), pianist and composer.
7. Jacques Offenbach (1819–1880), French composer.

230

To Wilhelm Bracke (in Brunswick)
London, January 21, 1877

Dear Bracke:
Good luck! on the latest example of the Social Democratic fighting forces in Germany![1] It made a great impression abroad, most especially in England, where the Berlin newspaper correspondents have for years done everything to mystify their British reading public over our Party affairs. But *"murder will out"* [in English], as John Bull says when he fails.

I would now like to know more (I did not want to trouble you with it during the election agitation) where I stand with Miss Isolde.[2] She had sent me the first proof sheets of the translation;[3] I wrote her that she is competent to do the work if she took time and did not rush, and I returned the four sheets. But at the same time I also sent her an extensive list of errors in the proofs.

This seems to have somewhat shocked the nerves of the little lady, for in her reply one glimpsed a certain petulance. Not misled by this, I wrote her that I considered her the chosen translator. Since then, weeks have passed and I have heard or seen nothing further. It is now absolutely necessary that the Fräulein decides, *oui ou non* [yes or no], and really delivers the work. Be so kind as to write her in this sense. Should she want to renege, one should try it with the Scheus,[4] although I am loath to have anything to do with Herr Scheu (which has nothing to do with this matter). There is no more time to be lost. If Isolde, the *Holde* [lovely], turns it down, she must return to me the French sheets.

Be so good as to make out a double contract—according to the conditions we agreed upon—one with your signature for Lissagaray and the other with his signature for you.
Salut.

Yours, K.M.

230

1. In the January 10, 1877, Reichstag elections the German Social Democratic Party polled 493,447 votes, or 9 percent of the total; its number of deputies increased from nine (as a result of the 1874 election) to twelve.
2. Isolde Kurz (1853–1944), German author and translator.
3. Prosper Olivier Lissagaray, *Histoire de la Commune de 1871* [*History of the Commune of 1871*] (Brussels, 1876); the German translation, under Marx's supervision, by Isolde Kurz was published by Wilhelm Bracke in Brunswick, 1877.
4. Andreas (1844–1927) and his brother Heinrich (1845–1926) Scheu, Austrian socialists who emigrated to England in 1874 and 1875 respectively.

231

To Wilhelm Alexander Freund (in Breslau)
London, January 21, 1877

Dear friend Freund:[1]
My New Year's greetings will unfortunately reach you and your dear wife belatedly, thanks to pressure of work and inflammation of the throat which I contracted during my last days at Karlsbad.[2] I was there in the situation of Martin Luther's peasant who mounted his horse on one side and fell off on the other side.

My daughter[3] sends her best regards to your wife and you. Among other things, she had sinned against a translation by Professor Delius[4] "The Epic Element in Shakespeare," printed by the local Shakespeare Society, of which she is a member and where she received great praises from Herr Delius. She begs me to ask you for the name of the Swabian anti-Shakespeare professor and the title of his work,[5] about which you spoke in Karlsbad. The matador of the local Shakespeare Society, Mr. Furnivall, absolutely does not want to miss the enjoyment of this opus.

The "Oriental Question" (which will end with a revolution in Russia, regardless of the outcome of the Russo-Turkish War [1877-1878] and the mustering of the Social Democratic forces in the Fatherland, will convince the German culture-philistines that there are more important things in the world than Richard Wagner's Music-of-the-Future.

With best regards for you and your dear wife.

Your amicably devoted, Karl

232

From letter to Wilhelm Bracke (in Brunswick)
London, April 21, 1877

Dear Bracke:
In the sheet I am enclosing, I am again noting the crudest mistakes by Kurz.

Months ago, when my correspondence with her ceased, I wrote Fräulein Kurz that—owing to lack of time—I can correct only factual errors,

---

231

1. Freund was a Breslau gynecologist and university instructor. *Freund* in German means "friend."
2..Marx was in Karlsbad from August 15 to September 15, 1876.
3. Eleanor Marx.
4. Nikolaus Delius (1813–1888), German philologist, Shakespeare scholar.
5. In his reply of July 19, 1877, Dr. Freund supplied the name of the author and title: Gustav Rümelin, *Shakespearestudien [Shakespeare Studies]* (Stuttgart, 1874).

such as are necessarily made by foreigners not familiar with French conditions, but not simple mistakes of translation.

Should she not proceed more carefully (I will sacrifice my time only for one or two more proof sheets), you must find an expert proofreader and deduct the payment from the translator's honorarium. . . .

Best regards.

Yours, K.M.

[Enclosed correction sheet]

p. 17 *Mandat tacite* is translated by the lovely [Isolde] as "*silent* mandate," which is nonsense. In German one speaks of "implied" contracts, but never of silent ones. But in the same sentence, "*démarche de Ferrières*" —referring to Jules Favre's trip to Ferrières, where Bismarck was—is translated as "Ferrières' step," thus transforming the *place* Ferrières into a *person*!

p. 18 "*Troohu . . . lui fit une belle Conférence.*" She translates: "made *him* a beautiful conference"; this is schoolboyishly literal, but makes no sense in German.

p. 20 *l'Hotel de Ville* is translated as "Town Hall"; the reference is to the September Government which resided in the "Hotel de Ville."

p. 20 *à ce lancé*—again schoolboyishly translated: "at *this throw* the whole mob roared." What does "at this (which?) throw . . . roared" mean in German? The word *lancé* must here be translated as "inflammatory cry."

p. 20 "*D'autres tocsins éclatent,*" is translated: "New (why not old?) tocsins were *drawn* (!)." The meaning of this is that more misfortune becomes loud. The very word "*éclatent*" and the whole connection of the sentence must have shown her that she wrote nonsense.

p. 25 Fräulein Kurz transforms "*Cordeliers,*" of the old French Revolution, into the nonexistent "*Franciscans.*" Not satisfied with that, she changes "*le prolétariat de la petite bourgeoisie*"—the proletariat of the petit bourgeoisie—into "the proletariat, the small bourgeoisie." This is nothing but slovenliness.

p. 26 *contre-maîtres* is translated as "*boatswains,*" whereas here it means "*foremen,*" and *chefs d'ateliers* are the "industrial managers."

p. 30 "*Paris capitulait avant le 15 sans l' irritation des patriotes.*" Kurz translates: "Paris capitulated before the 15th, without excitement on the part of the patriots." This would be correct, if the original stated:

"*Paris capitulait,* etc., *sans irritation de la part des patriotes*" (instead of "*sans l'irritation des patriotes*").

The sense is, therefore, the exact opposite, namely: "Without the excitement of the patriots Paris would have capitulated before the 15th."

In this very simple sentence, it is evident that we have here again the most unforgivable slovenliness.

p. 32 *"Jules Favre demandait à Trochu* sa démission."

Kurz translates: "Jules Favre demanded of Trochu *his dismissal."* Since a person cannot *dismiss* himself, but can only be dismissed by his superior, this sentence can only mean that Jules Favre wanted to be dismissed by Trochu. In fact, however, Jules Favre demanded Trochu's *resignation*, which is the literal translation of *"démission."*

233

To Frederick Engels (in Ramsgate)
London, July 18, 1877

Dear Fred:

In regard to Wiede,[1] I will answer him that (which is also the case) in my present state of health I am in no condition to be a contributor to any journal.

In reality, it would be very pleasant to see the appearance of a really scientific socialist journal. It would provide opportunity for criticism and countercriticism, wherein theoretical points could be discussed by us and the absolute ignorance of the professors and lecturers exposed, thereby at the same time bringing light into the heads of the *general public* [in English]—workers and bourgeois alike. But Wiede's magazine cannot be anything but *sham-scientific* [in English]; the same half-educated boors and half-ignorant literati who make the *Neue Welt*[2] and *Vorwärts*,[3] etc., so shaky, necessarily make up the greater part of his contributors. Ruthlessness—the primary condition of all criticism—is impossible in such a society, which, moreover, calls for constant consideration for superficiality, that is, articles for the ignorant. Think of a journal on chemistry which has for its basic assumption the readers' ignorance of chemistry! And apart from all that, the manner in which Wiede's contributors behaved in connection with the Dühring[4] affair, cautions one to stay away from those gentlemen as far as party-political relations allow. Their motto seems to be: He who criticizes his opponent through insults, has brains; but he who assails his opponent through real criticism, is an unworthy character.

233

1. Franz Wiede, editor of the Zurich monthly, *Die Neue Gessellschaft*, and co-editor of the Berlin semimonthly, *Die Zukunft*.
2. *Die Neue Welt*, an illustrated socialist journal, published in Leipzig.
3. *Vorwärts*, official organ of the German Socialist Workers' Party, published thrice weekly in Leipzig.
4. An attempt at the socialist congress in Gotha, May, 1877, to ban Engels' book, *Anti-Dühring*, a criticism of Eugen Dühring.

I hope that the insolences of the Russians in the Balkans[5] will rouse the Turks against their old regime. That the defeats of the Russians in European Turkey will lead directly to revolution in Russia, is now proved even to Lavrov[6] and Lopatin[7] through the outbursts in the Russian press, which the censorship could not control, because of the *failures* [in English] in Armenia. The tone of the Petersburg newspapers is more menacing than that of the German press at the time when the siege of Paris[8] did not proceed according to expectations.

For some days last week and the beginning of this one, insomnia and the accompanying chaotic mood of my head nerves had reached a hazardous stage. I feel better since yesterday.

With best regards from family to family.

Yours, K.M.

234

From letter to Frederick Engels (in Ramsgate)
London, July 25, 1877

Dear Fred:
Best thanks for the *billet doux* [love letter].

Another word about Neuenahr.[1] When one always goes to Karlsbad without interruption,[2] one always plays his last card. If, however, one takes refuge in a weaker spa, there still remains the last appeal, in case things assume a more precarious form. And one has to diplomatize with his *corpus* as with other things....

What do you say to the workers of the United States? This first outbreak against the *associated capital* [in English] oligarchy that has arisen since the Civil War,[3] will of course be smashed but it could serve as the beginning of the establishment of a serious labor party. Two favorable circumstances

---

5. On April 24, 1877, Russia declared war on Turkey, which was defeated in the Balkans.
6. Pyotr Lavrovich Lavrov (1823–1900), Russian Populist, sociologist, friend of Marx.
7. German Alexandrovich Lopatin (1845–1918), cotranslator of *Das Kapital* into Russian.
8. The Prussians besieged Paris from September 19, 1870, to January 28, 1871.

234

1. The sick Marx, with his ailing wife and daughter Eleanor, went for a cure to Bad Neuenahr, Germany, where they stayed from August 8 to September 27, 1877. See Letter 235, Marx to Engels, August 17, 1877.
2. Marx had gone to Karlsbad three consecutive summers, 1874, 1875, and 1876.
3. In July, 1877, a strike began by Baltimore and Ohio Railroad workers and, spreading over seventeen states, led to violence and the intervention of Federal troops.

enter here. The policy of the new President[4] will make the Negroes and the peasants [*sic*] of the West, who are already discontented over the great expropriations of land (*exactly of the fertile land* [in English]) in favor of the railroad, mining, etc., companies, allies of the workers. So that a nice sauce will brew over there, and the transfer of the center of the [First] International to the United States will provide there special opportunities *post festum* [after the event].[5]...

Salut.

Yours, Mohr

235

To Frederick Engels (in Ramsgate)
Bad Neuenahr, August 17, 1877

Dear Fred:

I would have written you sooner, but the daily stipulations of the whole human being—*a posteriori* [empirically], as a result of the trip to here and consolidated by the first week's mineral water drinking—make a man extremely incapable of action. Not much to report from here. A true idyll; moreover, owing to partly unfavorable weather (although, despite rain and storm spots, the air remains laudable) and to the continuing business crisis, the number of visitors here has dropped from three thousand to seventeen or eighteen hundred. Fortunate Ahr valley. It has as yet no railroads; but it is already surveyed, and by next year it is threatened by the *commencement d'éxécution* [start of the work] of railroad construction from Remagen to Ahrweiler, whence it will not go down the Ahr valley but leftward to Trier.

I have found here a very good physician. Dr. Schmitz[1] (born in Siegen), who is clever enough, despite the fact that he owns a house and garden here, to practice medicine in the winter (from the end of October on) in Italy. He has traveled much around the world, among other places, in California and Central America. In habits and manners, he reminds one of the old Dronke in his best period.

He has essentially confirmed what I have already written you from London. My liver no longer shows any traces of distention; the digestive

---

4. Rutherford B. Hayes (1822–1893), U. S. President, 1877–1881.
5. At The Hague congress of the First International, in September, 1872, Marx had proposed the successful motion that the General Council, its governing body, be transferred to New York, to save the organization from Michael Bakunin and his European Anarchist followers.

235
1. Richard Schmitz (1834–1893).

apparatus is somewhat disordered; but the real evil is nervous in nature. Schmitz told me again today that after a three-weeks stay here, I must spend time outdoors in the Black Forest, enjoying mountain, hill and forest air. *Nous verrons* [we will see]. He prescribed the same for my wife, who, moreover, must take medicines and has come here at the proper time, before her illness got worse. Tussychen's[2] appetite is gaining, which in her is the best symptom.

In Neuenahr, the mountains are somewhat too far away from the baths, at least for those who are accustomed to Karlsbad.

We are worried not to have received a blessed word about the adventures of the Longuet family.

How is your wife? I hope she feels better. Is your weather as capricious as here? In the Ahr valley, people are not accustomed to such weather.

In the casino [*Kurhaus*] (where one takes the baths, including here, as elsewhere, the drinking of the alkaline waters) there is a *Reading Room* [in English], which has, in addition to German and Dutch papers, the *Times*,[3] *Galignani's Messenger*,[4] *Figaro*, and *Indépendance Belge*,[5] that is, more than I need, since I am trying to avoid reading the newspapers. I see with regret that the Turks—at least to my layman's view—are again losing time [against Russia].

One drinks little wine here, and precisely the Walporzheimer and other red Ahr wines are forbidden to most guests (including myself).

Schorlemmer has promised to come here; but hitherto no "report" from him, as Richard Wagner puts it.

And now, *old boy* [in English], with best regards from family to family.

Yours, Mohr

236

From letter to Friedrich Adolph Sorge (in Hoboken, N.J.)
London, October 19, 1877

Dear Sorge:
... The workers themselves, when, like Herr Most[1] and Co., they give up work and become professional literati, always breed "theoretical" mischief

---

2. Eleanor Marx.
3. *The Times* of London.
4. An English-language publication, appearing in Paris three times weekly, then every week.
5. Brussels daily.

236
1. Johann Most (1846–1906), German Anarchist who emigrated to the United States in 1882.

and are always ready to join muddleheads from the allegedly "learned" caste. Utopian socialism, in particular, which for decades we have been sweeping out of German workers' heads with so much effort and labor—their freedom from it making them theoretically (and thereby also practically) superior to the French and English—this utopian socialism, the chimerical game played with the future structure of society, is again spreading in a much more futile form; it is not to be compared with the great French and English utopians, but with—Weitling.[2] It is natural that utopianism, which *before* the age of materialist-critical socialism concealed the latter within itself *in nuce* [in a nutshell], coming now *post festum* [after the event] can only be silly—silly, stale and basically reactionary. . . .

Satis superque [more than enough]!

Yours, Karl Marx

237

From letter to Wilhelm Blos (in Hamburg)
London, November 10, 1877

Dear Blos:[1]
. . . I "begrudge not" (as Heine says[2]), and neither does Engels. We two do not give a fig for popularity. As proof of my aversion for all cult of personality, I mention that during the period of the [First] International, I never permitted the numerous maneuvers of approval from various countries with which I had been molested to be made public, and I never replied to them except with rebuke here and there. When Engels and I first joined the secret Communist League [in 1847] we did so under condition that everything that furthered the superstition of authoritarianism be removed from the statutes (Lassalle, later, operated on exactly the opposite principle). . . .

Totus tuus [Entirely yours], Karl Marx

---

2. Wilhelm Weitling (1808–1871), German utopian communist, rejected by Marx.

237

1. Wilhelm Blos (1849–1927), German Social Democratic journalist, historian, later member of the Reichstag.
2. Heinrich Heine, *Lyrisches Intermezzo [Lyrical Intermezzo]*, Poem 18.

238

From letter to the Editor of the Petersburg literary-political journal, Otechestvennye Zapiski, [Homeland notes] *c. November, 1877, in reply to Nicolai K. Mikhailovski's article, "Karl Marx before the Tribunal of Mr. J. Zhukovski," published in the October, 1877, issue of that journal.*[1]

...What application for Russia can my critic make of this historical sketch [the original accumulation of capital in the West European economy]? Only this: if Russia strives to become a capitalist country along the West European model—and in recent years it has exerted a great deal of effort in that direction—it will not be able to do so without having first transformed a large portion of the peasantry into proletarians; and then, once plunged into the vortex of a capitalist economy, it will have to endure the inexorable laws of that system, exactly like other profane nations. That is all. But it is too little for my critic. He must by all means transform my historical sketch of the development of capitalism in Western Europe into a historical-philosophical theory of universal development predetermined by fate for all nations, whatever their historic circumstances in which they find themselves may be, in order finally to achieve that economic formation which with the highest upswing of the productive forces of social work assures mankind its most universal development. But I beg his pardon. (That [view] does me at the same time too much honor and too much insult.) Let us take an example.

In many passages in *Capital* I point out the fate which overtook the plebeians in ancient Rome. Originally they were free peasants, each cultivating his own piece of land. In the course of Roman history they were expropriated. The same kind of development, the separation from their means of production and subsistence, took place not only in the formation of large landownership but also in large-scale money capitalism. So one fine day you had on the one side free men who were deprived of everything, except their labor power, and on the other side, for the exploitation of that labor, the owners of all the acquired riches. What happened? The Roman proletarians did not become wage workers but an idle *mob*, even more contemptible than the so-called "poor whites" of the Southern United States, and from them there did not develop a capitalist production system but one based on slave labor. Thus events of a striking analogy, because they took place in a different

---

[1]The letter, written in French, was never sent; discovered by Engels after Marx's death, it was published in Russian in the Number 5 (1886) issue of the *Vestnik Narodnoyi Volyi* [*Herald of the People's Will*] and in German in the *Sozialdemokrat* of June 3, 1887.

historic milieu, led to entirely different results. If one studies each of these developments by itself and then compares them with each other, one will easily find the key to each phenomenon, but one would never thereby attain a universal key to a general historical-philosophical theory, whose greatest advantage lies in its being beyond history.

239

Postcard to Jenny Longuet (in Malvern)
London, September 16, 1878

My dear child:
I hope that the improved reports about Johnny[1] continue. You must send me bulletins every day and always the exact truth. The little man is the apple of my eye. Above all, he must be treated indulgently, hence not too much movement (passive or active) out of his home. If he continues to make progress, as I hope, it would perhaps be better to leave Saturday[2] (instead of Friday). For another day of rest and recovery is very important in his case.

Engels sailed today for Hampton [Littlehampton] with Madame Renshaw and Pumps,[3] who already has the air of the "*princesse régnante*" [reigning princess] and whose behavior has been put on, together with her five guinea mourning dress, which however has only increased her barely concealed "delight." Tussy[4] will write you further details about these peculiar goings-on.[5]

According to news from Liebknecht, the Bismarck Law[6] is failing or is executed only with modifications that pull its sting.

My best love to you and your Mama [in English]. Puppy[7] is very improved, the good little fellow.

Yours, Mohr

239
1. Marx's two-year old grandson, Jean-Laurent-Frederick Longuet.
2. September 21.
3. Mary Ellen Burns, niece of Engels' recently deceased mistress, Lydia ("Lizzy") Burns.
4. Eleanor Marx.
5. See also Letter 240, Marx to his wife, September 17, 1878.
6. The anti-Socialist law enacted by the Reichstag on October 19, 1878.
7. Henry (Harry) Longuet (1878–1883), Marx's infant grandson.

240

From letter to Jenny Marx (in Malvern)
London, September 17, 1878

Dear Jenny:[1]

Enclosed a post office order for £3, as we had agreed when I left.[2] If it is not enough under the changed conditions, let me know immediately.

After my return I have suffered from extreme headaches; but this has improved since I received from dear Jennychen the reassuring letter about Johnny;[3] and your good news today—I hope that it continues—was balsam to me.

On the doings at No. 122 Regent's Park Road,[4] I will not enter further,[5] since Tussy[6] is your regular chronicler for it, and I do not want to skim the fat off her soup. But I cannot resist telling you of an incident which, in its originality, reminds one both of Balzac and of Paul de Kock at the same time. As Tussy, Mrs. Renshaw,[7] and Pumps[8] (she is now knighted; Engels now calls her Pumpsia) sorted out the possessions of the deceased,[9] Mrs. Renshaw, etc., found a small packet of letters (about eight, of which six were from members of the Marx family and two from Williams[7] [Ramsgate]) and as Mrs. Renshaw was at the point of handing it over to Mr. Chitty,[7] who was present at the proceedings, Engels said: "*No, burn them! I need not see her letters. I know she was unable to deceive me*" [in English]. If Figaro (I mean the real one, in Beaumarchais) *trouvé cela* [had found this]? Later on, Mrs. Renshaw said to Tussy: "*Of course, as he had to write her letters, and to read to her the letters she received, he might feel quite sure that these letters contained no secrets for him—but, they might do so, for her*" [in English]. . . .

I hope that you and Jennychen recover a bit more during this week, continue your excursions steadily, wind, weather, and the health of the child permitting—*ensemble* [together]; if exceptionally it does not work out that

---

240
1. Mrs. Marx.
2. Marx had been in Malvern, with his wife and daughter Jenny, from September 4 to 14, 1878.
3. Jean-Laurent-Frederick Longuet.
4. Engels' residence in London.
5. See also Letter 239, Marx to Jenny Longuet, September 16, 1878.
6. Eleanor Marx.
7. Unidentified.
8. Mary Ellen Burns.
9. Lizzy (Lydia) Burns (1827–1878), Engels' mistress who had died recently.

way, *you yourself* must never stop the excursions, but I do hope that the little one [Johnny] will participate and so also his much-suffering mother. Best regards for Jennychen. Kiss for Johnny.

Adio.

Yours, Mohr

241

To Maxim Maximovich Kovalevsky[1] (in Moscow) [text found only in Russian]
London, April, 1879

[No salutation]
The work of Mr. Kareyev[2] is excellent. But I do not entirely share his view of the Physiocrats. Let us consider the theory of capital, that is the modern order of society. Beginning with Petty[3] and up to Hume,[4] this theory was developed in separate pieces, according to the period in which the author lived. Quesnay[5] was the first to put political economy on its real, that is, capitalist basis, and it is strange that he proceeded like a tenant farmer of a landowner. Mr. Kareyev is completely wrong when he says that the Physiocrats counterposed only one branch of production of society, namely agriculture, against another, that is, industry and commerce, but that, unlike Smith,[6] they never went so far as to counterpose the classes of society against each other. If Mr. Kareyev would recall the fundamental idea of the Preface to Ricardo's famous work,[7] where he distinguishes among three classes of society (landowners, capitalists, and workers through whose labor the land is cultivated), he would be convinced that the first discovery of the three classes in the economic sphere and their reciprocal relationships could have been made only in agriculture, as Quesnay did. Beyond that, the writer [on economics] must distinguish between what a particular author actually says and what he believes he says. This applies even to philosophical systems—what Spinoza considered the cornerstone of his system, namely, that what he thinks and what really is are two different things entirely. Hence it is not to be wondered at that some of Quesnay's followers, such as, for example, Mercier de la Rivière,[8] saw the essence of his total system in his [Quesnay's]

241

1. Maxim Maximovich Kovalevsky (1851–1916), a Russian historian.
2. Nicolai Ivanovich Kareyev (1850–1931), a Russian historian.
3. Sir William Petty (1623–1687), an English statistician, founder of modern political economy.
4. David Hume (1711–1776), English philosopher and historian.
5. François Quesnay (1694–1774), a French economist, founder of the Physiocratic school.
6. Adam Smith (1723–1790), classic Scottish economist.
7. David Ricardo, *On the Principles of Political Economy, and Taxation* (London, 1817).
8. Paul Pierre Mercier de la Rivière (1720–1793), a French Physiocratic economist.

paraphernalia, while the English Physiocrats, who wrote in the year 1798, were the first to prove, on the basis of Quesnay and in contrast to A. Smith, the necessity for the elimination of private property in land.

[Unsigned]

242

To Frederick Engels (in London)
St. Aubin's,[1] Trafalgar Hotel, August 14, 1879

Dear Fred:

I am sending this to your London address, since—according to your letter to my wife—I am not sure that after this date you still belong to the Eastbourne folk.

Enclosed a letter from Hirsch[2] to me, ditto a letter from Louise Juta to Pumps.[3]

Our trip to Jersey from Southhampton was too much dampened by a violent rainstorm; we arrived dripping at St. Hélier, where it also "poured" violently. Since then, the weather, after some hither-and-yon changes, has been very good. In Jersey, the peasants believed that the world was coming to an end; they claimed never to have experienced such a bad spring and summer. Tomorrow we move to the Hotel de l'Europe, in St. Hélier. We are giving up St. Aubin's because Tussy and I have a horror of a monotonous daily lamb and mutton diet, as a result of which I have become a reluctant vegetarian in the last few days. Other rooms here—and we looked around a great deal—were not to be found. When we arrived in Jersey, it was still relatively empty, but in time came masses of immigrants, including *Frenchies* [in English]. When we inquired for rooms this morning at the Hotel de l'Europe, we were fortunate in that fifty Frenchmen were preparing to leave, while the *steamers* [in English] heavily loaded with new passengers had not arrived yet.

At our departure from London, at Waterloo Station, we met Harney who came to see his wife off to Jersey. Fortunately, they already had the ticket for first class, while we took second class. We met again on the *boat* [in English]. Mrs. Harney, like ourselves, does not suffer from seasickness but is otherwise unwell. Upon landing, we separated, but received from her the address of her brother, with whom she is staying. We have paid her there a short "condolence" visit. The woman is altogether *impracticable* [in English].

242

1. Marx and his daughter Eleanor (Tussy) were in St. Aubin's and St. Hélier, on the Isle of Jersey, from August 8 to 20, 1879.
2. Carl Hirsch (1841–1900), German socialist journalist.
3. Mary Ellen Burns.

Although a Jersey native, she could give us no information, other than what is printed in the *Guide* [in English]. A good woman, but not just the *person* [in English] for people who travel for fun. For some time now I have again been sleeping regularly, but have not yet got rid entirely of my cold, which I caught as a result of the *abominable* [in English] weather. But this should quickly go away in this mild air. Tussy is all right.

Two tenant farmers from Derbyshire, father and son, have been our table mates here in Trafalgar Hotel. The day before yesterday they made an excursion to St. Malo by sailboat, and "having been in France" for the first time in their lives, they returned with an unequally greater respect for themselves. The father was now of half a mind to make a Mediterranean *trip* [in English] with his son, but he thought it was "too hot" there. "*By no means,*" the son, who is the *booklearned man* [in English] corrected him; "*by no means, there it is now—winter*" [in English]. The older man (in any case, in his prime, and *a sharp fellow, with the true business-eye* [in English]) also informed me that St. Malo lies on the southwest coast of France. But they are the more conversant with agriculture and other *farmers questions* [in English].

Tussy finds no noticeable difficulties with the baths, has hitherto taken them alternately in St. Brelade's and St. Hélier's bay; and currently she alternates between the latter and St. Clement's bay.

From my wife's letters, I see that Schorlemeyer[4] has arrived [in London] as an invalid; I hope to hear better news from him soon.

Since my arrival here, I have looked at no newspapers and have read nothing at all, except Carleton's *Traits and Stories of the Irish Peasantry, first volume* [in English].[5] It was work enough to peruse the first volume, the second one I am preserving for a better time. These are *unconnected tales* [in English], illustrating Irish peasant life now from one side, now from the other, and hence not designed to be consumed in one sitting. Nevertheless, it is a book which one should acquire and keep, in order to taste now this and now that dish, *à fur et mesure* [as called for]. Carleton is neither a good stylist nor a good composer, but his originality lies in the truth of his pictures. As an Irish peasant's son, he knows his subject better than do men like Lever[6] and Lover.[7]

With the best regards from Tussy and myself to all of you,

Yours, Mohr

---

4. Marx meant Carl Schorlemmer.
5. William Carleton (1794–1869), Irish author whose two volume *Traits and Stories* was published in London, 1853.
6. Charles James Lever (1806–1872), English author.
7. Samuel Lover (1797–1868), Irish-born English author.

243

To Jenny Longuet (in Ramsgate) [in German, French, and English]
St. Hélier, August 19, 1879

My darling beloved Jennychen:
Hurrah for the little world citizen![1] *Il faut peupler le monde de garçons d'autant plus que la statistique anglaise montre un excès de filles.*[2] I am glad that the catastrophe [the delivery] has come off happily, alas under difficult conditions. The arrangement which Mamma has made seems to me far from the most convenient. At all events, Tussy and myself leave tomorrow for London and then I shall be very soon *at your side* and everything will be quietly settled. Here the rainy time—otherwise so unknown to this delicious island—has again set in, so that we had already commenced discussing our departure, the whole aspect of our sojourn here having changed with the climatic and meteorologic changes. The Hôtel de l'Europe is excellent and one day we must go here together, *toute la famille* [the whole family].

I can hardly expect tomorrow morning when the boat will start from here to Southampton. I feel so anxious with you and little Johnny.

In the meantime my best compliments to Mamma and Longuet. Don't fret or worry or become melancholy, my child, everything will be all right.

Your faithful, Old Nick

You must excuse the brevity of these lines, as the letter has to be mailed immediately.

244

To Frederick Engels (in Eastbourne)
Ramsgate,[1] 62 Plains of Waterloo, August 25, 1879

Dear Fred:
My letter from Jersey[2] and yours from Eastbourne must have crossed each other.

243
1. On August 18, 1879, Jenny Longuet gave birth to a boy, Edgar, in Ramsgate.
2. It is necessary to populate the world with boys, the more so as English statistics show an excess of girls.

244
1. Marx and his ailing wife were in Ramsgate from August 21 to September 17, 1879.
2. Letter 242, Marx to Engels, August 14, 1879.

After the news of the catastrophe[3] in Ramsgate reached us tele-graphically, we set out the following day, last Wednesday,[4] for London. I was sorry for Tussy's[5] sake to cut short her stay in Jersey, but knew that my presence in Ramsgate had become necessary for various reasons. I arrived there on Thursday amid thunder, lightning and rainstorms. On Friday it was beautiful, on Saturday *it rained dogs and cats* [in English] from morning to evening, but yesterday it has been beautiful again, today wavering prospects. Many Jews and bedbugs hereabouts.

The main thing is that Jennychen[6] has fortunately come through the nine days of trial and finds herself quite well, *considering the circumstances* [in English]. For the time being, she nurses the child herself; it is desirable that this would continue to remain feasible. My wife is improving, although slowly.

My head is still not *all right* [in English]. Yesterday I saw *experimentally* certain mathematical notebooks I had brought with me, but soon had to give up the premature *job* [in English], it was only a—*test* [in English].

I did not and do not take any sea baths, but only warm baths. Specifi-cally, as a result of the dreadful weather at our arrival in Jersey, my throat condition had worsened, to which was added a sudden toothache, neither of which is as yet eliminated, although alleviated, reminding me on and off that they always lurk in the background.

Hirsch is in London; he left his visiting card in my house, but I could not go to see him anymore (he lives with Lessner[7]) on account of my sudden departure from London. The enclosed letter from Kaub[8] will indicate to you the highly peculiar circumstances of Hirsch's repeated expulsions from Paris.

I hope that Schollymeyer [Schorlemmer] feels better. Best regards to him and Pumps, to whom Johnny sends special greetings.

Have you read the opening speech of Allman, or whatever his name is?[9] I managed to do it, although not being a man of science.

Adio, *old boy* [in English].

Yours, Mohr

The head of the Massachusetts Labor Statistics Bureau, Wright,[10] has sent me various *reports from* [in English] 1874–79 (knows nothing of Harney's previous

---

3. The "catastrophe" refers to Marx's daughter, Jenny Longuet, giving birth to a son, Edgar, on August 18, 1879.
4. August 20.
5. Eleanor Marx.
6. Jenny Longuet.
7. Friedrich Lessner (1827–1910), German communist tailor in London, friend of Marx.
8. Karl Kaub, a German refugee worker in London.
9. George James Allman (1812–1898), English biologist.
10. Carroll Davidson Wright (1840–1909), American statistician.

consignments), together with a compendium of the Massachusetts Census, informing me at the same time that *"he shall be pleased, in future, to send you our publications as soon as issued"* [in English].

Such "phenomena of decency" arrive only from Russia and the United States.

My old *patron Dana called last Friday at Maitland Park.*[11] *Tussy*[12] sent me his card [in English].

245

To Bertha Augusti[1] (in Koblenz)
London, October 25, 1879

Dear Frau Bertha:
I have a visitor (tedious) sitting right here, but I do not want to miss the opportunity of expressing to you in great haste my thanks for the enjoyment I derived from reading your novel in the *Kölnische.*[2] Great talent is detectable by anybody, but the achievement is a surprise to him who knows under what narrow conditions, cut off from the outside world, you work. Moreover, permit me to add that in regard to German novels I am a heretic, think nothing of them, very spoiled by the best French, English and Russian novelist-poets, and that I began to read your *Verhängnisvollen Jahres* with the usual mistrust.

With the best wishes for your wellbeing,

Your amicably devoted, Karl Marx

246

From letter[1] to Friedrich Adolph Sorge (in Hoboken, N.J.)
London, November 5, 1880

Dear Sorge:
My long silence is to be explained by (1) the pressure of much work, and (2) by the dangerous illness of my wife which has lasted now more than a year.[2]...

---

11. Marx's London address (41 Maitland Park Road, N.W.) from 1875 to his death in 1883.
12. Eleanor Marx.

245

1. Bertha Augusti (1827–1886), German novelist.
2. Bertha Augusti, *Ein Verhängnisvolles Jahr. Roman in zwei Teilen* [*A Fatal Year. Novel in Two Parts*], in *Kölnische Zeitung*, September 6 to October 31, 1879.

246

1. Original in New York Public Library, Manuscript Division.
2. Mrs. Marx died, of cancer, on December 2, 1881.

In Russia, where *Das Kapital* is more read and appreciated than anywhere else,[3] our success is even greater. On the one hand, we have the *critics* (mostly young university professors, part of them personal friends of mine, and also some writers for reviews); on the other hand, the *terrorist Central Committee*,[4] whose *program*, secretly printed and issued recently in Petersburg, has aroused great fury among the anarchist Russians in Switzerland who publish *The Black Redistribution* (this is the literal translation from the Russian[5]) in Geneva. They—mostly (not all) people who had left Russia *voluntarily*—constitute the so-called party of propaganda, in contrast to the terrorists who risk their skins. (In order to carry on propaganda *in Russia*—they move to Geneva! What a *quid pro quo* [tit for tat]!) These gentlemen [in Geneva] are against all political revolutionary action. Russia is to leap by somersault into the anarchist-communist, atheist millennium! In the meantime they are preparing for this leap with the most tedious doctrinairism, whose so-called *principes courent la rue depuis feu Bakounine* [principles are being hawked about in the street since the late Bakunin].[6]

And enough for now. Let's hear from you soon. Best regards from my wife.

Totus tuus [Entirely yours], *Karl Marx*

I would be very glad if you would get together for me something worthwhile (in content) about the economic conditions in California, *of course at my expense* [in English]. California is very important to me, because nowhere else has the upheaval through capitalist centralization been carried out—with such haste.

247

To Achille Loria (in Mantua) [in French]
London, November 13, 1880

Dear Mr. Loria:[1]
Family worries, caused by my wife's very dangerous illness, have delayed my reply to your letter of September 14.[2] I regret that the inadequacy of my

---

3. For Marx's comment on the Russian translation, see Letter 180, Marx to Kugelmann, October 12, 1868.
4. Of the secret society, *Narodnaya Volya* [The People's Will].
5. Russian: *Tchorny Peredel.*
6. Michael Bakunin died in 1876.

247

1. Achille Loria (*c.* 1857–*c.*1943), Italian sociologist and economist.
2. In his letter, Loria wrote that he wanted to study English conditions in London, and asked for help either in journalism or as Marx's secretary.

personal means do not permit me to assure your stay in London, the more so as I have the best opinion of your talents, your knowledge and your scholarly future.[3]

Since I live a somewhat retired life and avoid contact with the English press, I have very little influence and few connections, to be helpful to you. I know from experience that the Italian competition in London is as *overdone* [in English], be it in regard to contributing to the press, or in the field of private teaching, as in all other spheres of the struggle for existence.

Nevertheless, at the reopening of Parliament—until then, everybody, that is, *the upper ten thousands* [in English] of the metropolis, is bored—I will ask *some well-meaning and influential men* [in English] for advice. Meanwhile, let me know if you speak French and a little English.

Faithfully yours, Karl Marx

248

From letter to Nicolai Frantzevich Danielson (in Petersburg) [in English]
London, February 19, 1881

Dear Sir:
... I wrote you some time ago that if the great industrial and commercial crisis England has passed through went over without the culminating financial crash at London, this *exceptional* phenomenon was only due to—French money. This is now seen and acknowledged even by English routiniers. Thus the "*Statist*" (January 29, 1881) says: "The money market has only been so easy as it has been during the past year *through an accident.* The *Bank of France* in the early autumn permitted its stock of gold bullion to fall from £30 million to £22 million.... *Last autumn undoubtedly there was a very narrow escape.*"(!)

The *English railway system* rolls on the same inclined plane as the European *public debt system.* The ruling magnates amongst the different railway-net directors contract not only—progressively—new loans *in order to enlarge their networks,* i.e., the "territory" where they rule as absolute monarchs, but they enlarge their respective networks *in order to have new pretexts for engaging in*

---

3. Loria, *La Rendita Fondiaria e la sua Elisione Naturale* [*Funded Income and its Natural Elision*] (Milan, Naples and Pisa, 1880), an advance copy of which the author sent to Marx at the end of November 1879.

new loans which enable them to pay the interest due to the holders of obligations, preferential shares, etc., and also from time to time to throw a sop to
the much ill-used common shareholders in the shape of somewhat increased
dividends. This pleasant method must one day or another terminate in an
ugly catastrophe.

In the *United States* the railway kings have become the butt of attacks,
not only, as before this, on the part of the farmers and other industrial
"entrepreneurs" of the *West*, but also on the part of the grand representative of
commerce—the *New York Chamber of Commerce*. The octopus railway king and
financial swindler *Gould* has, on his side, told the New York commercial
magnates: You now attack the railways, because you think them most vulnerable considering their present unpopularity; but take heed: after the railways *every sort of corporation* (means in the Yankee dialect *joint stock company*)
will have its turn; then, later on, *all forms of associated capital*; finally *all forms of
capital*; you are thus paving the way to—*Communism* whose tendencies are
already more and more spreading among the people. M. Gould *"a le flair bon*
[has a good nose]."

In *India* serious complications, if not a general outbreak, are in store for
the British government. What the English take from them annually in the
form of rent, dividends for railways useless to the Hindus; pensions for
military and civil servicemen, for Afghanistan and other wars, etc., etc.—
what they take from them *without any equivalent* and *quite apart* from what
they appropriate to themselves annually *within* India,—speaking only of the
value of the commodities the Indians have gratuitously and annually to *send over*
to England—it amounts to *more than the total sum of income of the 60 millions of
agricultural and industrial labourers of India!* This is a bleeding process with a
vengeance! The famine years are pressing each other and *in dimensions* till now
not yet suspected in Europe! There is an actual conspiracy going on wherein
Hindus and Mussulmans co-operate; the British government is aware that
something is "brewing," but these shallow people (I mean the governmental
men), stultified by their own parliamentary ways of talking and thinking, do
not even desire to see clear, to realize the whole extent of the imminent
danger! To delude others and by deluding them to delude yourself—this is:
parliamentary wisdom in a nutshell! *Tant mieux!*

Yours very truly, Karl Marx

249

To Ferdinand Domela Nieuwenhuis¹ (in The Hague)
London, February 22, 1881

Honored Party Comrade:
My long silence, in not answering your letter of January 6,² was due to my working on a list of changes you might want to make in case of a second edition of your *Kapitaal en Arbeid*.³ As a result of domestic vexations, unforeseen tasks, and other interruptions, I am not yet done, but am sending you these lines without enclosing the list, since my continued silence might be misinterpreted on your part. The changes that seem to me to be necessary concern details; the main thing, the spirit of the book, is there.

I thank you for the friendly dedication,⁴ since you thereby have personally thrown the gauntlet in the face of the bourgeois antagonists.

The author⁵ of *Mannen van Beteekenis*,⁶ *schoolinspector or something of that sort* [in English], had written me for material on my biography, and through his [book]⁷ dealer he has also applied to my brother-in-law Juta to induce me to accede to his request, something I usually decline. The gentleman—the author of *Mannen*—wrote me he does not share my views, but recognizes their importance, expressing respect, etc. The same individual then had the effrontery to incorporate in his brochure a libelous fabrication of the notorious Prussian spy Stieber, and likewise—probably under the inspiration of a Bonn academic socialist—deliberately to falsify citations, whereby the honorable man did not make the effort to read my polemic against the worthy Brentano⁸ in the *Voksstaat*,⁹ where he would have seen that Brentano, who had originally denounced me for "formal and material falsification" in the *Concordia* (journal of manufacturers [published in Berlin]), subsequently

249

1. Ferdinand Domela Nieuwenhuis (1846–1919), founder of the Dutch Social Democratic Party.
2. In his letter of January 6, 1881, Nieuwenhuis had asked Marx what political and social action socialists should take if they seized power.
3. In 1881, Nieuwenhuis published *Karl Marx. Kapitaal en Arbeid [Capital and Labor]*, an abbreviated exposition of *Das Kapital* in Dutch.
4. The dedication read: "To Karl Marx, the bold thinker, the noble fighter for the rights of the proletariat, this book is dedicated by the author as a token of respectful esteem."
5. Arnold Kerdijk (1846–1905), Dutch journalist.
6. *Men of Distinction*, a series of books published in Haarlem, 1870–1882; Volume X contains a biography of Marx by Kerdijk.
7. Word damaged in MS.
8. Lujo Brentano (1844–1931), German economist.
9. Socialist publication in Leipzig.

weaseled out of the lie, he had understood it differently, etc.[10] To chastise the "schoolinspector," a Dutch journal wanted to open its columns to me, but as a matter of *principle* I do not reply to such flea bites. Even in London I have never paid the slightest attention to similar literary yapping. Otherwise, I would have had to kill the best part of my time with rectifications of stories from California to Moscow. When I was younger, I occasionally struck out lustily, but age brings enough wisdom to avoid useless *dissipation of force* [in English].

The "question" before the forthcoming Zurich Congress,[11] which you report to me, seems to me to be a blunder. What is to be done *immediately* at a given, exact moment in the future depends entirely on the historical circumstances. The question you pose exists in a Never-Never land; it is actually a phantom problem to which the only answer must be a critique of the question itself. We cannot solve an equation which does not include the elements of its solution in its data. For the rest, the dilemmas of a government that suddenly emerges as a result of a popular victory are in no way specifically "socialistic." On the contrary. The victorious bourgeois politicians feel immediately embarrassed by their "victory," while the socialist can at least proceed without embarrassment. Of one thing you can be sure—a socialist government does not come to the helm of a country without such developed conditions that it can take the necessary measures to intimidate the bourgeois mass, so that the first desideratum—time for lasting action—is won.

You may perhaps point out to me the example of the Paris Commune; but apart from the fact that this was merely a revolt of a city under exceptional conditions, the majority of the Commune was in no way socialistic, and could not be. Nevertheless, with a minimum quantity of *common sense* [in English], it could have achieved a compromise with the Versailles government useful for the whole mass of the people—which was then attainable. The appropriation of the Banque de France alone would have put a fearful end to the Versailles machinations, etc., etc.

The general demands of the French bourgeoisie before 1789 were, *mutatis mutandis* [with necessary changes], approximately as well founded as the present-day demands of the proletariat in all countries with a capitalist form of production. But the way the demands of the French bourgeoisie were carried out—did any Frenchman of the eighteenth century have, *a priori*, the slightest idea about it? The doctrinal and the necessarily fantastic anticipation of the action program of a revolution of the future emerges only from contemporary struggle. The dream of the imminent destruction of the world

10. Brentano's two articles, accusing Marx of falsifications, appeared in *Concordia*, May 7 and July 4, 1872. Marx replied in *Volksstaat*, August 7, 1872.
11. The socialist world congress met from October 2 to 4, 1881, in Chur, Switzerland, having been refused permission by the Zurich Canton.

inspired the early Christians in their struggle with the Roman world empire and gave them a certainty of victory. Scientific insight into the unavoidable and continuing disintegration of the dominant order of society, constantly visible before our eyes, and the increasingly passionate whipping of the masses by the old government specters, as well as the gigantically advancing positive development of the means of production—all this serves as a guarantee that at the moment of outbreak of a real proletarian revolution, its very conditions (even if surely not idyllic ones) will directly produce the next *modus operandi* [operating method].

According to my conviction, the critical conjuncture of a new international workers' association does not yet exist; I therefore consider all labor congresses, particularly socialist congresses, insofar as they are not related directly to specific conditions in this or that nation, as not only useless but also harmful. They will always be dissipated in a lot of chewed-over general banalities.

Your most devoted, Karl Marx

250

To Vera Ivanovna Zassulich[1] (in Geneva) [in French]
London, March 8, 1881

Dear Citizeness:

A neurasthenic illness that has plagued me periodically for ten years has prevented me from answering your letter of February 16.[2] I regret not being able to give you concise information, destined for the public, on the question that you have done me the honor of asking. Months ago, I promised the St. Petersburg Committee[3] to write an essay on the subject. Still I hope that a few lines will suffice to free you from any doubt regarding the misunderstanding of my so-called theory.

In the analysis of the genesis of capitalist production, I wrote: "As the basis of the capitalist system is the radical separation of the producer from the means of production. . . .[4] The foundation of this whole development is *the*

250

1. Vera Ivanovna Zassulich (1851–1919), a Russian revolutionist and later Menshevik (in opposition to Lenin's Bolsheviks).
2. In her letter of February 16, 1881, Vera Zassulich asked Marx, whose *Das Kapital* was popular among Russian revolutionists, to give his opinion on Russia's future development, particularly the village communes. Marx wrote four drafts, the one given above being the shortest.
3. The Committee of the revolutionary organization, *Narodnaya Volya* [People's Will].
4. The dots indicating elisions are by Marx.

expropriation of the agricultural producers. This was first carried out radically in England. . . . But *all other countries of Western Europe* pass through the same movement." (*Le Capital, édit. française,* p. 315).

The "historical inevitability" of this movement is, thus, *expressly* confined to the *countries of Western Europe.* The reason for this limitation is stated in the following passage in Chapter XXXII:

"*Private property*, which is based on personal work . . . , will be replaced by *capitalist private property*, which is based on the exploitation of the labor of others, on wage-labor" (l.c., p. 341).

In this movement in the West, what is involved is the *transformation of one form of private property into another form of private property.* In the case of the Russian peasants, on the contrary, *their communal property will be transformed into private property.*

Thus, the analysis presented in *Das Kapital* contains no proofs—neither for nor against the viability of the village commune, but a special study which I have made and for which I acquired material from original sources, has convinced me that this village commune is the fulcrum for the social regeneration of Russia; but in order that it can be effective in this sense, one must first eliminate the disruptive influences which storm upon it from all directions and assure it the normal conditions of its natural development.

I have the honor to be, dear Citizeness,

Your very devoted, Karl Marx

251

From letter to Jenny Longuet (in Argenteuil)
London, April 11, 1881

My dear Jennychen:
It is dull since you all left—without you and Johnny[1] and Harra[2] and Mr. "Tea"![3] I sometimes run to the window when I hear children's voices that sound like those of ours, forgetting momentarily that the little fellows are across the Channel!

One consolation is that you have good living quarters, suitable for the children; otherwise everything seems *rather worse* [in English] than in London—with the exception of the climate, the beneficial effect of which, in regard to asthma too, you will discover *by and by* [in English].

251
1. Five-year old grandson, Jean-Laurent-Frederick Longuet.
2. Three-year old grandson, Henri (Henry) Longuet.
3. Two-year old grandson, Edgar Longuet.

I have a new doctor again for Mother, recommended by Professor Lankester[4]—namely, Dr. Donkin; *he seems a bright and intelligent man* [in English] but for Mother's sickness it seems to me that *one man* [is] *as good, and perhaps better, than another man* [in English]. However, the *change of medical advisers* [in English] is a distraction for her, and in the first period—which generally does not last long—she is full of praise for the new Aesculapius. Longuet's eyeglasses turned up soon after you left, they were in fact in your bedroom. Hirsch has been chosen to bring them back, but this gossip hunter seems unable to tear himself away from London at a time when there is so much to pry out. The "great" Most[5] affair alone is an inexhaustible source of fresh (if by no means "joyously sparkling") water for that Hirsch. Now he threatens not to leave before April 18. And then he has found a pal in Kautsky[6]—against whom he had grumbled so darkly; even Engels has taken a much milder view of this *Kautz*[7] since the latter has shown great talent as a drinker. When this charmer first visited me—I mean the little *Kautz*—the first question that escaped my lips: Are you like your mother?[8] But absolutely not, he assured me, and I silently congratulated his mother. He is a mediocrity, with a petty outlook, a smart aleck (only twenty-six years old), a know-it-all, in a certain sense industrious, busies himself with statistics but makes little sense out of them, belongs by nature to the tribe of philistines, but is otherwise a decent fellow in his own way; if possible, I turn him over to *amigo* Engels.

The day before yesterday the Dogberry Club was here; yesterday, in addition to the two Maitland girls[9]—and for a while Lankester and Dr. Donkin—an invasion by Hyndman[10] and spouse [Mathilda], both of whom have too much staying power [*Sitzfleisch*]. I can stand the woman, for she has a brusque, unconventional and decisive way of thinking and speaking, but it is comical to see how admiringly her eyes hang on the lips of her self-satisfied, garrulous husband! Mother was so tired (it was nearly 10:30 in the evening) that she withdrew. But she was amused by one *byplay* [in English]. Tussy[11] had discovered among the Dogberries a new *Wunderkind*, a certain Radford;[12] this youngster is already a barrister-at-law, but despises the *jus*

---

4. Sir Edwin Ray Lankester (1847–1929), English biologist.
5. Johann Most, a German Anarchist sentenced in London, June 16, 1881, to sixteen months in jail for praising the assassination attempt on Czar Alexander II.
6. Karl Kautsky (1854–1938), socialist theoretician.
7. A pun on Kautsky's name, *Kauz* meaning screech owl in German.
8. Romantic novelist Minna Kautsky (1837–1912).
9. Dolly (Dollie) Maitland and her sister, English actresses.
10. Henry Mayers Hyndman (1842–1921), English socialist.
11. Eleanor Marx.
12. Ernest Radford, a young man with whom Tussy occasionally went to the theater. She wrote to her sister Jenny, June 18, 1881: "He is a very nice young fellow. We all like him very much—& he has one great virtue—he is wonderfully like Irving."

[law] and is working in the same line as Waldhorn.[13] *He looks well, cross* [in English] between Irving[14] and the late Lassalle (though he has nothing in common with the cynical, oily-obtrusive, phony-Baronial Jew-manners of the latter), *an intelligent and somewhat promising boy* [in English]. Well, this is the nub of story—Dolly Maitland flirts with *him* violently, so that mother and Tussy constantly winked at each other during supper. Finally Mr. Maitland arrived, fairly sober, and had a wordy duel with his instructive table companion—Hyndman—about Gladstone, in whom the spiritualist Maitland believes. I—*rather irritated by a bad throat—felt glad when the whole lot vanished. It is a strange thing that one cannot well live altogether without company, and that when you get it, you try hard to rid yourself of itself* [in English]. . . .

Kiss the children a hundred times for me; regards for Longuet. Write me, dear child, about your health. Adio.

Yours, Old Nick

Dear Johnny, how do you like France [in English]?

252

From letter to Jenny Longuet (in Argenteuil) [in English]
London, April 29, 1881

My dear Jenny:
I congratulate you on the happy delivery;[1] at least I assume that everything is in order, as you took the trouble to write yourself. My "women" expected that the "new earth citizen" would increase "the better half" of the population; personally, I prefer the "male" sex among children who will be born at this turning point in history. They have before them the most revolutionary period that men have ever experienced. It is bad nowadays to be so "old" as to have to foresee instead of see. . . .

Yours, Old Nick

---

13. Unidentified.
14. Sir Henry Irving (1838–1905), English Shakespearean actor.

252

1. Marcel Longuet, Marx's grandson, who lived into the middle of the twentieth century.

253

From letter to John Swinton (in New York) [in English]
London, June 2, 1881

Dear Mr. Swinton:
... As to the book of Mr. Henry George,[1] I consider it as a last attempt—to save the capitalistic regime. Of course, this is not the meaning of the author, but the older disciples of Ricardo—the radical ones—fancied already that by the public appropriation of the rent of land everything would be righted. I have referred to this doctrine in the *Misère de la Philosophie* [*The Poverty of Philosophy*] (published in 1847, against Proudhon).

My wife sends her best regards. Unfortunately her illness assumes more and more a fatal character.

Believe me, dear sir,

Yours most sincerely, Karl Marx

254

From letter[1] to Friedrich Adolph Sorge (in Hoboken, N.J.)
London, June 20, 1881

Dear Sorge:
... Before I received your copy of Henry George I had received two others, one from Swinton[2] and one from Willard Brown;[3] I therefore gave one to Engels and one to Lafargue. Today I must confine myself to a very brief formulation of my opinion of the book. In theory, the man is totally *arrière* [backward]. He understands nothing about the nature of surplus value, and so he wanders about in speculations that follow the English pattern, but are even behind the English in the portions on surplus value that have attained independent existence, that is, the relationship of profit, rent, interest, etc. His fundamental dogma is that everything would be all right if land rent were paid to the state. (You will also find payment of this kind among the transitional measures included in the *Communist Manifesto*.) This idea originally belonged to the bourgeois economists; it was first put forward (apart from a similar demand at the end of the eighteenth century) by the earliest radical disciples of Ricardo, just after his death. I said of it in 1847, in my book

---

253

1. George, *Progress and Poverty* (New York, 1880).

254

1. The original is in the New York Public Library, Manuscript Division.
2. See Letter 253, Marx to John Swinton, June 2, 1881.
3. Willard Brown, an American socialist journalist.

against Proudhon:[4] "We understand such economists as Mill (the elder, not his son John Stuart, who also repeats this in a somewhat modified form), Cherbulliez,[5] Hilditch,[6] and others demanding that rent should be handed over to the state to serve in place of taxes. That is a frank expression of the hate the industrial capitalist bears toward the landed proprietor, who seems to him a useless thing, an excrescence on the total body of bourgeois production."

We ourselves, as I have already indicated, adopted this appropriation of land rent by the state among numerous other transitional measures, which, as is likewise stated in the *Manifesto*, are and must be self-contradictory.

But the first one to turn this desideratum of the radical English bourgeois economists into the socialist panacea, to explain this procedure as the solution of the antagonisms inherent in the present mode of production was Colins,[7] a Belgian-born ex-officer of Napoleon's Hussars, who in the latter days of Guizot[8] and the early days of Napoleon the Little [Napoleon III] favored the world with fat tomes from Paris about this "discovery" of his, which is like his other discovery, namely, that even if there is no God, there is an "immortal" human soul and that animals have "no feelings." For if they had feelings, that is, souls, we would be cannibals and a kingdom of righteousness could never be established on earth. His "antilandownership theory," together with his theory of the soul, etc., has been preached monthly for years in the Paris *Philosophie de l'Avenir*[9] by his few remaining followers, mostly Belgians. They call themselves "*collectivistes rationnels*" ["rational collectivists"], and have praised Henry George.

After them, and along with them, among others, the Prussian banker and former lottery collector Samter from East Prussia, a blockhead, spun out this "socialism" in a fat tome.[10]

All these "socialists" since Colins have this in common, that they leave wage labor, and thus capitalist production, untouched, and deceive themselves or the world into believing that through the transformation of land rents into a state tax, all the evils of capitalist production would disappear by themselves. The whole thing is thus merely a socialistically embellished attempt to save the capitalist rule, and, indeed, to establish it anew on an even wider basis than the present one.

This cloven hoof which is at the same time an ass's hoof, also unmistakably peeps out of the declarations of Henry George. It is the more unforgiva-

---

4. *The Poverty of Philosophy.*
5. Antoine Élisée Cherbulliez (1797–1869), Swiss economist.
6. Richard Hilditch, English economist.
7. Jean Guillaume Hippolyte Colins (1783–1859), French economist.
8. François Guizot (1787–1874), French historian and statesman.
9. *La Philosophie de l'Avenir, Revue du socialisme rationnel*, appeared monthly from 1875 to 1900.
10. Adolph Samter, *Social-Lehre. Über die Befriedigung der Bedürfnisse in der menschlichen Gesellschaft* [*Social Doctrine. Concerning the Satisfaction of Needs in Human Society*] (Leipzig, 1875).

ble in him, since he, on the contrary, should have asked the question: How did it happen that in the United States, where relatively—that is, compared to civilized Europe—land was accessible to the great masses of the people and to a certain degree (again relatively) still is, the capitalist economy and the corresponding enslavement of the working class have developed more rapidly and more shamelessly than in any other country?

On the other hand, George's book, like the sensation it has made among you, has importance in that it is a first, even though disappointing, attempt at emancipation from orthodox political economy.

Moreover, H. George does not seem to know about the earlier *American Anti-Renters*,[11] who were more practical than theoretical. He is otherwise a writer of talent (with a Yankee talent for advertising too), as, for example, is shown by his article on California in the *Atlantic*.[12] He also has the repulsive presumption and arrogance that invariably characterize all such panacea-hatchers.

My wife's sickness, between us, is unfortunately incurable. In a few days I am going to seaside at Eastbourne.

Salut fraternel [Fraternal greetings].

Yours, K. Marx

255

To Frederick Engels (in London)
Argenteuil,[1] 11 Boulevard Thiers, July 27, 1881

Dear Engels:
I cannot write in greater detail today because I have a mass of letters to expedite and the little folk[2] rightly commandeered me on the first day.

The trip from London to Dover went as well as was to be expected; that is, my wife, who was very sick[3] when we left Maitland Park, noted no unfavorable change during the trip. On board ship she immediately went to the ladies' cabin where she found a splendid sofa to lie down. The sea was absolutely calm, and the weather at its best. She landed in Calais in better condition than when she left London and decided to continue the journey.

---

11. A tenant-farmer movement of the 1840s.
12. The reference is probably to George's article, "The Kearney Agitation in California," in *Popular Science Monthly*, August, 1880.

255

1. Marx and his wife (she for the last time) stayed with their daughter, Jenny Longuet, at Argenteuil, France, from July 26 to August 16, 1881.
2. Marx's grandchildren: the four Longuet boys.
3. Jenny Marx had an intestinal cancer of which, in fact, she died within four months after this letter was written.

The only stations where our *tickets* [in English] allowed us to break the trip were Calais and Amiens. The latter (*about two hours* [in English] from Paris), she thought was too close to stop off. Between Amiens and Creil, she felt the approach of diarrhea and a strong churning of the bowels. In Creil the train stopped only three minutes, but she just barely managed to make the necessary call. In Paris, where we arrived at 7:30 in the evening, Longuet received us at the station. But the direct train from here to Argenteuil left too late for us to wait for it. So, after inspection of the trunks by the *douaniers* [customs officers], we went by cab to St. Lazare Station, where, after some wait, we took the railway to the place of destination, where we arrived only *about 10 o'clock* [in English]. She was in great pain, but this morning (at least now, *about 10 o'clock* [in English]) she feels better than used to be the case in London at the same time of day. In any case, the return trip will be much shorter.

Longuet introduced me today to his doctor,[4] so that in case of a recurrence of the diarrhea, steps would be taken immediately.

We found everyone well here, only Johnny and Harry,[5] owing to the change in temperature (the extremely hot days have affected all the children, especially Johnny), with somewhat of a cold. As a *summer house*, which it had obviously once served as for some *richard* [rich man], the lodging is brilliant.

With best regards for Pumps [In English].[6]

Yours, Mohr

Tussy,[7] it seems, has written her Paris correspondent[8] about my arrival, and, Longuet tells me, it has become practically an open secret. The "Anarchists," he says, will ascribe malicious election maneuvers to me. Clemenceau[9] told him I have absolutely nothing to fear from the police.

256

From letter to Frederick Engels (in Bridlington Quay)
Argenteuil, August 3, 1881

Dear Fred:
It is painful for me to press so hard on your *Exchequer* [in English], but the anarchy which has invaded my house in the last two years and caused all

---

4. Dr. Dourlen, a physician of Argenteuil, France.
5. Grandsons Jean-Laurent-Frederick and Henri Longuet.
6. Pumps was Mary Ellen Burns.
7. Eleanor Marx.
8. Carl Hirsch (1841–1900), German socialist journalist living abroad.
9. Georges Clemenceau (1841–1929), French journalist and statesman; at the time of Marx's visit to France, Clemenceau was the publisher of *La Justice*, a Paris daily of which Charles Longuet was one of the editors.

sorts of arrears, has weighed upon me for a long time. On the fifteenth of this month I must pay £30 in London,[1] and this has oppressed me from the day we left there.[2]

It is in no way certain when we will return. We go through here the same changes from day to day as in Eastbourne,[3] the only difference being that here frightful pains afflict her suddenly, as happened yesterday. Our Doctor Dourlen, who is an excellent physician and fortunately lives close by, took immediate steps and applied one of the heroic opium doses, which Donkin[4] had deliberately kept in reserve. This resulted in a good night for her, and today she feels so well that, for a change, she was up already at eleven o'clock in the morning and is diverting herself with Jenny[5] and the children. (The *diarrhea stopped* [in English] within two days of our arrival. Dourlen said at the beginning: if it is only an *accident* [in English], it was not important; but it could be a symptom of the fact that the bowels themselves are infected. Fortunately, this was not the case.)

The temporary "improvements" do not, of course, slow up the natural progress of the evil [cancer], but they deceive my wife and confirm Jenny— despite my protest—in her belief that our stay in Argenteuil must be prolonged as much as possible. I know the situation better and have, therefore, the greater anxiety. Last night, *in fact* [in English], was the first time that I have had an approximately reasonable sleep. I feel as dumb in the head as if a millstone were turning there instead.[6] For this reason, I have remained exclusively in Argenteuil, visiting neither Paris nor writing any person to encourage him to visit me. Hirsch has already expressed his surprise to Longuet in the office of *La Justice*[7] about this "abstention."

In the last five days there took place here a Kotzebuish[8] drama *into the bargain* [in English].

Jenny had as a cook *a very lively young girl from the country* [in English], with whom she was satisfied in every way, as she also treated the children most kindly. From her last *mistress* [in English], the wife of Dr. Reynaud (also a doctor in Argenteuil), Jenny had only the "negative" testimonial that the girl had left her employ *voluntarily* [in English]. Old *mother* [in English]

256

1. Engels replied, August 6, 1881: "Don't get any gray hair over the paltry £30. I will send a check for this amount to Tussy *in time*. . . . If you need more, let me know."
2. On July 26.
3. Marx and his ailing wife were in Eastbourne for their health from the end of June to July 20, 1881.
4. The Marx family doctor in London.
5. Jenny Longuet.
6. A paraphrase from Goethe's *Faust* (Act I, section 4): "*Ich fühle mich im Kopf so dumm, als ging ein Mühlrad drin herum.*"
7. Paris daily, of which Longuet was one of the editors.
8. August Friedrich Ferdinand von Kotzebue (1761–1819), German writer of melodramas.

Longuet,[9] who, so far as possible, tries to exercise a dictatorship over Jenny, was in no way satisfied with this and had nothing better to do than to write to Mrs. Reynaud on her own.

Madame Reynaud is a handsome coquette and her husband is a wild jackass; hence things happen in their house which cause a lot of gossip in Argenteuil. *They did not know that their erstwhile maid had found employment again in the same town*, and with M. Longuet to boot, an intimate friend of Dr. Dourlen, whose wife is an intimate enemy of Madame Reynaud! *This was to be looked after* [in English].

And so one fine forenoon Madame Reynaud—until then personally unknown to Jennychen—arrives, and tells her that the maid had had unclean affairs with males (and Madame?), but, what was worse, she was a thief, *dans l'espèce* [in particular], that she had stolen a gold ring from her; she assured Jenny she wanted to settle the matter, etc., *en famille* [in the family circle], without having recourse to the "authorities." In short, Jennychen *summons the girl* [in English], Madame Reynaud babbles at her and *at the same time* [in English] threatens the girl, who returns the ring—*whereupon* Dr. Reynaud denounces the unfortunate girl to the *juge de paix*.[10] *Upshot* [in English]: yesterday she was taken to Versailles before the *juge d'instruction* [examining magistrate]. You know that in the residue of Roman law, where *familia = servi* [family equals slaves], the Code assigns such petty crimes, which customarily go before the correctional police, to the Assizes.

In the meantime, Jenny took all possible steps before the *juge de paix*, a very decent man, but the thing was out of his hands the moment the girl was officially denounced. Still, Jenny's testimony, which he took down in writing, and the extrajudicial procedure of the Reynauds, which were also put into the protocol, will benefit the girl.

Jenny's defense of the girl surprised the *juge de paix*, but he took it humorously. He asked her: *Mais vous ne voulez pas défendre le vol?—Mais non, Monsieur, commencez par arrêter tous les grands voleurs d'Argenteuil, et de Paris par dessus le marché!*"[11]

The immediate result has been that she [Jenny] is without a cook. The dumb girl from London—sister of our erstwhile Carry[12]—*is good for nothing in that line* [in English], and, moreover, has her hands full with four children. . . .

Salut.

Yours, Mohr

---

9. Felicitas Longuet, Charles Longuet's mother.
10. Justice of the Peace.
11. "But you do not want to defend theft?"—"No, sir, but begin with arresting all the big thieves in Argenteuil, and those of Paris above all."
12. Unidentified.

257 _____

To Laura Lafargue (in London)
Argenteuil, August 9, 1881

Dear Laurachen:
I can only write a few lines, since the mail pickup is at hand.

Mama's condition is critical on account of increasing debility. Hence (since we can travel only in small stages) I wanted to leave this week under all circumstances, and so informed the patient. But she has thwarted my plan, in that she sent out our laundry yesterday. So we cannot think of leaving until the beginning of next week.

Perhaps—depending on her condition—we can stay a *few days* in Boulogne. The doctor thinks (under otherwise favorable conditions) that the sea air might momentarily be invigorating for her.

Next time (but you must write me *immediately* your next address) a more detailed report. Best regards for Paul.[1]

Yours, Old Nick

258 _____

From letter to Jenny Longuet (in Argenteuil)
London, December 7, 1881

My dear good Jennychen:
You surely will find it natural that at this moment I am not in a mood for "writing" and that, therefore, I write only now these few words. As I could not leave the sickroom at all, the doctor's interdiction of my participation at the burial was inexorable. I complied, as, a few days before her death,[1] on the occasion of the nurse asking her if anything ceremonial had been neglected, the dearly departed said: *"We are no such external people"* [in English].

Schorlemmer came from Manchester at his own initiative.

I still have to undergo the iodine-tattoo treatment on the chest and neck, etc., and its regular repetition produces a quite troublesome and painful skin burning.[2] This operation, executed merely to prevent a relapse dur-

---

257
1. Paul Lafargue, Laura's husband.

258
1. Jenny Marx died of cancer on December 2, 1881; Marx was too ill to attend her funeral.
2. Marx was suffering from bronchitis complicated by pleurisy.

ing the healing (actually accomplished, except for a bit of a cough), is thus of great service to me now. For mental suffering, there is only one effective antidote, and that is, physical pain. Put the destruction of the world on one side and a man with an acute toothache on the other!

I am now extraordinarily happy that despite much hesitation we had dared the trip to Paris![3] Not only the time itself which the unforgettable one spent with you and the children—"hardly" disturbed by the picture of a certain domestic bully and kitchen-Mirabeau—but also the reliving of that period during her last days of illness! It is quite certain that in this period your and the children's actual presence could not have diverted her as intensively as did the ideal occupation with all of you!

Her resting place is quite close to the dear "Charles."[4]

I have one consolation, that her energy collapsed in time. Thanks to the extraordinarily rare condition of the tumor—so that it was mobile—the characteristically unbearable pains began only in the very last days (and even then still controlled with injections of morphine, which the doctor deliberately reserved for the catastrophe, as with longer application it loses all effect). As Dr. Donkin had told me in advance, the course of the sickness took on the characteristics of a gradual wasting away, as in weakness of old age. Even in the last hours, there was no *death struggle*, but a gradual passing away; her eyes were fuller, more beautiful, more radiant than ever! ...

Just now I received the December 7 issue of *Justice*[5] and found therein, under the rubric *"Gazette du Jour,"* an obituary note which, among other things says:

"On devine que son (the reference is to your mother) *mariage avec Karl Marx, fils d'un avocat de Trèves, ne se fit pas sans peine. Il y avait à vaincre bien des préjugés, le plus fort de tous était encore le préjugé de race. On sait que l'illustre socialiste est d'origine israélite."*[6]

[From here to the end of this letter, Marx writes almost entirely in English.]

Toute cette histoire [All this history] *is a* simple invention; *there was no* préjugés à vaincre [*prejudice to overcome*]. *I suppose I am not mistaken in crediting*

---

3. Marx and his gravely sick wife visited their daughter Jenny in France from July 26 to August 16, 1881.
4. Jenny's ten-month-old son who died in July 1874; he is buried in the family grave in London's Highgate Cemetery.
5. *La Justice*, a Paris daily, of which Charles Longuet was one of the editors.
6. "One conjectures that her *marriage* to Karl Marx, son of a lawyer of Trier, *did not take place without difficulties.* It was necessary to overcome *quite a few prejudices, the strongest of which was race prejudice.* One knows that the illustrious socialist is of Jewish origin." The words in italics were underlined by Marx. Longuet's obituary note, despite Marx's furious reaction to it, was historically correct, as he undoubtedly must have heard it from his mother-in-law.

Mr. Ch. Longuet's inventive genius with his literary "enjolivement" [*embellishment*]. *The writer when speaking of the limitation of the working day and the factory acts, mentioned in another number of* La Justice— *"Lassalle and Karl Marx," the former having never printed or spoken a syllable on the matter in question. Longuet would greatly oblige me in never mentioning my name in* his *writings.*

The allusion to your Mama's occasional anonymous correspondence (in fact in behalf of Irving)[7] *I find indiscreet. At the time she wrote to the* Gazette de Francfort *(she never wrote to the* Journal de Francfort *as the* Justice *calls it—a simple reactionary, and philistine paper) the latter (the* Gazette) *was still on more or less friendly terms with the socialist party.*

As to the "von Westphalen," *they were not of Rhenish, but of* Braunschweigerischer Abkunft [*Brunswick descent*]. *The father of your mother's father was the factotum of the* berüchtigte [*notorious*] *Duke of Brunswick (during the "Seven Years' War"). As such he was also overwhelmed with favours on the part of the British government and married a near relative of the Argyll's. His papers relative to war and politics*[8] *have been published by the Minister von Westphalen.*[9] *On the other hand,* "par sa mère" [*on her mother's side*], *your mother descends from a small* Prussian *functionary and was actually born at Salzwedel in the Mark. All these things need not be known, but knowing nothing of them, one ought not pretend correcting* d'autres [*other*] *"biographies."*

And now, my dear child, send me a long description of the doings of Johnny[10] *et Co. I still regret that Henry*[11] *was not left to us at the time he went on so well. He is a child who wants a whole family's attendance being singly, exclusively concentrated upon him. As it is, with so many other little ones requesting your care, he is rather an impediment.*

With many kisses to you and your "little men."[12]

Your devoted father, K.M.

---

7. The *Frankfurter Zeitung* published a number of articles by Jenny Marx on the London theater, starring her admired Sir Henry Irving: "From the London Theater World" (November 21, 1875); "London Season" (April 4, 1876); "English Shakespeare-Studies" (January 3, 1877); "Shakespeare's *Richard III* in London's Lyceum-Theater" (February 8, 1877); "About the London Theater" (May 25, 1877). The articles were written anonymously.
8. Christian Heinrich Phillip von Westphalen, *Geschichte der Feldzüge des Herzogs von Braunschweig-Lüneburg* [*History of the Campaigns of the Duke of Brunswick-Lüneburg*], 2 vols. (Berlin, 1859).
9. Jenny Marx's half-brother, Ferdinand Otto Wilhelm von Westphalen (1799–1876), Prussian Minister of Interior (1850–1858).
10. Five-year old Jean-Laurent-Frederick Longuet.
11. Three-year-old Henri (Harra, Harry) Longuet, who died in 1883.
12. Jenny Longuet's four sons.

259

Postcard to Johann Philipp Becker (in Geneva)
London, December 10, 1881

Dear Friend:
You will perhaps have learned from the newspapers about the death of my wife (she expired on December 2). You will find it natural that during the first days of this irreparable loss I was in no way in a frame of mind to correspond; in fact, except for her brother, Edgar von Westphalen, in Berlin, you are the *only one* to whom I have until now personally reported; the other friends and acquaintances have been informed by my youngest daughter.

My wife remained until the last moment a loyal friend, and rightly grumbled that the party has not alleviated your and your loyal mate's struggle for existence, the long-standing, unshakable, and heroic champion that you are.

I myself am still a patient, but on the way to recovery; pleurisy, complicated by bronchitis, have seized upon me so gravely that the doctors for a moment, i.e., many days, doubted whether I would pull through. Farewell, dear friend. Greetings to your wife.

K.M.

260

To Friedrich Adolph Sorge (in Hoboken, N.J.)
London, December 15, 1881

Dear Sorge:
From the communication which your son [Adolph] brought you from here, you must surely have been prepared for the news of the death of my dear, unforgettable life-companion (on December 2). I myself was not yet sufficiently restored to show her the last honours. I am in fact chained to the house, but should go to Ventnor (Isle of Wight) next week.

I am emerging from the last sickness doubly crippled, morally because of the loss of my wife, and physically because of a thickening of the pleura and a greater irritation of the trachea windpipe.

I will, alas, have to lose considerable time with health-restoring maneuvers.

A new German edition of *Das Kapital* has become necessary. It comes at a very inopportune time.

Your Henry George reveals himself more and more as a humbug.[1]

I hope that Sorge Junior has arrived in good health; give him my regards.

Yours, K.M.

The English have recently begun to occupy themselves more with *Capital*, etc. Thus in the last *October* (or November, I am not quite sure) number of *Contemporary* there is an article by *John Rae* on German Socialism.[2] (Very inadequate, full of mistakes, but "fair," as one of my English friends told me the day before yesterday.) And why fair? Because [from here on, the letter is chiefly in English] *John Rae does* not suppose *that for the forty years I am spreading my pernicious theories I was being instigated by* "*bad*" *motives.* "*Seine Grossmut muss ich loben* [*I must praise his generosity*]*!*" *The fairness of making yourself at least sufficiently acquainted with the subject of your criticism seems a thing quite unknown to the penmen of British philistinism.*

Before this, in the beginning of June, there was published by a certain Hyndman *a little book:* England for All. *It pretends to be written as an exposé of the program of the* "*Democratic Federation*"—*a recently formed association of different* England Scottish *radical societies, half bourgeois, half* prolétaires. *The chapters on Labor and Capital are only literal extracts from or circumlocutions of the* Capital, *but the fellow does neither quote the book, nor its author, but to shield himself from exposure remarks at the end of his preface:* "*For the ideas and much of the matter contained in Chapters II and III, I am indebted to the work of a great thinker and original writer, etc., etc.*" *Vis-à-vis myself, the fellow wrote stupid letters of excuse, for instance, that* "*the English don't like to be taught by foreigners,*" *that* "*my name was so much detested, etc.*" *With all that his little book—so far as it pilfers from* Capital—*makes good propaganda, although the man is a* "*weak*" *vessel, and very far from having even the patience—the first condition of learning anything—of studying a matter thoroughly. All these amiable middle-class writers—if not specialists—have an itching to make money or name or political capital* immediately *out of any new thoughts they may have got at by any favorable windfall. Many evenings this fellow has pilfered from me, in order to take me out and to learn in the easiest way.*

Lastly, there was published on the first December last (I shall send you a copy of it) in the monthly review Modern Thought *an article:* "*Leaders of Modern Thought: No. XXIII—Karl Marx. By Ernest Belfort Bax.*"

260
1. See Letter 254, Marx to Sorge, June 20, 1881.
2. John Rae, "The Socialism of Karl Marx and the Young Hegelians," in *The Contemporary Review*, October, 1881, pp. 585–607.

Now that is the first English publication of that kind which is pervaded by a real enthusiasm for the new ideas themselves and boldly stands up against British philistinism. This does not prevent the biographical notices the author gives of me from being mostly wrong, etc. In the exposition of my economic principles and in his translations (i.e., quotations of the Capital) *much is wrong and confused, but with all that the appearance of this article, announced in large letters by placards on the walls of West End London, has produced a great sensation. What was more important for me, I received the said number of* Modern Thought *already on the thirtieth of November, so that my dear wife had the last days of her life still cheered up. You know the passionate interest she took in all such affairs.*

261

To Jenny Longuet (in Argenteuil)
London, December 17, 1881

My dear child:
Just now Tussy, *supported by* [in English] Engels, is taking a cab with the Christmas box for our little ones to the Parcel Company. Helen[1] asks me that I especially indicate that her gifts are: one little coat for Harry,[2] one for Eddy,[3] and a woolen one for Pa;[4] in addition, for the same Pa, a "little blue coat" from Laura; from me a *sailor's suit* [in English] for my dear Johnny.[5] Möhmchen [Mama] had laughed gaily in her last days when she told Laura how you and I went to Paris with Johnny and there chose for him a suit that made him look like a little *bourgeoisgentilhomme* [bourgeois-gentleman].

The letters of condolence which I received from persons of various nationalities, professions, etc., from far and wide, all express appreciation of Möhmchen's spirit of truthfulness and deep sensitivity rarely found in such conventional communications. I explain it on the ground that everything about her was natural and genuine, artless and unaffected; hence the impression she made on third persons as vital and luminous; thus even Frau Hess writes: "in her, nature has destroyed its own masterpiece, for in my whole life I have never encountered another such spirited and amiable woman."[6]

261
1. Helene Demuth.
2. Henri Longuet.
3. Edgar Longuet.
4. Charles Longuet.
5. Jean-Laurent-Frederick Longuet.
6. Sibylle Hess (1820–1903), widow of Moses Hess; she wrote to Marx, December 11, 1881.

Liebknecht writes that without her he would have succumbed to the misery of exile,[7] etc.

How extraordinarily strong she was by nature, despite her daintiness, is seen from the fact that, to the great surprise of the doctors, not a blemish was found on her body despite her long confinement in bed; whereas during my own recent illness my body was sore in some spots after only two weeks in bed.

As the weather has been very bad since the end of my illness, I am under house arrest, but next week, on the doctor's advice, I am going to Ventnor (Isle of Wight) and afterward further South. Tussy is going with me.

You will receive (by the same post from here) an article about me in the monthly, *Modern Thought*.[8] It is the first time that an English critique enters into the subject with such ardor. Möhmchen was cheered by it. Wherever the quotations from the German "text" are too poor (*I mean* [in English] too poorly *done into English* [in English]), I have had Tussy insert corrections in the few copies reserved for friends. The errors, under the category of "Life," are indifferent.

And now, my dear child, the best service that you can do me is to keep well yourself! I hope still to spend many a beautiful day by your side and to fulfil my function as a grandpa in a worthy manner.

With a thousand kisses for you and the little ones,

Ever yours, Old Nick

I have a good deal to tell you about Vivanti,[9] etc., but I believe that Tussy is reserving that for herself.

---

7. Wilhelm Liebknecht to Marx, December 12, 1881: "The news of the death of your wife shook me deeply. What more can I say? You know what this gallant woman meant to me— it is thanks to her that the misery of the London exile did not destroy me."
8. Ernest Belfort Bax, "Leaders of Modern Thought: No. XXIII—Karl Marx," in *Modern Thought*, December 1, 1881.
9. Anna Vivanti, sister of German author Paul Lindau.

THE LAST YEAR
January, 1882 • January, 1883

The last year of Marx's life can only be described as desperate. His coughing and insomnia were virtually unrelieved. He spent the year 1882 mostly outside air-polluted London. In search of clean air and sunshine, he went abroad, spending about four months on the Mediterranean, including Algiers, and almost half a year in France and Switzerland. Frequently, instead of sunshine, he found only rain. Nothing seemed to help his infected lungs, laryngitis, and sick liver. His last attempt at finding relief was made on the Isle of Wight, where he stayed about six weeks, returning to London on January 12, 1883, at the shocking news of the death (of cancer) of his oldest daughter, Jenny Longuet.

Marx survived his most beloved daughter by only two months. On March 14, 1883, he died while sitting in an easy chair in his London home. He was not yet sixty-five years old. The immediate cause of death, apart from unrelieved bronchitis and laryngitis, was probably a lung tumor which began to bleed.

Marx's letters of his last year constitute a remarkably detailed medical record of a great man dying.

262

To Laura Lafargue (in London)
Ventnor, Isle of Wight, January 4, 1882

Dear Laurachen:
Today is the first sunny and bearable day in Ventnor. They say the weather was excellent—until our arrival.[1] From then on, *gales every day* [in English], wind storms, and howling all night long; mornings, the *sky overcast, leaden, London-like* [in English]; temperature significantly colder than in London and, furthermore, what is worse, much rain. (The air itself, of course, was "purer" than in London.)

Under such conditions it was natural that my cough, in fact, the bronchial catarrh, should worsen rather than improve. Despite all that, some progress, insofar as I could sleep naturally part of the night, that is, without opium, etc. Still, the general condition not yet so good that I could work. Today, when the first week of our visit comes to an end, a reversal seems to take place. With warmer weather, this would surely be a splendid place of recovery for my sort of reconvalescence.

My companion[2] (this *entirely between us*) is practically not at all; suffers from severe nervous spasms; reads and writes all day long, insofar as she is not occupied with shopping for necessary provisions or taking short walks; is very laconic, and seems indeed to bear the stay here with me only out of a sense of duty, as a self-sacrificing martyr.

Is there still no recent news from Jenny, regarding the Christmas box?[3] The thing disquiets me.

You understand, my child, that from here, where until now I have had only negative experiences, I can report nothing positive—unless it be the great discovery that local literature is represented here by three newspapers; that there is here even *a school of art and a science institution* [in English], where next Monday evening a great lecture is to be given *on the cases and "métiers" of India* [in English].

Today I received a letter from Reinhardt[4] in Paris wherein he writes in the most sincere and most sympathetic manner about our great bereavement.[5]

262
1. Marx, accompanied by his daughter Eleanor, was in Ventnor from December 29, 1881, to January 16, 1882.
2. Eleanor Marx.
3. See Letter 261, Marx to Jenny Longuet, December 17, 1881.
4. Richard Reinhardt (1829–1898), German poet in Paris, once a secretary to Heinrich Heine.
5. Jenny Marx's death on December 2, 1881.

The vehemence with which the bourgeois newspapers in Germany have announced either my death or that of one inevitably close to me, has amused me much, and to please them, I, "the man destroying the world," must now necessarily become active again.

Willard Brown has written to Tussy from New York, he has commissioned a very intimate and competent friend in New Orleans to look into your house affair;[6] the latter *writes that at first sight* [in English] great swindles had taken place, but that he must make more detailed investigations to attain factual evidence.

I am enclosing as a curiosity for Paul[7] an excerpt from the *Money article* in *The Times* [of London] (December 29, 1881), which manifestly has been inserted by Messrs. Say[8] and Rothschild.[9] (Give my regards to Paulum[10] and Helen.[11])

Adio, my dear child. Write soon.

Yours, Old Nick

263

From letter to Frederick Engels (in London)
Ventnor, 1 St. Boniface Gardens, January 12, 1882

Dear Engels:
I will, experimentally, remain here[1] another week (the third from today); until now, no change of the weather for the better, rather the contrary. Tussy[2] is going to London on Monday[3] for a theatrical performance, in which she participates, but will then return here again.

When I left London, I had to spend on unavoidable things somewhat less than £20 of the £40 you gave me. Rent costs me here two guineas weekly, and, together with coal and gas, and apart from other extras, about £2/15 shillings; the rest of the weekly expenses, about four guineas. It is an expen-

---

6. The Lafargue family had some property in New Orleans.
7. Paul Lafargue, Laura's husband.
8. French economist Jean-Baptiste Say (1826–1896).
9. Alfons Rothschild (1827–1905), head of the family bank in France.
10. Paul Lafargue.
11. Helene Demuth.

263

1. In search for fresh air as relief for his bronchitis and other respiratory troubles, Marx, accompanied by his daughter Eleanor, went to Ventnor, Isle of Wight, on December 29, 1881, and remained there until January 16, 1882.
2. Eleanor Marx.
3. January 16.

sive place for this climatic hole. Including traveling expenses, I have already spent about £17, and have only £5 left. This will not suffice for the last week (incl. Tussy's *incidental London trip* [in English] and our probable return next week). I would, therefore, appreciate it if you would send me *some* [in English] £4 by Monday next, if possible.

As for later, Tussy is above all to be discarded in the role of a companion (in general, if I should move again, I will do without an attendant). The child is under *mental pressure* [in English], which entirely undermines her health. Neither travel, nor *change of climate* [in English], nor *physicians can do anything in this case* [in English]. The only thing one can do for her is to yield to her will and let her take theatrical *lessons* [in English] with Madame Jung.[4] She burns with the desire to open for herself, as she believes, an independent, active, artistic career, and one must admit she is right in any case in this, that at her age,[5] she has no more time to lose. I would not for anything in the world have the child imagine that she is to be sacrificed on the family altar in the form of a "nurse" to an old man. In truth: I am convinced that Madame Jung can be her only doctor *pro nunc* [for now]. She is not candid; what I now say is based on observation, and not on her utterances. What I have just mentioned is in no way a contradiction that the disturbing symptoms, namely at night, are, as Miss Maitland (she was here for two days) told me, frightening—and of a hysterical nature. But against this, too, no other means are available for her but pleasant and absorbing activity. I have a few conjectures about the affairs of her "*Gemüt*"[6] [mind or heart], but the subject is too delicate to be treated in black and white.

I received a letter from the Sorge family, written by Sorge Senior [Friedrich Adolph], countersigned by Frau [Katharina] Sorge and Sorge Junior [Adolph], in which they propose to me *to turn over a new leaf* [in English], that is, to settle with them in New York.[7] Anyhow, they mean well! . . .

Yours, K.M.

---

4. Real name: Jane Elisabeth Vezin (1827–1902), English Shakespearean actress.

5. Born in 1855, Tussy was then twenty-seven years old.

6. For years Eleanor Marx had been in love with the French journalist Prosper Lissagaray, a relationship which Marx adamantly opposed because he distrusted the Frenchman's character and reputation. Eleanor bowed to her father's will, but her yearning for Lissagaray severely affected her health, a delicate situation which Marx did not, or pretended not to, understand.

7. On December 27, 1881, after Jenny Marx's death, the Sorge family, living in Hoboken, N.J., wrote to Marx: "Come over to us, old friend, and become one of us! We will offer you as good a home as we can, and new surroundings and old work will in time alleviate your sorrow and sustain you."

264 _____

To Pyotr Lavrovich Lavrov (in Paris)
London, January 23, 1882

Dear Friend:

Enclosed a few words for the Russian edition of the *Communist Manifesto*; since they are to be *translated* into Russian, they are not as stylized as it was necessary for its publication in the German vernacular.

I have returned to London only a few days ago. The pleuritis and bronchitis from which I suffered have left me with a chronic bronchial catarrh, which my doctor [Donkin] hoped to eliminate by my going to Ventnor (Isle of Wight), a place usually warm even in winter. But this time—during my three-weeks stay there—Ventnor had cold-wet, fog-gray weather, while at the same time in London there was almost summer, which, however, disappeared when I returned.

It is now being planned to send me somewhere south, perhaps to Algiers. The choice is difficult, because Italy is not accessible to me (in Milan, a man was arrested because his name was similar to mine); I cannot even go by steamer from here to Gibraltar, because I have no passport, and even the English need one there.

Despite all medical pressures, as well as those closest to me, I would under no circumstances have agreed to such time-wasting operations, if this accursed "English" sickness did not affect one's brain. In addition, a relapse, even if I recovered from it, would cost me even more time. Withal, I still want to do a bit of experimenting here.[1]

I am sending you a copy of *Modern Thought* with an article about me;[2] I do not have to tell you that the author's biographical notice is completely false. My daughter—your correspondent Eleanor, who sends her regards—has undertaken to correct the incorrect passages incorrectly cited in English in the copy of *Capital* sent to you. But no matter how poorly Mr. Bax—I hear that he is a very young man[3]—may have translated, he is at any rate the first English critic who shows a genuine interest in modern socialism. One is struck by the sincerity of his language and tone of real conviction. A certain John Rae—I believe he is a teacher of political economy in some English university—has published an article on the same theme in the *Contemporary*

264

1. Up to here the letter was written in German; the rest was written in English, but is given here from a German translation.
2. Ernest Belfort Bax, "Leaders of Modern Thought, No. XXIII—Karl Marx," in *Modern Thought*, December 1, 1881.
3. Bax was then twenty-eight years old.

Review a few months ago;[4] very superficial (although he pretends to cite many of my writings, which he evidently never even saw), and full of pretensions to that superiority with which the true Briton, thanks to a special gift for stupid ignorance, is filled. At the same time he makes an effort to assume, in his generosity, that it was out of conviction, and not from selfish motives, that I have been misleading the working class with false doctrines for the last forty years! In general, people here, after a bit of knowledge of socialism, are beginning to demand nihilism and so forth. Ireland and the United States on the one side, and on the other side the imminent struggle between tenants and landowners, between agricultural workers and tenants, between capitalism and landownership; a few symptoms of the revival of the workingclass in industry, as, for example, in some recent by-elections for the House of Commons, where the official candidates of the workers (especially the renegade from the International, the miserable Howell[5]) were offically proposed by the acknowledged leaders of the Trade Unions and by Mr. Gladstone, "the people's William," and contemptuously rejected by the workers. The demonstratively radical clubs originating in London, which are composed largely of workers, English and Irish mixed, are absolutely against the "Great Liberal Party," *official* trade-unionism, and "the people's William," etc., etc.—all this presently induces the British philistine to learn something about socialism. Unfortunately, the journals, magazines, newspapers, etc., are exploiting this "demand" in that they "offer" the readers the adulterations of venal, ignorant, time-serving penny-a-liners (even granting they were shilling-a-liners).

A "weekly" called *The Radical* appears here, full of praiseworthy aspirations, bold in language (the boldness lies in the *sans-gêne* [unceremoniousness], not in vigor), which attempts to tear up the web of lies of the British press, but despite all that it shows a weak performance. What the paper lacks are animated editors. These people wrote me several months ago. I was then in Eastbourne with my dear wife, then in Paris, etc., so that they have so far not had any conversation with me. I consider it useless. The more I have read about their paper, the more I am convinced that it is incorrigible.

My daughter reminds me that it is about time to end this letter, since only a few minutes are left for mailing it.

Salut.

Karl Marx

---

4. John Rae, "The Socialism of Karl Marx and the Young Hegelians," in *The Contemporary Review*, XL (1881), 585–607.

5. George Howell (1833-1910), English bricklayer, trade union leader, a founder of the First International.

265

To Frederick Engels (in London)
Marseilles, Hôtel au Petit Louvre, Rue de Cannebière,
February 17, 1882

Dear Fred:

Tussy[1] must have written you a few lines yesterday. Originally, I wanted to leave Paris only next Monday,[2] since my *state of health was rather not improving.*[3] *I took at once the resolution of removing to Marseilles, and thence at once, on Saturday, to sail for Algiers* [in English].[4]

In Paris, accompanied by my Johnny,[5] I visited only one mortal, namely Mesa.[6] (In fact, Mesa *solicited* [in English] me too much to twaddle, and moreover, I returned too late to Argenteuil, about seven o'clock in the evening; I was sleepless the whole night.) I tried to persuade Mesa that the friends, namely Guesde,[7] should please *postpone* our rendezvous until *my return from Algiers. But all that in vain. In fact, Guesde is so much on all parts assailed just now, that it was important for him to have an "official" meeting on my side* [in English]. This much one has to grant the party. So I gave them an appointment, and Guesde and Deville came with Mesa to the Hôtel de Lyon et de Mulhouse, 8 Boulevard Beaumarchais, about five o'clock in the afternoon. I received them first in the dining room, where Tussy and Jennychen came with me from Argenteuil (Wednesday afternoon).[8] Guesde was somewhat embarrassed because of Jennychen, because he had just written a bitter article against Longuet, *although she (Jennychen) did not take any regard whatever to that incident* [in English]. As soon as the little ladies went away, I went with them first to my room, where we twaddled for about one hour, then down—Mesa having enough time to be annoyed—to the restaurant, where they paused enough to consume a bottle of Beauve with me. By seven o'clock they "all" had it. With all that, although I went to bed at nine, there was such an uninterrupted diabolical traffic noise until one o'clock that (about one o'clock) I again had a *vomissement* (vomiting), having chattered too much again.

265

1. Eleanor Marx.
2. February 20.
3. Marx, suffering from carbuncles, insomnia, and severe bronchial infection, spent most of the year 1882—the last full year of his life—in search of fresh air and a sunny climate.
4. Marx was in Algiers, hoping for sunny weather, from February 20 to May 2, 1882.
5. Grandson Jean Laurent Frederick Longuet.
6. José Mesa y Leompart, (1840–1904), Spanish Marxist socialist.
7. Jules Guesde (1845–1922). French Marxist socialist leader.
8. February 8.

The trip to Marseilles, on a beautiful day, was all right somewhere after the Lyons station. First, there was a one and a half [hour] *arrêt* [stop] at Cassis because of the distemper of the locomotive; then again the same *malheur* [misfortune] with the machine at Valence, although this time the *arrêt* did not last as long. In the meantime, it was bitter cold and an angry, biting wind. Instead of *some time before* twelve o'clock midnight, we arrived at Marseilles only after two o'clock in the morning; I was more or less, despite all covering, somewhat freezing and found an antidote only in "alcohol," [and] again and again resorted to it. The final annoying *épreuve* [ordeal] took place in the last quarter-hour (or more) in the *gare* [railroad station] de Marseille, open, windy-cold, and a very long procedure of delivering the luggage.

Today it is sunny in Marseilles, but the wind is not yet warm. Dr. Dourlen advised me to stay in the above-named hotel, whence I am departing tomorrow (Saturday), at five o'clock in the afternoon. The office of *"Paquebots à Vapeur des Postes Françaises"* ["French Postal Steamships"] is located here in the *same hotel* where I am staying, so that I immediately bought a ticket (for 80 francs, first-class) for the steamer *Said;* the baggage is equally enregistered here, so everything is as convenient as possible.

Apropos. Here I picked up a *Prolétaire* (*L'Égalité* is also sold here); that Lafargue always seems to me to multiply useless incidents, wherein the details are perhaps far from exact. *As to his characterizing Fourier a "Commun-ist," he is now that they make fun of him obliged to explain in what sense he might have called Fourier as a "Communist"* [in English]. This kind of "intrepidity," one can put aside, "put apart," or "put under"; it is even worse that such petty facts have to be saved at all. I find that he oraculates much too broadly.

My best compliments to Laura; I shall write her from Algiers. There is one single man sufficient as patron; it is a long letter written by Longuet to his friend Fermé [in English],[9] who has brought it so far as to become, from having once been deported to Algeria (under Napoleon III), a *juge d'appel* [appellate judge] in Algeria. There is no question about a passport or such things. On the passenger ticket, nothing is written except the Christian and family names.

My regards also to Lenchen[10] *and the other friends* [in English].

Adio!

Old Mohr

---

9. Fermé was a French judge in Algiers.
10. Helene Demuth.

266

To Frederick Engels (in London)
Algiers, Hôtel d'Orient, February 21, 1882

Dear Fred:
I left Marseilles Saturday, February 18, five o'clock in the afternoon, on the *Said, excellent steamer* [in English]; the passage was quick, so that at three-thirty in the afternoon on Monday (February 20) we arrived at Algiers. The sea voyage was nevertheless cold, and despite all the *comforts* [in English] of the ship, the diabolical noise of the machinery, wind, etc., made me spend two sleepless nights in the cabin.

What awaited me here, *mutatis mutandis* [all things considered] was the same *quid pro quo* [conditions] as on the Isle of Wight![1] This time the *season* [in English] is exceptionally cold and wet in Algiers, while, on the other hand, Nice and Mentone now lure most visitors. At any rate, I had some premonition insinuated more than once that I should, *d'abord* [first] begin with the Riviera. But this seems to be *fatalité* [fate]! The worthy *juge*[2] received me yesterday most cordially; Longuet's letter had prepared him a day before I arrived; he visited me today to consult over further decisions. The letters to France and England do not go off daily.

Write me under my own name and: care of Monsieur Fermé, *juge au tribunal civil*, No. 37 Route Mustapha Supérieur, Alger.

[no signature]

267

To Frederick Engels (in London)
Algiers, Hôtel Pension Victoria, Mustapha Supérieur, Boulevard Bon Accueil, March 1, 1882 (You can now send your letters to me direct at the above address.)

Dear Fred:
Telegram to you anticipated postcard, because the latter would have caused some useless worry. The fact is that thanks to the piling up of a number of unpleasantnesses (including the sea voyage), I landed in Algiers on February 20 with a corpus delicti frozen inside.

The month of December had been frightful in Algiers, in January the weather was better, February cold and wet. I caught the coldest three days of

---

266

1. Marx, with daughter Eleanor, was there from December 29, 1881, to January 16, 1882.
2. Judge Fermé, a Frenchman, friend of Charles Longuet and Paul Lafargue.

February (20, 21, 22). Sleepless, without appetite, strong cough, somewhat helpless, not without occasional attacks of *profunda melancolia* [deep melancholy], like the great Don Quixote. To return to Europe *at once then* [in English] back, things unaccomplished here, with the *faux frais* [unnecessary expenses], in addition the prospect of two nights torture in the cabin through the scandalous machinery dins! Otherwise, sure of escaping the *quid pro quo* by an immediate trip to Biskra, right on the Sahara Desert? But considering the means of communication and transportation, requiring seven to eight days more travel—a difficult matter—and, after consulting those familiar with the conditions, in no way harmless for a *pro nunc* [temporary] invalid who may expect similar *incidents* [in English] before arrival at Biskra!

Since in the *aprèsmidi* [afternoon] of February 22 the thermometer promised favorable weather forthwith, and since upon my arrival I had already, in the company of the good Judge Fermé, spied out the Hôtel-Pension Victoria, I left the Grand Hôtel d'Orient (where *bedded* also the *abominable philosophical radical* [in English] Ashton Dilke[1]—*by the by* [in English] in *Le Petit Colon*[2] and other *petits journaux Algériens* [minor Algerian journals], every Englishman *is a lord, even Bradlaugh*[3] *figures here as Lord Bradlaugh* [in English]) with baggage on *une des collines en dehors de la fortification, du côté de l'Est de la ville* [one of the hills outside the fortification, on the east coast of the city]. Here there is a splendid view, from my *chambre* [chamber] you see the Mediterranean Bay, the port of Algiers, villas rising on the *collines* [hills] like amphitheatres (*des ravines au dessous des collines, d'autre collines au dessus* [the ravines below the hills, other hills above]; further in the distance, *des montagnes, visible* [mountains, visible], etc., the snow-peak *derrière Matifou, sur les montagnes de Kabilie, des points culminants du Djurdjura* [behind Matifou, on the Kabilie Mountains, culminating in the peaks of Djurdjura]. (All the above mentioned *collines* are limestone.) In the morning, at eight o'clock, there is nothing more magical than this panorama, air, vegetation, the wonderful European-African *mélange* [mixture]. Every morning, from ten or from nine to eleven *thereabouts my promenade* [in English] between *des ravines et les collines situées au dessus de la mienne* [the ravines and hills above those of mine].

With all that [in English], one lives only in dust. *In first instance from* [in English] February 23 to 26, the only *really excellent change* [in English]; but now (although I am still so *frozen* that my clothing, *even then* [in English], *differs* from that of my clothing in the Isle of Wight and the city of Algiers in that until now in the villa I have replaced my rhinoceros overcoat with a light

---

267
1. Ashton Wentworth Dilke (1850–1883), English journalist and Member of Parliament.
2. An Algerian daily.
3. Charles Bradlaugh (1833–1891), English anti-Socialist journalist.

coat, leaving everything else unchanged) began (and lasts perhaps nine days, since February 27) the so-called *tempête, c'est à dire le tapage du vent sans de tonnerre et sans d'éclairs* [the uproar of the wind, without thunder and without lightning], *dangerous and treacherous time much feared by the natives* [in English]. Thus, in effect, only three really good days.

Meanwhile, my cough got worse *from day to day* [in English], *le crachement abominable* [the spitting abominable], little *sleep, above all a certain nasty feeling that my left side is once for all deteriorated by the perish, and my intellectual state most dejected. Thus I summoned Dr. Stephann*[4] *(best Algiers doctor). I had two interviews yesterday and today. What to do? I am just to go to Algiers to make prepare his prescriptions given; they are, after he had very seriously examined me* [in Marx's own idiosyncratic English]:

1. Collodion cantharidal, with *pinceau* [brush] tattooed;

2. Arseniate of soda, with specific quantum of water: one soupspoonful at every meal;

3. in case of need, nights during coughing, a soupspoonful mixture of codeine and lime julep.

He will come again in eight days; he prescribed my *bodily exercises, to keep within very moderate limits; no real intellectual work except some reading for my distraction* [in English]. So in fact I am not a *bit (rather a less* [in English]) better off than at London! *Hence a man ought never delude himself by too sanguine views* [in English].

I must stop, because I have to go to town to the apothecary. *By the by, you know that few people more averse to demonstrative Pathos; still, it would be a lie* [not] *to confess that my thought to great part absorbed by reminiscence of my wife, such a part of my best part of life! Tell my London daughters*[5] *to write to Old Nick instead of expecting him to write himself first* [in English].

How is Pumps[6] *going on in that serious work of man creating? Give her my best compliments.*

Give my compliments to Helen;[7] *ditto Moore,*[8] *Schorlemmer.*

Now, old good fellow [in English].

Yours, Mohr

Apropos! Dr. Stephann, like my dear Dr. Donkin, does not forget—the cognac [in English]!

---

4. German-born physician in Algiers.
5. Laura Lafargue and Eleanor Marx.
6. Mary Ellen Burns, wife of Percy Rosher, gave birth to a daughter, Lilian.
7. Helene Demuth.
8. Samuel Moore (*c.* 1830–1912), English lawyer, cotranslator of *Das Kapital*. Volume I.

268

To Frederick Engels (in London)
Algiers, March 3, 1882

Dear Fred:
Yesterday I received your letter, dated February 25, together with the *Daily News cuts* [in English] (O.N.[1] tragi-*comical* English State-and heart-secret). I hope that Tussy will at long last not frivolously dissipate her health any further; that my Cacadou, alias Laurachen,[2] is always blooming, despite many physical exertions. Have received no answer as yet from Paris.

The tempest—*c'est ici l'expression sacramentale* [this is here the decisive expression]—has continued since February 26, although under constantly *variable aspects* [in English].

On March 2, there was for me, as for all the other fellow-lodgers, general house arrest *for the whole day* [in English]; pouring rain from *early morning* [in English] out of a sky of London color, grey in grey; but now for the first time accompanied by windstorms with thunder and lightning; at four o'clock in the afternoon *again* [in English] an azure blue sky; later, a wonderfully beautiful moonlit evening. Brief changes of weather all day long, the temperature now rising, now falling. Meanwhile I began, among other things, the tattooing-treatment anew; *a remarkable improvement setting in* [in English] immediately in the next night. *This morning*, March 3, tattooing, the first act of the day; not *intimidated* [in English] by the wind, I found the promenade in balsam sea air from nine o'clock until *about* [in English] a quarter to eleven *most delightful* [in English]; came back just before a renewed, angry wind burst. *In a few minutes* [in English] I will be *summoned to* [in English] *déjeuner* [lunch], and am using this decisive moment these *few lines send to you* [in English].

Yours, Mohr

269

To Jenny Longuet (in Argenteuil)
Algiers, Hôtel Victoria, March 16, 1882

My dear child:
After receiving your letter through Fermé, I sent a messenger to the Hôtel d'Orient for an inquiry and there they handed him your letter of February 24.

268

1. Olga Alexeyevna Novikova (1840–1925), a Russian journalist living in England and in the Gladstone period serving as a diplomatic agent for her country.
2. Cacadou was Marx's nickname for his daughter Laura (Laurachen) Lafargue.

I will now give you a brief report about the state of my health.

As my cough is very pertinacious, expectorations violent, sleep-lessnesses, etc., I had Dr. Stephann (who also treats other fellow-lodgers) visit me, and has treated me since February 26. He is a resolute, sharp man. He found that since my departure from Paris my left side has been weakened by pleurisy and, as a result of an accumulation of unfavorable influences, is functioning abnormally. The main treatment for this is the *vésicatoires* [blisters] (water drawn through tattooing the left back and left chest with collodion cantharidal), which does me good, and other "mollifying" medicaments for the cough, and finally arsenate (tasteless like water) after every meal. So long as the weather permits, I am to continue my moderate morning promenades.

Unfortunately (with good weather the violence of the cough would ... [1] have disappeared of itself), a blood-spitting began on March 6, but after the March 8 and 9 violent ... [1], there were light after-pains until the twelfth, and by the thirteenth every trace of this hemorrhage had disappeared. In sum, the week of this disagreeable episode, Dr. Stephann took energetic steps: all movement (promenading, of course) forbidden; almost ditto all talk; hot foot-baths, etc., together with drastic medicaments. During this period I have been treated with *vésicatoires*, at the same time as tonics against the cough, etc., and in fact the coughing has extraordinarily diminished. The weather, too, has gradually taken a turning point, although it is not yet altogether *comme il faut* [as it should be]. In my villa on the hill (Hôtel Victoria)—the bay before me and nearby amphitheatrically rising villas— ... [1] even without promenading; in the small gallery of my and adjoining other *chambres* [rooms] there is a veranda, the entrance to the first floor. The doctor will give me permission to promenade again as soon he has examined the *corpus delicti*. To remark: Recently, not only has the appetite returned but also sleep. (Since February 16, *in fact since the night in the Hotel* [in English], in Paris, the insomnia has lasted uninterruptedly until the above-mentioned period.)

[The following two paragraphs were written in English.]

Take now all in all, the upshot is, as I too reported to London,[2] that in this foolish, ill-calculated expedition [to Algiers], I am now just arrived again at that standard of health when I possessed it on leaving Maitland Park.[3] I must, however, say that many visitors here too passed, and are passing still through the same trial. Since ten years Alger [Algiers] had no such a failure of the winter season. Myself had had some doubts; there was the experience of the Isle of Wight[4] and other corners, but Engels and Donkin fired each other mutually into African furor, neither one nor the other

---

269

1. Words indecipherable.
2. See Letters 267 and 268, Marx to Engels, March 1 and 3, 1882.
3. Marx's London address.
4. Marx was there from December 29, 1881, to January 16, 1882.

getting any special information, considering that in regard to temperature this year was extraordinary. I had now and again by innuendo given to understand to begin at least by Mentone (or Nizza: Nice) as Lavrov had received from Russian friends very favourable news, but all this was ruled down by my sanguine good old Fred[5] who, I repeat it, I say it amongst you and myself, may easily kill someone out of love.

I must tell you that in this Villa-Hotel, the two ladies, its managers, did everything in my service, no care nor attention neglecting. And as to the operations relating to the vésicatoires, *a young* Pharmacien *[pharmacist], Mr. Casthelaz (with his mother he is here as a patient ever since December) is so kind as to tattoo me, then open the* wassergefüllten Blasen *[water-filled blisters], then put linen on the somewhat rough skin, etc. He does all such things in the most genteel way, and offers these voluntary services in the most delicate manner.*

Nothing could be more magical than the city of Algiers, even more the *campagne* near this city during [and] before summertime; 1000 and 1 nights would be the mood, specifically—assuming good health—if one had the loved ones (not forgetting the grandsons[6]) around one. I am always enchanted when I receive from you news about the little ones; Tussy also writes me that she cannot get the little children out of her mind and yearns to have them near her. [It is] hardly four weeks before I can leave here, for I must see Dr. Stephann's treatment fundamentally to the end, and then begin (assuming that *all then as to weather altogether settled* [in English]) the air-treatment proper.)

I have seen nothing of *Justice*[7] (Polemic with "Citoyen") and also nothing whatever of Paris newspapers, except *Égalité.*[8] I am very pleased to learn from your letter that Tussy has tactfully solved her catastrophe.[9] When Lissagaray publishes his "Bataille," send me the first issues; *I do not believe in a great result* [in English]; *mais qui vivra verra* [he who lives will see].

During my very first days (still in Hôtel d'Orient), good Fermé pestered me, I mean, left me to go alone through hill and town, at the same time *overtalk*[ed] me. *All this I put at once an end to this, making him understand that I was an invalid* [in English]. But he meant well; now he knows that quiet, solitude, silence are my civic duty.

Kiss all the little ones. Greet Longuet. And many kisses for you, dear child.

Yours, Old Nick

---

5. Frederick Engels.
6. Edgar, Henri, Jean, and Marcel Longuet.
7. *La Justice*, Paris daily, of which Charles Longuet was an editor.
8. *L'Égalité*, Paris socialist daily.
9. On February 24, 1882, Jenny Longuet informed Marx that his daughter Eleanor (Tussy) had finally broken off her long-standing engagement to the French journalist, Prosper Lissagaray, a relationship that Marx steadily opposed.

270

To Paul Lafargue (in Paris) [Written originally in French, of which the text has been preserved in Russian, which has been translated into German. The text here is a translation from the German.]
Algiers, Hôtel Victoria, March 20, 1882

My dear Paul:
Your dear letter of March 16 was delivered to me today (twentieth); obviously it did not take by far as long to come here as mail does from London.

To begin with, my brave Gascon, "what is the meaning of Mustapha supérieur?" Mustapha is a name like John. When one leaves Algiers along the rue d'Isly, one sees a long avenue extend before one; on one side at the bottom of the hill are Mauritanian villas, surrounded by gardens (one of these villas is the Hôtel Victoria); on the other side, houses border along the road leading down from the terraces. All this together is called "Mustapha supérieur." Mustapha inférieur begins at the declivity of Mustapha supérieur and extends to the sea. Both Mustaphas form a community (Mustapha), whose mayor (this man has neither an Arabic nor a French name, but a German one) from time to time provides his inhabitants with information through official placards. You can thus see that there is a mild regime here. In Mustapha supérieur new houses are being constantly built and old ones torn down, etc., and even though the workers employed in this are healthy men and natives, they fall victim to fever after the first three days of work. Hence a part of their wages consists of a daily dose of quinine, given them by the entrepreneurs. The same custom can be observed in various regions of South America.

My dear Augur, you are very well informed (so you write): "You must gulp down all the French newspapers which are sold in Algiers." In reality, I do not even read the few newspapers which the other guests at Hôtel Victoria received from Paris; my whole political reading is confined to the telegraphic despatches in the *Petit Colon* (a small Algerian sheet like the Paris *Petit-Journal*, the *Petite République Française*, etc.). That is all.

Jenny wrote me that she is sending me Longuet's articles, which you also mention, but which I have not yet received. The only newspaper I receive from London is *L'Égalité*, but one cannot call that a newspaper.

St. Paul, you peculiar Saint, where did you hear or who told you that I must have "iodine poultices"? You will interrupt me and tell me that this is a trifle, but herein lies buried your method of "material facts." *Ex ungue leonem* [You can tell a lion by his claws]. In reality, instead of your "iodine poultices," I have to have my back daubed with collodion cantharidal, so that the liquid can be drained out. The first time I saw my left side (chest and back) thus worked over, I was reminded of a watermelon field in miniature. Since March 16, when I wrote to Engels, not a single dry spot is to be found either on my back or on my chest (which are next to be daubed) for the repetition of this treatment, the latter of which is not to be resumed until the twenty-second.

You say: "Enclosed is an invitation which will make you laugh." *Es regular* [To be sure]. But how can I laugh when the "enclosed" invitation is still in your hands? When the occasion arises, I will remind Mr. Fermé of his quondam Proudhonist comrade Lafargue. For the moment, however, so long as the doctor[1] does not allow me to go out, I would perfer to permit nobody to pay me long visits or carry on extensive conversations.

It rains as before; so capricious is the weather that it changes from one hour to another, runs the whole gamut or falls suddenly from one extreme to another. Despite all this, there is a continuing tendency toward improvement, we must wait. And withal, since my departure from Marseilles, the weather in Nice as well as in Mentone has been uninterruptedly magnificent until now. But this African sun and the local wonder-working air—have been an *idée fixe*, for which the responsibility is not mine. . . .

My sleep gradually returns. He who has not suffered from sleeplessness cannot appreciate the beneficent feeling one experiences when the fear of sleepless nights finally fades.

Heartiest regards for my dear Cacadoù[2] and all the others!

Your K. Marx

271

To Frederick Engels (in London)
Algiers, March 28–31, 1882

Dear Fred:
March 28: Annoying rain character this day in the early morning hours—concluded with it the short letter to Tussy.[1] After it was mailed, a storm developed, for the first time well executed; not only howling of the wind, pouring rain, thunder, but also continuous lightning *into the bargain* [in En-

270
1. Dr. Stephann.
2. Laura Lafargue.

271
1. Eleanor Marx.

glish]. This lasted deep into the night, and, as usual, at the same time a steep drop in temperature. Interesting, the color formation in the waves of the practically eliptical, beautiful bay: snow-white surf girded by seawater changing from blue to green.

March 29 (Wednesday): Annoying rain over the country, no less annoying the groaning wind blasts; cold-wet temperature.

This day, before *déjeuner* [lunch] (which takes place a *quarter past* [in English] or half-past eleven), Dr. Stephann came for the express purpose of "devoting" himself to the tattooing of the lowest parts of the back and chest which he had diagnosed and had preserved for himself. Preceded, as in every other visit, by a thorough examination; found a much better *status* [in English] on most of the left side; the *lowest* parts, still emitting a dull murmur, instead of Helmholtz's[2] musical tone, but can by and by be brought to order again (the bad weather prevents a more rapid progress). Stephann told me today for the first time—candidly, because he thinks me so far repaired that he can speak to me ruthlessly—that when I arrived in Algiers I had brought with me a serious *rechute* [relapse]. Only through the *vésicatoires des épanchement* [discharge of the vesicles] could it be contracted. It went better than he could have expected. Still, I will have to treat myself carefully for years. He will give me a written consultation—when I leave Algiers—specifically, for my London doctor. With people of my age, an experiment with *rechutes* is in no way to be repeated. A few hours after lunch, the *Tableau* [painting] on my skin began in grim earnest; it felt like one whose epidermis has become too short and who wants to burst out of it; painful the whole night long; I was absolutely forbidden to scratch.

March 30: At eight o'clock in the morning, my *assistant-doctor, my helpmate* [in English],[3] appears before my bed. Turned out that, in consequence of spontaneous movements, the blisters *generally* [in English] burst; a veritable flood, wetting the sheet, flannels, shirt, developed during the night. The tattooing thus brought about the *proper effect on the points of attack*. My amiable *help* [in English] promptly bandaged me up, so that it would not only prevent rubbing against the flannel but also make the subsequent absorption of the water possible and comfortable. This morning (March 31), Mr. Casthelaz found that the *suction* [in English] has finally ended and the drying up practically over. In this case, I could probably undergo another tattooing within one week (beginning March 29). *Tant mieux* [So much the better].

March 30 (yesterday): Weather became warm and pleasant around twelve noon, whereupon I went for a walk in the Gallery; later I slept a little, to make up for the restless night, which I will also do today, since the

---

2. Hermann von Helmholtz (1821–1894), pioneering Berlin University professor of physics.
3. The "helpmate" was Maurice Casthelaz, a French pharmacist.

rigorous avoidance of scratching at night continues, even though, as in the night of March 30–31, without pain.

Weather dubious today (March 31); at any rate, has not rained yet; will perhaps be relatively "good" around twelve noon, which is approaching.

Nothing more to add to the health-bulletin; in general, everything satisfactory.

Received a letter from Tussy today.

Apropos, some time ago she sent me the enclosed letter; I cannot decipher the signature; you will be able to do it. At any rate, a peculiar phenomenon: a Quedlinburg lawyer with his own philosophy! Only one thing is unclear to me: Did the copy of the man's "book" arrive at Maitland Park,[4] or does he want my exact address, so that it should reach me safely? In the first case, Tussy is to acknowledge receipt of his book; in the second case, she is to send him my "positive" address.

Mon cher [My dear], you, like the other *family members* [in English], will be struck by the errors of orthography, construction, false grammar; this happens to me always only *post festum* [later]—only in my still very great absent-mindedness. *Shows you* [in English], that a *sana mens in sano corpore* [a healthy mind in a healthy body] is still something to be rattled. *By the by* [in English], mending is bound to take place.

Just now the *tocsin* [in English] *pour déjeuner* [for lunch], and afterward this little letter has to be ready for the messenger going to Algiers. And so, greetings and for all.

Yours, Mohr

272

To Frederick Engels (in London)
Algiers, April 8, 1882

Dear Fred:
Yesterday, at four o'clock in the afternoon, examination by Dr. Stephann. Despite the change of weather, which caused a recurrence of my constant cold, it was very satisfactory. He found that the *épanchement* [discharge] on the lower spot (the left side of the chest) has entirely disappeared; but more resistance in one place (lower left) in the back. The latter was given a special going over by him through skin tattooing with collodion cantharidal. In consequence, very acute pains, a sleepless night (from April 7 to 8), thanks to this "painting," but this morning also a *most effective pumping of water* [in English] from the built-up blisters. Hence I do not doubt that this point of

---

4. Marx's London address.

attack, too, will soon give in. My assistant-doctor, Mr. Casthelaz, had to work on my green watermelon field for half an hour; then I had to lie in bed until *déjeuner* [lunch] at eleven-thirty; for, after being bandaged, the consequent water withdrawal [from the blisters] by drops is more comfortable that way.

On the other hand, Stephann found the cough stronger (but only *relatively*, since the coughing had sunk to a very low niveau) as a result of the insipid weather. During this week, I could exploit *morning hours* for walks on four days; since yesterday afternoon, the rain has not yet stopped; last night and today the rain assumed the *"caractère torrentiel"* [torrential character]. Today, a weak attempt to heat the dining hall, but actually this chimney does not seem to have been made for such a purpose, *but only for show's sake* [in English].

After lunch, I hit the pillow at two o'clock, to get some compensation for last night, but as the devil would have it, this and next week are *court-vacations*. Hence my plan was frustrated by the otherwise very amiable judge, Fermé, who let go of me only about five o'clock P.M., when dinner time was approaching. Among other things, Fermé told me that during his career as justice of the peace (and this a "regular" one), a species of *torture* to extort confessions was applied to Arabs; of course, the "police" do this (as the English do in India); the judge *is supposed to know nothing about all of it* [in English]. In other cases, he told me, when an Arab gang commits murder, mostly for the purpose of robbery, and the real culprits are caught after a time, and are sentenced and decapitated, this does not satisfy the injured colonist's family as expiation. They demand *into the bargain* [in English] *at least* half a dozen *innocent Arabs*. But here the French judges resist, specifically the *cours d'appel* [courts of appeals], while here and there a single, isolated judge's life is occasionally threatened by colonists, if he does not allow (his competence goes no further) a dozen innocent Arabs to be jailed as suspects of murder, robberty, etc., and to begin an investigation. But we know that where a European colonist settles, or even visits for business, among the "lower races," he considers himself in general more invulnerable than the Handsome Wilhelm I.[1] But the Britons and the Dutch surpass the French in shameless arrogance, pretentiousness, and cruel Moloch-propitiation-rage against the "lower races."

Pumps'[2] *Family Mission* [in English] is greatly promising; against it, one has to regard Hyndman's political mission of a problematical nature. That your short letter annoyed him, serves the fellow right, the more so in that his

---

272

1. German Emperor William I.
2. Mary Ellen Burns Rosher, who gave birth to a daughter, Lilian.

insolence toward me was based on the calculation that out of "propaganda considerations" I could not publicly compromise him. This he knew in fact.

The *Kankanus* [gossip] Bodenstedt,[3] and the sewer-aesthete Friedrich Vischer,[4] are the Horace and the Virgil of Wilhelm I.

Apropos! The *Kölnische Zeitung* article on Skobelev[5] is highly interesting.

This scrap of paper does not go off today (Saturday), because no *paquebots* [mail boats] sail on Mondays, Wednesdays and Saturdays to Marseilles; but, for an exception, one leaves Algiers on Sunday, at one in the afternoon and letters for this purpose must already be delivered at the post office by eleven in the morning (Sunday). The Hôtel Victoria, Algiers, sends the *messenger* [in English] with letters *early* Sunday *morning* already. On other days, the *paquebots* sail from Algiers to Marseilles at five-thirty in the afternoon.

But I wanted to send off these lines tomorrow, because Dr. Stephann's last examination was so specially favorable.

Best regards for all.

Yours, Mohr

273

From letter to Laura Lafargue (in London)
Algiers, April 13, 1882

Dearest Cacadou:
I make myself reproaches that I have not yet written you again, not that there is anything special to report from here. How often I think of you, at Eastbourne, of the sick bed of my Jenny,[1] and the daily devoted visits so cheering to the cantankerous Old Nick. . . .

It is one o'clock P.M., and I have promised, together with Madame Casthelaz, her son [Maurice], and another one of our colodgers, Madame Claude (of Neufchâtel), to visit the *Jardin du Hamma* or *Jardin d'Essai*. We have to be back before dinner (six o'clock P.M.), after which later *every effort at writing never as yet dared upon by me* [in English]. . . .

---

3. Friedrich Bodenstedt (1819–1892), German poet and translator.
4. Friedrich Theodor Vischer (1807–1887), philosopher of aesthetics.
5. In a speech in Paris on February 17, 1882, Russian General Michael Skobelev declared Germany to be the archenemy of the Slavic nations and prophesied the inevitability of a war with Germany.

273
1. From late June to July 20, 1881, Marx and his sick wife were in Eastbourne, where they were visited by daughter Laura.

April 14 [Letter continued, in English]

I commence this letter at the moment *when I have a few lines to be added to the foregoing, that is to say at about* one o'clock P.M. *The day ended yesterday as fine as that of the twelfth. Both* the evenings *twelve and thirteen (about eight hours* P.M.) *were warm—quite exceptional this—but cool (relatively) at the same time, hence really delightful. This morning the warmth a little more "heavy," and just since two hours the wind blows violently, probably the "orage" [tempest] predicted yesterday from fourteen–fifteen.*

Yesterday at one o'clock P.M. *we went down to Inferior Mustapha whence the tram brought us to* Jardin Hamma *or* Jardin d'Essai, *the which used for "Promenade Publique" with occasional military music, as, "pépinière" [plant nursery] for the production and diffusion of the indigenous vegetables, at last for the purpose of* scientific botanical experiments *and as a garden of* "acclimatation." *This all encloses a very large ground, part of which is mountainous, the other belonging to the plain. In order to see more minutely, you would want at least a whole day, and beside being somebody with you a* connaisseur, *for instance like M. Fermés friend and old Fourieriste, M. Durando, professor of botanics, who is the leader of a section of the "Club Alpin Français" on its regular Sunday excursions. (I very much regretted that my bodily circumstances and the Dr. Stephann's strict prohibition till now did not yet allow me to share in these excursions, having been three times invited thereto.)*

Well, before entering the "Jardin d'Essai" we took coffee, of course in the free air, a Mauresque "café." The Maure [Moor] *prepared it excellently, we were on a bank. On a rough table, in inclined positions, their legs crossed, half a dozen Maure visitors . . .* ² *were delighted in their small "cafétières," (everyone gets one of his own) and together playing at cards (a conquest this on them of civilisation). Most striking this spectacle: Some these Maures were dressed pretentiously, even richly, others in, for once I dare call it* blouses, *sometime of white woollen appearance, now in rags and tatters—but in the eyes of a true Musulman such accidents, good or bad luck, do not distinguish Mahomets children.* Absolute equality in their social intercourse, *not affected; on the contrary, only when demoralized, they become aware of it; as to the hatred against Christians and the hope of an ultimate victory over these infidels, their politicians justly consider this same feeling and practice of absolute equality (not of wealth or position but of personality) a guarantee of keeping up the one, of not giving up the latter. (Still they go to the devil without a revolutionary movement.)*

In regard to the plain part of the Jardin d'Essai *I remark only: It is cut by* three great longitudinal "allées" *of a wonderful beauty; opposite to the principal entry is the* "allée" *of the platenes* [plane trees]; *then the* "allée des palmiers [palms]" *ended by an oasis of immense seventy-two "palmiers," limited by the railway and the sea; at last the "allée" of the magnolia and a sort of figues* ([figs] *(ficus roxburghi). These three great "allées" are themselves cut by many others crossing them,*

---

2. Indecipherable.

such as the long "allée des bambous [bamboos]" *astonishing, the "allée" of* "pal-miers à chanvre [*hemp palms*]," *the "dragonniers [dragon trees]," the "eucalyptus" (blue gum of Tasmania), etc. (the latter are of an extraordinary quick vegetation).*

Of course, these sorts of allées *are not reproducible in European* "Jardins d'acclimatation."

[The following was written in German]:

In a large circle surrounded by plane trees, there was military music in the afternoon; a noncommissioned officer, in the usual French uniform, was the music director; by contrast, the musicians— (common soldiers)—wore wide red knickers (Oriental cut), white woolen shoes, tied to the knickers; a red fez on the head.

In the garden I did not mention (the nose, however, partly took great pleasure in this) orange trees, lemon trees—also almond trees, olive trees, etc.; still less did I mention cactus and aloes, which also grow wild (as do also the olive and almond) in the heath where our residence is.

Much as this garden enchanted me, I must remark on the existence, on this and similar excursions, of the abominable, the unavoidable *lime dust*; although I felt well in the afternoon and after returning home at night, nevertheless, there was a certain amount of cough irritation, thanks to the dust.

I still expect Dr. Stephann today, but cannot delay sending off this letter; the rest will be reported to Fred[3] later.

Finally, as Mayer of Swabia[4] used to say: Let's rise a little to a higher historic standpoint. Our nomadic Arabs (in many respects very degenerated, but who have retained some solid qualities through their struggle for existence) remember that they had once produced great philosophers, scholars, etc., and that the Europeans scorn them because of their present ignorance. Hence the following, brief Arabic wisdom-fable:

A philosopher boards a small ferry to take him across a storm-tossed river. The following dialogue ensues:

Philosopher: Ferryman, do you know *history*?

Ferryman: No!

Philosopher: Then you have lost half your life!

Philosopher, again: Have you studied mathematics?

Ferryman: No!

Philosopher: Then you have lost more than half your life.

Suddenly the storm capsized the ferry and threw both of them into the water.

---

3. See Letter 274 to Engels, April 18, 1882.
4. Karl Mayer (1819–1889), editor of the Stuttgart *Beobachter*.

Ferryman: Can you swim?
Philosopher: No!
Ferryman: Then your *whole* life is lost.
This will somewhat charm you Arabically.
With many kisses and greetings.

Old Nick

Best compliments to all [in English].

274

To Frederick Engels (in London)
Algiers, Tuesday, April 18, 1882

Dear Fred:
Received your letter yesterday, ditto Tussy's,[1] also the *"kayserlich"* ["imperial"][2] money.

In my last letter to Laurachen,[3] I announced the appearance of "two of
the most beautiful days"; but even before the letter was finished, sirocco (the
official weather reports, like other French publications, spell it now with one
"c" and now with two) announced himself, and his uproar served as an
overture to the predicted *"mouvements atmosphérique intenses"* ["intense at-
mospheric movements"]. I confessed to Laura that I am tired of this thing, am
in fact "Africa weary," and have decided to turn my back on Algiers as soon
as Dr. Stephann *did no longer "want me"* [in English].

Since April 14 (afternoon) until April 17, gusts of wind, storm, down-
pours, blaze of sun, continuous alternation (almost from hour to hour) between cold and hot. Early this morning it was beautiful; but now at 10 A.M.,
the wind again whistles its irksome melody. In its report yesterday, the
meteorological office assured—rather, predicted—an *"intense mouvement atmosphérique"* for May 7–8 (further into the future it does not penetrate *pro nunc*
[for now]); in addition, it promised *so-called* [in English] *"seismiques mouvements"* for the first week of the same May (these *"seismiques"* are supposed to
have a periodic connection with secret earthquakes).

Dr. Stephann came on the sixteenth (Sunday); after a tapping examination, he said: no more trace of the *"pleurésie"* [pleurisy] (*as far as to* [in English]
"rechute" [relapse]); on the other hand (also on the left side), he was less
satisfied with the bronchial condition than during his last examination.

274

1. Eleanor Marx.
2. This is a pun on the Kayser & Co. bank through which Engels sent Marx money.
3. See Letter 273, Marx to Laura Lafargue, April 13, 1882.

Meanwhile, he tattooed with great energy (from Sunday [April 16] afternoon and night until early Monday morning [April 17], I had plenty of damned time to praise his energy!). For the rest, Dr. Stephann was entirely in agreement with me that bronchitis was inseparable from this weather; under these conditions, a longer stay here would have an unfavorable effect. He believes he will be able to release me, with written instructions, at the end of April, if nothing unexpected occurs, for example, a brilliant change in the weather or, what is not probable, a worsening of my condition. And so, on May 2, I will take the same *Said* under the same Captain Mace (a very nice fellow) that brought me to Algiers, back to Marseilles, whence I will try my luck in Cannes, Nice, or Mentone. Hence do not send either letters or newspapers from London, *unless you do it just after the receipt of these lines* [in English]. In the meantime, should the plans change, I will write you all immediately.

I fear that "iron" will arrive in Algiers, after not only I but also the family Casthelaz have left Africa; the whole world prepares itself for flight [the meaning of this whole sentence is unclear].

You must excuse the meagerness of this missive [in English]. On account of the energetic tattooing, I spent a sleepless night, April 16–17; from April 17 to 18, no pain, because yesterday, at seven in the morning, the *assistant-doctor* [in English][4] has performed his duties; but the itching of newly healing skin made the second night also sleepless. As I have enjoyed the morning promenade very early today (for two hours), *"üw begrijp"* [Dutch: "you understand"] (I no longer know how the Dutch spell it, but *ü begreip!*—the devil knows how much it has to do with the "concept"—but it still sounds like Zalt-Bommel, coming from the mouth of my cousin,[5] now divorced from Parson Rothhaus[6])—in one word, you will understand that I must lie down on my ear and ferret out some compensation for sleep. In the meantime: Sleep, what more do you want! Now I must mention a nasty trick which the French authorities played on a poor robber, a poor professional multiple murderer of Arabs. Only at the very end, or as the infamous Cockneys say, on the moment *"to launch"* [in English] the poor sinner *"into eternity"* [in English] did he discover that he would not be shot but guillotined! *This was contrary to their agreement*! Contrary to their promise! Despite their agreement, he was guillotined. But this is not all. His relatives expected the French, according to their usual custom, to hand them over the body together with the head, so that they could sew the two together and then bury "the whole." *Quod non* [Nothing doing]! Screams and curses and fumings; the French authorities refused, flatly, and for the first time ever! When the torso

---

4. The "assistant-doctor" was Maurice Casthelaz.
5. Antoinette (Nannette) Philips.
6. Rothhaus—old spelling of *Rothaus*, "Red House"—is Marx's satiric Germanization of the name Roodhuizen, the Dutch clergyman to whom his cousin Nannette had been married.

enters paradise, Mohammed asks: Where did you lose your head? Or, how did the head break off from the torso? You are unworthy to be in paradise! Go and have your hair cut to be like a Christian dog! And so wail the relatives.

Yours, Old Mohr

At closer examination—I have not asked anything until now—Stephann told me that, although completely ignorant of German, he is the son of a German. His father had emigrated to Algiers from the Palatinate (Landau).

275

To Frederick Engels (in London)
Algiers, Friday, April 28, 1882

Dear Fred:
Received your letter and the [in English] copies of the *Kölnische Zeitung.*

This letter is merely to report that on May 2 (Tuesday) I will leave Algiers on the same *Said* and with the same commandant, Mr. Mace, "*lieutenant de vaisseau*" [naval lieutenant], which had brought me to Algiers. Last Wednesday I visited the French squadron of six ironclads; of course, I inspected the admiral's ship, *Le Colbert*, where a noncommissioned officer, a handsome and intelligent fellow, showed and demonstrated to me everything in detail. Genuinely French, he told me when I left that he was tired of this boring service and hoped *bientôt* [soon] to receive his discharge. I and my companions (three of the *co-locataires* [fellow guests] of the Hôtel Victoria) had received permission for admission only after the end of the "service." We watched everything from the boat, alias skiff, observing the maneuvers of the admiral's ship and the five ironclads. Tomorrow afternoon there is a "ball" on the *Colbert*; I could have received an invitation through Fermé, but had no time for that. Specifically, on Tuesday (April 25) the last examination by Dr. Stephann; the collodion-tattooing is over: *quo ad* [with it] the pleurisy relapse *altogether absolved* [in English]. On the other hand, tomorrow (Saturday), at three o'clock in the afternoon, I go to visit him to receive his written consultation and take farewell from him. The weather is now partly hot, but *in fact* [in English] the hurricane—storms dancing the sirocco—(at night altogether and repeatedly gusty every day) has continued the whole week (also *today* [in English]). It is the reason why my cough has not relented; *hence* [in English] my seasonable flight from Algiers.

Best regards for all.

Yours, Old Mohr

Apropos. Before the sun, I put away the prophet's beard and the wig, but (since my daughters would like it better this way) I had myself photographed before sacrificing the hair on the altar of an Algerian barber. I will receive the photographs next Sunday (April 30). I will send you specimens from Marseilles. You will see from it that, *considering* [in English] the continuing collodion-painting (in the style of Ludwig of Bavaria) for eight whole weeks (during which time one did not have a single full day of repose), *j'ai fait encore bonne mine à mauvais jeu* [I still made a good face at a bad situation].

276

To Frederick Engels (in London)
Monte Carlo, Hôtel de Russie, May 8, 1882

Dear Fred:

A sea storm was meteorologically predicted two to three weeks before my departure (early May) from Algiers.[1] In fact, during my final African days, the sirocco raged, and with it great heat, but corrupted by gusts of wind, dust storms, and momentary, even if rapidly disappearing, unexpected cooling. My bronchial catarrh became more violent during that period and has not yet abated sufficiently. The storm (in the night of May 4 to 5) at sea made itself also felt by a draft in the cabin. I arrived in Marseilles (the morning of May 5) in a heavy rain, which continued until I reached Nice. I imported *one day of rain* (yesterday) also to Monte Carlo; today splendid weather. You see, I remain consistent, for before my arrival it has not rained for months in Nice and Monte Carlo. But this time, it is mere raillery, not as serious as in Algiers.

In Nice, where I remained on the fifth and sixth, I soon found that the wind is capricious, and that a constant uniformity of temperature was by no means to be expected. Today, Dr. Delachaux, *médecin-chirurgien* [surgeon] (residing in Interlaken), who stays in this hotel, confirmed my brief experience. On his vacation trip, he visited Nice, the surrounding places and generally the most famous spots of the Riviera, *so far with an eye to business as to ascertain which places he might best recommend to sufferers of lung diseases, bronchial catarrh of a chronic character, etc. He declared decidedly against Nice, but preferred Monte Carlo even to Mentone* [in English]. Dr. Delachaux is returning today to his Swiss homeland.

Of the charm of the local natural beauty, you know *everything* [in English], either from personal observation, or from print or painting. In many of its features it reminds me vividly of Africa.

In general, one will soon have to give up hope for "warm, dry air" anywhere. The sun spots prophesy intensive action of the rays, and in France there is fear of a drought.

276

1. Marx left Algiers on May 2, and stayed in Nice and Monte Carlo from May 5 to June 3, 1882.

For conscience sake [in English], I will consult tomorrow the German Dr. Kunemann here. I have with me a written consultation from Dr. Stephann (from his visiting cards, I noticed that Dr. Stephann is also *professeur suppléant à l'École de Médecine* [assistant professor at the School of Medicine] on the Algiers faculty), which spares me further chatter. As soon as Stephann declared the pleurisy to be over, I began, at his advice, to rub tincture of iodine on the upper parts (left side) of the chest and back. From the embarcation until *today* [in English], I interrupted these operations, which, moreover, are "difficult" to execute on one's own back, although Dr. Delachaux advised me to try it with the help of a mirror. *Qui vivra verra* [He who lives will see]; at any rate, I want to talk to Dr. Kunemann beforehand. For I want to move about as much as possible.

In the Reading Room of the Casino of Monte Carlo there is an almost complete collection of Parisian and Italian newspapers; German papers are quite well represented, very few English ones. From the *Petit Marseilles* of today's date, I saw "l'assassinat de Lord Cavendish et de Mr. Burke."[2] But the local public, for example, the *table d'hôte* comrades of the Hôtel de Russie, are much more interested in what happens in the *salles de jeu* [gambling rooms] of the Casino (*tables de roulette et de trente-et-quarante* [roulette and other gaming tables]). I am particularly amused by a son of Great Britain, thoroughly morose, sullen, demented, *and why* [in English]? Because he lost a certain amount of gold pieces, whereas he had been completely determined to "pilfer" them. He did not realize that Fortune itself is not "*to bully*" [in English] even by British rudeness.

These lines must come to an end, as letters can be sent only by messenger to the post in Monaco.

Best regards for all.

Yours, Mohr

277

To Jenny Longuet (in Argenteuil)
Monte Carlo, Hôtel de Russie, May 8, 1882

Dear Jennychen:
This *Monte Carlo*, when these lines are being addressed to you, is one of the three places (lying next to each other), whose trinity constitutes the state of "Monaco" (Monaco, Condamine, and Monte Carlo). Its situation is beautiful, the climate superior to that of Nice and even Mentone.

Naturally, I had this comical consistency of importing *the first two rainy days* (since January) into this area; they seemed only to have waited until my

---

2. On May 6, 1882, the Chief Secretary for Ireland, Lord Frederick Cavendish, and his deputy, Thomas Henry Burke, were assassinated by terrorists in Dublin's Phoenix Park.

arrival from Algiers. Otherwise, however, I encountered splendid weather.

As you know from my last letter, my pleurisy is over; the bronchial catarrh can go away only gradually. For the rest, the air will soon be dry and warm *everywhere*; but then the intensity of the action of the sun's rays will prevail the more as the former is dotted with big spots. Hence everywhere there will soon be weather useful to me.

As [it is] uncertain how long I will remain here, I want to know immediately from Paris *where* I will find you; it would be best to telegraph me here, since a telegram of three or four words can inform me sufficiently.

Many kisses for the children.

Yours, Old Mohr

278

To Frederick Engels (in London)
Monte Carlo, Hôtel de Russie, May 20, 1882

Privately

Dear Fred:

It would be useless to communicate this to the children, as it would alarm them unnecessarily. But I have to report the latest experiences to *somebody at least* [in English].

In the last letter (I am not exactly sure whether I wrote it direct to you or to Tussy or to Laura[1]), I wrote that I would report particulars after meeting with Dr. Kunemann.[2] This took place on May 8; he is an Alsatian, trained scientifically (medically); for example, he shared with me Dr. Koch[3] on bacilli, before the arrival of your letter; a man of great practice; has at least fifty-two to fifty-four years on his hump, as he was a student at the university in Strassburg in 1848; in politics, he finds in the newspaper, *Le Temps*, the organ corresponding to his temperament; science has convinced him that everything moves "slowly"; no revolutionary overthrow—compelled to march after it just as much "backward" (as, for example, in the Echternacher Procession[4]); the education of the masses and "nonmasses," a primary condition, etc. *In one word, politically, a republican philistine* [in English]; all of which explains why I did not let myself in for a discussion with him on this subject, except a mention of the "Machiavellian" policy of Charles III, absolute tyrant of Monaco. He considered me a 48'er, and except for this date, I gave him no other dates about my normal *public activity* [in English].

278

1. The letter was written to Engels on May 8, 1882.
2. German doctor in Monte Carlo.
3. Robert Koch (1843–1910), founder of science of bacteriology.
4. A medieval procession, involving complicated steps, taking place at Whitsuntide in Echternach, Luxembourg.

Now to the point. Originally, he concluded from my visiting card, which mentions Dr., and which I remitted to him through his domestic servant, that I was a Dr. med., about which he was further convinced by Dr. Stephann's card, which I handed to him; ditto, that of my new doctor acquaintance from Interlaken;[5] also the card of Dr. Donkin, whom I mentioned as a friend of my friend, Prof. Ray Lankester, since he wanted to know who had treated me in London, etc. Then I gave him Stephann's *consultation écrite* [written consultation].[6]

Thus, while he considered me as a Dr. med. colleague, *either theoretically or practically* [in English], he gave clearance to the liver, after auscultating and percussing me. And to my alarm—the *pleurisy is back*, even though in a lesser degree, *on one spot, on the left, in the back*; but the bronchitis is more or less *chronic*! He thought one or two *vésicatoires* would put an end to the thing (pleurisy); on May 9 (Tuesday), first *vésicatoire*; on May 13 (Saturday), second *vésicatoire* was prescribed after a visit to Kunemann, but it could be applied only on May 16 (Tuesday), after drying up; on May 19, I visited him (Friday); auscultation and percussion; found it better, namely, the *épanchement* [effusion] slightly reduced; he thought (since these doctors feared the patient would lose patience during this whole week, being *plus ou moins* [more or less] tainted and tortured at each visit) it would not be necessary to go on further with the *vésicatoires*; I could content myself with only a rubbing of tincture of iodine (prescribed for me by Stephann against bronchitis) on the upper *and also lower* spots on the left side of the chest and back. Whereupon I declared that if the *épanchement* did not disappear entirely, I preferred the *vésicatoire* again (for May 23, Tuesday); from Dr. Stephann I knew that when it comes to pleurisy, tincture of iodine is a weak, uncertain, and drawn-out means. For Kunemann it was clearly more agreeable that I decided on a heroic remedy; I hope now that on May 26 or 27 he will tell me that this *second relapse* is now final (*pro nunc* [for now]).

In fact, "fate" has manifested itself this time consistently, and even almost, as in Dr. Müllner's tragedies,[7] horribly. Why did Kunemann (and I must have "discovered" this before) declare the bronchitis to be "chronic"? Because on the whole Riviera the weather has been uncommonly bad and abnormal; but he thought it was perhaps normal insofar as there was too little rain, almost none, from *January to the beginning of May*; too-warm weather must have brought about a reaction. I declared to him more simply that it was all the fault of my coming here from Algiers; on May 4, I brought rain to Marseilles, and after some resistance, the weather—*mutatis mutandis* [barring

---

5. Dr. Delachaux; see Letter 276, Marx to Engels, May 8, 1882.
6. See Letter 275, Marx to Engels, April 28, 1882.
7. The plays of the German dramatist, Amandus Gottfried Adolf Müllner (1774-1829), assigned to man an inexorable, predestined fate.

minor differences]—assumed the character of the Algerian "stormy weather" in the place of my present stay. It requires much patience, especially also on the part of my letter addressees. Such *repetitio* are too tedious. A useless, meaningless, and also expensive way of life!

Tomorrow, I am writing to Tussy,[8] since I had not replied to her last letter. Today I am uncomfortable, as, in bending, the new skin made by the *vésicatoire* has the tendency to rub itself painfully against the jacket or linen. *Notabene*: What I shall write to the children is the truth, but *not the whole truth*. Why distress them?

Yours, Mohr

Dr. Kunemann's mistake about my character as a *"medical" colleague* was cleared up when he refused a fee on my first visit; he was the more sweet when he was informed that I was a *layman*, and hence to be "bled."

279

To Eleanor Marx (in London)
Monte Carlo, Hôtel de Russie, May 28, 1882

Dear Tussychen:

Bebel's letter was neither in Engels' letter nor in yours, which I received last night. It must have been inadvertently left out in London. *At all events, I wash my hands of it* [in English].

Today, 24 degrees in the shade, as in general the summer heat has begun since my postal card to you[1] (even though the sky is not as absolutely cloudless as the local connoisseurs demand). Under such circumstances, "good intentions" do not coincide with a detailed report; at any rate, much good is not lost thereby.

In regard to the sea voyage from Algiers, it can only be remarked that it took place in unfavorable weather conditions; on the night of May 4 to 5 a violent storm which transformed my cabin (which, furthermore, I had to share with a Lyons merchant philistine) into a veritable wind cavern. In the morning (May 5) we found ourselves before Marseilles in a strong, cold rain. The steamer did not land directly; passengers and baggage were transported by boat, only to wait several hours in a drafty *douane purgatorio* [customs purgatory] for the train to Nice. These cold-producing "moments"

---

8. See Letter 279, Note 1, Marx to his daughter Eleanor, May 21, 1882.

279

1. Marx to Eleanor Marx, May 21, 1882: " . . . I really had the intention of writing you today (Sunday) a long letter, but man proposes, the thermometer disposes. Today is a perfectly beautiful day, but *exceptional*."

détraquaient plus ou moins de nouveau ma machine [put my organism more or less out of order], threw me anew *entre les mains d'un Esculape* [into the hands of an Aesculapian] in Monte Carlo, who found that in regard to the "bronchial business" I need no other treatment than what was prescribed by Dr. Stephann. In a few days (perhaps next Tuesday, May 30), I expect to be dismissed by Dr. Kunemann.[2] In any case, I do not expect to leave this robbers' nest before early June. Whether or not to remain longer, Dr. Kunemann is to decide. The sensitivity of persons suffering respiratory diseases (that is, those liable to relapses) is heightened in a normally favorable climate. For example, who in the North would dream of immediately getting pleurisy, bronchitis, etc., at an unexpected draft, yet in Algiers the French philistine must always watch out for it. A Madame Fleury, a guest in this Hôtel de Russie, was sent from Paris to Cannes on account of pleurisy; in March and April she completely recovered there, zestfully climbed mountains, etc. For an after cure and distraction, she then left Cannes for Monte Carlo, caught cold during that short, two-hour ride—at the railroad station in Antibes—and is now worse than she had been in Paris. One hears of visitors who did not come here for pleasure or gambling, among whom surely nine out of ten are victims of *"rechutes"* ["relapses"].

When Goethe speaks of man "casting off" the old snake skin in the process of rejuvenation,[3] he probably does not mean the artificially produced *"fausses peaux"* ["fake furs"].

Some time when it is not as "torrid" as today, I must tell you a little about this Gerolstein principality (even the Offenbach music is not lacking, nor Mademoiselle Schneider, nor the ornamental and adorned carabinieri ((hardly 100)).[4] Nature here is splendid, further improved by art—I mean the magical gardens on barren rocks that slope from steep heights all the way down to the blue sea, like the hanging terraces of Babylonian gardens. But the economic basis of Monaco-Gerolstein is the gambling Casino; if it should close up tomorrow, Monaco-Gerolstein would go into the grave—all of it! I do not like to visit the gambling hall. Think of it, at the table d'hôte, in cafés, etc., one speaks and whispers about nothing but the roulette and trente-et-quarante tables. Here and there one wins; for example, a young Russian lady (a Russian diplomat-agent's wife, who is a guest in the Hôtel de Russie) won 100 francs and then lost 6,000 francs; another gambler lost his return fare home; still others gamble away great family fortunes. Very few take anything away from this robbery—I mean very few gamblers, and among them almost exclusively—the rich. Reason, calculation, etc., do not come into question at

2. A German doctor practicing in Monte Carlo.
3. From Goethe's poem, *"Zahmen Xenien,"* V.
4. An ironic reference to Offenbach's operetta, *The Duchess of Gerolstein*, in which the famous diva Hortense Schneider played the leading role in Paris.

all; one can only calculate on the favorable probabilities of "chance" if one has adequate means to risk. Still I understand that it attracts the *beau sexe* [fair sex]; the *mondaines* [worldly ladies] no less than the *demi-mondaines* [ladies of the evening], *schoolgirls* [in English] as well as bourgeoises, *all push on* [in English], with eyewitnesses around them. I believe that in addition to Monaco-Gerolstein, which would sink without the gambling Casino, Nice—the aristocratic and adventurous world in the winter months—would also not survive as a fashionable center without the Monte Carlo Casino. And withal, what child's play is the Casino compared to the stock exchange!

(This pen and this ink should be renewed; it is truly an art to write with them—they force this exclamation from me!)

To the right of the Casino (which contains the gaming tables) and close to it is the Café de Paris and near it a kiosk; on it there waves a daily poster, not printed but written, signed with the initials of the author: for 600 francs one receives from him, black on white, the mysteries of science; for 1,000 francs, the promise of winning one million at the roulette and trente-et-quarante tables. Even on this pinnacle, by no means exceptional customers are to be found. In reality, the great majority of gamblers, male and female, believe in the science of this pure game of hazard; gentlemen and ladies sit in front of this Café de Paris or on benches in the wonderful garden which belongs to the Casino, hold little tablets (printed) in their hands, head bent, scratching and calculating, or one explains importantly to the other "which system" he prefers, whether one is to play in "series," etc., etc. One has the impression of seeing inmates of a lunatic asylum. Grimaldi of Monaco[5] and his principality Gerolstein and his gambling lessee thrive among them and are after all, Offenbach-speaking, "more interesting" than the swindled ones.

Should my residence change, *I will telegraph* you. The return trip to Paris, at any rate, will take place in stages and "carefully."

Best regards for all,

Old Nick

280

To Frederick Engels (in London)
Monte Carlo, May 30, 1882

Dear Fred:
Since the May 23 application (the third of Monte Carlo) of *vésicatoire* [blistering plaster], I had late today an appointment with Dr. Kunemann, but only in connection with the "bronchiatical." *Quod-ad Pleurésie* [in regard to

---

5. Charles III (1818–1889), Prince of Monaco, 1856–1889.

pleurisy], on the other hand, I had a long final examination today; the *épanchement* [discharge] is *gone*; what remains is so-called *dry pleurisy*; there is no longer any moisture on the way, but there remains a rustle from one skin to the other, to express it in a falsely popularized way. He believes it useful to apply a *vésicatoire* today for the last time, then to emigrate to Cannes for a few short days, to be able to toddle off to Paris afterward.

He believes that I contracted the pleurisy quite accidentally; likewise, by the same token, with my solid, normal build, I should never have let it catch me for the last forty years—accidentally! To get rid of it is the more difficult because of the chances of a relapse.

Since I had to parade before him fore and aft in my naked beauty, he called my attention to the fact that the left side had earlier swelled against the right because of the pleurisy; now, on the contrary, the left side (what is involved is the damaged spot) has shrunk in contrast to the right, and that as a consequence of my treatment. The complete working off of the last traces, the souvenir marks, so to speak, of the pleurisy, would be attainable *later* by a stay in the mountains, where a thinner air prevails. Through such a gymnastic, forced upon them by the milieu, the lungs must again "adjust" themselves. I could follow the details the less, in that he tried to explain them to me in a French frequently mixed with Alsatian German, as well as some Yankee English. But still it was clear what Dr. Stephann had told me on the first day: Your chest remains the way it is; should, therefore, an artificial tissue replace and restrict one of the lungs, the lungs must satisfy themselves with a smaller space. To the extent that the tissue is removed, the lungs expand again.

I have just returned from Kunemann, that is, nearly six o'clock in the evening, which (six o'clock) is the last postal hour *for today* [in English]. *Tomorrow*—owing to the final application of the *vésicatoire* tonight—writing is *out of the question* [in English]. The day after tomorrow I must recuperate, and so all of you will "hardly" get further news from me before the second or third of June.

With best regards.

Old Mohr

281

Postcard to Jenny Longuet (in Argenteuil) [in English]
Cannes, June 4, 1882

Dearest Child:
I will come on *one of the first days of the week that begins June 6*. I cannot yet be more precise; it will depend on circumstances that cannot yet be foreseen exactly. Hence you would *do me a favor* if you did not worry about the exact

day or hour of my arrival. Until now, I have always experienced that *nothing hurts me more than when somebody waits for me at the railroad station.* Tell nobody (including the *Gascon*,[1] the Russian,[2] and Hirsch) that I am expected in that week. I need absolute quiet *alone with your family, No. 11 Boulevard Thiers.*

Yours, Old Nick

Under "quiet," I understand "family life," the "noise of children"—this "microscopic world" that is much more interesting than the "macroscopic" one.

282

To Frederick Engels (in London)
Cannes, June 5, 1882

Dear Fred:
On 30th May [in English] (pro Monte Carlo), last brand mark on the back; on May 31, the postoperations kept me under house arrest; on June 3, I was emancipated from [Dr.] Kunemann and left on the same day.[1] He advised me under all circumstances to spend a few days at Cannes,[2] as a necessity for the "drying" of the wounds.

Thus I had vegetated the whole month in this *repaire* [den] of the genteel idlers or *adventurers* [in English]. Nature is splendid, otherwise a desolate nest; it is "monumental," in that it consists of nothing but hotels; here there are no plebeian "masses," apart from the *Lumpenproletariat* [proletariat trash] of the *garçons d'hôtels, de café* [waiters of hotels, cafés], etc., and the *domestiques* [servants]. The old robbers' nest on the towering cliff, surrounded by the bay on three sides, that is, *Monaco*, at least a fragile old medieval type of a little Italian town; on the other side, *Condamine*, mostly below at the sea, between the "city" of Monaco and the *maison de jeu* [casino] (that is, Monte Carlo), which is growing rapidly. *Monaco, in the strict sense* [in English], is the "politics," the "State," the "government;" *Condamine* is the ordinary "petit bourgeois" society; but Monte Carlo is *"the pleasure," and thanks to the* banque de jeu [gambling bank] *the financial basis of the whole trinity* [in English]. Strange how these Grimaldis became important; formerly they lived from piracy, and one of them,[3] for instance, wrote to Lorenzo de Med-

281
1. Paul Lafargue.
2. Peter Lavrov.

282
1. Marx had been in Monte Carlo for nearly a month, from early May to June 3, 1882.
2. He remained in Cannes for two days, until June 5.
3. Lamberto Grimaldi (d.c. 1494), Prince of Monaco, 1457–1494.

ici[4] that his territory was narrow and in addition, barren; nature, therefore, destined them for piracy on the seas; Lorenzo should, therefore, be so generous as to guarantee them a yearly "present," since they did not "dare" to chase Florentine ships. Lorenzo, consequently, paid them a small annual stipend. After the victory of the Holy Alliance over Napoleon I, Talleyrand,[5] who had selected the arch-bum, the ex-tyrant of Monaco,[6] as his boon companion among the émigrés, as a lark "restored" the father of Florestan I[7] "*au nom du principe de la légitimité*" ["in the name of the principle of legitimacy"]. These two restorations—the one of Hesse-Kassel[8] and the other of Monaco—this *couple* [in English] deserves to figure in a new edition of Plutarch; at the same time, what a contrast between the Genoese (above all, emerging out of financial robbery) and the German "patriarch."

Our Dr. Kunemann has a quiet sorrow that, owing to his liberal principles which gave offense, he was replaced as the personal physician of His Serenissimus, the stone-blind Charles III, by an Englishman (Dr. Pickering). *The survival of the best—that is, as a personal physician to a duodecimal little tyrant—to a Britisher, of course, warranted by the nature of the beast! And that is the worst; this same Dr. Pickering, before being called by natural selection, he had dangerously fallen ill at Monaco, was treated and cured by Dr. Kunemann* [in English]. There are many such doleful fatalistic dramas in this world!

Peculiarly enough, this hot weather has aggravated rather than improved my bronchial cough. Naturally, the more "pretexts" for catching cold! For the rest, Kunemann (and the man is a first-rate doctor, knows English, German, as well as French medical literature, is a specialist on lung and chest diseases) does not share your view in regard to my return to Paris. I should not do it with interruptions. The weather is now hot, not only during the day but is also warm at night. This would be a main cause for catching cold on the railroad stations; the more frequent the trip's interruption, the greater the possibility for a relapse. On the contrary, I am to carry from Cannes two bottles of good old Bordeaux for the trip. He, like Dr. Stephann, goes down to fundamentals: in the treatment of pleurisy, the stomach is to be viewed in the same way as bronchitis, etc.; good and much food; "to get accustomed" to it despite oneself; "good" "drinking" and distraction during the voyage, etc.; little walking or climbing; thinking as little as possible, etc.

So following these "instructions," I am on the best way to "idiotism," although the bronchial catarrh still hangs on.

---

4. Lorenzo de Medici (1449–1492), ruler of Florence.
5. Charles Maurice de Talleyrand-Périgord (1754–1838), French statesman and diplomat.
6. Honoratus IV (1758–1819), Prince of Monaco, 1814–1819.
7. Florestan I (1785–1856), Prince of Monaco, 1841–1856.
8. Wilhelm I (1743–1821), Elector of Hesse-Kassel, 1803–1807 and 1813–1821.

The Old Garibaldi,[9] to console me, joined "eternity" from bronchitis. Naturally, at a certain age, it is altogether indifferent how one is *"launched into eternity"* [in English].

I have been here three days and am leaving this evening. In Nice, and exceptionally, too, at Cannes, there is *a strong wind (although warmer) and a dust storm*. Nature also has its philistine humor (in the manner of the "Old Testament," where the snake's fodder is to be dirt, and Darwin's dirt diet of worms,[10] humoristically viewed). Such natural witticisms run through the whole local press of the Riviera. For example, on May 24 there was a dreadful storm at *Mentone*; lightning struck *auprès de la gare* [near the railroad station] (of Mentone) and at the same time knocked the shoe off a wandering philistine, leaving the rest of the philistine intact.

With best regards for all.

Old Mohr

Only after a few days of my arrival in Paris will I let friends know about it. As little "contact with people" as possible. I find Dr. Dourlen a good physician to consult.

283

Postcard to Laura Lafargue (in London)
Argenteuil, 11 Boulevard Thiers, June 17, 1882

Private and confidential

Best Child:
I have previously arranged with Engels—as I have already orally informed Paul[1]—that as soon as I can go to Switzerland (probably in the latter half of July), *you accompany me*. I will in fact hardly venture to travel alone anymore.

---

9. Giuseppe Garibaldi died on June 2, 1882, three days before this letter was written.
10. Charles Darwin, *The Formation of Vegetable Mould, Through the Action of Worms, with Observations on their Habits* (1881).
283
1. Paul Lafargue.

You see that it is *plus ou moins votre devoir d'accompagner le vieux de la montagne* [more or less your duty to accompany the Old Man of the Mountain].[2]

As I have still to remain here at least three weeks because of sulfur cure at Enghien, I hope that Helen[3] and Tussy will come here on a short trip during this period. I have written to Helen and Tussy in that sense.

Lafargue has been invited by Jennychen for tomorrow.

Adio.

Old Nick

284

To Frederick Engels (in London)
Argenteuil,[1] July 4, 1882

Dear Fred:

Actually, summer began only July 1 (*or rather on the second only* [in English]). I have had until now two sulfur baths *with douches*, tomorrow the third. I have experienced nothing more lordly than the *Spritzbad* (alias *douche*); from the bath one steps on a raised board, in the "altogether"; the bath attendant uses the hose (the size of a firehose) the way a virtuoso does his instrument; he commands the movement of the body and bombards alternately all *parts* [in English] of the corpus (*save the head* [in English]: *the skull case*) for 180 seconds (alias three minutes), now strongly, now weakly, up to the legs and feet, and always advancing crescendo.

You can see how little desire a man has to write here. At eight-thirty in the morning I have to be at the *railway* [in English] (that is, *this the time of leaving exactly for Enghien* [in English]), return to Argenteuil about *twelve o'clock* [in English], *déjeuner* [lunch] soon after, *après* [thereafter] greatly needed rest, as the sulfur debilitates one in every way; then into the open, etc. In the *inhalation* [in English] hall the *atmosphere* [in English] is dark with sulfur vapor; here one remains thirty to forty *minutes* [in English]; every five minutes, at a table, one sucks in a special, pulverized, sulfur-heavy vapor (from pipes [zinc] with faucets); every person is mummified in rubber from head to foot, then each marches behind the other around the table; an innocent scene from Dante's Inferno.

Remember me to Schorlemmer. I am keeping for him a photograph of me from Algiers.

Lafargue poses here as an *important oracle* [in English]. Paris is for him *the only place of the world worth manhood* [in English].

[unsigned]

---

2. Laura Lafargue accompanied her father on his Swiss trip.
3. Helene Demuth.

284

1. Marx visited his daughter Jenny Longuet in Argenteuil, from June 6 to August 22, 1882, at the same taking the sulfur bath treatments at nearby Enghien-les-Bains.

285

To Frederick Engels (in London)
Argenteuil, Thursday, August 10, 1882

Dear Fred:
Next Tuesday I will know from Dr. Feugier[1] whether I am definitely to leave Enghien or remain a few more days for the cure.

Unfortunately, I am obliged, in case I leave here (with Laura[2]) for Switzerland[3] (Vevey or a similar place has been recommended), to ask for some *monetary subsidy* [in English]. Specifically, I discovered *accidentally* that Jenny[4] is cruelly pressed by the *landlord* [in English] for the rent (and they don't joke about this here), and I had enough trouble to have her take the money and settle the thing.

Furthermore, I hope (the *only resistance comes from Longuet*, who couldn't care less whether this would be a relief for Jennychen or of use to Johnny)[5] that Johnny goes to London with Tussy,[6] whom I would give some money so that she and the boy could go to the seashore for two weeks. The main excuse of Herr Longuet was that he did not want to leave Johnny with us for half a year and that a stay at the seashore in Normandy, where he would take him to Madame Longuet[7] in Caen, would be necessary for Johnny's health.

In reality, Johnny is growing up wild here, has forgotten the little reading and writing that he knew, has become uncivil out of boredom (that is, out of nonoccupation), and causes Jennychen more trouble than the other three little ones.[8] Herr Longuet does "nothing" for the child, but his "love" consists of not removing the boy from him, for the few moments that he is visible here, as he spends his forenoons in bed while in Argenteuil and returns to Paris at five in the afternoon.

Given Jennychen's pregnancy,[9] it is absolutely impossible to control young Johnny. Tussy is an *excellent disciplinarian* [in English], and she can bring him to order. Longuet, therefore, can have no excuse that the boy

---

285
1. Marx's doctor in Enghien.
2. Laura Lafargue.
3. Accompanied by his daughter Laura Lafargue, Marx traveled in Switzerland, including Lausanne and Vevey, from August 23 to September 25, 1882.
4. Jenny Longuet.
5. Jenny Longuet was then suffering from cancer and had, in fact, only about five months to live; she could not, therefore, take care of her four little children—a fact that distressed her father.
6. Eleanor Marx.
7. Felicitas Longuet, Charles Longuet's mother.
8. In addition to Jean, six, the three other Longuet children were Henri, aged four; Edgar, aged three Marcel, aged one.
9. On September 16, 1882, Jenny Longuet gave birth to her last child, a daughter also named Jenny, who lived until 1952.

cannot go to England (where Tussy would also send him to school) because he has to be at the "seashore"; he should go to the "seashore," but in England.

 With the above expenses and the doctor's fee, as well as various necessary purchases, I will have little left for the trip to Switzerland. I find it very disagreeable to press you this way, but it is necessary, if I am not to return to London immediately.

 Salut.

Mohr

The news in the French papers, that is, Parisian, first in *Le Temps*,[10] that Liebknecht is going to Paris to "make contacts with German workers there and to visit the socialist Karl Marx, who after his return from Algiers now lives in Argenteuil"—I say, this note in this form smelled "of the police" and is too tactless even for Liebknecht. If he should still find me here, I will give him a piece of my mind over his "tactlessness" (it grows out of his urge to show off).

286

Postcard to Frederick Engels (in London)
Vevey,¹ Hôtel du Léman, September 4, 1882

Dear Fred:
Laura² will write you in detail about our happenings, or rather nonhappenings, since we live here as in Lubberland. We had *trips* [in English] on the *lake* [in English], like other people.

---

10. *Le Temps*, August 6, 1882.

286

1. Marx was in Vevey, Switzerland, from August 27 to September 25, 1882.
2. Laura Lafargue to Frederick Engels (in London)
Paris, September 28, 1882
Dear General:
"I have been quite unable to write to you before this, though I much wanted to report progress. Our departure from Vevey took place on Monday the twenty-fifth, up to which date we were weather-bound. We reached Geneva in the afternoon of Monday, spent the whole of Tuesday with poor old Becker and said good-bye to beautiful Switzerland on Wednesday morning. Paris we reached last night at half-past eleven P.M., put up for the night at the Hôtel du Chemin de Fer and are now—early in the morning—sitting amid my own household gods (that look anything but divine) in the Boulevard de Port-Royal. Words are quite powerless to describe the state of filth and disorder in which I find these rooms of mine and so I will waste as few of them as possible on that subject. You will wonder perhaps that we should have turned tail so precipitately from Geneva, but had we

On August 31, I received Jennychen's[3] letter with the enclosure of your letter and the check; I have transmitted the latter to the local banking house, Genton et Co. in Paris, for *encaissement* [cashing].

August 31, and September 1, 2, and 3, brilliant weather (yesterday too hot). Today, storm and rain, hopefully it will not degenerate into a general heavy rain. Peculiar, that I still cough; I believe I am the only person in Vevey who coughs; at least I met no other one. But my *general state* [in English] is very satisfactory; without any oppression of the chest, I climbed, with Laura, the local vineyards, as well as even the higher ones at Montreux.

Mr. Songeon, *président du conseil municipal de Paris* [president of the municipal council of Paris], called on me at our hotel; he is one of the *refugiés* [refugees] I knew in London in 1849–1850. He honored me with his official report to the Paris *conseil municipal* on the delegation (Songeon among them) to Rome for the apotheosis of Garibaldi;[4] what is involved here primarily is "Songeon's" own apotheosis, as he was the spokesman of the French delegation. Showed me also a copy of *Kapital*, which is supposed to accompany him in his lonely wandering through the forest, not far from here.

With the English in Egypt,[5] hitherto not yet as rapid a success as Wolseley had "predicted."

Herr Virchow, as I saw from yesterday's *supplément de Journal de Genève*,[6] has again demonstrated that he "despises" Darwin endlessly and, therefore, also organic chemistry and is, in fact, the only scientific man.

[unsigned]

---

stayed there another day, Papa would have had a relapse and all the good work that had been done at Vevey would have been undone.

"Trudging about on foot through the streets of Geneva with a vile wind blowing and a blinding rain drenching you is by no means what suits Papa's condition and it says much for his improved state of health that he could hold out for a day without being materially affected for the worse.

"I have much to say to you about Paul and his aberrations but all that must stand over. Papa has the incorrigible habit of wanting to talk and be talked to as soon as ever I take pen in hand and consequently I write these lines under a running fire of wit and wisdom which is quite stultifying. I hope you will forgive me if under the circumstances I am rather more confused than usual. I will add a postscript to this in a day or two. Pray write a line at once to say what sort of weather you are having, as Papa's coming movements depend on that. We go to Argenteuil this morning. Paul is the Lord knows where. However, I had asked him to send me the key of our rooms so that I am as free as a latchkey can make me. Affectionately, dearest General, Yours, Laura."

3. Jenny Longuet.

4. On June 11, 1882, there was a great commemorative celebration in Rome in honor of Giuseppe Garibaldi, who died on June 2, 1882.

5. On September 13, 1882, British forces under Sir Garnett Wolseley defeated the Egyptians at Tel el-Kebir, and on September 15, they occupied Cairo.

6. Supplement of the *Geneva Journal*, a conservative daily.

287

To Frederick Engels (in London)
Paris, September 30, 1882

Dear Fred:

Just here (that is, Gare St. Lazare) from Argenteuil, to await Laura[1] to have dinner with her in Paris and take her with me back to Argenteuil; before leaving, the *facteur* [postman] caught me with your letter and enclosure. Laura will arrive here in about a quarter of an hour, probably with your letter to her.

Dr. Dourlen examined me today in Jennychen's presence. The *râlement muqueux* [mucous throat-rattling] has *disappeared*; some *whistling* is left, but the best point is to end this stubborn catarrh, which has already changed its character substantially. My general *habitus* [condition] is extraordinarily improved; I have also become "fatter."

Under no circumstances, does he [Dr. Dourlen] want me to remain in London more than fourteen days, or, in very good weather, three weeks. He fears moderate cold less than humid air. Under no circumstances, should I travel by express train through Calais at night; I should go to Calais by day, and take the morning steamer next day.

For the rest, he considers it premature to begin the *campagne de l'hiver* [winter campaign] in the Isle of Wight, Jersey, Morlaix (Brittany), or Pau. Moreover, he does *not* like me *to stay too far in the South*, except *in case of need* [in English], hence he found Vevey better for me than the warmer Montreux. He assumes that the normal temperatures, etc., will not suddenly rebel again because of my arrival. Finally, he will give me *definite* "permission" to leave for London *only* after he has satisfied himself with the meteorological *bulletin* [in English] for the next days. (French doctors have a severe prejudice against the London climate.) He is now sure of a complete cure, if no mistakes are made. Hence I will not leave before Tuesday[2] at least.

If the French government—*as represented by the swindling financier* [in English] Duclerc[3]—(particularly in the absence of the Chamber [of Deputies])—knew about my presence here, it would perhaps send me packing without Dr. Dourlen's permission, since the "Marxists" and "Anti-Marxists," in their respective socialist congresses at Roanne and St. Étienne,[4] *both sorts,*

287
1. Laura Lafargue.
2. October 3.
3. Charles Théodore Eugène Duclerc (1812–1888), French journalist and statesman.
4. The Marxist-socialist congress met at Roanne, September 26 to October 1, 1882; the non-Marxists ("Possibilists") met at St. Étienne, on September 25.

did their best to spoil my stay in France. I am somewhat compensated in this by the fact that the Alliance gang—Malon,[5] Brousse,[6] etc.—saw themselves "very" disappointed in their hope, *as if* (our Bruno's [Bauer] favorite expression) their "quiet" insinuation: Marx is a "German," alias "Prussian," hence also the French "Marxists" are traitors—caught on with nobody anymore, and nobody even dared for a moment to become "public." *C'est un progrès* [That's a little progress].

Clemenceau has been gravely ill, and is not yet fully recovered. He took with him, for the period of his sickness, a copy of *Kapital*. Seems to be the fashion now for *French real or would-be "advanced" leaders—if "the Devil be sick* [in English]."[7]

Best regards for all, not forgetting Jollymeyer.[8]

The Mohr

I will write or telegraph before leaving France.

288

To Laura Lafargue (in Paris)
London, October 9, 1882

Dear Cacadou:
The weather is not bad today, that is, a few hours are good enough while the sun shines brightly; for the rest, cloudy skies and rain squalls from time to time; on the whole not cold, and the well-known fogs mornings and evenings.

On Sunday, Schorlemmer came to London, only for a friendly good-bye; this evening he has to return to Manchester, where he has to "perpetrate" a lecture tomorrow. He sends you his regards.

Engels is very annoyed that he has not received *L'Égalité*[1] for months; my copy is likewise no longer being sent here. What is the cost of a subscription of *Citoyen*[2] and the postage to London? I forgot it when I left Paris;[3] and I will send you a money order as soon as I hear from you.

---

5. Benoît Malon (1841–1893), French radical, Communard, Anarchist.
6. Paul Louis Marie Brousse (1844–1912), French socialist doctor and politician.
7. "The Devil was sick,—the Devil a monk would be;
The Devil was well,—the Devil a monk was he."
8. Carl Schorlemmer.

288
1. Paris socialist newspaper.
2. *Le Citoyen*, Paris socialist newspaper, of which Paul Lafargue was one of the editors.
3. Early in October, 1882.

Yesterday we were at Engels' for dinner. Pumps with baby[4] and Percy[5] of course were also there. The baby is very lively, her conversation incomparably brighter than that of her mama—at any rate.

Last evening [Dr.] Donkin came to visit me, but will examine me medically only later this week; he found my looks better. He thought that the Isle of Wight was best for me in the approaching *fog time of England* [in English].

Johnny[6] is gay and generally "happy," although he often speaks of his *maman* and Harry movingly.[7] Under Tussy's guidance, he has again become accustomed to washing himself every morning from head to foot in cold water. His "well-being" leaves nothing to be desired; the regular early sleeping hour (eight o'clock in the evening) also agrees with him. His scholarship has reached to the "big letters," ditto the making out of the big Roman numerals and watches.

I am very anxious to receive from you news about Jenny's state, personal and household. Has the Longuet family returned?[8]

The great agitator St. Paul[9] is of course again enthroned on the battlements of the Boulevard de Port-Royal. Write me about his adventures; but above all, about yourself, how it goes, how things are.

My cough is still troublesome, more as *memento* [warning] that I must get it off my neck, in order to be able to work *altogether* [in English] again.

Lenchen[10] and Johnny send their regards.

Be well, my dear and devoted travel-companion[11] Cacadou.

Old Nick

---

4. Mary Ellen Burns Rosher and daughter.

5. Percy Rosher, Mary Ellen's husband, English businessman.

6. Six-year-old Jean-Laurent-Frederick Longuet.

7. His mother, Jenny Longuet, Marx's oldest daughter, and Henri, a four-year-old brother. Jenny was then gravely ill in France with cancer, of which she died three months later.

8. Charles Longuet and his three young sons, Henri, Edgar and Marcel.

9. Paul Lafargue, carrying on socialist agitation in France.

10. Helene Demuth.

11. For about a month, from August 23 to September 25, 1882, Laura accompanied her ailing father on a tour in Switzerland.

N.º 231.   des Geburts-Aktes.

Im Jahr achtzehn Hundert achtzehn am _____ des Monaths May
um _____ Uhr des _____ erschien vor mir Civilstands-Beamter der Bürgermeisterei
im Kreis _____ der Herr Heinrich Marx
wohnhaft zu _____ alt _____ Jahr, (Stand) Profession _____
und zeigte mir ein Kind von _____ Geschlechts vor, und erklärte, daß dasselbe in _____
am _____ des Monaths May um _____ Uhr des _____ von dem
Herrn Heinrich Marx (Stand) Profession _____
wohnhaft zu _____ und seiner Frau _____
erzeugt worden sey, daß dieselbe diesem ihrem Kinde den Nahmen _____ Carl
geben wollten. Nachdem gedachte Vorzeigung des Kindes und obige Erklärung in Gegenwart zweyer Zeugen,
nämlich: des _____
Jahr, (Stand) Profession _____ wohnhaft zu _____ und des _____
_____ alt _____ im Jahr, (Stand) Profession _____
_____ wohnhaft zu _____ geschehen war, so habe ich über alles dieses in
Gegenwart des Vorzeigers des Kindes und der Zeugen gegenwärtigen Akt in doppeltem Original aufgesetzt,
welche nach Vorlesung derselben vom Vorzeiger des Kindes, den Zeugen, und mit unterschrieben wurden.

Also geschehen zu _____ am Tag, Monath und Jahr wie oben.

*"Carl" Marx's birth certificate, Trier, May 5, 1818, 2 A.M. One of the
certificate's signers was his father*

(Right) Bonn University, which Marx attended from October, 1835, to August, 1836. (Below) Alte Leipziger Strasse, Berlin, where Marx lived in the winter of 1837, as a student at the University there

Berlin University (Friedrich Wilhelm Universität), where Marx was a student from October, 1836, to March, 1841

Marx's ("Carolo Henrico Marx") Doctor of Philosophy diploma, in Latin, Jena University, April 15, 1841

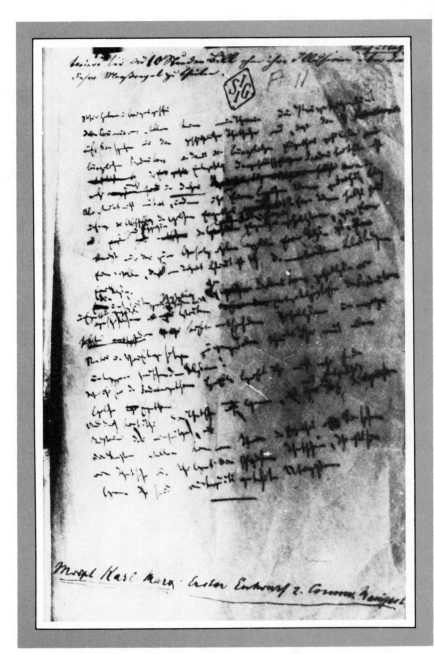

The only preserved page of Marx's draft of the Communist Manifesto, *written in December, 1847*

"Charles" Marx's French passport (good for one year), issued in Paris, August 24, 1849, the day he was expelled from France

Marx's letter of thanks to Engels, August 16, 1867, the night he completed correcting the last page proofs of Das Kapital

Ferdinand Flocon's invitation to Marx, in the name of the Provisional French Government, to return to France, March 10, 1848

Marx's letter to Friedrich Adolph Sorge (in Hoboken, New Jersey), June 20, 1881, criticizing Henry George

Marx's death certificate, recorded in Somerset House, London, March 16, 1883 (he died on March 14)

Marx's residence in Brussels, 5-7 rue d'Alliance, where he lived from May, 1845, to May, 1846

Marx's last London residence, 41 Maitland Park Road, where he lived from March, 1875, to his death on March 14, 1883

289

To Frederick Engels (in London)
Ventnor,[1] November 8, 1882

Dear Fred:

What do you say to Deprez's experiment in the Munich Electricity Exposition?[2] Almost a year has already gone by since Longuet promised to get for me the works of Deprez (especially in proof that electricity permits the transmission of power for long distances through simple telegraph wires). Specifically, an intimate friend of Deprez, Dr. D'Arsonval,[3] is a collaborator on *La Justice*[4] and has published a number of things on the former's researches. Longuet forgot every time, as usual.

With great pleasure I saw in the *"paper"* [in English] you sent me how Sherbrooke and Rivers Wilson[5] parade as *"trustees in London for the Bondholders"* [in English]! Yesterday, in the *Standard,*[6] *House of Commons debates* [in English], Gladstone was badly mauled on account of these trustees, since the above-named Rivers Wilson still occupies a high (that is, well-paid) post in the English *Public Debts* [in English] Administration. Gladstone, clearly embarrassed, first sought to *pooh-pooh* [in English] it, then at the announcement of a threatening *motion* [in English] against Rivers Wilson, Gladstone lied that he knew nothing about the Galveston and Eagle, etc., Railway Co.[7] No less gloriously did *our saintly grand old man* [in English] [Gladstone] play in the Gibraltar "Extradition."[8] One recalls that this same Gladstone had not gone through in vain his apprenticeship alongside a Graham,[9] etc., in the tricky bureaucratic oligarchy under Sir Robert Peel.

For inept lies, stupid word-twisting, rotten evasions, in the Egyptian affair,[10] Sir Charles Dilke[11] is entirely in place. He has neither the pietistic

289

1. On October 30, 1882, Marx went to Ventnor, Isle of Wight, where he remained until January 12, 1883; this was his last tour in search of health.
2. At the Exposition in 1882, the French physicist, Marcel Deprez, demonstrated the long-distance transmission of electricity from Munich to Miesbach, about forty kilometers away.
3. Jacques Arsène D'Arsonval (1851–1940).
4. The Paris daily, of which Charles Longuet was a staff member.
5. Charles Rivers Wilson (1831–1916), English colonial official.
6. London conservative daily.
7. Reference to a current political scandal in the House of Commons.
8. In August, 1882, three Cuban revolutionaries, led by Antonio Maceo, having fled from their Spanish prison in Cadiz, were extradited from Gibraltar back to Spain.
9. Sir James Graham (1792–1861), British Whig statesman.
10. The occupation of Cairo in September, 1882.
11. Sir Charles Wentworth Dilke (1843–1911), English politician and writer, was undersecretary in charge of Britain's Egyptian affairs.

casuistry of Gladstone nor the gay scorn of *quondam* Palmerston. Dilke is a simple, ill-bred parvenu, who makes himself out to be big in his churlishness.

Since I get *The Standard* here, I saw the telegram from Frankfurt you mentioned.

Apropos. I would be glad if Bernstein[12] would send me the *Yearbook*, which contains the article by Oldenburg (at least I think this is the author's name) on my theory of value.[13] Although I do not need it, still it would be better if I had before me that which was then argued. When I wrote to the little parson,[14] I was ready for everything; but in-between there had been my entire illness and the loss of my wife—a period of long mental eclipse.

The violent wind storms continue to rage here, particularly evenings and nights; early mornings are mostly rainy or at least *gloomy* [in English]; during the day, there are always good intervals, which one must catch; with it, inconstant, capricious weather. For example, last Sunday,[15] at four o'clock, I went on the Downs and walked on the bicycle path along Bonchurch, whose highest houses, rising on terraces, reach up to the path (the lowest ones are close to the sea); the path snakes, now up, now down, between the height of the Downs and the shoal at the sea. (Last time, when I was here with Tussy,[16] I did not dare climb up to the path.) Here one can stroll for hours, enjoying mountain and sea air together. It was as warm as in the summer; the sky pure blue, with only a few transparent, white little clouds; suddenly *cold rain, sky suddenly overcast* [in English]. To this I have to thank the muscle-rheumatism (on the left side of the chest, near the old *corpus delicti*); it was so violent Monday night that on Tuesday, despite my reluctance, I had to call a doctor. My *old spinster* [in English] MacLean,[17] upon my inquiry, told me that two doctors came to her house. The greatest, the most fashionable man was "*I. G. Sinclair, Physician to the Royal Hospital for Consumption*" [in English]. I asked *whether he be the old fogey whose coach I had had the displeasure of meeting almost daily before the door of her house. Indeed, he was the man* [in English]. He visits especially an *old lady* [in English] who lives here constantly, "*with whom nothing serious it was the matter,*" but "*she liked to see the doctor at least three times in the course of a week*" [in English]. I denied myself this patron. But the second doctor, whom the other lodgers consult, was, in contrast, a younger man. *Dr. James M. Williamson.* I called him; *indeed, he is a nice young*

---

12. Eduard Bernstein (1850–1932), German socialist editor and theoretician.
13. Heinrich Oldenburg, "*Die Grundlage des wissenschaftlichen Sozialismus*" [*The Foundation of Scientific Socialism*], in *Jahrbuch für Sozialwissenschaft und Sozialpolitik,* 1880.
14. Ferdinand Domela Nieuwenhuis; see Letter 249, Marx to Nieuwenhuis, February 22, 1881.
15. November 5.
16. Eleanor Marx.
17. The landlady.

fellow, nothing priestly about him [in English]. In fact, he had nothing to prescribe to me except a liniment for rubbing in. (This muscle-rheumatism,
while it lasts, causes difficulties, since it provokes unpleasant sensations,
especially when coughing.) For the rest, he apologized for the bad weather.
In regard to the cough, particularly recently also in London, when it assumed a disagreeable spasmodic character, I am my sole medical adviser, and
hope soon to get rid of it without a doctor med.

So that I should not depend too much on the capricious wind and
temperature-change when I stroll in the open air, I am obliged again to carry
with me a *respirator* [in English] in *case in need* [in English].

A great scandal was caused here by the letter in *The Standard* and in the
Globe,[18] *to that effect* [in English] that Ventnor is a *central head of typhoid fever* [in
English] and that many people have fallen victim to it in recent times. Now
there are official and unofficial answers to this "*libel*" [in English] in the local
press. But what is most comical is that the Ventnor municipal philistine
wants to make *a libel-case* [in English] against the letter writer!

Salut.

The Mohr

290

To Eleanor Marx (in London)
Ventnor,[1] 1 St. Boniface Gardens, November 10, 1882

My dear Tussychen:
[First paragraph in English] *On the whole, I cannot at all complain of Ventnor. The
weather was unsettled, tempestuous, alternately rainy, dry, sunny, chilly, etc., but
with all that very seldom foggy, a good deal of pure air, and, except a few days,
generally always a few hours fit for longer promenades. Yesterday and today the air
rather cold, but from eleven to two o'clock on the sea shore (where children are playing,
and reminding me of poor Harry)[2] and on our Undercliff walk,[3] and up to the railway
station, and even to the down, no want of sunshine.*

You must not forget, dear child, that I arrived here in no way *all right*
[in English]. On the contrary; almost continuous spasmodic coughing, much
expectoration, increasingly unsatisfactory nights in the last two weeks, in no

---

18. *The Globe and Traveller*, London conservative daily.

290

1. Marx, in search of health, was in Ventnor, Isle of Wight, from October 30, 1882, to
January 12, 1883. His health got worse.
2. Four-year-old grandson Henri Longuet.
3. When Marx was with Eleanor on the Isle of Wight, from December 29, 1881, to January
16, 1882, they used to promenade in Ventnor and St. Catherine's Point.

way a sense of well being. This could not change in one day, but there is a tendency for improvement.

At bottom, it was pleasant that in consequence of a rheumatism of the muscle, I found refuge in Dr. Williamson,[4] before Donkin's prescription could arrive from London (today). The rheumatism is so close to the old spot of my *iterated pleurisy* [in English] that the doctor, through percussion and auscultation, could convince me that *all was still right* [in English]—since the last examination by Donkin. The coughing has decreased, but Williamson at his visit today (the second) persuaded me to take another medicine; he said it would shorten the transition period up to the stage when, through fresh air and much moving about outside the house, full reconvalescence is to be expected.

With all that, I have not yet got to the point of real work, but have occupied myself with this and that, in preparation for work.

Do you have William Langland's *Complaint of Piers the Ploughman?*[5] If not, could you borrow it from Furnivall,[6] or, as it is not expensive, I could buy it from the Early English Text Society.

Furthermore, you will see if under the (old style) *Égalités* (I mean the former weekly-*Égalité*) on my table near my bed you will find an article, rather a report, on the glorification of cheap Chinese labor in Europe by *the official Paris economists*. I don't know whether the issue of Malon's former *Revue*[7] (it lies behind the sofa on a shelf of my library) treats the same Chinese subject. If so, you can send it to me, in case the *Égalité* is not found.

How is my Johnny? No more cough? Regards for him and Lenchen. And how is your own health?

I must finally write to poor Jennychen. It is painful to me; I feel that she cannot endure this pain.

Salut.

Old Nick

291

To Frederick Engels (in London)
Ventnor, November 11, 1882

Dear Fred:

I am returning the *Prolétaire*[1] to you. Hard to say who is the greater man— Lafargue, who has poured his oracular inspirations into the bosoms of Malon

---

4. James M. Williamson.
5. *The Vision of Piers the Plowman*, a fourteenth-century English poem.
6. Frederick James Furnivall (1825-1910), English philologist.
7. Benôit Malon's *La Revue Socialiste*.

291

1. *Le Prolétaire*, a Paris weekly of non-Marxist socialists ("Possibilists").

and Brousse, or these two heroes, double stars, who not only lie consciously but also lie to themselves that the outside world has nothing better to do than to "intrigue" against them, while in reality, the whole world has a skull of the same construction as this noble pair.

Lafargue has the usual stigma of the Negro tribe:[2] *no sense of shame*, I mean thereby no modesty about making himself ridiculous.

Still, the time has come, if the journal[3] is not to be wantonly ruined, unless it is the *intention* (which would be incredible) that it *should* be buried through a government lawsuit—that Lafargue put an end to his childish braggings about his future revolutionary atrocities. This time he is handsomely duped by himself. Naturally scared that some denunciatory paper might have reprinted the dreadful, antipolice, Anarchistic excerpts from the suppressed *Étendard*,[4] the latter even "more far-reaching" than Paul Lafargue, that patented oracle of *socialisme scientifique* [scientific socialism]—scared by such revolutionary rivalry, Lafargue quotes himself (and recently he has become handsomely accustomed not only to let his oracles fly into the world, but also to have "fixed" himself through self-quotations) as proof that *Étendard*, that is, *Anarchism* itself, had only copied the wisdom of Lafargue & Co., but that its realization was untimely and immature. Thus it goes with oracles sometimes; what they believe to be their own inspiration is, on the contrary, very often only a reminiscence that remained stuck in memory. And what Lafargue has written and "cited" from himself—is in fact only a reminiscence of a Bakuninist prescription. Lafargue is in fact the last pupil of Bakunin, believing in him earnestly. He should reread the pamphlet on the Alliance[5] that he wrote in collaboration with you and it would become clear to him whence he got his most recent ammunition. It took much time, in fact, before he understood Bakunin, and has misunderstood him into the bargain.

Longuet as the last Proudhonist and Lafargue as the last Bakuninist! *Que le diable les importe* [May the devil take them]!

A beautiful day today and I must go into the open (it is still only half past ten in the morning).

In my last letter[6] I wrote you I wanted to get rid of the cough without the *medical men* [in English]; but Dr. Williamson called my attention *d'une manière autoritaire* [in an authoritative manner] that despite all that I have to swallow the medicaments. In truth, the brew agrees with me; the main element in it is

---

2. Paul Lafargue, Marx's son-in-law, was a mulatto born in Cuba.
3. *L'Égalité*, a Paris socialist (Marxist) daily.
4. *L'Étendard Révolutionnaire*, a French Anarchist weekly published in Lyons.
5. In 1873, Lafargue, in collaboration with Engels and Marx, wrote *L'Alliance de la Démocratie Socialiste et l'Association Internationale des Travailleurs*, a pamphlet exposing Bakunin's machinations against the First International.
6. See Letter 288, Marx to Engels, November 8, 1882.

Quinine disulphuricum; the rest: morphine, chloroform, etc., never was absent in the previous brews.

How is it with Hartmann's[7] invention woes?

Salut.

The Mohr

292

To Frederick Engels (in London)
Ventnor, December 4, 1882

Dear Fred:

Enclosed Bebel's letter, which interested me very much. I do not believe that an industrial crisis is so imminent.[1]

On the whole, the November weather has been good, although very changeable. The first December days brought raw cold, alternating with dirty-mild dampness. Today it is fine, but despite this, I am condemned to house arrest. As I have had a trace of hoarseness (surely not as a result of talking), an unpleasant feeling in the esophagus, increased coughing, and little sleep, despite my regular, unexposed, and long walks, I had to summon the doctor again. One cannot get rid of these gentlemen so easily! It is only a catarrh in the throat; nevertheless, he believes it necessary that I keep to my room until the inflammation has gone away. In addition to some medicaments to be swallowed, he had me breathe vapors of benzine (somewhat mixed, it seems to me, with a bit of chloroform). Today—for the third time since my arrival here—he again ausculated and percussed me, and found everything otherwise in order. In a few days he will leap in again to see if the house arrest can be lifted.

What is remarkable about the article in *Plebe*[2] about my theory of value is that all three of its opponents—Laveleye,[3] Cafiero,[4] and Candelari[5]—prattle

---

7. Lev (Leo) Hartmann (1850–1908), Russian revolutionist and Populist.

292

1. On November 14, 1882, Bebel wrote to Engels from his prison in Leipzig that he could think of only two events that would bring about a revolution and do away with Bismarck's anti-Socialist laws; one event was a European war, the other a "commercial and industrial crisis."

2. *La Plebe*, an Italian newspaper in Lodi.

3. Émile Louis Victor de Laveleye (1822–1892), Belgian economist.

4. Carlo Cafiero (1846–1892), Italian Anarchist, published a condensation of *Das Kapital* in Italian.

5. Romeo Candelari, Italian journalist.

The articles by Candelari on radical economics and by Laveleye on Marx's theory of surplus value were published in *La Plebe*, October 8 and 15, 1882. The articles by Cafiero appeared in the same paper, October 22 and 29, and November 5 and 12, 1882. In the November 12 article, Cafiero cited Benoît Malon on Marx.

the same twaddle, *l'un contre l'autre* [one against the other]. The quotation on my theory of value, which Candelari cites from Malon's *Histoire Critique de l'Économie Politique* [*Critical History of Political Economy*] (Lugano, 1876), really surpasses in insipidity all these three high-flyers.

I hope that all's right in [in English] 41, Maitland Park Road.[6] I expect a few words from there, but I know that *poor* [in English] Tussy[7] is *overworked* [in English].

Salut.

The Mohr

293 _____

To Laura Lafargue (in Paris)
Ventnor, 1 St. Boniface Gardens, December 14, 1882

Dearest Cacadou:
I received *all* your letters at the right time, still I—great sinner, I!—write only now, when the General's[1] letter, just arrived, informed me of Paul's[2] arrest. The General enclosed Paul's and your letters, so that I am *au fait* [informed]. Paul will assuredly be free again in a few days.

Why did I not write to you before? Because I did not have anything especially cheerful to report, and otherwise you knew from the General's correspondence that personally I am by no means doing *badly*, and that my house arrest began only some fourteen days ago as a result of a *tracheal catarrh*, without, however, a pleurisy or bronchitis complication. *All this is very encouraging, considering that most of my contemporaries, I mean fellows of the same age, just now kick the bucket* [in English] in gratifying numbers. There are enough young jackasses to keep the old ones alive.

Recently, Paul has written *his best things*—with humor and impudence, with solidity and sprightliness—whereas *before*, a certain ultrarevolutionary phraseology here and there annoyed me; for that always appeared to me to be "hollow," and our own people should leave this specialty to the the so-called Anarchists, who in reality are supporters of the present system and want to upset nothing—these poor infantile heads are from birth, *ce n'est pas leur faute, le chaos* [it is not their fault, chaos]. Presently they come to the aid of the "*affaires véreuses cabinet*" [the "Black Cabinet," for governmental snooping into private correspondence] as "*péril social*" ["social danger"]. The worst about it

6. Marx's London address.
7. Eleanor Marx.

293

1. Frederick Engels.
2. Paul Lafargue.

is that if there were such a thing as an objective "investigating judge," he would have to proclaim publicly that they are entirely "undangerous!" One could forgive the Anarchists everything, if only they were not so too "innocent!" This does not make them "saints." It was a good joke on the part of a Pope [Julius II] who, when asked by Henry VII (the victorious antagonist of Richard III) to make a Saint out of Henry VI, replied that just because a man is an "*innocens*" (alias "idiot") he is not thereby entitled to be called "*sanctus*" ["holy one"].

Here, my child, one finds in any case better weather than in most other regions, including France and Italy. I live here as a hermit, have no contact with anybody save the visits of Doctor Williamson.

Well, child, as soon as your duties allow it (for *Paul's gallant fight with the powers that be make the man sympathetic, to use this, a French penny-a-liner's phrase* [in English]), *come here and live here with me!*

Some recent Russian publications, *printed in Holy Russia, not abroad, show the great run of my theories in that country.[3] Nowhere my success is to me more delightful; it gives me the satisfaction that I damage a power, which besides England, is the true bulwark of the old society* [in English].

Yours, Nick

294

To Frederick Engels (in London)
Ventnor, December 18, 1882

Dear Fred:
Retour des MSS [Return of the manuscript];[1] *very good!*

Doctor has just been here again; I cannot say that I see any progress, rather the contrary. It is not cold outside, but rainy, damp, and the doctor maintains he cannot permit me to go out until there is a nice day; otherwise he would take no responsibility.

Au diable! il faut patienter [Devil take it! One must have patience]!
Salut.

The Mohr

---

3. The reference is probably to V. P. Voronzov's Preface to his book, *Sudby Kapitalisma v Rossyi* [*The Fate of Capitalism in Russia*] (St. Petersburg, 1882), in which he speaks of the Marxist influence on Russian socialists.

294

1. Engels, *Die Entwicklung des Sozialismus von der Utopie zur Wissenschaft* [*The Development of Socialism from Utopia to Science*], which he completed in September, 1882.

295

Postcard to Eleanor Marx (in London)
Ventnor, 1 St. Boniface Gardens, December 23, 1882

Dear Child:
From Laura's letter (which Engels forwarded to me today),[1] I see that Jennychen has again been afflicted with a virulent inflammation. I fear the worst, if it is neglected. We must consider (and do speak about it to Lenchen[2] before you leave for here) whether we should not relieve her of Harry[3] or even have him come here, in case of necessity. How can Jennychen find time for curing her illness, with all these babies together? And will our Johnny[4] be neglected (sanitarily) if another one, instead of him, leaves there?

Harry is an additional burden to the already difficult condition of poor Jennychen.

Bring along the *Physiology* (I don't know if it is by *Rank* or *Ranke*[5]). In addition, the *booklet* by Freeman[6] (*History of Europe*), which contains chronological tables; it is in my bedroom, on the shelves with newspapers, etc.

[no signature]

296

To Eleanor Marx (in London)
Ventnor, 1 St. Boniface Gardens, January 8, 1883

Dear Tussychen:
On Saturday, I received a few lines from Dr. Williamson, with an enclosure of a letter to Williamson from Dr. F. Bayshawe, dated January 4, 1883, 5 Warrior Square, St. Leonards on Sea, wherein it says:

"*We had a week of almost continuous rain or moist air, which gave place on the second to dry weather, of varying direction. Since that we have had sunshine each afternoon, tho' not much of it. I will endeavour to send you some further statistics*

295

1. On December 21, 1882, Laura Lafargue wrote to Engels: "Jenny is in a very precarious condition.... The inflammation she suffers from was rather worse than better when I saw her and she is altogether out of spirits. I am doing all I can to get her to see the doctor again."
2. Helene Demuth.
3. Henri Longuet, Jenny's second son.
4. Jean-Laurent-Frederick Longuet.
5. Johannes Ranke (1836–1916), a professor of physiology and anthropology at the University of Munich.
6. Edward Augustus Freeman (1823–1892), an English historian.

tomorrow. I believe we may say generally that the climate of Hastings is dryer than much of the South Coast, tho' this may be at the expense of some warmth, etc." [The whole paragraph in English].

Here, on Saturday (January 6), we had good weather during the noon hours; yesterday the weather was dry, but cooler; it is always sunniest on the Esplanade. Yesterday and the day before yesterday, I took walks; the weather promises to be good today. In general, it is coolish outside the direct sunshine. At any rate, there is a prospect for a crescendo of better temperature.

Hastings still remains a possibility, when prospects here are disappointing. Apart from that, there comes a moment when a change of locations is useful in and for itself. This much we know now, that the change from Ventnor to Hastings does make some sense, but not other places on the South Coast where conditions are like those of the Isle of Wight.

I still have a hard struggle with the accumulation of mucus. On Saturday morning, when I got out of bed, I even had a spasmodic attack, so that for some seconds I vainly gasped for air. I believed it came from nervous irritation; the anxiety over Jennychen! I don't have to say anything more about it. I would have hurried over to Argenteuil *immediately*, but to place the burden of perhaps another sick guest on the child! For nobody can guarantee me that the trip *would* not *have punished me with a relapse* [in English], which I have hitherto happily escaped. But it remains hard not to be able to go to the child.

With best regards, Old Nick

297

From letter to Eleanor Marx (in London)
Ventnor, January 9, 1883

My dear good child:
How dear of you to write so often and in such detail; still I do not wish to *encroach on the very little "free" time you have to dispose of* [in English]. I received your letter after sending off mine, after the return from my walk along the seashore. From Paris I have no further news.

Today I was at the point of "strolling on foot" again—*despite the noise of the wind* [in English]—when my doctor came; he ordered me to remain indoors, since it was cold outside. He examined me again. Everything is the same, insofar as the cold in the head is *chronic* (hence the continuing hoarseness), but from a "higher" standpoint my condition is better in that the suspicious spots are not affected. The semipermanent cough was already burdensome enough, but it is now loathsome because of the daily *vomissements* [vomitings]. This makes any kind of work often impossible, and the doctor believes—he still believes, *and that is something* [in English]—he will be able to cure me of this torment (with a little remedy which he has just prescribed). *Qui vivra, verra* [He who lives will see].

Apropos! In my bedroom somewhere, or on my work table, in the briefcase or in some *little box* [in English], there must still be a few copies of the Algerian photograph. *If you find them, you might send me two photographs. One of them I have promised to Madame Williamson* [in English]. . . .

Kiss my grandson¹ for me [in English].

Farewell [in English], *Old Nick*

298

Marx's Last Letter to Engels, Written About Two Months Before His Death

To Frederick Engels (in London)
Ventnor,¹ January 10, 1883

Dear Fred:
It was very good of you to send me immediately Lafargue's letter;² it very much set my mind at rest, the more so as today I received at the same time a letter from Lafargue which indicates an improvement in [Jenny Longuet's] health. I am entirely in accord with you that *under no circumstances* must Johnny³ now leave [London]. This does not come into the question until Jenny is fully recovered.⁴ It would be unforgivable to make the child's condition more difficult. I am writing directly to Longuet about it today. I would appreciate it if you yourself would write a few words to Jennychen to the same effect. Johnny will thereby not yet be lost to the *armée territoriale.*⁵

It is remarkable how every nervous excitement immediately attacks my throat, as the Red [Ferdinand] Wolff did his brother, the grain speculator. Shortly before, at the first shock from the bad news from Paris, I had a

297

1. Seven-year old Jean-Laurent-Frederick Longuet, who was in Eleanor's care in London while his mother was dying in Argenteuil.

298

1. Marx, in his continued search for a cure, again went to Ventnor, Isle of Wight, on October 30, 1882, and remained there until January 12, 1883, leaving upon the news of the death of Jenny Longuet, his favorite daughter, in France on January 11, 1883.
2. On January 6, 1883, Paul Lafargue wrote to Engels about Jenny Longuet's grave illness and about the efforts of his wife, Laura Lafargue, to help her dying sister in Argenteuil.
3. Six-year-old Jean-Laurent-Frederick Longuet, Marx's favorite grandson.
4. She died the day after Marx wrote this letter.
5. Territorial army, meaning Parisians. "Johnny" Longuet actually lived well into the twentieth century, dying in 1938, after having been a leader of the French socialist party.

spasmodic coughing attack, feeling as if I were choking to death. Poor Jennychen must have often experienced similar highly *distressing feeling* [in En-
glish] during her asthma attacks.

In regard to "Hepnerchen,"[6] my view is to treat him in a "businesslike"
way. He is, after all, free to publish our Preface in his Leipzig edition, and to
point out that last year the Russians published a new translation.[7] If he does
not consider it worth the effort to print the *Manifesto without a new Preface by
us*, then let him do or not do as he pleases. For "our crowd," it is second
nature "to point a pistol at the breast," so one must consider Hepnerchen's
behavior as self-evident.

I received the annual account of 1881 from *poor* [in English] Meissner; it
seems to have been a bad year, which is of little importance since, according
to his own report, the edition[8] was being "exhausted" in the year 1882; the
less he sold in 1881, therefore, the more he must have sold in 1882. My long
silence must have appeared to him as a will-o'-the-wisp. Mohammed finally
comes to him; alas, not yet, what he would have most preferred would have
been a package of newly revised sheets.[9] Since the beginning of my long and
only occasionally interrupted "house arrest," in consequence of my continuing sickness—or to use a South German *aesthetic* expression, à la Madame
Karl Blind, formerly Cohen, as a result of my daily "puking" (from the
coughing)—I have been little able to make any progress with the revision.
Still I believe that with patience and pedantic self-control I shall be able to get
on the track again.[10]

The Mohr

299

To Eleanor Marx (last letter) (in London)
Ventnor, January 10, 1883

Dear Child:
The enclosed letter from Lafargue (be so good as to return it to me later) has
put my mind at ease about Jennychen,[1] even though Lafargue presents the

---

6. Adolf Hepner, a German socialist editor.
7. A Russian edition, *Manifest kommunistitcheskoy Partii* [*Manifesto of the Communist Party*], appeared in Geneva in 1882.
8. Volume I of *Das Kapital*.
9. For the third German edition of *Das Kapital*.
10. Marx never completed Volumes II and III of *Das Kapital*, which were published after his
death by Engels.

299
1. Jenny Longuet.

matter perhaps too optimistically for my sake; still, it seems as if the immediate danger is over.[2]

The reports about Wolf,[3] Pa[4] (*who is now the idolater of* [in English] Wolf), etc., are charming.

Under present circumstances (and in this Engels also agrees with me), the moment is not favorable for sending Johnny back to Argenteuil. He *must not go back*, until Jenny is again in a condition to keep house. One must keep in mind, not the secondary considerations, but only the main things, which are those that had nearly killed Jenny. A few months more or less do not matter, entirely apart from the fact that the poor lad would sink into disorder there.

I hope, Tussychen, that you will immediately write to Jennychen in the sense of these lines. I will send a few words to Longuet today, to the office of *La Justice* .

You must report to Johnnychen[5] the news about his siblings; *of course* [in English], you will also report the main contents of Lafargue's letter to Lenchen.[6]

Yesterday the weather was frightful; today, too, it is far from "brilliant;" wet. Nevertheless, I think of taking my "constitutional" [in English] today. . . .

[The letter is broken off here.]

---

2. On January 11, one day after this letter was written, Jenny Longuet died of cancer in Argenteuil.
3. Nickname for grandson Edgar Longuet.
4. Nickname for grandson Marcel Longuet.
5. Seven-year-old grandson Jean-Laurent-Frederick Longuet, who was staying with Eleanor in London.
6. Helene Demuth.

LETTERS
TO AND ABOUT
FERDINAND
LASSALLE
(1849 - 1868)

INTRODUCTION

Ferdinand Lassalle was a noted historic figure who should be better known than he is in the English-speaking world, which is the reason for the inclusion of these Marx letters to and about him.

A brilliant jurist, orator, scholar, and labor organizer, Lassalle, as a young man, was close to Marx and his communist circle (although never a communist himself) in Brussels and Cologne. Subsequently, while Marx lived in penurious exile in London, Lassalle pursued his triumphant, albeit flamboyant, career in Germany, culminating in his founding of the first German national labor party—*Allgemeiner Deutsche Arbeiterverein*—in 1863. Later, the *Arbeiterverein* merged with other labor organizations to form Germany's powerful, Marxist-oriented Social-Democratic Party. At the age of thirty-nine, Lassalle, after a long-standing relationship with a loyal older woman, Countess von Hatzfeldt, was killed in a duel—which Marx and Engels considered silly—over a nineteen-year-old girl.

Marx's attitude toward Lassalle, who was seven years his junior, was characterized by love-hate feelings. While Lassalle admired and helped Marx whenever asked, the latter was clearly jealous of the power, fame, influence, and wealth achieved by Lassalle through sheer talents and guts. Deeply envious, and yet admiring, Marx indulged in scathing anti-Semitic remarks about Lassalle ("Nigger-Jew," etc.) in his private letters, as can be seen in the following pages.

300

From letter to Ferdinand Freiligrath (in Cologne)
Paris, July 31, 1849

Dear Freiligrath:
I confess that Lassalle's behavior surprises me very much. I had applied [for financial assistance] to him personally,[1] and as I had at one time lent money to the Countess herself,[2] and as I know Lassalle's affection for me, I was far from anticipating such compromising [publicizing Marx's distress]. I had, on the contrary, recommended to him the highest discretion. For me, the biggest embarrassment is preferable to public begging. I wrote him to that effect.[3]

The whole story irritates me inexpressibly....

Yours, K. Marx

301

From letter to Ferdinand Lassalle (in Düsseldorf)
London, February 23, 1852

Dear Lassalle:
I would still like to know whether my second letter has also failed to reach you.[1] I know that you are exact in your replies, and thus I must ascribe the delay of news from you to some mischance.

Since my last letter, the state of my health has again improved, although I still suffer greatly from eye trouble. Social conditions, on the other hand, have worsened. I have received a definite refusal from the publisher for my

---

300

1. The penniless Marx was then under orders of expulsion from Paris, which he left for London on August 24, 1849.
2. Sophie von Hatzfeldt, Lassalle's client and mistress; as a successful lawyer in Düsseldorf, he won a divorce for her after a lengthy and notorious battle through thirty-six different tribunals.
3. Marx to Freiligrath, London, September 5, 1849: "Lassalle seems to be insulted by my letter to you and the one that I wrote to him. This was surely far from my intention, and I would have written him so, if my present situation [as a new refugee utterly without means] did not make letter writing a real burden."

301

1. These letters have not been found.

book on economics;[2] my anti-Proudhon manuscript, which has been wandering in Germany for a year, has likewise failed to reach harbor;[3] the financial crisis has at last reached a height comparable to the commercial crisis now felt in New York and London. Unfortunately, unlike the gentlemen merchants I do not have the resource of bankruptcy. Herr Bonaparte was in a similar situation when he risked his *coup d'état*.[4] ...

    Salut.

K. Marx

302

From letter to Frederick Engels (in Manchester)
London, August 26, 1854

Dear Engels:
... I have received a letter from Lassalle in which he triumphantly announces that the seven- or eight-year-old Hatzfeldt war is over.[1] *Enfin* [At last]! With a "triumphant" settlement for the Old Lady,[2] whose virtue and, even more, her purse seem to have come out of the battle equally "vierge" ["virginal"]. Lassalle now intends to move his residence to Berlin, but has already heard intimations of police difficulties....

Totus tuus [Entirely yours], *K.M.*

303

To Ferdinand Lassalle (in Paris)
London, July 28, 1855

Dear Lassalle:
I have been in the country for some weeks now, in the cottage of a friend,[1] who had to make a trip to Scotland. So it came about that your letter reached

---

2. In February, 1845, Marx made a contract for a two-volume work on economics with the Darmstadt publisher Karl Wilhelm Leske, who canceled it two years later.
3. The German translation of Marx's *Poverty of Philosophy* was not published until 1885.
4. Louis Bonaparte (Napoleon III) made his *coup d'état* on December 2, 1851.

302

1. The battle over the Hatzfeldt divorce, marked by scandal and flamboyance, lasted from 1846 to 1854.
2. Countess Sophie von Hatzfeldt was then forty-nine years old, Lassalle twenty-nine.

303

1. Peter Imandt, in whose cottage in Camberwell, a London suburb, Marx stayed from July to September 12, 1855.

me only yesterday. For the rest, I have taken measures that letters should be forwarded to me immediately from the city.

I am, of course, surprised to know you to be so near to London without thinking of coming over here for a few days. I hope you will come and discover how short and inexpensive the trip from Paris to London is. If the doors of France were not hermetically closed to me, I would surprise you in Paris.

I have a few friends in Paris, but (at this moment I am not writing from the city) I can send you their addresses only when I get back to Soho, where they are kept.

Bacon says that really important people have so many relations with nature and the world, so many objects of interest, that they easily console themselves for every loss. I do not belong to these important people. The death of my child[2] has deeply shaken my heart and brain, and I feel the loss as keenly as on the first day. My poor wife is also completely *downbroken* [in English].

If you see Heine again, give him my regards.

Yours, K.M.

304

From letter to Ferdinand Lassalle (in Düsseldorf)
Manchester, November 8, 1855

Dear Lassalle:

You receive this very belated reply. On the one hand, I received your letters later because I was in Manchester and they were in London, and my wife did not know exactly whether or not I had left Manchester. On the other hand, I have been so afflicted by the most atrocious toothaches that what happened to me was what Hegel demanded of sensuous consciousness, namely, that at the railroad station, where this was to pass over in the self-consciousness, my hearing and sight vanished, and thus also my writing.

In regard to your question about the book by Coffinières, entitled, *Les Mystères de la Bourse*,[1] I believe that this miserable concoction is still among my books left behind in the Fatherland. During my first stay in Paris[2] I was misled by the title to buy the book. Herr Coffinières is a lawyer who, *au fond*

---

2. Edgar Marx ("Musch"), Marx's only son, who died on April 6, 1855, at the age of eight.

304

1. Antoine Simeon Gabriel Coffinières, *De la bourse et des spéculations sur les effets publics* [*The Stock Exchange and the Speculations in Stocks*] (Paris, 1824).
2. Marx lived in Paris from the end of October, 1843, to February 3, 1845.

[at bottom], knows nothing about the stock exchange and warns against the "juristical" frauds of the *"agents de change"* [money-changers]. Hence there is nothing to be learned from the book, neither facts nor theory, not even entertaining anecdotes. Furthermore, it is thoroughly dated. "Let him go, fair Donna"—that is, Coffinières—"He is not worth your wrath."

Weerth is now, after a long trip across the Continent (he returned from the West Indies at the end of July), back in Manchester. In eight days he will again sail for the tropics. It is very amusing to listen to him. He has seen, experienced and observed much. Crossed most of South, West, and Central America. On horseback across the pampas. Climbed the Chimborazo. Also stayed in California. If he no longer writes feuilletons,[3] he now speaks them and the listener has the additional advantage of live action and roguish laughter. For the rest, he raves about the life in the West Indies and has nothing good to say about the human sweepings and the weather of the local Northern climate. And, indeed, it is bad, very bad....

Yours, K.M.

305

From letter to Frederick Engels (in Manchester)
London, March 5, 1856

Dear Frederic:
...*Levy.*[1] Sent here by the Düsseldorf workers[2] with a dual mandate. (1) *Denunciation of Lassalle.* And after a *very sharp* examination, I believe *they are right.* Since the countess received her 300,000 taler [as her divorce settlement], Lassalle has completely changed; deliberately repulsing workers, sybarite, flirting with the blue bloods. Furthermore, they reproach him with constantly exploiting the Party for his *private muck* and wanting to utilize the workers themselves in *private crime* in the interest of the [Hatzfeldt] case.

The case came to an end thus: Count Hatzfeldt's[3] business manager, Stockum, who, you know, was later sentenced by the Court of Assizes to five years in jail, quarreled with the Count. He let Lassalle know that he possesses documents that would put the count in jail for perjury, forgery, etc. Lassalle promised him [Stockum] 10,000 taler. Lassalle, furthermore, per-

---

3. The poet Georg Weerth contributed feuilletons and other articles when he was on the staff of the *Neue Rheinische Zeitung*, of which Marx was editor-in-chief in 1848–49.

305
1. Gustav Levy, German socialist.
2. Members of the Communist League.
3. Edmund, Count von Hatzfeldt-Wildenburg, Sophie's husband.

suaded Chief Procurator Kösteritz (who was compelled to resign because of this affair) to let Count Hatzfeldt know that a bill of indictment against him was pending. Hatzfeldt fled to Paris, when Lassalle handed him over the embarrassing papers and took back the bill of indictment upon his *signing the agreement* with the countess. (Kösteritz naturally acted purely as an instrument.) Thus, not his [Lassalle's] juristic acumen but a thoroughly dirty intrigue brought a sudden end to the case. The 10,000 taler to Stockum, he did not pay, and the workers say rightly that such a breach of faith can be excused only if he handed over the money to the Party instead of producing it for the countess. They are telling a mass of private dirtiness, which I cannot recount because I have forgotten one after the other. Among other things: Lassalle gambled with foreign government securities, for which the Düsseldorf man Scheuer advanced him money. They lost. Scheuer went bankrupt. Lassalle wins the case. Scheuer demands the money he had advanced him. Lassalle refers him mockingly to Paragraph No. 6 of the code, which prohibits gambling on the foreign stock exchanges. The workers say that they would have let Lassalle do anything, on the pretext that he were honorably involved in the case.

Now that he won the case, instead of asking to be paid by the countess and making himself independent, he lives disgracefully under her yoke as *homme entretenu* [kept man], *without any pretext whatever* [in English]. He had always boasted about what he would do when he won the case. Now he deliberately put this aside as demanding, superfluous instruments. On New Year's Day, he attended a (private) meeting, where a French colonel was present. To everybody's surprise, in the presence of sixty workers, he spoke of nothing but the "War of Civilization Against Barbarism," of Western nations against Russia. His plan was to go to Berlin, to play the great lord there, and to open a salon. Upon his return from there, he promised the countess, in Levy's presence, to create for her "a court of literati." Again in Levy's presence, he has constantly expressed his "hankerings for dictatorship" (he appears to view himself far differently from the way we view him; he considers himself world conquering, because he had been ruthless in a private intrigue, as if a really important man would sacrifice ten years to such a bagatelle), etc., etc. An example of how dangerous he is: In order to smuggle a man from the Workers' Party into the police as an alleged spy, he *gave him one of my letters*, of which he [the spy] was to say that he had stolen it from Lassalle, so as to legitimate himself. Furthermore, the workers say: Considering his diplomatic manner, he would never have appeared so rough against them if he did not intend to go over to the bourgeois party. Still, he feels he has enough influence so that in a moment of insurrection he could talk the masses out of it by climbing on the table and haranguing them, etc. Levy says that the hatred for him is so great that, no matter what we may decide, the workers would massacre him if they now found him in the movement in Düsseldorf. For the rest, they are convinced that he would act differently in time, should anything suspicious reach his ears.

All these are details, overheard, and partly written down. The *whole* has made a *definite* impression on me and Freiligrath, despite my affection for Lassalle and my mistrust of workers' gossip. I told Levy: It is naturally impossible to come to a conclusion on the basis of a one-sided report; suspicion is useful in all circumstances; one should continue to watch the man, but for the time being avoid any public sensation. Perhaps we will find the occasion to force Lassalle to take a clear position, etc., etc....

The second object of Levy's mission was to bring me information on the condition of the workers in the Rhine Province....

Salut.

Yours, K.M.

306

From letter to Frederick Engels (in Manchester)
London, May 8, 1857

Dear Frederick:
... Enclosed Lassalle's letter,[1] which you should return to me early next week, after reporting it to Lupus. How should I act toward the fellow? Answer or not? The comical vanity of the lad, who wants to be famous by force and who, without any reason, writes seventy-five sheets on Greek philosophy,[2] will amuse you.[3] ...

Yours, K.M.

307

To Ferdinand Lassalle (in Düsseldorf)
London, December 21, 1857

Dear Lassalle:
Of the various letters you mention, I received only the one you sent via Freiligrath. I did not answer, or rather I waited for a private opportunity to

306

1. Not available.
2. Lassalle, *Die Philosophie des Herakleitos des Dunkeln von Ephesos* [*The Philosophy of Heraclitus the Obscure of Ephesus*], 2 vols. (Berlin, 1858).
3. Engels to Marx, May 11, 1857: "Herewith Lassalle's letter. Through and through the silly Jew ... That there is nothing to the fellow, we of course know, but it is difficult to find positive ground on which to break with him directly, particularly since one has heard nothing further from the Düsseldorf workers."

reply—for reasons that are not to be reported properly in writing. In addition, I remark that it was you who *first* broke off our correspondence, in that you did not answer my letter from Manchester[1] for more than a year.

My thanks for [in English] *Heraclitus.*[2] I have always had a great tenderness for that philosopher, whom, among the classics, I prefer to all others except Aristotle. The [later][3] philosophy—Epicurus (especially he), the Stoics and Skeptics, I had made an object of *special* study,[4] but more out of [political] than philosophical interest. While I [express] my thanks, [I say] that I have *not* yet received the book. [Nutt] will send it as soon as he...[text damaged].

... write you about the Ministry. You know my views of Palmerston which I have not changed. Apart from that, I am not familiar with the newspaper, since no Austrian journal is to be found here, hence I do not know its general tendency. By all means, I would be interested in receiving a few issues.[5]

I live here very isolated, since all my friends have left London. Moreover, I do not want any contact. *Relativement parlant* [relatively speaking], Freiligrath is doing tolerably well as manager of a Swiss bank, and he is the same invariably amiable, worthy chap. Lupus and Engels are, as always, in Manchester. We are still mourning the loss of Weerth.

The present commercial crisis has spurred me to work seriously on the Outline of Political Economy[6] and to prepare something on the current crisis. I am compelled to kill the day ... with work for a living. Only the night is left for *real* work but indisposition [intervenes] to interrupt. Have not yet ... looked around for a bookdealer. ... I cannot write you any news, since I live as a hermit. My wife has been very ill last winter and summer, but has now recovered somewhat.

If you have Dr. Elsner's address, send him my regards.

307

1. See Letter 304, Marx to Lassalle, November 8, 1855.
2. Lassalle, *Die Philosophie des Herakleitos des Dunkeln von Ephesos* [*The Philosophy of Heraclitus the Obscure of Ephesus*].
3. This bracketed word and other elisions throughout the balance of the letter indicate damaged paper in the original.
4. Marx's doctoral dissertation: *Difference Between the Democritean and Epicurean Philosophy of Nature* (1841).
5. In his letter of December 17, 1857, to Marx, Lassalle included an invitation to Marx from his cousin, Max Friedländer, to contribute to the Vienna daily, *Die Presse*, of which the latter was editor. Marx temporarily refused, but began to write for it on October 25, 1861, continuing to do so for over a year.
6. Marx published his first book on the subject, *Critique of Political Economy*, in 1859.

The old jackass Ruge has made, as I hear, an attempt to renew his *Deutsche Jahrbücher.*[7] History will not go back so far as to make this possible.

Yours, K.M.

308

From letter to Frederick Engels (in Manchester)
London, December 22, 1857

Dear Frederick:

You have triumphantly saved me from the claws of the fisc,[1] and praised be thy name—Hallelujah!

Enclosed a letter (with another enclosure) from the great Lassalle,[2] in which he informs me positively that he has begun to become seriously known by his fame in Berlin. These effusions of a beautiful spirit will delight you and Lupus. The worthy Lassalle has worked on philosophy, the *Heraclitus*, the way he had on the Hatzfeldt case and finally won it, if he is to be believed. It seems, in fact, that the Old Ones—philologists and Hegelians— were surprised to witness such a *posthumous* blossoming of a past epoch. But we will see the thing ourselves, and even though a gift horse, will look deep into its mouth—on the express condition, of course, that the Heraclitus does not smell of garlic. *Fancy only this fellow going up and down the streets of Berlin and "asking for himself" strutting like a peacock, a stride and a stand: biting his lips, with "a political regard" as who should say: "This is the man who has written Heraclit* [in English]." Perhaps the lad can be useful to us in digging up book pub- lishers, assuming that he does not fear that his fame, which he is also seeking in the economic field, would suffer from competition and a loss of renown. I wrote to Friedländer through Herr Lassalle that I am also "anti-French," but not less so than "anti-English" and that I could least of all write for "Lord Pam" [Palmerston]. Thus, I have turned down the thing. If Friedländer sends me a copy of *Die Presse* so that I can see whose spiritual child it is, and if

---

7. Arnold Ruge had published *Deutsche Jahrbücher für Wissenschaft und Kunst*, a learned journal, in Leipzig from 1841 until its suppression by the censorship in January, 1843.

308

1. See Letter 74, Marx to Engels, December 18, 1857, appealing for money to pay his taxes.

2. On December 17, 1857, Lassalle informed Marx that he had asked his cousin Max Friedländer, editor of the Vienna *Presse*, to invite him as a contributor to the paper.

those fellows want me to write weekly merely a *money article*, for which, of course, they must shell out, then I could at any rate agree. In this *case* [in English], there can be no question of politics.

I have written Lassalle briefly and cooly.[3]...

Yours, K.M.

309

From letter to Frederick Engels (in Manchester)
London, February 1, 1858

Dear Frederick:
... *Heraclitus the Obscure* by Lassalle the Bright is basically a very flabby piece of work. With each of the many images by which Heraclitus works out for himself the unity of affirmation and negation, in steps Lassalle and takes the opportunity of presenting us, always at full length, with some extract from Hegel's *Logic*, which hardly gains by this process; he is like a schoolboy who has to prove in his lesson that he has his "essence," "appearance," and "dialectical process" down pat. And when the schoolboy has acquired such speculation, one may be sure that despite all he will be able to carry on this process of thought only according to the prescribed recipe and in the sacred forms. That is exactly the case with our Lassalle. The fellow *[Kerl]* seems to have tried to make Hegel's *Logic* clear to himself through Heraclitus and never to have tired of perpetually starting this process anew. In regard to erudition, we have here an enormous exhibition of it. But every expert knows how easy it is to compile this sort of display of quotations, when one has the time and money, and, like Lassalle, can have the Bonn University library sent direct to his house whenever he likes. One can see what a singular swell the fellow appears to himself in this philological finery, moving with all the grace of a chap who wears fashionable dress for the first time in his life. Since most philologists do *not* have the speculative mind which predominates in Heraclitus, every Hegelian has the indisputable advantage of understanding what the philologist does not understand. (It would, at any rate, be strange if a fellow, just because he had learned Greek, became a philosopher in *Greek* when he was not one in *German*.) But instead of simply taking all this for granted, Mr. Lassalle treats it in a quasi-Lessing manner. In long-winded legal terminology, the Hegelian interpretation is justified against the false

---

3. See Letter 307, Marx to Lassalle, December 21, 1857.

constructions of the philologists, false because of their lack of special knowledge. So that we have the double pleasure, first, of seeing dialectical things, which we had almost forgotten, reconstructed for us in all their amplitude, and secondly, of having this "speculative heritage" vindicated against the unspeculative philologists as the particular philological and juridical craftiness and erudition of Mr. Lassalle. For the rest, despite the fellow's boast that Heraclitus has up to now been a book with seven seals, he has added absolutely nothing new, in the main point, to what Hegel has said in his History of Philosophy. He only brings out in detail what naturally could have been done amply enough in two printer's pages. Still less does it occur to this bloke [*Bursche*] to betray any critical ideas on dialetics itself. If all the fragments of Heraclitus were printed together, they would hardly fill half a printer's sheet. Only a bloke who prints books at the expense of that dreadful "person" [Countess von Hatzfeldt], can afford to give to the world two volumes of sixty sheets on such a pretext.

There is a sentence in *Heraclitus the Obscure* where, in order to explain the change of all things into their opposites, he says: "So gold changes into all things, and all things change into gold." Gold, says Lassalle, in this context means money (which is correct) and money is value. Therefore, the Ideal is the Universal; the One (value) and Things are the Real; the Particular is the Many. He utilizes this startling insight in order to give us, in a lengthy note, an earnest account of his discoveries in the science of political economy. Every word is a blunder, but presented with extraordinary pretentiousness. From this one note I can see that the fellow is proposing to present political economy in the Hegelian manner in his second big opus.[1] He will learn, to his regret, that to bring a science by criticism to the point where it can be dialectically presented, is a totally different thing from applying an abstract, ready-made system of logic to mere inklings of such a system.

But as I wrote you soon after his first self-enraptured letter, the old Hegelians and philologists must in reality have been pleased to find such an old-fashioned character in a young man who passes for a great revolutionary. In addition, he flatters and curtseys in all directions in order to ensure a favorable reception. As soon as I have run through the stuff I will send it to you.

Salut.

Yours, K.M.

309

1. In 1864, Lassalle published his book on political science: *Herr Bastiat-Schulze von Delitzsch, der ökonomische Julian, oder: Kapital und Arbeit* [*Herr Bastiat-Schulze von Delitzsch, the Economic Julian, or Capital and Labor*] (Berlin, 1864).

310

To Ferdinand Lassalle (in Düsseldorf)
London, February 22, 1858

Dear Lassalle:
Nutt[1] sent me *Heraclitus*. As soon as I have read it, I will report to you my opinion.[2] But you must be patient for some time, as at this moment I have extraordinarily little free time. Personally I had not investigated the Stoics' relations to Heraclitus from the aspect of the philosophy of nature, because it seemed to me to be immature. In Epicurus, on the other hand, one can demonstrate that, although he starts out from the Democritean philosophy of nature, he turns the points upside down everywhere. One can hardly blame Cicero and Plutarch that they did not understand this, since even gifted persons like Bayle and even *ipsissimus* [his very own self] Hegel had not detected it. Moreover, one cannot expect from the latter, who was the first to comprehend the whole history of philosophy, that he be a wood carver in details.

You will see in the newspapers that Palmerston has been overthrown. Those who knew the old rascal best are mostly inclined to the view that his recent blunders have been *deliberate* in order to facilitate his exit pro tempore. They say that it has been *le dernier but de toute sa vie* [the highest aim of his life] to bring about a war between England and France, which he now believes to have achieved, so that other hands can occupy themselves with the execution of *his* plan and that when the imbroglio has advanced sufficiently, *the nation will be forced to call again upon him* [in English]. The latter view may be too crafty, but it seems to be certain that Pam [Palmerston] in no way resigned *unwillingly*.

In regard to your cousin,[3] I am prepared for one thing, but which I presume the *Presse* is not ready to accept—namely, that all I could engage myself for would be *one* weekly article on commerce, finance, etc., in the three countries, England, France, and the United States of America, depending upon the interest of the moment. This is the *most possible* form for also attacking Bonaparte.[4] It is, moreover, the form in which I would have absolutely nothing to do with the *Presse* politically. At this moment, a great deal of ignorance of *French* financial conditions and French economic conditions in general seems to me to prevail. The question is whether this matter interests

310
1. David Nutt (d. 1863), English publisher and bookdealer.
2. See Letter 312, Marx to Lassalle, May 31, 1858.
3. Max Friedländer, editor of the Vienna daily, *Die Presse*.
4. Napoleon III.

the *Presse*, or rather its readers, sufficiently. I would ask £1 for such a weekly article. In addition, I must receive some back numbers of the *Presse*, so that I can see whether my principles will altogether permit me to work for the paper. However that may be, thank your cousin in my name for being so kind as to think of me.

I want to tell you the state of my work on political economy. I have been in the process of completing it for several months. But the thing moves very slowly, because subjects one has made the chief aim of one's studies, at the moment that one is ready for conclusions, show new aspects and solicit rethinking. Added to that, I am not master of my time, but rather its slave. Only the nights are left for myself, but frequent liver attacks and relapses disturb this night work. In view of all these conditions, it would be most agreeable for me to publish the whole work in piecemeal issues [*Heften*]. This would perhaps also have the advantage of more easily finding a publisher with small working capital who would not be stuck in the enterprise. You would of course oblige me if you find such an enterpreneur in Berlin. When I speak of *Heften*, I mean ones like Vischer's *Aesthetics*.[5]

The work to which I am referring is *Critique of Political Economy*, or, if you like, the system of bourgeois economy critically presented. It is at once a presentation and, thereby, a critique of that system. I am by no means clear as to how many printed sheets the whole thing will make. If I had the time and the means to finish the whole before giving it to the public, I would condense it greatly, since I have always liked the method of condensing. This way, however—perhaps better for the understanding of the public, but certainly to the harm of the format—printed in serial *Heften*, the matter necessarily becomes somewhat attenuated. *Notabene*: As soon as you know that the thing is to be undertaken in Berlin *or not*, be so kind as to write me, since if it does not go in Berlin, I will try in Hamburg. Another point is that I have to be paid by the publisher—a necessity that may frustrate the matter in Berlin.

The presentation, I mean the style, is entirely scientific, hence not repugnant to the police in the ordinary sense. The whole is divided essentially into six booklets. 1. Capital (contains some introductory chapters). 2. Landed property. 3. Wage labor. 4. The State. 5. International trade. 6. World market. Of course, I cannot help making occasionally critical comments on other economists, specifically a polemic against Ricardo, insofar as he, *qua* citizen, is compelled to commit blunders *even from a strictly economic viewpoint*. Altogether, however, the critique and history of political economy and socialism is to constitute the subject of another work. Lastly, the brief *historical sketch* of economic categories and relationships, to make a third

5. Friedrich Theodor Vischer, *Aesthetik oder Wissenschaft des Schoenen* [*Aesthetics or Science of the Beautiful*], 4 vols. (Reutlingen, Leipzig, and Stuttgart, 1845–1857).

[book]. After all, I have the misgivings that now, having brought fifteen years of study so far, stormy movements from the outside are likely to interfere. *Never mind* [in English]. If I finish too late to find the world interested in such things, the fault is clearly *my own* [in English].

The notice about Rudolfus Schramm has amused me greatly. Unfortunately, a better Schramm, Konrad Schramm, brother of the above and one of my best friends, died of consumption in Jersey about four weeks ago. The deaths of Weerth, Schramm, and Dr. Daniels in recent years have been hard on their friends, among whom I have been fortunate to be included.

The times that loom before us are stormy. If I could consult only my private inclination, I could wish that the peace on the surface would continue for a few more years. This is, at any rate, the best time for scientific undertakings, and in the end, after the experience of the last ten years, the contempt of the masses, as of individuals among rational human beings, must have grown to such an extent that *"odi profanum vulgus et arceo"*[6] is a practically forced wisdom of life. But all this is merely a philistine mood that will be swept away by the first stormy weather.

Yours, K.M.

The connection between the latest events in France and the commercial crisis is clear to perhaps few people. It becomes evident, however, when one considers: (1) the real economical state in France produced by the last crisis; and (2) asks the question, and answers it *consciencieusement* [conscientiously], why the *attentat*[7] produced such effects that *apparently stood in no proportion whatever, and even in no necessary relation to the alleged cause* [in English].

311

To Ferdinand Lassalle (in Berlin)
London, March 11, 1858

Dear Lassalle:
You letter found me bedridden, [hence][1] the delay in my reply. I am now again all right. *D'abord* [to begin with], whether the negotiation[2] [started][1] by you end favorably or not, I want to express my warmest thanks for your

---

6. "I hate the common mob and resist it," from Horace's *Odes*, Book III.
7. The attempt on the life of Napoleon III by the Italian nationalist Felice Orsini on January 14, 1858, for which the latter was executed.

311
1. Paper damaged.
2. Negotiation with Franz Gustav Duncker for the publication of Marx's *Critique of Political Economy*.

effort, the value of which increases by 100 percent because of your illness. I hope that you are now fully recovered. After Petersburg and Madrid, Berlin is the most unhealthful capital in Europe, as friend Quételet[3] has estimated, but which I, as a five-year resident in Berlin, can also personally confirm, compared to London, Brussels, and Paris.

Now as to business, permit me, in answer to the questions addressed to me, to begin backward, with No. 4.

(1) The publisher is to have the right to break off publication *after the second installment*. But he must give notice in time. He is to make a special contract with me—in case he wants to print *more than one* issue, with the third *Heft*.

(2) In regard to the honorarium, in case of necessity I would set the minimum for the first *Heft* as—O, as surely I cannot write the whole work for nothing, but even less to see the publication given up because of money difficulties. I absolutely do not know the German rate for writers. If, however, you think that 30 taler per sheet is not too much, then ask for it. If the sum seems too high to you, then reduce it. Once the thing is launched, we shall see under what conditions the publisher can and wants to continue it.

(3) Minimum of installments, say, four sheets; maximum, six. It would, of course, be desirable that every installment constitutes a relatively whole one. But the various sections are of entirely different lengths.

The first installment must, under all circumstances, be a relatively whole one, and since it contains the foundation for the whole development, it can hardly be done in less than five or six sheets. I will know about it in the final elaboration. It contains: (1) Value, (2) Money, (3) Capital in general (the process of production of capital, the process of circulation of capital, the unity of both of capital and profit, rents). This constitutes an independent brochure. You yourself will have found in your economic studies that Ricardo got into contradictions between the development of profit and his (true) determination of value, which led in his school to a complete giving up of fundamentals or to the most revolting eclecticism. I believe I have brought the matter into the clear. (Of course, at closer investigation the economists will find that *altogether it is a dirty business* [in English].)

(4) In regard to the total number of sheets, I am actually very unclear about it, since the material of the book is found in my *Heften* only in the form of monographs, which often go into great details that disappear in the summary version. Nor is it in any way my intention to work out simultaneously all the six books into which I divide the whole, but only to give in the last

---

3. Lambert Adolphe Jacques Quételet, *Sur l'homme et le développement de ses facultés* [*On Man and the Development of His Faculties*] (Paris, 1835); Marx used the English edition published in Edinburgh in 1842.

three books merely the outlines; while in the first three, which contain the basic economic development, expositions cannot be avoided everywhere. I believe that the whole will hardly be possible to do in less than thirty to forty sheets.

With best regards.

Yours, K.M.

P.S. If the publisher agrees, the first installment could reach him about the end of May.

312

To Ferdinand Lassalle (in Berlin)
London, May 31, 1858

Dear Lassalle:
Post tot discrimina rerum [After so many misfortunes] at last again a sign of life. Since my wife's letter to you,[1] my story has been simply this:

After I have been totally unable to write, not only *in a literary, but in the literal sense of the word* [in English], for several weeks and have made vain efforts to rebel against the illness; after I have been inundated with medicaments and all *to no use* [in English], my doctor informed me positively that I must have a change of air, secondly must all *intellectual labour drop for some time* [in English], and finally must ride a horse as my main cure. In and for itself, my sickness was not dangerous—elongation of the liver, but this time with specifically repulsive symptoms which furthermore has malignant meaning in my family, since it had been the start of my father's fatal illness. Well, with

---

312

1. Jenny Marx to Ferdinand Lassalle, April 9, 1858: "Dear Herr Lassalle: Since Karl last wrote you [March 11, 1858], his liver ailment from which he already suffered then and which unfortunately recurs every spring, had so worsened that he had to medicate himself constantly, and today he felt so incapable of writing that he commissioned me to express his warmest thanks for your many kind efforts on his behalf. I, too, cannot refrain from expressing my pleasure over the fortunate realization of the contract [for Marx's book, *Critique of Political Economy*], and I see from this that you have not yet entirely lost yourself in theoretical work and that, alongside your immersion in *Heraclitus* (which I also dip into), you have preserved your practical skill, and have remained "a clever manager," as the English say. Karl would have written you about your work some time ago, but any writing is so difficult for him. The mental anxiety and agitation because of his inability to bring his work to a rapid conclusion, naturally contributes greatly to a worsening of his condition; likewise the burdensome work for the 'daily bread,' which of course cannot be postponed. Nevertheless, we hope that he will be able to deliver the manuscript on time. As soon as Karl feels better, he will write you, and so for the time being content yourself with these lines and accept the warm regards of *Jenny Marx*."

great reluctance I finally yielded to the urging of the doctor and the family and went to Engels in Manchester,[2] devoted myself to riding and other physical exercises, and after four weeks there I returned to London fully restored. The sickness, in my circumstances altogether a very costly *luxury* [in English]—was the more inconvenient in that it held up the copy of the first *Heft* [of *Critique of Political Economy*] for publication. I will now get to it diligently. From your friendship I expect that you will give the publisher precise information about these *adventures* [in English]. You can easily imagine what my frame of mind has been during that illness when you realize that these liver pains induce hypochondria and then also all kinds of household conditions and the publication problem, to disgust me with life. Now I am again restored to my usual humor.

During the period of my illness, I studied your *Heraclitus* and found your restoration of his system out of scattered fragments masterful; I have also been no less impressed by the acuteness of the polemic. My reservations are merely those relating to form. I believe that the presentation could have been condensed without endangering the content. I would have wished, furthermore, to see in the book itself *critical* indications of your relationship to the Hegelian dialectic. Much as this dialectic is absolutely the last word in all philosophy, it is nevertheless necessary to free it from the mystical semblance it has in Hegel. Finally, I do not agree with you in a number of specific details, for example, your interpretation of the Democritean philosophy of nature. All these, however, are nonessential. The difficulties that you had to overcome in your work are the more clear to me as, about eighteen years ago, I had made a similar study of a much easier philosopher—Epicurus[3]—namely, the construction of a total system out of fragments, a system which, I am convinced, existed only *in itself* in the writings of Epicurus but not in any known systematics—as is also the case with Heraclitus. Even among philosophers who gave their work systematic form, Spinoza for example, the real internal structure of a system is entirely different from the form in which he consciously presented it. Moreover, what I do not understand is where, in the midst of all your other labors, you found the time to acquire a knowledge of so much Greek philology.

On the whole, the present period is agreeable. History has patently in mind *to take again a new start* [in English], and the signs of dissolution *everywhere are delightful for every mind not bent upon the conservation of things as they are* [in English].

Salut.

Yours, K.M.

---

2. Marx was with Engels in Manchester from May 6 to 24, 1858.
3. Marx's doctoral dissertation: *Difference Between the Democritean and Epicurean Philosophy of Nature*, begun in 1838 and completed in March, 1841.

313

From letter to Frederick Engels (in Manchester)
London, June 7, 1858

Dear Frederick:
... Enclosed a letter from Lassalle. It is a highly curious history.[1] I cannot answer until I get your and Lupus' opinion. Hence I wish that you two would consult each other immediately and send me your views right away.[2] My opinion is that Lassalle should not enter into the duel with the donkey Fabrice, and that, even from a duel standpoint, the attack upon him by the two gentlemen from the "*Landgerichte*" [Provincial Court] has made any dueling out of the question. Generally it is my opinion—of course, it is ridiculous to consider whether dueling *in itself* is consonant "*with* principle"—that under *present circumstances, at this peculiar juncture* [in English], etc., etc., in world history, men of the revolutionary party should answer their *private enemies* [in English] with canes, fists, and kicks, but should not let themselves get involved in duels. ...
Salut.

Yours, K.M.

314

To Ferdinand Lassalle (in Berlin)
London, June 10, 1858

Dear Lassalle:
You should have received a reply to your letter by return mail. But I thought it fit not to formulate my own views, but, *tres faciunt collegium* [three making a

---

313

1. Lassalle was ambushed by two officers of a Düsseldorf court, Fabrice and Bormann, and provoked to a duel by Fabrice; it was, as Engels put it, an attempt to "murder him furtively." Lassalle consulted Marx about how to respond to the challenge.
2. Engels replied June 9, 1858: " ... When two simultaneously attack *one*, you are dealing with canaille with whom honour and fair play stops ... , so that an honourable fight between two, a fair duel, cannot be fought with them ... Our [Engels' and Wolff's] opinion is the same as yours: that (1) for revolutionists duels are altogether inappropriate, and that (2), since Lassalle had declared himself as opposed to duelling in 'principle,' he would expose himself to ridicule if he now dueled. Hence our opinion is that you can easily write to Ephraim *Gescheit* [Ephraim the Smart: an anti-Semitic tag for Lassalle] that he should not fence, but that he should cheerfully resume his 'unshatterable resolution,' get drunk, and possibly soon again take the world by the teeth and for the hundredth time risk annihilation. As for the discovery that he possesses an adequate supply of vanity, we had best, I think, congratulate him in private."

board], to report the case to Engels and Lupus in Manchester and get their judgment. As their views coincide with my own on all points,[1] you can consider the following as our common opinion:

1. *From the Standpoint of the Duel.* It is as clear as daylight that the two gentlemen, the *Intendanturrat* [supervisor councillor] and the *Assessor* [assistant judge], by their cheap assault on you, have already thoroughly put themselves in a position where the only duel one *can* permit oneself with such lads has already *taken place* in the beating itself. When two fellows ambush a third and *both* attack him, we do not believe that any dueling code in the world *permits* dueling with such a pack. If Herr Fabrice wanted to provoke a duel with his riding whip, Herr Bormann should have simply stood by as a *witness* or should have been altogether superfluous. But when two assail *one* simultaneously and one of them attacks the victim from the rear, then you deal here with riffraff who prove that a fair duel, an honorable fight between two individuals, is not possible with them.

2. *The Principle of the Duel.* We do not believe that, in general, such a relative affair as a duel can be subsumed under the category of *good* or *bad.* There is no doubt that the duel itself is not rational, still less that it is a relic of a bygone stage of culture. Nevertheless, it shows the one-sidedness of *bourgeois* society that, in self-contradiction, it asserts the right to certain feudal forms of individualism. The law of the duel in the United States of America proves this most strikingly. There, individuals can get themselves involved in such an unbearable collision that the duel comes to appear to them to be the only solution. But such a deadly tension is in fact not possible against an indifferent subject such as a superintendent or assessor or a lieutenant. Dueling involves a serious personal relationship. Otherwise it is a farce. It is always a farce when it takes place with an eye to so-called "public opinion."

3. Hence we view the duel as something depending on circumstances, which, *pis aller* [at worst], can be resorted to in exceptional cases. In the present case, however, the circumstances are decisively against it, apart from the fact that the street assault on you has put it altogether out of the question.

4. The first decisive circumstance is that you are not only opposed to all dueling in principle but also that you have stated this principle in the presence of Fabrice. You would, therefore, incur ridicule if you now dueled out of fear of "public opinion."

5. In the present case, the duel has absolutely no meaning other than the carrying out of a recognized *conventional* form of the privileged ranks under certain circumstances. Our Party must take a resolute stand against this ceremony of those ranks and reject with cynical derision any arrogant

314

1. See Letter 313, Marx to Engels, June 7, 1858, and Engels' reply, June 9, 1858.

demand for its observance. The conditions of the time are altogether too serious to indulge now in such infantilism, and it would be pure childishness to duel with Herr Fabrice just because he is a "superintendent" and belongs to the dueling clique, whereas, for example, if a tailor or a cobbler has assaulted you on the street, you would simply have left the matter to the courts, without injury to your "honor." In the present case, you would duel not merely with Fabrice the individual, who means nothing to you, but with the "Board of Managers" [*Intendanturrat*]—a maneuver that would be absurd. In general, the demand of those fellows that any conflict with them be settled by means of the duel as a *privilege* belonging to them—and all fashionable duels belong in this category—must be absolutely laughed away. The recognition of the duel would be directly counterrevolutionary.

Here, then, are our views *in nuce* [in a nutshell]. We will be interested in hearing the further development of the story.

Salut.

Yours, K.M.

315

From letter to Frederick Engels (in Manchester)
London, July 2, 1858

Dear Engels:

... I have not heard from Ephraim *Gescheit*[1] for two weeks. As I was, of course, convinced that my letter[2] was in no way destined to be used by him discreetly, I formulated it carefully, *so that it will be extremely difficult for him to abuse it* [in English]. Apart from the special *circumstances* [in English] of the *case* [in English], about which I have quite literally repeated your views, I attacked the duel only insofar as, *sub specie* [in essence], it is used as a caste privilege by fellows who believe that insults to them *must* be punished differently from those of tailors, cobblers, etc. Against such silly lads' pretensions, it is revolutionary to take a "philistine standpoint" and "German student code" position. Moreover, I answered Ephraim's trampling on principles by saying that the duel belongs in the category that Aristotle designated as "indifferent," that one can do or leave alone, He is, of course, right that it is a relic of a decayed stage of development, but that given the "one-sidedness and narrowmindedness of bourgeois relationships, individualism can sometimes be asserted in feudal form." ...

Salut.

Yours, K.M.

315
1. Lassalle.
2. See Letter 314, Marx to Lassalle, June 10, 1858.

316

From letter to Frederick Engels (in Manchester)
London, August 8, 1858

Dear Engels:
... Enclosed a letter from Lassalle. Ephraim *Gescheit*[1] is a curious fellow. While he demands from me *an immense amount of discretion* [in English] and acts with endless mysteriousness, the whole mess appears, in essentials, in the *Kölner Zeitung*. A ridiculous braggadocio runs through the man's letters. "Thus I sent a razor-sharp memoir, etc." "I activated Böckh and Humboldt." Humboldt wrote "a fulminating letter." "I myself sent to the Prince[2] a strong petition written in EXTREMELY pure German." "Truly thunder-striking complaints against the Minister." "Entirely confidential." "My big pistol." "Hopeless." "DEEPEST silence and discretion." "If this is not good for the bedbugs, etc." ...

Yours, K.M.

317

To Ferdinand Lassalle (in Berlin)
London, November 12, 1858

Dear Lassalle:
Post tot pericula [After so many dangers]. My reply to your last letter has been delayed by an atrocious toothache. I did not answer your letter from Frankfurt because you did not give me a return address.

D'abord [first]: *Beatus ille* [Blessed is he] who is not seen through Köster's[1] eyes but sees with Köster's eyes. Freiligrath and I have told Köster himself at great length that I have been unable to work practically the whole summer because of a most virulent liver ailment. In regard to my "splendid situation," Freiligrath and I had found it seemly to show an average German citizen [visitor] the brightest side and to conceal the darkest, as both of us were of the opinion that even the best citizen of this sort takes malicious satisfaction in seeing the real living conditions of the *"fuorusciti"* ["refugees"]. *So far* [in English] Köster.

316
1. Lassalle.
2. The Prince of Prussia.

317
1. Heinrich Köster (unidentified).

As for the postponement in sending my manuscript,[2] I was, first, prevented by illness and, secondly, I had to devote myself to remunerative labors. But the real reason is this: The material was before me; and it was only a question of form. But in the style of everything I wrote I smelled the liver illness. And I have a double reason not to allow this work to be spoiled on medical grounds:

(1) It is the product of fifteen years of research, that is, the best period of my life.

(2) It presents, for the first time, an important view of social relationships scientifically. Hence I owe it to the Party that the matter be not marred by a dull and wooden style that is peculiar to a sick liver.

I am not striving for an elegant presentation but only to write in my usual style, which has been impossible for me to do during the months of my illness, although in that period I wrote, because I had to, at least two volumes of English editorial articles *de omnibus rebus et quibusdam aliis* [about all knowable and some other things].

I believe that if this matter were explained to an even less astute person than Herr Duncker is supposed to be, he could only approve my procedure which to him as a publisher comes down to the fact that I am trying to deliver the best commodity money can buy.

I will finish in about four weeks, as I have only just begun the writing proper.

Another circumstance, which, however, you will have to explain upon the arrival of the manuscript: It is probable that the first part, "Capital in General," will take up two *Hefte* [installments], since, as I find in working over the subject, which involves the presentation of the most abstract aspect of political economy, that too much conciseness would make it indigestible to the public. On the other hand, however, the second part must appear *simultaneously*. The inner coherence requires it and the total effect depends upon it.

Apropos. In your Frankfurt letter you did not write me about your own economic work.[3] As for our rivalry, I do not believe that there exists in this field an *embarras de richesses* [embarrassment of riches] for the German public. In fact, economics as a science in the German sense is still to be created, and this will require not only us two but a dozen others. At least I hope that as a result of the success of my own work, a number of better brains will be devoted to this field of research.

---

2. *Critique of Political Economy*.

3. Lassalle, *Herr Bastiat-Schulze von Delitzsch, der ökonomishe Julian, oder Kapital und Arbeit* [*Herr Bastiat-Schulze von Delitzsch, the Economic Julian, or Capital and Labor*]. See Letter 320, Marx to Engels, February 25, 1859. Lassalle's book was not published until 1864.

I would be greatly in your debt if from time to time you would write to me about Prussian conditions and send me the appropriate newspaper clippings.

My wife sends her regards and fears that Köster has been as mistaken about "her beauty" as he was about her husband's health.

Freiligrath also sends his regards. He is busy head over heels in his banking career. Hence you must not hold his silence against him.

Salut.

Yours, K.M.

318

To Ferdinand Lassalle (in Berlin)
London, February 2, 1859

Dear Lassalle:
The manuscript[1] was sent out from here on January 26; on January 31, the receipt of its arrival was back *here* from Berlin. The Parcel Society received the receipt from its correspondent. On the other hand, your letter notifying the nonarrival of the manuscript is dated January 31. *In any case*, the Prussian government—perhaps friend Stieber—has rummaged through the manuscript for three days. So far as I know, they had a legal right to see whether the parcel contained Brussels lace, and not to bother about the other packages. Who can guarantee that some bureaucratic underling did not have fun in using one or two pages as paper matches?

In its own interest, I assume that the Prussian government has taken no false steps with my manuscript. Otherwise I would bring about a devilishly violent storm in the London press (the *Times*, etc.).

I will write you a *real letter* tomorrow or the day after.[2] This is only a business notification, before the post closes.

By the by [in English], I have been extraordinarily pleased with your writing.

Best regards from my wife, who imagines that since the dismissal of her *cher frère* [dear brother][3] it is safe to send at least manuscripts to Berlin.

Salut.

Yours, K.M.

318

1. *Critique of Political Economy.*
2. See Letter 319, Marx to Lassalle, February 4, 1859.
3. Ferdinand von Westphalen, Jenny Marx's half-brother, who was dismissed as Prussian Minister of the Interior (Police) in October, 1858.

It is possible that I will manage to arrange for an *English translation* of the first installment. Duncker must put on the title page: "The author reserves to himself the right of translation" [in English].

319

From letter to Ferdinand Lassalle (in Berlin)
London, February 4, 1859

Dear Lassalle:
Still no notification from Duncker of the receipt of the manuscript, and I am not sure that it has not been left in the hands of the authorities. From the enclosed scrap you can see that it has left London January 26.

Ad vocem bellum [In regard to war]: The general view here is that the war in Italy is unavoidable.[1] This much is sure: Herr Emmanuel[2] is serious about it, and Herr Bonaparte[3] was serious about it....

The war will of course lead to serious results and in the end surely to revolution. Above all, it maintains Bonapartism in France, drives back the internal movement in England and Russia, restores the pettiest nationalist passions in Germany, etc., and will, therefore, in my view, serve as counter-revolutionary in all directions.

However it may be, from the local emigration expect—*nothing*. With the exception of Mazzini, who is at least a fanatic, it consists entirely of industry knights whose entire ambition consists of squeezing money out of the English. Herr Kossuth[4] has thoroughly degenerated into a traveling lecturer who peddles the same imbecility in various provinces of England and Scotland and always repeatedly sells to a new audience.

The dogs here have all become conservative, so that actually they deserve to be amnestied. For example, Herr Gottfried Kinkel publishes here a weekly called *Hermann*, compared to which even the *Kölnische Zeitung* appears to be an audacious and intelligent journal. (Owing to all kinds of flirtation with aesthetic Jewesses, it is supposed that the sweet, melodramatic parson [Kinkel] caused his wife to fall out of the window and break her neck. Freiligrath, in his good nature, through the sorrowful scenes let himself be moved to write a poem on the deceased Johanna Mockel,[5] but in a few days he

---

319

1. The war between France and the Kingdom of Sardinia (Piedmont) against Austria, which lasted from April 29 to July 8, 1859.
2. King Victor Emmanuel II of Sardinia.
3. Napoleon III.
4. Louis Kossuth (1802–1894), Hungarian patriot.
5. Kinkel's wife, about whom Ferdinand Freiligrath wrote a poem, "*Nach Johanna Kinkels Begräbnis*" ["After Johanna Kinkel's Burial"], a copy of which the poet sent to Marx on December 6, 1858, and which was published in *Die Neue Zeit*, December 11, 1858.

realized that the pain was *faked* and that Herr Gottfried never felt *so free and easy* [in English] as after the death of his wife.) The fellow preaches "Optimism" in murmuring, hat-doffing, soft-breathing form. His journal should be called *"Gottfried."* For my part, I would prefer to write under the yoke of Manteuffel than under the German philisitinehood in London City. But for Herr Kinkel the yoke is the more sweet and light in that actually he does not even have an infinitesmal part of character or insight of these philistines....

Salut.

Yours, K.M.

320

From letter to Frederick Engels (in Manchester)
London, February 25, 1859

Dear Engels:

I am writing you again this evening because time presses. I am morally certain that Duncker, after my letter to Lassalle, will accept the brochure.[1] Jew-boy Braun[2] did not, of course, write me about my manuscript,[3] although four weeks have already elapsed. For one thing, he has been busy with the publication of his own immortal "flaming" work[4] (still, the Jew-boy, even his *Heraclitus*, although miserably written, is better than *anything the democrats can boast of* [in English]), and then he will probably have to take over the final correction of my own scrawl. For another, my analysis of money has given him indirectly a frightful blow on the head which may have stunned him somewhat. Specifically, he had made the following remarks in *Heraclitus*, which I quote literally despite their interminable length (you must read it yourself too)....

[The quotation, on money, omitted here.]

Naturally, I have not paid the slightest regard for this Talmudic wisdom, which abuses Ricardo on account of his monetary theory, which, by the way, is not his but derives from Hume[5] and Montesquieu.[6] Lassalle may feel himself personally insulted by this. In itself, there was nothing to it, for in my book against Proudhon[7] I myself accepted Ricardo's theory. But Jew-boy Braun wrote me a very ridiculous letter in which he stated that he was

---

320

1. Engels, *Po und Rhein* [*Po and Rhine*], published by Duncker, April 1859.
2. Marx's anti-Semitic tag for Lassalle.
3. *Critique of Political Economy*.
4. Lassalle, *Franz von Sickingen. Eine historische Tragödie* [*Franz von Sickingen. An Historical Tragedy*] (Berlin, 1859).
5. David Hume (1711–1776), English philosopher.
6. Baron de Montesquieu (1689–1755), French political philosopher.
7. Marx, *The Poverty of Philosophy* (Paris and Brussels, 1847).

"interested in the forthcoming publication of my book, *although* he himself is in the process of writing a great work on National Economy,"[8] to which he "is devoting two years." However, if I "took away too much new stuff from him, he would perhaps give up the whole thing." Well! I replied that there was no rivalry to fear, that in this "new" science there was room for him, for me, and for a dozen others.[9] From my treatment of the subject of money, he must realize that either I know nothing about it, although the whole history of monetary theories would then founder with me, or that he is a jackass who, with a few abstract phrases such as "abstract unity," etc., presumes to pass judgment on empirical matters that one has to study, and study for a long time *into the bargain* [in English], to be able to talk about them. For this reason, he is not altogether green in the innermost corner of my heart at this moment. But, and this is the point I want to stress, Lassalle has, first, too much serious interest "in the thing," and, secondly, he is too much "Ephraim the Smart" not to side with us *coûte que coûte* [cost what it may], the more so because of his brawl with the Düsseldorfers.[10] At the same time, his residence in Berlin has convinced him that for an energetic fellow like himself there was nothing doing with the bourgeois party there.[11]

Therefore, with clever *management* [in English] on our part the man would belong to us hide and hair, no matter how many "inflammatory" billy goat leaps he may make and no matter how he may chastise, with lengthy commentaries, Heraclitus as the most succinct philosopher. For the same reason, I am *sure*, he will *force* your brochure[12] on Duncker *en cas de besoin* [in case of need]. For the rest, I have so formulated my letter to him that he can show it to Duncker. It was, in fact, written for Duncker, not for Lassalle, although Ephraim, despite his smartness, will hardly notice that.

Hence I consider it *certain* that Duncker will accept the brochure and now the important thing is that you immediately proceed to write it, for this is like a newspaper article. There is no time to lose. For the same reason, and for purposes of direct influence, I believe you must confine yourself to no more than four or five sheets (if that much is necessary). Hence consider yourself entirely rid of your task of writing for the *Tribune* (unless some war event, which is not likely, comes up before your brochure is completed) until you have finished. The *wisest* thing would be if you suddenly became ill and stayed away from the office in order to write the thing uninterruptedly.

---

8. Lassalle, *Herr Bastiat-Schulze von Delitzsch* (Berlin, 1864).
9. See Letter 316, Marx to Lassalle, November 12, 1858.
10. See Letter 305, Marx to Engels, March 5, 1856.
11. In a letter to Marx, January 31, 1859, Lassalle complained about the cowardice and vacillations of the liberal bourgeoisie grouped around the Berlin daily, *Volks-Zeitung*.
12. Engels, *Po und Rhein*.

Amicus Engels Senior, *amicus Ermen (Gotofredus!), sed magis amicum*
τὸ φρονεῖν.[13]
"φεῦ, φεῦ, φρονεῖν ὡς δεινόν 'ἔνδα μὴ τέλη
λυει [λύῃ] φρονοῦντι."[14]
Your Old Man may say the latter to you, as did Teiresios to King
Oedipus, to which you would reply that he is
"ἐν τοῖς χέρδεσι [κέρδεοιν]
μόνον δέδορχε, τὴν τέγνην [δέδορκε, τὴν τέχνην] δέφυ
τυφλός."[15]
Salut.

Yours, K.M.

321

From letter to Ferdinand Lassalle (in Berlin)
London, March 28, 1859

Dear Lassalle:
Ad vocem [regarding] *financial need: D'abord* [To begin with], my best thanks
for your willingness. In the meantime, I have sought another way, writing to
my mother if she would lend me the money for a few weeks. *Je verrai* [I will
see]. Here in London, a promissory note could have been arranged only
through Gerstenberg. But this one, Kinkel's patron and an inflated little man,
is not to have the pleasure of my contacting him, even for a purely formal
favor.

Ad vocem Duncker: Next Wednesday (the day after tomorrow), the man
will have had the manuscript[1] nearly nine weeks. So far, only *three proof sheets*
have been sent to me. Speaking frankly among ourselves, it seems to me that
Duncker regrets having undertaken the matter and, therefore, drags it out in
the best procrastinating style of the Wetzlar Chancellery.[2] If he continues in
this manner, the book will not appear even for Easter. It causes me another
embarrassment. I am in negotiation with an Englishman for an English
translation of the first installment. That, of course, depends on its publication in German, and since in London everything is done under steam pres-

---

13. "I like the Old Engels, I like Ermen (Gottfried!), but I like science more."
14. "Alas! It is dreadful to be wise where wisdom brings no reward to the sage." (Sopho-
cles, *King Oedipus*).
15. "Sharp-sighted enough when it comes to his private profit, but blind in carrying out
his trade [or prophecy]" (*King Oedipus*).

321
1. *Critique of Political Economy.*
2. The Court of the Holy Roman Empire, which sat in Wetzlar from 1693 to 1806, became
a byword for notorious procrastination and venality.

sure, the Englishman is beginning to be suspicious. You absolutely cannot explain to an Englishman the German way of doing business....

Ad vocem your correspondence for the [Vienna] *Presse*: I am absolutely of the opinion that you should do it. For you as a *Prussian* it is, to be sure, "indecent" to write for an *Austrian* paper. In principle, however, we must, as Luther said of dear God, "strike one scamp with another,"³ and, when an opportunity opens for the general dissolution, contribute to the confusion. *Before* the troubles that have now begun, I would neither have written for the *Presse* myself nor advised you to do so. But the process of ferment has started, and now everyone must do what he can. Infiltrating poison wherever possible is now advisable. If we should confine ourselves to writing for papers that share our *general* point of view, we would absolutely have to adjourn all journalistic activity. Should one let only counterrevolutionary things be pumped into so-called public opinion?

Ad vocem Tribune:⁴ You surely have misunderstood me when you thought that I asked of you consideration for the subscribers of the *Tribune*. The matter is this: My proper business with the *Tribune* consists of writing leading articles, on whatever subject I like. In this, England plays the main role, France in second place. A good portion [of the articles] has economic content. But since the change of regime in Prussia⁵ I have given myself the personal pleasure of writing from time to time as a "Berlin" correspondent, and the "inner" connection with the Hohenzollern Fatherland brought it about that I could write about the conditions there with great assurance. Among the subscribers to the *Tribune* are many Germans. The German-American newspapers, whose name is legion, plagiarize it. Hence it was important to give the occasional articles I wrote from "Berlin" local color, in order to continue my polemic with the Prussian State in the New World. For such color, some gossip is indispensable. Added to that, the history of Prussia is now made up essentially of *chronique scandaleuse* [scandalous chronicle]. *Hinc illae lacrimae.*⁶ In this respect, your last letter has done me a good service.

Salut.

Yours, K.M.

---

3. Martin Luther, *Von Kauffshandlung und Wucher* [*On Trade and Usury*] (1524).
4. *New-York Daily Tribune*, of which Marx was London correspondent from 1851 to 1862.
5. In October, 1858, Prince William (later William I) became Regent of Prussia, replacing his deranged brother Frederick William IV.
6. "Hence those tears": Terence, *Andria*, Act I.

322

To Ferdinand Lassalle (in Berlin)
London, April 19, 1859

Dear Lassalle:
I have not specially acknowledged the receipt of £14/10 shillings because the letter was registered. However, I would have written sooner if my damn "cousin from Holland"[1] had not visited me and *in the most cruel manner* [in English] taken up my surplus working time.

He is now gone [in English], and so I breathe again.

Friedländer wrote me.[2] The conditions are not as favorable as you originally informed me, but still *"respectable"* [in English]. As soon as a few secondary points have been settled between us—and I think this will happen in the course of this week—I will write him.

Here in England the class struggle is making most gratifying progress. Unfortunately, there is at the moment no Chartist newspaper, so that for about the last two years I have had to discontinue my literary collaboration in this movement.

I now come to *Franz von Sickingen.*[3] *D'abord* [first], I must praise the composition and the action, and that is more than can be said of any other modern German drama. *In the second instance* [in English], leaving aside all purely critical attitude to this work, it greatly excited me on first reading and will, therefore, produce this effect in a still higher degree on readers who are more dominated by their feelings. And now this is a second, very important aspect.

Now *the other side of the medal* [in English]: First—this is purely formal— since you have written in verse, you might have worked over your iambs a little more artistically. However much *professional poets* may be shocked by such carelessness, I nevertheless consider it on the whole an advantage, since our spawn of poetical epigones have retained nothing but formal gloss. Secondly: the deliberate collision is not merely tragic but is the tragic collision that destroyed the revolutionary party of 1848–49, and rightly so. Therefore, I can only express my highest agreement in making this the pivotal point of a modern tragedy. But I ask myself whether the theme you treat is suitable for

---

322

1. Johann Carl Juta.
2. See Letter 321, Marx to Lassalle, March 28, 1859.
3. Franz von Sickingen (1481–1523), a German knight, led a nobles' revolt during the Reformation. He was joined by the poet and humanist Ulrich von Hutten. They were defeated by the feudal lords, as were the peasants in the Peasants' War (1524–25).

a presentation of this collision. Balthasar can actually imagine whether Sickingen, if he had raised the banner of opposition to imperial power and declared open war against the Princes, instead of hiding his revolt behind a knightly feud, he would have been victorious. But can we share this illusion? Sickingen (and with him Hutten,[4] more or less) did not go down because of his cunning. He succumbed because as a *knight* and as a *representative of a declining class* he rebelled against what already existed, or rather against its new form. Strip Sickingen of his individuality and his particular training, natural bents, etc., and what is left is—Götz von Berlichingen. In this last-named *pitiable* fellow is embodied in adequate form the tragic contrast between knighthood on the one side and emperor and princes on the other, and that is why Goethe rightly made a hero of him.[5] Insofar as Sickingen—and even Hutten himself to a certain extent, although with him as with all ideologists of a class such expressions must be considerably modified—fights against the princes (after all, he takes the field against the Emperor[6] only because he transformed himself from an emperor of the knights to an emperor of the princes), he is in reality only a Don Quixote, even though an historically justified one. That he began the revolt under the guise of a knightly feud, means nothing more than that he began it in a *knightly* fashion. If he had begun it otherwise, he would have had to appeal directly, and at the very outset, to the cities and peasants, that is, to precisely the classes whose development negated knighthood.

If, therefore, you did not want simply to reduce the collision to that presented in Götz von Berlichingen—and that was not your plan—then Sickingen and Hutten had to succumb because they imagined they were revolutionaries (this last cannot be said of Götz) and, just as the *educated* Polish nobility of 1830, made themselves exponents of modern ideas, on the one hand, while in reality representing reactionary class interests, on the other.[7] The *noble* representatives of the revolution—behind the slogans of unity and freedom, there still lurked the dream of the old Empire and law of the jungle—in that case, should not have absorbed all interest, as they do in your play, but the representatives of the peasants (particularly they) and the revolutionary elements in the cities should have formed a significantly important active background. You could then also, and to a much greater extent, have given voice to the most modern ideas in their most naïve form, whereas now, apart from *religious* freedom, the main remaining idea is *civil* unity. You yourself would then have had to *Shakespearize* more, while I chalk up against

---

4. Ulrich von Hutten (1488–1523), German humanist poet of the Reformation.
5. Johann Wolfgang von Goethe, *Götz von Berlichingen* (1831).
6. Charles V (1500–1558), Holy Roman Emperor, 1519–1556.
7. In November, 1830, Polish aristocrats led an unsuccessful uprising against Czarist Russian occupation of Poland.

you, as your most important shortcoming, your *Schillering*[8] that is, your transforming of individuals into mere speaking tubes of the spirit of the times. Did not you yourself fall into the diplomatic error, like your Franz von Sickingen, of placing the Lutheran-knightly opposition above the plebeian-Münzerian[9] opposition?

I miss, moreover, what is characteristic in the characters. I except Charles V, Balthasar,[10] and Richard from Trier.[11] And had there ever been a time that had more rough characters than the sixteenth century? For me, [your] Hutten is too much a mere representative of "exaltation," which is a bore. Was he not also intelligent and witty, and was not a great injustice done to him?

How much your Sickingen, whom by the way you depict much too abstractly, suffers from the collision which was independent of his personal calculations, is seen in the manner in which he has to preach to his knights friendship for the cities, etc., on the one hand, while arbitrarily exercising law of the jungle justice in the cities, on the other.

In particulars I must here and there criticize the exaggerated reflections of individuals on themselves—which derives from your love for Schiller. Page 121, for example: When Hutten tells Marie his life story, it would be highly natural to have Marie say: "The whole gamut of feelings," etc., up to—"And it weighs more heavily than my years."

The verses that precede this—from "They say" up to "aged"—could *then* follow, but the reflection, "The virgin ripens into womanhood in one night" (although it shows that Marie knows more than the mere abstraction of love), is entirely useless. At the very least, Marie should begin with the reflection of her own "aging." After she has said all that she has related in "one" hour, she could give general expression to her feelings in the sentence on her aging. Furthermore, in the following lines I am shocked by: "I consider it a *right*" (namely, happiness). Why is the naïve viewpoint, which up to that time Marie claims to have had of the world, to be punished as lies while it is transformed into a doctrine of rights? Perhaps I will explain to you in detail my meaning another time.

I consider the scene between Sickingen and Charles V particularly successful, although the dialogue has somewhat too much pleading on both sides; also the scenes in Trier. Hutten's sentences about the sword are very beautiful.

And now enough for this time.

---

8. Friedrich von Schiller (1759–1805), German poet, dramatist and philosopher.
9. Thomas Münzer (*c.* 1490–1525), German Anabaptist mystic.
10. Balthasar Slör, participant in German Peasants' War of 1525.
11. Richard von Greifenklau (1467–1531), Archbishop and Elector of Trier, opponent of the Reformation.

In my wife you won a special fan for your drama, only with Marie is she not satisfied.

Salut.

Yours, K.M.

Apropos. In Engel's *Po und Rhein* there are serious typos, a list of which I am putting on the last page of this letter.

323

To Ferdinand Lassalle (in Berlin)
London, May 5, 1859

Dear Lassalle:

From the enclosed letter, dated April 12,[1] which I want you to return, you will see that there is a substantial difference between the conditions offered by your cousin and those you originally reported to me.[2] Nonetheless, I accept by *return post.* I only remarked: (1) that I cannot lay out the money for the telegrams, something that you, for that matter, understood and anticipated in your letter; (2) that it would be desirable for me (I did not, however, make this a *conditio sine qua* [indispensable condition]) if an arrangement could be made, as is the case with the *Tribune,*[3] that I could draw on a banker here after the articles have been sent out, etc.

Since then I have received no answer, which is strange. In case the editorial office decided on somebody else, good manners require that I be informed. You know that I had in no way pushed myself forward in this matter. But once I had undertaken it, I made some preparatory moves among English newspapers, etc., and I do not quite want to be compromised with these people and other acquaintances, to whom I had reported the matter. That on my part I have not yet despatched any article is, of course, due to the fact that there has been no definite engagement.

The elections here, alas, did not turn out sufficiently Tory.[4] In the latter case, a revolutionary movement would have begun *by and by* [in En-

---

323

1. Max Friedländer to Marx, April 12, 1859.
2. See Letters 321 and 322, Marx to Lassalle, March 28 and April 19, 1859; see also Letter 85, Marx to Engels, April 16, 1859.
3. *New-York Daily Tribune*, for which Marx was the London correspondent.
4. In the Parliamentary elections of late April/early May, 1859, the Whigs won a majority.

glish]. Palmerston's return to the Foreign Ministry, *after some shuffling* [in English], can now be considered certain[5] and so Russia will again direct English policies.

Salut.

Yours, K.M.

324

From letter to Frederick Engels (in Manchester)
London, May 6, 1859

Dear Frederick:

... *Ad vocem* [in regard to] *business* [in English]. The jackass Friedländer wrote me on April 12 but forgot the main thing, that is, to indicate a banking house. Instead of that, he spoke of an "advance." The latter is *nonsense* [in English]. Every week it is necessary to have eight to ten, often fifteen, pounds sterling for the telegrams. I wrote that to the jackass.[1] So far, no answer, although he sends me the Vienna *Presse* (which I see has now 26,000 subscribers) regularly. Yesterday I wrote a thunderous letter to Lassalle.[2] I see in the *Presse* that Lassalle began his correspondenceship and telegraphing to that newspaper with great zeal, even if little talent. But he accepted this position only after I "gave him the permission" in writing[3] that whatever he writes he should not risk it politically without my *consent* [in English]. Would it not be a comical story if the whole transaction [with the Vienna *Presse*] only amounted to Lassalle's installing himself there? But there is a possibility that the delay is caused by the difficulty Friedländer has in making arrangements, due to the present money troubles in Vienna. *Meanwhile* [in English], in my impatience I work on algebra.

Salut.

Yours, K.M.

---

5. In June, 1859, Palmerston became Prime Minister for the second time. Marx was convinced that he always pursued pro-Russian policies.

324

1. Marx to Friedländer, May 16, 1859: "I have received no answer to my letter ... to you. If the derangements in the Vienna money market [due to a major bank bankruptcy on May 5, 1859] prevented the intended arrangement, *I beg you to inform me by return post*, since, having made certain arrangements with local newspapers about telegraphing which involved financial obligations, I must immediately break them off."
2. See Letter 323, Marx to Lassalle, May 5, 1859.
3. See Letter 321, Marx to Lassalle, March 28, 1859.

325

To Frederick Engels (in Manchester)
London, May 18, 1859

Dear Engels:

Lassalle's letter contains many points for which I am going to give him a drubbing. *D'abord* [first], the youngster[1] speaks of what he "should do for me." But I did not demand anything from him except that, having inaugurated the whole thing and my seeing his correspondence constantly in the [Vienna] *Presse*,[2] he explain to me the mysterious silence from Vienna.[3] That was *his business* [in English]. Secondly, he pretends that he corresponded with the *Presse* only after a hard struggle and at "my" urging. But in the same letter he confesses that he began to correspond with Vienna *before* I declared myself ready to be a correspondent there. But then he turns the "relationship" upside down. When he wrote me about Friedländer's offer, he burned up two pages on whether or not he should write to Vienna, leaving the decision to me. It was, to begin with, self-evident that if I found a *Presse* correspondence-ship good enough for me, I would not consider it too bad for Lassalle. In addition, I saw from his letter how he was chewing his fingernails for my *consent* [in English]. Why, then, this bragging distortion of the causal nexus? What he says about the paper's "tendency," about which, he writes, he "reprimanded" Friedländer, is nonsense. For an Austrian paper, under present conditions, the Vienna *Presse* is edited ably and decently, with much more tact than Lassalle would be able to muster. Finally, I did not ask the youngster to lecture me on what would be "worthy" or not for me. I find it *rather arrogant* [in English] for him to impart advice to me. If Friedländer can settle the money matters, I will stick to my decision, which will in no way be affected by Friedländer's not seeming to find Lassalle's correspondence agreeable. From the last issue of the *Presse* I see that it has reached 27,000 subscribers.

Lassalle's pamphlet[4] is an *enormous blunder* [in English]. The publication of your "anonymous" pamphlet[5] does not let him sleep. The position of the revolutionary party in Germany at this moment is, of course, difficult, which is, however, clear in any critical analysis of the *circumstances* [in English]. In regard to the "governments," it must be apparent from all points of view that

---

325

1. The "youngster" Lassalle was then thirty-four years old.
2. See Letter 85, Marx to Engels, April 16, 1859.
3. See Letter 323, Marx to Lassalle, May 5, 1859.
4. Lassalle, *The Italian War and the Task of Prussia, A Democratic Voice*.
5. Engels, *Po und Rhein*.

in the interest of Germany's *existence*, demands must be put upon them that they should *not be neutral*, but, as you rightly say, *patriotic*. But the revolutionary points should be made simply in stressing more strongly the opposition *against* Russia than against Boustrapa.[6] Lassalle should have done this in the face of the anti-French outcry in the *Neue Preussische Zeitung*. It is also *this* point that the course of the war will in practice drive the German governments to treason against the *Reich*, where one will be able to catch them by the neck. For the rest, when Lassalle presumes to speak in the name of the Party, he must be prepared in the future either to be disavowed by us, as conditions are too important for considerateness, or, instead of following the mixed metaphors of fire and logic,[7] he must become aware of the viewpoint of other people besides himself. We must now thoroughly stick to Party discipline, or everything will end in the muck....

Salut.

Yours, K.M.

326

From letter to Frederick Engels (in Manchester)
London, June 10, 1859

Dear Frederick:

Received two manuscripts today. *A splendid one*, yours on "Fortification," for which I really feel pangs of conscience at so having claimed the little spare time that you have. *A grotesque* one, namely Lassalle's reply to me and you on his *Sickingen*.[1] A whole forest of closely written pages. Inconceivable how a man in this period and under these world-historical conditions not only finds time himself to write suchlike but also to assume that we have time to read it....

Ad vocem Lassalle.

Re the gigantic manuscript, in which he casually also mentions the "anonymous one"[2] that he wrote "in the name of the Party," I replied to him

---

6. Nickname for Napoleon III.
7. Words which Lassalle used about his pamphlet, in a letter to Marx written in the middle of May, 1859: " ... in the course of recent days ... I have sought to weave a fabric out of logic and fire, which at any rate ... will not fail to have an effect on the people."

326

1. See Letter 322, Marx to Lassalle, April 19, 1859. On May 18, 1859, Engels also wrote Lassalle a long critique of *Sickingen* (not included in this volume).
2. In May, 1859, Lassalle published in Berlin an anonymous pamphlet, *The Italian War and the Task of Prussia, A Democratic Voice*, in which he defended the Prussian position of neutrality in connection with the Italian war of 1859.

today in a letter about the size of this one.³ In regard to the pamphlet, I only remarked: "By no means our view. Superfluous to write about it, since we will comment on it publicly in print."

Salut.

Yours, K.M.

327

From letter to Ferdinand Lassalle (in Berlin)
London, June 10, 1859

Dear Lassalle:
Since the time I have not written you, I have made fifteen proof sheets ready for delivery to the English-American *Cyclopaedie* in New York.¹ This work was no joke. Today is my article day for the *Tribune*.² Hence no time at all. I am writing only so that you know that I have received your letters and pamphlet.³

Here only this much:

Ad vocem Sickingen:⁴ I will read it and write you as soon as I have time.

Ad vocem the *pamphlet*: In no way my view or that of my Party friends in England. For the rest, it is probable that we will express our own views in print.

Ad vocem Duncker: I wrote him that I am sorry if my letter wounded him.⁵ Moreover, the delay unheard of. It is already five weeks since I received the last proof sheets. You cannot expect that I—*after having made the contract*—should comport myself toward, and let myself be treated by, the publisher as if he printed the thing out of "favor" to you. He has already accomplished this much—that I have lost my *English* publisher until further notice....

Ad vocem Proudhon: Is said to have gone crazy and been put away in an insane asylum in Brussels.

Salut.

Yours, K.M.

---

3. See Letter 327, Marx to Lassalle, June 10, 1859.

327

1. In 1858–59, *The New American Cyclopaedia* published sixteen articles by Marx and Engels, mostly on military personalities. For list, see Saul K. Padover, *Karl Marx: An Intimate Biography* (McGraw-Hill, New York, 1978), p. 651.
2. As London correspondent to the *New-York Daily Tribune*, Marx sent in articles twice weekly, Tuesdays and Fridays.
3. Lassalle, *The Italian War and the Task of Prussia*.
4. Lassalle, *Franz von Sickingen. An Historical Tragedy* (Berlin, 1859).
5. See Letters 87 and 88, Marx to Duncker, May 28 and June 2, 1859.

328

From letter to Ferdinand Lassalle (in Berlin)
London, October 2, 1859

Dear Lassalle:
It was decent of you that despite the bad appearance that speaks against me, you were the first to take up the pen, particularly in a matter concerning my own interest.

In regard to my silence, briefly the following:

First, I received both your letters only many weeks after they were mailed, specifically, after my return to London from a trip through Manchester to Scotland, which I made for business reasons.[1] Events in the meantime marched so rapidly that they broke off the points, so to speak, of our debate. For the point in question did not deal, and between us could not deal, with the nationality question, but with the fittest policy for the revolutionary-German side to pursue vis-à-vis its own governments and abroad.... And since it is "the curse of an evil deed that it must constantly produce new evils,"[2] my silence itself created a new obstacle for breaking it. In addition—and I beg you not to consider this a rhetorical figure of speech—a whole series of bourgeois, not yet fully eliminated, entanglements that effectively did away with all moods for writing. So much for the silence, which despite all *appearances to the contrary* [in English], had no evil intent.

Now in regard to Duncker.

When I returned to London, I found a letter from him[3] which made it impossible for me to turn to him for a continuation of my work.[4] In addition, as I have not written you for such a long time, I could not suddenly begin to write you about my own affairs. So I let the matter drop on the tacit assumption that if I did not hear from Duncker up to a certain time, I would turn to another publisher.

From one of your earlier letters, it seemed to me, to be sure, that Duncker had engaged himself to publish two *Hefte*, the first part of which ("Capital in General") to be printed in full. On the other hand, the first *Heft* was much larger than intended in the original plan, and I was thus little

---

328

1. On June 12 Marx went to Manchester, and then to Scotland, to discuss with a few communist friends the publication of *Das Volk*, a German-language weekly, of which Marx became editor on July 3 but which suspended publication for lack of funds on August 20, 1859.
2. Schiller, *Wallenstein*.
3. Duncker to Marx, June 25, 1859.
4. *Critique of Political Economy*, published June 11, 1859.

disposed altogether to have him as "publisher *malgré lui*" ["despite himself"]. It would, of course, be desirable that both parts of the first *Heft*, which form a whole, would be issued by the same publisher.

I must now work the whole thing over entirely, as the manuscript of the second *Heft* is already one year old; and since my situation does not allow me at this moment to devote too much time to it, I hardly believe that I would finish it before the end of December. This, however, is the *most extreme time limit.*[5]

I am busy working over the *English* version,[6] which is likewise interrupted by bourgeois thunderstorms. At any rate, in England I am sure of a better reception than in Germany, where, so far as I know, not a single rooster has crowed over the thing. I only wish that at least the *first part* were entirely available to the German public. Should it go on like this that no further notice is taken of the work, then I intend to write all the subsequent parts in English and no longer bother with the German philistines.

Vale faveque [Be well and devoted].

K.M.

329

From letter to Ferdinand Lassalle (in Berlin)
London, November 6, 1859

Dear Lassalle:
You would have received an answer from me sooner if a mass of disgusting household affairs had not entirely absorbed my spare time.

1. I thank you for your efforts with Duncker.[1] You are mistaken, however, if you think that I expected laudatory recognition from the German press or that I give a farthing for it. I expected attacks or criticism, but not a complete ignoring, which must also hurt the sales. They had so thoroughly reviled my communism on various occasions, that it was to be expected that

---

5. Nothing came of the plan. By 1861, Marx decided to recast the whole structure of his economic work, which resulted in *Das Kapital*, published, not by Duncker in Berlin, but by Otto Meissner in Hamburg (1867).
6. The first English edition of *Critique of Political Economy* did not appear until 1909, more than a quarter of a century after Marx's death.

329

1. For the publication of the continuation of the *Critique of Political Economy*, a project dropped by both publisher and author.

they would let loose their wisdom on its theoretical foundations. Professional economic journals, after all, do exist also in Germany.

In America, the edition has been thoroughly discussed in the whole German-language press, from New York to New Orleans. My only fear is that the book would be considered too theoretical for the labor public there....

Salut.

Yours, K.M.

P.S. Disagreeable as it may be for me to speak of it: My financial conditions are in a very dangerous crisis, so much so that I hardly have the time for my *Tribune* articles, and even less for the *Economy*. In the next eight to ten weeks, I will have more than £40 income. But the important, the decisive, point for me is to *anticipate* this income. Can you be helpful to me with a promissory note in this matter? In eight, or at most ten weeks, I will be good for £50.

330

From letter to Ferdinand Lassalle (in Berlin)
London, November 14, 1859

Dear Lassalle:
I reply briefly by return post.

What is involved is not that *you* supply the money, but only a promissory note transaction. Will you allow me to draw one on you for three months? *In that case*, you will get the reimbursement (guaranteed not only by me *but also by Engels*) *before* the note falls due. What is involved is an accommodation bill, or in crude German, a note riding. It is, of course, still questionable *if* I can bring it off to negotiate such a note. But it would be a *chance*. Engels would have provided what is necessary, if his liquid assets were not tied up in a court case involving physical damage to an Englishman.[1]

The affair costs over £100, and from London, accommodation bills on Manchester are possible only among businessmen....

Salut.

Yours, K.M.

330

1. Engels to Marx, September 22, 1859: " ... An unknown Englishman in a pub insulted me, I struck him with an umbrella, the point of which hit his eye. The fellow went to his lawyer, I did the same. ... Now the *Schweinhund* threatens court action; and when it comes to that, the affair will cost me £200.... "

331

From letter to Frederick Engels (in Manchester)
London, February 9, 1860

Dear Engels:
... *Well* [in English], what a *fuss* [in English] the beast makes over this![1] How the fellow flaunts himself against Liebknecht morally![2] This same fellow who had used the most brazen means and associated with the most shameless persons in the service of la Comtesse de Hatzfeldt![3] Does the beast forget that, although I had wanted to have him admitted into the [Communist] League, a unanimous decision of the Central Committee in Brussels did not accept him because of his notoriety? *In fact* [in English], out of delicacy, I had kept this a secret from the man, as I also did not tell him that a few years ago a Düsseldorf workers' delegation was sent to me with a report of the most scandalous, largely irrefutable, information against him.[4] Now look at the swaggering ape! Hardly does he—looking at us through his Bonapartist-colored eyes—think that he detects a weakness in us, when he puffs, oraculates, throws himself into farcical postures. On the other hand, how anxious he is that I have not let myself be cast into the background by Vogt without further ado, to *the benefit of my tender friend Lassalle* [in English]—how all his juridical instincts come out of him! How he contradicts himself! How cheap he becomes! One should not "touch" the thing [the Vogt affair] further. "It" would not be "received well." Not received well! *Man* [in English]! For the sake of his small-beer wisdom, I should let myself be kicked around by schoolmaster Squeer, alias Zabel![5] I now have Mr. Lassalle's number....

Yours, K.M.

331

1. Marx, involved in a Berlin court case with a man called Karl Vogt, was angry at Lassalle who wisely advised him to moderate himself in his rage against Vogt, about whom he wrote a furious polemic, *Herr Vogt* (1860). For the whole irrational episode, see Saul K. Padover, *Karl Marx: An Intimate Biography* (1978), Chapter XVIII.
2. In January, 1860, Lassalle advised Marx to have no Party contact with Wilhelm Liebknecht, because the latter was a correspondent for the conservative daily, *Allgemeine Zeitung*.
3. Countess Sophie von Hatzfeldt, whom Lassalle represented in her scandalous divorce.
4. See Letter 58, Marx to Engels, March 5, 1856.
5. Friedrich Zabel, editor of the *National-Zeitung*, a liberal Berlin daily.

332

From letter to Frederick Engels (in Manchester)
London, April 16, 1860

Dear Engels:
... Received from Lassalle another lengthy effusion, together with a printed essay (on Fichte's political testament) for Walesrode's political pocketbook, which is yet to appear.[1] From Lassalle's letter, it appears that he has read your brochure,[2] and hence that it has *come out in Berlin.* The publisher will probably announce it with the Easter eggs. Lassalle's letter, purely foolish. He is sick again. He is again writing a "great work." In addition to this great work, he has three other great works, among them one on "National Economy," clearly composed in his soul already, and he is also studying six or seven unnamed sciences, with "productive intentions." The countess, he writes, has suffered great money losses, on account of which he must go to Cologne. Probably fraudulent railroad, etc., speculations....

Yours, Mohr

333

From letter to Ferdinand Lassalle (in Berlin)
London, January 16, 1861

Dear Lassalle:
D'abord [First], my best, although belated, wishes for a happy New Year.

My wife is now convalescing. I myself became seriously ill because of her illness, and am now suffering from an inflammation of the liver. A fine New Year's present. Until now the pain has been chronic. Now it becomes acute.

This explains my silence, despite my deep empathy, as well as that of my wife, for your illness. I hope that in your next letter you will be able to report an improvement. If you would send me a *thoroughly detailed* report of your illness, I would consult a doctor whom I consider a true Aesculapian *genius.*[1] He does not live here, but in Manchester....

332
1. Lassalle, "Fichte's Political Testament and the Most Recent Times," in Ludwig Reinhold Walesrode's *Demokratische Studien* (Hamburg, 1860).
2. Engels, *Savoy, Nice, and Rhine* (Berlin, April, 1860).
333
1. Dr. Eduard Gumpert.

I rarely read German things. But recently I came across A. Bastian's *Der Mensch in der Geschichte*,[2] etc. I find the book bad, formless and pretentious. His claim to establish a "natural history" foundation of psychology remains a pious wish. Furthermore, the "psychological" foundation of history proves that the man knows neither what psychology nor what history is.

Very significant is Darwin's book[3] and suits me as a natural-history basis of the historical class struggle. The crude English manner of development, one must naturally include in the deal. Despite all deficiencies, here for the first time we have not only the death blow of "teleology" in natural history, but also the rational sense of the same explained empirically.

Recently I have seen more German newspapers. It is abominable stuff. Withal, a smug mediocrity, which is actually *nauseous* [in English].

Can you send me the second series of Eichhoff's *Polizei-Silhouetten?*[4] Not to be obtained here.

I have now also read Walesrode's *Todtenschau.*[5] Fine stories in it! But feeble portrayal, which, however, is to be excused considering the time of publication.

With my best wishes for your health and regards from my wife,

Yours, K.M.

334

From letter to Frederick Engels (in Manchester)
London, January 29, 1861

Dear Engels:
... Enclosed a letter from Lassalle ... In regard to the proposed new publication of a *Neue Rheinische Zeitung*[1]—Hatzfeldt, whose note I am enclosing, has 300,000 taler at her disposal—so I myself would grasp at this straw in the present circumstances, but the waves in Germany do not yet beat high enough to carry our boat. It would be aborted from the first....

Salut.

Yours, K.M.

2. Adolf Bastian, *Der Mensch in der Geschichte. Zur Begründung einer psychologischen Weltanschauung* [*Man in History. On the Foundation of a Psychological World View*], 3 vols. (Leipzig, 1860).

3. Charles Darwin, *On the Origin of Species by Means of Natural Selection* (London, 1859).

4. Karl Wilhelm Eichhoff, *Berliner Polizei-Silhouetten* [*Berlin Police-Silhouettes*] (Berlin, 1860).

5. Ludwig Reinhold Walesrode, *Eine politische Todtenschau* [*A Political Death View*] (Kiel, 1859).

334

1. Marx was editor-in-chief of the *Neue Rheinische Zeitung* in Cologne, June 1, 1848, to May 19, 1849. On January 19, 1861, Lassalle wrote to Marx: "*Once more*, I put the question to you: (1) How much capital would be *necessary* to found a newspaper here [in Berlin]? (2) Who among the erstwhile editors of the *Neue Rheinische Zeitung* would return here eventually for such a purpose?"

335

From letter to Frederick Engels (in Manchester)
London, February 14, 1861

Dear Frederick:
... I have not yet written to Lassalle. The best solution might be a weekly, but, on the other hand, how much would be risked in view of the tactlessness of our friend, when he sits on the spot, is chief editor, and is thus in a position to ride us all! He himself would naturally stress the thing as a Party organ, and thus we would share the responsibility for all the stupidities and spoil our position in Germany even before we have won it back. This is to be considered most seriously....[1]
Salut.

Yours, K.M.

336

From letter to Ferdinand Lassalle (in Berlin)
Zalt-Bommel, March 7, 1861

Dear Lassalle:
... I have no passport except an old French expulsion pass of 1849. To go to the Prussian embassy in London goes against the grain. To have myself naturalized as an Englishman (as Freiligrath, Bucher, Zimmermann,[1] etc., did) and to travel with an English passport, I also did not want. The question now is as follows: In 1845, when the Prussian government persecuted me in Belgium, I obtained through my brother-in-law[2] an emigration certificate from Prussia. Under the pretext that I ceased to be a Prussian subject, I was, as is known, expelled by the Prussian government in 1849. Legally, however, all refugees living ten years outside the country also ceased to be Prussian "subjects." I have never let myself be naturalized abroad. Furthermore, pursuant to the decision of the Preliminary Parliament in 1848—a decision accepted as valid by all German governments at the election to the Frankfurt Parliament—refugees, even those who, like Vogt, etc., had become naturalized abroad could again claim their right as German citizens and be elected

---

335

1. For a discussion of Lassalle's plan for a newspaper publication in Berlin, see Letter 338, Marx to Engels, May 7, 1861; in the end, Marx, with Engels' advice, decided to turn down the whole idea.

336

1. Ernst Wilhelm Eduard Zimmermann, German refugee in London.
2. Wilhelm Robert Schmalhausen, a Dutch lawyer married to Marx's oldest sister Sophie.

everywhere to the Parliament. Based on this, I requested in 1848 that my Prussian citizenship be reintegrated. The then Prussian Ministry rejected the request, but dared to treat me as a foreigner only after the revolution was defeated....

...You know that I want to arrange here complicated money problems with my uncle[3] (who administers my mother's estate and who had previously often made considerable advances on my share of the inheritance). The man is tough, but is vain about my authorship. Hence in your letter to me you must speak of the success (*lucus a non lucendo* [woods of no light, that is, an explanation by contrary example] of my recent writing against Vogt, of common newspaper plans, etc., and altogether to structure the letter in such a way that I should be able to show the Herr Uncle "the confidence" of showing it to him. In addition, you must not omit to report something about politics. *Vous m'entendez, mon cher* [You understand me, my dear].

My best regards to you and the Frau Countess.

Yours, K. Marx

337

To Antoinette ("Nannette") Philips (in Zalt-Bommel) [in English] Berlin, 13 Bellevuestrasse (Lassalle's residence), March 24, 1861

My dear Cousin:

I cannot thank you enough for your precious letter which fails only in being too short, although you have acted up to the English rule of packing the best things in the smallest compass.

I arrived at Berlin on Sunday last (eighteenth March), at seven o'clock in the morning. My travel was not marked by any incident save a six-and-a-half hours' delay at Oberhausen, an abominably tedious little place. Lassalle who lives in a very fine house, situated in one of the finest streets of Berlin, had everything prepared for my reception, and gave me a most friendly welcome. The first hours having been talked away and my railway fatigue chased by some rest and some refreshments, Lassalle introduced me at once to the house of the Countess of Hatzfeldt who, as I soon became aware, dines every day in his house at four o'clock P.M., and passes her evenings with him. I found her hair as "blonde" and her eyes as blue as formerly, but for the remainder of her face I read the words imprinted in it: twenty and twenty make fifty-seven. There were in fact wrinkles full of "vestiges of creation," there were cheeks and chin betraying an embonpoint which, like coal beds, wants much time to be formed, and so forth. As to her eyebrows, I was at

---

3. Lion Philips.

once struck by the circumstance that they had improved instead of deteriorating, so that art had by far got the better of nature. On later occasions I made the general remark that she perfectly understands the art of making herself up and of finding in her toilette-box the tints no longer derived from her blood. Upon the whole, she reminded me of some Greek statues which still boast a fine bust but whose heads have been cruelly "beknappered" by the vicissitudes of time. Still, to be not unjust, she is a very distinguished lady, no blue stocking, of great natural intellect, much vivacity, deeply interested in the revolutionary movement, and of an aristocratic *laissez aller* very superior to the pedantic grimaces of professional *femmes d'esprit*.

On Monday, my friend Lassalle drew up for me a petition to the chief of the Prussian police for my restoration to the civil rights of a Prussian subject. On Tuesday, Lassalle himself, who is a man of extraordinary audacity, carried the petition to Herr von Zedlitz (*Polizeipräsident* [Police president], partisan of the *Junkerpartei* [Junker Party] and the king's confidant) and, what with menaces, what with flatteries—Zedlitz considering this direct appeal to himself, instead of to the subaltern authorities, as a compliment paid to his person—he has so far succeeded that today the ministerial paper—"*Die Preussische Zeitung*"—announces my return to the "fatherland." Still I have not yet received an official answer in regard to my re-naturalization.[1]

On Tuesday evening Lassalle and the countess led me to a Berlin theater where a Berlin comedy, full of Prussian self-glorification, was enacted.[2] It was altogether a disgusting affair. On Wednesday evening I was forced by them to assist at the performance of a ballet in the Opernhouse. We had a box for ourselves at the side—*horribile dictu* [horrible to relate]—of the king's "loge." Such a ballet is characteristic of Berlin. It forms not, as at Paris, or at London, an *entrejeu* [intermezzo—that is, an interpolated entr'acte], or the conclusion, of an opera, but it absorbs the whole evening, is divided into several acts, etc. Not a syllable is spoken by the actors, but everything is hinted at by mimicry. It is in fact deadly—dully. The scenery, however, was beautiful; you assisted for instance at a sea-voyage from Livorno to Naples; sea, mountains, a seacoast, towns, etc., everything being represented with photographical truth.

On Thursday Lassalle gave a dinner in honour of my return, gentlemen and ladies being invited. Among the celebrities there were the old general

---

337

1. The petition for the restoration of Marx's Prussian citizenship was rejected in June, 1861.

2. *Die Journalisten*, a comedy by Gustav Freytag. In Letter 97, Marx to Engels, May 10, 1861, Marx described it thus: "A most repulsive Hamburg-Westphalian patois, words chewed up quickly behind one another, not a single well constructed or completed sentence."

von Pfül,[3] "*Schlachtenmaler*" [Battle Painter] Bleibtreu,[4] Hofrath Förster[5] (a known Prussian historiograph and formerly called the "*Hofdemagog*" ["court demagogue"], he being a personal friend of the late king) and so forth. Hofrath Förster brought out a toast on my humble self. I was seated at table between the countess and Fräulein Ludmilla Assing,[6] the niece of Varnhagen von Ense,[7] and the editor of Varnhagen's correspondence with Humboldt. This Fräulein, who really swamped me with her benevolence, is the most ugly creature I ever saw in my life, a nastily Jewish physiognomy, a sharply protruding thin nose, eternally smiling and grinning, always speaking poetical prose, constantly trying to say something extraordinary, playing at false enthusiasm, and spitting at her auditors during the trances of her ecstasies. I shall today be forced to pay a visit to that little monster which I treated with the utmost reserve and coldness, giving her to understand by friend Lassalle that the power of attraction works upon myself always in a *centrifugal* direction and that, when I happen to admire a person very much, I am very apt to steal altogether out of its presence.

The state of things here is illboding for the powers that be. The Prussian Exchequer labours under a deficit, and all the old parties are in a movement of dissolution. The chamber of deputies will have to be re-elected during this season, and there is every probability that, during the process of its reconstitution, a great movement will pervade the country. This may, as my friend Lassalle thinks, be the proper moment for starting a newspaper here in the Prussian capital, but I have not yet come to a firm resolution. The necessity of waiting for the official answer of the authorities to my petition may prolong my sojourn beyond the term originally contemplated.

You see, my dear child, I have seen much during a few days, but still you may be sure that I always wish myself back to Bommel.

With my best compliments to yourself, your father, and the whole family, believe me always,

Your most sincere admirer, Charles Marx

338

From letter to Frederick Engels (in Manchester)
London, May 7, 1861

Dear Frederick:
Habet confitentem reum [You have a confessing defendant]. But the *circonstances attenuantes* [extenuating circumstances] for my not writing to you were as

---

3. Ernst Heinrich Adolf von Pfül (1779–1866), a Prussian general and Minister of War in 1848.
4. Georg Bleibtreu (1828–1892), German battle scenes painter.
5. Friedrich Christoph Förster (1791–1868), a Prussian historian.
6. Ludmilla Assing (1821–1880), a writer and friend of Lassalle.
7. Karl August Varnhagen von Ense (1785–1858), a German literary critic.

follows: To begin with, you know that I spent the greatest portion of my time in Berlin in Lassalle's house,[1] and there it was *impossible* for me to write you without communicating the letter to Lassalle, and *that did not serve my purpose* [in English]. Later I was constantly en route, from Berlin to Elberfeld, Cologne, Trier, Aachen, Bommel, Rotterdam and Amsterdam....[2]

Now to political business.

... It would be quite timely if we could publish a newspaper in Berlin next year, disagreeable though the place is to me personally. With the help of Lassalle, some 20,000 to 30,000 taler could be raised. But *hic jacet* [here is the rub]. Lassalle made me a direct offer. At the same time he confided to me that alongside with me, he must also be editor-in-chief. And Engels? I asked him. "Well," he replied, "if three are not too much, then Engels can also be editor-in-chief. But you two must not have more votes than I, otherwise I would be outvoted every time." He gave the following reasons why he wanted to be co-editor-in-chief: (1) that in the eyes of the public he was closer to the bourgeois party than I, and he could, therefore, raise money more easily; (2) that he had to sacrifice his "theoretical studies" and theoretical peace, and must have some compensation therefor, etc. Nevertheless, if we did not agree, he added, "I will be prepared, as before, to help the paper in a pecuniary and literary way; it would be an advantage for me; I would have the use of the paper without the responsibility," etc. This was, of course, only sentimental talk. Blinded by the esteem which he enjoys in certain circles because of his *Heraclitus* and in others by spongers because of his good wine and cuisine, Lassalle does not know, of course, that he is in disrepute in the eyes of the larger public. Besides, there is his disputatiousness; also his sticking fast in "speculative concepts" (the fellow even dreams of a new Hegelian philosophy of the second potential, which he wants to write); his infection with the old French liberalism; his wide-ranging pen; his obtrusiveness, tactlessness, etc. As one of the editors, if under severe discipline, Lassalle could perform services. Otherwise, only discredit. But you can see that, in view of the cordiality he showed me, I was in a great quandary in regard to speaking to him frankly. Hence I confined myself to a general vagueness, telling him I could not decide without a prior discussion with you and Lupus. (That was the main reason why I did not write you from Berlin, since I did not want to get a reply from you on this point.) If we decide in the negative, then the countess and Lassalle plan to start on a year's trip to the Orient or to Italy. *But here is the rub* [in English]. He expects now an answer from me which I can no longer postpone. *Qu'en dis-tu,* [What do you say]?

The fellow is frightfully pathetic, and hence I had no choice but to maintain toward him a constant irony, which injured his egotism the more as

338
1. Marx stayed with Lassalle in Berlin from March 17 to April 12, 1861.
2. Marx did not return to London until April 29, 1861.

thereby the countess, whom he had impressed as a universal genius, began to develop a serious hankering for emancipation from this Buddha. Strangely enough, at certain moments the Hatzfeldt woman adopted from him a Jew-like [*jüdelnden*] tone of speech. . . .

Yours, K.M.

339

From letter to Ferdinand Lassalle (in Berlin)
London, May 8, 1861

Dear Lazarus:[1]
Post tot discrimina rerum.[2] My silence—during the trip,[3] then in London where during the first week I had to play Amphytrio [friendly host] to my Rotterdam cousin[4]—is the fault of the countess. She had promised me that in Zalt-Bommel [Holland] I would find her portrait and a letter from her. Since neither came and I stick strictly to *jus vindictae* [right of revenge], I also did not write. In addition, my time in Zalt-Bommel was completely occupied. On the one hand, I had business to transact with my uncle,[5] and on the other, I had to pay court to my girl-cousin.[6] *So, you see Sir, writing was out of the question* [in English]. My stay in Trier was useful insofar as my mother annulled some old promissory notes. For the rest, the old woman interested me also because of her fine spirit and unshakable equanimity of character. . . .

The day before yesterday I wrote to Engels about the newspaper plans[7] and expect to receive a reply from him in a few days. The American conditions [Civil War] make it probable that even if nothing comes of the newspaper undertaking, I would move to Berlin for one semester or so, *always supposed that I get my renaturalization. London, I can't deny it* [in English], possesses an extraordinary power of attraction for me, even though to a certain extent I live like a hermit in that gigantic nest.[8] . . .

And now, *mon cher*, I must finally express my heartiest thanks for the amiable friendliness with which you have received and entertained me, and

---

339
1. For the name Lassalle-Lazarus, see Letter 340, Marx to Engels, May 10, 1861.
2. "After so much caprice of fate": Virgil, *Aenead.*
3. Marx left Berlin on April 12, 1861, returning to England by way of Holland.
4. Jacques Philips.
5. Lion Philips.
6. Antoinette Philips.
7. See Letter 338, Marx to Engels, May 7, 1861.
8. Nothing came of the newspaper project, particularly since Mrs. Marx was vehemently opposed to the idea of living in Berlin or anywhere else in Germany.

particularly also tolerated my bad habits. You know that my head was full of worries, added to which I suffered from the liver. The main thing, however, remains that we both together laughed so much. *Simia non ridet* [The ape does not laugh], and so we have confirmed ourselves as consummate Buddhas.

Enclosed two small photographs. One for the countess, whom I send my regards, and one for you.

Yours, K.M.

340

From letter to Frederick Engels (in Manchester)
London, May 10, 1861

Dear Frederick:

... Apropos. Lassalle-Lazarus. In his great book on Egypt, Lepsius[1] has proved that the Exodus of the Jews from Egypt is nothing more than the history that Manetho relates about Egypt's expulsion of "the nation of lepers," headed by an Egyptian priest named Moses. Lazarus, the leper, is thus the prototype of the Jews and of Lazarus-Lassalle. But in our Lazarus, the leprosy lies in the brain. His illness was originally a badly cured case of syphilis. This resulted in caries in one of his legs, of which there are still traces, or, as his physician Frerich (I don't know how this famous professor writes it) says, neuralgia or something of the sort in one leg. To his own bodily detriment, our Lazarus lives as luxuriously as his counterpart, the rich man,[2] and this I consider a main deterrence to his cure. He has become generally so very superior that he would consider it a debasement, for example, to go to a beer hall. Strangely enough, he asked me at least four times whom I meant by Jacob Wiesenriesler in my *Herr Vogt*.[3] Still, in his really

---

340

1. Karl Richard Lepsius, *Denkmäler aus Ägypten und Äthiopien* [*Monuments from Egypt and Ethiopia*], 12 vols. (Berlin, 1849–60).
2. St. Luke 16: 19-25: "There was a certain rich man, which was clothed in purple and fine linen, and fared sumptuously every day: And there was a certain beggar named Lazarus, which was laid at his gate, full of sores.... And it came to pass, that the beggar died, and was carried by the angels into Abraham's bosom: the rich man also died, and was buried. ... And he cried and said, Father Abraham have mercy on me, and send Lazarus, that he may dip the tip of his finger in water, and cool my tongue; for I am tormented in this flame. But Abraham said, Son, remember that thou in thy lifetime receivedst thy good things, and likewise Lazarus evil things: but now he is comforted, and thou art tormented."
3. In his pamphlet, *Herr Vogt*, Marx referred to Ferdinand Lassalle as Jacob Wiesenriesler— meaning Jacob Sewage-Meadow.

"objective" vanity, this was merely a *usus naturae* [natural]. He will send to all of us his new juristic masterpiece (Dharma).[4]...

Totus tuus [Entirely yours].

K.M.

341

To Ferdinand Lassalle (in Berlin)
London, May 29, 1861

Dear Lassalle:
I have written to a friend[1] in Germany, and I hope that in eight days *at the latest* he will send you the remaining £10 (67 taler). The matter is very annoying to me; but my uncle,[2] as is the case with such old gentlemen, while he thoroughly keeps his promises, does it with some obstacles for me.

My American correspondenceship,[3] owing to the conditions there, is suspended for the time being, until European affairs again become of interest to the Transatlantics.

In Paris, as a result of the American crisis, there prevails extraordinary ill luck among the workers. Ditto in Lyons.

The entire official English press is, of course, on the side of the *slaveholders* [in English]. These are the same fellows who had wearied the world with their anti-slavery philanthropism.[4] But *Cotton, Cotton* [in English]!

Engels visited me here for three days.[5] He is not yet ready to move [to Berlin]. If he did, he would have to give up his position, break his contract, hurt himself financially, and he says he does not want to do that *save in decisive times* [in English], but not, if after perhaps three months he should fall into the hands of the Prussian authorities *without doing good to anybody* [in English]. He does not consider conditions ripe as yet for a newspaper [in Berlin]. He thanks you for the *military maps* [in English].

In the letter which you transmitted to her, I wrote the countess *more exact* details about Bonaparte's[6] infamy against Blanqui, and *about the whole*

---

4. Marx's ironic name for Lassalle's scholarly work, *The System of Acquired Rights* (1861).

341
1. Carl Siebel.
2. Lion Philips.
3. For the *New-York Daily Tribune*.
4. The movement to abolish the slave trade.
5. From about May 20 to 23, 1861.
6. Napoleon III.

case [in English] in general. She will certainly inform you about it. My best regards for her. I hope that her health has improved.

I am curious to hear more about your *transactions* [in English] with the Prussian government. Thanks for your renewed zeal.[7]

In order to break my deep depression over my *in every respect unsettled situation* [in English], I am reading Thucydides. Those ancients at least always remain fresh.

Salut.

Yours, K.M.

342

From letter to Ferdinand Lassalle (in Berlin)
London, June 11, 1861

Dear Lassalle:

Be so kind as to hand over the enclosed letter to the countess.

Your book,[1] which arrived here a few days ago (I immediately sent the respective copies to Manchester), gratefully received. I began it backward, particularly with the Pelagian history, and then read about the right of inheritance in the front of the book, wherein I penetrated up to page 215. It is in every respect a significant work. Criticism and judgment, however, must await my reading through the whole.[2] Merely a few remarks in passing: Adoption is the main form in *India*. English law has taken an opposite direction from that of France. The absolute freedom of the testator (according to which no Englishman or Yankee can be compelled to leave a farthing to his family) dates back only to the bourgeois revolution of 1688 and has been formed in the same measure as "bourgeois" property has developed in England. But it would appear that the absolute freedom of the testator, of bequeathing in general, entirely apart from its specific Roman origin, etc., is a delusion, which must have its own roots, independent of the mythology, etc., in bourgeois society. . . .

Salut.

Yours, K.M.

---

7. In April, 1861, while Marx was in Berlin, he applied for a restoration of his Prussian citizenship; despite Lassalle's efforts, the application was rejected in November, 1861.

342

1. Lassalle, *Der System der erworbenen Rechte* [*The System of Acquired Rights*] (Leipzig, 1861).
2. See Letter 343, Marx to Lassalle, July 22, 1861.

343

From letter to Ferdinand Lassalle (in Berlin)
London, July 22, 1861

Dear Lassalle:
... I have read through the second part of your work[1] (when I wanted to begin the first part, my eye inflammation intervened) and derived very great pleasure from it. I began with No. 2 because the subject lay closer to me, which, however, will not prevent me from considering the matter in its totality.

You have to some extent misunderstood—and the fault lay with my mode of expression—the very brief marginal glosses in my last letter.[2] To begin with, under "testator's freedom" I did not understand the freedom to make a testament but the freedom to make it without any regard for the family. In England the testament itself is very old and there is not the slightest doubt that the Anglo-Saxons took it over from Roman jurisprudence. That the English quite early considered, not the intestate, but the right of inheritance based on a testament, appears from the fact that in the high Middle Ages, when the *pater familias* died *ab intestato* [without leaving a will], only the legal portions went to his wife and children, according to circumstances, but from one-third to one-half fell to the Church. For the parsons assumed that if he had made a will, he would have left a certain amount to the Church for the salvation of his soul. In this sense, it is quite understandable that in the Middle Ages testaments had a religious meaning and were made in the interest of the deceased and not of the survivors. However, the circumstance that I wanted to point out was that after the Revolution of 1688 the limitations on the family's right of inheritance (feudal property, of course, does not come into question here) were abolished and legally established in favor of the legatee. That this corresponds to free competition and a society based upon it, is , of course, little question; just as little as that Roman law, more or less modified, which modern society appropriated because of the legal conception that the subject had of free competition, corresponds to the Roman person (I do not want to enter here into the argument, which is very essential, that the legal conception of certain property relationships, insofar as it emerges from it, is not and could not be congruent with it).

That the appropriation of the original Roman testament (and insofar as the scholarly insight of jurists comes into consideration still) is based on a misunderstanding, you have demonstrated. From this, however, it does not follow that the testament in its modern form—no matter how contemporary

343
1. Lassalle, *The System of Acquired Rights.*
2. See Letter 342, Marx to Lassalle, June 11, 1861.

jurists may construe the misunderstandings of Roman law—is the misunderstood Roman testament. Otherwise it could be said that each achievement over an older period, which is appropriated by a later one, is the misunderstood old one. It is certain, for example, that the three unities, as the French dramatists under Louis XIV have construed them, are based on the misunderstood Greek drama (and on Aristotle as an exponent of same). On the other hand, it is equally certain that they understood the Greeks in precisely that way because it corresponded to their own artistic needs, and hence they clung to this so-called "classical" drama for such a long time, even after Dacier[3] and others correctly interpreted Aristotle for them. Or that all modern constitutions largely rest on the misunderstood English constitution; that they accept as essential precisely that which seems a lapse in the English constitution—and that now still exists in England *formally* only *per abusum* [by misuse]—for example, a responsible *Cabinet*. The misunderstood form is precisely the general one and suitable for general use in a particular stage of development of society.

The question, for example, whether the English would or would not have had their testament (which despite its direct descent from the Roman and its adoption in Roman forms is *not* Roman) seems to me to be unimportant. If I posed the question differently, it would be somewhat like this: Whether the *Legate* [legacies] (and the present so-called testament makes the main heir in fact only a *residuary legatee*) could have emerged by themselves from civil society, even without the prop of Rome? Or, instead of a legacy, a written disposal of property in general on the part of the *defuncti* [deceased one]?

It seems to me not yet *proven* that the Greek testament was imported from Rome, although, of course, probability favors it. . . .

Yours, K.M.

344

From letter to Ferdinand Lassalle (in Berlin)
London, April 28, 1862

Dear Lassalle:
Old Boy [in English], you will be furious with me, and justly so, but at the same time also most unjustly. I have postponed writing you from day to day because I hoped daily to have regulated my affairs far enough to be able to pay you at least the debt of £10, as well as to have the *peace of mind* to write to you. Instead, the situation has worsened daily. The *Tribune*,[1] with which I

---

3. André Dacier (1651-1722), French philologist, translator of the Greek classics.

344

1. *New-York Daily Tribune*.

had resumed my connection even though it reduced my income to one-third, has finally *done away with* all foreign correspondents. Thus I am now completely in a *vacuum* [in English]. I do not want to sing any litany to you; it is a wonder that I have not gone altogether *mad*. I mention this muck only because I do not want your misunderstanding in addition to my other troubles. . . .

As for *my book*,[2] it will not be finished for another two months. In the last few years, in order not to die of hunger, I had to perform the meanest tasks and often for months I could not write a single line of the "thing." Added to that is my peculiarity that when I look over something I wrote four weeks earlier, I find it unsatisfactory and begin to rewrite the whole thing anew. At any rate, the work loses nothing thereby, and the German public is, after all, occupied *pro anno* [for the year] with incomparably more important affairs.

Ad vocem [In regard to] your book,[3] which, of course, I have now read in its entirety and individual chapters over again, it occurred to me that you seemed not to have read Vico's *New Science*.[4] Not that you would have found anything in it for your specific purposes, but as philosophical conception of the spirit of Roman law in contrast to the jurist philistines. You would hardly be able to work your way through Vico's original, as it is written not merely in Italian but in a highly intricate *Neapolitan* idiom. Against this, I recommend the French translation: *La Science Nouvelle* (Paris, 1844). To whet your appetite, I cite the following passages. . . .

[Quotations from Vico omitted here.]

After Wolf (Homer)[5] and Niebuhr (Roman history),[6] Vico contains the germ of the foundations of comparative linguistics, and also heaps of genius. Hitherto I have never been able to get hold of his juristic writings.

In the circumstances in which I now find myself (and have been for nearly a year), I have been able to get to a critique of your book *by and by* [in English]. Against this, I would appreciate it, *not for my sake* but for that of my wife, if, before I send you the equivalent, you would indicate the Brockhaus publication of the first part of your book on economics.[7]

The English middle class (and aristocracy) has *never* more shamelessly disgraced itself than in the great [Civil] war that is now taking place across the Atlantic. In contrast, the English *working class* [in English], which alas suffers most from the *bellum civile* [civil war], has never shown itself more heroic and

2. *Das Kapital*, which Marx began in 1861 and did not complete until 1867.
3. Lassalle, *The System of Acquired Rights*.
4. Giambattista Vico, *Principii di Scienza Nuova* (1725); new edition, Naples, 1859.
5. Friedrich August Wolf, *Prolegomena ad Homerum* [*Prologues to Homer*] (Halle, 1795).
6. Barthold Georg Niebuhr, *Römische Geschichte* [*Roman History*], 2 vols. (Berlin, 1827 and 1830).
7. Lassalle, *Herr Bastiat-Schulze von Delitzsch* . . .

more noble. This is to be admired the more when one knows, as I do, the means used here and in Manchester to move them to a demonstration. The only big organ which they still have, the scoundrel Reynolds's *Newspaper*,[8] has been bought by the *Southerners* [in English], as well as the most important *lecturers. But all in vain* [in English]! . . .

My best regards for the countess. She will soon receive a letter from me. I hope that such trivialities as not writing will never mislead her about my constant devotion and admiration for her.

Yours, K.M.

345

From letter to Ferdinand Lassalle (in Berlin)
London, June 16, 1862

Dear Lassalle:
Bucher did indeed send me three copies of *Julian Schmidt*,[1] but none of the other writings you mentioned.[2] The *Herr Schmidt* (a copy of which I sent to Engels and Wolff each) was the more welcome as it found me in a by-no-means happy mood. Moreover, although I have read little of it but only leafed through it, the fellow was repulsive to my soul as the epitome of such disgusting middle-class snobbism even in literature. You rightly make it clear that your attack is indirectly aimed at the middle-class culture mob. In this case, it signifies: You beat the donkey, but you aim at the pocket. Since for the time being, we cannot directly "crop" the ears of that purse, it becomes more and more necessary that we knock off the head of their loudest and most arrogant culture donkeys—with the pen, although poor Meyen in the *Freischütz*[3] found this "literary guillotine game" childish and barbaric.[4] Above all, I was most delighted by the *Schwabenspiegel*[5] and the "seven" wise men, I almost said, the "seven Swabians" from Greece.[6] Incidentally, since one will perceive Julian

---

8. *Reynolds's Newspaper*, a London weekly.

345

1. Lassalle, *Herr Julian Schmidt der Literaturhistoriker* [*Herr Julian Schmidt the Literary Historian*] (Berlin, 1862).
2. Lassalle to Marx, June 9, 1862: " . . . In the meantime you will have received through . . . Bucher my *Julian*, my *Fichte* [*Die Philosophie Fichtes* (Berlin, 1862)] and my speech on the constitution. . . ."
3. *Der Freischütz*, a literary newspaper in Hamburg, 1825–1878.
4. Eduard Meyen, "Berliner Brief" ["Berlin Letter"], in *Der Freischütz*, April 23, 1861.
5. A pun on *Sachsenspiegel*, a thirteenth century Saxon land and feudal inventory.
6. The "seven wise men" of ancient Greece were Solon, Bias, Pittacus, Cleobul, Chilon, Myson, and Thales, who lived in the seventh to sixth centuries, B.C. To these, Julian Schmidt added the later sages Democritus, Pythagoras, and Heraclitus.

the Grabowite[7] in Julian Schmidt (which is, however, unjust, because it appears to be a sarcastic remark aimed at the Apostate,[8] or at least some ridicule of the other Julian)—..., I can comment that the *Sophos* [Greek: Sage] as the proper character mask (but here the mask in a good sense) of Greek philosophy has occupied me very much earlier in life. First, the seven Swabians or Wise Men as the forerunners, the mythological heroes, then Socrates in their midst, and finally the *Sophos* as the ideal of the Epicureans, Stoics, and Skeptics. Furthermore, I was amused to see a comparison drawn between the *Sophos* and its caricature (in some respects) in the French "sage" of the eighteenth century. Then the *Sophistas* [Sophist] as a necessary variation of the *Sophos*. For moderns, it is characteristic that the Greek connection between character and knowledge, which is contained in the *Sophos*, has been preserved in the national consciousness only in the Sophists.

In regard to Julian, not Julian the Grabowite but Julian the Apostate, I recently had an altercation with Engels, who, as soon became apparent at the opening of the row, was essentially correct. But so specific is my aversion for Christianity that I have a bias in favor of the Apostate and could not identify him either with Frederick William IV or any other romantic reactionary, not even *mutatis mutandis* [with necessary changes]. Do you not feel the same?...
Salut.

Yours, K.M.

346

To Frederick Engels (in Manchester)
London, July 30, 1862

Dear Engels:
From the enclosed scraps you will see in part how I am bothered. The landlord, hitherto appeased, was paid £25. The piano man, who should have received the £6 installment on the rental of the piano last June, is a crude ruffian. I have before me tax bills for £6. The school crap of about £10 I have fortunately paid already, since I do everything possible to spare the children direct humiliation. I paid off the butcher with £6 (and this was my total quarterly earning from the [Vienna] *Presse!*), but the fellow is dogging me again, not to mention the baker, *teagrocer, greengrocer* [in English], and whatever this devil's rabble are called.

The Jewish Nigger Lassalle, who fortunately departs at the end of this week, has luckily again lost 5,000 taler in a fraudulent speculation. The fellow would rather throw his money into the muck than lend it to a "friend," even if the interest and capital were guaranteed. In addition, he acts on the

---

7. An ironic reference to Wilhelm Grabow, a prominent Prussian politician.
8. The Roman emperor Julian, the so-called Apostate.

notion that he must live like a Jewish baron or baronized (probably by the countess) Jew. Think of it, this fellow, who knows my history with America,[1] etc., and is thus familiar with the crisis in which I find myself, has had the effrontery to ask me if I would give one of my daughters to the Hatzfeldt as a "companion" and if he should arrange for me the patronage of Gerstenberg! The fellow cost me precious time, and, so thought this animal, now that I have "no business" but am merely engaged in "theoretical work," I could just as well kill time with him! In order to keep up certain appearances in the presence of this lad, my wife had to take to the pawnshop everything that was not riveted or nailed-down!

If I had not been in my present frightful position and if I had not been irked by the parvenu's rattling the moneybag, I would have been royally amused by him. In the year since I have seen him, he has become quite crazy. His stay in Zurich (with Rüstow,[2] Herwegh, etc.) and his subsequent trip to Italy, together with his *Herr Julian Schmidt*,[3] etc., have completely turned his head. He has now emerged as not only the greatest scholar, the deepest thinker, the most gifted researcher, etc., but also as a Don Juan and a revolutionary Cardinal Richelieu. Added to this, the continuous prattling in the falsetto voice, the unaesthetic theatrical gestures, the didactic tone!

In deepest secrecy, he informed me and my wife that he had advised Garibaldi not to make Rome the object of his attack, but, instead, to go to Naples, declare himself dictator there (without wounding Victor Emmanuel's[4] feelings), and mobilize a people's army for a campaign against Austria. Lassalle had him hammer out a people's force of 300,000 men, and naturally the Piedmontese Army was to join them. And—after the plan was approved, as he says, by Herr Rüstow—a detached corps was to march on rather, to sail, to the Adriatic Coast (Dalmatia) and stir up insurrection in Hungary, while the main army under Garibaldi, avoiding the Quadrilaterals,[5] was to move from Padua to Vienna, where the people would immediately rise in revolt against the government. Everything would be finished in six weeks. As the lever of action: Lassalle's political influence or his pen in Berlin. And Rüstow at the head of a corps of German volunteers attached to Garibaldi. But Bonaparte[6] was paralyzed by this Lassallean *coup d'éclat* [brilliant coup].

346

1. Marx's loss of the *New-York Daily Tribune*'s correspondenceship due to the American Civil War.
2. Friedrich Wilhelm Rüstow, Garibaldi's chief of staff.
3. Lassalle, *Herr Julian Schmidt der Literaturhistoriker* [*Herr Julian Schmidt the Literary Historian*] (Berlin, 1862).
4. Victor Emmanuel II, King of Italy.
5. The four fortified cities: Verona, Legnago, Mantua, and Peschiera.
6. Napoleon III.

He has now also seen Mazzini and "he too" approved and "admired" his plan.

He appeared before these people as the "representative of the German revolutionary working class" and let them know (literally!) that he (Itzig[7]) through his "brochure on the Italian war prevented Prussia's intervention in it," and that *in fact* [in English] it was he who had shaped "the history of the last three years." Lassalle was extremely furious with me and my wife when we made fun of his plans and kidded him as an "enlightened Bonapartist," etc. He screamed, fumed, leaped in the air, and in the end became thoroughly convinced that I was too "abstract" to understand politics.

As to America [in English], he said, that is quite uninteresting. The Yankees have no "ideas." "Individual freedom" is merely a "negative idea," etc., the decayed sweepings of the old philosophy.

As I have said, under different circumstances (and if he had not disturbed me in my work) the fellow would have amused me royally.

In addition, the vulgar gluttony and the lecherous lustfulness of this "idealist."

It is now completely clear to me that he, as is proved by his cranial formation and [curly] hair—descends from the Negroes who had joined Moses' exodus from Egypt (assuming his mother or grandmother on the paternal side had not interbred with a *nigger* [in English]). Now this union of Judaism and Germanism with a basic Negro substance must produce a peculiar product. The obtrusiveness of the fellow is also *Nigger*-like [in English].

Incidentally, if Herr Rüstow invented the campaign from Padua to Vienna, then it seems to me he has one chevron too many.

Salut.

Yours, K.M.

One of the great discoveries of our *Nigger* [in English]—which he only confides to his "most trusted friends"—is that the Pelasgians[8] are descendants of the Semites. Main proof: In the Book of Maccabees the Jews send emissaries to Greece for help, appealing to the tribal family relationship. Furthermore, an Etruscan inscription was found in Perugia, and Privy Councillor Stücker and an Italian man have deciphered it simultaneously and have independently resolved the Etruscan alphabet into the Hebraic.

So that we no longer would have to supply him with "Blue Books,"[9] he bought (under Lothar Bucher's guidance) £20 worth of them.

He converted Bucher to socialism, as he claims. Bucher is quite a delicate, even if confused, little man, and in any case I cannot believe that he

---

7. Anti-Semitic tag for Lassalle.
8. An ancient Greek people.
9. Official British Government publications; this reference, of interest to Lassalle, was to : *Papers relating to proposed annexation of Savoy and Nice to France and memorial on the relations between Switzerland and Savoy as a neutral* (3 parts, London, 1860).

has accepted Lassalle's "foreign policy." Bucher is the "female typesetter" in *Julian Schmidt*.

If you had come here for only a few days, you would have accumulated enough stuff to make you laugh for a year. That is why I wanted so much to have you here. Such an opportunity does not come every day.[10]

---

10. Excerpt from Mrs. Karl Marx, *Kurze Umrisse eines bewegten Lebens* [*Short Outlines of a Stirring Life*], written about 1865. "In July, 1862, we had a visit from Ferdinand Lassalle. He was almost crushed under the weight of the fame he had achieved as a scholar, thinker, poet and politician. The laurel wreath was fresh on his Olympian brow and ambrosian head, or rather on his stiff, bristling Negro hair. He had just victoriously ended the Italian campaign—a new political coup was being contrived by the great man of action—and fierce battles were going on in his soul. There were still fields of science that he had not explored! Egyptology lay fallow: 'Should I astonish the world as an Egyptologist or show my versatility as a man of action, as a politician, as a fighter, or as a soldier?' It was a splendid dilemma. He wavered between thoughts and sentiments of his heart and often expressed that struggle in really stentorian accents. As on the wings of the wind he swept through our rooms, perorating so loudly, gesticulating and raising his voice to such a pitch that our neighbors were scared by the terrible shouting and asked us what was the matter. It was the inner struggle of the 'great' man bursting forth in shrill discords. He was in London when he received news of his father's serious illness. He parted with his faithful companion Lothar Bucher, who during the exhibition of 1862 performed for him the duties of messenger, informer, errand boy and entertainer....

"Having found little sympathy for his great man's ideas among us, Lassalle hastened away to Switzerland where he found more receptivity and greater admiration in the society of 'great men' that his soul was hankering for. There he found a congenial atmosphere among sycophants and parasites. He returned to Berlin and instead of showing his worth as an Egyptologist, a soldier, a politician, a poet or a thinker, he chose to follow the yet untrodden path of the Messiah of the workers. Years before, [Hermann] Schulze-Delitzsch had led a savings-bank working people's movement. He was attacked and there began the 'new era of the emancipation of the workers, a movement such as Europe had never seen, the great and only liberation of the oppressed classes through direct suffrage and equality for all.' As a Messiah and an Apostle, Lassalle went over the whole of Germany; pamphlet followed pamphlet and a working-class movement took shape which, being a godsend for the government's political fight against the rather annoying aspirations of the Progressive Party, was silently tolerated and thus indirectly favored by that government.

"As for his 'Lassallean doctrines,' they consisted of the most brazen plagiarisms of the doctrines that Karl had developed twenty years before and a few additions of his own which were frankly reactionary, the result being an astonishing mixture of truth and fiction. And yet all this impressed the working class. The best among the workers kept to the correct kernel of the cause and the crowd of boorish philistines supported with fanatic admiration the new doctrine, the deceptive glamour of the affair and the new Messiah for whom there arose a cult the like of which history has never known. The incense of the boors inebriated half of Germany and even now that Lassalle lies in a quiet Jewish cemetery in Breslau after being shot in a duel in Geneva by a Wallachian youth, the waving of censers, flags, and laurel wreaths still persists. Lassalle left a testament in which he made Countess Hatzfeldt his principal legatee and bestowed considerable legacies on his 'new Swiss friends.' This will be contested by his mother and sister, and the lawsuit is still going on. At the same time he declared Bernhard Becker to be his successor in the management of the affairs of the working class."

347

From letter to Frederick Engels (in Manchester)
London, August 7, 1862

Dear Engels:
The *landlord* [in English] was here on Monday[1] and told me that, after his long patience, if I did not pay him in the shortest possible time he would turn over the matter to a *landagent* [in English]. Then the *broker* [in English] was here. Likewise—peculiarly enough on the same day—I received the tax bill, as well as letters from the *épiciers* [grocers], mostly acquainted with the landlord, complaining and threatening to refuse me *provisions* [in English].

Lassalle left Monday evening. I saw him after *all these events* [in English] had taken place. He saw from my *dejected* [in English] appearance that the crisis, long known to him, had led to a catastrophe *of any art* [*sic*, in English]. He asked me. After I told him, he informed me he could let me have £15 until January 1, 1863; also that promissory notes for any desired *amount* [in English] could be drawn on him, provided that you or somebody else would promise to pay the sum over and above the £15. He cannot do more in his straitened circumstances. (I believe it, since he needed here £1/2 shillings *daily* for *cabs* [in English] and cigars alone....

Itzig [anti-Semitic tag] told me further that he would perhaps establish a newspaper in Berlin, when he returned there in September. I told him I would become the English correspondent for it for *good pay*, without assuming any *responsibility* [in English] or political *partnership* [in English] since politically we agree on nothing except a few remote objectives....

Salut.

Yours, K.M.

348

To Ferdinand Lassalle (in Zurich)
London, August 20, 1862

Dear Lassalle:
I think that despite your rovings through the High Alps and Italy you are spending a few days in Zurich or at any rate receive letters there *poste restante* [General Delivery]. For greater safety, I informed Herr Rüstow that I have written you "*poste restante* Zurich."

347
1. August 4, 1862.

Despite my "situation," I would have made the whole transaction retroactive, if the note had not already been in the hands of the "Brothers Meyer" in Berlin. This was, of course, to some extent against the stipulation that Borkheim had originally promised me, to keep the note at hand until your return to Berlin. Nevertheless, I saw nothing deceitful in the matter, as I considered the use of your name as a mere *formality* in this first note, and had no idea that it would have any connection with your "civic existence" or that it would lead to a collision in some sort of civic drama.

Specifically, I believed that Engels' guarantee of "a sum" of 400 taler was itself sufficient "in case of accident or death"; and as regards the "due-date," I knew that Engels was a man of *absolute* "punctuality and promptness" in money matters, particularly in promissory notes. Otherwise I would not have involved you in this *business* [in English].

Since the matter can no longer be undone, without disgracing Engels and me with Borkheim, I will send you Engels' bond tomorrow.[1] It takes three days from Manchester to here and back. *As soon as you have received it*, it would be a good idea to write to "Brothers Meyer" (this is the name of the firm in Berlin which has Engels' bill of exchange), that you will accept it *upon your return*.

Again, regretting very much to have involved you in the matter—a rashness, due to the ignoring of various premises on your part and mine—I remain

Yours, K.M.

349

To Ferdinand Lassalle (in Berlin)
London, November 7, 1862

Dear Lassalle:

Today Freiligrath sent me £60 to cover the note. Its *renewal*, as I pointed out at the beginning of the operation, occurs only in that Borkheim has received a note from me on you, *for two months post datum* (dated from November 6, and hence payable around January, 1863) for 100 taler or £15.

From the few words that you have written me from time to time, I see that your grievance continues, and the form of your writing indicates it too.

348

1. Engels to Lassalle, August 21, 1862: "At your request, I confirm hereby (what is self-evident in itself) that eight days before the due date of my promissory note of 400 taler to you, per November 13, 1862, I will pay it in Berlin; and if you will let me know to which banker to pay, I will provide the money by November 5."

The long and short of the story is that you are both right and wrong. You demand that I should send a copy of your letter from Baden. For what purpose? So that you can make sure that your letter could be made as an *excuse* for mine to Zurich?[1] With all the *power of analysis* [in English] given you, could you find out with *your own* eyes that which *my* eyes had read, specifically, could you read from it the circumstances under which my own eyes had read? In order to prove to me that I had read wrongly, you must first equalize the readers and then the conditions of the readers, an equalization that you, as Lassalle, would have to undertake under Lassallean circumstances, and not as Marx under Marx's circumstances. Hence, nothing but stuff for new controversy could come out of this. From your letter, I see how little the power of analysis helps you in these actions. Specifically, you ascribe to me what I had never *intended*. The latter I ought to know best under all circumstances. The *literal words* of the letter might prove you right, but the *sense* hidden behind the words, I know *de prime abord* [from the first] better than you. What made me fly into a passion, you could not even imagine. It was the notion that I deduced from your letter (*unjustly*, as a rereading in colder blood has convinced me) that you *doubted* whether I acted with Engels' approval. I concede to you that I did not mention this in my letter and that, apart from my personal relationship, and considered purely factually, this was a tasteless presupposition. Still it appeared so to me at the moment I wrote to you. Conceded further: that this did not express my real grievance, perhaps was not even hinted at in my letter, and that that issue was, rather, based on a false point. Such is the sophistication of all passion.

You are, at any rate, in error in the way you interpret my letter; I am in error, because I wrote it and provided the *materia peccans* [the cause of error].

Ought we, therefore, to become positively estranged? I believe that the substance in our friendship is strong enough to bear even such a shock. I confess to you, *sans phrase* [without circumlocution], that I, a man on the powder keg, permitted a control of the circumstances over me that is un-seemly in an *animal rationale* [rational being]. In any case, it would not be magnanimous on your part, as a jurist and procurator, to hold against me this *status animi* [mental state] in which I would rather have put a bullet through my head.

Thus I hope that our old relationship, "despite everything," will con-tinue undisturbed.

Since that time, I have been on the Continent, in Holland, Trier, etc.,[2] to regulate my [financial] situation. *J'ai abouti à rien* [I accomplished nothing].

349

1. See Letter 348, Marx to Lassalle, August 20, 1862.
2. Marx visited Zalt-Bommel (Holland) and Trier, from August 28 to September 7, 1862.

I wanted to send you the Roscher book,[3] but found that the postage—ten shillings—was the price, though not the value of the book. Still I hope to find another occasion.

My cousin from Amsterdam[4] writes me that your book[5] will be discussed comprehensively, at his instigation, in the Amsterdam journal of jurisprudence.

Salut.

Yours, K.M.

For approximately the last six weeks I have been entirely prevented from working on my book,[6] and am working on it now only with interruptions. Still it is coming to an end *by and by* [in English].

350

From letter to Frederick Engels (in Manchester)
London, January 2, 1863

Dear Frederick:
... Received letter from Itzig [anti-Semitic tag for Lassalle], including the brochures.[1] Contents of the letter: I should return the Roscher[2] to him. *Content of the brochures*: Continuation of the lecture on the Prussian constitution.[3] *Core*: Lassalle is the greatest political figure of all time, especially his own time. It is Lassalle, *and no mistake* [in English], who has discovered, from the purely unhypothetical and purely hypotheticalless theory, that the real constitution of a country is not the written one, but consists of the actual "power relationships," etc. Even the *Neue Preussische Zeitung* and Bismarck and Roon,[4] as he demonstrates in his citations, pay homage to "his" theory. His listeners can, therefore, depend on it, that just as he has discovered the real theory, so he possesses also the real solution for the "moment." And the solution is: "Since the government, despite the decisions of the Chamber,

---

3. Wilhelm Roscher, *System der Volkswirtschaft* [*System of National Economy*], Vol. I (Stuttgart and Augsburg, 1858).
4. August Philips.
5. Lassalle, *The System of Acquired Rights*.
6. *Das Kapital*.

350
1. Lassalle, *What Now? Second Lecture on Constitutionalism* (Zurich, 1863).
2. Wilhelm Roscher, *System of National Economy*.
3. Lassalle, *On Constitutionalism*.
4. General Albrecht Theodor Emil Count von Roon (1803–1879), Prussian statesman and field marshal.

continues its military expenditures, etc., and since therefore the existence of a constitutional regime is a *lie*, etc., the Chamber should suspend its sessions until the government declares those expenditures stopped." This is the power of the "voice of reality." To save the Chamber the labor, he has immediately formulated for it the proper decree.

The Old Heimann[5] has been happily gathered to the bosom of Abraham. Greetings and *compliments of the seasons to the ladies* [in English].[6]

Yours, K.M.

351

From letter to Frederick Engels (in Manchester)
London, April 9, 1863

Dear Frederick:

...Itzig [Lassalle] has already published another two brochures on his trial,[1] which fortunately he did *not* send me. On the other hand, on the day before yesterday he sent me his "Open *Reply*" to the Central Labor Committee of the Leipzig Workers (read: Congress of *philistines[2]*). He comports himself—self-important, throwing around phrases borrowed from us—entirely as the future workers' dictator. The question of wages and capital, he solves in "a playful, easy way" *(verbotenus)* [literally]. Specifically: the workers must agitate for universal suffrage, and then send men like him, armed "with the shining weapon of science," to Parliament. Afterward they would build workers' factories, for which the State would advance capital, and these institutions would extend throughout the whole country *by and by* [in English]. This, at any rate, is surprisingly new! I will cite one passage:

"That the question of a German workers' movement is already being discussed today, whether the *Association is to be conceived in his[3] or my sense*—that is in large part *his* achievement; that is, of course, his *true* achievement, and it cannot be estimated too highly.... The cordiality with which *I recognize this achievement* need not prevent us, etc." *Ça ira* [That will do]....

Salut.

Yours, K.M.

---

5. Heimann Lassal, Ferdinand's father, died in 1862.
6. The ladies were Mary and Lizzy Burns, two sisters who lived in Engels' house.

351

1. Lassalle, "The Lassallean Criminal Case" (Zurich, 1863); and "The Criminal Sentence Against Me ... " (Leipzig, 1863).
2. Lassalle's "Open Reply" to the Leipzig Committee was written on March 1, 1863.
3. Franz Hermann Schulze-Delitzsch (1808–1883), German economist and politician.

352

From letter to Frederick Engels (in Manchester)
London [British Museum], May 29, 1863

Dear Frederick:
... In regard to Itzig [anti-Semitic tag for Lassalle], he dared Freiligrath—as the latter confidentially informed me (he showed me Itzig's letter)—to write a poem on the new movement,[1] meaning a eulogy to Itzig. But he did not succeed with Freiligrath. In his letter, Lassalle wrote, among other things: "Daily hundreds of newspapers carry my name to the remotest corners of Germany." "My proletarians! etc." Since Freiligrath did not eulogize him, he found another poet. Here is an example:

> *Herbei, du deutsches Proletariat!*
> *Herbei, lass' ferner Dich nicht fruchtlos mahnen!*
> *Hier steht ein Mann, bereit den Weg zu bahnen*
> *Zu Deinem Wohlsein. Rüste Dich zur Tat!*
> *Er sitzet nicht im hohen Parlamente,*
> *Stolzieret nicht mit seinem Worttalente;*
> *Einfach, verständlich spricht er für uns Alle,*
> *Der Mann des Volkes, Ferdinand Lassalle!*[2]

Macte puer! [Hail, Stripling!] Is this not good for the bedbugs? ...

Yours, K.M.

353

From letter to Frederick Engels (in Manchester)
London [British Museum], June 12, 1863

Dear Engels:
...Itzig [anti-Semitic tag for Lassalle] has sent me (perhaps also to you) his speech before the court on *direct taxes*. There are some good things in it, but

---

352
1. On May 23, 1863, Lassalle founded the General German Workers' Association.
2. Freely translated:
> This way, thou German proletariat!
> This way, do not let thyself be summoned in vain!
> Here stands a man, ready to prepare the way
> to thy welfare. Arm thyself for the deed!
> He does not sit in a high Parliament,
> does not flaunt his talents for words;
> simply, clearly, he speaks for us all,
> The man of the People, *Ferdinand Lassalle!*

the whole thing is, first of all, unbearably pushy, boastful, and *written* with the most ridiculous erudition and self-importance. In addition, it is *essentiale-ment* [essentially] the bungled exercise of a "schoolboy" who is in a hurry to proclaim himself a "solidly learned" man and independent researcher. Hence it teems with historical and theoretical *blunders* [in English]. One example may suffice (in case you have not read the stuff yourself). He wants—in order to impress the court and the public—to present a species of retrospective history of the polemic against indirect taxes, but backtracks diagonally by citing from Boisguillebert and Vauban to Bodin,[1] etc. Here the arch-school-boy is revealed. He leaves out the *Physiocrats*, but clearly does not know that everything that Adam Smith, etc., had said on the subject had been copied from them, and they were in general the heroes on that "question." Equally altogether schoolboyish is his idea of "indirect taxes" conceived as "bourgeois taxes," which they were "in the Middle Ages," but not today (at least not where the bourgeoisie is developed), as he could learn from Herr Robert Gladstone[2] & Co. in Liverpool. The jackass seems not to know that the polemic against "indirect" taxes is a slogan of the English and American friends of "Schulze-Delitzsch" and Company, hence, at any rate, a slogan *against* them, I mean the Free Traders. Altogether *schoolboyish* in his *application* of a sentence by Ricardo to Prussian ground rents. (Hence fundamentally false.) It is touching how he informs the court of "*his*" discoveries, made in the deepest "science and truth" during frightful "night hours," specifically:

that in the Middle Ages there existed landed real estate,

that in modern times there exists "capital," and now

the "*principle* of the workers' estate," of "labor," or of "*the moral principle of labor*";

and on the same day that he reported his discovery to the philistines, *Oberregierungsrat* [Government Councillor] Engel[3] (without knowing about him) reported it to a refined public in the [Berlin] Academy of Song.[4] He and Engel mutually congratulated each other by "letter" on their "simultaneous" scientific findings.

The "workers' estate" and the "moral principle" are, indeed, the grand achievements of Itzig and the *Oberregierungsrat*.

353

1. French political philosopher Jean Bodin (1530–1596).
2. Cousin of British statesman William Ewart Gladstone.
3. Prussian statistician Ernst Engel (1821–1896).
4. On February 15, 1862, Ernst Engel delivered a lecture, "The Censuses, Their Position in Science and Their Task in History," before the Berlin Academy.

I have not been able to bring myself to the point of writing to the fellow since the beginning of the year.

If I should criticize his stuff, it would be a loss of time; in addition, he appropriates every word as a "discovery." To hit him in the snout with his plagiarism would be ridiculous, since I do not want to take away from him our things [ideas] in the form that he has smeared them up. To give recognition to those boastings and *tactlessnesses*, would not do either. The fellow would immediately take advantage of it.

Hence there is nothing left for us to do until his anger finally bursts out. Then I would have a very fine excuse for saying, as he always (like *Oberregierungsrat* Engel) remarks himself, this is not *"communism."* I would then answer him that his repeated protestations, if I must take notice of them, have forced me to do this:

(1) To show the public how and where he has copied us;

(2) how and where we differ from his stuff.

In order not to derogate "communism" and not to hurt him, I would completely ignore him.

Incidentally, the fellow makes all this noise out of sheer vanity. In 1859, he belonged entirely to the Prussian liberal bourgeois party. Now he may find it more convenient under the *auspices of government* [in English], to let loose on the "bourgeois," instead of on the "Russians." To revile the Austrians and to rave for the Italians, has always been something specifically Berlinish, rather than keeping one's mouth shut against the Russians, as does our brave youth [Lassalle].

Salut.

Yours, K.M.

354

From letter to Frederick Engels (in Manchester)
London, July 6, 1863

Dear Engels:
...Itzig [anti-Semitic tag for Lassalle] has sent me a new brochure,[1] his speech in Frankfurt. Since I am now spending, ex officio, ten hours a day on economics, it is not to be expected that I should kill my spare hours with the

---

354
1. Lassalle, "A Workers' Reader," speech delivered on May 17 and 19, 1863.

reading of the thoughts of this schoolboy. Hence I shelved it for the time being. In my free time, I pursue differential and integral calculus....
Salut.

Yours, K.M.

355

From letter to Frederick Engels (in Manchester)
London, August 15, 1863

Dear Frederick:

...The same Itzig [anti-Semitic tag for Lassalle] keeps on collecting for his manure factory those pieces of party excrement that we had discarded twenty years ago, with which to fertilize world history. Thus, for example, he had arranged publication in the *Nordstern*[1] the adhesion piece by "Herwegh" (who surely has preserved his *Platonic* love for the "principle of labor"). This *Nordstern* is edited by the tramp Bruhn,[2] whom Lassalle had bought from Blind. In this way, Itzig has nominated "Moses Hess" to be his "Governor of the Rhine Province," etc. And he still cannot rid himself of the *idée fixe* that Freiligrath should eulogize him in song. Freiligrath gives him the Bronx cheer.[3] Specifically, by holding out before Freiligrath the good example of G. Herwegh, he has summoned him urgently through his Leipzig "Governor." If he only knew how Freiligrath and I had laughed over this new attempt!

O Itzig, O Itzig, was hast du gedenkt,
Das Du Dich an den Herwegh und den Moses H[ess]gehenkt[4]...
Salut.

Yours, K.M.

355

1. Pro-Lassalle Hamburg daily.
2. Karl von Bruhn (b. 1803), German communist journalist.
3. See Letter 352, Marx to Engels, May 29, 1863.
4. Literally translated:
    "O Itzig, O Itzig, what didst thou think,
    That thou on Herwegh and Moses H[ess] got hanged!"

356

To Jenny Marx (wife) (in Brighton)
London, September 2, 1864

Dear Jenny:

Yesterday I received a letter from Freiligrath—copy to follow—wherein you will see that Lassalle has been fatally wounded in a duel at Geneva.[1] The news has dismayed us, as Lassalle was after all too good a man to have been destroyed this way. Upon receipt of the letter, I went to see Freiligrath, that is, to his home, since I knew that Ida[2] was away. He was "pleasantly" surprised by my visit. His daughter Louise was with him. The rest of the gang returns at the end of this week. Louise had been with Franziska Ruge[3] in Brighton for two weeks. In view of the Freiligrath-Ruge relationship, etc., you should be careful with your Baroness[4] visiting cards. Ruge is the kind of fellow to make [hostile] use of this.

Freiligrath is in no way "moved," as he claims to be in his letter, but made his little jokes as before, even at Lassalle's expense. He told me that his bank[5] is in crisis, and that the Geneva affair[6] and particularly Fazy's role in it, are doing it great harm. Finally, Tussy's[7] *last* [in English]. As it appeared from Freiligrath's letter that Lassalle's duel was caused over a lady whom he wanted to marry,[8] Laura[9] recalled that he told every lady that "he could love her only for six weeks." So, said Tussy, *he is warranted for six weeks*" [in English].

Jennychen[10] works like mad *in her greenhouse* [in English]. All are well and send their regards.

The Old One [in English]

356

1. For details of the duel, see Letter 357, Marx to Engels, September 7, 1864, and the latter's comment in Note 1.
2. Freiligrath's wife.
3. Daughter of Marx's enemy, Arnold Ruge.
4. Mrs. Marx (Jenny von Westphalen) was the daughter of a German baron and hence entitled to call herself Baroness, as she did, in some defiance, on her visiting cards.
5. Freiligrath was the manager of the London branch of General Bank of Switzerland.
6. In the August, 1864, election for the Geneva city council, there was rioting on the part of the followers of Fazy after he lost his reelection bid.
7. Nickname of Marx's youngest daughter, Eleanor.
8. Helene von Dönniges.
9. Marx's daughter Laura.
10. Marx's daughter Jenny.

357

From letter to Frederick Engels (in Manchester)
London, September 7, 1864

Dear Frederick:
Lassalle's misfortune[1] has been going through my head in a damnable way in the last few days. He was after all one of the *vieille souche* [old tribe] and an enemy of our enemies. Added to that, the thing came as such a surprise that it is hard to believe that this noisy, *stirring, pushing* [in English] man is now dead as a mouse and his mouth shut altogether. His death is one of the many tactless things he committed in his life. *With all that* [in English], I am sorry that our relationship had been troubled in the last years, indeed through his own fault.[2] On the other hand, I am glad that I resisted incitements from various quarters to attack him in his " Jubilee-Year."[3]

The devil knows, the group becomes smaller, no new ones are coming up. For the rest, I am convinced that if Lassalle had not associated with the military adventurers and revolutionaries *en gants jaunes* [in kid gloves] in Switzerland, he would never have met with that catastrophe. But he was fatally attracted to this Koblenz[4] of the European revolution.

The "Bavarian ambassador's daughter"[5] is none other than the daughter of the Berlin Dönniges,[6] the university codemagogue of Rutenberg and Con-

---

357

1. On August 30, 1864, Ferdinand Lassalle was fatally wounded in Geneva in a duel with a Rumanian pseudo-prince, Janko von Racowitza, over a girl, Helene von Dönniges. Engels commented about it in a letter to Marx, September 4, 1864: "You can imagine how the news surprised me. Personally, historically, scientifically, Lassalle may have been what he was, but politically he was surely one of the most outstanding fellows in Germany. For us he was an uncertain friend in the present, quite certainly an enemy in the future, but nevertheless it hits one hard to see how Germany destroys all moderately capable men of the extreme party. What joy there will be among the manufacturers and the Progressive pig-dogs [*Schweinhunden*], Lassalle having been after all the only man in Germany whom they feared. But what an extraordinary way to lose one's life: To fall seriously in love with a Bavarian ambassador's daughter—this would-be Don Juan—to want to marry her, to come into collision with a dismissed rival who was at the same time also a Wallachian swindler, and to let oneself be shot to death. Such a thing could only happen to Lassalle, that strange mixture of frivolity and sentimentality, Jewishness and chivalric bravado that was peculiarly his own. How could a political man like Lassalle get himself into a duel with a Wallachian adventurer!"
2. See Letter 358, Marx to Sophie von Hatzfeldt, September 12, 1864.
3. The year 1863, when (in May) Lassalle was chosen president of the General German Workers' Association, which he had founded.
4. During the French Revolution, in the 1790's, Koblenz was the center of the anti-Revolutionary royalists.
5. Helene von Dönniges, the nineteen-year old girl over whom Lassalle fought the duel that killed him.
6. Franz Alexander von Dönniges.

sorts, belonging originally to the *jeunes gents* [young gentlemen], or rather, since they were no gentlemen, to the *jeunes gens* of the little *Rabunzel* [twerp] Ranke, the editor of the dreadful German Imperial annals,[7] etc. What the little dancing dwarf Ranke considered to be intellect—his playful anecdote-mongering and his referring of all great events to trivialities and lousinesses—was strictly forbidden to these *young men from the country* [in English]. They were expected to stick to "objectivity" and leave ideas to their Master. Our friend Dönniges was considered a rebel to a certain extent, since he challenged Ranke's monopoly on ideas, at least factually, and showed through various *ad oculos* [eyewitnesses] that he is as good a born "lackey" of "history" as Ranke.

I am wondering what will now become of Lassalle's organization.[8] Herwegh, this Platonic friend of "labor" and practical friend of the Muses, is not the man to take over. In general, all the lesser leaders in it are *rubbish* [in English]. Liebknecht writes me that the Schulze-Delitzsch Society in Berlin has hardly forty members.[9] You can judge its state when you realize that our Wilhelm Liebknecht is a consequential political personage in it. Should Lassalle's death lead fellows like Schulze-Delitzsch, etc., to insolences against the deceased, it would be desirable that the former's adherents behave in such a way as to make it possible to enter the arena on their side, if necessary. I must now find out who has his literary remains. I will immediately get out an injunction—since the Memoir-vultures like Ludmilla [Assing], etc., are sniffing closely around those remains—against having a single line of mine or yours published. In Prussia, one can force this through the courts, if necessary. . . .

Salut, *old boy* [in English].

Yours, K.M.

358

To Sophie von Hatzfeldt (in Berlin)
London, September 12, 1864

My dear Countess:
You can understand how the unexpected news of Lassalle's death has surprised, shocked, and shaken me. He was one of the people of whom I

---

7. Ranke, ed., *Jahrbücher des Deutschen Reichs unter dem Sächsischen Hause* [*Annals of the German Empire under the Saxon Dynasty*].
8. The General German Workers' Association.
9. The Berlin Workers' Association, founded in January, 1863, by the economist Franz Hermann Schulze-Delitzsch.

thought a great deal.[1] This is the more unfortunate for me as we had not been in contact in recent years. But the reason was *his silence*—because he began it, not I—and an illness of more than a year's duration, of which I am rid only in the last few days. There are additional reasons, which I would have to report to you orally, not in writing. But be sure that nobody can be more deeply pained by Lassalle's passing than I. And above all, I feel for you. I know what the deceased has meant to you, what his loss is to you.[2] Be glad of one thing. He died young, in triumph, like Achilles.

I hope, my dear countess, that you will bear this stroke of fate with your noble and brave spirit, and accept the expression of my complete devotion.

Your sincere friend, Karl Marx

359

To Sophie von Hatzfeldt (in Berlin) [copy of a fragment]
London, October 16, 1864

My dear Countess:
I have been so seriously ill in the last few weeks that I had to stay in bed, and, alas, postpone a reply to your friendly letter of October 1 until now.

I assure you that I still cannot make myself accept Lassalle's death as a *fait accompli!* So full of life, spirit, energy, projects, so thoroughly youthful as I visualize him, and now suddenly dead—I lack the connecting links, the transitions, and this fact weighs on me like a disordered and monstrous nightmare.

You are quite right when you suppose that nobody could recognize the greatness and importance of Lassalle more than I. He himself knew that best, as his letters to me prove. So long as we maintained our correspondence, I always expressed my warmest recognition of his achievements, on the one hand, and my critical frankness about what appeared to me to be dubious here and there, on the other.

In one of his last letters to me he expressed his satisfaction with this in his own powerful way. But apart from all his achievements, I loved him *personally*. The worst of this is that we mutually concealed this from each other, as if we would live forever. . . .

[no signature]

358
1. See Letter 357, Marx to Engels, September 7, 1864.
2. Marx to Wilhelm Liebknecht, September 20, 1865: " . . . Old Hatzfeldt is staying in Paris, where she is intriguing with the 'horned' father of 'socialism,' Moses [Hess], her most submissive slave. . . . She is now engaged in cooking up with him the 'apotheosis' of her late 'Oedipus' [Lassalle]. . . . "

360

From letter to Frederick Engels (in Manchester)
London, November 4, 1864

Dear Frederick:

...You must return all the enclosed papers as soon as you have read them. *I still need them.* So that I do not forget what I wanted to report, I number them.

(1) *Lassalle and Countess Hatzfeldt.*

The copious document is a copy of a circular which Herwegh's wife (*honny* [sic] *soit qui mal y pense*)[1] Emma sent to Berlin immediately after the catastrophe,[2] so that extracts from it could be used in the newspapers. In it you can see how skillfully Emma [Herwegh] has placed herself and her flabby husband at the beginning, middle and end of the affair; how the account avoids two important points: first, the meeting of Rüstow[3] with Dönniges and his daugher,[4] wherein the latter must have *turned down* Lassalle before the scene which Emma relates took place; secondly, how it came to the duel. Lassalle wrote the insulting letter. But something followed this, which is *not* being told and which led directly to the duel.[5]

The suppression of two such important turning points raise critical doubts about the trustworthiness of the account.

(2) *The Hatzfeldt Letter.*

Upon her return to Berlin, I sent her a brief letter of condolence[6] through Liebknecht. He wrote me[7] that she complains that "I have left

---

360

1. "Shame on him who thinks evil of it": motto of the Order of the Garter.
2. The duel which led to Lassalle's death on August 31, 1864.
3. Friedrich Wilhelm Rüstow (1821–1878), German officer on Giuseppe Garibaldi's staff.
4. Helene von Dönniges, the nineteen-year-old girl over whom Lassalle fought the duel.
5. Engels took a much more cynical view of the affair. He wrote to Marx, November 7, 1864: "I am returning the stories about Herwegh and Hatzfeldt. What kind of a further provocation, which injured the Wallachian [the duelist Janko von Racowitza] and which Emma is supposed to have suppressed, are you referring to? Lassalle obviously went *kaputt* because he did not immediately throw the dame [Helene von Dönniges] on the bed in the lodging-house and screwed her properly; she did not want his beautiful mind but his Jewish jock. It is again the same story that could only happen to a Lassalle. That he forced the Wallachian to a duel was doubly crazy."

Some years later, on August 22, 1868, Engels again wrote to Marx about Lassalle: "The more one gets to know the details of the Lassalle tragicomedy, the more one sees the comic side of it.... Poor Baron Itzig! Comical in the exalted moment when he gives his alter ego, Rüstow, the order to sleep, if necessary, with the beautiful Helene *per procura* [in his place]—he knew well how little danger there was in that—as little, he thought, as in the duel when the Wallachian shot off his nuts. Poor Itzig! To be shot by a Wallachian in the 'gelding'!"
6. See Letter 358, to Countess von Hatzfeldt, September 12, 1864.
7. On September 30, 1864.

Lassalle in the lurch," as if I could have done the man a better service than to keep my mouth shut and leave him to his own devices. (In his last speech before the Düsseldorf Assizes,[8] he played the Marquis Posa to Philip II's Handsome William,[9] whom he wanted to induce to a suspension of the present constitution, to a proclamation of direct universal suffrage, and to an alliance with the proletariat.) You can see what is behind Hatzfeldt's letter and what she wants from me. I have answered her in a very friendly way, but warded her off diplomatically.[10] The modern savior! The person and the sycophants who surround her are mad. . . .

Salut.

Yours, K.M.

361

To Ludwig Kugelmann (in Hanover)
London, February 23, 1865

Honored Friend:

Yesterday I received your very interesting letter and will now reply point by point.

First of all, I shall briefly describe my attitude toward *Lassalle*. During his agitation, our relation was suspended: (1) because of the self-praising braggadocio, to which at the same time he added the most shameless plagiarism from my writings, etc.; (2) because I *condemned* his political tactics; (3) because, even *before* he began his agitation, I fully explained and "proved" to him here in London that direct *socialist* action by the "State of *Prussia*" was nonsense. In his letters to me (from 1848 to 1863), as in his personal encounters, he always declared himself to be an adherent of the Party which I represent. As soon as he had convinced himself, in London (at the end of 1862), that he could not play his games with me, he decided to put himself forward as the "workers' dictator" against me and the old Party. Despite all this, I recognized his services as an agitator, even though at the end of his short life the agitation itself appeared to me more and more in an ambiguous light. His sudden death, old friendship, sorrowful letters from Countess Hatzfeldt, indignation over the cowardly insolence of the bourgeois newspapers toward one whom in his lifetime they had so greatly feared, all that induced me to publish a brief statement against the wretched Blind [Karl],

---

8. His defense in court, June 27, 1864.
9. King William I of Prussia: Marquis Posa was a hero in a Schiller play who thought he could convince Philip II of the rightness of his cause.
10. See Letter 359, Marx to Countess von Hatzfeldt, October 16, 1864.

which, however, did not deal with the content of Lassalle's actions (Hatzfeldt sent the statement to the *Nordstern*[1]).

For the same reasons, and in the hope of being able to remove the elements that seemed to me to be dangerous, Engels and I promised to contribute to the *Social-Demokrat* (it has published a translation of the "Address,"[2] and at the editors' request, upon Proudhon's death, I wrote an article about him)[3]; and, after Schweitzer had sent us a satisfactory program of his editorship, we allowed our names to be used as contributors.[4] An additional guarantee for us was that Liebknecht was an unofficial member of the editorial board. Nevertheless, it soon became apparent—the proofs fell into our hands—that Lassalle had in fact betrayed the Party. He had entered into a formal contract with Bismarck (of course without having in his hand any kind of guarantee). At the end of September, 1864, he was to go to Hamburg and there (together with the crazy Schramm and the Prussian police spy Marr) "force" Bismarck to annex Schleswig-Holstein, that is, to proclaim its incorporation in the name of the "workers," etc., in return for which Bismarck promised universal suffrage and a new socialist charlatanism. It is a pity that Lassalle could not play the comedy through to the end! The hoax would have made him look damned ridiculous! And all efforts of this kind would have been put to an end for good!

Lassalle went astray because he was a *"Realpolitiker"* of the type of Herr Miquel[5] but cut on a larger pattern and with stronger aims! (By the by, I had long ago sufficiently seen through Miquel to explain his role by the fact that the National Union[6] offered an excellent excuse for a petty Hanoverian lawyer to make his voice heard outside his own four walls by all Germany, and thus, by its reaction at home, validate the enhanced reality of himself in the Hanoverian homeland, playing the "Hanoverian Mirabeau" under Prussian

---

361

1. Marx, "Letter to the Editor of the *Beobachter* at Stuttgart," published in *Nordstern*, December 10, 1864.
2. Marx, "Inaugural Address of the Workingmen's Association," written October 21–27, 1864; published in *Social-Demokrat*, December 21 and 30, 1864.
3. Marx, "On P. J. Proudhon," letter to Johann Baptist von Schweitzer, January 24, 1865; published in *Social-Demokrat*, February 1, 3, and 5, 1865.
4. Liebknecht, on November 4, and Von Schweitzer, on November 11, 1864, asked Marx to contribute to the *Social-Demokrat*, to which Marx (together with Engels) agreed in the hope of turning it in a revolutionary direction. The Marx-Engels statement of their collaboration with the paper was published in its issue of March 3, 1865. They broke with the paper about two weeks later: on March 19, 1865, the *Social-Demokrat* printed Marx's "Statement" of the break.
5. Johannes Miquel (1828–1901), a German lawyer, erstwhile communist, later a leader of the National Liberal Party.
6. The German National Union, founded in 1859, dissolved in 1867.

protection.) Just as Miquel and his present friends snatched at the "new era" inaugurated by the Prussian Prince Regent, in order to join the National Union and to latch on to the "Prussian top," just as they developed their "civic pride" under general Prussian protection, so Lassalle wanted to play the Marquis Posa of the proletariat with Philip II of Uckermark [i.e., Wilhelm I], Bismarck acting as intermediary between him and the Prussian kingdom. He only aped the gentlemen of the National Union. But while they invoked the Prussian "reaction" in the interest of the middle class, Lassalle shook hands with Bismarck in the interest of the proletariat. Those gentlemen had greater justification than Lassalle, insofar as the bourgeois is accustomed to regard the interest immediately before his nose as "reality," and as in fact this class has generally achieved a compromise everywhere, even with feudalism, while in the nature of things, the working class must be sincerely *"revolutionary."*

For a theatrically vain nature like Lassalle's (who was not, however, to be bribed by paltry things like office, a mayoralty, etc.), it was a most tempting thought: an action directly on behalf of the proletariat, executed by Ferdinand Lassalle! In fact he was too ignorant of the real economic conditions connected with such an action to be critically true to himself. The German workers, on the other hand, were too "demoralized" by the despicable "practical politics" which had induced the German bourgeoisie to tolerate the reaction of 1849-59 and the stupefying of the people, not to hail such a quack savior, who promised to get into the promised land in one leap! ...

Yours, K.M.

362

From draft of a letter to Johann Baptist von Schweitzer (in Berlin)[1]
London, October 13, 1868

Dear Sir: ·
...*D'abord* [To begin with], in regard to the Lassalle Association,[2] it was established in a period of reaction. After a fifteen-year slumber, Lassalle reawakened the workers' movement in Germany—and this remains his immortal service. But he committed great mistakes. He permitted himself to be dominated too much by the immediate circumstances of the time. He made a

---

362

1. Johann Baptist von Schweitzer.
2. The General German Workers' Association, founded by Lassalle in Leipzig on May 23, 1863; he was its president until his death, on August 31, 1864.

small starting point—his opposition to a dwarf like Schulze-Delitzsch—into the central point of his agitation: State-help versus self-help. Thereby he merely took up again the slogan which Buchez,[3] the leader of Catholic social-ism, had propounded in 1843 and subsequently against the real workers' movement in France. Much too intelligent to regard this slogan as anything more than a temporary *pis-aller* [makeshift], Lassalle could justify it only on the ground of its (alleged) immediate practicality. For this purpose, he had to maintain that it could be carried out in the *near* future. Hence *the* "State" became transformed into the Prussian State. Thus he was forced into con-cessions to the Prussian monarchy, the Prussian reaction (feudal party), and even the clericals. With Buchez's State aid for associations he combined the Chartist cry for universal suffrage. He overlooked the fact that conditions in Germany and England were different. He overlooked the lessons of the Second Empire with regard to French universal suffrage. Moreover, from the outset—like every man who maintains that he has in his pocket a panacea for the sufferings of mankind—he gave his agitation a religious and sectarian character. In fact, every sect is religious. Furthermore, precisely because he was the founder of a sect, he denied all natural connection with the earlier movement in Germany, as well as abroad. He fell into the same error as Proudhon, and instead of looking among the actual elements of the class movement for the real basis of his agitation, he tried to ascribe its course to these elements according to a certain dogmatic recipe.

Most of what I am saying here *post festum* [after the event] I predicted to Lassalle in 1862, when he came to London and invited me to place myself with him at the head of the new movement....

I promise you,[4] under all circumstances, my impartiality, which is my duty. On the other hand, I can promise nothing ... [if] someday I ... may want to explore in open criticism ... Lassallean superstitition, as I once did in the case of Proudhon.[5]

Assuring you of my best personal wishes,

Faithfully yours, K.M.

---

3. Philippe Joseph Benjamin Buchez (1796–1865), French politician and historian.
4. Schweitzer succeeded to the presidency of the German Workers' Association upon Lassalle's death.
5. Marx, *The Poverty of Philosophy* (1847).

LETTERS from HEINRICH MARX to HIS SON KARL as a STUDENT in BONN and BERLIN · *1835-1837*

In October, 1835, Karl Marx matriculated in Bonn University. He was then a boy of seventeen, the oldest son in a family of eight siblings and the glowing hope of his parents. His father, Heinrich Marx, a prominent lawyer in Trier, a small historic town in Rhenish Prussia, where Karl was born in 1818, considered him the most gifted of his children and one with the brightest future. "I wish to see in you," he told Karl, "what I could have become if I had come into the world under the same favorable auspices as you." To his mother, Henriette Pressburg Marx, a poorly educated woman born in Holland, Karl, whose name she pronounced in the Dutch way: "Kar-rel," was a *Glückskind*—a Child of Fortune.

In Bonn, Karl entered the Faculty of Jurisprudence, since it was his father's hope that he would become a lawyer. He registered in six courses, three in law and three in poetry and art. For the first three weeks he did not write home at all. It did not seem to have occurred to him that his overprotective father would be concerned about his studies and his doting mother would be worried about his always delicate health. Six weeks after his matriculation, his father complained: "It is amazing that we do not even have your address yet." In the first three months Karl wrote home only twice, hurried and hardly legible notes asking for money. Those letters, as well as others of the period, have been lost.

Karl plunged ebulliently into the gay life of the roistering students, with their carousing, drinking, and dueling. He joined a student *Landsmannschaft* (regional fraternity), of which he became a leader, and carried a dueling weapon, for which he was arrested once in nearby Cologne. Together with other students, he indulged in "nightly uproarious disturbances of the peace and drunkenness," to quote the remarks on his Leaving Certificate from Bonn, for which he spent twenty-four hours in the University *Karzer* (student prison).[1] Sometime in the summer of 1836 he fought a duel and was wounded near the right eye. And all the time he spent money lavishly and, to the dismay of his father, piled up debts.

Karl's riotous living shocked his conservative, provincial father. On July 1, 1836, Heinrich Marx sent a brief, official note to Bonn: "I not only grant my son Carl[2] Marx permission but also [express] my intention ... that he transfer to the University of Berlin in the next Semester." In August, Karl left Bonn for Trier, where he spent his vacation and where he became secretly engaged to Jenny von Westphalen, his childhood sweetheart who was four years his senior and regarded as the most beautiful girl in Trier. Jenny, daughter of a local aristocratic family, had to go through seven years of anxiety and torment before she and Karl could get married (June 19, 1843).

The following letters of Marx's parents seem to be the only ones to have been preserved.

1

To Karl Marx (in Bonn)
Trier, November 18, 1835

Dear Karl!
First, a few words about my [previous] letter, which may possibly have vexed you. You know that I do not stand pedantically on my authority and that I would admit even to my child when I am wrong. I had, in truth, told you that you should write home only after you have looked around you more

---

1. For details, see Saul K. Padover, *Karl Marx: An Intimate Biography* (McGraw-Hill Book Co., New York, 1978), Chapter III.
2. Carl—with a "C" —was the name on Marx's birth certificate and other official documents.

closely. Still, you should have taken my words less literally, particularly since you know how anxious and worried your good mother is. But enough of this chapter.

Your letter, which was hardly legible, has given me great pleasure. You may be sure I entertain no doubts about your good will and your diligence, and also not about your determination, to do something that is excellent. In the meantime, I am delighted that the beginning is agreeable and easy for you and that you are acquiring a taste for your vocation.

Nine courses seem to me to be somewhat too many, and I don't want you to do more than body and soul can bear. Still, if you do not find it too difficult, then it might be all right. The field of knowledge is immeasurable, and the time is short. In your next letter you will surely give me a report in greater detail. You know how everything that concerns you intimately interests me.

With the juridical courses you need not...[1] be melodious and poetic. The material does not allow it.... To poetry you will have to accommodate yourself and ... find the deepest values. Excuse ... special subjects.

What can I say more? Preach to you? Tell ... what you do not know? Although nature has ... sufficiently endowed you, so that when you truly ... your clear understanding, your pure feelings, your uncorrupted ... inform you not to stray from the straight path ... , and what I hope for, you know very well. I only want ... to obtain what under less favorable circumstances ... I could not. I wish to see in you what perhaps I could have become if I had come into the world under the same favorable auspices as you. You can fulfil or destroy my finest hopes. It is perhaps unjust and unwise to build the finest hopes on another human being and thereby possibly undermine his own peace of mind. Nevertheless, what else but nature can be responsible for the fact that men who are not otherwise weak are yet weak fathers?

To you, dear Karl, has been allotted luck such as few youngsters of your age have. In the first important years of your life, you have found a friend, a very estimable friend,[2] older and more experienced than you. Know how to appreciate this stroke of luck. Friendship, in the real classical sense of the term, is the finest gem in life, and, at your age, for life. It would be the best touchstone of your character, your mind and heart, yea, of your morality, if you retain that friend and remain worthy of him.

That you remain morally good, that I do not really doubt. Still, a great lever for morality is the pure belief in God. You know I am anything but a fanatic. But this belief is for man, early or late in life, a genuine need, and

---

1

1. Throughout the letter, ellipses indicate words missing or torn out.
2. Ludwig von Westphalen, the father of Marx's future wife, Jenny.

there are moments in life when even an atheist [*Gottesleugner*] is drawn to pray to the All-Highest. And it is a commonplace . . . , for that in which Newton, Locke and Leibniz believed in, everybody . . . must submit to.

Herr Lörs[3] took it amiss that you did not say good-bye to him. You and Clemens[4] were the only ones [who didn't]; he . . . Herr Schlick. I had to resort to an innocent lie and tell him . . . we visited him during his absence. The association . . . grouped with Clemens pleased me little.

Herr Lörs has been appointed second director, and yesterday Herr Brüggemann, the commissioner, was here for his installation. There was a big . . . ceremony, where Herr Brüggemann and Herr Loers spoke. At noon, Herr Lörs gave a big dinner, which I also attended. There I spoke to many who inquired about you, and many congratulated me that Herr Wienenbrügge[5] is your friend. I am truly desirous to make his acquaintance, and I would be pleased if both of you visit us for Easter and, it goes without saying, stay with us. This would be a particular proof of his friendship for you.

And so, dear Karl, farewell, and when you have given your mind strong and healthy nourishment, do not forget that in this miserable world the body is its first companion and conditions the well-being of the whole machine. A sickly scholar is the unhappiest being on earth. Therefore, do not study any more than your health permits. Add to it, daily exercise and abstinence, and I hope to embrace you every time more strengthened in mind and body.

Your devoted Father, Marx

Apropos. I have read your poem word for word. I confess to you with complete frankness, dear Karl, that I do not understand it, neither its true sense nor its tendency. In daily life, it is an unchallenged truism that with the fulfillment of the most ardent desires, the value of the latter strongly declines and often disappears altogether. That you did not mean to say. It would also have been very heartening as a moral basis, as, guided by such thoughts, one banishes immoral enjoyments, and postpones even moral ones, in order to retain the desire in the postponement or achieve a heightened enjoyment. Kant has felicitously said something of the sort in his anthropology.

Do you want to find bliss only in abstract idealizing (something analogous to ecstasy)? In brief, do give me the key, I confess my limitation.

[*On the left margin of the first page*]
At the ceremony for Herr Lörs, I found the position of the good Herr

---

3. Vitus Lörs (*d.* 1862), Marx's Latin teacher in the Gymnasium.
4. Heinrich Clemens (*c.* 1818–1852), Marx's fellow-student in the Gymnasium and in Bonn, later, a notary in Saarlouis.
5. Christian Hermann Wienenbrügge (*c.* 1817–1851), a Bonn philosophy student, who lived there in the same house as Marx; he later became director of a girls' school in Trier.

Wyttenbach[6] extremely painful. I could have wept over the humbling of this man, whose only fault is too much generosity. I did my best to show him my esteem and told him, among others, how you too are devoted to him and that you wanted to write a poem in his honor, but that you did not have the time. That made him happy. Would you do me a favor and send me a few verses for him?

[*Postscript on top right of the first page*]
P.S. Your dear Mother was prevented, and so it went until today, November 29th. Amazing, that we still do not know your exact address yet.

[*Mother's Postscript, written November 29*][7]
Greatly beloved dear Carl!

with much pleasure I take the pen to write to you the letter of your dear father is long already and always I am prevented, so that I could already have had a letter from you, which would attest to your well-being for you can believe me that I really very much long for you thank Heaven we are all quite healthy everything is active and diligent also Eduard[8] toils so that we hope yet to make an efficient man out of him now you cannot ascribe it to the weakness of my sex if I am curious to know how you arranged your small household, if frugality plays the main role in big as well as in little household expenses which is an indispensable necessity, in addition I permit myself to remark dear Carl that you must never regard cleanliness and orderliness as unimportant because health and cheerfulness depend upon them see to it punctually that your rooms are scrubbed often set a regular time for it—and scrub my beloved Carl weekly with sponge and soap—how goes it with the coffee Do you fabricate it yourself or what, I beg you to report to me everything about the housekeeping, your amiable Muse will not feel offended by the Prose of your Mother, tell Her that through the inferior the superior and the better are attained, and so keep well if you have a wish for Christmas that I can satisfy I am prepared for it with pleasure so keep well my beloved Carl be worthy and good and always keep God and your Parents before your eyes adieu your loving Mother Henriette Marx.

All the children send their greetings and kisses and as it always used to be you are the kindest and the best.

---

6. Johann Hugo Wyttenbach (1767–1848), the director of the Gymnasium that Karl Marx attended, of whom the Prussian Government was suspicious because of his liberalism. Vitus Lörs was appointed deputy director in order to keep an eye on him and on liberal students.
7. Punctuation and syntax have been preserved more or less as in the original German, but not the spelling.
8. Karl Marx's brother Eduard was born on July 30, 1824, and died on December 14, 1837.

2

To Karl Marx (in Bonn)
Trier, early 1836

Dear Karl:

If the account of your condition[1] was not somewhat poetic—and I hope it was—then it was very much designed to disquiet us. I hope that your sad experience will at least show you the necessity of being somewhat more careful with your health. After a good conscience, that is the highest good of humanity, and the sins of youth in regard to every immoderate or even harmful gratification in and by itself, revenge themselves frightfully. A tragic example of this we have here in Herr Günster.[2] There is no question of vice in his case, to be sure, but smoking and drinking have shattered his already weak chest, and he will hardly survive the summer. His life itself is a torment, and in him a fine spirit will be lost.

Even immoderate studies are an insanity in such a case. Moderate actions, on the other hand, such as walking, even riding occasionally but not madly, are beneficial, but a gay spirit and a putting aside of all capriciousness are even better.

Your financial account, dear Karl, is à la Karl, without coherence, without result. It would have been shorter and more to the point to put the figures in regular columns, if the operation had been very simple, and one also demands *order* in a scholar, particularly in a practical jurist.

I find nothing to object to, on the whole, but I believe that at this moment the acquisition of many books is purposeless and burdensome, especially big historical works.

Your trip was purposeful if it benefited your health, but you should have written a few words about it in advance.

Despite *both* your letters (you see, they can be counted), I am still not familiar with your plan of study, which of course must be of great interest to me. So far as I can see, you are not taking any natural-history courses, and if physics and chemistry are so badly taught, then you would by all means do better to attend them in Berlin. Only the Introduction to financial economics [*Kameralistik*], it seems to me, would be purposeful, for it is always good to have an overview of the subject in which one is to work.

2

1. In one of his two letters home, Marx informed his parents that his health had broken down.
2. Günster, like Heinrich Marx, was a lawyer in Trier.

Apropos! Herr Gratz from here[3] sent me an introduction to Herr Walter.[4] I sent it on to him with a letter—have you heard anything about it? I would be pleased about it because precisely that professor appealed to you so well.

Your small circle, believe me, appeals to me more than the pub. Young people who find pleasure in such a gathering are necessarily educated persons and are more conscious of their worth as future outstanding citizens than those who find their worth in conspicuous coarseness.

You do well to delay publishing. A poet, a literateur, nowadays must have something excellent to offer if he is to make a public appearance. Otherwise he may simply pay homage to the Muses. This always remains one of the noblest homages to women. But if everywhere the debut into the world is largely decisive, it is especially so in the case of these demigods. Their superiority must be evident in the first verses, so that everybody immediately recognizes the divinely gifted. I tell you frankly that your talents please me deeply, and I expect much from them, but I would be grieved to see you make your appearance as a little poetaster [*Poetlein*], merely adequate for deification in your immediate family circle. Only the first-rate has the right to claim the attention of a pampered world—which Schiller had, and which poetical minds would probably call "Gods" had.

I thank you, moreover, dear Karl, for your filial remark that you would first submit your first work to my criticism. This is the more tender of you as you know how little poetry nature has inoculated me with, how in all my life I have been unable to compose even a tolerable poem, even in the sweet days of first love. Nevertheless, I will think about it and wait to see if this was a mere compliment.

How come, dear Karl, that your trip does not figure among your expenses? You did not, I hope, make your way with fencing?

I am enclosing a bank draught for 50 talers and can only tell you on this occasion that you should carry your own responsibility for your studies and, insofar as you need nothing more, refrain from further caprices. The hope that some day you might be a support for your siblings is too attractive, and is too enticing for a generous heart, for me to deprive you of it.

For the time being, I have nothing more to add and recommend to you repeatedly to guard and maintain your health. There is no more pitiable being than a sickly scholar and no more unhappy parents than those who see

---

3. Peter Alois Gratz (1769–1849), former professor at the Catholic Theological Faculty at Bonn, was a school councillor at Trier.
4. Ferdinand Walter (1794–1879) was professor of law at Bonn University.

a son brought up with hope and sacrifice fading away. Take this to heart. I can only appeal to your heart, for I believe it is good and noble. Embracing you with his soul,

Your father, Marx

Mother's Postscript to letter of early 1836:
[*Syntax, structure and punctuation left unchanged*]
dear beloved Carl! Your sickness has troubled us all, but I hope and wish that you will be restored again—and even though I am very anxious in regard to the health of my dear children, I am nevertheless convinced that if you dear Carl act sensibly you can reach a high old age—but to do that you must avoid everything that can aggravate the sickness, you must not get too hot and should not drink much wine and coffee and not consume sharp stuff like much pepper or other sorts of spices, you ought not to smoke tobacco or stay up too late at night and get up early. Beware also of catching cold and don't dance dear Carl until you are fully recovered, it will seem to be ridiculous to you dear Carl that I thus make like a Doctor you don't know how parents feel in their hearts when their children are not well and how this has already caused us many a troubled moment—only see to it that you children remain morally and physically healthy and don't worry about the rest, the dear father thank heaven has been well the whole winter and there is no lack of work and all of us have been right well—how do you like my native town?[5]— its location is really beautiful and I hope that it has inspired you so that it gave you material for a poem write real soon dear Carl better little [than nothing] but don't let too much time pass adieu your loving [mother] I kiss you in thoughts dear Carl

your mother, Henriette Marx

3

To Karl Marx (in Berlin)
Trier, December 28, 1836

Dear Karl:
...But I repeat, you have undertaken great responsibilities,[1] and, dear Karl, at the risk of offending your susceptibilities, I will speak my mind in my usual somewhat prosaic way. With all the exaggerations and exaltations of love in your poetic soul, you cannot restore the peace of mind of that being to whom you have totally given yourself; on the contrary, you run the danger of

---

5. Christmas, 1835, Karl Marx, for the first time, visited Nijmegen, Holland, where his mother was born on September 20, 1788.

3

1. His secret engagement to Jenny von Westphalen.

shattering it; only through the most exemplary conduct and through manly and firm striving, and at the same time of a nature beneficial to the welfare of humanity, can you succeed in straightening out your relations with her, raise her in her own and in the world's esteem, and reassure her.

I have spoken to Jenny and I wish I could have entirely reassured her. I did my best, but not everything can be reasoned away. She still does not know how her parents will receive the news of your relationship. The opinion of relatives and the world, too, is no small matter. I fear your not-always-justified sensitivity and leave it, therefore, up to you to evaluate the situation yourself....

She brings you an invaluable sacrifice—she displays a self-denial which can be properly estimated only by cold reason. Woe to you if you ever could forget this in your whole life. But now only you can take effective action.[2] From you alone must come the certainty that despite your youth you are a man who deserves the world's respect, who conquers it with giant steps....

Your devoted father, Marx

4

To Karl Marx (in Berlin)
Trier, February 3, 1837

Dear Karl!
Your last letter[1] has pleased me greatly, because it proved to me that you have put aside your petty weaknesses which had disquieted me, that you recognize your situation, and that you are striving with energy and dignity to assure your future. Still, dear Karl, do not fall into the opposite extreme.

Apart from the fact that sociableness has great advantages for the amusement, recreation and further development of a young man, nevertheless prudence requires—and this you must not neglect, now that you are no longer alone[2]—that one should procure some support in an honorable and dignified way. *Neglecting* [potentially important individuals], especially if one is not always inclined to seek out the most honorable way of doing so, is something that eminent persons or those who think themselves to be such do not easily forgive, and particularly not when they have condescended to a certain extent. Messieurs Jaehnigen[3] and Esser[4] are not only able men, but for

---

2. A firm promise to pursue a practical career.

4

1. Not found.
2. A reference to his engagement to Jenny.
3. Jaehnigen, whom Heinrich Marx knew as a judge in Trier, was a judge in the Court of Appeals in Berlin after 1836.
4. Esser was a judge in the same Court in Berlin.

you probably important men, and it would be highly unwise and rude to neglect them, especially since they have received you very handsomely. At your age and position, you cannot demand reciprocity.

The body, too, should not be neglected. Health is the highest good for everybody, and even more so for scholars.

Do not exaggerate. With your natural talents and your present diligence you will attain a goal, and in this, a single semester does not matter.

No matter how much experience I may have, I cannot prescribe to you a plan to serve as a clear survey with all its shadings.

Indeed, it seems to me beyond doubt that your intent to train yourself in scholarship is good and appropriate for you, provided you do not overlook a trifle—that of developing your voice somewhat.

But of course all this may take too much time, and in the nature of things it might be desirable to find a remedy. In this connection, therefore, nothing else is left but *authorship*. But how to go about it? This is a difficult question, which itself is preceded by another one: Will it be possible immediately to win the confidence of a bookdealer? For that might well be the hardest. Should you succeed in that—and you are altogether a Child of Fortune [*Glückskind*]—then the second question comes up. Philosophical or juridical subjects, or both together, seem preferable for laying a foundation. Genuine poetry can well take second place, and it never hurts one's reputation, except in the eyes of some pedants. Light verse is the most useful, if original and in a novel style, and with a good name you can reasonably and surely await a professorship, etc., etc. But you have to make a firm decision—if not this second, then certainly this year, and once made, it should be kept firmly in mind and pursued unswervingly. The difficulty you face cannot be at all compared to that faced by your Papa when he decided to become a lawyer.

You know, dear Karl, that out of love for you I have got into something which does not fit my character and which at times depresses me. But for me no sacrifice is too great when the welfare of my children demands it. I have also won the boundless confidence of your Jenny. But the good, kind girl torments herself constantly—fears to harm you—to lead you to undue exertion, etc., etc. It is oppressive to her that her parents do not know [of her engagement to Karl] or, as I believe, do not want to know. She herself cannot understand how she, who believes herself to be an entirely reasonable being, could have let herself be so carried away. There may be some human shyness underneath all this.

A letter from you to her—which you may enclose to me—can bring consolation, but it should not be dictated by a visionary poet. It should, on the contrary, be full of tender, devoted feelings of pure love, which I do not of course doubt, but it must clearly keep in mind your relationship and must elucidate and illuminate your prospects. Your express hopes must be laid out clearly and with firmness, so that they carry conviction.

The letter must firmly state the assurance that your relationship [to Jenny], far from doing you harm, will have the happiest effects on you, and in a certain sense I believe this myself. On the other hand, you must demand with firmness and with masculine assertion, which will assure the poor child, that she must not waver or look back, but look forward to the future with serenity, confidence and a firm eye.

What do you say to your father? Do you not find that astonishingly I qualify as a shady dealer? If my action were known, how askance many a person would look at me! What impure motives would perhaps be ascribed to me! But I make myself no reproaches—may Heaven grant its blessing, and I will feel myself very happy thereby.

It would be proper to visit Herr Eichhorn,[5] but I leave that to you. But, I repeat, I do wish that you visit Messieurs Jaehnigen and Esser more often.

It would do no less good to seek contact at least with some of the more influential professors.

Have you not seen young Schriever[6] anymore? Since we maintain very good relations and Miss Schriever will probably marry your friend Karl von Westphalen, I would be pleased if you sought him out a few times, especially as he is to visit here soon.

Have you heard nothing more about Dr. Kleinerz? I would like to hear something about him.

I am enclosing a letter of credit. It is for more than you yourself asked for. But I did not want to change it, because I now have confidence in you that you will not use more than you need.

Now, please God, dear Karl, write soon, if you have not yet mailed a letter equivalent to the one I recommended here. Write also about your landlord, who interests me very much.

Herr von Notz[7] told me you intend to come home for the fall vacation. I do not agree to this at all, and if you reflect on your relationship [to Jenny] and to the persons dear to you, you must agree with me. But it is possible that I would come to Berlin. What do you say to that?

Your devoted father, Marx

P.S. I am sending my best regards to my dear friend Meurin[8] and his amiable wife. Tell him that he would do me a favor if he gave me a few minutes of his time.

---

5. Eichhorn was a councillor at the Rhenish Court of Appeals in Berlin.
6. The Schrievers were a Trier family, the head of which was a government official.
7. Heinrich von Notz (*ca.* 1818–1848) was Karl Marx's fellow-student in Trier and at the University of Berlin.
8. A judge of the Rhenish Court of Appeals in Berlin.

It would not be amiss, dear Karl, if you wrote something readable.

Jenny I see rarely; she is not free to do as she pleases. But you can rest assured that her love remains true. If you have written her, as I wish you did, then I will ask her for a reply.

5

To Karl Marx (in Berlin)
Trier, March 2, 1837

Dear Karl!
It is remarkable that I, who am by nature a lazy writer, should become inexhaustible when I come to write to you. I do not want to and cannot hide my weakness from you. From time to time, my heart revels in the thoughts of you and your future. And yet, from time to time, I cannot escape the sad, suspicious, fearful thoughts that strike like lightning: Does your heart match your head and your talents? Does it have room for the earthly but gentler feelings that are such an essential consolation to the sensitive human being in this vale of sorrows? Is the Daemon, which is clearly not given to or dominated by everybody, of a celestial or a Faustian nature? Will you—and this is not the least painful doubt in my heart—ever be susceptible to human, domestic happiness? Will you—and this doubt is not the less tormenting since I came to love a certain person[1] as if she were my own child—be capable of bringing happiness to those nearest to you?

You will ask, What brought me to this train of thought? I have had such melancholy thoughts often before, but I gladly drove them away, for I always had the need to embrace you with all the love and respect of which my heart is capable, and I forget myself all over easily. But I see in Jenny a striking phenomenon. She, who is so totally devoted to you with her childlike, pure soul, occasionally and against her own will shows a kind of fear, a misgiving-induced fear, which does not escape me and which I do not know how to explain, every trace of which she tries to eradicate in my heart as soon as I call her attention to it. What is it, what can it be? I cannot explain it, but unhappily my personal experience does not permit me to be easily deceived.

Your rise in the world, the flattering hopes of seeing your name in great renown, as well as your earthly well-being, do not merely lie in my heart but are long-nourished illusions that have nestled deeply. At bottom, however, these feelings belong to a large extent to a weak man and are not entirely free from the usual dross: pride, vanity, egoism, etc., etc. But I can assure you

---

5

1. Jenny von Westphalen.

that the realization of these illusions would not be enough to make me happy. Only when your heart remains pure and beats purely humanly, and no daemonic genius alienates your heart from finer feelings—only then would I find the happiness through you that I have dreamed about for many years; otherwise, I would see the noblest objectives of my life shattered. But why mollify myself too much and perhaps sadden you? At bottom, of course, I do not doubt your filial love for me and your good, dear Mother, and you know very well where we are most vulnerable.

Now I move over to the positive. A few days ago, after she received your letter through Sophie,[2] Jenny visited us and spoke about your plan. She seems to approve your reasons, but feared the step itself, which is very understandable, I, on my part, consider it good and commendable. As she indicated, she will write you not to send the letter direct—I cannot agree with her opinion. To set her mind at rest, you write us eight days in advance on what day you will post the letter. The good girl deserves every consideration, and I repeat, as compensation for what she has already suffered she deserves a long life full of tender love, also for what she is yet to suffer, for she has to deal with strange pietists.

Regard for her is primarily what makes me wish that you would soon take a fortunate step into the world, because this would bring her peace of mind, at least I think so. And I affirm to you, dear Karl, that without this I would strive to restrain you from taking any practical steps at present, rather than urge you on. But you see, the witch has somewhat unsettled my old head, and above all I wish to see her at peace and happy. This, only you can do, and the objective is worthy of your whole attention, and perhaps it is a good and wholesome thing that, despite all the daemons, the moment you enter the world you are also compelled to humane consideration, prudence, foresight, and mature deliberation. I thank Heaven for this, as I always want to love the humane in you, and you know that I, a practical man, am not altogether so unpolished as to be insensitive to the Noble and the Good, but nonetheless I do not willingly withdraw from the earth, where I have a base, exclusively into the ethereal spheres, where I have no firm ground. All this causes me to ponder, more than I would otherwise do, over the means that stand at your disposal. You have laid hold of the theater, and, indeed, there is much truth in it. But will all its importance, with all its great fanfare, there is also naturally the danger of failing in it. And not always—especially in big cities—is it necessarily the intrinsic worth that is decisive. Intrigue, cabals, jealousies—perhaps among those who mostly thrive on them—often outweigh the Good, particularly when it is not elevated and maintained by a well-known name.

---

2. Karl Marx's oldest sister.

What, then, would be the wisest thing? As far as possible, to take into consideration that the great attempt be preceded by a smaller one which is tied up with less danger, but which is still important enough to carry off a not inconsiderable reputation in case of success. Should a small effort achieve this, the material, the subject, the circumstances should nevertheless contain something substantial. I have long brooded over such a subject, and the following ideas seem to me to be appropriate.

The subject should be taken from a period in Prussian history—not so advanced as is required by epics but a tense moment, where fate tilts the scales decisively.

It must be an honorable one for Prussia and contain the possibility of assigning a role to the genius of the monarchy—perhaps through the spirit of the very noble Queen Louise.

Such a moment is the great battle of Belle Alliance-Waterloo. The danger immense—not only for Prussia, its monarch [Frederick William III], but also for all of Germany, etc., etc., etc. In truth, Prussia here delivered the great blow—you can do that perhaps through an ode in the great style, or some such, which you understand better than I do.

In and by itself, the difficulty would not be too great. The greatest perhaps would be squeezing a big picture into a small frame—and to seize the great moment felicitously and aptly. But if it is patriotic, full of feeling, and worked over in the German spirit, such an ode would suffice to establish a reputation, to consolidate a name.

But I can only propose and advise; you have outgrown me, and on this point you excel me altogether, and so I must leave it to you to decide.

The subject proposed by me has the great advantage that it can be quickly carried out, since the anniversary [of the Battle of Waterloo] is on June 18. The costs are not very significant, and if necessary, I would bear them. I want very much to see the good Jenny at peace and in a position to look up proudly. The good child ought not to fret. And if you succeed in this—and the task is not beyond your powers—then you are secure and can give up your hothouse life.

In reality, that moment cannot fail to arouse enthusiasm, for if it [Waterloo] had miscarried, mankind and particularly the human spirit would have been placed in perpetual chains. Only today's mongrel liberals can idolize a Napoleon. Under him, in truth, no person had dared speak out aloud those ideas that are now daily published and without hindrance, in all of Germany and particularly in Prussia. And he who has studied history and the mad expression of ideology, may with good conscience greatly celebrate his [Napoleon's] fall and the victory of Prussia.

Give my hearty regards to friend Meurin. Tell him that until now I have not been able to take the walk he suggested. I have had the grippe for eight days, and I dare not yet go to anything else but meetings.

Your devoted father, Marx

6

To Karl Marx (in Berlin)
Trier, September 16, 1837

Dear Karl!
Your last letter,[1] which was received some eight days ago, makes me expect a greater addendum soon, and I would have gladly waited for the whole. But it might be painful for you to wait [for my answer] that long, the more so since it involves a plan which may perhaps affect the next steps.

You know me, dear Karl, I am neither obstinate nor prejudiced. Whether you prepare yourself for this or that career is, at bottom, a matter of indifference to me. The only concern of my heart for you is that you choose what is more appropriate for your talents. From the first, one thought of the obvious [law]. Such a career, however, seemed to be repugnant to you, and I confess that, suborned [*bestochen*] by your early opinions, I yielded and agreed that you choose your profession, be it jurisprudence or be it philosophy, and in the last analysis I preferred the latter. I was sufficiently familiar with the difficulties of such a career, having had recently an occasion, in Ems, to make the acquaintance and to see much of a professor from Bonn. On the other hand, it is not to be overlooked that a person could play a great role in Bonn as a professor of jurisprudence, and that it is easier to be sent from Berlin to Bonn, with some connections, of course. Poetry could provide such connections for you. But it would also require much luck and many years, and your special situation presses urgently upon you.

Let us look at the other side (and it is important that, with good classical training, a professorship in that field be kept in your mind as a final object). Does a practical career advance that fast? As a rule, no; and experience proves that only too well. Here, too, connections have a great deal to do with it. Without connections, you would not even be able to complain if, after completing your studies, you become an assistant judge [*Assessor*] without salary and remain such for many years. But even with the strictest morality and the most tender sensibility, it is permissible to acquire some connections through one's own merit, the protégé's excellence persuading the patron, in good conscience, to prefer and promote him. Nature has, indeed, equipped you with such gifts as are appropriate for this. How to make the best use of this, is up to you, and for a third person it is difficult to weigh this, the more so since individual character comes into consideration here. And whatever you may decide upon, you must look at it from this viewpoint and apply *the* proper measure, for you are in a hurry, as you feel it and I feel it.

6
1. Not found.

In some respects, all this is, of course, to be regretted, but even the most beautiful painting has its shadowy sides, and here resignation must enter. Such resignation, however, is based on such brilliantly luminous parts, and has its origin entirely in one's own will, guided by the heart and by reason, that it is to be regarded more as enjoyment than as sacrifice.

But I return to this: What shall I advise you? To begin with, in regard to your plan to become a drama critic, I must start by admitting that on the subject itself I have no special competence. Dramatic criticism requires much time and great range. As art, such work may be, in our time, the most meritorious. As fame, it may lead to a learned diploma.

How would it be received? With more hostility than favor, I believe; and the good, learned Lessing, so far as I know, walked little on roses, but lived and died as a poor librarian.

Will such a career produce special financial advantages? The question merges with the above, and I am in no position to answer categorically. But I still believe that excellent individual works, a fine poem, a solid tragedy or comedy, would be more appropriate to your own purposes. But you have paved your own path, and you may continue to go on this way. I can only send up one wish to heaven, that, in some way, you may attain your proper goal as soon as possible.

But I still want to add this. If, after three years of study, you no longer ask for any financial help from home and thereby, out of necessity, do things which may be damaging to you, than let destiny govern and I would rather offer my own sacrifices, no matter at what cost, than see you harmed in your career. Should you finally settle on a career reasonably and without neglect, you would, of course, give me great relief, because since the separation of the court [where Heinrich Marx practiced] and the peddling of the young, [my] income has declined in proportion to the heavy increase in expenditures. But, as I said, this consideration should not be a disturbing one to you.

When you discuss a practical career, why do you not mention at all government service [*Kameralia*]? I do not know whether I am wrong or not, but it seems to me that the art of poetry and literature finds patrons in the bureaucracy easier than in the department of Justice, and a singing government-councillor [*Regierungsrat*] seems to me to be more natural than a singing judge. And, at bottom, what else does *Kameralia* require than what you already need as a real jurist, except natural science? The latter, however, you must by no means neglect, it would be irresponsible to do so.

But you are at the source where you can get information, and precisely for that aspect which under normal conditions you would not have honored for a long time—*the vital question of one's own significance*, which presses upon you and which you must, therefore, ponder, examine, and treat. I am not worried that these considerations, even though they are pressing ones, would ever lead you to vulgar, sneaking actions. Despite my whitened hair and somewhat bowed spirit and full of worries, I would still defy and despise vulgarity. Such a thing cannot possibly occur to you, with your unparalyzed vitality and loaded with Nature's blessings. To a proud youth, in the fullness of his vigor, some things may seem to be demeaning when viewed from cleverness and duty, but are an imperative command when one has assumed the well-being of certain persons as a duty. It is, to be sure, too much to ask that a 19-year old be worldly-wise, but he who is 19—[crossed out].

I did not show your last letter to the Westphalen family. These very good people are a peculiar sort; they talk about everything so extensively and unceasingly, that it is better to provide them with as little nourishment as possible. Since your studies this year are the same as last year, I see no reason why I should give them material for new fantasies.

Jenny is not here yet, but will come soon; that she does not write to you, is—I have no other words for it—childish, capricious. That she enfolds you with the most self-sacrificing love, of that there can be no doubt, and she was not far from sealing it with her death.

Once she has got it into her head that it is unnecessary to write, or whatever other obscure notion she may possess in this regard, one must say there is something original about her; and, you will ask, what good does that do? You may be sure, as I am (and you know, I am not a credulous person), that not even a prince would ever be able to take her away from you. She clings to you with body and soul—and you must never forget this—and at her age she brings you a sacrifice, the like of which ordinary girls would be incapable. Thus if she has the notion of not wanting, or not being able, to write to you, for Heaven's sake let it pass. For, at bottom, writing is only a symbol, and one can forgo it when one is sure of the substance. Should the occasion arise, I will speak to her about it, although reluctantly.

This last year I have been happy at the thought of seeing you, and so one lives in eternal disappointment. The only thing that does not disappoint is a good heart, the outflow of the heart—love—and in this respect I can count myself among the rich; for I possess the love of an incomparable wife, the love of good children.

Do not again let us wait such a long time for letters. Your good mother needs cheering up, and your letters have a wonderful effect on her spirit. This summer she suffered much, and only a person entirely forgetful of her own self could have stood up under it, but it still goes on. May God deliver us soon out of this long struggle! Write occasionally a few lines to Eduard,[2] but do so as if he were completely well again.

---

2. Karl's younger brother.

If you could, without undue familiarity, make closer contact with Herr Jaehningen, you would do me a great favor; I desire it very much. For you, above all, relations with Herr Esser would be very advantageous, and from what I hear he is a friend of Meurin's.

Furthermore, I beg you to go to Herr Privy Justice-Councillor Reinhard and appeal to him in my name to expedite my case. Win or lose, I have enough worries, and would like to have this one out of my mind.

Now, my dear good Karl, I believe I have written enough. I do little portioning out, believing that warmed-over portions do not compare with fresh ones. Farewell, and don't forget, when thinking of your old father, that you have young blood; and when you are fortunate enough, protect it from stormy and devastating passions, but then revitalize it at least with youthful gaiety, cheerful spirit, and youthful pleasures that go with heart and reason.

You are embraced with heart and soul, by

Your faithful Father

Mother's Postscript to letter of September 16, 1837
[*Syntax, structure, punctuation left unchanged*]
Dear beloved Carl
That dear Heaven keep you healthy is surely my most ardent wish in addition that you be moderate in your course of living be it as much as possible in your wishes and hopes since you have achieved the most essential, you can act with more calm and composure. Frau von W[estphalen][3] has spoken with the children[4] today. [Jenny is expected][5] to come today or tomorrow, she writes, she yearns so much for Trier and is eager to hear from you, I believe that Jeny [*sic*] her silence toward you is due to maidenly shame which I have often observed in her which is certainly not to her disadvantage and which enhances her other charms and qualities even more. Edgar[6] will probably go to Heidelberg continue his studies...[7] to be feared—That your well-being and thriving in whatever you undertake lies close to our heart you are convinced let the Almighty and the Benevolent only point out the right way to what is beneficial for you we will pray only have courage and...will be crowned I kiss you warmly in thought....for the fall will make a jacket to protect you against the cold. write real soon dear Carl you eternally loving Mother Henriette Marx.

Also write once to Hermann[8] a few lines include them to us he is doing very well one is satisfied with him.

---

3. Jenny's mother.
4. Karl Marx's siblings.
5. Paper damaged.
6. Edgar von Westphalen, Jenny's only full brother, who was Marx's fellow-student in the Trier Gymnasium.
7. Indecipherable word.
8. Hermann Marx (1819–1842), Karl's brother who died of tuberculosis.

7

To Karl Marx (in Berlin)
Trier, December 9, 1837

Dear Karl!

When one recognizes one's weakness, one has to take measures against it. If I were to write you coherently as usual, my love for you would lead me astray into a sentimental tone, and everything preceding it would be lost, the more so as—at least so it appears to me—you never read a letter a second time, and consistently so, since your reply is never an answer.

Hence I want to exhale my complaints in aphorisms, for they are real complaints I am making. In order to make them clear and have you swallow them like pills, I state questions which I am inclined to solve entirely à posteriori.

1. What is the task of a young man whom nature has indubitably endowed with unusual talents, particularly

(a) when, as he claims and I moreover believe, he honors his father and idealizes his mother;

(b) when he, without considering his youth and his position, chains one of the noblest girls to his fate, and

(c) thereby puts a very honorable family in the embarrassing position of having to approve a relationship which would appear, according to normal worldly conditions, to be full of dangers and gloomy prospects for this beloved girl.

2. Did your parents have any right to demand that your behavior and your mode of life bring them joy, or at least joyful moments, and possibly avoid gloomy ones?

3. What have been the fruits of your splendid endowments in relation to your parents?

4. What have been those fruits in relation to yourself?

Properly speaking, I could and should end here, and leave the entire answers to you. But here I fear every poetic vein. Despite the danger of appearing too prosaic to my Mr. Son, I will answer prosaically, from real life, as it is.

The mood in which I find myself is in reality less than poetic. With a cough that every year depresses me and my business more and more, and combined as it is with a recently incurred gout, I find myself more out of sorts than reasonable and am chagrined at my weakness of character, and so, of course, you can expect only the complaints of an aging and peevish man, who frets over eternal disappointments and particularly over the fact that he has to hold up to his idol a mirror full of caricatures.

Replies, respective complaints

1. To deserve gifts, postulates gratitude; and as splendid natural gifts surely are the most excellent, they require gratitude in a higher degree. But nature lets itself be shown gratitude only by the proper use of those gifts, and if I may use a common expression, it is usurious with its pound [of flesh].

I know well how one should and must answer this in a somewhat nobler style, namely, that such gifts should be used for one's own ennoblement, and this is certainly not what I am disputing. Yes, one should use them for one's ennoblement. But how? One is a man, a spiritual being, a member of society, and a citizen. Hence physical, moral, intellectual, and political ennoblement. Only when there is harmony in one's efforts to achieve these great objectives, can a beautiful and attractive Whole be produced, pleasing to God, men, parents and one's girl, and which can be called a genuinely plastic picture with more truth and naturalness than the meeting again of one's old school comrade.

But as I said, only the effort of extending the ennoblement in measured and equal relationships to all parts manifests the will to show oneself worthy of one's gifts; only in the symmetricalness of this division can be found the beautiful picture, the true harmony.

Yea, limited only to individual parts, even the most sincere exertion does not bring forth by itself any good results, nay, it produces caricatures: coxcombs physically, eccentric visionaries morally, intrigants politically, and educated bears spiritually.

(a) Yea, if a young man really wants to bring joy to his parents, whose merits are left to his heart to honor, he must make a special effort, particularly when he knows that they have placed their finest hopes in him;

(b) Yea, he must reflect that he has undertaken a duty, which is the more sacred as it is possibly beyond his years, to sacrifice himself for the well-being of a girl, who, in view of her splendid qualities and social position, has brought him a great sacrifice when she gave up her brilliant position and prospects for a faltering and gray future in tying herself up to the fate of a young man. To create a future for her is the simple and practical solution—to be worthy of her in the real world, not in the smoke-filled room with a reeking oil-lamp by the side of a barbarian scholar;

(c) Yea, he has to pay a great debt, and a noble family demands great retaliation for the well-grounded hopes surrendered by their beautiful child with her splendid personality. For truly, thousands of parents would have denied their approval. And in gloomy moments, your own father almost wishes that they had done so—for so deeply in my heart lies the well-being of the angelic girl, whom I love as if she were my own daughter and for whose happiness, therefore, I am so anxious.

2. All of these duties together form a tightly woven bond which by itself would suffice to banish all evil spirits, to chase away all aberrations, to make good all deficiencies, and to develop newer and better impulses; to make an orderly man out of a barbarized boy, a solid thinker out of a negative genius, a social human being out of a dissolute leader of a circle of dissolute boys; to make out of him a man who, while retaining enough pride not to bend and wiggle like an eel, would still have enough practical sense and tact to feel that only in contact with moral people can one learn the art of showing the world one's most agreeable and advantageous side, to win attention, love, and respect as soon as possible, and to make practical use of the talents that Mother Nature has in truth endowed him with in profusion.

This, in brief, was the *task*. How is it solved?

God help us!!! Disorderliness, stupefying dabbling in all the sciences, stupefying brooding at the gloomy oil lamp; barbarousness in a scholar's dressing gown and unkempt hair instead of the unruliness at a beer glass; frightening unsociableness with a disregard for all decorum and even all consideration for the *father*. The art of intercourse with the world confined to a filthy room, where, perhaps in the supreme disorder, the love letters of a Jenny and the well-meaning and possibly tear-drenched admonitions of a father to *fidibus* [trust], which, to be sure, is better than if they should fall into the hands of the even more irresponsible disorder of third hands. And in that workshop of senseless and pointless erudition, do you expect a ripening of the fruit that would refresh you and your beloved, a reaping of the harvest that would fulfil your sacred obligations?

3. Despite my resolution, I am oppressed by the deep feeling that I am hurting you, and my weakness [for you] comes upon me already again, but, in order to help me—quite literally—I take the prescribed actual pills, swallow everything, for I want to be hard for once and breathe out my complaints. I do not want to become soft, because I feel I have been too indulgent, that I have not complained enough, and that thereby I have become to a certain extent your accessory in guilt. I want and must tell you that you have given your parents much displeasure and little or no joy.

Hardly have the wild doings in Bonn come to an end, hardly has your debt book been canceled—and it was truly such in manifold ways—when, to our consternation, the love anguish began; and with the kindheartedness of genuinely romantic parents, we became its heralds and cross bearers. But, feeling strongly that herein your life's happiness was concentrated, we endured the inevitable and perhaps played unsuitable roles ourselves. You were estranged from your family while so young and, looking for a beneficent influence on you through the eyes of parents, we hoped to see good effects developing soon, as in fact reflection and necessity equally spoke for it. But what harvest did we reap?

Never have we had the pleasure of a sensible correspondence, which is usually the consolation for absence. For correspondence assumes a consistent and continuous exercise, pursued interlacingly and harmoniously by both sides. Never did we receive any answer to our letters; never did a letter of yours have any connection either with your preceding one or with any of ours.

When we received from you the news of a newly made acquaintance, it was once and for all gone forever, like a stillborn child.

What our beloved son actually does, thinks, acts—no sooner has he thrown an occasional rhapsodic phrase when the valuable report shuts as if by magic.

Often we have been for months without a letter and the last one was when you knew that Eduard[1] was sick, your mother suffering, I ailing, and cholera raging in Berlin; and as if all this did not even require an apology, your next letter did not mention a word about any of this but contained a few poorly written lines and an extract from the diary, entitled *"Besuch"* [Visit], which, frankly, I would rather have shown the door than received, a crazy concoction that only proved how you squander your talents and stayed up nights to produce monsters; that you followed in the footsteps of the new fiends who screw up their words so that they cannot hear them themselves; that a deluge of words, reflecting no ideas or merely disordered ones, are christened a product of genius.

Yea, the writing did contain something—complaints that Jenny does not write, overlooking the fact that at bottom you were convinced that you were favored on all sides—at least there was no basis for despair and pessimism—but this was not enough; the dear ego longed for the pleasure of reading what was known (which, of course, in the given case is quite fair), and that was practically everything that Mr. Son had to say to his parents, whom he knew to be suffering and whom he had afflicted by his senseless silence.

As if we were men made of gold, Mr. Son, against all agreements and practices, disposes of nearly 700 taler in one year, while the richest people hardly spend 500. And why? I will do him the justice of believing that he is no debauchee and no wastrel. But how can a man who discovers new systems every eight or fourteen days and must tear up the old ones that had been so laboriously built—how can he, I ask, bother with trifles? How can he fit himself into a petty order of things? Everybody has his hand in his pocket, and everybody imposes on him, so long as his circle is kept from being disarranged—and a new cheque is soon written. Little people like G.R. and

---

7

1. Eduard Marx, Karl's eleven-year-old brother, who died five days after this letter was written.

Evers may worry about such things, but they are common chaps. In their simplicity, they may, to be sure, try to digest the lectures—even if only the words—and to make well-wishers and friends again, for at the examination there are men, professors, pedants, and occasionally vengeful scoundrels, who would gladly humiliate an independent [student];...[2] the greatness of man lies only in that he creates and destroys!!!

Those poor young fellows [G.R. and Evers, etc.], to be sure, sleep peacefully at night, except occasionally when they have given half or the whole night to pleasure, while my efficient, talented son spends his nights in miserable vigil, wears out his mind and body in serious study, forgoes all pleasures, in order to create solid abstractions, but what he builds today he demolishes tomorrow, and in the end he has destroyed his own without absorbing those of others. In the end, the body becomes sickly and the mind confused, while the ordinary little people glide along unhindered and occasionally reach their goal better, or at least more comfortably, than those who disdain their youthful joys and ruin their health in order to snatch at the shadow of learning, which they probably would have conjured up better in one hour of social intercourse with competent persons, and have had social pleasure into the bargain!!!

I am closing, for in my quickened pulse beats I feel that I am at the point of falling into a mellow tone, and today I want to be merciless.

I also have to report to you complaints from your siblings. From your letters one can hardly tell that you have any; and as for the good Sophie,[3] who has suffered so much for you and Jenny and who is so boundlessly devoted to you, you never think of her unless you need her.

I have paid your cheque for 160 taler. I can hardly charge it to the old academic year, as it probably has its full load. And for the future, I don't want to expect many more such.

For you to come home now, would be folly! I know, to be sure, that you care little for lectures—for which you probably pay—but I want at least to observe decorum. I am certainly not a slave to [public] opinion, but I also don't like gossip at my expense. You can come for Easter vacation—even fourteen days before, I am not that pedantic—and despite my present letter, you can be sure that I will receive you with open arms and that there will beat for you a father's heart, which is now ailing from overstimulation.

Your father, Marx

---

2. Unclear.
3. Sophie Marx (1816–1883), Karl's oldest sister.

Appendix II

CHRONOLOGIES

THE MARX FAMILY*

Karl Marx's Parents

Heinrich Marx	Born, Sarrelouis, France, April, 1777 Died, Trier, Germany, May 10, 1838
Henriette Presburg (or Pressburg)	Born, Nijmegen, Holland, September 20, 1788 Married Heinrich Marx, Nijmegen, November 22, 1814 Died, Trier, Germany, November 30, 1863

Karl Marx's Siblings**

Sophie	Born, Trier, November 13, 1816 Married Wilhelm Robert Schmalhausen, Maastricht, July 12, 1842 Died, 1883
Hermann	Born, Nijmegen, August 12, 1819 Died, Trier, October 14, 1842
Henriette	Born, Trier, October 28, 1820 Married Theodor Simons, Trier, September 3, 1844 Died, Oberhausen, January 3, 1856
Louise (Luise)	Born, Trier, November 14, 1821 Married Johann Carl Juta, June 5, 1853 Died, c. 1893.

*See also Biographic Index
**Karl Marx: Born, Trier, May 5, 1818; married Jenny von Westphalen, Kreuznach, June 10, 1843; died, London, March 14, 1883.

Emilie	Born, Trier, October 24, 1822 Married Johann Jacob Conradi, October 22, 1859 Died, Trier, October 24, 1888
Caroline	Born, Trier, July 30, 1824 Died, Trier, January 13, 1847
Eduard	Born, Trier, April 7, 1826 Died, Trier, December 14, 1837.

Karl Marx's Children

Jenny (Jennychen)	Born, Paris, May 1, 1844 Married Charles Longuet, London, October 10, 1872 Died, Argenteuil, France, January 11, 1883
Laura	Born, Brussels, September 26, 1845 Married Paul Lafargue, London, April 2, 1868 Died, Le Perreux, France, November 26, 1911 (suicide)
Edgar ("Musch")	Born, Brussels, December 17, 1847 Died, London, April 6, 1855
Heinrich Guido ("Föxchen")	Born, London, November 5, 1849 Died, London, November 19, 1850
Franziska	Born, London, March 21, 1851 Died, London, April 14, 1852
Eleanor ("Tussy")	Born, London, January 16, 1855 Died, London, March 31, 1898 (suicide)

Karl Marx's Grandchildren

(1) *Lafargue*
(Child of Laura and Paul Lafargue)

Charles-Étienne ("*Schnappy*," "*Schnaps*")	Born, London, December 31, 1868 Died, Madrid, July, 1872

(2) *Longuet*
(Children of Jenny and Charles Longuet)

Charles	Born, London, September, 1873 Died, London, July, 1874

Jean-Laurent-Frederick	Born, London, 1876
(Johnny)	Died, France, 1938
Henri (Harry)	Born, London, 1878
	Died, London, 1883
Edgar ("Wolf")	Born, Ramsgate, August, 18, 1879
	Died, Paris, 1950
Marcel	Born, Argenteuil, 1881
	Died, 1949
Jenny	Born, Argenteuil, 1882
	Died, Paris, 1952

KARL MARX: HIGHLIGHTS OF HIS LIFE

1777

April Birth of Heschel (Heinrich) Marx, Karl's father, in Sarrelouis, France (now West Germany), whence the Marx family moved northward to Trier when he was a young boy.

1788

September 20 Birth of Henriette Presburg, Karl's mother, in Nijmegen, Holland.

1814

February 12 Birth of Jenny von Westphalen, Karl Marx's future wife, in Salzwedel, Prussia.

November 22 Marriage of Heschel Marx and Henriette Presburg, Karl's parents, in Nijmegen, Holland.

1818

May 5 Birth of Karl Marx in Trier, No. 664 Brückengasse (now No. 10 Brückenstrasse).

1824

August 26 Karl Marx's baptism, together with seven siblings (Sophie, Hermann, Henriette, Luise, Emilie, Karoline, and Eduard), in Lutheran church. The Marx family had been Jewish.

1830

October Karl Marx enters Friedrich Wilhelm Gymnasium in Trier, which he attends for five years.

1835

September 24 Graduates from the Gymnasium.

October 15 Matriculates in Bonn University, Faculty of Jurisprudence. Address: 1 Stocken Strasse, then 764 Joseph Strasse.

1836

August Fights a student duel.

August 22 Leaves Bonn for Trier, where he becomes secretly engaged to Jenny von Westphalen.

Mid-October Goes by post coach to Berlin, taking up quarters first at 61 Mittelstrasse, then 50 Alte Jacobstrasse.

October 22 Matriculates in Berlin University, Faculty of Law, studying philosophy, jurisprudence, literary and art history. He remains in Berlin four and a half years, until March 30, 1841.

1837

Reads Hegel, other philosophers, jurists, and historians; writes plays, fifty-six poems ("Book of Love" and "Book of Poems," dedicated to Jenny von Westphalen; and "Wild Songs," dedicated to his father); meets Young Hegelians, the so-called *Freien*; has a nervous breakdown.

1838

May 10 Death of Heinrich Marx, Karl's father, in Trier.

1839–1840

Marx studies classic Greek philosophers in the original and works on his doctoral dissertation, *Differenz der demokritischen und epikureischen Naturphilosophie* [*Difference Between the Democritean and Epicurean Philosophy of Nature*].

1841

March 30 Officially completes his studies at Berlin University.

April 15 Receives Ph.D. degree from Jena University, in absentia.

Mid-April Leaves Berlin for Trier, where he remains until early July.

May 4	Declared unfit for Prussian military service because of affected lungs.
Early July– Mid-October	Lives in Bonn in vain expectation of a university professorship.

1842

January 15– February	Writes critique of Prussian censorship for Arnold Ruge's *Deutsche Jahrbücher*; owing to censorship difficulties, article is not published until February, 1843, in Swiss-based journal, *Anekdota zur neuesten deutschen Philosophie und Publicistik*, Volume I.
March 3	Death of Ludwig von Westphalen, Jenny's father, who was friendly to young Marx.
May 5	Begins a series of six articles on freedom of the press, in *Rheinische Zeitung* (Cologne), May 5, 8, 10, 12, 15, 19.
August 9	Publishes "The Philosophical Manifesto of the Historical School of Law," in *Rheinische Zeitung*.
Mid-October	Becomes editor-in-chief of *Rheinische Zeitung* and moves from Bonn to Cologne.
October 16	Publishes first article on communism in *Rheinische Zeitung*.
October-early 1843	Begins study of French utopians: Fourier, Cabet, Proudhon, etc.
November	Marx and Frederick Engels meet for the first time in office of *Rheinische Zeitung*.
Late November	Breaks with Young Hegelians over critical *Rheinische Zeitung* policies.

1843

January 1-16	Publishes a series of seven articles on the suppression of *Leipziger Allgemeine Zeitung*, in *Rheinische Zeitung*, January 1, 4, 6, 8, 10, 13, 16.
March 17	Resigns from *Rheinische Zeitung*, which is closed by censorship on April 1.
June 10	Marries Jenny von Westphalen, in Kreuznach.
Summer	Writes "Critique of Hegel's Philosophy of Right," and "On the Jewish Question."
Late October	Moves to Paris: 41 Rue Vaneau; becomes co-editor, with Arnold Ruge, of *Deutsch-Französische Jahrbücher*.

1844

Late February   Publishes first—and last—double issue of *Deutsch-Französische Jahrbücher*, containing his two articles, "Critique of Hegel's Philosophy of Right," and "On the Jewish Question."

March 23   Meets Russian revolutionist Michael Bakunin in Paris.

April–August   Works on *Economic and Philosophic Manuscripts of 1844* (first published, in Berlin, 1932).

May 1   Birth of daughter Jenny (later Jenny Longuet), in Paris.

July   Meets French social theorist Pierre Joseph Proudhon in Paris.

August 28   Meets Engels for the second time, spend ten days together, decide upon literary collaboration, and strike up what became an intimate lifelong friendship.

September   Begins to meet French radical workingmen's groups and to study economic and socialist theorists.

1845

Mid-January   Receives order of expulsion from France.

February 3   Moves to Brussels: 4 Rue d'Alliance, outside Porte de Louvain.

February 24   Publication of *Die Heilige Familie [The Holy Family]*, a polemic against former Hegelian friend Bruno Bauer and colleagues, written in collaboration with Engels.

Spring   Writes brief "Thesis on Feuerbach" (first published by Engels in his *Ludwig Feuerbach*, in 1888).

September   Begins work on *Die Deutsche Ideologie [The German Ideology]*, in collaboration with Engels.

September 26   Birth of daughter Laura (later Laura Lafargue).

December 1   Gives up Prussian citizenship.

1846

Early in year   Founds, with Engels, Communist Correspondence Committee in Brussels.

March 30   Vehement confrontation with German radical Wilhelm Weitling.

Late April	Meets German radical Wilhelm Wolff, who becomes lifelong friend.
May	Moves to hotel Au Bois Sauvage, 19/21 Plaine St. Gudule.
Summer	Completes *The German Ideology* (not published until 1962).

1847

January 3– February, 1848	Writes for *Deutsche-Brüsseler-Zeitung*, a radical German-language semi-weekly in Brussels.
Mid-January	Moves to new address: 42 Rue d'Orléans, Fbg.de Namour, Brussels.
January–April	Works on *Misère de la Philosophie [Poverty of Philosophy]*.
Early June	Organizes, with Engels, German Communist League, in Brussels.
Early July	Publication, in French, of *Misère de la Philosophie*, subtitled, *Réponse à la Philosophie de la Misère de M.Proudhon [Reply to the Philosophy of Poverty by M.Proudhon]*, in Paris and Brussels (a German edition came out posthumously in 1885).
Late August	Founds, with Engels, German Workers' Association, for propagation of communist ideas.
November 29	Participates, with Engels, in international meeting of Fraternal Democrats in London.
November 29– December 8	Participates in London congress of Communist League, which commissions him to draw up the *Communist Manifesto*.
December 13	Returns to Brussels from London.
December 17	Birth of son Edgar.
Late December	Lectures before German Workers' Association on *Wage Labor and Capital*, published as a pamphlet in 1884, 1891, and 1925.

1848

Late January	Completes, with Engels, *Manifesto of the Communist Party*—known as the *Communist Manifesto*—in German, and sends it to London to be printed.
February 24	Publication of the *Manifesto*.

March 1	Receives invitation from French Provisional Government to return to Paris, after outbreak of revolution there in February.
March 3	Receives order of expulsion from Belgium.
March 4	Arrested in Brussels and expelled with his family.
March 5	Arrives in Paris; address: 10 Rue Neuve Ménilmontant (Boulevard Beaumarchais).
March 12	Elected president of Communist League.
March 21–29	Writes, with Engels, "Demands of the Communist Party in Germany."
April 6	Leaves Paris, with Engels, to participate in revolution in Germany which had broken out there following the February example of France.
April 11	Arrives in Cologne; address: No. 7 Apostelstrasse.
Mid-April	Works on plan to establish a new radical daily, *Neue Rheinische Zeitung*.
June 1	Publishes first issue of *Neue Rheinische Zeitung*, subtitled *Organ der Demokratie* [*Organ of Democracy*]. It opened with 6,000 subscribers, and appeared until May 19, 1849.
August 3	Denied citizenship application by Prussian Government.
September 25	Outbreak of revolution in Cologne.
September 26– October 5	Suspension of *Neue Rheinische Zeitung* under martial law.
November	Meets American newspaperman Charles Anderson Dana, who is later (1852) to appoint him London correspondent of *New-York Daily Tribune*.
December 6	Indicted on charges of *lèse majesté* and incitement to rebellion.
	1849
February 7–8	Tried in Cologne court and acquitted by jury.
May 16	Receives order of expulsion from Prussia.
May 19	Publishes last issue of *Neue Rheinische Zeitung*, in inflammatory red ink.
June 3	Arrives in Paris.
July	Joined by wife and their three children (Edgar, Jenny, Laura); address: 45 Rue de Lille.

July 19	Receives order of expulsion from Paris.
August 24	Leaves Paris for London, where he was to spend the rest of his life.
Late August	Helps to reconstitute Communist League in London.
September 17	Arrival of pregnant wife and their three children; live in rooming house on Leicester Square.
November 5	Birth of son, Heinrich Guido, called "Föxchen," because he was born on Guy Fawkes Day.
November 10	Arrival of Engels in London.
December	Works with Engels on plans for a new journal, *Neue Rheinische Zeitung. Politisch-Ökonomische Revue.*

1850

March–November	Publishes, with Engels, *Neue Rheinische Zeitung. Politisch-Ökonomische Revue* (six issues).
July	Begins study of Political Economy in British Museum.
November 30	Publication of English translation of *Communist Manifesto.*

1851

August 7	Receives invitation from Charles Anderson Dana to write for *New-York Daily Tribune.*
June 23	Birth of Frederick Demuth, Marx's illegitimate son.

1852

January–May	Publication, in two installments, of *The Eighteenth Brumaire of Louis Bonaparte*, in German, in New York City.
End May– Mid-June	In Manchester, visiting Engels.
August 21	Publication of first article (translated by Engels) in *New-York Daily Tribune.* (His last *Tribune* piece appeared March 10, 1862.)
November 17	Dissolution, at Marx's suggestion, of Communist League.
December 14	Ill with hemorrhoids.

1853

Late January	Publication of *Revelations about the Cologne Communist Trial*, in Basel.

April 24   Publication of same, in German, in Boston, as a brochure.

October 19–   Publishes six articles, "Lord Palmerston," in
January 11, 1854   *Tribune*; this series, in eight installments, also appeared in *The People's Paper*, a Chartist publication.

1854

Mid-January   Publication of the satire, *Knight of the Magnanimous Consciousness*, in German, in New York.

September 9–   Publishes eight articles, "Revolutionary Spain," in
December 2   *Tribune*.

1855

January 2   Publishes first article in *Neue Oder-Zeitung* of Breslau. Altogether, Marx contributed 112 articles (some in collaboration with Engels) to that newspaper, the last one on October 8, 1855.

January 16   Birth of daughter Eleanor ("Tussy").

April 6   Death of eight-year-old son Edgar ("Musch").

1856

January–February   Hemorrhoids.

Early October   Moves from Soho to new house: 9 Grafton Terrace, Maitland Park, Haverstock Hill (the Marx family lived there until 1864).

1857

January–July   Illness (headaches, toothaches, earaches, throat aches, and, as Mrs. Marx said, "God knows what else") and inability to work.

September–   Writes sixteen articles (eight in collaboration with
April 1858   Engels) for *New American Cyclopaedia*, New York.

1858

February–May   Illness and inability to work.

August   Begins writing *Critique of Political Economy*.

November   Toothaches and inability to work.

1859

June 11   Publication of *Critique of Political Economy* in edition of 1,000 copies (first English translation, 1909).

1860

December 1 Publication of *Herr Vogt*, a bitter pamphlet against Karl Vogt, in London.

December Reads Charles Darwin's *Origin of Species by Means of Natural Selection* (Marx to Engels, December 19: "It is the book that contains the natural-history basis of our philosophy").

1861

January Inflammation of the liver.

March 17– Visits Ferdinand Lassalle in Berlin.
April 12

April 10 Applies for restoration of Prussian citizenship (rejected in November).

Early June Begins work on *Das Kapital*.

October 25 Publishes first article ("The North American Civil War") in *Die Presse*, a Vienna daily.

1862

March 10 Last article ("The Mexican Imbroglio") in *New-York Daily Tribune*.

1863

February–May Illnesses (eye inflammation, liver trouble, coughing) and inability to work.

September– Ill with carbuncles.
December

November 30 Death of mother, Henriette Marx, in Trier, Germany.

December 7– Trip to Germany and Holland (where he visited his
February 19, uncle, Lion Philips, in Zalt-Bommel).
1864

1864

March Moves to new house: 1 Modena Villas, Maitland Park (the Marx family lived here until 1875).

July 31– Ill with influenza and carbuncles.
August 31

July 20– On cure in Ramsgate
August 10

September 28	Attends founding meeting of International Working Men's Association (First International), at St. Martin's Hall, London; chosen member of Provisional Committee.
October 21–27	Drafts "Provisional Rules" and "Inaugural Address" of the First International (published, December 21 and 30).

1865

May–June 17	Writes "Wages, Price and Profit."
May–August	Ill with influenza, carbuncles, etc.
October 20– *November 2*	Visits Engels in Manchester.
Late December	Completes first draft of *Das Kapital*.

1866

Mid-January– *Mid-March*	Ill with carbuncles, unable to work.
March 15– *April 10*	On cure in Margate
Mid-April– *December*	Continued illnesses—carbuncles, toothaches, rheumatism, liver.

1867

Late March	Completes *Das Kapital*.
April 10	Leaves London for Hamburg.
April 12–16	Discusses publication of *Das Kapital* with publisher Meissner in Hamburg.
April 17–May 15	Visits Dr. Ludwig Kugelmann in Hanover.
May 19	Returns to London.
August 15–16	Finishes correcting proof of *Das Kapital*.
September 14	Publication of *Das Kapital* (Volume I).

1868

January– *Mid-May*	Festering carbuncles all over his body; arsenic treatment.
April 2	Marriage of daughter Laura to Paul Lafargue.
April 22	Begins intermittent work, for brief periods, on Volume II of *Das Kapital*.

August 21–24	In Ramsgate.
November 29	Engels offers Marx annuity of £350 to relieve him permanently of financial distress.

1869

Mid-February–Late May	Liver illness and carbuncles.
July 1	Engels gives up his business in Manchester.
Late July	Publication of second edition of *Eighteenth Brumaire* in Hamburg.
September 7–11	At Basel Congress of the First International, Marx is unanimously reelected to its General Council.
September 18–October 7	Visits, with daughter Eleanor, Dr. Kugelmann in Hanover.
October 8–9	Visits publisher, Meissner, in Hamburg.
October 11	Returns to London.
Late October	Begins to study Russian language.

1870

Mid-January–April	Liver inflammation, carbuncles, abscesses; undergoes two operations.
May 23–June 23	With daughter Eleanor, visits Engels in Manchester, to prepare publicity for *Das Kapital*, which is largely ignored by reviewers in Germany.
July 19–23	Writes "First Address of the International on the Franco-Prussian War," which is published, in German and French, in an edition of 30,000 copies.
August 9–31	On cure for sciatica at Ramsgate, 36 Hardres Street.
September 6–9	Writes "Second Address of the International on the Franco-Prussian War," protesting annexation of Alsace-Lorraine by Prussia.
September 16	Writes last letter to Engels in Manchester.

1871

January on	Continued illnesses—bronchitis, coughing, sleeplessness.
March 18	Establishment of Paris Commune.
April 18–May 29	Writes *The Civil War in France*, a pamphlet defending the Paris Commune, published in English in London, in German in Leipzig (July), and in a later edition by Engels in 1891.

June–December	Organizes financial assistance for Paris Commune refugees in London.
July 3	Gives interview to R. Landor, correspondent of *The New York World* (published in *World*, July 18; and in *Woodhull & Claflin's Weekly* [New York], August 12.
August 16–29	On cure in Brighton, Globe Hotel, Manchester Street.
September 17–23	Participates in London conference of the International.
September 28– October 3	On cure in Ramsgate with Mrs. Marx and Engels.

1872

January– Early March	Works, with Engels, on the anti-Bakunin circular "Fictitious Splits in the International."
March 27	Publication of first foreign translation—in Russian—of *Das Kapital* (translation begun by Bakunin, completed by Nicolai F. Danielson). Of an edition of 3,000 copies, 900 were sold out in first six weeks.
April–May	Edits French translation of *The Civil War in France*, published in June in Brussels, 2,000 copy edition.
July 9–15	On cure in Ramsgate, with Engels.
July	Publication in Leipzig of new German edition of *Communist Manifesto*, with introduction by Marx and Engels.
Mid-July	Publication of first part of second German edition of *Das Kapital*.
Late August	Chosen delegate to congress of the International in The Hague.
September 1	Arrives, with wife and daughter Eleanor, in The Hague.
September 2-7	Participates actively in the congress and in the struggle with the Bakuninists which led to dissolution of the International.
September 17	Returns to London. Publication of first installments of French translation of *Das Kapital*.
October 10	Marriage of Jenny Marx to French socialist Charles Longuet.

1873

January 24	Writes Epilogue for second German edition of *Das Kapital*.

May–June	Corrects and retranslates French edition of *Das Kapital*.
May 22–June 3	Visits Dr. Eduard Gumpert (for medical consultation) and other friends, including Carl Schorlemmer and Samuel Moore, the cotranslator of *Das Kapital* into English, in Manchester.
Early June	Publication of second German edition of *Das Kapital*.
November 24– December 15	On cure in Harrogate, with daughter Eleanor.

1874

February–April	Continued illnesses.
Mid-April– May 5	On cure in Ramsgate, 16 Abbott's Hill.
Mid-July– Late July	On cure in Ryde, Isle of Wight, 11 Nelson Street.
August 4–9	In Ramsgate, with sick daughter, Jenny Longuet.
August 24	Rejection of British citizenship application.
August 19– September 21	On cure in Karlsbad, Hotel Germania, with daughter Eleanor.
October 3	Returns to London.
October 28– December 18	Serial publication in Germany—in *Der Volksstaat*, a Social-Democratic journal appearing twice weekly in Leipzig—of *Revelations About the Cologne Communist Trial*; it was published as a brochure in 1875.

1875

March	Moves to 41 Maitland Park Road (or Crescent), N.W., where he is to live until his death in 1883.
May 5	Sends *Critique of the Gotha Program* to Wilhelm Bracke for the Social-Democratic congress in Gotha, Germany.
August 15– September 11	Second time, on cure in Karlsbad, Hotel Germania.
September 20	Returns to London, after visiting several European cities.
Late November	Publication of French edition of *Das Kapital* (translation begun by Joseph Roy, corrected by Marx, completed by Charles Keller and others).

1876

August 16–
September 15   Third time, on cure in Karlsbad, Hotel Germania, with daughter Eleanor.

1877

March 5   Completes first part of Chapter 10 for Engels' book, *Anti-Dühring*.

Late March   Resumes intermittent work on second volume of *Das Kapital*.

August 8   Completes second part of Chapter 10 for *Anti-Dühring*.

August 8–
September 27   On cure, with sick wife, in Bad Neuenahr, Germany: Hotel Flora.

1878

September 4–14   On cure, with wife and daughter Jenny Longuet, in Malvern.

1879

August 8–20   On cure in St. Helier and St. Aubin's, Isle of Jersey: Trafalgar Hotel.

August 21–
September 17   On cure, with sick wife, in Ramsgate: 62 Plains of Waterloo.

1880

January–December   While ill, works intermittently on second and third volumes of *Das Kapital*.

Early August–
September 13   On cure, with wife and children, in Ramsgate.

1881

Late June–
July 20   On cure, with sick wife, in Eastbourne: 43 Terminus Road.

July 26–
August 16   With dying wife, visits daughter Jenny Longuet, in Argenteuil, France: 11 Boulevard Thiers.

October 13–
Mid-December   Gravely ill.

December 2   Death of wife, Jenny Marx, of cancer; Marx too ill to attend funeral.

December 29–
January 16, 1882   On cure in Ventnor, Isle of Wight: 1 St. Boniface Gardens.

1882

January 21 Writes (with Engels) preface to Russian translation (by G. Plekhanov) of *Communist Manifesto*; preface published in Russian weekly, *Narodnaya Volya*, February 5.

February 9–16 Visits daughter Jenny Longuet in Argenteuil, on route to cure for pleurisy and bronchitis in Algiers.

February 20–
May 2 On cure in Algiers: Hotel Victoria.

Early May–
June 3 In Nice and Monte Carlo. Hôtel de Russie.

June 3–5 In Cannes.

June 6–
August 22 Visits daughter Jenny Longuet in Argenteuil, taking sulfur baths at Enghien-les-Bains.

August 23–27 Visits Lausanne, with daughter Laura Lafargue.

August 27–
September 25 Visits Vevey, Switzerland, with daughter Laura.

October 30–
January 12, 1883 On cure in Ventnor, Isle of Wight; 1 St. Boniface Gardens.

1883

January 11 Death of Jenny Longuet, of cancer, in Argenteuil, causing Marx to return to London from Ventnor.

January 11–
March 14 Gravely ill with laryngitis, bronchitis, lung tumor, etc.

March 14:
2:45 P.M. Dies at home in London, sitting in an easy chair.

March 17 Buried in family grave, Highgate Cemetery, London.

1890

November 4 Death of Marx family lifelong housekeeper, Helene Demuth, in Engels' home.

1895

August 5 Death of Engels.

1898

March 31 Suicide of Eleanor Marx.

1911

November 26 Suicide of Laura and Paul Lafargue.

1929

January 28   Death of Frederick Demuth, Marx's illegitimate son.

FREDERICK ENGELS: BRIEF CHRONOLOGY

1820

November 28   Born, Barmen, Rhenish Prussia, son of Friedrich Engels, a manufacturer, and Elisabeth Franziska Mauritia

1837

Left Elberfeld Gymnasium, to work in a business firm in Bremen, Germany

1842

November   Went to Manchester, England, to work in his father's business firm.

1844

August   Met Marx in Paris and struck up a lifelong friendship and collaboration.

1845

Published, in German, *The Condition of the Working Class in England* (English translation: 1892).

February 24   Published his and Marx's book, *The Holy Family.*
April   Joined Marx in Brussels.

1846

February   Published, in collaboration with Marx, *Communist Manifesto*, in German.
September   Collaborated with Marx on *The Germany Ideology.*

1848

June 1   On editorial staff of Marx-edited *Neue Rheinische Zeitung*, Cologne.

1849

May   Indicted in Germany, fled abroad.
November   Joined Marx in London.

1850

March to   Copublished with Marx *Neue Rheinische Zeitung.*
November   *Politisch-Ökonomische Revue.*

November	Left London to work in his father's textile firm in Manchester, where he was to spend the next twenty years.

1870

September 22	Moved to London, 122 Regents Park, N.W., to be near Marx.

1878

Published his book, *Anti-Dühring*.

1882

Published *Development of Socialism from Utopia to Science* (English title: *Socialism, Utopian and Scientific*, 1892).

1884

Published *Origin of the Family Private Property and the State*.

1884–1895

Devoted his last years to preparing the final volumes of *Das Kapital*.

1885

Brought out Volume II of *Das Kapital*.

1888

Published his last book, *Ludwig Feuerbach and the End of Classical German Philosophy*.

1894

Brought out Volume III of *Das Kapital*.

1895

August 5	Died, in London, of throat cancer.
August 11	Ashes scattered, as provided in his will, on the sea.

FERDINAND LASSALLE: BRIEF CHRONOLOGY

April 11, 1825	Born in Breslau, Germany, the son of a wealthy Jewish silk merchant, Heimann Lassal.
1843–1846	Attended Breslau and Berlin universities, studying philology, jurisprudence, history, and philosophy.

1846–1854	Fought for Sophie von Hatzfeldt's divorce, a case that became notorious throughout Germany but which culminated in success and a lifelong income (7,000 taler) for Lassalle.
1854	Settled in Berlin, where he moved in the most powerful political and social circles.
1857	Published a two-volume scholarly book, *The Philosophy of Heraclitus the Obscure of Ephesus*.
1861	Published his major juridical work, *The System of Acquired Rights*, in two volumes.
1861–1864	Carried on dramatic labor-organizing agitation, for which he was jailed occasionally.
August 31, 1864	Died from duel in Geneva, Switzerland.

BIBLIOGRAPHY

Except for the handful of letters written by Marx in English and French, all the letters in this volume are translations from the German original. The translations are all by me.

There are few books containing Marx's personal letters in English. Those that do exist are mainly political and are, moreover, devoted not to Marx alone, but to Marx and Engels. One of the rare exceptions is *Letters to Dr. Kugelmann* (International Publishers, 1934), a book that contains a number of personal, in addition to political, letters. There are fourteen letters written by Marx in English (such as it was) to members of his family, published in the *Annali* of the Istituto Giangiacomo Feltrinelli (Milan, 1958); they have been reprinted in Wolfgang Schwerbrock's paperback, *Karl Marx Privat* (Paul List Verlag, Munich, 1962).

The writings of Marx (and Engels) are to be found in many German collections. Foremost of these is the *Marx-Engels Werke* (thirty-nine volumes plus two volumes of Supplement), prepared by the Moscow Institute of Marxism-Leninism and published by Dietz Verlag, Berlin (East), 1964–1968. The letters in this collection (by Marx and Engels) are contained in nine volumes (XXVII–XXXV).

There are other, briefer, German collections of Marx's letters. Among them:

Blumenberg, Werner   *"Ein Unbekanntes Kapitel aus Marx's Leben: Briefe an die Holländische Verwandten"* ["An Unknown Chapter Out of Marx's Life: Letters to the Dutch Relatives"], in *International Review of Social History*, I (1956), pp. 54–111.

Blumenberg, Werner   *"Marx' und Engels' Briefwechsel mit Franz Duncker"* ["Marx's and Engels' Correspondence with Franz Duncker"], in *ibid.*, X (1965), pp. 105–19.

Eckert, Georg   *Wilhelm Liebknecht Briefwechsel mit Marx und Engels [Wilhelm Liebknecht Correspondence with Marx and Engels]*, The Hague: Mouton & Co., 1963.

Häckel, Manfred   *Freiligrath's Briefwechsel mit Marx und Engels [Freiligrath's Correspondence with Marx and Engels]*, 2 vols. Berlin: Akademie Verlag, 1968.

Mandelbaum, Kurt   *Die Briefe von Karl Marx und Friedrich Engels an Danielson (Nikolai-on) [The Letters of Karl Marx and Friedrich Engels to Danielson (Nikolai-on)]*, Leipzig: Rudolf Liebing Verlag, 1929.

Marx-Engels Briefwechsel [Marx-Engels Correspondence], Berlin: Dietz Verlag, 1949

Mayer, Gustav   *Lassalle's Briefwechsel [Lassalle's Correspondence]*, Vol. III, subtitled: *Der Briefwechsel zwischen Lassalle und Marx [The Correspondence between Lassalle and Marx]*, Stuttgart and Berlin: Deutsche Verlagsanstalt, 1922.

Mehring, Franz   *"Freiligrath und Marx in ihrem Briefwechsel"* ["Freiligrath and Marx in their Correspondence"], in Supplement to *Neue Zeit*, April 12, 1912, pp. 1–56.

Müller, Manfred   *Familie Marx in Briefen [The Marx Family in Letters]*, Berlin: Dietz Verlag, 1966.

Letters in English translation are also to be found in The Karl Marx Library, seven volumes, edited by Saul K. Padover and published by McGraw-Hill Book Co., New York, as follows:

Marx On Revolution (1971), pp. 130–31, 381–407, 510–37.
Marx On America and the Civil War (1972), pp. 36–49, 247–78.
Marx On the First International (1973), pp. 366–583.

Marx On Freedom of the Press and Censorship (1974), pp.159–75.
Marx On Religion (1974), pp.231–57.
Marx On Education, Women, and Children (1975), pp.135–52.
Marx On History and People (1977), pp. 15–53, 144–46, 159–61, 164–65, 171–73, 177–78, 183–88, 192–94, 197–207, 215–19, 223–35, 246–47, 252–53, 276–84, 292–96, 298–99, 304–05, 309–12, 315–18, 320–23.

For a select English bibliography of Marx's writings—in addition to his letters—see Saul K. Padover, *Karl Marx: An Intimate Biography* (McGraw-Hill Book Co., New York 1978), pp.646–47.

BIOGRAPHIC INDEX

SUBJECT INDEX